D1603982

American Jewish Orthodoxy in Historical Perspective

American Jewish Orthodoxy in Historical Perspective

by

Jeffrey S. Gurock

KTAV Publishing House, Inc.
1996

Library of Congress Cataloging-in-Publication Data

Gurock, Jeffrey S., 1949–
   American Jewish Orthodoxy in historical perspective / by Jeffrey S. Gurock.
      p.   cm.
   Includes bibliographical references and index.
   ISBN 0-88125-567-X
   1. Orthodox Judaism—United States—History. 2. Orthodox Judaism—New
York (State)—New York—History. 3. Jews—Cultural assimilation—United
States—History. I. Title.
BM205.G87   1996
296.8'32'0973—dc20   96-9364
                                                                          CIP

Manufactured in the United States of America
KTAV Publishing House, Inc.
900 Jefferson St., Hoboken, NJ 07030

For
Rabbi Avraham Weiss
friend, colleague and teacher

Contents

Acknowledgments

Last year, my colleague, Professor Yaakov Elman and Mr. Bernard Scharfstein of KTAV Publishing House suggested that scholars, students, and a significant general reading audience would benefit from having my writings on American Jewish Orthodoxy available in one readily accessible volume. This present work has brought together some fifteen of my most important studies with a new introduction which sets this body of literature within its appropriate historiographical context.

I am grateful to the eleven different journals and organizations that hold copyrights on these articles for their granting me permission to republish my work. The names of the institutions and the original bibliographical citations are listed in the front matter to this volume. I am also grateful to the many scholars who over the years have read early drafts of these articles before they were accepted for publication in academic journals. Here, I am especially thankful for the assistance of Professors Benjamin R. Gampel of the Jewish Theological Seminary of America and Marc Lee Raphael of the College of William and Mary who have helped improve the quality of so much of my writing. I am also pleased to note the excellent assistance Dr. Richard White of KTAV has given me in seeing this present volume to completion.

As with everything I write, and everything I do, I am inspired and strengthened by the support lavished upon me by Pamela Gurock, and Eli, Rosie and Michael Gurock. It is also a source of great pride for me that Eli designed the cover of this book. The work is dedicated with respect and affection to my friend, colleague and teacher Rabbi Avraham Weiss.

Grateful acknowledgment is made to the various editors and publishers who have granted permission to reprint the following:

"Resisters and Accommodators: Varieties of Orthodox Rabbis in America, 1886–1983." *American Jewish Archives*, (November, 1983): 100–187. Reprinted in *The American Rabbinate: A Century of Continuity and Change, 1883–1983.* (New York: KTAV Publishing House, Inc., 1985), pp. 10–97.

"The Orthodox Synagogue," *The History of the Synagogue in America*, Jack Wertheimer, ed. (New York and London: Cambridge University Press, 1988), pp. 37–84.

"Jacob A. Riis: Christian Friend or Missionary Foe? Two Jewish Views," *American Jewish History*, (September 1981): 29–47.

"Why Albert Lucas Did Not Serve in the New York Kehillah," *Proceedings of the American Academy for Jewish Research*: v. 51 (1984): 55–72.

"The Winnowing of American Orthodoxy," *Approaches to Modern Judaism II* (Chico, CA 1984), pp. 41–54.

"From Exception to Role Model: Bernard Drachman and the Evolution of Jewish Religious Life in America, 1880–1920," *American Jewish History* (June 1987): 456–484.

"The Americanization Continuum and Jewish Responses to Christian Influences on the Lower East Side, 1900–1910," *Christian Missionaries and Jewish Apostates*, Todd Endelman, ed. (New York: Holmes and Meier, 1987), pp. 255–271.

"A Generation Unaccounted For in *American Judaism*," *American Jewish History* (December 1987): 247–259.

"The Ramaz Version of American Orthodoxy," in *Ramaz: School, Community, Scholarship and Orthodxy*, Jeffrey S. Gurock, ed. (Hoboken, NJ: KTAV Publishing House, Inc., 1989), pp. 40–82.

"A Stage in the Emergence of the Americanized Synagogue Among East European Jews, 1890–1910," *Journal of American Ethnic History* (Spring 1990): 7–25.

"Time, Place and Movement in Immigrant Jewish Historiography," in *Scholars and Scholarship: The Interaction between Judaism and Other Cultures* (New York: Yeshiva University Press, 1990), pp. 169–185.

"In Search of the Other Jewish Center: On the Writing of the Social History of American Orthodoxy, 1900–1910," in *Reverence, Righteousness, and Rahamanut: Essays in Memory of Rabbi Dr. Leo Jung,* Jacob J. Schacter, ed. (Northvale, NJ: Jason Aaronson, 1992), pp. 131–146.

"How 'Frum' Was Rabbi Jacob Joseph's Court? Americanization Within the Lower East Side's Orthodox Elite, 1886–1902," *Jewish History* (Winter 1994): 1–14.

"Consensus Building and Conflict over Creating the Young People's Synagogue of the Lower East Side," *The Americanization of the Jews,* Norman J. Cohen and Robert Seltzer, eds. (New York: NYU Press, 1995), pp. 230–246.

"American Orthodox Organizations in Support of Zionism, 1880-1930." in *Zionism and Religion,* Samuel Almog, Jehuda Reinharz and Anita Shapira, eds. (in press).

Introduction:
The Historiographical Context

The freedom America has always granted its Jews, through the legal separation of Church and State, to either practice their religion or to voluntarily abandon connections with their faith, has posed unparalleled challenges to the continuity of Judaism in this country. The unequaled openness of American society and the desire of Jews who came to and advanced in this country to live harmoniously with their Gentile neighbors has, likewise, made difficult the perpetuation of Judaism. How Jews have defined these challenges and difficulties and have attempted to reconcile or preserve unchanged the traditions they remembered, or were told about, from Europe has been the underlying theme of all serious historical research that has examined Jewish religious activity in the United States.

The bulk of scholarship has focused on the reconcilers, the rabbis and lay leaders who attempted to find ways to accommodate Judaism to the powers of the American environment. Generally, that interest has translated itself into examinations of the Reform, Conservative and the Reconstructionist movements. After all, these liberal denominations have offered new approaches to how and when prayer services might be conducted in response to the needs of acculturating congregants and the perceived demands of the host culture. They have, likewise, tendered their own, modern understandings of Jewish law and tradition explaining, if not justifying, their innovative approaches. When analyses of these activities and views have been well executed, they have taken into account the efforts of neighboring Christian groups to maintain their own faith and faithful within a secular American society. The most useful works have also been sensitive to comparable styles and degrees of change that took place contemporaneously in European lands that influenced Jews here.

A few students of American Judaism have looked closely at the rabbis and other synagogue officials who have made every effort to resist changing the teachings and practices of the faith despite the pressures placed upon them by the host culture. In writing about resistance, and in identifying that response solely with Orthodox Judaism, these authors have examined the extent to which both Americans and other American Jews have permitted those who would not change to deviate from general society. Such historians have been sure to highlight how leaders of that traditional denomination have remained loyal to old patterns of thought and behavior even at the expense of losing many adherents to their cause. Studies of Orthodoxy have also frequently focused on the lack of tolerance that these preservers harbored towards other co-religionists who made very different types of peace with America.

My own analyses of American Judaism have strongly indicated that attitudes favoring reconciliation or accommodation, no less than the stance of resistance, have characterized Orthodoxy's encounter with America. I have argued, for example, that at every point in American Jewish history, different groups of rabbis, each calling themselves Orthodox, harbored fundamentally different views of how staunchly they should advocate or demand traditional observance from their congregants. Moreover, as my views and understanding of the history of Orthodoxy in this country has sharpened and deepened, I have pointed out that even as it is very useful to speak of Orthodox Jews as either resisters or as accommodators to America, it is almost as important to carefully calibrate both the degrees of deviance and the levels of acceptance that have characterized that group's response to America.

Not every rabbinic opponent of acculturation was equally committed to blocking out America and modernity from his life and from the lives of those who would follow him. Similarly, not all those who professed the viability of accommodation to America within traditional strictures were of the same mind as to how far their reconciliations might go. Variant approaches between and among rab-

binic resisters and accommodators often had much to do with
where they were trained. American-trained Orthodox rabbis usually
were more lenient than their European-born counterparts. Strict-
ness also had a lot to do with where the rabbi and his congregation
were situated in America. Typically, rabbis in large Eastern urban
centers were more dogmatic in their attitudes than colleagues who
worked in smaller Jewish communities. But even these very worth-
while educational or geographical determinants were not uniformly
predictive of how rabbis, in fact, behaved and performed in America.
Needless to say, the variety of responses among Orthodoxy lay leadership and its synagogued rank and file have been even more variegated, making their responses to the challenges of America even
more difficult to categorize.

What I have established as a conceptual framework for identifying
and interpreting the spectrum of Orthodox responses to America
might also be applied to the study of Conservative, Reform and
Reconstructionist Judaism. Although the accommodationist dimensions of these modern expressions of Judaism may be readily iso-
lated, liberal Jews and their leaders too have developed their own
multiple sets of strategies to preserve some—or most—of the basics
of Judaism's past. If anything, it can be argued that within each
denomination, at different times and places, a variety of determina-
tions have been made about how accommodating or resisting Jews
must be in response to America's challenges. Such considerations,
in their own way, make it clear that as much as denominational definitions are useful in classifying many synagogue, lay and rabbinic
activities, these labels are not always unqualifiably helpful in categorizing the myriad of American Jewish religious experiences.

I have arrived at these views of how the history of American
Orthodoxy and American Judaism in general should be conceptual-
ized as a result of close to twenty years of study which began when I
first recognized that what I had uncovered about the religious experience of one specific American Jewish community raised serious
questions about certain generally accepted historiographical traditions.

When I started work on *When Harlem Was Jewish, 1870–1930* (1978), I assumed, based upon my reading of the few standard and highly influential works in this field, that late nineteenth–early twentieth century American Orthodoxy evolved along one predominant path and direction, in a way that was altogether different from incipient Conservative Judaism; a movement with which it supposedly differed fundamentally. The regnant sociological--historical studies that had been composed during the 1950-early 1960s, all agreed that Orthodoxy during the era of East European migration was widely and determinedly antagonistic to change under America's impact. The generally-accepted story was that during the 1880–1920 period, those among the migrating masses who were sincere in their religious commitment aspired, under the guidance of their own rabbis from Russia and Poland, to transplant to these shores an Orthodoxy that resisted modernity and acculturation and was unqualifiably opposed to other forms of Judaism that were trying to reach immigrants and their children. So disposed, these rejectionists denigrated innovative efforts through the modern talmud torah to offer an educational model different from the transplanted heder or yeshiva. Similarly, they gave no support to initiatives to Americanize the synagogue, preferring their old-world *shtibls* instead. And, of course, the resisters had nothing but contempt for the leaders and philosophy of the Conservatives' Jewish Theological Seminary which was then finding its way in attempting to offer an American alternative to the forms of Judaism that these new arrivals were trying to perpetuate.

The four major works and the one seminal, oft-referenced article that established this historiographical tradition included Moshe Davis, *The Emergence of Conservative Judaism: The Historical School in Nineteenth Century America* (Philadelphia, 1963), Nathan Glazer, *American Judaism* (Chicago, 1957), Marshall Sklare, *Conservative Judaism: An American Religious Movement* (Glencoe, Ill., 1995), Will Herberg, *Protestant-Catholic-Jew: An Essay in American Religious Sociology* (Garden City, 1955) and Abraham J. Karp, "New York Chooses a Chief Rabbi," *Publications of the American Jewish Historical Society* (March, 1954): 127–198.

This historical school of thought did note a contemporaneous, indigenous brand of tolerant, acculturated Orthodoxy of Sephardic and Western European extraction that existed in communities far removed geographically, socially and attitudinally from the immigrants' world. In speaking of these religious uptown Jews, particular note was taken of the outlook and activities of Henry Pereira Mendes, rabbi of New York's Congregation Shearith Israel, America's oldest congregation, who was both a founder, in 1886, of the Jewish Theological Seminary and, a decade later, the first president of the Union of Orthodox Jewish Congregations of America. But, Mendes and his small coterie of rabbinic and lay colleagues, which included, among others, Rabbis Sabato Morais and Bernard Drachman and Lewis N. Dembitz were denominated as Orthodox in name alone.

These Americanized traditional Jews were, in fact, ultimately acclaimed as representatives of Historical School Judaism; categorized as implicit spokesmen for what would, in time, emerge as Conservative Judaism. For historian Moshe Davis, in particular, Mendes and his associates could never have been truly Orthodox because they neither feared enlightenment nor modernity, were optimistic about the capabilities of American Jews to find formulas for the perpetuation of Judaism, and were convinced that "*Klal Yisrael* is the historic basis for the unity of the people at all times and places." Davis was much more comfortable describing those who loosely constructed the traditional teaching that "Judaism can be adapted to changing conditions according to biblical and talmudic teachings' even as they adhered strictly to the "the traditional *mitzvot* [as] the basic condition . . . for a Jewish way of life" as a cooperative right-wing of a widely-embracing Historical School.[1] In all events, the Lower East Side and other comparable immigrant hubs, remained for these historians, the locus of the predominant, unmediated form of Orthodoxy. Downtown was the home of the old-world social and theological system that retained some currency within the immigrant generation but was ill-equipped to meet the religious needs of second generation Jews. Sociologist Marshall Sklare understood Orthodoxy's persistence in the ghetto as derived from its sturdy stance as "a cultural constant in the life of the disoriented newcomer, as a haven in the stormy new environment." But, he pointed out that as the integration of the immigrants proceeded, as they and their children aspired to be good neighbors with other Americans even as they achieved "unparalleled social mobility," they lost their affinity for East European ways and transplanted institutions. His fellow sociologist Will Herberg argued comparably that "because religion and immigrant culture were so thoroughly fused as to seem almost indistinguishable, the East European immigrants came up against a shattering crisis as they confronted the second generation, their American sons and daughters [who were] desparately anxious to become unequivocally American."[2]

For historian Abraham J. Karp, Rabbi Jacob Joseph symbolized resistance to America and his tragic career as Chief Rabbi of New York exemplified the impossibility of re-creating on voluntary American soil the traditions remembered from Eastern Europe. As Karp explained, Rabbi Joseph was given the unenviable and unattainable task of convincing a disorganized Orthodox community to follow his lead, to respect his ordinances and most importantly, to rally immigrants and their children to adhere to traditional ways even as American goals and mores forcefully lured them away from their parents' faith.[3]

Fortunately, it was said, for the ultimate survival of Judaism, as immigrants, and especially as second generation Jews acculturated, aspired to middle class status, and felt an intensifying disinclination for unmediated Orthodoxy, Conservative Judaism offered itself as a religious alternative to assimilation. For Sklare and his fellow sociologists Herberg and Nathan Glazer, the early suburban—or third settlement areas—of the 1920s were the place and time for the first sustained efforts on the part of those who advocated a highly practical mixture of Jewish traditions and American mores. And while Glazer, particularly, was quick to note that Jewish religious identification declined during the inter-war period, he also asserted that the denomination that the Seminary spawned offered a thoughtful and useful program to the disaffected. By emphasizing Jewishness more than Judaism for wavering second generation Jews, Conservative leaders, whether in their Americanized synagogues or their modern religious schools, were able to maximize their potential constituency as East European adjustment to America reached completion. These efforts also created a solid base for Conservative denominational hegemony during the "Jewish [religious] revival" of the subsequent, post-World War II era.[4]

I first became apprehensive that such neat chronological ranges and certain geographical settings and, above all, these tight denominational labels obscured the greater complexity and fluidity of American Jewish religious life when these static conceptualizations did not apply to Jewish Harlem in the first decade of this century. There, long before the 1920s, a second generation Jewish community evolved in a locale one step removed from downtown, that responded to disaffection with innovative Jewish educational and congregational programs. Moreover, the anti-assimilation forces in this second settlement community were led by a heterogeneous group of rabbis and lay people who defied easy categorization. Harlem's Uptown Talmud Torah, for example, which characterized itself as an Orthodox educational institution, was also the early home of the Teachers' Institute (T.I.) of the Jewish Theological Seminary and drew its own teachers from that professional training program. The principal of the T.I. was Rabbi Mordecai M. Kaplan, a 1902 graduate of the Seminary, who had served in an American Orthodox congregation attended by East European Jews in neighboring Yorkville. There he had associated harmoniously with Rabbi Moses Sebulun Margolies (Ramaz), who though officially a spokesman for the transplanted East European rabbinate, not only supported the modernization of synagogue activities in his congregation and but also served on the Board of Education of the Harlem talmud torah. In that latter capacity, Ramaz sat and deliberated with, among others, Reform lay worthies Louis Marshall and Jacob Schiff as well as with Dr. Israel Friedlander, an early spokesman for Conservative Judaism.[5]

A close examination of a second Harlem religious organization, the Institutional Synagogue, founded in 1917 by Rabbi Herbert S. Goldstein, again pointed to the existence of Americanized Orthodox synagogue life, fostered by East European Jews in a neighborhood outside of the immigrant enclave. There on 116th Street and Lenox Avenue, a determined Orthodox rabbi, who could boast both of *semicha* from a downtown colleague of Rabbi Jacob Joseph and of rabbinic ordination from the Seminary, established a congregation that honored and maintained all the strictures of the traditional religious service even as it created and promoted a myriad of ancillary American social, recreational and cultural activities to attract youngsters and their parents to synagogue life. In other words, up in Harlem before the 1920s, there was an Orthodox prototype of the very popular third settlement or suburban synagogue center that would later be roundly identified with the Conservatism of the inter-war or post-war periods. Thus, the histories of the Uptown Talmud Torah and the Institutional Synagogue had given me every indication that not all transplanted East European rabbis were advocates of resistance and that Orthodoxy had, in the pre-1920 period, a vibrant accommodationist strain—I would call it American Orthodoxy—that was cooperative with, but distinctive from, those who, early on, identified with Conservative Judaism.

It remained for "Resisters and Accommodators: Varieties of Orthodox Rabbis in America, 1883–1983" for me to speak broadly and comprehensively about the history of this distinctive American Orthodoxy. In that article, I readily accepted the notion that most transplanted East European rabbis opposed Americanization. Rabbi Jacob Joseph was for me too the paradigmatic nineteenth century resister. And I emphasized that avowed rejectionists both greater and lesser than the Chief Rabbi himself played fundamental roles in articulating Orthodox reactions in this new world. What was path-breaking about my study was its demonstration that throughout this entire century, Orthodoxy in this country harbored an alternative, tolerant and reconciled approach to Jewish group acculturation. Here, I differed fundamentally with Davis, for example, in arguing that even if Mendes and his friends differed from Rabbi Joseph in their social outlooks and shared the Historical School members' appreciation of American mores, they were never among the forefathers of twentieth century Conservative Judaism. Rather, they were the originators of their own independent American

Orthodox movement and were role models for American born or trained Orthodox rabbis of East European descent who, from the 1920s on, competed with Conservative spokesmen for the allegiances of second generation Jews and their children.[6]

Five years after the appearance of "Resisters and Accommodators," I applied an analogous conceptual framework to writing a historical overview of "The Orthodox Synagogue" in America and argued, once again, for a recognition of a long, independent history for American Orthodoxy. In that article, I asserted that from the very start of this country's life, Orthodox congregational spokesmen and functionaries have been of two minds in determining the stance their institutions would take towards the majority of American Jews who led lives clearly in variance from Orthodoxy's rendering of traditional law and behavior. Some leaders determined that their synagogues must neither accept nor accommodate those who did not recognize and obey past traditions. They sometimes denied synagogue rights to those publicly known to be less observant than the rule setters. Others within the Orthodox camp, on the other hand, have traditionally turned a blind eye to the heterogeneity of potential communicants. Needless to say, when officials of what I called "exclusionary" congregations engaged a rabbi, they usually opted for a religious guide who resisted Americanization. For their part, heads of "inclusionary" congregations have attempted to attract the largest number of Jews to their fold and usually favored a tolerant rabbi who would help them in their quests. And they have often purposefully instituted novel—but to their minds religiously permitted—liturgical, sermonic and ancillary synagogue activities. These congregations have frequently resorted to the same outreach techniques that liberal Jewish denominations, and even Christians, have used to present themselves as relevant to acculturated constituencies.

In making the case for the long-standing "inclusionary synagogue," I questioned Sklare, Herberg and Glazer's designation of Conservative Judaism as initially alone and then, as supreme in addressing the religious needs of immigrant Jews from Eastern Europe. I indicated that long before the suburbia of the 1920s and even before Harlem in the 1910s, efforts were made on the Lower East Side to fashion a Judaism that was fully faithful to traditional doctrine even as it related to American mores. I also emphasized that since the 1920s, these distinctive American Orthodox synagogues often competed successfully against their liberal Jewish counterparts for mass allegiances in all sorts of outer-city and suburban neighborhoods.

In the years that spanned the appearance of these two seminal articles and during the subsequent decade, I have refined my definitions of resistance and accommodation and have sharpened the periodization for understanding the evolution of American Judaism. As a result of sustained research, I would now argue that while most transplanted East European rabbis of the 1880–1920 period resisted Americanization, neither they nor their Agudath ha-Rabbanim (Union of Orthodox Rabbis of the United States and Canada, founded 1902), the organization to which hundreds of them belonged, were ever fully resolute in their desire to recreate in America the religious world they remembered from Rusia. Even Rabbi Jacob Joseph and his closest supporters harbored some noticeable ambivalencies towards the cause. Some actually gestured support for those with different views of how to properly perpetuate Jewish life in this country. Moreover, both the Chief Rabbi and most of his twentieth century successors, supported Zionism, always in its religious form and sometimes also in its secular dimensions. In so doing, these rabbis aligned themselves with a Jewish national movement which, in the minds of the clear majority of East European religious authorities was modernism incarnate. Each of these findings has also suggested to me how essential it is to understand the changing nature and decline of traditional Jewish communal life in Eastern Europe itself to fully comprehend the course of Orthodox resistance in America.

Meanwhile, my work on Albert Lucas, the Lower East Side's formest anti-missionary fighter, has showed me that while American Orthodox leaders of the early twentieth century were generally unified in their mission to address the religious needs of Americanizing youth, these accommodationists were of several minds in defining their priorities. They also differed widely in their willingness or unwillingness to work with Reform Jewish leaders in advancing their cause. For example, Lucas, the Orthodox Union's first Executive Secretary, believed wholeheartedly in the use of modern educational methodologies to teach traditional Jewish values. For him, it was one of the only ways of saving community children from the clutches of conversionists. Lucas was, however, just as strident in his belief that since the city's German Jewish elite shared neither his Orthodox understanding of Jewish tradition nor his anger and concern over the threat of missionaries, they could not be trusted allies. So disposed, Lucas and his small coterie of friends would have nothing to do with the German-dominated New York Kehillah, the 1910s Jewish communal umbrella organization. They preferred to work alone on their focused pursuit of missionaries. Other Orthodox Union officials set Lucas' concerns aside and worked comfortably with Schiff, Marshall and other uptowners in the larger campaign to rescue the next generation from the drift towards assimilation. In staking out his position, the British-born, English-speaking Lucas proved to be less of an accommodationist than the Russian-born, Yiddish-speaking Ramaz.

A decade and a half of continued investigations has also reinforced my appreciation that the Lower East Side at the turn of the century was the place and the time for the emergence of second generation Jews who had significant assimilation problems that were addressed by, among others, the lay and rabbinic leadership of American Orthodoxy. Through my biographical study of Bernard Drachman and in my explicit critiques of Glazer's periodization and of Sklare's and Herberg's stereotypical depiction of the nature of Jewish religious identity downtown, I have emphasized that by 1900, a full generation or more had passed since the beginnings of large scale East European Jewish migration to these shores. Enough time had passed for the emergence of what was then called "the rising generation in Israel," young American Jews who wanted to be comfortable in religious settings but who were estranged from their parents' old-world synagogues.

These needy young people were ministered to by friends of theirs from the downtown neighborhood, many of whom were then students at the Jewish Theological Seminary. During that era, though the Seminary was led by Conservative theologians and spokesmen, most of its students adhered to Orthodoxy and planned careers in service of that more traditional religious community. In doing their "field placements" among their own kind, these rabbis-in-training experimented with new ways of conducting the Orthodox services and in transmitting Jewish education under the watchful eyes and inspiration of senior American Orthodox rabbis like Drachman and Mendes. Most of these efforts were linked organizationally to the then-nascent Orthodox Union and were bankrolled by a new elite of East European origins. Some of these lay leaders who promoted modern Jewish education and the accepting and innovative synagogue within their own immigrant community had themselves arrived before 1881. They had, by 1900, begun to amass tidy fortunes and were anxious—like the German Jews before them—to be the acknowledged leaders of their community. The young rabbinical students who worked downtown carried these American Orthodox ideas and goals to second settlement areas in the 1910s and ultimately to inter-war suburbia even as many of their fellow Seminary classmates applied what they had learned on the Lower East Side to 1920s-1930s Conservative congregations across this country.

In shedding additional light on this critical time and place in Jewish denominational history, two of my historical case-studies have specifically addressed one of the more salient issues surrounding American Orthodoxy's rise: How receptive or how unreceptive—or how accepting or how resistant—were different Orthodox elements living and working in the downtown neighborhood to these incipient modern synagogue efforts. In "A Stage in the Emergence of the Americanized Synagogue among East European Jews, 1890–1910," I examined the religious life of, among others, some of the major *baalbatim* who, in the decade before they would support those young Seminary activists, moved their own synagogues away from the immigrant *shtibl* roots and towards acculturated stances. My "Consensus Building and Conflict . . ." detailed the efforts of the Jewish

Endeavor Society, the youth wing of the early Orthodox Union that was closely aligned with the Seminary, to permanently establish themselves downtown despite the opposition of those who were threatened by or jealous of their efforts.

Finally, two works of mine have raised questions about the fate of American Orthodoxy in the post-World War I period. These articles have followed that denomination's ongoing saga to almost the present day. "The Winnowing of American Orthodoxy" took its own critical look at Glazer, Sklare and Herberg's periodizations, specifically their understandings of where and how Conservatism rose to ascendancy as a popular alternative to old-line Orthodoxy and to assimilation. My study suggested that American Orthodoxy long persisted as a competitive religious option in a variety of geographical settings, particularly since the lines of demarcation between itself and Conservatism were largely blurred in the eyes of acculturated second and third generation congregants.

My explication of the educational philosophy and program of the school that since 1936 has carried Rabbi Margolies' name placed its own highly accommodationist orientation within the spectrum of American Orthodox attitudes of the past fifty years. Both of these efforts are also, in many ways, suggestive of the rich research possibilities that continue to exist in exploring American Orthodoxy, and American Judaism in general, during the eras that followed the close of mass East European migration to this country.

Resisters and Accommodators: Varieties of Orthodox Rabbis in America, 1886–1983

Introduction: Orthodox Rabbis and Institution Building, 1886–1887

On January 31, 1886, Orthodox Rabbis Sabato Morais of Philadelphia, Abraham Pereira Mendes of Newport, Henry Schneeberger of Baltimore, and Bernard Drachman of New York attended a meeting in the vestry rooms of Manhattan's Spanish-Portuguese Synagogue Shearith Israel hosted by Rabbi Henry Pereira Mendes, minister of that oldest Jewish congregation in America. They were brought together to plan an institutional response to the growth of the American Reform movement. Specifically they were concerned with the emergence of Hebrew Union College as a training center for American rabbis and with the liberal denomination's adoption of its 1885 Pittsburgh Platform, "designed," in the words of one contemporary critic, "to deal a mortal blow to Orthodox Judaism."[1] They were joined at this and subsequent deliberations by, among others, New York Rabbis Alexander Kohut, Aaron Wise, and Henry S. Jacobs, Philadelphia's Marcus Jastrow, and Baltimore's Aaron Bettelheim. The latter clerical figures, though possessed of rabbinical training similar in style to that of their Orthodox colleagues, had by the time of these conclaves publicly articulated, and were perceived as supporting, interpretations of Judaism at variance with contemporary Orthodox teachings:[2] These men also served in congregations which deviated liturgically from Orthodox practice. They represented what later denominational leaders and historians would describe as Conservative Judaism in nineteenth-century America.[3]

The Jewish Theological Seminary of America was the final product of their cooperative labors; a "Jewish Institute of Learning" which its first president, Sabato Morais, prayed would preserve "Historical and Traditional Judaism . . . by educating, training and inspiring teachers-rabbis who would stand for the 'Torah and Testimony.'" Graduates would use "their knowledge of Jewish learning, literature, history, ideals and Jewish Science" to instruct American Jewry how "to live as a power for human uplift and as a factor in the evolution of world civilization in both Americas."[4]

Institution building was also in the air several blocks south on New York's Lower East Side when just a year later the Association of American Orthodox Hebrew Congregations met at Norfolk Street's Beth Hamedrosh Hagodol to search for a chief rabbi for the city. They were desirous of putting an end to the disorganization and lack of discipline which characterized religious life in the ghetto. Perhaps inspired by the publication that same year of immigrant Rabbi Moses Weinberger's lament on contemporary non-observance and call for an authoritative religious officialdom as a key solution to the dilemma, this group of Orthodox laymen looked to Western and Eastern European seats of learning both for guidance and ultimately for a candidate. They hoped to find a zealous fighter of uncommon ability who would stop "open and flagrant desecration of the Sabbath, the neglect of dietary laws, and the formation of various shades of Orthodoxy and Reform." Most specifically, "his mission" would be "to remove the stumbling blocks from before our people. . . through his scrupulous supervision with an open eye the *shohatim* and all other matters of holiness." After much deliberation and some politicking on both sides of the Atlantic, an agreement was reached in April, 1888 between the association and Rabbi Jacob Joseph of Vilna. Three months later, the downtown community rejoiced when the renowned sage and preacher assumed his post in America.[5]

Central figures in each of these institutional initiatives called themselves Orthodox rabbis.[6] But they shared little in common. The most striking difference between the more traditional element in the Seminary coalition and the chief rabbi chosen by the downtown religious association was their respective educational backgrounds. The East European-born Rabbi Jacob Joseph received the traditional heder and yeshiva schooling in his hometown of Krohze, Lithuania, where he showed great promise as a scholar and potential religious leader. His quest for advanced training led him to the Volozhin Yeshiva, where he became a disciple of Rabbi Hirsch Leib Berlin and Rabbi Israel Salanter. Rabbi Joseph's homiletic and literary skills made him an accomplished speaker and writer in Hebrew and Yiddish. He was not exposed to formal education in the secular culture of the land of his birth. Not so his Sephardic counterparts, Morais and the Mendeses. A large part of their educational training was not in the world of the rabbis but in the realm of general knowledge. The Italian-born Morais attended the University of Pisa, while the younger, British-born Mendes studied first at University College, London, and then earned a medical degree at the University of the City of New York. Still, from early youth they were destined to become rabbis. Family traditions, or in Morais's case, close association with a leading rabbi of the home country provided the basis for their interest in and training for the Orthodox ministry of Western Europe and finally of America.[7]

On the other hand, the road to the Orthodox rabbinate of American-born Bernard Drachman and Henry W. Schneeberger was by no means pre-ordained. Drachman was born in New York City in 1861 to Galician and Bavarian parents and was raised in Jersey City, New Jersey, in a community which then housed but twenty or thirty Jewish families. By his own account, his earliest experiences in life were "very much like that of any American child in an ordinary American environment. He attended the local public schools and received his primary Jewish education first from a private tutor and later in a small talmud torah. A gifted student in both secular and religious studies, Drachman gained admission to Columbia University from where he graduated in 1882. He was recruited after grade school to be one of the first students at the Emanu-El Theological Seminary. This Reform-run "prep school" was designed "to give youths preliminary training required for the [Reform] rabbinate." "English-speaking rabbis," Drachman later recalled, "were then very rare in

America and members of the organization were desirous of supply-
ing this deficiency." Drachman was destined not to fulfill his patrons'
expectations, for upon graduation from Columbia and Emanu-El, he
shocked the religious school's officials by declaring that while he
intended to travel to Germany to study for ordination, it would not
be, as planned, at Geiger's Reform *Lehranstalt,* but rather at the
more traditional, Frankel-founded Breslau Seminary. Drachman
remained at Frankel's institution, which he defined as "in fundamental harmony on the basic concepts of traditional Judaism and its
adjustment to modern conditions," and received ordination in
1885. He then returned to New York and began his career as a spiritual leader who "insisted on maintaining the laws and usages of
traditional Judaism," possessed both of a rabbinical degree conferred
upon him by Dr. Manuel Joel of the Breslau Seminary and of that
city's Neue Synagogue and a Ph.D. from the University of Heidel-
berg.[8]

Henry W. Schneeberger, Drachman's colleague in the American-
born rabbinate, was born in 1848, also in New York City. The son of
a prosperous merchant from Central Europe, he attended New
York's public schools and Columbia Prep before enrolling in the university in 1862. His early religious training also paralleled Drachman's; he received his primary Jewish education from private tutors,
among whom was the famous anti-Christian polemicist Professor
Selig Newman. Upon graduation from Columbia in 1866, he too set
off for Europe, but in his case to study with Rabbi Azriel Hildesheimer; a man who, according to his student, stood for "moderate
orthodox views and its conservative principles." Schneeberger dedicated himself to his mentor's philosophy of uniting "an unimpaired
culture of the Jewish national religious sciences with a firm and
solid fundamental general education . . . to make . . . good Jews and
at the same time furnish them with social accomplishments that
can make them useful to society." Schneeberger returned to New
York in 1871 not only with Hildesheimer's ordination but also with
a Ph.D. from the University of Jena.[9]

These differences in training were strongly reflected in the way
each rabbi looked at the broader Jewish and general worlds around

him. The Sephardic rabbis were raised and educated not only among non-Jews but with Jews of every denomination and ethnic expression. Morais and Mendes were thus inured to interdenominational cooperation when they joined in the establishment of the Seminary. And although their work there was intended to stop Reform theological progress, they still perceived the Cincinnati-led group as an equal partner in community wide campaigns against common outside threats like the omnipresent missionary problem.[10] Schneeberger and Drachman had even less difficulty working with the forerunners of the American Conservative movement. After all, Schneeberger and his Conservative counterpart Aaron Wise had both been ordained by Hildesheimer, and Drachman, like Kohut, had been trained at Breslau. And although Wise and Kohut had broken with what Drachman and Schneeberger still defined as Western European Orthodoxy, they were still considered valuable colleagues in the battle for "the harmonious combination of Orthodox Judaism and Americanism which [for Drachman] was the true concept of the ancient faith of Israel."[11] Not surprisingly Drachman and Schneeberger too viewed Reform leaders as allies against outside threats.

Rabbi Jacob Joseph did not share these perceptions. Even if he could accept the legitimacy of the ordination of his more liberal Orthodox associates, he certainly had no time for, or interest in, those who had broken from the Orthodox fold.[12] From his European background, he knew of but one expression of Judaism, and it was to help save the faith from America that he had come to this country. Sabbath observance, the supervision of kosher meats, and the provision of immigrant children with a Jewish education were all in sorry disarray. He viewed it as his high task to lead a religious renaissance dedicated to the re-creation on voluntary American soil of the traditions left behind in Europe.[13]

Rabbi Jacob Joseph's more Americanized Orthodox counterparts shared his concern for the upgrading of traditional Jewish communal functions. Drachman later became head of an Orthodox Jewish Sabbath Alliance, which endeavored to convince Jewish shopkeepers to close their establishments on Saturday and petitioned the state legislatures to repeal blue laws which undermined the economics of traditional behavior.[14] But the motivation which drove and directed Drachman and his fellows' efforts stemmed from an altogether different understanding of the unique role to be played by Orthodox rabbis in America. They were trained to believe that resistance to modernization, in this case Americanization, was futile, and that any attempt to approximate in this country that which existed in the Old World was destined to fail. It was thus the job of the Orthodox rabbi in America to help his people mediate between their willing acceptance of the demands of acculturation and the increasingly problematic requirements of their ancestral identity. To them alone was given the task of creating a viable, truly American traditionalist alternative to the attractions of reformers. Rabbi Jacob Joseph, to their minds, was not equipped to address these issues.[15]

On a practical level this meant that while Rabbi Jacob Joseph harangued his listeners over their noncommitment to the Sabbath, Drachman worked to change American law to facilitate increased Jewish comfortableness with traditions. And while the East European spent most of his time supervising the meat markets, the Americanized expended their energies primarily in bolstering and modernizing Jewish education.[16] When Rabbi Joseph and his generation of downtowners looked at the heder, they would lament the low level of learning achieved by students and bemoaned the pitifully poor salaries paid to *melamdim*.[17] His Americanized counterparts too were appalled by the ineffectiveness of Jewish education, but for them, the solution began with the elimination of the European form of pedagogy and the providing of decent salaries to American-trained Jewish educators, who would teach a traditional Judaism relevant to the needs of new generations.

These categories of difference so apparent here among individuals and groups of rabbis each piously declaring themselves to be Orthodox has continued to characterize that denomination's rabbinate over the last one hundred years.[18] With certain notable exceptions or important subtle variations, training, institutional affiliations, and personal attitudes toward both emerging events and outside organizations have polarized the American Orthodox rabbinate into two camps: resisters and accommodators. The former have attempted to reject acculturation and disdained cooperation with other American Jewish elements, fearing that alliances would work to dilute traditional faith and practice. The latter have accepted the seeming inevitability of Americanization and have joined arms with less-traditional elements in the community so to perpetuate the essence of the ancestral faith. While the central issues facing each generation were different and the relative strength of each point has fluctuated, the basic split within the denomination has remained constant and from all contemporary indications will long endure.

The Issue of Immigrant Adjustment

If in 1887 Rabbi Moses Weinberger acknowledged and respected uptown traditional society, and Rabbi Jacob Joseph was at least ambivalent toward Drachman, Mendes, and their cohorts, East European Orthodox rabbinic opinion by 1902 was decidedly opposed to and strident in its nonrecognition of the Americanized Orthodox rabbinate. On July 29 of that year a group of sixty Orthodox rabbis hailing from Russia, Poland, and Austria-Hungary met in the auditorium of the Machzikei Talmud Torah on New York's East Broadway to formalize the creation of the Agudath ha-Rabbanim (Union of Orthodox Rabbis of the United States and Canada).[19] These clerical representatives of immigrant Jewish communities from Montreal, Toronto, Bangor, Omaha, and Denver were summoned to New York by Rabbis Asher Lipman Zarchy, Yehudah Leib Levine, Moses Sebulun Margolies (Ramaz), and Bernard Levinthal of Des Moines, Detroit, Boston, and Philadelphia, respectively. The mid-westerners had already, in a circular letter to their colleagues in July 1901, expressed their distress over "the constant desecration of the Torah" and spoke of a divine "obligation to unite and form a union of Orthodox rabbis."[20] The easterners helped concretize this declaration several months later when, in May 1902, they chaired a meeting of predominantly New England-based rabbis at Ramaz's Boston home.[21] There they drew up an agenda of concerns and set a tentative date for a national Orthodox rabbinic conclave for July in New York.[22]

The sobriety of this call was matched only by the somberness of the delegates as the deliberations began. The meeting was convened on the day of Rabbi Jacob Joseph's funeral. The senior rabbi had been a broken man from years of struggle to bring order to immigrant Jewish religious life and died a relatively young man of fifty-nine the very day representatives arrived for the conclave. And yet it seemed somehow appropriate that the business of the rabbis continued through the days of mourning, for theirs was the task of solving through a national organization the same problems which had confounded and, to a great extent, defeated their late, revered teacher.[23]

The assembled rabbis sought means of recalling back to Judaism immigrants and their children who were daily drifting from the faith and practices of the past. Jewish education, they determined, had to be upgraded, individuals and institutions had to be encouraged to observe the Sabbath more punctiliously, kashruth supervision had to be more scrupulously monitored, and the all-too-often abused marriage and divorce laws had to be upheld. The delegates also declared which individuals were qualified to lead this religious revival by restricting membership to "those rabbis ordained by the well-known scholars of Europe" who were "spiritual leaders of Orthodox congregations in the United States (and Canada)." In addition, all educationally prepared candidates had to abide by the association's regulations, which provided, among other stipulations, that no rabbi occupy a pulpit in a city served by a fellow member without the approval of the organization's executive board. The prevention of encroachment of a different kind was in the delegates' minds when they further resolved that "if an unqualified person settles in a community and poses as a rabbi, the *Agudah* will attempt to quickly influence him to leave. If. . . unsuccessful then the annual convention will determine his future."[24]

Under these provisions, three types of self-declared Orthodox rabbis were to be denied leadership roles in Agudath ha-Rabbanim's efforts to reach immigrant generations as well as the mutual aid and charity benefits of organizational ties.

1. *The unqualified rabbi.* The Reverend Samuel Distillator; who advertised his varied talents of *shohet, mohel,* and *mesader kidushin* in local New York newspapers around the turn of the century, typifies the unwanted entrepreneurial rabbi who seemingly served constituencies without benefit of clerical certification.[25]

2. *The politically uncooperative rabbi.* It is noteworthy, but not surprising, that at least two of Rabbi Jacob Joseph's contemporaries, Rabbis Hayim Yaacov Widerwitz of Moscow and Joshua Segal, were not charter members of the Agudath ha-Rabbanim. The former was educated "at Hasidic yeshivas" and served in Moscow for fifteen years until 1893, when he settled in New York. His colleague, the so-called Sherpser Rov, arrived in the United States in 1875 and lived out his life in the metropolis. These men were better known by their respective American titles of "Chief Rabbi of the United States" and "Chief Rabbi of the Congregations of Israel," "counter"-chief rabbis who opposed Rabbi Jacob Joseph's hegemony, particularly in the area of kosher meat supervision, in the 1890s. Men like Widerwitz and Segal were less than beloved to those who had mourned Rabbi Jacob Joseph's passing. And for their part, they had little interest in surrendering their autonomous authority, including their control of numerous abattoirs and butcher shops, to any ecclesiastical committee.[26]

3. *The American Orthodox rabbi.* By 1902 Rabbis Drachman, Schneeberger, and Mendes had been joined in the Americanized Orthodox rabbinate by Western European-trained colleagues Joseph Asher, David Neumark, and Henry S. Morais, and by men like Joseph Hertz, Herman Abramowitz, Julius Greenstone, and Mordecai M. Kaplan of the first pre-1902 generation of Seminary graduates.[27] None of these clerical figures was invited to join the Agudath ha-Rabbanim. But they were not written out of organizational affiliation because of the place and method of their ordination; the Agudath ha-Rabbanim's own house historian declared in 1902 that "the first students that graduated from there [the Seminary] were full-heartedly for the faith of Israel and its Torah."[28] Their nonacceptance was predicated, more directly, upon their divergent views on how to best solve the problems articulated by the Agudath ha-

Rabbanim and upon their perceived attempt to undermine immigrant confidence in ghetto rabbinic authority. The Agudath ha-Rabbanim's policy of nonrecognition of and noncooperation with the American Orthodox rabbinate was expressed most emphatically two years after its founding when it announced its opposition to the Union of Orthodox Jewish Congregations of America, a synagogal association founded by Mendes and his Americanized associates just six years earlier.[29]

The Orthodox Union was called into existence in 1898 to protect "Orthodox Judaism whenever occasions arise in civic and social matters . . . and to protest against declarations of Reform rabbis not in accord with the teachings of our Torah."[30] Practically this meant that Drachman, Mendes, and some younger colleagues fought against blue laws, protected the rights of Sabbath observers, advocated the modernization of Jewish educational techniques, and argued that they, far more than the uptown Reform forces, had the best Jewish interests of the immigrants at heart. The Agudath ha-Rabbanim was unimpressed by their activities. To them, the Orthodox Union was a poorly disguised agent of Americanization which preached a synthesis of Jewish and American methods and values which threatened the continuity of the faith. To Agudath ha-Rabbanim minds, Orthodox Union leaders, bereft of their own constituency uptown, where Reform held sway, were sweeping into the ghetto and—not unlike the universally despised Christian missionaries—were seeking to wean East European Jews away from their traditional religious commitments.[31]

The Agudath ha-Rabbanim was probably most disturbed by the Orthodox Union's understanding of and approach to meeting the crisis of turn-of-the-century Jewish education. For the downtown rabbis, the American heder and yeshiva system had only to be faulted for its failure to produce scholars who would continue the intensive study of rabbinic law and who would ultimately produce talmudic novellae on American soil. The Jewish community had to be severely chastised for its unwillingness to support these traditional institutions of study. It refused to grant all due respect to the scholars from Europe who labored unnoticed in the intellectual wasteland of America. Probably most Agudath ha-Rabbanim members knew little of their Christian contemporary Hutchins Hapgood's writings on ghetto civilization. But had they read him, they undoubtedly would have agreed with his assessment of the life of "the submerged scholars" of the ghetto, men who "no matter what . . . attainments and qualities" were unknown and unhonored "amid the crowding and material interests of the new world."[32] The Agudath ha-Rabbanim attempted to solve this dilemma by approximating in America the internal conditions which sustained the great East European yeshivas they had left behind. Yiddish, they thus asserted, should be the preferred language of religious instruction, since it is "the language of the children's parents." English would be used only "when necessary," such as in communities where no Yiddish was spoken. The attainment of a solid, albeit separatistic, yeshiva education was deemed the goal for all Jewish pupils. Indeed, the Agudath ha-Rabbanim's Yeshiva Committee was called upon to "supervise the . . . subjects taught in the yeshiva . . . lest the students regard the yeshiva simply as a stop over before they pursue advanced secular studies."[33]

Advocates of modern Jewish education shared none of these perceptions or prescriptions. Drachman expressed their position best when he defined the goals of Jewish education as the training of Jewish boys and girls through English-language instruction "to perform all the duties, to think all the thoughts and to feel the emotions which are the historical heritage of those of the household of Israel." This love for the Jewish heritage, he further emphasized, was unobtainable either in the heder, through private tutors, or through the all-day Jewish parochial school system. He spoke strongly for what would later be called "released time," an "ideal program" which would reach the disaffected and unaffiliated children of immigrants "during the day when children are awake and interested." But his greatest dream was of an efficient Jewish after-public-school program, "a great system of Jewish public schools housed in their own buildings and equipped with all pedagogic requirements to supplement the general public school system." There, of course, the traditions of the past would be transmitted through the language of the new land.[34]

Agudath ha-Rabbanim leaders also witnessed with great concern the efforts of Orthodox Union members to modify the trappings and change the aesthetics of Orthodox synagogue life. It was the American Orthodox rabbis' perception that a major cause of the disaffection from Judaism of immigrants and even more of the second generation was their uncomfortableness with the noisy and undignified *landsmanshaft* synagogue service. These congregations, linking Jews from the same hometown or region, offered the opportunity to pray and socialize in an Old World setting. For Agudath ha-Rabbanim members, the *landsmanshaft* synagogue represented the institutional expression of religious identity steeped in their European traditions.

But Orthodox Union members argued that "*landsmanshaft* Judaism" was in deep trouble. The immigrant synagogue undeniably helped succor the newly arrived in encountering America by providing him/her with the familiar ritual and social flavor of the other side. However, as the immigrant inevitably progressed in this country, and became infused with new American mores, this Judaism rooted in what Union people felt was only nostalgia for the past was declared devoid of any chance of surviving the external societal pressure upon them to live and act as Americans.

The Jewish Endeavor Society (JES), founded in 1901 by the early students and first rabbis produced by the pre-Schechter Seminary, sought to address this socioreligious dilemma. As students and later as ordained rabbis, Herman Abramowitz, Julius Greenstone, and Mordecai M. Kaplan were among those inspired by their teacher Drachman to offer acculturating immigrants on the Lower East Side, and later on in Harlem and Philadelphia, Jewish educational and cultural programs and "dignified services" designed to "recall indifferent Jewry back to their ancestral faith." The "young people's synagogues" established under the auspices of the JES held services on Sabbaths and holidays, more often than not in the late afternoon, probably to attract those who had been working until evening on these Jewish holy days. The society's leaders characterized their ser-

vices as Orthodox, an assertion buttressed by their use of the traditional prayerbook and their insistence upon the separation of the
sexes. But in other ways, the services differed dramatically from
those in the *landsmanshaft* synagogue. Recognizing the growing
unfamiliarity of Jews with Hebrew, they instituted supplementary
English-language prayers and considered the substitution of English
translations for standard prayers. A weekly English sermon on topics related to the American Jewish experience was standard. Congregational singing in English and Hebrew was encouraged. And all
overt signs of commercialism were eliminated from congregational
life.[35]

Not surprisingly, these youthful efforts gained the quick and active
support of rabbis associated with the Orthodox Union. Henry S.
Morais, H. P. Mendes, Joseph M. Asher, David Newmark, and of
course Drachman all lectured to the JES membership and taught
society-run classes. Indeed the Jewish Endeavor Society could be
fairly described during its nearly ten years of existence as the "youth
division" of the Orthodox Union.[36]

This new approach to synagogue life was neither rapidly nor universally accepted by downtown society and its rabbinate. The itinerant preachers *(maggidim)* who spoke to crowds of worshippers on
Sabbath and holiday afternoons did not appreciate the society's
competition for synagogue space. More respected and established
Agudath ha-Rabbanim constituents had more profound philosophical differences with the movement and its leaders. Foremost was the
fear that the infusion of American-style trappings and social activities was simply the first step toward the abandonment of traditional
Judaism's theological teachings. Secondly, but almost as important,
they were concerned that the leaders of the Orthodox Union, in
their zeal to promote their Americanization-Judaism synthesis, con-
sorted with Reform Jews who engaged in similar methods with the
purpose of weaning immigrant Jews from their religious past. In
April 1904 the Orthodox Union, which supposedly stood for "protest
against declarations of Reform rabbis," sat with leaders of the
Reform Emanu-El Brotherhood, Temple Israel, and the West Side
Synagogue to consider a report drafted by the interdenominational

Board of Jewish Ministers to coordinate the endeavors of the several young people's synagogues which had sprung up since 1900. In the Agudath ha-Rabbanim's view, the Orthodox Union was at best lending unfortunate recognition to deviationist Jewish movements and at worst threatening the continuity of the faith through cooperation with the liberals.[37]

The Agudath ha-Rabbanim's nonrecognition of the Orthodox Union also led to the seemingly unnecessary duplication of efforts on issues of common concern. Rampant nonobservance of the Sabbath, for example, was a problem which exercised traditional leaders of all stripes. The Agudath ha-Rabbanim placed Sabbath preservation beside educational improvement as its highest communal priority and maintained a standing Sabbath Committee "to strengthen its observance among our people." The Orthodox Union also spoke out both institutionally and individually for the cause. Drachman specifically served for more than a quarter century as president of the Jewish Sabbath Observers Association, founded in 1894. But there is no evidence of the Agudath ha-Rabbanim and the union working together to promote the Sabbath cause during the organizations' first generation of activity.[38]

This evident lack of teamwork, however; did not lead to large-scale waste through the duplication of communal energies. The Agudath ha-Rabbanim and the Orthodox Union each attacked the problem somewhat differently, reflecting their own unique understandings of the functions of the Orthodox rabbinate in leading the immigrant community. Downtown leaders perceived as a prime concern the identification for the truly observant of those establishments, particularly butcher shops and bakeries, which violated the Sabbath. They encouraged their followers not to patronize such concerns and exhorted both these public violators and the Jewish community at large to return to traditional behavior. The Agudath ha-Rabbanim initiated forays for the cause outside its own circumscribed constituency when it appealed to Jewish trade unionists to make "Sabbath-day off" a demand in owner-worker negotiations. And it hoped to influence "Jewish charitable organizations to set up divisions to seek employment for Sabbath observers." But it stayed away from external community-directed efforts, the hallmark of the Orthodox Union actions.[39]

The American rabbis disdained preacherlike exhortations and addressed themselves to American conditions which encouraged religious violations. They communicated with Jewish businessmen and employers, but their primary brief was with the American legislative system, which grudgingly retained discriminatory blue laws. These regulations prevented Jews from trafficking on Sunday, forcing them to desecrate their Sabbath to work an economically viable week. The Orthodox Union also spoke out clearly against the practice of holding State Regents, school, and civil service examinations only on Saturday. And they protected Jewish children destined to be punished for skipping school on Jewish holidays. The members of the Jewish Sabbath Observers Association worked hardest to promote traditional practice through Albany legislation. The leaders of the Agudath ha-Rabbanim held sway more comfortably on East Broadway.[40]

The Orthodox Union rabbis' self-perception as public protectors of the immigrant's religious rights in America also led them to the forefront of campaigns against school sectarianism and outright missionary activities. To be sure, Henry P. Mendes's interest in these concerns clearly predated the founding of his organization. He was instrumental in the creation in 1880 of the Envelope Society, which helped sponsor the Hebrew Free School Association, established to fight missionary successes downtown. As leader of the Orthodox Union, he presided over organizational deputations to public school officials to eliminate Christian celebrations from the schools. The Orthodox Union would ultimately sponsor a successful boycott of the New York schools in 1906. Mendes, Drachman, and Asher were among the names always associated with the establishment of Jewish mission schools in the ghetto to combat the Christian mission homes. Through its lay leadership the Orthodox Union went so far as to join hands with a Catholic priest in fighting Protestant so-called nonsectarian influences in the poor Jewish and Catholic areas.[41]

The Agudath ha-Rabbanim did not criticize these activities, but it neither joined the union's antisectarianism fight nor initiated any parallel campaign of its own. Its more narrow, internally-looking communal agenda spoke to other issues—problems which, significantly, the Americanized rabbis did not emphasize.

Ultimately, the Agudath ha-Rabbanim was less concerned that American law respect the immigrant Jew and more interested that the new American continue to respect Jewish law. The organization's view of the problems of immigrant Jewry was probably best summed up by Rabbi Jacob David Willowski of Chicago. Earlier in his life Willowski had declared from Europe that "America is a *treif* land where even the stones are impure." Nonetheless he eventually found his way to these shores, and in 1904 he wrote: "All [these problems] are to be blamed on the land [of freedom] where groups with varying viewpoints and opinions came to be settled and no one recognizes any authority."[42]

So disposed, Agudath ha-Rabbanim members worked to reinvigorate the transplanted rabbis' authority in voluntaristic America as a means of leading immigrant Jews back toward greater observance of traditional Jewish law, often clearly in resistance to the pressures of Americanization. Orthodox Union rabbis formulated their labors based on the assumption that the clerical figure who saw Judaism as a faith in opposition to America would fail to sustain both himself and his community. Rather it was the job of the American rabbi to help present the essence of Jewish identity to the immigrant, regardless of his degree of traditional religious practice, as compatible with the inevitable American identity. And as we will presently see, Orthodox Union rabbis also recognized that they could not do the job alone.

In the winter of 1909, the opportunity for Orthodox rabbis to cooperate with Jews of varying stripes in reinvigorating the immigrant's sense of belonging to his community came to hand in the form of the New York Kehillah. This citywide umbrella organization was initially called into existence as a response by Jews—both immigrants and established Americans—to anti-Semitic allegations of Jewish criminality on the Lower East Side. It soon began to address itself to the broader questions of Jewish religious and cultural survival. High on its list of communal priorities was the creation of the Jewish "public school system" Drachman and others had earlier called for; attractive to new immigrants and capable of calling back to Jewish identification those who were rapidly assimilating. Temple Emanu-El's Rabbi Judah L. Magnes served as the chairman of the movement, which numbered such German-Jewish Reform lay worthies as Jacob H. Schiff, Felix Warburg, Daniel Guggenheim, and Louis Marshall as its major financial backers. As the Kehillah idea moved closer to realization, Orthodox rabbis were faced with the following dilemma: could they work with, indeed trust, Reform Jews in the development of their own Orthodox institutions in America? Cooperation with the rich philanthropists would bring significant sums to the impoverished field of Jewish education. But would cooperation eventually lead to co-optation, as Reform Jews forced both American and assimilatory ideologies upon the consciousness of Jewish youth?[43]

The American Orthodox rabbis associated with the Orthodox Union did not fear association with the Kehillah. Though loyal to their union's mandate to "protest against declarations of Reform rabbis not in accord with the teachings of our Torah," they had no predisposition toward opposing all efforts led by Reform Jews solely because of their denominational label. True to this formula, the Orthodox Union lent support to the Kehillah in 1909, albeit with some reservations, arguing that the institution should be given a chance "if the Kehillah can help not merely Judaism but Orthodox Judaism." They agreed with the Kehillah's plan to make the talmud torah system a bastion of both Americanization and Judaism, so long as instruction would be in keeping with Orthodox traditions when Judaism was taught. And if they harbored fears that their liberal brethren did not really understand the faith's requirements, they kept their apprehensions to themselves. Besides, they trusted their own ability to monitor the educational activities from within. Drachman and Mendes were charter members of the Jewish Community's ruling executive committee, and Mordecai M. Kaplan served on the Kehillah's first education committee.[44]

The East European-born Orthodox rabbinate—primarily but not exclusively those affiliated with the Agudath ha-Rabbanim—was initially highly suspicious of the Kehillah's designs. They feared that this American institution, led by unreliable Reform leaders and lay-men, would ultimately seek "to undermine the Orthodox institu-tions of the Jewish Quarter." Soon after the Jewish Community became a reality, however; Agudath ha-Rabbanim leaders recog-nized that Kehillah power and money might be utilized, ironically, to strengthen their hold as religious authorities in the ghetto. As thoughts of a tenuous *modus vivendi* began to be expressed in East European Orthodox circles, some rabbis even started to consider the possibility of their co-optation of the citywide construct.[45]

This change of attitude stemmed directly from the Kehillah Execu-tive Committee's call in December 1909 for the establishment within its multifarious city-wide structure of a Vaad ha-Rabbanim, "a committee of recognized and authoritative rabbis for the control of the whole matter of kashruth and shechita and other religious matters." Perceptive Agudath ha-Rabbanim members immediately understood that in its desire to bring all groups of Jews and all Jew-ish issues under its banner, the Kehillah was willing to formally rec-ognize men like them as the officialdom in charge of "all matters such as kashrus, milah, mikveh (etc.), concerning which no differ-ences of opinion as to the *Din* exist." An infrastructure was being created, albeit by the "wrong people," which could ultimately lead to the resuscitation of the traditional Jewish community, with pow-erful rabbis at the head, in religiously-barren voluntaristic America. If direction of Jewish education could only be wrested away from the Kehillah's acculturationist cum assimilationist Reform Jewish founders and their American Orthodox rabbinic supporters, they could emerge from this initial limited partnership in effective control of the New York Jewish community. Through these most round-about of means, the dreams of Rabbi Weinberger and the hopes of Rabbi Jacob Joseph would be fulfilled. So disposed, twenty-three of the Agudath ha-Rabbanim's forty-six New York-based members joined the thirty-two-member Kehillah Vaad ha-Rabbanim, founded in 1912. Their game-plan was to use the threat of immediate withdrawal from the Kehillah to extend their influence in the field of education, a strategy which Kehillah officials staunchly resisted.[46]

With all its inherent weaknesses and potentialities for conflict, this tenuous marriage of interests could not have even been considered without the efforts of two highly influential pre-World War I Orthodox leaders who simply did not fit the mold of the transplanted East European rabbi, Rabbi Philip Hillel Klein of Harlem's First Hungarian Congregation Ohab Zedek and Ramaz (Rabbi Moses Sebulun Margolies) of Yorkville's Congregation Kehilath Jeshurun. The basic sympathies of these exceptional men were with the harmonization of Judaism with American values, and they perceived American Orthodox rabbis, if not Conservative rabbis and Reform leaders, as worthy colleagues. But as astute communal politicians, they still aspired to maintain influence in all religious power bases, even going so far as to stand at the head of avowed anti-Americanization institutions. Accordingly, both of these men were leaders of the Agudath ha-Rabbanim. Ramaz was its long-time president, and Klein, for several years, was an honorary president. Yet while both stood at the helm of an organization which opposed the Kehillah's Americanization assumptions and which seemingly did not recognize other rabbis as equal colleagues, they simultaneously served as members of the Kehillah's governing executive committee. In the latter capacity, Ramaz and Klein served with Drachman and Mendes on the committee of religious organization, which developed the Vaad ha-Rabbanim proposal. And in 1911, Ramaz participated in the Executive Committee's Educational License Bureau, a committee which included Rabbi Mordecai M. Kaplan, then principal of the Jewish Theological Seminary's Teachers Institute, a Dr. Langer, principal of the German Reform-run Educational Alliance School, and Dr. Samson Benderly, director of the Kehillah's own Bureau of Education.[47]

These seemingly conflicting affiliations surprised no one who had followed either man's American career. The Hungarian-born Klein arrived in the United States in 1890, eleven years after his ordination by Rabbi Azriel Hildesheimer. Possessed also of a Ph.D. from the University of Jena, Klein, as rabbi of a growing, prestigious immigrant congregation, found he had much in common with the Western European-trained Rabbis Drachman, Asher; Henry Morais, and Mendes. His shared interests and concerns led him to join in the founding of the Orthodox Union in 1898. And yet six years later; he emerged as an early member of Agudath ha-Rabbanim, which did not recognize his friends and opposed their organization. In fairness, one might suggest that Klein, by virtue of his "modern" Orthodox training with Hildesheimer and his secular university degree, may not have initially agreed with the Agudath ha-Rabbanim's philosophy. This conceivably marginal member of Agudath ha-Rabbanim was indeed not among the American-based European rabbis called to the initial gathering of the Agudath ha-Rabbanim. But election to that rabbinic body did not change him. In fact, as he rose in the organization, he continued to work with the American Orthodox rabbinate. And finally, in 1909, when his own congregation moved up from downtown's Norfolk Street to Harlem and attracted both new immigrants and more acculturated and second-generation Jews to his pulpit, he agreed to work with Drachman as his rabbinic associate. Klein preached in Yiddish and Hungarian, primarily to the older generation; his colleague spoke in English. No greater recognition of the reliability of the American Orthodox rabbinate could be given by a leader of Agudath ha-Rabbanim than to share his pulpit with the Orthodox Union's "second in command."[48]

Ramaz's activities and associational patterns also belied his position as a head of the Agudath ha-Rabbanim. Rabbi Margolies was born and raised in Kroza, Russia. He attended yeshivot in his hometown, Bialystock, and Kovno before serving as rabbi in Slobodka (1877–99). He migrated to America in 1899 and served as unofficial chief rabbi of Boston. It was, strikingly, in his New England home that the agenda for the founding of the Agudath ha-Rabbanim was drawn up. Though seemingly in accord with his organization's definition of rabbi, upon assuming the post of rabbi of an affluent, uptown New York pulpit in1905, he acceded to working with Rabbi Mordecai M. Kaplan, a graduate of the pre-Schechter Seminary and a major spokesman for the Jewish Endeavor Society. As in the case of Klein and Drachman, Margolies and Kaplan shared ministerial duties. Margolies appealed to the older generation; Kaplan began building his career of youth-centered activities.[49]

Ramaz also broke with the Agudath ha-Rabbanim's policies when he served on the board of education of the Uptown Talmud Torah, beginning in 1908. By 1911 he had become head of that group, which included Rabbi Israel Friedlaender of the Seminary and German Reform lay leaders Schiff and Marshall. This organization advocated, even before 1910, many of the American educational innovations which Drachman wanted and which ultimately became part of the Kehillah's programming. Thus, it was quite natural that Ramaz, like Klein, informed by almost a decade of cooperation with Jews of varying stripes in searching for American Jewish solutions to the problems of immigrant identification, would find his way into the leadership of the Kehillah. How and why he and Klein remained powerful in the rejectionist Agudath ha-Rabbanim is a separate question.[50]

The hoped-for working alliance between the Vaad ha-Rabbanim and the Kehillah did not, however; long survive. Magnes's group zealously protected their authority over Jewish education. They stated categorically in 1912 that while the Kehillah would "at all times welcome every recommendation that may be made to it. . . by the Vaad ha-Rabbanim," it would not bind "itself to same." The Vaad, for its part, led by Rabbi Shlomo Elchanan Jaffe of Norfolk Street's Beth Medrosh Hagodol and East Harlem's Rabbi Samuel Glick, held its ground as ritual authority and worked to extend its influence to education. Its activities prompted Israel Friedlaender to quip "that it was in bad taste to connect the matter of kashrus with that of education."

As time went on, even the powers granted the Vaad did not go unchallenged. In December 1912 Mendes stated that "while the rabbis of the Board were perfectly competent to deal with the matters of schechita and kashrus, there were other subjects, such as 'get,' Sabbath legislation, and milah which required the activities of rabbis and laymen who were in better touch with conditions in this country." By 1914, its dream of communal co-optation now dead, the Vaad's leaders decided it had no stake in the Kehillah. Contending that "the session or time allowed for daily instruction by the [Kehillah's Education] Bureau, for the schools affiliated with it, was insufficient for effective religious training," Vaad members seceded from the Jewish Community and began working independently.[51]

Leading the Vaad out of the Kehillah were the very men who had brought it in initially, Rabbis Klein and Margolies. In August 1914 both resigned from the executive committee. Klein cited "poor health" and complained that the committees he served upon did not "call upon [his] specialized sphere of knowledge." Ramaz resigned with the allegation that in "all matters pertaining to religion [that] should be referred to the Board of Rabbis to be acted upon. . . the Board of Rabbis was ignored entirely."[52]

The departure of Klein and Margolies from the Kehillah did not mark a decline in their dedication to the spirit of the Kehillah's endeavors or to participation in Americanization efforts. It certainly did not end their close collegial association with American Orthodox rabbis. Klein continued to work harmoniously with Drachman in the Ohab Zedek pulpit through the beginning of the 1920s. Ramaz continued to serve on the Uptown Talmud Torah's board of education even as that school became one of the Kehillah's flagship institutions. This institution was the home of the Seminary-run, Kehillah-financed Teachers Institute, which Mordecai M. Kaplan directed. Most significantly, in 1913, after some three years of serving alone in his synagogue's pulpit, Ramaz agreed to the appointment of Rabbi Herbert S. Goldstein, an American-born and trained rabbi, possessed of a unique dual ordination. He had been ordained as an Orthodox rabbi by Rabbi Shlomo Elchanan Jaffe, an Agudath ha-Rabbanim worthy, and in 1913 he had received a rabbinical diploma from the Seminary, where he had been a student of Kaplan's.[53]

Significantly, Goldstein's Schechter-era Conservative ordination did not disqualify the Columbia University-educated cleric, one of the last of the Drachman-Schneeberger generation of Orthodox rabbis, in Ramaz's eyes. The senior rabbi was also seemingly untroubled by Goldstein's outspoken public criticism of the social capabilities of the East European Orthodox rabbinate. In a front-page editorial in the *Hebrew Standard,* published in June 1915, Goldstein declared that the preservation of "the Judaism of the future" lay solely in the hands of "the young, university-trained Orthodox rabbi." Only they, he argued, could assist the "scientifically-trained, skeptical young Jew, reconcile what he learned in the public school and college with the ancient doctrines of his faith." Only those "reared on American soil, who have breathed the ideal of American democracy, who have been born and bred like other Americans," could minister to the acculturated intent on breaking down the ghetto walls to "live as their neighbors, their fellow citizens, the Americans."[54]

Ramaz overlooked Goldstein's difference in training and tacitly accepted his social orientation, because to a great extent he agreed with his colleague's understanding of Judaism's requirements in America. Ramaz and Goldstein apparently worked harmoniously in the Kehilath Jeshurun pulpit for five years. Ramaz ministered to the first generation, Goldstein attended their children. Finally, in 1917, ambition and the drive for even greater youth-directed programming led Goldstein to leave Yorkville to found the Institutional Synagogue in neighboring Harlem.[55]

Though Rabbis Klein and Margolies were the most renowned East European-born and trained clerics who willingly and consistently cooperated with Jews of differing theological confessions both within the Kehillah and without, they were not the only New York-based immigrant Orthodox rabbis to lead lives dedicated to the harmonization of Jewish tradition with Americanization. The thoughts and activities of Rabbis Shmarya Leib Hurwitz and Zvi Hirsch "Harris" Masliansky also departed forcefully from the patterns of rabbinic attitude and behavior promoted by the Agudath ha-Rabbanim. Masliansky was generally recognized as the most outstanding Yiddish-language preacher on the Lower East Side at the turn of the century. But he did not share the common proclivity of the downtown *maggidim* to oppose religious innovation. Born in 1856 in Slutzk, Minsk, Russia, into a rabbinic family, he was educated in yeshivot in Mir and Volozhin. Ordained in 1880 by Rabbi Isaac Elchanan Spektor of Kovno and Rabbi Samuel Mohilever of Bialystock, he spent the early years of his rabbinate as a teacher and preacher in Eastern Europe. There he worked enthusiastically to increase popular support for the then nascent Zionist cause. Banished from Russia in 1894 for his controversial public utterances on Jewish nationalism, he migrated to the United States and immediately began to speak out for Zionism and for the Jew's need to acculturate to America short of abandoning tradition.[56]

Masliansky's attitude toward Americanization soon became known to German-American Jewish leaders, who in 1898 appointed him the first official lecturer in Yiddish at the Educational Alliance. Masliansky's appointment represented a signal departure from the Americanizing institution's earlier policies of disdaining the cultural-linguistic baggage of its immigrant clients. Now, through him, the Alliance sought to begin bridging the widening chasm between Yiddish-speaking parents and their quickly acculturating children. Similar awakened sensitivities led Louis Marshall, four years later, to call upon Masliansky's assistance in launching his *Yiddishe Welt* as an organ dedicated to encouraging rapid acculturation through the medium of the Yiddish tongue.[57] It is thus not surprising to find Masliansky at the founding of the Orthodox Union in 1898, in the forefront of supporters of the Jewish Endeavor Society in the early 1900s, and as a consistent supporter of the Kehillah from its inception to its ultimate decline. Masliansky publicly expressed his approach toward cooperation with the Drachmans and Mendeses of the Jewish community, not to mention the Marshalls and Schiffs, when he declared in homiletic fashion that before Orthodox Jews vocally opposed the miscasting of Jewish tradition represented by the Reform movement, let them first learn from their liberal colleagues how to organize communal life, "how to honor leaders, and how to give charity." "There will come a time," he prophesied, "when Judah [Orthodoxy] and Ephraim [Reform] will be united, but first let Judah be united in its own territory."[58]

Shmarya Leib Hurwitz also had credentials as a preacher from Eastern Europe, but he built his reputation in this country primarily as a Jewish educator who, possessed of an impeccable Orthodox pedigree, accepted the modern pedagogic methods promoted by the Kehillah. Hurwitz was born in the town of Kritchev in the province of Mogilev, Russia, in 1878. A scion of a Chabad Hasidic family, he attended yeshivot in Mstislav and Shamyachi before serving as a rabbi in Yekaterinoslav from 1899 to 1906. Arriving in New York, he quickly earned a reputation in downtown society as an able preacher. Saturday- and holiday-afternoon services in major ghetto-based synagogues were spiced by his addresses to the appreciative crowds. In 1908 he moved to Harlem's Congregation Bnei Israel Anshe Sameth, lured uptown by real estate operator Joseph Smolensky, who reportedly enticed Hurwitz with a lucrative contract which spared him "from the poverty which most rabbis find themselves in." In 1909 Hurwitz moved to create the Rabbi Israel Salanter Talmud Torah to meet the educational needs of the thousands of children residing on the outer ridge of Jewish Harlem who were then untouched by modern Jewish education. By 1910 the talmud torah was home to 350 children in twelve different after-school classes.[59]

When the Kehillah became a reality, Hurwitz gave it his full-hearted support. He backed the founding of the Bureau of Education, supported its "model school" program, and permitted the creation of a boys' preparatory junior high school on its premises.[60]

Significantly, Hurwitz's advocacy of modern pedagogic methods and his association with non-Orthodox Jews did not endear him to all the members of his congregation. But then again, they probably had problems with his views of Orthodox synagogue life in general. In April 1912 Hurwitz declared, in an article entitled "The Necessity to Found Synagogues Here in America," that so long as synagogues were dirty, the services too long, disorderly and basically unintelligible, and the sermons dealt with esoteric midrashic and talmudic subjects, youngsters would not find Judaism attractive. Indeed Hurwitz severed his connections with his immigrant congregation and preferred to work with his patron Smolensky to help strengthen American Judaism primarily through the talmud torah system.[61]

Finally, the career of Philadelphia's Rabbi Bernard Levinthal suggests that the pre-World War I clerical ability to serve the Agudath ha-Rabbanim while personally promoting the harmonious synthesis of Judaism with Americanization through cooperation with Jews of varying theological opinions was not entirely a metropolitan New

York area phenomenon. His multifarious communal activities, ranging from the founding of a modern, communal talmud torah to charter membership in both the German-dominated anti-Zionist American Jewish Committee and the later Zionist American Jewish Congress, to early leadership of the Federation of American Zionists and the Orthodox Union, led one sympathetic biographer to describe him as "the most Americanized of the strictly Orthodox rabbis in the country." All these distinctions were achieved while he served as a longtime honorary president of the Agudath ha-Rabbanim.[62]

The so-called chief rabbi of Philadelphia (he oversaw the activities of some six congregatons) predicated his activities upon his understanding that "a rabbi is a rabbi of all Israel, not merely of Orthodox, Conservative or Reform." He reportedly declared that in communal work, one has to "stand above all positions and denominations."[63]

As with his fellows, particularly Margolies and Klein, Levinthal was not simply a seeker after communal influence and honor regardless of ideological inconsistency, though none of these men was immune to the pursuit of power and self-aggrandizement. They were, rather; strident Americanizers who used their connections to promote their perception of Judaism's requirements. As such, they were destined to serve as role models for a new generation of American-born Orthodox rabbis—trained at the Rabbi Isaac Elchanan Theological Seminary (RIETS) and elsewhere—who emerged after World War I.[64]

The Challenges of Interwar American Judaism (1920–1940)

The Agudath ha-Rabbanim, for all its ideological difficulties with Orthodox Union rabbis in the pre-World War I period, had to admit that its Americanized opponents almost always displayed deference to their East European colleagues as the recognized officialdom in ritual matters.[65] This authority was more than merely a source of honor or responsibility or even power in the American Jewish community. It was, specifically in the areas of kosher supervision, a most important source of steady income for many an immigrant rabbi seeking financial stability, if not economic advancement, in this country. Rabbis Asher Lipman Zarchy, Hirsch Grodzinski, and Moses Matlin did not migrate to Des Moines, Iowa, Omaha, Nebraska, and Sioux City, Iowa, respectively, with the primary goal of building great Jewish communities in these areas. Rather, they were drawn by the large stockyards of these cities and the pecuniary rewards to be earned as overseers for companies which distributed kosher meats throughout the United States. Others did not have to trek that far to find gainful rabbinic employment. There were religious constituencies desirous of a "chief rabbi" to bring order to religious practice within cities that were but a few hours from the major immigrant centers.[66] That control of Jewish industries rested solely within the East European rabbinate did not mean, however, that colleagues did not frequently compete with each other for a given city's meat stipend. The most celebrated instance of pre-World War I rabbinic rivalry was the challenge to Rabbi Jacob Joseph by Rabbi Widerwitz and Rabbi Segal. Their attack upon his control of New York's meat and poultry abattoirs and butcheries and their emergent counter-chief rabbinate effectively undermined whatever authority Rabbi Joseph had in communal affairs. Indeed, the Agudath ha-Rabbanim was set up to some degree to remedy this problem. But it had only limited success. The 1903 Chicago battle between Rabbis Jacob David Willowski and Zvi Album was probably that era's most striking case of rabbinic noncooperation. Album was a charter member of the Agudath ha-Rabbanim, and Willowski, one of late-nineteenth-century world Jewry's most renowned rabbinic writers, was honored as *zekan ha-rabbanim* ("elder rabbi") by the Agudath ha-Rabbanim in 1903, the year of his immigration. Both were committed to upholding their organization's policy of non-encroachment by one rabbi upon a colleague's territory. Yet Willowski's attempt, as the newly elected chief rabbi of Chicago, to impose his suzerainty upon the butcheries under Album's domain led to a citywide battle punctuated not only by vicious polemics between angry supporters of each faction but by fistfights in local synagogues.[67]

Kashruth competition was even more acute among Orthodox rabbis not bound by Agudath ha-Rabbanim strictures. In 1906 Rabbi

Luntz fought Rabbi Selzer in Paterson, New Jersey, creating two chief rabbinates there. Rabbi Gabriel Z. Margolis, chief rabbi of Boston beginning in 1907, battled Rabbi Federman, the city's incumbent kosher meat overseer. And while Agudath ha-Rabbanim leaders sought to use kashruth supervision as a weapon in Kehillah negotiations over Jewish education, other East European rabbis publicly challenged their authority to represent Orthodox Jewry in the area of meat regulation.[68]

Internecine rivalries over kashruth control were already quite commonplace when, in the 1920s, a new generation of American-born and/or trained rabbis entered the fray. These modern rabbis neither shared the East Europeans negativism toward Americanization nor consistently deferred to their elders, as had the previous generation, in matters of Jewish ritual regulation. For Agudath ha-Rabbanim members the emergence of a new group of English-speaking Orthodox rabbis was undoubtedly a source not only of consternation but also of embarrassment. Ironically, these rising leaders were products of an institution which the Agudath ha-Rabbanim had been instrumental in founding and maintaining—the Rabbi Isaac Elchanan Theological Seminary, [RIETS].

This school, later and better known as the affiliate of Yeshiva University dedicated to the training of American Orthodox rabbis, was organized in 1897. It grew out of the desire on the part of several graduates of Yeshiva Etz Chaim, the first elementary-level all-day yeshiva in the United States, for further and more intensive talmudic study combined with a modicum of general studies. Lithuanian-born kosher wine supervisor Rabbi Yehudah David Bernstein, a founder of Etz Chaim, and Rabbi Moses Matlin, the father of an Etz Chaim student, joined with layman David Abramowitz in inaugurating the institution. In its early years, RIETS was decidedly not "a rabbinical training seminary in the modern and professional sense of the term."[69] A goodly number of its early students were already ordained rabbis or ritual slaughterers from Russia who saw in RIETS a European-style yeshiva overwhelmingly dedicated to the advancement of rabbinic scholarship.[70] It was thus understandable that the delegates would rally to the cause when Rabbi Bernstein rose at the

Agudath ha-Rabbanim's second convention, in 1903, to propose formal recognition and support for RIETS. It was also not surprising that Agudath ha-Rabbanim members would champion the acute fund-raising needs of RIETS. After all, several early Agudath ha-Rabbanim members—Rabbis Matlin, Bernstein, Avraham Alperstein, and Kaplan—were among the first *roshei yeshiva* (talmud instructors) at the school.[71]

Three years later the ongoing relationship between school and rabbinical association was cemented when a Semicha Board was created at RIETS under the control of the Agudath ha-Rabbanim, specifically through members Margolies, Klein, Levinthal, and Samuel Z. Wein. This authority would ordain men who had the same training and qualifications for the rabbinate as candidates back in Europe. To this point little official thought had been given to the very different prerequisites for service in an American pulpit.[72]

Soon, however, the question of what types of competencies a man needed to possess in order to serve effectively as a rabbi in America became a major point of dispute at RIETS. The student body's composition had been changing as the first decade of the twentieth-century passed. By 1908, according to one contemporary estimate, the majority of students were native-born sons of immigrants.[73] For these students, attendance at RIETS was their or their families' answer to the public school-heder/talmud torah educational marriage. They wanted the intensive talmudic education on the European model offered by a traditional yeshiva. But they simultaneously desired improved secular studies to permit them to ultimately compete with fellow Jews and other Americans in the marketplace, universities, and professions of this land. Only a few of these new-style students sought careers as rabbis in America, but they too sought to be competitive.[74] They entered RIETS hoping to become knowledgeable in the ways of American science and civilization and equipped as English public speakers comfortable with homiletic messages attractive to fellow new Americans.

The pressure to Americanize RIETS peaked in 1908, when the students struck the institution. They demanded a broader, more systematic secular curriculum, instruction in the English language and "in the art of public speaking" as well as in the "softer" Jewish disciplines of Hebrew literature and Jewish history. The yeshiva's predominantly lay directors ultimately recognized the potency of the ideology which backed this demonstration and responded by electing the student-sympathetic Ramaz as their new president.[73] That change began a protracted process which, through Ramaz, Levinthal, Klein, and significant Orthodox lay support, redefined the RIETS mandate. From that point on, RIETS evolved to ultimately stand as an institution of "Torah and *hakhma* (secular knowledge)," capable of training Orthodox spokesmen "according to the spirit of the times." The battles of 1908 ultimately led to the reincorporation of a merged RIETS and Etz Chaim in 1915 as the Rabbinical College of America under Rabbi Dr. Bernard Revel.[76]

Dr. Revel stood unequivocally in favor of "Torah and *hakhma*." His own life story was proof of the possibilities in the harmonization of Torah scholarship with the secular. Born in Kovno in 1885, young Revel earned the reputation of an *illui* (budding talmudic "genius") at the Telshe Yeshiva, where he was ordained. But Revel's purview went beyond talmudic erudition. While still in Russia he evinced much interest in the Western-oriented disciplines of the *Wissenschaft des Judenthums.* He also, interestingly, demonstrated a passing interest in the ideology of Bundism (Jewish Socialism), a highly un-Orthodox modern expression of Judaism.[77]

This uncommon young Orthodox rabbi migrated to the United States in 1906 and quickly found RIETS hospitable to his need to continue rabbinic learning. New York University simultaneously met his desire for intensified secular studies, and he graduated with an M.A. degree in 1909. From there, Revel's quest for higher study in the world of Jewish Science brought him to Dropsie College, America's first nontheological Jewish academic institution. This institution, which was destined to develop close spiritual and personal ties with the Jewish Theological Seminary, graduated Revel as its first Ph.D. in 1912.[78] Thus, when called back to RIETS in 1915 to assume the presidency, at the age of thirty, Revel had achieved, through his own initiative and perseverance, what the school hoped to provide succeeding generations of American Orthodox rabbis. He was an "immigrant" rabbi comfortable both in his parents' universe and in the ways of America, capable of training students and colleagues to aid Jews in their harmonization of conflicting cultural and traditional values.

To help Revel in his labors were the two "grand old men" of American Orthodoxy, Rabbis Mendes and Drachman. The former was appointed professor of homiletics; the latter, as professor of pedagogy, "acted in various instructional capacities," teaching both Hebrew studies and the German language. Several years later, Mendes's spot on the faculty was assumed by Herbert S. Goldstein, one of the most renowned Orthodox preachers of his era. For Mendes and Drachman the reorganization of RIETS undeniably represented a new start for the "seminary idea" of 1887, which to their minds had been waylaid by the liberalizing innovations of Schechter. True advocates of traditional Judaism in America would now again be produced, theologically prepared and socially competitive in the marketplace of American ideas and denominational expressions.[79]

For members of the Agudath ha-Rabbanim, the reorientation of RIETS forced a most troubling major policy decision. Could they continue to support and service an institution which now did not mirror the desire to recreate an East European yeshiva environment in America and instead strove to reflect the immigrant's attempted accommodation of Judaism with America? For men like Ramaz, Klein, and Levinthal, who had manned the RIETS Semicha Board from 1906 and/or the Agudath ha-Rabbanim's Rabbinical College Committee set up in 1917 to monitor the school's activities, support for the changes was a natural extension of their philosophy of positive acculturation. But what of the aforementioned Rabbi Jaffe, also a member of the 1917 committee, who had previously avoided frequent institutional association with Drachman and Mendes and Americanization efforts in general? And what of the less-famous committee members like Eliezer Preil of Trenton, Eliezer Silver of Harrisburg, and Israel Rosenberg of Jersey City, not to mention the rabbis who held classes at RIETS? None of these men had previously championed Margolies/Klein/Levinthal policies. How could they rec-

oncile the apparently sharp deviation from the long-standing organizational policy of non-recognition of Americanization programs?[80]

Several factors may have contributed to the Agudath ha-Rabbanim's acceptance of the change in RIETS. First was the recognition that in member Revel the American Orthodox seminary was
being led by a man of impeccable rabbinic training who, whatever
his acculturating proclivities, understood the feelings of his colleagues. Second, they perceived that the idealized old-style yeshiva,
for all its scholarly grandeur, could not compete effectively for
American-born students, or ultimately for Jewish souls, against the
traditionalism of the Jewish Theological Seminary. They were forced
to move somewhat from their position of almost complete nonac-
commodation. They decided to stay with RIETS as its "rabbis,"
working in typical Agudath ha-Rabbanim style from within to
achieve their organization's ultimate goals. They would be the traditional teachers of the next generation of rabbis, bulwarks against all
except the most necessary changes. They would ordain students
whose loyalty they hoped to retain.[81]

However, it was not long before Agudath ha-Rabbanim members
recognized that many of the ordainees did not intend to remain obe-
dient disciples. RIETS produced during its first generation some fifty
trained-in-America rabbis.[82] While the vast majority found positions in the metropolitan area either as pulpit rabbis or as heads of
large communal talmud torahs, some ventured to other venues and
to smaller Jewish communities previously served only by one or two
East European rabbis, creating an immediate potentiality for rabbinic competition.[83]

Such was the case in 1931 when a young RIETS graduate, hired
by a Portland, Maine, congregation for the Passover holidays, began
to "buy his community's *chometz*" and received a stipend for his services. The resident Agudath ha-Rabbanim rabbi, who depended
upon holiday honoraria for his economic survival, was outraged. He
complained to the Agudath ha-Rabbanim that "this young chick
whose eyes have not yet opened has pushed me aside after my ten
years in the community. Please declare his rulings void and his ordination nullified."[84]

An even more vexing incident took place that same year in Massachusetts when another RIETS-trained rabbi "overruled" the chairman of the Agudath ha-Rabbanim-backed Council of Orthodox Rabbis in a matter of kosher meat slaughtering. The younger rabbi characterized the Agudath ha-Rabbanim decision as "foolish." And when asked if he knew the chairman of the rabbinic council he "acted as if the Chairman wasn't worth knowing and he boasted that he had no desire to be a member of an organization such as the Agudath ha-Rabbanim."[85]

The Agudath ha-Rabbanim responded to these charges and to the more generalized complaint that the American rabbis were undermining old-line authority in Jewish localities.[86] Under the leadership of its new president, Rabbi Eliezer Silver (elected in 1923), deputations and protests were addressed to Revel urging him not to send yeshiva graduates to communities led by Agudath ha-Rabbanim members without the specific permission of the resident senior rabbi. Secondly, Silver launched a program to bring the already ordained American rabbis into the Agudath ha-Rabbanim's fold and under its control.[87] He offered them organizational collegiality and mutual aid, provided that they could pass the more stringent *yadin yadin* ordination required of members.[88]

Silver drew heavily upon his own wide experience as a rabbi in the field in tendering this plan. Born in the Lithuanian town of Abel in 1881, he had gained his earliest training from his father, Rabbi Bunim Tzemah Silver, before receiving advanced rabbinical training in Dvinsk, Vilna, and Brisk. He was awarded ordination from Rabbis Hayim Ozer Grodzinski and Shalom Ha-Kohen of Vilna. Unlike so many of his Orthodox rabbinical colleagues, Silver, upon his arrival in the United States in 1906, did not settle in New York. Rather, with the assistance of Rabbi Levinthal, he established himself in Harrisburg, Pennsylvania, where he remained until 1925. He then moved on to Springfield, Massachusetts, for six years before assuming a pulpit in Cincinnati, Ohio, a position he would hold until his death more than fifty years later.[89]

From his vantage points "outside of New York," Silver witnessed and participated in numerous controversies over kashruth and over all communal control in the smaller Jewish communities. He understood the fears of the rabbanim threatened by insurgent rabbis and dedicated himself to clerical unity under the Agudath ha-Rabbanim's banner.

Rabbi Revel, for his part, was desirous of maintaining good relations with the Agudath ha-Rabbanim. Their continued approbation of his graduates lent all-important legitimacy to the institution. The promise of membership in the Agudath ha-Rabbanim for his students was also welcome. Accordingly, Revel took steps in the early 1930s to develop a rabbinical curriculum that would prepare his yeshiva men for the more advanced degree. But at the same time, he recognized that Silver's demands threatened the very existence of his school. To Revel, RIETS had been reorganized to offer American-born youth the opportunity to become American Orthodox rabbis. They were to compete effectively with Seminary-trained Conservative ordainees for leadership of an Americanized Jewish community. But how attractive could his school be to potential students if they knew that their ultimate job placement was to be effectively controlled by a coterie of East European-oriented rabbis? Faced with such a conflict, Revel seemingly adopted a fence-straddling policy. He was officially sensitive toward the Agudath ha-Rabbanim's position when specific conflicts arose, and simultaneously encouraged East European rabbis to accept his younger generation. He also tried to sensitize his disciples to respect the provinces of their elders.[90]

Revel's American-trained rabbis were not captivated by the Agudath ha-Rabbanim's offers, nor did they share their mentor's seeming great concern over RIETS's institutional legitimacy. First, few were then qualified for full membership in the Agudath ha-Rabbanim, and fewer saw the necessity for more advanced study to enter the lists. More importantly, the younger clerics viewed the senior rabbinic alliance as out of touch both structurally and ideationally with contemporary issues, unable to serve the rapidly emerging second-generation Jewish community of the interwar period. The Agudath ha-Rabbanim was, to their minds, an organization which preached rabbinical unification to standardize Jewish ritual practice and yet was rife with discord both from within and from without. Its combative members were seen as unaware of the negative impact their often notorious behavior made upon masses of acculturated Jews. And the popular perception of the Orthodox rabbinate was, for RIETS graduates, no mean issue. While the older immigrant laity which backed the Agudath ha-Rabbanim rabbis knew and "understood" the roots of these internecine rivalries, their children did not. And it was precisely these younger Jews, whom Agudath ha-Rabbanim members were ideologically and sociologically unable to reach, that they were seeking to influence. Membership in the Agudath ha-Rabbanim would be of little help to the American-trained Orthodox rabbi, then in the early throes of competition with the rising Conservative rabbinate, in projecting himself as a legitimately modern traditional pastor.

These critical evaluations of the East European rabbinate took permanent organizational form in 1935 with the founding of the Rabbinical Council of America (RCA).[91] This new organization was in truth an amalgamation of two separate but similar-thinking organizations, the Rabbinical Council of the Orthodox Union and the Rabbinical Association of RIETS. The former organization was formed in 1926 by, among others, the rabbis of three of Manhattan's most established modern Orthodox synagogues: Herbert S. Goldstein of the Institutional Synagogue, David De Sola Pool, Mendes's successor at Shearith Israel, and Leo Jung, who replaced now Reconstructionist Rabbi Mordecai M. Kaplan at The Jewish Center. These men, who were reminiscent of, if not identical to, the earlier Drachmans and Mendeses in their rabbinical training and orientation, sought to help bring American concepts of standardization to the kashruth industry through the OU symbol.[92] The Orthodox Union brought together RIETS men who either could not qualify for the Agudath ha-Rabbanim or did not want to join it. Chaim Nachman, H. Ebin, Ben Zion Rosenbloom, and Joseph H. Lookstein sought both to help their alma mater and to assist themselves in pulpit placement and congregational problems.[93] The amalgamation of these groups into the RCA constituted a signal enduring link between two generations of American Orthodox rabbis.

The RCA set as its dual mandate the bureaucratization and standardization of kashruth and the promotion of its own brand of American traditional Judaism above and beyond the power of the Conservative movement. Toward the first goal, the RCA fought for more than a generation, and with only a modicum of success, to end the practice of individual rabbis negotiating the right to oversee a particular product's kashruth. As the RCA saw it, this chaotic system of sometimes secret agreements lowered public esteem for the rabbinate when it did not encourage imposters or unscrupulous supervisors in the field. The RCA campaigned for the concentration of all kashruth under the OU banner; a public statement that control of this industry was a communal responsibility and not an individual rabbi's sinecure. The RCA commissioned and controlled competent supervisors and publicized the OU symbol as authoritative. It also sought to encourage the greater observance of kashruth both by the Jewish public and by national Jewish organizations, then notorious in Orthodox minds for their unkosher-catered meetings and banquets.[94]

The actuation of these plans required that RCA members surrender their autonomy to the national body, a personal and financial concession to communal priorities that many were loath to make. Indeed, it was not until 1954 that the RCA could officially prohibit its members from granting personal certifications. And even then compliance was not uniform either within or without the organization. Certainly Agudath ha-Rabbanim rabbis and innumerable other unaffiliated rabbis unbound by this bureaucracy resented the undermining of their authority. But then again, the RCA's methods in the second major area of its interest, the battle against Conservative Judaism, elicited even less Agudath ha-Rabbanim support.[95]

The Conservative movement had emerged during the interwar period as American Jewry's numerically predominant religious denomination. Offering its communicants a sociologically sophisticated mixture of liturgical traditionalism and ideological liberalism, it attracted vast numbers of second-generation Jews uncomfortable with their parents' European-looking Orthodoxy and put off by the "church-like" religious radicalism of Reform. American Jews were good family men who wanted to pray seated next to their wives and family. And they found in Conservatism a theology and practice attuned to the slowly developing suburban life-style, prepared to make religious accommodations to America's work clock and transportation revolution and yet still remain philosophically and practically within older Jewish traditions. Masses of Jews saw in the Conservative rabbi an adroit mediator between the ancestral faith of the past and the exigencies of the American future. These leaders could communicate their approach in impeccable English understandable to Jews and Gentiles alike. Orthodox rabbis, in their view, did not truly understand the demands of the acculturated, and Reform rabbis had yet to be sensitized to their fears of assimilation and of intermarriage.[96]

Agudath ha-Rabbanim rabbis, whose policies of resistance to Americanization possessed little currency with most second-generation Jews, had little to offer the acculturated in response to Conservatism's appeal, except well-articulated contempt for its perceived corruption of rabbinic tradition. The innumerable proclamations against and excoriations of the Conservative rabbinate, for all their intensity, had little practical effect.[97] The Yiddish-speaking followers of the Agudath ha-Rabbanim, those who knew and were influenced by the organization's ordinances, were Jews with relatively little interest in Conservatism's American social appeal. And those attracted to the liberal-traditionalists were drawn from among those disinterested in and unaware of old-line proclamations and attitudes.

RCA rabbis, on the other hand, staunchly believed that they could compete effectively against the Conservative rabbinate for spiritual leadership of the next generation. Through a tripartite policy of simulation, inclusion, and cooperation, they sought to prove that the American Orthodox rabbinate and its laity could be as attuned to American mores as their more liberal brethren without doing violence to the tenets of the ancestral faith.

RCA board member Joseph H. Lookstein of Manhattan's Congregation Kehilath Jeshurun was probably the organization's staunchest advocate of simulation. The Orthodox synagogue could be as architecturally modern, its services as decorous and appealing, its liturgy as linguistically intelligible, and its English-language sermon as compelling as any Conservative temple. Born in 1902 in the province of Mogilev, Russia, Lookstein was brought at age seven to the United States and settled with his family first on the Lower East Side and then in the Brownsville section of Brooklyn. He received his basic Jewish and secular education at the all-day Rabbi Jacob Joseph School on Henry Street and then moved a few blocks over on the Lower East Side to the Talmudical Academy, the RIETS "prep school." Significantly, while studying for ordination, Lookstein pursued an advanced secular degree at City College of New York. It was during his university years that this talented and culturally versatile young man was called to assist Ramaz as student rabbi in the Yorkville pulpit previously occupied by Mordecai M. Kaplan and Herbert S. Goldstein.[98]

Ordained by RIETS in 1926, Lookstein served as assistant to Ramaz during the last ten years of the senior rabbi's life. While in thispost, he earned graduate degrees from Columbia University, was appointed by Revel professor of homiletics and practical rabbinics at Yeshiva University, and emerged as a leading spokesman for the RCA. Blessed with a gift for English sermonizing and possessed of an impressive academic and professional resume, Lookstein bore witness that a RIETS graduate could be as worldly and Americanized as any of his seminary counterparts.[99]

One sympathetic family biographer has suggested that Lookstein's simulation idea grew out of his rejection while an adolescent of "the noise, the tumult and the general disarray of the Orthodox *shuls.*" Impressed by the aesthetics and dignity that were characteristic of Reform and Conservative synagogues, he "strove to combine warmth with dignity, the enthusiasm of Orthodoxy with the aesthetics of Reform, the tradition of four thousand years of Jewish practice with the modern active tempo." That meant weekly English-language sermons, prayers in English as well in Hebrew, special-theme Sabbaths, and guest speakers. In 1937, Lookstein even invited Judah Magnes, then chancellor of the Hebrew University in Jerusalem, to speak from the Kehilath Jeshurun pulpit on Kol

Nidre night. All these policies and programs dated back to Drachman and the beginnings of American Orthodoxy at the turn of the century and to Goldstein in the 1910s. But by Lookstein's time these activities were more characteristic of the Conservative synagogues.[100]

Lookstein was also a prime exponent of simulation in Jewish education. Clearly disdaining the Agudath ha-Rabbanim's concept of a yeshiva and taking Drachman's early idea that Orthodox Jewish education should emulate the public schools, Lookstein, in 1937, founded the Ramaz School, the prototype of many of today's modern day schools. Lookstein believed he could simulate the best aspects of the integrationist, acculturationist philosophy of the public schools in a homogeneous Jewish school environment. The student at Ramaz would receive the intensive Hebraic and Judaic training unobtainable in released-time or supplementary programming, while learning with equal intensity the values and mores of American society. Lookstein argued that the Jewish school calendar should correspond directly to the public school schedule; there would be no classes on Sundays, and Christmas vacation, renamed winter vacation, was instituted to permit maximal social integration with non-Jews and less Jewishly committed co-religionists.[101]

Unfortunately for the RCA, not all Orthodox rabbis possessed Lookstein's leadership capabilities or served congregations as content as the Yorkville synagogue with his aesthetic innovations and nondoctrinal changes.[102] Far more frequently, the interwar-period American Orthodox rabbi found himself in conflict with congregants who wanted to attend an "Orthodox" synagogue, defined here as a synagogue served by an American-trained Orthodox rabbi, but at the same time wanted to adopt the egalitarian mixed seating characteristic of Conservative temples. And when they were not debating pew patterns, conflicts raged over the equally crucial question of standardizing the time of Friday evening services. RIETS men serving such congregations had to deal with frequent lay requests that the synagogue precincts be used on weekday evenings for mixed dancing congregation-sponsored socials. They also had to decide whether men known to be public nonobservers of the Sabbath could be allowed the honor of leading services, as well as whether a man married to a non-Jew could be accepted into full synagogue membership. They even had to take positions on such seemingly less compelling problems as whether and when pulpit flowers might be used in the synagogue.[103]

For many rabbis the answer to all these queries was yes, sometimes unabashedly, sometimes reluctantly. To compete against the more liberal traditionalists, many rabbis felt they would have to accommodate congregational pleasures and take simulation beyond the limits of theological acceptability, although without formal or programmatic assent. At the same time, these rabbis wished to see themselves as Orthodox rabbis and as members of the RCA, and to be so considered by their colleagues.[104]

This approach to synagogue life and congregational ritual was particularly prevalent among those rabbis serving in midwestern pulpits, graduates of either RIETS or the relatively new Chicago-based Hebrew Theological College (HTC). The latter seminary was founded in 1922 by a group of Midwest-based rabbis to train local youths for rabbinic pulpits. Committed from its inception to producing "modern leaders of Orthodox Jewry," its curriculum emphasized not only "intensive study of the Talmud and the Codes . . . and mastery of the *Tanach* [Bible] but also a thorough knowledge of Jewish history and literature and a comprehensive grasp of the problem of contemporary Jewish life." As such, this rabbinic training school had much in common with the early pre-Schechter Seminary while sharing many of the ideological perspectives of the Revel-organized RIETS. It stood for little that would satisfy the Agudath ha-Rabbanim's understanding of the goals and methods of a yeshiva. In any event, its modern ordained rabbis, far removed from the metropolitan hub, fought the "battle for Orthodoxy" against powerful Reform and Conservative forces. They almost universally acquiesced at least on the issue of mixed seating. Still, as graduates of an American Orthodox training center, they sought RCA membership, posing a critical policy dilemma for the national organization.[105]

The RCA adopted a policy of inclusion both for HTC graduates and for those RIETS alumni who led what would come to be known as "traditional" congregations. Undoubtedly faced with a choice between accepting the situation of their colleagues, as it was, or driving them into the arms of the Conservative Rabbinical Assembly (RA) and the United Synagogue of America, the RCA by 1942 opted for inclusion. Its articulated policy was to admit all rabbis ordained at RIETS, HTC, or any other recognized Orthodox institute or authority. National office-holding in the organization, however; was to be reserved for rabbis serving in separate-seating congregations.[106]

The RCA strove to garner additional respect for Orthodoxy and its rabbinate through cooperation with more liberal Jews on interdenominational issues. In 1936, in a move highly reminiscent of Drachman and Mendes's willing participation in the New York Kehillah, the RCA became a constituent member of the Synagogue Council of America, an amalgam of Conservative, Reform, and Orthodox groups which dealt, *inter alia*, with church-state concerns and problems of anti-Semitism, issues upon which seemingly all denominations could agree. Ten years earlier the Orthodox Union and its Rabbis Goldstein and Pool had been among the founders of the council. And in 1939, RCA leaders sat down with Central Conference of American Rabbis (CCAR) and RA spokesmen to explore their mutual concerns over "the secularization in the Jewish centers and federations." To be sure, the usual fears were expressed that cooperation on nonreligious or interreligious matters would lead to theological co-optation. But to many RCA people, the possibility of projecting themselves as leaders not only of their community but of the entire Jewish community was all too compelling.[107]

These RCA policies, to be sure, did not sit well with the Agudath ha-Rabbanim. Harkening back, as always, to the European model which dominated its perspective and fueled its energies, the Agudath ha-Rabbanim contended that the rabbi's job was primarily to lead and not to be the servant of his community. Jewish law, it countered, set certain standards which may be neither suspended nor abridged on the basis of the popular will. And those clerics who would undermine the immutable halakha had no place in the Orthodox rabbinate. The Agudath ha-Rabbanim could see no social, political, or religious legitimacy to American colleagues serving in mixed-seating synagogues. And the RCA apologia that once ensconced in his pulpit a rabbi would hopefully change things for the "better," held for no currency for its members. Indeed, they even had difficulty with the seemingly innocuous simulation idea that Orthodox synagogues could hold Friday-evening lectures on "secular" topics to attract the uncommitted, because it emulated Conservative practice.[108]

Acting on these beliefs, the Agudath ha-Rabbanim in 1939 called upon the seventeen men who maintained memberships in both the Agudath ha-Rabbanim and the RCA to leave the American association in protest over its articulated policies. The resignation of these distinguished rabbis from the RCA, it was hoped, would effectively undermine that clerical body, leading to the reestablishment of a separate RIETS alumni society clearly under the hegemony of the Agudath ha-Rabbanim.[109]

One year later, the Agudath ha-Rabbanim sought to assert its rabbinical suzerainty in a far more dramatic way, through a takeover of RIETS. The death in 1940 of Bernard Revel, at the age of fifty-five, left Yeshiva in disarray. Gone was the synthesizer who had fused, for students and American Orthodox rabbis alike, the positive goals of acculturation with the maintenance of the Old World faith. American Orthodoxy was bereft of the spokesman who could crystallize and articulate its distance from Conservative Judaism and its differences with the Agudath ha-Rabbanim brand of Orthodoxy. With Yeshiva at bay, some rabbinical students gravitated toward the Seminary. Meanwhile, the Agudath ha-Rabbanim tried to step into the vacuum. Rabbi Silver suggested to the RIETS board that an Agudath ha-Rabbanim committee be appointed to administer the school. With his men in charge, Silver could monitor the types of men leaving RIETS and the pulpits they were to assume[110]

Yeshiva's board politely but firmly sidestepped Silver's initiative. Instead they appointed a primarily in-house executive board to manage the school while a search for a new president could be conducted. In 1943, Rabbi Samuel Belkin emerged as a worthy successor both to Revel's post and as expositor of his philosophy. A thirty-one-year-old professor of classics at Yeshiva College and Talmud instructor at RIETS, Belkin was in personal background, educational training, and philosophical orientation remarkably similar to his predecessor. Like Revel, Yeshiva's new president had been recognized while a child as a potentially, prodigious talmudic scholar. He was ordained at age seventeen at the yeshiva of Rabbi Israel Meir Ha-Kohen Kagan in Radun, Russia. Like Revel, Belkin also manifested a voracious appetite for secular humanistic learning. His quest for the latter form of scholarly training led him to the United States and to American universities, where in the years between his arrival in this country and his appointment to Yeshiva's faculty, Belkin not only mastered the English language but earned a Ph.D. in classics at Brown University and was elected to Phi Beta Kappa. In him, Yeshiva had once again found a leader whose life spoke to its commitment to living harmoniously in both the world of Jewish faith and the universe of secular knowledge and society. It would be Belkin's agenda through his more than thirty years at Yeshiva's helm to expand the purview of the university and to deepen the parameters of Revel's message. He would sit atop of a theological seminary that aspired to produce a type of rabbi who was truly conversant with, if not comfortable in, the American environment. RIETS graduates would continue to be occasionally objectionable to the Agudath ha-Rabbanim.[111]

It was RCA leaders who played a large role both in blocking the Agudath ha-Rabbanim takeover and in the selection of Belkin, thus ensuring that Yeshiva stayed Revel's course. Having asserted their independence from the respected East European rabbis, they lobbied hard to maintain their alma mater as an institutional bastion of support for their ideas and activities.[112] While that struggle raged, the RCA proceeded to place even greater distance between itself and the senior rabbis by creating its own Halacha Commission. Through this agency, which responded to questions on religious law and practice submitted to it by individual members, the American rabbis formally asserted that as a group they were competent not only to teach Judaism in this country but also to adjudicate problems of ritual observance. No longer would American-born rabbis have to defer to the learning of the members of the Agudath ha-Rabbanim. Through the Halacha Commission, a statement was implicitly and explicitly made that a man trained in the ways of the modern Jewish world as well as the world of Torah was better equipped to apply precedent and procedures to the needs of the Americanized lay majority. It was to this committee that questions regarding mixed dancing, the permissibility of autopsies to advance medical science, and the use of microphones during Sabbath and holiday services were submitted, and authoritative answers were rendered.[113]

The RCA, however; probably could not have made, or sustained, this broad assertion of its authority in American Jewish life without the philosophical backing and practical support of another uncommon East European-born rabbi, Joseph B. Soloveitchik.[114] The "Rov," as he came to be known to his disciples within and without Yeshiva University, emerged in the 1940s as the towering ideologue of American Orthodoxy.

Soloveitchik was born in 1903 into a world-renowned rabbinic family. His grandfather, Rabbi Hayim Soloveitchik, the so-called Brisker Rov, is credited with revolutionizing the methodology of talmudic study in the East European yeshivot. The "Brisker method," in the words of one of its present-day exponents, "relied upon an insistence on incisive analysis, exact definition, precise classification and critical independence." Soloveitchik learned this system under the close tutelage of his father, Rabbi Moses Soloveitchik, with whom he studied almost exclusively through his teen years. While still a young man, Joseph Soloveitchik came to believe that a systematic knowledge of general philosophy would enhance his understanding of the Torah and its applicability to the modern condition. He enrolled in the University of Berlin in 1925 and studied there for six years under the Neo-Kantian philosopher Heinrich Maier, earning a Ph.D. in 1931 with a dissertation on the philosophy of Hermann Cohen.[115]

While the younger Soloveitchik sought his own road to more advanced religious understanding, Rabbi Moses Soloveitchik was recruited by Revel to head the RIETS faculty in 1929. His appointment did much to solidify the traditional talmudic and codes core of the rabbinic training at RIETS, while Revel introduced mechanisms for the ancillary skill development so much required of an American cleric. With Rabbi Moses Soloveitchik on the faculty, few could effectively question the scholarly reliability of men who studied at RIETS.[116]

In 1932 Rabbi Joseph Soloveitchik migrated to these shores, was accepted as unofficial chief rabbi of Boston, and affiliated with the Agudath ha-Rabbanim. During his early American years, Soloveitchik, bred in a tradition that emphasized the intellectual rather than the pastoral functions of the rabbinate, devoted himself primarily to the dissemination of Torah scholarship through public and private lectures and through the creation of the first Hebrew day school in New England, Boston's Maimonides School. This school's approach and curriculum more closely resembled those of the recently founded Ramaz than the older Etz Chaim.

It was not until 1941 and the death of his father that Rabbi Joseph Soloveitchik brought his talmudic excellence and affinity for the study of philosophy to Yeshiva University.[117] The Agudath ha-Rabbanim asked Rabbi Soloveitchik to head up the RIETS Talmud faculty. His acceptance assured the rabbinic body that a high level of rabbinic scholarship would continue to characterize Yeshiva while it went through the throes of replacing President Revel, but, as time went on, Soloveitchik's political nonalignment with the Agudath ha-Rabbanim in its dealings with the younger Orthodox rabbis led the organization to be less than satisfied with him.[118]

For RIETS students and their more senior alumni colleagues in the RCA, Rabbi Soloveitchik's emergence came to mean something entirely different.[119] Here was a man possessed of the highest East European rabbinical credentials and yet philosophically and psychologically capable of relating "the ideal *halakhic* system to the basic realities of human life" and able to formulate "a creative philosophy, conservative and progressive, keeping intact our Jewish tradition even as he was developing it further" who would become their spiritual guide and legal mentor.[120]

In practical terms this ultimately meant that Rabbi Soloveitchik not only understood and accepted the forces and pressures which had created the RCA tripartite approach to religious life—simulation, inclusion, and cooperation—but was prepared to assist in setting authoritative parameters for each of these policies. In the sociological realm of simulation, Soloveitchik granted those who sought his advice the widest latitude. He applauded those who could show "the American Jew that it is possible to have a synagogue conform to the *Shulkan Aruk* . . . and at the same time . . . excel as far as good behavior, cultivated manners and beautiful sermons are concerned." And in certain specific situations, he acceded to a RIETS graduate accepting a pulpit in a mixed-seating congregation, if that congregation demonstrated a willingness to be convinced to conform to Orthodox strictures. In one case, after being informed that a mixed-seating congregation was willing to install a temporary *mechitza* during the trial Sabbath of an RCA member, Soloveitchik, in his own words, "inclined to take the more liberal view of the situation. . . [but] only to a situation in which there is at least a vague probability that the visit of the rabbi might pave the way for bringing that synagogue into the fold." At the same time, as adviser to the RCA's Halacha Commission in the 1940s and as its chairman in the early 1950s, Soloveitchik vigorously opposed so-called Orthodox congregations which adopted the Conservative practice of having the cantor face the congregation rather than the ark in prayer and/ or showed no interest in moving in the direction of separate seating. He also rendered a final, negative opinion on the issue of the permissibility of a microphone at Sabbath and holiday services. That decision further distinguished the Orthodox from the more liberal congregations.[121]

Finally, he staunchly supported the RCA policy of cooperation with the less traditional in broad communal agencies. In a poignant statement on the need for Jewish unity against hostile outside forces, Soloveitchik declared:

> When representation of Jews and Jewish interest *klapei chutz* [towards the outside world] are involved, all groups and movements must be united. There can he no divisiveness in this area for any division in the Jewish camp can endanger its entirety. . . . In the crematoria, the ashes

of Hasidim and Anshe Maseh [pious Jews] were mixed with the ashes of radicals and free thinkers and we must fight against the enemy who does not recognize the difference between one who worships and one who does not.[122]

At the same time he advised RCA members to tread warily when dealing with Conservative and Reform rabbis on issues affecting theinternal life of the Jewish community.

Although Rabbi Soloveitchik's leadership did much to legitimize the RCA's approach toward meeting the problems of mid-twentieth-century American Jewish denominational life, his influential voice did little to effectively reconcile Agudath ha-Rabbanim and RCA disagreements. If anything, the Soloveitchik years (ca. 1940 to the early 1990s) witnessed the widening of the gap between groups of Orthodox rabbis operating in America. RCA stalwarts, possessed of the Rov's imprimatur and thus confident of their authenticity, have organizationally resisted, although with some notable individual exceptions, the gravitational pull of the East European-trained rabbis. At the same time, the Agudath ha-Rabbanim has become more and more attuned to a very different Torah voice which has solidified and further formalized its resistance to the harmonization techniques characteristic of the American Orthodox rabbinate. This new era of immigrant Orthodoxy, which we will presently discuss, began on a large scale during and after World War II, and to a great extent its adherents have eclipsed the indigenous prewar Agudath ha-Rabbanim leaders as the staunchest resisters of Americanization. In so doing, they have challenged the assumptions of both the Agudath ha-Rabbanim and the American Orthodox rabbinate.

A New Era of Immigrant Orthodoxy (ca. 1940–1980)

Through all its early years of disagreement and conflict with American Orthodox rabbis, the Agudath ha-Rabbanim proudly projected itself as the institutional bastion of resistance against Americanization's inroads into traditional faith. But not all East European rabbis who shared the Agudath ha-Rabbanim's basic point of view aligned themselves with that organization. In its earliest days, some Gali-

cian- and Hungarian-born or trained rabbis disdained affiliation
with the predominantly Lithuanian rabbinic alliance on ethnic
grounds.[123] For others nonalignment with the rabbinical association meant continued freedom to pursue their own pecuniary interests in the kashruth field.[124] Finally and most significantly, there
were rabbis who believed that the Agudath ha-Rabbanim's anti-
acculturation and antimodernization policies did not go far enough.
They looked askance at the Agudath ha-Rabbanim's continued support for RIETS, especially as creeping Americanization slowly transformed that East European-style yeshiva into Yeshiva University.
And they had theological difficulties with the organization's consistent backing of modern Jewish nationalism, albeit through the
somewhat separatistic Mizrachi (Religious Zionist) movement.

Rabbi Gabriel Z. Margolis was one individual who opposed the
Agudath ha-Rabbanim both practically and philosophically. And in
the early 1920s, he unified varying strains of East European rabbinic disaffection with Agudath ha-Rabbanim into a competing
organization, Knesset ha-Rabbonim ha-Orthodoxim (Assembly of
Hebrew Orthodox Rabbis). The Vilna-born Margolis, scion of a
Lithuanian rabbinical family, had served communities in the Russian Pale cities of Dubrovno, Horodno, and Yashinovka for close to
forty years before migrating to the United States and settling in Boston in 1908 at the age of sixty. This senior scholar, the reputed
author of several European-published rabbinic tracts, quickly elected
chief rabbi of several New England-area congregations, saw little
personal value in affiliating with the still relatively new rabbinic
organization.[125] If anything, he recognized the Agudath ha-Rabbanim as an organizational establishment which stood in the way of
his economic and rabbinic-political advancement through the
kashruth industry. Indeed, upon his removal to New York in 1912
to head up the Adath Israel Congregation and burial society, and
upon his recognition that the kashruth industry in the metropolis
was then under Agudath ha-Rabbanim control through its rabbinic
officialdom of Klein, Ramaz, and Jaffe, he undertook a decade-long
campaign to undermine the reliability of Agudath ha-Rabbanim
within New York Orthodox circles. Not only did he speak out

against the Agudath ha-Rabbanim's move toward cooperation with the Kehillah, he charged his opponent Ramaz with incompetence in his monitoring of slaughtering procedures. And he also pointedly accused Jaffe of falsely certifying unkosher products. Finally, Margolis violently opposed the Agudath ha-Rabbanim's support for a 1919 strike by the Butcher Workmen Union and the Union of Live Poultry Workers. This dispute gave him the opportunity to declare that the Agudath ha-Rabbanim was itself a "union" designed to prevent competent competitive rabbis from establishing themselves in the United States. But despite all his efforts, Margolis was unable to effectively wrest kashruth control from the incumbent supervisors.[126]

In the early 1920s it became clear that Margolis's difficulties with the Agudath ha-Rabbanim went well beyond questions of money and rabbinic power and propriety. Margolis was, firstly, troubled by his opponents' support for Zionism. As he saw it, Jews had no right to actively participate in their own political redemption. God alone would decide when the exile should end, and therefore no true-believing Orthodox Jew could associate with that modern national movement. Using the traditional liturgical rendering of Maimonides' Creed as his source, he announced that "God will send at the end of days his redeemer to save those who wait for him. For God and for no one else. And as he took us out of Egypt, so he will show us miracles soon and in our own day."[127]

Margolis also had difficulty with the Agudath ha-Rabbanim's continued association with the Americanized RIETS. Rabbi Isaac Elchanan Spektor; he declared, "would turn over in his grave if he knew that a seminary had been built bearing his name where [general] philosophy, the humanities and all other meaningless matters were taught." RIETS, he believed, had lost its way as it sought, under Dr. Revel, to emulate Columbia University and the hated Jewish Theological Seminary of America.[128]

These philosophical concerns, coupled with his long-standing practical opposition, led Margolis in 1920 to organize some 135 like-minded critics of the Agudath ha-Rabbanim into the Knesset ha-Rabbonim ha-Orthodoxim. This assembly placed high on its agenda of priorities the reformation of what it called "the politics of kashruth." And not unlike the organization it opposed, the Knesset called for the strengthening of traditional Jewish education in the United States, the greater observance here of the Sabbath, and help for afflicted Jews across the seas. Not surprisingly, it also adroitly refrained from recognizing Zionism as an international Jewish reality in this post-Balfour period. But for all the noise and furor of their criticism and protests, Margolis and his followers failed to unseat the Agudath ha-Rabbanim as the most representative voice of the East European rabbinate in America.[129]

Rabbi Yehudah Heschel Levenberg's contemporaneous, quiet institutional challenge of the Agudath ha-Rabbanim, on the other hand, was ultimately of tremendous, enduring significance. In the 1910s and the early 1920s, the Slabodka-trained chief rabbi of New Haven organized the Beis Ha-Medrash Le-Rabbanim (Orthodox Rabbinical Seminary), the first European-style yeshiva in the United States offering no secular studies.[130] This inaugural institutional statement that Torah Judaism need not, on any level, accommodate Americanization attracted to its faculty such future luminaries as Rabbis Moses Feinstein, Yaacov Ruderman, and interestingly enough, the young, newly arrived Samuel Belkin.[131] Although the school would survive but a few years—it declined precipitously when Levenberg moved himself and his school to Cleveland—it set an ideological standard which at least Rabbis Feinstein and Ruderman would uphold in their respective yeshivas, Mesivta Tifereth Jerusalem of New York and Baltimore's Ner Israel, both founded in the 1930s.

These schools were two of the five enduring institutions formed or transformed during the interwar days which challenged the RIETS/ Agudath ha-Rabbanim monopoly on rabbinic training and leadership, and their shared, if somewhat strained, assumptions about the limits of Americanization. Williamsburg's Mesivta Torah Vodaas, led by Rabbi Shraga Feivel Mendlowitz, Rabbi David Liebowitz's Brooklyn-based Yeshiva Chofetz Chaim, and Brownsville's Yeshiva Rabbi Chaim Berlin, headed by Rabbi Yitzchok Hutner, joined their Manhattan- and Baltimore-based colleagues in standing four-square against the combination of advanced secular and religious studies within one institutional setting. But significantly, none actively opposed their students attending schools like the City College of New York at night. These yeshivas were not producing American Orthodox rabbis, as was RIETS. Rather, they were educating Orthodox rabbis in America who would acquire their advanced degree of integration with the host society in other, secular institutions. Such were the limits of the approaches to religious educational life even in the circles that were the most resistant to Americanization during the pre-World War II days. There was no rabbinical group or individual who would or could attempt to shut out America totally from the lives of religious students.[132]

The coming of World War II broadened tremendously the limits of Orthodox rabbinic resistance to Americanization. Hitler's invasion of Poland in 1939 and of Russia two years later forced to these shores a new breed of Orthodox Jews to a great extent previously unseen in America. These were men and women who during the period of mass migration had heeded the words of Rabbi Israel Meir Ha-Kohen Kagan (the Hafetz Hayim): "Whoever wishes to live properly before God must not settle in these countries."[133] They were now entering this country—when immigration laws permitted—only because the Europe they knew was in the process of being destroyed. Individually this meant that people who had not broken to any great extent with the traditional past to seek their fortune and new world in America were reinvigorating the Orthodox community. The desire to become like all other Americans was far less pronounced among them than it had been among those who preceded them. Obversely, their zeal to recreate European institutions on American soil was far more emphatic than that of the immigrant Orthodox of the turn of the century. Institutionally, this new migration came to mean the settlement and sustaining in America of two new religious organizational forms, the refugee yeshiva and the leader-oriented sect.

Cleveland's Telshe Yeshiva and the Beis Medrash Govoha in Lakewood, New Jersey, best represent the Torah institutions founded or reestablished in this country by rabbis, students, and their followers who successfully, and in some cases miraculously, escaped the European Holocaust. In the former case, Rabbis Elya Meir Bloch and Chaim Mordecai Katz led their community halfway around the world from western Russia through Siberia to Japan and then to Seattle, Washington, before reassembling their lives and yeshiva in 1941 in an Ohio suburb. There, on American soil, they proceeded to recreate almost intact both the methodology of talmudic study and the insulated spirit of their old-country home. Two years later, Rabbi Aharon Kotler formerly head of the Polish Kletzk Yeshiva, after a similarly arduous journey, resettled in America. Possessed of an even greater drive to recreate the Jewish religious world then being destroyed by the Nazis, he founded his yeshiva in a rural New Jersey community. There, theoretically removed from the assimilatory influences of the metropolis, an institution was built which would not only block out America but would even deemphasize the "utilitarian" goal of training young men for the active rabbinate. His school stood for the East European ideal of "Torah for its own sake." Men would study there not so much for ordination but for the love of learning. American talmudic scholars would there be produced worthy of what would have been Lithuanian Jewry's highest scholarly accolades.[134]

The arrival in America of leader-oriented Orthodox immigrant groups was also a product of the dislocations which accompanied and followed the Second World War. In 1939 Rabbi Joseph Breuer moved from Frankfurt am Main, by way of Belgium, to New York's Washington Heights, bringing with him the Orthodox traditions of Samson Raphael Hirsch and quickly attracting to his new residence a considerable following of German immigrant Jews. In 1940, Rabbi Joseph Isaac Schneersohn, the leader of the Lubavitcher Hasidim, made Brooklyn's Crown Heights his home, beginning a process which led thousands of wartime and postwar Russian Hasidic refugees to that locality. The year 1946 witnessed the settlement of Hungarian Satmar Rebbe Joel Teitelbaum and his followers in Brooklyn's Williamsburg. And these years and the next decade witnessed Hasidic groups from Romania, Hungary, and Galicia following their leaders to these shores. The Hasidic groups differed from each other somewhat in matters ritual, social, and ideological, and overall the approach of the East European Hasidim to religious life certainly varied significantly from the teachings of the Hirschian Western European contingent. But what they all held in common was the Orthodox community structure, resistant of rapid Americanization, rooted in their allegiance to their respective chief rabbis.[135]

Unlike poor Rabbi Jacob Joseph, who after his arrival in the United States searched for a constituency which would resist the inroads of the new land, Rabbis Breuer, Schneersohn, Teitelbaum, and the others led their followers to America with their individual authority and power remaining intact. Committed to recreating the lost communities of Europe on American soil and resisting, each to its own degree, the pressures of immigrant acculturation, these leader-oriented groups quickly established their own networks of schools, self-help charitable institutions, and social organizations. Chief rabbinates were now truly being established in this country, but with one major difference. None of these men, with the possible exception of the Jewish-proselytizing Lubavitcher Rebbe, attempted to extend their formal suzerainty beyond the community of their true believers.

These new, growing, and confident Orthodox elements impacted dramatically on the status, thinking, and practice of such indigenous Orthodox groups as the Agudath ha-Rabbanim. No longer were these long-time Orthodox rabbis in America the most strident force against Americanization. Though the circumstances that brought the newcomers to America were entirely different from those which directed the earlier generation, they were nonetheless showing that traditional faith could progress in this country without any accommodation to the host environment. This meant, for example, that an Americanized RIETS/Yeshiva University, even in its most traditional of incarnations, was not, to their minds, a necessary evil to attract a lost generation back to the ancestral faith. Why, Lakewood or Telshe devotees asked rhetorically, trim one's ideological and social sails to represent the entire, seemingly uncaring American Jewish community, when there now existed a strong, ever developing, committed religious population which accepted the law of the Torah and wanted only those rabbis trained as in the past to lead and guide them?[136]

This newly arrived Orthodox leadership also questioned the Agudath ha-Rabbanim's long-standing commitment to Zionism, as expressed through its support of the Mizrachi movement. Many, if not all of the newcomers were backers of the Agudath Israel. That religio-political party, founded in Central and Eastern Europe in 1912, linked in its opposition to Zionism a diverse group of Hirschians, Hasidim, and Lithuanian yeshiva spokesmen. At its inception the Agudath Israel criticized modern Jewish nationalism on strong theoretical and practical theological grounds. In its view, Jewish tradition had ordained that the Jews were in exile for their sins and were destined to remain in Diaspora until Providence willed their miraculous return. Accordingly, the contemporaneous Zionist manifestation was a false messianic movement, led mostly by men and women who had broken with the Jewish religious past, which threatened the continuity of the people's existence. Significantly, the Agudath Israel was particularly strident in its upbraiding of Mizrachi religious Zionists, seeing them as the worst transgressors of all. They spoke and behaved daily like Orthodox Jews and yet they supported the apostate movement.[137]

The cataclysmic and climactic events of the 1930s and 1940s, which witnessed Zionism's emergence not only as a major political reality but more significantly as a practical refuge of necessity, caused the Agudath Israel to modify its position. It had become increasingly difficult to oppose this projected sovereign refuge haven for one's people in a Hitlerian world, even when one opposed the Zionist movement. Accordingly, the Agudath Israel deemphasized its theological difficulties with Jewish nationalism and refocused its attention on the fact that Israel was being built by secular Jews unconcerned with and unbridled by the law of the Torah. Now occupying an ideological position still significantly different from the Mizrachi's—the latter had always considered itself the "watchdog" for Judaism *within* the Zionist movement—the Agudath Israel in the 1930s and 1940s charted its own separatist role in "building Eretz

Yisrael in accordance with Torah and the guidance of the
Practically this meant that it would remain outside of the
political system, while creating its own religious institutic
fighting for greater traditional religiosity in the Yishuv. By World
War II's end only a small minority from the original Agudath Israel
coalition, the Naturei Karta of Jerusalem and their Satmarer cous-
ins, remained opposed to the rise of Israel.[138]

The Agudath Israel in its original form—Rabbi Gabriel Z. Margolis
notwithstanding—made no appreciable impact upon the Orthodox
rabbinate in America through the mid-1930s. Agudath ha-Rabbanim and RCA members seemingly shared leadership in the relatively small but vibrant American Mizrachi movement. Indeed, an
American branch of the Agudath Israel did not appear until 1938.
And even then, under the guiding hand of the Agudath ha-Rabbanim's president, Eliezer Silver, a major goal of the American
branch was to find mechanisms for all Orthodox Jews concerned
with the Yishuv to cooperate in promoting their religious institutional life.[139]

The Torah-world leaders who arrived during and after World War
II rejected this cooperating, seemingly half-hearted approach. Transplanting the European Agudath Israel's position to America, they
endeavored to chart a course for their movement in line with their
group's worldwide position. Rabbis Kotler, Bloch, Katz, and Grozovsky all became, as early as 1941, part of the Council of Torah
Sages, an Agudath Israel presidium in America which effectively
replaced the indigenous American-born leadership. Implicit here
was the newcomers' critique of the old-time American rabbis' non-
adherence to uncomprising principles.[140]

The Council of Torah Sages also championed, and with characteristic intensity, long-standing Agudath ha-Rabbanim causes. The
older organization had from its inception argued that Yiddish was
the most appropriate language for Jewish religious instruction. But
it allowed, however, that English might be used as a secondary
tongue, particularly in geographical areas where Yiddish had been
forgotten. In 1947 Rabbi Kotler declared that Yiddish must be the
sole language for teaching the tradition. "Mass assimilation among

the gentiles," he pronounced, "will result if we utilize the language of the land. Our Jewish children will then emulate non-Jewish practice."[141]

The council's 1956 categorical condemnation of Orthodox rabbis cooperating with their Conservative and Reform counterparts in the Synagogue Council of America and on local boards of rabbis gave another of the Agudath ha-Rabbanim's old-line principles its fullest articulation. In a ban signed by eleven *roshei yeshiva*—including Rabbis Kotler, Feinstein, and Ruderman, two Mesivta Torah Vodaas instructors, Yaacov Kamenetsky and Gedalia Schorr, and two refugee RIETS scholars, Lifshitz and Zaks—colleagues were "forbidden by the law of our sacred Torah to be members" of such organizations. Significantly, Rabbi Eliezer Silver, still president of the Agudath ha-Rabbanim, did not sign the proclamation. For him, such a written testament, despite his basic philosophical agreement with its thrust, would effectively cut off Yeshiva University men whom he still hoped to influence both from his organization and from the wider, growing yeshiva world.[142]

Men like Eliezer Silver were undoubtedly filled with bittersweet sentiments by the rise of this new era of immigrant Orthodoxy. While they could only applaud the rapid and comprehensive growth of a truer-than-ever Orthodox community in this country which was seemingly well-resisting America's pressures and recreating reasonable facsimiles of Old World life-styles, they had to be saddened that the realization of that which they had originally set out to do was being achieved by others. Indeed, by the mid-1950s, long-time Agudath ha-Rabbanim members could not help notice that even their organization was no longer in their hands. In 1958, the majority of the organization's members were wartime immigrant rabbis, and the Agudath ha-Rabbanim's presidium was now controlled by Council of Torah Sages men like Kotler, Feinstein, Kamenetsky, and Lifshitz among others. The strictest of the Orthodox of one generation had been eclipsed by the new yeshiva world with its army of new immigrants. In 1960, the Agudath ha-Rabbanim officially opposed members belonging to mixed rabbinical groups. It solemnly declared that any rabbi who belonged to such organizations as the Synagogue Council and/or the New York Board of Rabbis (NYBR) would forfeit his membership. And with an eye toward the Orthodox Union/RCA it declared that "all Orthodox rabbis must also resign from the Board of Rabbis."[143]

This new generation of immigrant Orthodox rabbis also made its impact on the thoughts and behavior of RCA members. Although the Council of Torah Sages denigrated their education and deplored their outlook, some RCA men have been either unwilling or unable to ignore the new immigrant rabbis' teachings and influence. This sensitivity to what renowned, transplanted European figures were thinking and saying was seen most graphically in the RCA's reaction to the aforementioned 1956 ban. With Rabbis Kotler, Feinstein, and others officially on record as opposed to their membership in the Synagogue Council, and/or the NYBR, a group of RCA spokesmen led by then President Rabbi David Hollander argued that the RCA had no choice but to submit to higher Torah law. Although Hollander's view never acquired the majority necessary to change RCA policy, the influence of the council had made inroads. Its uncompromising position had detached from the American Orthodox rabbinical ranks a segment willing, after a generation of struggle for independence, to surrender its autonomy to a body of immigrant rabbis.[144]

The yeshiva world has influenced the American Orthodox rabbinate in other ways, less easily documented, but equally significant. As one contemporary sociologist discovered, the RIETS student of today is far different from his counterpart of prewar days. He too has felt the impact of the yeshiva world's uncompromising ideology. Indeed, many have come to redefine our term "simulation" to mean the attempt to approximate the talmudic learning environment of a Chaim Berlin or a Lakewood while participating to an ever decreasing degree in a university setting. And while all RIETS men revered Rabbi Joseph Soloveitchik, and a goodly proportion still evince an interest in the secular, for some the rabbinic role-model was a Rabbi David Lifshitz (a signatory of the 1956 ban) or any number of younger *roshei yeshiva* who have themselves sought to emulate the East European rabbinical style. Significantly, RIETS has responded to

these demands and proclivities through the establishment, beginning in the 1950s, of its own Kollel (postgraduate, "Torah for its
own sake") programs, as well as, in 1970, the *yadin yadin* program,
first conceived of by Revel two generations ago. Finally, although
Rabbi Haskel Lookstein, following in his own father's footsteps, may
have been assigned by RIETS to teach students homiletics, many
present-day rabbinic candidates believe that their ability to rise in
congregational life is predicated less on their capacity to deliver
articulate English-language sermons and more on their reputation
as a talmudic scholar attractive to an increasingly learned Orthodox
laity.[145]

Reflections on the Current Generation of Accommodators (ca. 1940–1980)

For all the inroads immigrant Orthodox rabbis have made during
the post-World War II years upon the thinking and practices of their
American-trained colleagues, the traditions begun by Drachman
and Goldstein,[146] institutionalized by Revel and Belkin, formalized
by Lookstein, and delimited and crystallized philosophically by Rabbi
Soloveitchik have by no means disappeared. The current generation
of RCA rabbis still constitutes for the most part a hard core of support for the established principles of simulation, inclusion, and cooperation. For some, continued backing for the idea that Orthodox
rabbis must represent the entire community, and should cooperate
with and include less-traditional colleagues to the extent that they
can, is an exigency of life as a minority denomination in the subur-
banized contemporary Jewish community. This point of view was
clearly apparent in the reaction of rabbis serving communities far
removed from the New York metropolis to Hollander's anti-SCA
position. "A local rabbi who would follow Hollander's intolerant
footsteps," one Colorado-based source declared, "would be hooted
out of town or consigned to obscurity.[147] But for most of the rabbis
who tacitly ignored the 1956 ban, the decision to avoid self-segrega-
tion was less a product of necessity and more an act of faith. Indeed
RIETS produced, from the late 1930s to the 1950s, a coterie of

graduates who not only supported umbrella defense and interdenominational organizations but personally rose to leadership positions in these cooperative institutions.

Significantly, men like Rabbis Emanuel Rackman (RIETS, '32), Israel Miller (RIETS, '41), and Herschel Schacter (RIETS, '42) were all initiated into the practical world of Jewish intragroup cooperation as chaplains in the United States Armed Forces during the Second World War. As volunteers willing to serve both their country and all its Jewish elements, they entered the military already predisposed toward representing a broad ethnic polity. Their close observation, if not eyewitnessing, of Hitler's atrocities sensitized them further to Rabbi Soloveitchik's message that Jew-hatred drew no ideological lines.[148]

Returning to America in the late 1940s, all three of these men built multifaceted careers as leaders of second-generation American congregations, spokesmen for the RCA and for Religious Zionism in America, and as Orthodox representatives in a myriad of intragroup organizations. Each has served in the Executive and other high-ranking capacities in the Jewish Agency, the American Zionist Federation, and the World Zionist Organization. Miller and particularly Schacter were among the first to join the community-wide battle for Soviet Jews.[149] Rackman was president of the New York Board of Rabbis from 1955 to 1957. And not surprisingly each has served as chairman of the Jewish Welfare Board's Commission on Jewish Chaplaincy. Most significantly, in 1968 Schacter was elected chairman of the Conference of Presidents of Major American Jewish Organizations, the first Orthodox rabbinical leader to speak for that umbrella organization. The principle of cooperation was thus fully articulated as a RIETS/RCA man represented to the American and world governments the interests of some thirty Jewish organizations running almost the gamut of Jewish commitments and postions. In 1974–76 Miller served in this powerful and prestigious post. And in 1982, Rabbi Julius Berman, a 1959 graduate of RIETS and president of the Orthodox Union, became the third Orthodox-based chairman.[150]

Architectural, sermonic, and ancillary congregational simulation is also still advocated by most RCA members. And in the most recent decade, Orthodox simulation has added an additional dimension, for at least some RCA members, through their advocacy of increased women's participation in all aspects of synagogue life. The rise of the feminist movement has impacted substantially upon American Jewish denominational life. Dramatic change has both taken place and has been resisted in the more liberal movements. Women are now trained and ordained as rabbis at the Reform Hebrew Union College-Jewish Institute of Religion, at the Reconstructionist Rabbinical College, and at the Jewish Theological Seminary's rabbinical program. On the local level, Conservative women have struggled for greater liturgical access and participation, and both Conservative and Reform women have petitioned for increased control over the political dimensions of synagogue life.[151]

Americanized Orthodoxy, too, has not been immune to these currents of change. Although a goodly proportion of the RCA membership has resisted to date either debate over or concession to women's goals, another smaller contingent has been searching, textually and sociologically, for the limits to which they can accommodate within the Orthodox reading of Jewish law that which is becoming part of the more liberal Jewish theological/sociological world. Accordingly, many Orthodox congregations now permit their women to serve on lay boards of trustees, and some even permit female membership on synagogue ritual committees. Most strikingly, a few rabbis have placed their imprimatur upon separate women's tefilot (prayer services) within their communities. Interestingly, by 1982 this latter initiative had become pervasive enough for the Agudath ha-Rabbanim to declare in a tone somewhat reminiscent of eighty years ago:

> God forbid this should come to pass. A daughter of Israel may not participate in such worthless ceremonies that are totally contrary to Halacha. We are shocked to hear that "rabbis" have promoted such an undertaking which results in the desecration of God and his Torah. We forewarn all those who assist such "Minyonim," that we will take the strictest measures to prevent such "prayers," which are a product of

pure ignorance and illiteracy. We admonish these "Orthodox rabbis":
Do not make a comedy out of Torah.[152]

In 1976, Rabbi Norman Lamm was elected Yeshiva University's
third president. A self-described disciple of Rabbis Belkin and
Soloveitchik, this American-born and Yeshiva College-trained,
RIETS-ordained leader was in his early career a junior colleague of
Joseph Lookstein at Yorkville's Kehilath Jeshurun and later served as
successor to Leo Jung at the West Side, New York, Jewish Center.[153]
During his administration, Lamm has committed himself forcefully
to many of the now century-old principles which have directed the
Americanized Orthodox rabbinate. But, as we have seen, the Orthodox world in America today is quite different from the one his predecessors first knew. The refugee-yeshiva/leader-oriented communities,
now in their own second generation, are strong, resolute, and growing. The simulators and cooperators seem to be represented more in
his own generation than in the one being trained and emerging
from his own theological seminary.

Lamm, for his part, has urged lay and rabbinical leaders "to
broaden our horizons beyond our immediate needs and the concerns of our narrow constituency to embrace all of the Jewish community throughout the world." And he has spoken out in a
historical vein against "right wing . . . authoritarianism which . . .
has largely abandoned the fierce intellectual independence which
had always been the hallmark of the European yeshiva scholar in all
segments of religious life." On a more philosophical level he has
declared similarly:

> We are committed to secular studies, including all the risks that this
> implies, not only because of vocational or social reasons, but because
> we consider that it is the will of God that there would be a world in
> which Torah be effective; that all wisdom issues ultimately from the
> Creator and therefore it is the Almighty who legitimizes all knowledge.

Finally, he has charged his fellow Americanized Orthodox rabbis to
take their unique message, different from what is offered both by the
more liberal denominations and by the world of transplanted
Europe, to the larger American Jewish community as teachers, rab-

bis, and communal leaders. Time will tell how strongly his voice will be heard both within and without the American Orthodox seminary that he champions.[154]

2

The Orthodox Synagogue

Introduction: Exclusion and Inclusion in the Orthodox Synagogue

In March 1847, New York's Congregation Shearith Israel, America's oldest congregation, adopted a position on one of this country's most enduring Jewish communal problems. In an amendment to organizational bylaws, congregational trustees ruled that "no seat in our holy place of worship shall hereafter be leased to any person married contrary to our religious law and no person married contrary to our religious law shall be interred in any of the burial places belonging to this Congregation." Religious legislators hoped that the fear of exclusion from the faith's most basic privileges would deter young Jewish men from intermarriage. Such, however, proved not to be the case. Jews continued to marry non-Jews out of love, the unavailability within the severely limited Jewish marriage pool of suitable spouses, or the desire for socioeconomic advancement through familial linkage with society's dominant culture. This American synagogue, lacking its medieval European counterpart's communal power of prior restraint through effective excommunication (*herem*), could not legally or forcibly prohibit a co-religionist in a free society from doing what he pleased. It could only punish after the fact, imposing sanctions that may or may not have troubled the resolute intermarrying Jew. This piece of modern ecclesiastical legislation did, of course, assure that a Jew who intermarried—still a member of that faith community in the eyes of its own religious law—would be immediately and permanently lost to his people.[1]

Ostracism, however, was not the only possible organizational response to rampant exogamy. Indeed, prior to 1847, the synagogue had had a long history of official disinterest in members' marital choices and was tacitly accepting the intermarried Jew as both a seat-holder and even as a congregational elector. This latter policy was informed by the understanding that no matter what one's deviation from accepted religious norms, an offending Jew remained a member of the synagogue. There were, however, congregational critics of this early "lenient attitude," which was designed, as one historian of this synagogue has characterized it, "as a means of keeping those intermarried in the fold." Trustee Jacob Abrahams, for one, demurred: "To give such a person the rights of a member will have a baneful influence on the welfare of the congregation. . . by encouraging the young men of our persuasion to marry those of another faith. "[2]

This episode in nineteenth-century congregational history points to a dilemma that has confronted Orthodox[3] rabbinic and lay leaders of synagogues throughout this country's history: What stance should their religious institution take toward the majority of American Jews, who, owing to the open and secular nature of general society, lead lives clearly in variance with Orthodox rendering of traditional law? In general, Orthodox synagogue spokesmen and functionaries have adopted two opposing views on this question: Some have argued that the Orthodox synagogue must neither accept nor accommodate those who do not recognize and obey the past traditions. This exclusionary policy, found mainly in the early phases of American Jewish history, prescribed formal reading out through the denial of synagogue rights and honors to those publicly known to be less observant than the rule setters. Later on, these same excluders often chose—when they were not forced to do so—to remove themselves from their own indigenous congregations. When some congregations began to overlook violations by worshipers and when in the mid-nineteenth century many synagogues voted to abandon, officially, Orthodox ritual, those who wished to maintain the old standards separated themselves from institutional life and established competing Orthodox institutions. More frequently, particularly during the period of Jewish immigration from Eastern Europe, the reluctance or inability to modify, update, or Americanize synagogue ways to satisfy worshiper demands led Jewish masses to voluntarily abandon Orthodoxy, at least the form transplanted from Russia or Poland.

Others within the American Orthodox camp have traditionally turned a blind eye to the heterodoxy of potential communicants. These includers have attempted, particularly in the twentieth century, to attract the largest number of Jews to their fold. They have often purposefully instituted novel—but to their minds religiously permitted—liturgical, sermonic, and ancillary synagogue activities.

The excluders have often deemed that the includers' efforts to make the Orthodox synagogue more appealing to the less, or no longer observant, were at best a major sociological blunder and at worst a fundamental theological deviation. At the same time, the includers have characterized their opponents as unknowingly consigning traditional Judaism to oblivion in an American Jewish world of rampant nonobservance. To a great extent, these positions have been crystallized and strengthened by the postures taken by America's more liberal denominations. But this division within Orthodoxy, as is already apparent, preceded the rise of the Reform and Conservative movements. In many instances, this difference of approach has had little to do with what other organized Jewish groups have said or done.

The Era before the Rise of Reform Judaism (circa 1800–1850)[4]

Shearith Israel was not the only American congregation in the first half of the nineteenth century to vacillate between exclusionary and inclusionary policies toward its religiously nonconforming congregants. Beginning in 1798, Philadelphia's Congregation Mikveh Israel officially withheld membership and "religious rights and privileges" from any Jew who intermarried. But twenty-eight years later, it voted down a similar motion to deny intermarrieds "all synagogue honors and privileges." Its sister congregation in Philadelphia, Rodeph Shalom, behaved similarly when it first ruled in 1826 that "no member married to a non-Jew could share in honors and privileges." Three years later, the synagogue backed off and decided that exogamists who pledged to raise their children as Jews would not be expelled.[5]

In the 1840s exclusionary forces in Baltimore led by Abraham Rice, the first ordained rabbi to serve in the United States, articulated a more stringent set of requirements for synagogue integration. Here the Rabbi ruled that known Sabbath violators should be denied Torah *aliyot.* But Rice and his backers too were quickly forced to backtrack. In the late 1840s, Sabbath violators were granted *aliyot,* but congregants were instructed by clergy not to recite "amen" to the nonconformist's blessing. But in 1853, this practice was effectively quashed. No congregation was willing to maintain a law that would effectively destroy their institution by reading the majority of its worshipers out of the synagogue.[6]

This perspective also motivated New Orleans's first congregation, Shanarai-Chasset, to legislate in its original bylaws that not only intermarried Jews, but also their "strange women" (non-Jewish spouses), could be buried in the Jewish cemeteries, albeit in a special section. This very lenient position arose from the recognition that over one-half of the Jews then marrying in the Bayou chose Gentile mates. "Congregational leaders," historian Bertram Korn has suggested, "tried to keep these men from feeling alienated from their ancestral faith and how profoundly they hoped that the children of these marriages might be saved for Judaism."[7]

Still, even these most lenient synagogue leaders did not adapt customs and practices to counteract the broader alienation felt by nineteenth-century American Jews. In the most celebrated instance of intrasynagogal strife of that era, the request of congregational insurgents that certain synagogue procedures be modified "to bring back under your immediate protection and influence [a number of Israelites] whom are now wandering gradually from the true God and . . . the faith of their fathers," was met with a resounding no.[8]

In 1824, forty-seven memorialists submitted their now famous petition to the president and adjunta of Charleston, South Carolina's K. K. Beth Elohim, calling for changes in the synagogue's life within Orthodox tradition.[9] Although they were aware that much of what they were suggesting closely resembled the demands of members of the early German Reform Movement, they nonetheless averred that they wished "not to abandon the institutions of Moses, but to understand and observe them."[10]

These petitioners probably could not have chosen to convince a more unyielding group of synagogue leaders. Beth Elohim was on record in the 1820s as denying membership to both intermarrieds and Sabbath violators. Furthermore, it had sought to control congregants' behavior through the levying of fines for innumerable offenses both within and without synagogue precincts. Thus, in a move totally consistent with the policies of their then most exclusionary American synagogue,[11] "the miscreated front among our people," as one trustee characterized the memorialists, were denied even a hearing on their submission. Asserting that Jewish tradition "prescribed a certain fixed mode of service, established at the destruction of the second Temple," the *Parnassim* (trustees) held out no hope that innovations would be considered by this Orthodox congregation.[12]

Outright rejection did not prevent the insurgents from leaving the synagogue altogether and establishing their own Reformed Society of Israelites. This early experiment in Reform Judaism, as it has been frequently called, lasted but nine years. In 1833, the combined forces of familial and social pressure (the last informal, modern, remnants of medieval Jewry's once official power of excommunication), the absence of trained liberal Jewish functionaries, and the removal from Charleston of the Reformed Society's foremost spokesman brought the offending minority back into the Beth Elohim fold. The victory of the unbending exclusionists was short-lived. When, a decade or so later, a new Beth Elohim majority under the direction of Hazzan Gustav Poznanski ruled that an organ was admissible for use in synagogue services, its now minority of Orthodox members decided to secede from their no-longer traditional congregation. This remnant founded Congregation Shearith Israel, which was open to those who still adhered to Orthodox teachings and procedures.[13]

Charleston's Shearith Israel was the only early nineteenth-century Orthodox congregation founded by those unwilling to acquiesce to their home synagogue's liberal drift. It was not, however, the only congregation of this period to have been formed by exclusionist minorities who were uncomfortable with the heterodox religious practices of fellow congregants and displeased with inclusionary policies of the synagogue leaders. In New York, Shearith Israel's reign of more than a hundred years as that city's sole congregation came to an end, in part, because it was unwilling to control, beyond periodic anti-intermarriage legislation, the religious deportment of congregants. In striking out on their own, B'nai Jeshurun's founders moved that their synagogue would enroll as a member only "he [who] adheres to our religion as regards the observance of our holy Sabbaths and Holidays."[14] However, in New York, unlike Charleston, exclusionary sentiments were not expressed by long-standing members demanding liberalization. Rather, they were voiced by new immigrants who felt uncomfortable with the processes and practices of this American synagogue.

Although to this day Shearith Israel proudly proclaims itself the Spanish-Portuguese synagogue, long before the nineteenth century it housed a mixed Sephardic-Ashkenazic constituency. Only its liturgy remained uniquely Sephardic.[15] The arrival of a new, large contingent of German Polish Jews beginning in the 1820s upset this unified or homogeneous synagogue-community.'[16] Displaying an attitude that would characterize the response of Jewish immigrants for the next 125 years, the new Americans, coming from lands where religion pervaded every Jew's life, were struck by the marginality of the synagogue. As another historian has aptly put it, "the established burghers" that the immigrant encountered "wanted an orderly and undemanding Jewish church which would affirm their respectability without interfering with their life style." This type of religion, which consisted of Judaism in the synagogue and Americanism at home and in the streets, was unacceptable to the new arrivals. For these still unacculturated Jews, exclusionary policies grew out of a program for recreating on these shores a familiar and encompassing synagogue life. Liturgy, synagogue governance, and social controls were all to be reconstituted according to the norms of homelands where obeisance to Jewish law was, or had been, legally mandated.[17]

But once having ordained that prayers in B'nai Jeshurun should follow a particular variant of the Ashkenazic *minhag,* the new congregation soon discovered elements within their own mixed Dutch, Polish, and German constituency partial to an alternate rendering of the liturgy. In this case, although the congregation was prepared to *include* these ritually observant Jews as members, they could not change their services to meet every individual's liturgical tastes. Consequently, unaccommodated congregants chose to *exclude* themselves from New York's second synagogue to form newer congregations that practiced one or another version of the Orthodox rite. Thus in 1828, some Dutch, Polish, and German Jews left B'nai Jeshurun to form Anshe Chesed. In 1839, other Polish Jews from B'nai Jeshurun and Anshe Chesed left to organize Shaarey Zedek. Divisions over rites and disagreements over the distribution of synagogue rights and honors continued through the 1840s until there were no fewer than fifteen types of Polish, Bohemian, Dutch, English, German, and, of course, Sephardic-Ashkenazic synagogues in New York City by 1850.[18]

The propensity of new immigrants to follow their own Orthodox liturgy, which was based on their European country of origin, led to the proliferation of synagogues in other American cities: In 1841 a German congregation, Beth Ahabah, was established in Richmond, Virginia; in 1842 K.K. B'nai Jeshurun was established in Cincinnati by members who believed that "the mode of worship in the established synagogue of our beloved brethren K. B. Israel is not in accordance with the rites and customs of the German Jews"; and in 1847 Baltimore's Bavarian Nidhei Israel (also known as the Baltimore Hebrew Congregation) joined another German congregation, Oheb Israel, in meeting the needs of Orthodox Jews. All in all, by 1850, six American cities housed multi-congregational communities, split along national lines.[19]

But for all the ethnic-cum-liturgical differences that splintered congregations, and despite significant differences of opinion over how much control synagogues should exert over those who sought their precincts, American congregations were united in one basic, overriding approach to institutional life. No congregation sought to recruit that large segment of American and Americanizing Jews who, disaffected from synagogues, cared little for the demands of synagogue discipline. For the German immigrant groups, comfortable only with transplanted Old World ways, their inactivity was largely preordained by their lack of understanding of this new country. In the Sephardic synagogues, a combination of Hidalgo Jewish pride coupled with organizational resistance to change precluded experimentation with service revision.[20]

This era of complacency ended in the 1850s, for within their own organizations, voices arose urging reforms that would accommodate Judaism to American society. Orthodoxy's monopoly over synagogues ended. From then on, Jews possessed more than just the option of following established procedures or abandoning synagogue life. The Orthodox synagogue now had to determine to what extent its definition of Jewish law permitted ritual change to counter Reform Judaism. As might be expected, significant differences in opinion emerged.

Orthodox Institutions (circa 1850–1880)

In 1848, New York's Emanu-El Congregation took its first hesitant steps on the road toward becoming one of America's flagship Reform synagogues. A German hymnal was introduced to supplement the traditional Siddur used by the two-year-old congregation. In so doing, Emanu-El joined Baltimore's Har Sinai Congregation, formed just a few years earlier by members of the city's Hebrew congregation, which had been unhappy with its Orthodox rabbi's leadership. However, it was not until the 1850s that this first "self-declared Reform congregation in America" abandoned all Orthodox forms and practices. Nor did reform come overnight to the initially Orthodox congregations in Buffalo, Chicago, and St. Louis. Important Orthodox traditions remained even as synagogues adopted mixed choirs, organs, and abridged services. Most significantly, even when reforms were initiated, they were justified as attempts "to preserve and advance in the path of Orthodox Judaism."[21]

Although slow and sometimes unsteady, American Judaism's drift toward liturgical and procedural liberalism continued unabated throughout the years 1850–1880 and affected both immigrant German and indigenous Sephardic congregations. By 1880, America's Orthodox congregations—which had numbered thirteen in 1840 and which grew to some 200 by 1860 when liturgical liberalism had just begun to gain mass popularity—were reduced to a mere handful of the some 275 synagogues serving this country's acculturated Jews in the years immediately preceding the period of Jewish immigration from Eastern Europe.[22]

The Americanization of synagogue laity, as one path-breaking historian has taught us, motivated liturgical and structural liberalism. As large numbers of German immigrants acculturated, adopting the work habits, dress, language, and overall life-styles of their fellow citizens, they desired to see their houses of worship adopt American norms. It was widely recognized that the Orthodox synagogue, rooted in European customs and prevented from change by archaic laws and practices, could not help Jews remain Jewish while integrating more and more with American culture. Or, to paraphrase another historian's earlier conceptualization, when nineteenth-century American Jews were asked whether it was possible for them to become part of a land that accepted them and still adhere to the 3,000-year Jewish tradition, they answered with a resounding no! Accordingly, the overwhelming response of initially Orthodox synagogues to calls for change from within their congregation was to accede. They tacitly agreed that Jewish law and Orthodox practice could not coexist with Americanization. Clearly, the moment of acquiescence differed from synagogue to synagogue, in accordance with the level of acculturation achieved by those affiliated, but the end result was the same.

Still, not all Orthodox congregations, or Orthodox minorities within changing synagogues, capitulated to the drive for liturgical liberalization. For example, in any number of American cities, Orthodox institutions were established by worshipers disaffected by their home congregation's adoption of mixed seating, an organ, or some other innovation. Sometimes protesters against synagogue reforms attempted to utilize America's civil courts to bolster their position. The disaffected obtained court injunctions barring reforms, arguing that reforms violated publicly filed articles of incorporation that services be conducted along Orthodox lines. Out-of-court settlements often provided traditionalists with financial assistance to establish new congregations.[24]

The survival rate of these breakaway Orthodox synagogues was not particularly high. Few remained Orthodox through the 1870s. Some were drawn into the Reform orbit. Others came to be comfortable with a hybrid religious ceremonial. They abandoned the Orthodox policy of separate seating, but did not adopt the Reform practices of mixed choir and organ music. Nor did they show interest in abridging the service and in utilizing a modern prayerbook, customs then characteristic of the nascent group of synagogues later to be categorized as Conservative.[25] All of these congregations were caught within the maelstrom of Americanization currents that so energized the Reform Movement. Thus, although they perceived Reform teachings and customs as too extreme for their liking, they were also uncommitted to Orthodoxy's personal demands. Although they may not have been attuned to Conservative liturgical departures, they still wanted to pray like good Americans, seated next to their wives and children even as they recited the traditional services.[26]

Breakaway synagogues that remained permanently within the Orthodox camp sometimes had to resort to extraordinary exclusionary policies to ensure that, no matter how small the Orthodox constituency might possibly become, the congregation's ritual would remain Orthodox. Such was the case for Baltimore's Chizuk Amuno. Its constitution boldly announced that "no change or alteration" could be made in divine services without the unanimous approval of all members. Moreover, "should any member offer a motion or resolution to change . . . , he shall ipso facto forfeit his membership. "[27] Still, Chizuk Amuno, and for that matter all other American Orthodox institutional remnants of this period, did move to accommodate, within the framework of Jewish law, the sociological wants of synagogue-goers. Like their Reform opponents, they, too, Americanized.

By the 1880s, the German vernacular had been widely replaced by English in prayer and discourse. The need to maintain decorum in services was strongly emphasized and in many places the often-riotous and always unsightly sale of synagogue honors was curtailed or abolished. What is most significant, in 1876 Chizuk Amuno called to its pulpit Henry W. Schneeberger, the first American-born Jew of any denomination to be trained as a rabbi. A definite statement was thus made that an acculturated German immigrant and his children could behave as Americans within the more up-to-date Orthodox synagogue.[28]

Orthodox synagogues of long standing, like New York's Shearith Israel, looked to strict exclusionary controls in synagogue governance to protect their denominational integrity. The Manhattan-based congregation, to ensure that its Orthodox majority would not be easily outvoted by any newly affiliating insurgents who might neither share their religious sentiments nor their sense of history, created a committee to investigate the religious opinions of potential members. Subsequently, a rule was passed that members had to be affiliated three years before they could be considered synagogue electors; and only electors could enact ritual changes.[29]

Baltimore's Shearith Israel, for its part, placed its hopes for survival on even stricter exclusionary policies. It officially denied membership to Jews known to be Sabbath violators and persisted with these policies well into the twentieth century. Richmond's Beth Shalom, too, resisted pressure to accommodate calls for synagogue modification, but its refusal to change its practices effectively led to institutional suicide. Slowly but surely, the synagogue's inertia toward religious liberalism induced congregants to move toward the Reform Beth Ahabah. In 1898, with nary a soul left to serve, Richmond's oldest congregation closed.[30]

Alone among its sister congregations, Philadelphia's Mikveh Israel consistently tried to do more than simply survive institutionally with its traditional liturgy intact. Not content to merely endure as an Orthodox remnant in a Reform-dominated country, it sought to fight back, to develop nationally acceptable programs, and to seek out alliances linking all those opposed to the denationalized, deritualized denominational foe. To do otherwise, reasoned its two famous nineteenth-century leaders, Hazzan Isaac Leeser (served 1829–1850) and Rabbi Sabato Morais (served 1851–1897), would be to abandon all but a handful of American Jews to a faith system so attuned to American ways that it threatened Jewish group continuity. Believing that even if Jews did not practice all of Orthodoxy's teachings they had to be kept away from Reform, these nineteenth-century Orthodox includers *par excellence* accepted as colleagues in the struggle to control the Americanization of the synagogue gone wild, individuals and groups that had themselves broken with Orthodoxy to some extent, either ritually or ideologically; these were predominantly the men and institutions that would later he credited with founding or inspiring the Conservative Movement.

Cooperation to combat a larger threat was evident as early as 1840 and soon thereafter, in 1855, when Mikveh Israel's Leeser joined with Isaac M. Wise and others in developing schemes for national religious unity.[31] The resultant Cleveland Conference of 1855 dealt programmatically with the quest for a universally acceptable *Minhag America* (American ritual) but also directly addressed the radical reforms advanced by David Einhorn. Some thirty years later, Mikveh Israel and Sabato Morais were instrumental in bringing together another coalition. This one was dedicated to combat the antinationalistic, antitraditional ritual, and nonceremonial postures assumed by the Reform Movement in its 1885 Pittsburgh Platform. On January 31, 1886, Morais led Chizuk Amuno's Schneeberger, H. P. Mendes of Shearith Israel (New York), Bernard Drachman of the newly established Zichron Ephraim,[32] and other Orthodox synagogue spokesmen into a meeting with, among others, Rabbis Marcus Jastrow of Philadelphia's Rodeph Shalom, Alexander Kohut of Ahawath Chesed (New York), and Aaron Bettelheim of San Francisco's Ohabei Shalom—soon to be rabbi of Baltimore's Hebrew Congregation—all leaders of congregations that had adopted some reforms. These Orthodox and Conservative representatives pooled their energies to create the Jewish Theological Seminary of America, an institutional bulwark against the unfettered growth of Reform.[33]

Mikveh Israel was also there as a guiding spirit in 1898 when some fifty congregations founded the Union of Orthodox Jewish Congregations of America. This national congregational association—an institutional alternative to the Reform Union of American Hebrew Congregations—was mandated to "protest against the declarations of Reform rabbis not in accordance with the teachers of our Torah."[34]

But for all these efforts to attract individuals and groups away from Reform, the ultimate reality remained that neither they nor their ideological opponents were particularly successful in halting defection from Judaism. Whatever its institutional strength in the 1880s and 1890s, Orthodoxy, like American Judaism in general, had a weak constituency. And even when acculturated Jews did attend the most traditional synagogues, they did not see those institutions as central to their lives. Lewis N. Dembitz, a founder of the Orthodox Union, probably said it best when he characterized most of his fellow Orthodox Jews as "persons who do not lead a Jewish life, but read the olden prayers." Fortunately for American Orthodoxy, and ultimately for the faith's survival in general in this country, their ranks were more than refilled by a new migration of Jews who brought a new vitality to that denomination. But then again, it would be years before these new arrivals would recognize their counterparts in the Orthodox Union as colleagues in battles against both assimilation and Reform Judaism.[39]

From *Shtibl* and *Landsmanshaft* to Young Israel and Synagogue-Center (1850–1920)

Distinctively East European synagogues began in the United States in the 1850s. Although numbers of Jews from the Czarist empire, Romania, Hungary, and their environs had found their way to America long before the mid-nineteenth century, it was only with the founding of New York's Beth Hamidrash in 1852[36] that this Jewish ethnic minority expressed its religious and cultural individuality by founding its own institutions. Prior to that time, "Russian" Jews, if they chose to affiliate, prayed and associated with co-religionists in congregations run along Central European, though increasingly Americanized, Orthodox lines.[37]

The circumstances surrounding the founding of the Beth Hamidrash and its successors were highly reminiscent of those that fostered their sister congregation in New York, B'nai Jeshurun, almost thirty years earlier. Newly arriving immigrants found synagogue practices in America foreign to them. Liturgical variations and modernizations were only part of the problem. Like all Jewish immigrants before and after them, these East Europeans recognized that their Americanized brethren viewed the synagogue as little more than a ceremonial center of minor significance in their lives. For them, the synagogue was central to the civilization they possessed in Eastern Europe.

Beth Hamedrosh Hagodol* provided its worshipers, in the words of its long-time member, historian Judah David Eisenstein, with a "socially religious [atmosphere]." Jews who affiliated there, he explained, "combine[d] piety with pleasure; they call[ed] their *shule* a *shtibl* or prayer-club-room; they desire[d] to be on familiar terms with the Almighty and abhor[red] decorum; they want[ed] everyone present to join and chant the prayers; above all they scorn[ed] a regularly ordained cantor." Although devotionals looked informal, the commitment of members to Judaism's traditions was quite serious. The religious reliability of the *shohet* (ritual slaughterer) employed by the synagogue was scrupulously monitored. And the congregation's baking of *matzot* was also overseen with strict care. "As an extra precaution," Eisenstein tells us, "every member personally supervise[d] the baking of the *matzot* for his own family use." Their *Hevrah Mishnayot* and a *Hevrah Shas* (Talmud study classes) also reflected staunch allegiance to tradition. Founded in the 1870s, they were maintained by the congregation every morning and evening. In all events and for all occasions, the synagogue endeavored to recreate for its members the world they had left behind.[38]

---

*The spelling of this institution varies in the extant sources. We are using Eisenstein's spelling used in his noted 1901 *PAJHS* article.

Four years later, the Romanian[39] Kehal Adath Jeshurun of New York's Allen Street joined the quest to transplant East European religious culture to America. Over the next two and a half decades, the period immediately preceding the mass migration of Russian Jews to these shores, a vanguard of more than twenty similarly mandated synagogues was established both in downtown New York and in at least six other American cities.[40] They ranged from Chicago's famous Beth Hamedrosh Hagodol U'Bnai Jacob (established 1867) and New York's renowned First Hungarian Congregation Ohab Zedek (established 1873) to Philadelphia's Chevrah Bikur Cholim (established 1861) and Boston's long-forgotten Congregation Shomre Shabbos (established in the early 1870s).[41] Each of these congregations offered their worshipers a comfortable sense of belonging as the immigrants slowly made their way in a new American world. In return, the synagogue requested—when it did not demand—that members continue to observe Judaism's teachings as brought over from Europe. The requirement, for example, that "every member . . . attend services on Sabbath and Holidays, and if found violating the Sabbath is to be expelled" was a common feature of these congregations' bylaws.[42]

It soon became abundantly clear that many immigrants were not living up to their end of the bargain. Although they needed and wanted the ethno-religious camaraderie that came with synagogue associations, they were uncertain how strongly or for how long they could continue to follow traditional behavior patterns when commandments conflicted with their drive for advancement in this country. So stated Rabbi Hirsch Falk Vidaver in his 1875 description of Boston's first East European congregation. Congregation Shomre Shabbos, he observed, was "founded by Russian Jews who observed the Sabbath and study the Talmud. Yet many of its members, though faithful to other Orthodox regulations nevertheless break the Sabbath."[43]

America's pressures threatened the very holding of services at New York's Ohab Zedek. In the late 1870s, synagogue leaders reported that "although the number of members was slowly increasing, the attendance at services kept dwindling. Ten men, therefore, were appointed each week to attend services under penalty." Inevitably also, Americanization played a significant role in the actual structuring of synagogue life. Like the Germans before them, the East European Jews desired to see their houses of worship reflect their new-found comfort. As soon as finances permitted, congregations looked to move from storefront *shtibls* to renovated former churches, newly built synagogue edifices or to buildings previously occupied by German congregations.[44]

In 1885, for example, Beth Hamedrosh Hagodol, which began in an attic on Bayard Street and which later called "an old Welsh chapel" its home, purchased the Norfolk Street Baptist Church and moved into this Gothic Revival building. Two years later, Kehal Adath Jeshurun, born on Allen Street, engaged the Herter Brothers, a Christian architectural firm, to build a Moorish-style sanctuary-center. During that same time period, Ohab Zedek took over the Norfolk Street Synagogue, which had previously been occupied by two West European congregations, Anshe Chesed and Shaarey Rachamim.[45]

Although services in these new precincts were conducted largely as they had been in the past, the demeanor of worshipers underwent a significant transformation. Men still sat separately from their wives; the siddur was followed without abridgement; and the time of prayers was not altered. However, gone now was the "prayer club room" intimacy that had earlier characterized synagogue life. Decorum, always the first demand of acculturating groups in making their religious regimen more intelligible and respectable to the world around them, was strongly emphasized. The maintenance of order was furthered by the assignment of seats or pews. This new formality was intensified further in the 1880s, when four of New York's landmark East European synagogues embarked upon what one historian has aptly described as "the chazan craze."[46]

As newly arrived immigrants, worshipers at Beth Hamedrosh Hagodol had "scorn[ed] a regularly ordained cantor. . . [with] his foreign melodies." A generation later, in 1877, now as Americanized Jews, the congregants of this same synagogue hired Rev. Judah Oberman for $500 per year. Three years later, Simhe Samuelson replaced him and was paid an annual fee of a thousand dollars. Not to be outdone, and also fearful of losing members to their Norfolk Street competitors, the Suvwalker Congregation and the Kalvarier synagogue quickly hired their own cantorial virtuosi. In 1886, Kehal Adath Jeshurun shocked downtown society by engaging Rev. P. Minkowsky for the then-staggering sum of five thousand dollars per annum. But Beth Hamedrosh Hagodol remained competitive by bringing "over the well-known cantor, Israel Michaelowsky . . . paying him a large salary."[47]

To the Americanizing immigrants—Eisenstein called them "the young reformers"—these cantors were well worth the investment. They brought a certain elegance to the services and created an aura of respectability. Contemporaries must have reasoned that a man who contributed beyond his means to support a famous cantor would certainly remain silent during the prayers. For synagogue leaders, failure to acquiesce to this new trend was tantamount to institutional suicide. Immigrants on the way up socially and economically would not pray in synagogues beneath their station.[48]

Although there was nothing in this new synagogue style that ran counter to Orthodoxy's teachings and traditions—who could object to quiet during services or fail to remember that renowned cantors were a fixture in the Orthodox synagogues of Europe long before the phenomenon hit America—the rise of congregational formalism did not receive universal, communal approbation. Downtown, Rabbi Moses Weinberger spoke for the chorus of critics when he argued that although no one "can deny that a sweet-singing *chazan* is pleasing to the ear the lust for great *chazanim* and larger and more magnificent synagogues . . . has taken our people ten steps backwards." Weinberger was explicitly troubled by the sight of Jews violating the Sabbath by carrying admission tickets to their packed-house prayer extravaganzas. Implicitly, he was disturbed by the changing attitudes toward synagogue life that departed from European modes. Jews were no longer attending services primarily to face God. Rather, they were there first and foremost to see and to be seen by other Jews and by society around them. But in his heart, Weinberger also probably understood that this synagogal accommodation to the acculturating immigrant's proclivity for conspicuous consumption, even in religion, was the price that was to be paid to maintain the Jews' loyalty to Orthodox ritual in the synagogue and allegiance to Judaism as they adjusted to this country.[49]

Besides, there is much evidence to suggest that only a small fraction of the rapidly Americanizing immigrants remained long enough within synagogue life to care about decorum, "edifice complexes," cantors, and the like. More frequently, the acculturating immigrant in his quest for greater mobility and social acceptance perceived the synagogue as an antiquated embarrassment and chose to break completely with the synagogue. He either assimilated or expressed his Jewishness through continued geographical propinquity to other Jews or through identification with any one of the myriad of modern Jewish ideological movements that made up ghetto civilization.[50]

America's East European Jewish congregations first faced up to the disaffection with synagogue life in 1879 when representatives of some twenty-four immigrant *shuls* from New York and other cities organized the Board of Delegates of United Hebrew Orthodox Congregations. In their "Call to Israel," these spokesmen complained that "while our material prosperity has been increased to a marvelous extent, . . . the disintegration process in our religious system . . . is appalling beyond description. 'All the glare and glamour of costly synagogues and temples," they declared, "cannot conceal [this] from our view." The association fervently believed that the way to counteract inroads against traditional commitments and observances was to recreate an enduring East European civilization on American soil. For them, that reestablishment began with the appointment of a powerful "Chief Rabbi . . . for all the congregations in the United States," who would guide, advise, and above all, rule over his community. An offer was soon tendered to Rabbi Meir Loeb ben Jehiel Michael Malbim, a famous East European scholar. Malbim accepted this call, but to the dismay of all concerned, Rabbi Michael passed away en route to this country and with him died this first attempt to bring drifting Jews back into the religious fold.[51]

Eight years later, in 1887, with the religious conditions of immigrant Jewry far from improved, a second initiative was undertaken. The arrival, beginning in 1881, of tens of thousands of refugees from Czarist pogroms and legislation, multiplied by ten to twentyfold the number of congregations in this country. Even so, this mass migration neither substantially nor permanently increased the numbers of unwavering, practicing Orthodox Jews. To be sure, by the mid-1880s, the interested worshiper, searching for a socially religious atmosphere that would remind him of home, had the option of praying not only in an East European-style synagogue but in a *landsmanshaft* congregation that perpetuated the particular customs of the ancestral home. An intricate *landsmanshaft* network grew out of this drive, as the synagogue succored the immigrant and provided a myriad of social and economic services.

But, as already mentioned, the affinity of worshipers for the fidelity to Orthodox ritual in this type of religious setting, more often than not did not carry over into personal religious behavior. Simply put, immigrant Jews went to *shul* Friday night to be among friends and to pray to God, but they went to work Saturday morning to advance themselves in America. And as European memories began to recede, as they made their way in America, social attachments to the *landsmanshaft* system inevitably loosened. Still, when they went to *shul*, they expected services to be authentically Orthodox as carried over from Europe.[53]

This form of religiously inconsistent behavior, based on nostalgia and the communal elements of synagogue life, was incomprehensible to the immigrants' children born in America, who were imbued early on with the quest for economic mobility and social acceptance. This was the dilemma that the Association of the American Orthodox Hebrew Congregations confronted when in 1887 it called to New York Rabbi Jacob Joseph of Vilna to serve as chief rabbi of the city.[54]

Although Rabbi Joseph survived his trip to America, his career on these shores was a disaster. He possessed authority and expertise, but he had no power in this country. Although his East European-style oratory packed Beth Hamedrosh Hagodol, the seat of his administration, he could not stop his audiences from desecrating the Sabbath. In addition, his Yiddish-language message said nothing to the next generation of Jews. It soon became clear to elements within the Orthodox community that transplanted institutional forms, which took no cognizance of the centrality of Americanization within the immigrants' consciousness, would not save Judaism. These new Orthodox spokesmen also understood that they could not alone successfully refashion synagogue life to recapture for the faith "the rising generation in Israel."[55]

So disposed, the lay, and a portion of the rabbinic, leadership of some of the earliest established East European synagogues cooperated with their Central European Orthodox brethren by founding the Orthodox Union (OU) in 1898. Even as Eisenstein of Beth Hamedrosh Hagodol, Yiddish newspaper editor Kasriel Sarasohn of Kehal Adath Jeshurun,[56] and Ohab Zedek's Rabbi Philip Hillel Klein[57] still supported the declining Rabbi Joseph, they also led a downtown contingent ready to talk with the officialdom of New York's Shearith Israel, Baltimore's Chizuk Amuno, and so on, with respect to establishing a united Orthodox front.[58]

All of these men had been in this country long enough before the founding of the Orthodox Union to understand the promises and pitfalls of Americanization. Significantly, they had themselves achieved a noticeable degree of acculturation without abandoning ancestral teachings and they wanted the same for their brethren. Thus, although the original mandate of the Orthodox Union said much about challenging "the declarations of Reform rabbis not in accord with the teachings of our Torah," it was clear from almost the very start, that the organization's focus would be more on helping immigrants balance their allegiance to Judaism with the drive to Americanize than on striking out against another denomination.[59]

The banker Sender Jarmalowski and businessman Jonas Weil of upper Manhattan's Zichron Ephraim shared their co-ethnics' and religionists' sentiments. These immigrants of long standing in this country had also arrived in the decades before 1881, so that, by the time the Orthodox Union was established, they had achieved not only a high degree of Americanization, but had also reached a remarkable level of affluence. They were able to move their families from the Lower East Side to residential Yorkville, and there established a decorous, architecturally impressive Orthodox synagogue. The plans of the Orthodox Union, as we shall presently see, fit well their understanding of Judaism's requirements in America. In 1889, Zichron Ephraim engaged Bernard Drachman, an American-born, university-trained rabbi. A man destined to be a major force in the Orthodox Union, he already possessed the linguistic and cultural capabilities to appeal to Americanized children of immigrants.[60]

This major personnel decision was soon emulated by Zichron Ephraim's Yorkville sister congregation, Kehilath Jeshurun, an affiliate of the Orthodox Union that had been founded in 1871 by economically advanced Central and East Europeans. In 1904, this congregation replaced its Yiddish-speaking rabbi with a Columbia University graduate, Rev. Mordecai M. Kaplan, a Drachman student and a recent ordainee of the early Jewish Theological Seminary of America.[61] When in 1906 Ohab Zedek moved uptown, they began to share Drachman with the Zichron Ephraim synagogue. The English-speaking rabbi shared a Harlem pulpit with the foreign language speaking, but American thinking, Rabbi Philip Klein.[62]

Twelve other East European congregations from nine other American and Canadian cities joined in the founding of the Orthodox Union. Their participation in, and cooperation with, the Union testifies that East European groups outside the metropolis also recognized that immigrant disaffection from Judaism had to be solved along American lines.[63]

The Orthodox Union moved upon its self-imposed mandate to "take action of a more positive nature to conserve the true intentions of Judaism" when, beginning in 1901, it tacitly adopted the Jewish Endeavor Society (JES) as its "youth division." The union believed that "congregations must have ministers and ministers to hold the young men and women must be acceptable." The JES, founded by the early students and first rabbis produced by the early Jewish Theological Seminary of America, was considered by the Union to be more than equal to the challenge.[64]

The Endeavor Society offered Jewish educational, social, and cultural programs to Americanizing immigrants on the Lower East Side, and later on in Harlem and in Philadelphia, and conducted "dignified services dedicated to recall indifferent Jewry back to their ancestral faith." They understood that if Judaism was to remain, or become once again, vital in the immigrants' life, the Orthodox synagogue had to recognize Americanization's pressures upon potential communicants. Accordingly, the "young people's synagogues" established under JES auspices generally held their Sabbath and holiday services in the late afternoons to attract individuals who had been working until evening. Society leaders, to be sure, characterized their services as Orthodox and buttressed their assertion by using the traditional prayerbook and insisting upon the separation of the sexes. But in many other ways, these services differed dramatically from those in the *landsmanshaft* synagogues. The Endeavorers sought to admit America into the Orthodox service as much as Jewish law would permit and to exorcise those customs that would embarrass and disillusion acculturating worshipers. Recognizing the growing unfamiliarity of Jews with Hebrew, they instituted supplementary English-language prayers and considered the substitution of English translations for standard prayers. A weekly English sermon on topics related to the American Jewish experience became standard, and Yiddish played no role in rabbinic discourse or lay discussion. In addition, all overt signs of commercialism were eliminated from synagogue life.[65]

The Union also supported a number of other independent youth synagogue initiatives. In 1902, reacting to the reported need for a "large well-constructed Orthodox synagogue' for acculturating Jews in Harlem, Mendes and Drachman assisted local leaders in establishing Congregation Shomre Emunah. Like the Endeavor Society, the organizers of this synagogue promised to conduct services loyal "to Orthodox ritual in an impressive, decorous manner. This up-to-date Orthodox synagogue sought to spare worshipers the unseeming distractions of noise, commotion, and blatant commercialism.[66]

Three years later, in 1905, Henry S. Morais, son of Seminary founder Sabato Morais and a leader himself of the OU, organized

Congregation Mikve Israel in Harlem. This synagogue took the Americanization of the cantor's role a significant step further. Morais and his followers rejected outright the *landsmanshaft*-style, untrained functionary who droned on as Jews prayed noisily at their own rate. But they also recognized that many young people were not comfortable in congregations where cantors sang solos, even in a quiet sanctuary. Instead, Mikve Israel leaders became the earliest advocates of congregational singing in the Orthodox service. Morais instructed his cantor to be a true "servant of the community" by chanting simple tunes that could be easily followed by worshipers. Lay people were encouraged to join in singing the prayers, so that traditional forms of prayer would become more meaningful. Congregational singing also helped synagogue leaders to maintain decorum; lay people who were actively participating had little time for idle gossip.[67]

Mikve Israel was also way ahead of its time in addressing the role and status of women within an Orthodox context. Although most congregations across all denominations kept women from synagogue office, relegating them to the women's auxiliary or sisterhood, two women were members of its original twelve-member board of trustees. Here, although females were precluded from leadership in prayer, they had an important voice in all other congregational activities.[68]

These groups' ambitious attempts to draw those disaffected from Judaism into the Orthodox synagogue were neither quickly nor universally accepted. Rabbi Jacob David Willowski (Ridbaz), the so-called Slutzka Rov, a leader of the immigrant Agudath ha-Rabbanim (Union of Orthodox Rabbis of the United States and Canada), was probably the most outspoken ideological critic of these changes. He was keenly aware of the difficulties transplanted East European synagogues were experiencing, but for him modifications in the sociology of synagogue life, if not tantamount to deviation from the faith's theological teachings, were the first step toward that eventuality. In his view, the ways of the past had to be better promoted and not abandoned, and no accommodation would be accorded those breaking with ancestral beliefs. The Ridbaz was particularly angry at congregational adoption of English-language sermons. If such practices persisted, he declared, there would be "no hope for the continuance of the Jewish religion."[69]

Willowski publicly punctuated his point of view in 1904 by demanding to deliver a Yiddish-language sermon at the High Holiday services of Yorkville's Congregation Kehilath Jeshurun, a leading synagogue in the modernization movement. This affront to the synagogue's English-speaking spiritual leader, Mordecai M. Kaplan, prompted one unimpressed contemporary to characterize the Slutzka Rov's action as an "insult to honest Orthodoxy."[70]

The Endeavorers and their cohorts also had difficulties with less respected elements in the immigrant Orthodox community who opposed their initiatives on more practical grounds. Saturday and holiday afternoons were a time often reserved in downtown synagogues for popular rabbinic discourses given by *maggidim*. These ghetto preachers sold tickets, before and sometimes during Jewish holidays, to their histrionic performances and did not appreciate the competition for synagogue space. They often succeeded in influencing synagogue leaders to refuse rentals to these young interlopers. As one Endeavorer regretfully put it: "Services were successful but unfortunately a *maggid* usually appeared on the scene followed by his hosts and naturally the services had to make room for the Yiddish preacher. "[71]

The Endeavorers and early youth synagogues ultimately did not survive the decade.[72] But it was not the Ridbaz's fulminations nor the *maggidim's* competition that defeated them.[73] Rather, Americanization, the lures of secularized society, effectively undermined these, as it would undercut all later Jewish reclamation efforts. Many second-generation Jews were simply unmoved by Endeavorer appeals, as they followed the road toward assimilation. These early youth-oriented Orthodox synagogues did, however, leave an important legacy: They were the forerunners of the enduring Young Israel and Institutional Synagogue movements that began after 1910.[74]

In 1913, with the problem of youth disaffection from Judaism unsolved, a new institutional initiative to "bring about a revival of Judaism among the thousands of Jews and Jewesses. . . whose Judaism is at present dormant" was inaugurated on the Lower East Side. Like the Endeavorers before them, the founders of this new Young Israel (YI) movement were students at the Jewish Theological Seminary. Not surprisingly, Moses Rosenthal and Samuel Sachs looked to their teachers Rabbi Mordecai M. Kaplan and Israel Friedlaender for advice in developing programming "to awaken Jewish young men and women to their responsibilities as Jews in whatever form these responsibilities are conceived." Their appeal was directed to "all . . . whatever be their views of Judaism, whatever be their social or economic status." Their activities were to consist of a balance of classes, educational forums and lectures, and Americanized Orthodox religious services.[75]

For the Seminary leadership, the Young Israel movement fit well the mandate set for that rabbinic institution by its president, Solomon Schechter. In his reorganization efforts, Schechter focused the Seminary's goals on training a new generation of American rabbis of East European heritage who would recapture their brethren for the faith. Although Kaplan and Friedlaender's own personal and institutional understandings of Judaism clearly deviated from that of Orthodoxy, they understood that their American-style services and activities would have to be strictly Orthodox if they hoped to receive the approbation of downtown society. Their sensitivity to the attitudes of potential downtown critics was so acute that when Rabbi Joseph Hertz (a pre-Schechter Seminary graduate and later chief rabbi of Great Britain) spoke at YI sabbath services, he lectured Friday night in English and Saturday morning in Yiddish.[76]

This careful approach had its rewards. Four downtown synagogues, including, not surprisingly, the Orthodox Union-affiliate Kalvarier and Kehal Adath Jeshurun, who had backed earlier Endeavorer efforts, trusted the Orthodoxy of the Young Israel and opened their doors to their activities. More significantly, the Orthodox *Morgen Zhurnal*, the downtown organ slowest to accept harmonization schemes of any kind, stamped its approval upon their initiatives.[77]

Whatever its Seminary connection, the strength of the early YI resided in its lay constituency of "young businessmen and professional people" who attempted "to arouse and intensify the Jewish consciousness of our young men and women and thus to close up the gap now existing between young and old." It was they who helped the YI grow beyond its original balance of educational and strictly religious programming toward the synagogue-center it became.[78] It was this objective that moved a contingent of YI men in 1915 to establish the first permanent Young Israel (Model) Synagogue. Layman Harry G. Fromberg explained the goals of this endeavor:

> [a model synagogue is to be created] where every atom of our time honored traditions could be observed and at the same time prove an attraction particularly to the young men and women; a synagogue where, with the exception of prayer, English would be spoken in delivering sermons and otherwise, complete congregational singing instituted, *schnoddering* eliminated and decorum to an extent of almost 100 percent maintained.[79]

Lay leaders of Young Israel also knew that modern, decorous services alone could not ensure institutional survival under the pressures of assimilation. Early on, the Young Israel linked itself with Drachman's Jewish Sabbath Observers Association, which had sought to find jobs for those loyal to Sabbath observers. It thereby hoped to undermine the economics of assimilation. Equally important, the YI defined its synagogue as a Jewish social center, where young men and women could meet. Dancing, boat rides, and athletics such as were standard at nonsectarian or Christian settlement houses were included as part of synagogue life. Fromberg, speaking for his organization in 1918, argued that:

> The time has come when the man and woman in America must be taught to feel that he or she need not be deprived of the innocent social pleasures so long as it is done in accord with Jewish rites and principles, it is the aim of the synagogue to make the young people feel that being Jews need not deprive them of their social activities and pleasure.[80]

Rabbi Herbert S. Goldstein could not have agreed more. His Institutional Synagogue in Harlem, even more than the YI movement, constituted the most consciously articulated attempt to approximate within the Orthodox synagogue the activities available in other Americanizing social settings. Goldstein came to this post with both an impressive rabbinic pedigree and with important early career experience. He was twice ordained; first by Rabbi Shlomo Elchanan Jaffe of Beth Hamedrosh Hagodol, a stalwart defender of downtown religious society, and later by the JTS, from which he was graduated as a rabbi in 1913. He thus knew both traditional ways and modern American Jewish plans.

While at the Seminary, Goldstein had been exposed to Kaplan's teachings that the synagogue had to offer the second-generation Jew more than modern services if it hoped to compete with assimilation. Settlement house and Young Men's Hebrew Association (YMHA) social programs had to be brought into the Orthodox synagogue. Synagogue life could now be entered through any number of portals. Ultimately, it was hoped, they would find their way toward religious dedication and identification.[81]

Goldstein first acted upon these ideas during his tenure as English-speaking rabbi of Yorkville's Kehilath Jeshurun. There, he was instrumental in the founding of the Central Jewish Institute (CJI), a prototype of the envisioned religious center. CJI became the institutional mecca for all social, recreational, and educational programs ancillary to Kehilath Jeshurun's Americanized Orthodox services. Still, its critics claimed that it possessed "all the elements of the synagogue center but only externally so. The three departments have no close contact because the synagogue element is not bold enough. The synagogue has not developed its full capacity and its influence is small." By 1917, convinced that he had taken that model as far as it could go, Goldstein severed his connection with the Yorkville congregation, brought together a group of fledgling Harlem youth organizations, and established his own Institutional Synagogue. There he was free to develop and to integrate all aspects of synagogue life. A year later, Kaplan followed his student's lead and created The Jewish Center of New York's West Side, which would also serve as a prototype for hundreds of Jewish synagogue centers organized around the country over the next decades.[82]

By the close of the First World War, youth-oriented Orthodox synagogues had come of age. The Young Israel and the Institutional Synagogue both boasted of several thousand members and followers. Both were economically stable and each would influence the establishment of similar initiatives in cities throughout the United States. But this was only a partial victory. As Kaplan pointed out in 1917,

> The synagogue has lost hold on more than one-half of the largest Jewish community in the world. . . . It is evident that the density of population, economic conditions and length of stay in this country have so rapid an effect upon synagogue affiliation that we cannot but infer that the synagogue owes its existence more to the momentum of the past than to any new forces created in this country for its conservation and development.[83]

What was true of New York was apparent in other smaller, and less ambitious and creative Jewish communities. In truth, none of the institutional forms of Orthodoxy—whether *landsmanshaft* synagogue, affiliating first-generation Orthodox Union congregation, Young Israel, or Institutional Synagogue/Jewish Center—succeeded in retarding assimilation. With the battle unfinished, the 1920s opened under a new threat to the Orthodox synagogue. Conservative and Reform Judaism began to seriously challenge Orthodoxy for the allegiances of those Jews of East European heritage who still wanted to adhere to some version of their faith as they advanced in America.

In Competition with Conservative and Reform Judaism (circa 1920–1945)

Reform and Conservative interest in East European constituencies began long before the 1920s. But neither the Reform-leaning People's Synagogue, founded in the 1890s, nor Reform Rabbi Stephen S. Wise's Free Synagogue, established in 1908 out of Clinton Hall, a part of Lillian Wald's Henry Street Settlement, captured the imagination of downtown Jewry. The immigrant generation, which was often ambivalent, when not downright antagonistic, toward Americanized Orthodox youth services, had no interest whatsoever in these foreign conceptions and expressions of Judaism. And the second-generation Jews, who could be attracted to services with an American flavor, perceived the Reform ritual and practice as too extreme a break with the faith of the fathers.[84]

Early twentieth-century Conservatives fared only slightly better. In fact, its United Synagogue of America (USA), founded in 1913, first demonstrated its potential strength only in the last years of the 1910s. At the same time that the Young Israel, Institutional Synagogue, and Jewish Center initiatives emerged within American Orthodoxy, less traditional congregations catering to the second-generation constituency appeared coast to coast. However, not all of its member synagogues were Conservative in practice. New York's and Kaplan's Jewish Center, the West Side's Pincus Elijah, and Young Israel of Brooklyn were just three that had retained strict Orthodox ritual and seating patterns, even as they joined this congregational association.[85]

Denominational competition for the allegiances of affiliating second-generation Jews began in earnest in the 1920s. The battlegrounds were the clean streets and fresh meadows of the outer boroughs, city limits, and early suburban neighborhoods of America's immigrant metropolises. The now-grown children of Jewish immigrants flocked to these areas in search of improved living conditions and as a reflection of their intensifying American identification. For some, the physical removal from their parents' transplanted East European environment facilitated their ongoing assimilation. Now on their own, making their way in American economy and society, they had no use for the synagogue, be it unreconstructed European, American Orthodox, Conservative, or Reform. For others, however, suburbia was the site of their continued efforts to harmonize Judaism with their newer cultural heritage, and there they found that the Conservative and Reform synagogues, possibly even more than American Orthodox, presented reasonable solutions to their religious dilemmas.[86]

Orthodox synagogues and their leaders were of several minds in their response to Reform and Conservative competition. For East

European-born rabbis serving immigrant inner-city congregations, the answer was a consistent categorical condemnation of liberal ritual practices. These clergymen also lent moral support outside their neighborhoods to Orthodox Jews who were within congregations moving toward Conservativism. In one celebrated case, the Agudath ha-Rabbanim went to court to stall a Cleveland synagogue's efforts to install family pews and to change the starting time of prayers. Then again, these rabbinic authorities also had difficulties with the halakhically innocuous goings-on in Young Israel and other American-style Orthodox congregations. These critics followed Willowski's old exclusionary tradition when they expressed grave reservations over Orthodox synagogues holding Friday night lectures on "secular" topics to attract the uncommitted because it seemingly emulated other denominations' practices.[87]

Old-line synagogue leaders could easily express their belief that modifications in the sociology of synagogue life were tantamount to theological deviations because they were, more often than not, geographically, linguistically, and culturally removed from the battle for the second-generation allegiances. Not so the Young Israel and the Orthodox Union synagogue, which defined itself as American, for they presented themselves as attuned to the identity problems of the acculturated. For some of these congregations, the answer was acquiescence to the burgeoning Conservative Movement. Not all newly affiliating United Synagogue congregations began de novo in the 1920s. Some, like the Cleveland Jewish Center noted above, started out as Orthodox congregations and, with Seminary men at the helm, moved slowly from the Orthodox Union to the United Synagogue. Other American-style Orthodox congregations disdained capitulation and chose instead to compete with their liberal brethren. In their search for followers, however, they understood that most potential members were not only moving from Orthodoxy in personal practice, as had already been the case twenty years earlier, but that there were other denominations that accepted their heterodoxy without question.[88]

The answer of interwar Americanized Orthodox synagogues was a two-pronged plan of modernization in the service and conscious inclusion in congregational life of all Jews regardless of their personal religious deportment. Synagogues made concerted efforts to push Orthodox ritual practice to its halakhic limits. A member's activities at home and in the streets were overlooked as long as he upheld Orthodoxy in the sanctuary. Most important, university-trained, English-speaking rabbis ordained primarily at the Rabbi Isaac Elchanan Theological Seminary (RIETS), later and better known as the rabbinical-training branch of Yeshiva University, were called upon to implement these policies.[89]

These American rabbis entered the field just in time. RIETS frequently received appeals from Orthodox Jews when synagogues contemplated adopting Conservative practices. They requested a capable Yeshiva graduate to hold the line. In 1929, a communal leader in Massachusetts wrote:

> If we do not get a Yeshiva man, I am quite sure that there will be a Seminary man. I am not saying this in the nature of a threat but I feel that the spirit aroused among the younger men is such that they feel the need for an English speaking rabbi and they will want it satisfied.[90]

Once installed in the pulpit, RIETS men endeavored to make Orthodoxy as acceptable and as inclusive as the liberal denominations. Some rabbis were highly successful. In the 1920s, men like Joseph H. Lookstein and Leo Jung came to Manhattan's Kehilath Jeshurun and the West Side's Jewish Center, respectively. There they led flagship Orthodox Union congregations, continued the traditions of Drachman, Goldstein, and early Kaplan and raised decorum and the Orthodox sermon to its highest level. They made, according to one historian, "Orthodoxy respectable" within their affluent, second-generation, albeit inner-borough, Jewish communities.[91]

Orthodox rabbis placed in outer-borough and suburban locales were as culturally refined as Jung and as homiletically proficient as Lookstein, but did not have the political sagacity to keep the liberalizing elements at bay. And they could do nothing about their synagogue's location away both from urban work areas and sometimes from members' homes. Clerical and lay synagogue leadership was faced with the same questions that had troubled Orthodox congregational officials a century earlier: Can a mixed-seating synagogue remain in the Orthodox fold? Should membership or synagogue honors be bestowed upon individuals known to be Sabbath violators? The evidence was, of course, right there. Members drove their cars from home to Orthodox service. Ultimately (here the question echoed Orthodox difficulties over two centuries), should a man married to a Christian be allowed to join the congregation?[92]

Many congregations responded affirmatively to some of these questions, creating, beginning in the 1920s, the so-called traditional Orthodox congregation. These hybrid synagogues were most prevalent in Midwestern and Southern Jewish communities far removed from Orthodoxy's New York hub, the home of the OU, YI, and, in 1935, the Rabbinical Council of America (RCA), which linked RIETS and other English-preaching Orthodox rabbis. This "Orthodoxy on the Periphery," as one Danville, Virginia, RIETS man described it, served those whose "practical observance (of mitzvoth) may have vanished from their lives to an alarming extent. Yet they want an Orthodox *shul* with Orthodox leadership." These Jews, in the words of a St. Louis-based rabbi, were at best a half-baked laity with a confused and distorted version of Judaism." They deported themselves as Orthodox only insofar as their ritual practices within synagogue precincts were closer to the old ways than the Conservatives in town.[93]

Still, the Orthodox Union and the RCA tacitly and even formally accepted these congregations as bona fide Orthodox synagogues. To do otherwise would have been to drive their rabbinic colleagues and lay constitutents into the arms of the USA and the Conservative Rabbinical Assembly (RA). The RCA, for example, voted in 1942 to admit to its membership all men ordained by RIETS or by any other Orthodox institution or authority. They did, however, reserve national officeholding for rabbis officiating at synagogues with separate seating. The Orthodox Union, for its part, never publicly defined its admission criteria. Still, many congregations with several hundred members, both within and outside New York, had mixed-pew synagogues.[94]

These heterodox synagogues battled for second-generation allegiances against both the liberal denominations and the threat of assimilation. In the former encounter, the American Orthodox synagogue (defined here as including YI and OU congregations of both mixed and separate-seat orientations) more than held its own. It survived American Jewry's move toward suburbia and offered an alternative to USA congregations. Indeed, in the 1920s and 1930s, YI and OU congregations in New York City's outer boroughs of the Bronx, Queens, and Brooklyn and suburban Long Island may well have outnumbered their Conservative counterparts. Just as eleven USA synagogues served Queens and Long Island during the 1930s, so did an estimated nineteen OU affiliates. Both offered potential members socioreligious attractions ancillary to the divine services. In the Bronx, eleven Conservative temples were matched by at least as many Orthodox synagogues. In Brooklyn's new Flatbush, Bensonhurst, and Borough Park neighborhoods, the Brooklyn Jewish Center and sixteen other Conservative congregations competed with fourteen Young Israel affiliates.[95]

Outside of New York, the Orthodox Union was not as popular, and the Young Israel was almost nonexistent.[96] In other American cities, Orthodox institutions were overwhelmed by liberal denominational power and influence. In Newport News, Virginia, for example, an Orthodox rabbi publicly deplored "the spiritual plight of the adolescent girls lured away from traditional Judaism by the confirmation ceremonies in Reformed and Conservative congregations." His New Orleans-based colleague understood his predicament quite well. The latter's report on "Orthodoxy in the South" indicated that "Orthodoxy does not seem to be in style. . . . There are a number of Orthodox congregations, which, in the interest of harmony, have no Sunday School of their own, but send their children to the Reform school." And from California came the news that "while Orthodox groups . . . do not feel qualified as yet to do constructive work, the Conservatives and their Reform colleagues are taking full advantage of their inactivity." Nonetheless, in 1938, the OU made the claim that it represented 900 U.S. congregations in at least 150 cities in an estimated 27 states (coast to coast), and constituted "the largest

Jewish religious group numerically in the United States. "[97] Whatever their success in battling the Conservatives and the less pervasive Neo-Reformers, it is clear that American Orthodoxy—and, indeed, Conservatism and Reform—did not accomplish its ultimate goal of recapturing assimilating Jewry back to the faith. The "one-half baked" congregants, about whom the St. Louis rabbi complained, were at least affiliated with synagogue life. Many others were simply uninterested. So great was the problem that in 1935 the OU willingly joined with its USA and Union of American Hebrew Congregations rivals in a "Back to the Synagogue" endeavor to reclaim Jews to religious life, whatever their denominational expression. However, even this cooperative effort was minimally successful.[98]

In 1940 American Orthodoxy was congregationally large but the practice of Orthodoxy beyond synagogue precincts was weak. Like their counterparts of the 1880s, even when most second-generation Jews attended the most traditional of American synagogues, they did not view that involvement as central to their lives. However, once again a new Jewish migration hit America's shores during and after World War II and quickly revitalized and transformed Orthodoxy's strength and orientation.

The American Orthodox Synagogue—Postwar and Beyond

A breed of Orthodox Jews, previously unseen in America, settled here beginning in 1933. Refugees first from Hitler's terror and later from Stalin's tanks sought this country because their European home communities had been, or were in the process of being, destroyed. During the period from 1880 to 1920 these Jews had harkened to the Hafetz Hayim's (Rabbi Israel Meir Ha-Kohen Kagan) admonition: "Whoever wishes to live properly before God must not settle in that country." Brought to America by tragic fate, they set out to make the best of an unwanted situation. They approached the reconstitution of the synagogue life and the religious civilization they had seen burned before their eyes with uncompromised zeal.

Far more than any prior wave of migrants, they remained true to the ideal of excluding America from their community's life.[99]

Their success in perpetuating European modes of worship and behavior, and in keeping the impulse to Americanize off their *shtibl's* agenda, is owed to a temporal power that for them is greater than America, that of their rebbes, or transplanted religious leaders.

Chief rabbis did predate the postwar period, but men like poor Rabbi Jacob Joseph were given the unenviable task by their lay employers of recapturing or luring immigrants and their children back to Orthodox Judaism after Americanization had severely affected their potential constituencies. Postwar religious leaders, ranging from the German community's Joseph Breuer to the Hasidic rebbes to the *roshei yeshiva* of transplanted Lithuanian yeshivas, gained and maintained powers that Rabbi Joseph never possessed. Their followers were immigrants who came to Washington Heights or to Williamsburg or to Lakewood, New Jersey, precisely to be with them and together to live the good Jewish life at a distance from this country.[100]

This intense, exclusionary orientation has, with only one noteworthy exception, not been exported to the wider American Jewish community. The proselytizing Lubavitcher Hasidim alone have attempted to extend their formal suzerainty beyond the community of true believers and toward third- and fourth-generation co-religionists disaffected with acculturated, middle-class life-styles. All other refugee communities have not been actively concerned with the assimilated. Indeed, in a most poignant commentary on his group's attitude toward Orthodox outreach, one Lakewood Yeshiva student told a contemporary sociologist that the best thing that he could do to bring other Jews closer to the Torah was to intensify his own study of the sacred texts: "We do not know what God's motives are and how he works. It is entirely possible that my keeping my *Gemora* [Talmud] open five minutes longer will result in God influencing someone to become a little more interested in religion."[101]

Although staying behind their own fences, these staunchly Orthodox elements have made a tremendous impact upon the indigenous American Orthodox synagogue movements. Those who have borne witness to the faith that traditional Judaism could progress in this country without accommodation to the host environment have, for example, undermined the original assumptions and redirected the priorities of the contemporary Young Israel movement. These youth synagogues of two generations ago were built by Jews unhappy with *landsmanshaft* Judaism and convinced that their parents' European rabbis could contribute little to the maintenance of their religious identity. Indeed, many early Young Israel congregations prided themselves on their ability to survive and conduct services without the benefit of professional clergy, rabbinic or cantorial. Finally, for the acculturated these synagogues were most comfortable conducting dances and mixed socials. They reasoned that it was far better for their generation to congregate under American Orthodox auspices than at competing events sponsored by the Young Peoples Socialist League (YPSL) or Christian settlement houses.

The postwar YI synagogues have been influenced by refugees who reject such an inclusionary approach. These synagogues are today almost always headed by a pulpit rabbi; pay more than nominal obeisance to transplanted East European authorities, even if their own spiritual leaders are American-born and English-speaking; and widely disdain ancillary synagogue activities. One sociologist has suggested that the watershed in the YI's drift toward the orientation of refugee Orthodoxy took place in 1963, when its national director—significantly a graduate of a transplanted European-style yeshiva—"urged a united Orthodox front which would turn to the *'Gedoley Torah'* (leading Orthodox sages in America) . . . and be bound not only by their decisions on purely halakhic matters, but also by their point of view on non-legal matters." In essence, this scholar contends, the YI was now turning for advice and direction to the same type of rabbis against whom their predecessors had tacitly rebelled. In recent years, when Young Israels have looked to reach out beyond their synagogue precincts, it has been in the promotion of kosher kitchens for Orthodox students at American universities or to the development of their movement's presence in the State of Israel.[102]

The rightward shift of Young Israel and other liked-minded OU synagogues has been spurred on by two other significant sociological developments: the growth of Jewish day schools and the limited acculturation of the refugee's children and grandchildren. During the interwar period, even the most traditionally observant members of YI or strictly Orthodox OU congregations attended American public schools and after-school Talmud Torah programs. Immigrant parents, with few exceptions, sent their children to the public schools and expressed their residual Jewish commitment by directing these pupils to afternoon congregational and communal schools. Those second-generation Jews, positively influenced by supplementary Jewish education, filled the rows of American Orthodox synagogues between 1920 and 1945.[103]

The proliferation of Jewish day schools after 1945, a result of the disenchantment of middle-class parents with the educational program offered at public schools coupled with increased confidence in their dual identities as Americans and as Jews, has changed Orthodox synagogue life. Third- and fourth-generation children generally know more of Jewish traditional teachings and practices than do their elders. Day school youth, many of whom by the time of this writing have themselves reached middle age, look at a rabbi not so much as a senatorial, homiletically proficient figure, but as a teacher who can help them expand their familiarity with tradition beyond the years of their formal education. Equally important, their social expectations of synagogue life are different from those of their parents. Younger worshipers do not cheek the synagogue calendar for socials and dances. They see the *shul* reestablishing its traditional role as house of assembly, study, and prayer.[104]

For the acculturated, these synagogues also have attracted some members of refugee Orthodoxy's second and third generation. American economics, technology, and higher education have today facilitated the emergence of affluent, scientifically trained, and sophisticated American-born Jews who are unimpressed, if not relatively untouched, by American societal values. These doctors, lawyers, accountants, computer scientists, and engineers feel more at home in their transplanted European yeshivas even as they seek higher general training at colleges, which, ironically, had been off limits to even their most assimilated of co-religionists a generation earlier. American universities, for their part, have permitted individuals to graduate from their schools without exposure to the assimilatory liberal arts—many even give some transfer credit for yeshiva talmud study—not only because the business of education has changed, but because America now is trying to train its best and brightest. Americanization, consequently, is no longer a requirement for advancement its American society.

Accordingly, the children and grandchildren of refugees have emerged from ghetto poverty to fashionable middle and upper-class status in urban and suburban neighborhoods without a concomitant break with immigrant culture and religion. There they have linked arms with and have significantly influenced their co-religionists trained in day schools in creating a contemporary synagogue life that is committed to the study and maintenance of traditional law. When these Jews talk about issues ancillary to the synagogue, their concerns are with eruvs (enclosures) permitting observant parents to wheel baby carriages to services on the Sabbath. Thus they ensure that the Orthodox family living in suburbia stays together, albeit on opposite sides of the synagogue's partition.[105]

Not all of the Orthodox Union's 1,000 congregations look to European-trained *gedolim* for inspiration. Nor are they led by day school graduates or products of the yeshiva world. For the majority of congregations, particularly those situated away from large metropolises and suburbias (still the homes of refugee Orthodoxy and its cultural epicenters), advanced-level Talmud class programming and *eruv* installation and maintenance arc the least of their problems. They are, rather, concerned with continuing their struggle for institutional survival against both assimilation and the now very powerful liberal denominations.[106]

In the postwar battle for affiliates, the Conservative and Neo-Reform approaches to synagogue life were well suited to the demography and sociology of the Jewish move to suburbia. However, for all the strength of liberal Judaism within these most contemporary Jewish frontiers, Orthodox synagogues for the not particularly observant have survived. (Indeed, the OU claimed as late as 1965 that it spoke for three million Jews and for 3,600 synagogues; an inflated figure.) Ironically, these synagogues, whatever their true numbers, have been successful with third and fourth-generation Jews for some of the same reasons that *landsmanshaft* synagogues were popular with their immigrant ancestors. "Non-observant Orthodox," as one sociologist has described them, opt for the more traditional congregations because they feel that Conservative or Reform synagogue-centers are "too cold, too large, or too formal" for their tastes. These somewhat nonconformist suburbanites seek the same familiarity with other Jews and with the Almighty that fueled the faith of their parents. "[107]

American Orthodox synagogues are divided more than ever between those accepting and accommodating Jews who do not privately follow traditional practices and those that arc founded and maintained by individuals who, more than any previous generation in American Jewish history, observe the Orthodox understandings of tradition. Yet, with religious lines clearly drawn, a new sociological force, that of women's rights and religious privileges, has entered the Jewish world and augurs to redefine again the terms *inclusion* and *exclusion* as applied to the Orthodox synagogue.

The rise of the feminist movement clearly has not made as profound an impact upon Orthodoxy as it has upon other Jewish denominations. Women have not appeared at Yeshiva University's portals demanding admission to RIETS. Nor have women served as cantors in even the most liberal Orthodox synagogues, as they do in Reform temples. Yet American Orthodoxy, too, has not been immune to currents of change. To date, the majority of Orthodox synagogues—across the denomination's spectrum—exclude their women from formal ritual and organizational leadership. However, an increasing number of congregations now include women on lay boards of trustees and some even permit female membership on synagogue ritual committees. What is most striking, a few let their women carry Torah scrolls around the synagogues as a regular, accepted part of the ritual. Moreover, these same congregations have placed their imprimatur upon separate women's *tefillot* (prayer groups) within their organization's precinct. Time will tell whether the Orthodox women so involved in these services will remain content with the changed but still limited access to the divine now accorded them. In all events, a history of the Orthodox synagogue in America written fifty years from now will undeniably begin with the fate of this social development within and outside Orthodoxy.[108]

3

How "Frum" Was Rabbi Jacob Joseph's Court? Americanization Within the Lower East Side's Orthodox Elite, 1886–1902

At the close of the nineteenth century, the Association of the American Orthodox Hebrew Congregations was the downtown group most intent on transplanting the religious civilization they remembered from Eastern Europe to the United States. It was they, representatives from some fifteen of the largest congregations on the Lower East Side, who attempted beginning in 1887, to "rouse" their "brethren" from their lethargy to create a great Torah center in America, to capitalize upon the "liberty [they enjoyed] to observe our religion, to study, teach, observe, perform and establish our Law." These were the holiest of Jewish traditions which immigrants and their children had, until that moment, "neglected and held in low esteem."[1]

The Association's appointment of a chief rabbi for New York was, of course, the key element in their scheme. Rabbi Jacob Joseph of Vilna, an ultimately tragic figure, was given the job of leading "the battle which must be waged in order to keep the next generation faithful to Judaism in spite of educational, social and business influences which, in America, are so powerful to make our sons and daughters forget their duty to the religion in which their ancestors lived and for which those ancestors died."

There was certainly much to be done to "correct abuses . . . which have been a reproach for us and a weapon for the enemies of Judaism." Orthodoxy in America had to put its own house in order. The constant squabbling over who controlled kashruth regulation had to end. Insufficiently trained rabbis or outright impostors, who made a mockery of the holy regulations of matrimony and divorce, had to be put out of business. And the "brazen outlaws," as one contemporary of Rabbi Joseph put it, the unobservant laymen who sometimes dominated synagogue life and politics, had to be upbraided and removed. But beyond each of these specific intolerable conditions, all part of the libertine and voluntaristic American world within which they found themselves, theirs was the ultimate mission of preventing "our children and grandchildren [from] straying." "For many are they," as the Association's first broadside put it, "who stray like sheep, listening to shepherds who bid them drink from broken cisterns that hold not the true water of life."[2]

To attract the "many who should be enlisted under its banner," in other words, to lead downtown youths back to their fathers' and grandfathers' orthodoxy, great stock was placed in the success of an educational system that would attempt to exclude American culture. The Yeshiva Etz Chaim, also established in 1887, was the ideal institution. Indeed, many of the Association's own people, who loyally supported the chief rabbi, were in fact the organizers of this small heder for boys. In one of his first acts as chief rabbi, Jacob Joseph visited the storefront school, examined the pupils on their knowledge of the Bible and Talmud and came away impressed with the strength of Etz Chaim's traditional curriculum. Secular subjects were only grudgingly imparted to the youngsters at the close of their nine hour school day. The Association and the rabbi's hope was, of course, that this school would be a viable alternative to public school permitting youngsters to steer clear of these temples of Americanization where disrespect for Jewish tradition was also routinely inculcated.[3]

And while they were on the subject of steering the impressionable away from those who did not respect their Jewish past, some Association people were also vocally antagonistic not only to radicals of all stripes who truly wanted to smash the vessels of the Torah's teachings, but also to other religiously-committed Jews who offered a somewhat different approach towards group continuity. One downtown rabbi who rejoiced at the founding of Etz Chaim, and who was instrumental in articulating the call that eventually went out to Rabbi Joseph, had the following to say about the Jewish Theological Seminary of America (JTSA) founded that same critical year of 1887. That Jewish educational institution had a mission too of reaching the disaffected youth of the immigrant ghettos. But to this critic, "the entire matter is nothing but imagination, exaggeration and deception . . . This entire thing neither was nor will be. And even if it should somehow rise and establish itself on one foot, it will never be of any value to the Jewish people."

An Orthodox newspaper editor on the Lower East Side, who strongly sympathized with the Etz Chaim efforts, was more specific in his upbraiding of the JTSA's work. The Seminary's most advanced students, he scoffed, had finished but 17 pages of Talmud and only segments of Rashi's Commentary on the Talmud in the course of an entire year of study. How could these undereducated rabbinical school graduates, he wondered out loud, taught by professors lacking in commitment to the Torah, lead the battle against assimilation. They were themselves part of the problem, not the solution.[4]

Predictably, the interest of Association people in transplantation, their rejection of American ways, and their abhorrence of the Seminary was transmitted to and through the early Yeshiva Rabbi Isaac Elchanan and the Agudath ha-Rabbanim (Union of Orthodox Rabbis of the United States and Canada), closely related institutions that followed in the footsteps of Etz Chaim and the chief rabbi. The rabbis who were parents of the graduates of the New York heder founded the yeshiva. Association members backed this initiative to train rabbis in this country just as they were educated in Russia. At its inception, students received no secular or English language training. Rabbis who were close colleagues and admirers of Rabbi Joseph formed the rabbinical union to continue as a group the holy work that their colleague had begun. High on its list of objectives was to define who was qualified to be respected as an Orthodox rabbi in the United States. They made an early determination that even the most pious graduates of the Jewish Theological Seminary could never be accepted. Not surprisingly, the early yeshiva, then an East European citadel on American soil, became the most favored institution of the Agudath ha-Rabbanim.[5]

Altogether, a chain of tradition can logically be constructed linking the Association, the chief rabbi, the rabbinical union and the elementary heder and advanced New York yeshiva as constituting a rejectionist front against the perceived evils of Americanization among East European immigrants. I [for one] have characterized them in several places as a stalwart group of transplanters, exclusivists and resisters; zealots who aspired to transplant European community conditions to America, resist acculturation and oppose other Jewish efforts to come to terms with the new world environment.[6]

While there is no denying these activists' efforts to recreate the European kehillah, their apprehension of modern ways, and their antagonism to opponents, a closer look at Rabbi Joseph's court—the first link in this chain of tradition—reveals, nonetheless, that some of these resisters of acculturation harbored noticeable ambivalences towards the cause. The Association, a loose combine of the faithful possessed of comparable or related views, was by no means monolithic. Resistance to America was embraced with varying degrees of commitment. Some members of that circle hinted at acceptance of those with different views of how to perpetuate Jewish life in America. Others went further and occasionally supported seemingly competing institutions. For any number of individuals within Rabbi Joseph's court, old European ways were essentially ideals towards which always to strive. But accommodations to American situations were often the order of the day. Less ambiguous rejection of American ways and of other Jewish expressions began in the years after the death of the chief rabbi.[7]

The Association's own inaugural broadside promulgated in April, 1888, provides the first hint that there could have been some room in their traditional world view for a modicum of modernity. In a three line sentence, tucked in the midst of paragraphs that explained why the organization was needed and detailing what was expected of Rabbi Joseph, there is a striking assertion that the Association was also founded to "create an intelligent Orthodoxy and to prove that *also in America* (emphasis mine) honor, enlightenment and culture can be combined with a proper observance of religious duty." In other words, here the Association, that ordinarily spoke so strongly about past ways, was tacitly declaring modern concepts like "honor, enlightenment and culture" as compatible with traditional faith commitments. There was even place in that terse pronouncement for the Association apparently to acknowledge that such basics of acculturation were not unknown to them from Eastern Europe. The striking phrase "also in America" suggests that the Association's people could be devoted transplanters and idealizers of the past and still recognize trends then arising within their former old-world homes that augured to integrate secular ideals with religious values. Remarkably, here downtowners were, in effect, being told that such new ideas, originating as they did within Eastern Europe itself, could theoretically find a home in the reconstituted kehillah they were seeking to create in America.[8]

However, this rhetorical warmth towards "honor, enlightenment and culture" did not carry over to Association activities. Its school, Etz Chaim, through its first two decades of existence, showed little interest in expanding its students' general educational horizons. Downtown heder boys rigorously learned traditional subjects from nine in the morning until mid-afternoon. General studies were offered unenthusiastically and haphazardly after three in the afternoon. That a secular education was tendered at all was due both to the pressures of American educational regulations and demands from students themselves who wanted to be taught more about the world around them. It was the desire of the youngsters to compete within American society and not the school's sympathy towards modern values, of any import, that brought secular training—minimal as it was—to this cloister.[9]

But even as the Association did not really countenance acculturation in its school,[10] it did, at the same time, clearly feel at home with a bearer of East European modernist affinities. One of the judges on Rabbi Joseph's court, a member of the Association's inner circle, was a product of the modernization and enlightenment then slowly changing life in Russian yeshivas; the very change hinted at in the group's broadside.

At first glance, Rabbi Israel Kaplan looked, spoke and, in most ways, acted like an old-time *rov*. For example, he never learned to speak English during his score of years in America. Nonetheless, this learned talmudist, who had studied in a number of East European yeshivas, including Volozhin where he might well have been a schoolmate of Rabbi Joseph—they were the same age—was also influenced by, if not, representative of newer Orthodox attitudes in Russia. Family tradition has it that while still a student, Israel Kaplan had already displayed "unusual liberal tendencies for a man whose background and training were entirely traditional." He was, to begin with, inquisitive about the world of secular culture outside the yeshiva and seemingly was persistent enough to earn "privileges [within yeshivas] not accorded to other students. He was permitted to read something of modern Hebrew literature and journalism." It is probable that while in the Volozhin yeshiva, he joined that circle of students who were attracted to the Haskalah, or Jewish Enlightenment. He certainly counted among his friends Samuel Joseph Fuenn, the famous *maskil* who, remarkably, provided Kaplan, upon his departure to America, with a letter of introduction to Professor Alexander Kohut care of the Jewish Theological Seminary.[11]

Israel Kaplan was no less conventional, and surely avant-garde, in his attitude towards the education of Jewish girls. In this respect he was far ahead of the Association that spoke longingly of the return of Jewish children to ancestral faith, but thinking as they did, solely of old European school models, established a heder for boys only. Kaplan, on the other hand, while still in Europe, had insisted that his daughter, Sophie, attend heder with the boys in their hometown of Swentzian because, as her brother would later recall, "that was the only way she would have the opportunity of learning Hebrew and understanding the Bible." This act alone, her brother also suggested, "probably classed father with the *Maskilim* or intelligentsia, who were suspect of heresy." Still, Israel Kaplan's reputation in the European yeshiva reportedly remained fast by virtue of his association with the town's rabbi, Isaac Reines, who was destined to be the leader of the Mizrachi (Religious Zionist) movement. This suggests that even if Kaplan behaved somewhat differently than most Orthodox scholars, his attitudes were not totally unique and were not deemed outside Orthodoxy's pale.[12]

In New York, Kaplan's problems, in this area, had nothing to do with the possibility of his being maligned as a free thinker for his efforts on behalf of Sophie. Rather, he faced a more prosaic dilemma of where and how to find a school for his daughter's continuing training. Indeed, the Association, for all its seeming devotion to old ways, was very tolerant of his patently idiosyncratic behavior. For example, he endured no apparent censure or criticism for his ongoing belief that he had much to discuss with all types of Jews— including the non-Orthodox. A frequent guest in Kaplan's New York home was the eminent biblical scholar, Arnold B. Ehrlich, a former apostate from Judaism, who before his return to Judaism, had assisted his German colleague Franz Delitzsch in translating the New Testament into Hebrew (1877) and in publishing a missionary newspaper. There Kaplan and Ehrlich would discuss the sources of various rabbinic passages relevant to Ehrlich's work.[13]

And then there was the matter of Kaplan's failure to keep his son for very long in Etz Chaim. In the Association's scheme of things, immigrant boys like Mordecai M. Kaplan, who were the sons of rabbis from Russia, were essential to the mission of transplanting European Judaism to American soil. If properly trained in the ways of the yeshiva world of Russia, these youngsters could be projected to their larger Jewish community as a learned, religious elite, living proof of what religious Jews could achieve in the unholy land of America. They would be role models to those who wavered, showing that young Jews could become, under the conditions of freedom, "zealous followers," as the Broadside put it, of the sacred past, despite all the lures of the world around them.

Young Kaplan, by pedigree and from earliest training in his native Russia, could have been that paradigmatic serious student of Judaism's hallowed traditional texts. But the lad stayed at Etz Chaim at most a year and a half before enrolling in public school. From there, the junior Kaplan's quest to learn more about Judaism and to be of service to his people led him to the Jewish Theological Seminary. Each of these acts betrayed the Associations fondest hopes. But here again, the Kaplans' behavior was not deemed inimical to the cause.[14]

Judah David Eisenstein, the Association's highly outspoken secretary, was surely not the one to take Israel Kaplan to task for his modernist views and for the rabbi's plans for his son. After all, currents of the Enlightenment had also touched Eisenstein while he still a youth in Eastern Europe. He would indicate in his memoirs, years later, that

> at the age of about fourteen, the spirit of knowledge began to stir within me and aided by youth of my own age I studied extensively the Bible and books of Enlightenment written in pure Sacred Tongue, and we corresponded in the Hebrew language. Besides this, with the help of a Christian teacher, I studied Russian and German and the rudiments of the sciences.[15]

Equally important, when his own son was born after Eisenstein's arrival in the United States, he readily sent him to the public schools of New York and complemented that secular training with "a private teacher for him to spend a few hours daily in Hebrew studies until he succeed[ed] in his study of the Written and Oral Torah and all books of our Sages." To be sure, Eisenstein made that decision about his son, Isaac, in 1881, five years before Etz Chaim opened its doors. An American heder education was not yet available. At the same time, Eisenstein's vision of what type of American Jewish youth his son could become with public school and private Torah training is still highly instructive. In a contemporaneous letter, Eisenstein boasted to his own father, Zeev Wolf Eisenstein, that he would "spare neither money nor effort" to ensure "that he may be an example to the children of his age in this country." Clearly, as he saw it, exposure to the world of Americanization would not ruin his religious youth's ability to be a role model for his contemporaries. If anything, Eisenstein dismissed his own father's "reprimand . . . that it is useless to know the language of the land grammatically." Comfortable with his decision and with his lifestyle, he continued:

> You support your argument by our fathers and their fathers, forgetting that they lived in the past; the present requires other measures. There

are many things that we did not do then, but nevertheless do so now in broad daylight. For necessity impels us, so that we may mingle with the people among whom we live.[16]

Here again, the ideals of the European past were reconsidered in light of American realities.

Eisenstein also had no problem whatsoever with the idea that the son of Rabbi Joseph's lieutenant might attend a modern rabbinical training school and not a yeshiva to acquire the skills necessary to lead his generation back to the Torah. In a detailed exposition on Jewish denominational life and the role of seminaries in America that he published in 1888 in the *New York Yiddishe Zeitung,* Eisenstein declared that seminaries were decidedly "good, useful and necessary" *(davar tov u-mo'il ve-nahutz)* because many of the immigrant rabbis were simply not up to the challenge of reaching the Americanized immigrants and their children. In this truly remarkable statement for one who supported the chief-rabbi initiative, Eisenstein asked: why must we continue to request rabbis from overseas—the Association's very own *modus operandi*—if we can produce our own in the United States who understand this country's environment? The rabbis who do come over here, he argued, often do not understand American culture nor the outlooks of those Jews born in America. They do not understand the language of this country. And some of these "rabbis" are corrupt impostors, "evil doers without any traits of decency." For Eisenstein, American graduates of a seminary built on these shores, on the other hand, would be known to all for their moral rectitude and properly screened from the very start of their training. They seemingly could deal better with the new American world.

Indeed, Eisenstein was so captivated with the job modern schools might do on behalf of disaffected generations that he allowed that, in theory, even a seminary like Hebrew Union College (HUC), established by Reform Jews for the service of all of American Jewry, could be a useful "trade school" for the contemporary rabbi. After all, a perusal of that college's curriculum revealed that "Torah and Nach with its Targumim, Mishnah, Talmud with Rashi and the Tosefot,

Midrash, [Maimonides'] Guide of the Perplexed, Mishneh Torah and Shulkhan Arukh" were all taught; subjects an Orthodox rabbi needed to know. The problem with the Cincinnati school, of course, was that although Isaac M. Wise projected HUC as a truly non-denominational institution—as Eisenstein explained it, theoretically, a graduate might choose to be either an Orthodox or a Reform rabbi—in reality, the Reform administration of the College "lead the students according to their religious views" *(al pi ruham)*.

Turning to the Jewish Theological Seminary, Eisenstein argued that it had a tremendous potential to help save American Jewry, if operated properly. It could train the type of Orthodox rabbi America needed. Clearly, at least in this exposition, he expressed the view that the types of transplanted schools his association was and would be founding were not his most favored institutions. And, in an even more remarkable turn in his analysis, Eisenstein suggested that the seminary was useful even if it produced *Conservative* (emphasis mine) as well as the best type of Orthodox rabbi.

These were the same "Conservatives" whom he had pilloried earlier in the essay, labeling them as not all that different from "the radicals" (i.e. Reformers). Radicals, he argued as a good spokesman for the Association, were open, honest and unabashed in their deviations from the Torah's truths. The hypocritical Conservatives were, rather, more patient and circumspect in their desire for change. And while they claimed to be a traditional Jewish group, "they lack authority because they do not rely on the Shulkhan Arukh but for a hall, or a third or a quarter of it." Or to put it another way, when Eisenstein looked carefully at the pronouncements of the Pittsburgh Platform, that 1885 Reform statement which ostensibly caused Conservative rabbis to part company fully with the Reformers, the ghetto critic determined, to his dissatisfaction, that Conservative rabbis actually subscribed to most of its points. And yet in the latter part of the essay, which praises the Seminary for its potential to produce both Orthodox and Conservative rabbis, Eisenstein, the Association's secretary, hinted at a measure of acceptance of a non-Orthodox expression of Judaism.

Of course, for the JTSA truly to fulfill its warranted functions "many changes had to be made place." It could not drift towards religious radicalism, as he believed it was doing. It had be set upright, as an American Orthodox school. To do so, the school must "not admit Radical congregations to its association because if their numbers increased over the course of time, they would overturn" the Seminary's mission. The faculty had to be faithful to Orthodox tradition. They had to "observe the conservative faith and be sure not to break with even the most minor mitzvah of the commandments of the Torah." Most specifically, these teachers had to instruct "with their heads covered and in all their teachings never to deviate from the strictures of the *Shulkhan Arukh.*" But once again it seemed that notwithstanding his advocacy of a modern Orthodox way of teaching and thinking, there was room in Eisenstein's ideal seminary both for men who would ultimately emerge as Conservative as well as Orthodox rabbis.[17]

To be sure, Eisenstein was pessimistic that his sort of American rabbinical school would ever really evolve at the JTSA. At the close of his treatise, he suggested that the sympathies of those who financially supported the school leaned more toward religious radicals than traditional Jews. Still, Eisenstein held out hope that the JTSA would possibly find the strength to move resolutely towards teaching Judaism's ancient truths in a modern American way.[18]

While Eisenstein pondered the fate of the JTSA and spoke positively of an approach to Jewish continuity that was different from the Association's, other less articulate, although no less significant, downtowners fully supported both the Association's program and the Seminary's mission. Immigrant banker Sender Jarmalowski's presence on the Seminary's founding Board of Trustees, even as he was the Association's treasurer in 1887, strongly evidenced his positive appreciation of the JTSA's role in the religious lives of his and of future generations. Here again, it seems that an active transplanter of East European Judaism could both revere past ways and still make allowances to meet America's religious demands.[19]

Jarmalowski was not the only Lower East Side lay leader to support or be linked to both the Association's activities and the Seminary initiative. Nathan Levin of East Broadway was both an Association vice president and a founding trustee of the JTSA.[20] And then there were Asher Germansky and Moses Bernstein who were both "subscribers" [i.e. financial contributors] to the Seminary and were among the founding trustees of the Yeshiva Rabbi Isaac Elchanan.[21] These astute community people also showed the capacity to support and pay homage to the hallowed East European past while looking favorably upon the Seminary's championing of the future.

There was, finally, one additional Association person, who twice quietly supported the Seminary. But his activity is not easily explained. In 1890 and then again in 1892, Rabbi Jacob Joseph himself is listed in the JTSA *Proceedings* as a "subscriber" to that modern rabbinical institution. Could the paradigmatic nineteenth-century resister of Americanization have had his own modernist leanings, even as he advocated the transplantation of European Jewish civilization to America? One possible explanation for Rabbi Jacob Joseph's uncharacteristic move is that it was an act of gratitude towards Seminary founders Rabbis H. P. Mendes and Bernard Drachman for their assistance in the chief rabbi's unending battles to regulate *kashruth* in New York. And the uptown rabbis had significant influence over the owners of wholesale butcheries. Unfortunately, the chief rabbi never did explain why he "subscribed" to the JTSA.[22]

A new era of more strident resistance to Americanization and entrenched opposition towards religious opponents began for the transplanted Orthodox rabbinate and its followers in the years that immediately followed the death of the chief rabbi in 1902.[23] In the new rabbinic-led environment, the delegitimization of the Seminary in the eyes of the immigrant Jewish community ranked high in the Agudath ha-Rabbanim's list of concerns. To be sure, the East European rabbis' condemnation of the Seminary centered upon its new, twentieth-century leadership that would slowly move that school towards becoming the flagship educational institution of Conservative Judaism in America. Professors like Orientalist Solomon Schechter and Talmudist Louis Ginzberg were castigated as "expounders of the Higher Criticism which is anything but Orthodox." But this policy of non-recognition also extended to the loyally Orthodox students of the Old (pre-1902) Seminary, pious senior students who were graduating even as the school was changing and who never really studied with those who would not have "a share in the world to come."[24]

These were the young men whom Eisenstein in 1888 was seemingly reaching out to as potential ministers to the next Jewish generation. And yet they were pilloried, not because they were allegedly theological deviants, but because of the Seminary's new leadership and because they of their training to preach in English. These rejectionist positions were expressed most dramatically in 1904 when the Agudath ha-Rabbanim's *zekan ha-rabbanim* (honorary Senior Rabbi), Jacob David Willowski, a renowned East European sage then sojourning in America, refused to preach in Yiddish in an uptown American Orthodox congregation if its young Seminary-trained rabbi, a devout Orthodox Jew, would be allowed to offer his own English language message.[25] One indicator of how rapidly Orthodox resistance was moving in this community was that Judah David Eisenstein partially defended the old world rabbi's stance, when the Anglo-Jewish newspaper the *American Hebrew* which was closely attached to the Seminary, accused Willowski of blatant intolerance. Although unwilling to object to all sermonizing in English—Eisenstein readily admitted, in another piece, that several of the Agudath ha-Rabbanim's members "often preach in English"[26]—he nonetheless criticized the quality and substance of the religious message that even an Orthodox Seminary graduate had been taught to offer. Comparing this American rabbi uncharitably to the *maggidim* (itinerant Yiddish preachers) who entertained and enlightened congregations both in America and in Europe, Eisenstein wrote:

> The few who enjoy the rhetoric of the English preacher prefer hearing a good *maggid*, especially those who are acquainted with the Jewish literature. They are tired of empty phrases in a golden tongue; they want something of substance; meat and wine in place of vegetables and water. It is to be regretted that the elements that constitute a good *maggid* are missing in the English speaking preacher.[27]

Poignantly, the object of the Agudath ha-Rabbanim's attacks, Willowski's objections, and the subject of Eisenstein's polemic was the son of Israel Kaplan, Mordecai M. Kaplan, whose eventual role in American Jewish life, religion, and culture was to prove so enduringly great.

4

American Orthodox Organizations in Support of Zionism, 1880-1930

A casual remark by the man considered the first American Zionist, dutifully recorded and amplified upon by both the earliest and more recent historians of Zionism, has been widely accepted as succinctly capsulizing the attitude of the most Orthodox of American Jews towards the Jewish national movement. In an 1889 article in the *Shulamith*, the short-lived Yiddish language organ of the early Hovevei Zion of New York, Isaac Jacob Bluestone wrote of opponents to his cause: "The very religious consider us heretics, who wish to bring redemption before its time."[1]

Bluestone's first biographer, Hyman B. Grinstein, drawing both on the *Shulamith* article and passing remarks in his subject's unpublished memoirs, accepted this complaint at face value:

> The history of *Hibat Zion* [sic] in the next decade [early 1880s–1890s] is vividly described in these memoirs. Difficulties beset the movement from the start. The ultra-Orthodox Jews would have nothing to do with what seemed to them an attempt to negate Messiahism [sic].[2]

Marnin Feinstein reiterated this theme of the ultra Orthodox versus incipient Zionism in America in his very focused study of early Zionism in America. He attributed the "slow progress" of the movement to, among other factors, the "opposition of Reform and Orthodox leaders" and wrote matter-of-factly of "the ultra-Orthodox Jewish element's bitter oppos[ition] to the resettlement of Zion."[3] Similar are the sentiments of Melvin Urofsky, author of a general history of Zionism in America. According to him, in 1897 "opposition of both Orthodox and Reform" stifled growth of Zionist clubs in Chicago and Philadelphia. He offered evidence of staunch Orthodox antipathy to

Zionism when he noted that in 1904, while world Jewry mourned Herzl's death, "at a meeting of rabbis in a small East Side synagogue, Rabbi Shlomo Jaffe, leader of an ultra Orthodox group prayed: 'Blessed is the Lord who struck him down.'"[4]

To be sure, these scholars have been quick to note that not all Orthodox Jews shared this uncompromising view. Urofsky, for one, in discussing the founding of the Federation of American Zionists in 1898, has pointed out that while "the alleged secularism of the Federation also upset many Orthodox Jews who held themselves aloof from the movement on the traditional religious grounds that restoration could not be man's work but God's alone," there were "many Orthodox Jews [who] did not object to man's efforts to save himself." Their problems were with the "secular emphasis of Herzlian Zionism." Urofsky locates these more modern Orthodox Jews within the nascent Orthodox Union, formed the same year as the Federation, and chronicles their shift from cooperation with the Federation towards an independent Mizrachi movement (a process completed finally in 1914) while deftly suggesting important differences on this issue between them and the ultra Orthodox. In short, extant scholarship has two basic themes: the existence of profound "ultra" Orthodox opposition to Zionism, and significant differences of opinion between the "ultras" and "moderns" on this highly charged issue.[5]

A closer look at the pronouncements and activities of Orthodox Jewish leaders during the first fifty years of Zionism's slow emergence in America (1880–1930) suggests very different stances and relationships. Both the East European rabbinate, first as individuals (until 1902) and then as an organized group through their Agudath ha-Rabbanim (Union of Orthodox Rabbis of the United States and Canada), as well as the Union of Orthodox Jewish Congregations, the organization of the Americanized Orthodox rabbinate and their lay supporters, largely supported Zionism. Moreover, support for Zionism—always in its religious incarnation, and sometimes also in its secular form—was the one area where there was consistent intra-Orthodox unity of opinion. Among the "ultras," resistance to American ways and rejection of accomodationist means did not usually carry over to vocal opposition to the modern Jewish national movement. Divergence from this unified view and profound differences of opinion would come after 1930.

The Agudath ha-Rabbanim was the seat of East European-born opposition to American modernity. The "ultras" organized this bastion in 1902 to resist the impact of secularism and Americanism on traditional observance. These transplanted old-world rabbis had learned from the sad experience of earlier critics of America—individuals like their revered Rabbi Jacob Joseph, late Chief Rabbi of New York City—that acculturation was too great a force for any one rabbi to battle. Still, they believed that together they could do much to recreate in America the religious world they remembered from Russia.[6]

Were they fully resolute in their world-view and campaign? Certainly their inaugural charter (of 1902) implicitly identified, for example, the undermining influence of free public education on the next generation's allegiance to Judaism. For them the ideal solution was the building of East European yeshivas in America, where the boys instructed in Yiddish and Hebrew, would be taught the lessons of the past and surely socialized into a reconstructed world fundamentally different from the rest of American society. At the same time they were very realistic about what could be accomplished within a society already so secularized that Jews had to be called back to traditional behavior. Thus, in their charter they said that "the Yeshiva committee should also supervise the secular subjects [albeit only 'necessary subjects'] taught in the yeshivot." In their recent East European experience, the questions of if, when, and how venaculars or secular subjects would be taught in a yeshiva were hotly debated.[7]

Such pragmatism about what could be achieved here and how it could be done appears again also when the Agudath ha-Rabbanim conceded that although "teachers are to translate [Hebrew texts] into Yiddish . . . when necessary the teachers may also utilize English." And "in areas where only English is spoken, it may be the basic tongue." While it felt that a strong yeshiva education was necessary for all boys, it realized that most "youth work or attend secular schools by day." Accordingly, the Agudath ha-Rabbanim called for the building of evening schools with an admittedly watered down curriculum of "Torah, ethical instruction and the basic history of the Jewish people." [8]

Notwithstanding the Agudath ha-Rabbanim's in-practice less than full rejection of modern American ways—United States "ultras" certainly pale in their enthusiasm for no change when compared with their European counterparts; after all they had made their own "break" by coming to America—it is still quite remarkable how accepting, active and continually supportive they were of Zionism. For advocacy of the Jewish national cause, particularly as it moved from its earliest Hibbat Zion phase in the 1880s to a full blown political and cultural movement in the 1890s, was modernism incarnate, a fundamental break with the view held by the clear majority of East European religious authorities. [9]

For evidence of the proximity of the Agudath ha-Rabbanim to Zionism in America one has only to look at the time and place of the meeting that called the rabbis' organization into being. According to the Agudath ha-Rabbanim's own chroniclers, the meeting of the nine rabbis who determined that the time had come "to raise the standard of Judaism in general and of Torah specifically . . . through the organizing of Orthodox Jewry", took place in May 1902 in the home of Rabbi Moses Sebulun Margolies (Ramaz) in Boston during the Federation of American Zionists Conference (FAZ). Five of these East European-trained rabbis—including their host—were either delegates to the Conference or, even more impressively, were members of the FAZ Executive Council. Five other charter members or early affiliates of the Agudath ha-Rabbanim were also delegates and/ or early leaders of the FAZ. In Boston and in other American cities, they deliberated with such seemingly unlikely colleagues as Reform rabbis Richard Gottheil, Stephen S. Wise and Abraham Radin and other non-Orthodox Jews as Rabbi Marcus Jastrow and Henrietta Szold, as well as secularized Zionists.

Quite early in its history the Agudath ha-Rabbanim itself indicated it was on the same wave length as other American Zionists. At its second annual conference (1903) "Zionism was unanimously accepted as part of the conference program," albeit with the unexplained proviso "that the Zionist society in America hold their meetings as literary and religious bodies and not as social clubs." The Agudath ha-Rabbanim also publicly mourned Herzl's death. Notwithstanding the above noted joy expressed by Rabbi Shlomo Jaffe and his rabbis "in an East Side synagogue," the organization of East European rabbis in America, upon "receipt of the news of Herzl's death", adopted a "resolution of respect," properly eulogized the fallen leader, and on the last evening of their meeting conducted "memorial services under the auspices of the Mizrachi wing of the Zionist organization."[10]

Remarkably, in each of these early expressions and activities, and particularly in its association with others of very different religious views, the Agudath ha-Rabbanim deviated significantly from its own expressed policies of not-recognizing liberal rabbis and not cooperating with their American Orthodox colleagues. To the Agudath ha-Rabbanim, rabbis of the Central Conference of American Rabbis, who embraced Americanization and rabbis of the Union of Orthodox Jewish Congregations who made their own social accommodations with this new land, were all misleading the people—albeit to different degrees—whose stances had to be opposed and with whom one should not associate. But their allegiance to Zionism, born, as we will presently see, primarily out of their continued allegiance to a particular brand of East European religious Zionist thought was so strong that they were willing to work with others.[11]

Whatever their motivation, the immigrant rabbis' supportive position was, understandably, applauded by American Zionists. As Richard Gottheil proudly said in 1901, the "mere fact that we have among the Zionists orthodox, good men [and] leading reformers . . . would be a sufficient refutation of all charges against Zionism." But the Agudath ha-Rabbanim's cooperation was probably most appreciated by the rabbis and lay leaders of the Union of Orthodox Jewish Congregations of America. During the years that OU President (and FAZ Honorary Vice President) Rabbi Henry P. Mendes, outspoken lay leaders like Lewis Dembitz, E. W. Lewin-Epstein (FAZ Executive Committee members) and Harry Friedenwald (future FAZ president and long-time OU Vice President) witnessed the Agudath ha-Rabbanim openly question their authority to represent Orthodoxy in America, it was undoubtedly warming to them to be recognized as equals and worthy coworkers by the East European sages.[12]

If Rabbi Mendes and the others were surprised by this comradeship, they could have been reminded that such understandings were not unprecedented within the East European rabbinic world Agudath ha-Rabbanim members had left behind. Such contemporary Torah scholars like Rabbis Isaac Elchanan Spektor, Naphtali Zevi Judah Berlin and Samuel Mohilever were all publicly identified with the incipient Hibbat Zion movement in Russia. All argued the appropriateness of all Jews laboring together in the national rebirth and they acted on their beliefs by attending important Hibbat Zion conferences, like Kattowicz (1884) and Druzgeniki (1887). In the former meeting, they met with and gained the respect of Leo Pinsker, a man far removed from tradition, but who appreciated the support emanating from those Orthodox authorities.[13]

The Agudath ha-Rabbanim members who staunchly advocated Zionism on these shores were keenly aware of Spektor, Berlin and Mohilever's teachings since many of them were literally their students. The younger America-based East European rabbis, the Agudath ha-Rabbanim members, were the generation that studied with the immediate spiritual predecessors of the Mizrachi (Religious Zionist) movement.

The views of Spektor, Berlin and particularly Mohilever, though the minority opinion among the rabbis of Eastern Europe, became the unquestioned majority view among the most Orthodox Jews in America, as it was the students of the early Hibbat Zion sympathetic Spektor and Berlin and the Religious Zionists' Mohilever who first made the trip to America and then within the generation of their teachers' deaths, formed the Agudath ha-Rabbanim. At least seven of the founders or early members of the Agudath ha-Rabbanim who were also either Honorary Vice Presidents, members of the Executive Committee or delegates to the early 1900-1906 meetings of the FAZ were students and/or were ordained by Spektor, Mohilever or Berlin. Two other America-based students of that illustrious triumvirate, who were important leaders in the FAZ did not join the Agudath ha-Rabbanim. Understandably, Rabbis Zvi Hirsch Masliansky, the famous East European rabbi as Americanizer and Shepsel Schaeffer, individuals whose general orientation beyond Zionism itself was more modern than the Agudath ha-Rabbanim, had even less difficulty cooperating with FAZ members. Rabbi Abraham Ashinsky of Pittsburg shared their views and their affinity for the FAZ. A disciple of Rabbi Eliezer Rabinowich and Hayyim Rottenberg, who have learned in Kovno, Ashinksy, uniquely and significantly, was both a member of the Agudath ha-Rabbanim and an early supporter of the Orthodox Union, putting him also squarely in the pro-modernity and Americanization camp.[14]

For itself, in cooperating with the FAZ, the Agudath ha-Rabbanim could also draw upon the precedent set for them locally just a few years earlier by Rabbi Jacob Joseph. Although the Chief Rabbi had his difficulties with the non-Orthodox character of early constituent organizations of the FAZ, in 1897 he was willing to help organize a pro-Zionist rabbinical conference in New York attended by a score of colleagues. That same year witnessed the founding of the Knesset Zion ha-Metzuyanet by local Orthodox rabbis "to strengthen the position of the Zionist movement among Orthodox Jews."[15] Thus in the decade before there was a Mizrachi, a cadre of rabbis sympathetic to the type of ideals the Mizrachi would soon stand for settled in this country, and while most of the East Europeans resisted Americanization, they set a modernist tone within their community on the question of the Jewish national revival.[16]

As a Mizrachi party formed in Russia in the first decade of the twentieth century, understandably Agudath ha-Rabbanim rabbis, followed the lead of that minority Eastern European religious authority, and found the American Mizrachi movement to be the right, independent, vehicle for expressing their nationalist sentiments. But they trailed their parent organization in their evolution by about a decade.

Initially, the American Mizrachi was, in fact, a creation of the FAZ and was publicly described in 1904 as "the conservative wing of the Zionist organization (FAZ)."[17] It was first set up, primarily through the efforts of Jacob de Haas in order to undermine an incipient, competitive group, the United Zionists. This latter predominantly-Orthodox and East European faction was headed by Rabbi Philip Hillel Klein. But interestingly enough, despite Klein, an early important leader of the Agudath ha-Rabbanim, the rabbinic organization did not rally to the United Zionist's banner. And when that ephemeral organization waned in 1905, there was Rabbi Klein within the FAZ's Mizrachi playing an essential role. Rabbi Klein became President of the early Mizrachi and five of the seven directors were Agudath ha-Rabbanim members. Moreover, the true split with the FAZ (at the beginning of the 1910s) was neither sudden nor dramatic. Significantly, Klein and member Rabbi Ashinsky served together on the FAZ Executive Committee along with Rabbi Bernard Levinthal, another leading Agudath ha-Rabbanim spokesman throughout that decade. Indeed, until the formal founding of the independent American Mizrachi in 1912 there was a Mizrachi-wing and/or Agudath ha-Rabbanim man in a leadership position in an organization that was, and would always remain, predominantly non religious, non-Orthodox and certainly non-East European Orthodox. East European. For himself, Zvi Hirsch Masliansky, that East European-born rabbinic gadfly, also a frequent member of the FAZ Executive, remained with that organization through its transformation into the Zionist Organization of America in 1917.[18] And the Orthodox Union through Friedenwald, Lewin-Epstein, Harry Fischel and, later on, Rabbi David De Sola Pool—maintained a tradition of American Orthodox participation within the general Zionist movement that would continue for another generation.[19]

During the succeeding decade and a half, Agudath ha-Rabbanim support and affinity for the Mizrachi was strong and resolute. On an organizational level their missions were intertwined in 1921 under Rabbi Meyer Berlin when the Agudath ha-Rabbanim's favored institution, New York's Rabbi Isaac Elchanan Theological Seminary incorporated the Mizrachi's fledgling Teachers Institute. In a move somewhat paralleled, but unequalled in Eastern Europe (significantly in Reines' own Lida yeshiva), a traditional transplanted yeshiva on American soil supported, albeit with some carping by *roshei yeshiva*, a teacher training program with a diverse Torah and *judische Wissenschaft* curriculum and a strong Zionist orientation.[20]

The Agudath ha-Rabbanim consistent cooperation with the world Zionist movement underscored how aligned they were with the Mizrachi world view. They bristled at charges that their rabbis were not outspoken enough in support of the larger movement. Presidium member Rabbi Israel Ha Levi Rosenberg of Paterson wrote for his group in 1914: "It is self-evident that support for the return to the land of Israel is one of the pillars upon which Orthodox Judaism rests." Asking the Agudath ha-Rabbanim to vote in favor of the return, he wrote, "is like asking them to vote for such basics as the sabbath and other mitzvoth. . . ." For him, human efforts to actualize the Jews' traditional yearning for the ingathering of the exiles was a fundamental article of faith. And he perceived and demanded an essential role for his and his rabbinical colleagues in advancing the modern national movement. "[If only] the influence of the Agudath ha-Rabbanim would increase," he declared, "they would be more influential in moving forward the work of Zionism, since most of the rabbis are its supporters."[21]

Thus it was totally in character for the Agudath ha-Rabbanim to receive news of the Balfour Declaration "with great joy and enthusiasm" and to react to the San Remo Mandate Conference of 1920 by sponsoring a parade in New York which attracted 10,000 marchers. "How beautiful a sight," one observer remarked, "rabbis, the shepherds of Israel leading a parade with [Zionist] flags at their heads."[22]

When the Agudath ha-Rabbanim supported the return to Zion, it did not mean only the religious institutions of the old yishuv. Its organizational historians claimed that:

If indeed the Agudath ha-Rabbanim expended most of its energies on behalf of the old *yishuv,* the truth is that we were among the first supporters of the national movement. The rabbis were among the first workers for the Keren Ha-Yesod and other institutions whose goal is the upbuilding of the land.

To take but one example, in 1925 every member rabbi was requested to devote at least one public appeal a year on behalf of the Jewish National Fund. In so doing, the Agudath ha-Rabbanim was reportedly willing to put aside their "unhappiness with the behavior of the Histadrut both here and in Palestine . . . [and] worked with individuals who on other issues were far removed from their position."[23]

If anything, the Agudath ha-Rabbanim's major complaint against rank and file Zionist and Palestine relief groups was that the secular Zionists did not do their fair share for religious institutions. Such was their complaint during World War I when the Temporary Organization for Support of the Yishuv designed to support, among other Zionist needs, the educational institutions in Palestine, ignored requests from the old *yishuv.* Apparently, the Joint Distribution Committee did the same causing the Agudath ha-Rabbanim to turn to the Central Relief Committee (the American Orthodox [predominantly OU] component in the JDC) with the demand that it work more strongly from within that umbrella organization for the survival of yeshivas and synagogues in Palestine.[24]

The Agudath ha-Rabbanim probably demonstrated its staunchest support for Mizrachi by its lack of enthusiasm for the ideology and political agenda of the Agudath Israel. America's East European rabbis were not unmindful of the alliance back home of Lithuanian roshei yeshiva, Hasidic rebbes and German Neo-Orthodox followers of Samson Raphael Hirsch in protesting the Zionist movement and showing profound disdain for Mizrachi policies of cooperation. Indeed, in 1913, a year after the Agudath Israel's formal founding in Kattowicz, America's Agudath ha-Rabbanim, at its own 11th annual meeting, voted "to establish branches of Agudath Israel in the U.S. wherever possible" and to "request that members travel to nearby cities to promote Agudath Israel." But the Agudath Israel that America-based rabbis were advocating resembled the European parent organization in but one aspect: promoting the growth and fate of holy institutions within Palestine. Their toned-down articulation of the Agudath Israel mission may have had much to do with the America-based rabbis long-standing desire to maintain the approbation and support of the East European Orthodox rabbinate. The dilemma was: how to do so without abandoning their own legitimate principles. To address that question, the Agudath ha-Rabbanim, accordingly, not only projected the Agudath Israel as an organization that shared Mizrachi goals and objectives but also tried their utmost to convince European leadership of the values of unity of purpose world-wide.[25]

Let us examine, for example, the resolution adopted by the Agudath ha-Rabbanim on Zionism at their annual meeting of May 1923. The positions reported by Rabbi Joseph Konvitz, chairman of the Eretz Yisrael committee, extended a "blessing upon God-fearing individuals who work together for the sake of heaven, particularly the organizations of Mizrachi and Agudath Israel, whose common goal is the building up of the land with the spirit of Torah and Mitzvoth" and opposed those who in building up Zion were acting contrary to the Torah. Specifically, they set as a goal the pressuring of the World Zionist Organization to increase support to Mizrachi institutions to improve the level of Sabbath observance. And they called upon both Mizrachi and Agudath Israel "to find means, to the extent that it is possible, to unify themselves and put their strength together to build up the land."

To press their point, the Agudath ha-Rabbanim delegated three of its members to attend both the 1923 Zionist Congress and the First World Congress of the Agudath Israel. At the former, secular gathering they were to urge officials to adopt legislation to curb the public desecration of the Sabbath in Tel Aviv. At the religious gathering they were to appeal for unity between Agudists and Mizrachiites, i.e., in essence for the curtailing of attacks against the Religious Zionists. The Agudath Israel would not hear of this call for moderation.[26]

Summing up its achievements in the area of Zionism and the Yishuv, the Agudath ha-Rabbanim would boast in 1926 that

if the old yishuv has survived until now, credit must go to [our] rabbis . . . We have also done much for the rise of the new yishuv. When the announcement came from San Remo, we joined the entire people in its

joy, tears welled up in our eyes. In our midst may be found both Mizrachi and Agudath Israel supporters., but the Agudath ha-Rabbanim
does not interfere in political matters. For us, it is clear: If we are to
have a land of Israel, we must have the Torah of Israel, if we have a
Jewish people, we must have a God of Israel.[27]

With all that has been said here of American Orthodox affinity for
much of the Zionist cause through the 1920s, can we not find any-
where a dissenting anti-Zionist opinion. In fact, there were individual Orthodox rabbis throughout this time frame who articulated
strong theological reservations. Gershon Greenberg has identified
men like Lithuanian-born Rabbi Shalom Isaacson and Hungarian
immigrant Rabbi Baruch Meir Levin who questioned the theological
right of Jews to return to Zion in a non messianic context and the
fate of Torah within the Zionist movement. Baruch Klein, probably
the most outspoken of these rabbis, saved his harshest words for the
Mizrachi, who, as Greenberg described it, "are used as pious fronts
by the secularists." But his strident words, as we have seen, had little effect on the policies of the Agudath Ha-Rabbanim, of which he
was a long-time minority opinion member.[28]

His views might have received a somewhat better hearing, begin-
ning in 1920, within the short-lived Knesset ha-Rabbonim ha-
Ortodoksim b'America, a rival on many areas and causes to the
Agudath ha-Rabbanim. This other organization of Eastern European
trained rabbis was founded as an extension of the views and work of
Rabbi Gavriel Z. Margolis (Reb Velvel).

Reb Velvel was born in 1847 and educated in yeshivas in Vilna
and Volozhin, receiving ordination from Rabbi Yaacov Beirat of
Vilna. He arrived in this country in 1907 after a distinguished
twenty-seven years as a rabbi in Grodno and became Chief Rabbi of
Boston, a position just vacated by Ramaz who had moved to New
York. Four years later, Reb Velvel would become rabbi of the Adath
Israel Society (United Hebrew Community of New York), an organization that had begun, just a few years earlier, as a burial society
and was then expanding into the areas of free loans, sick benefits
and, most importantly for us, shechita and kashruth supervision.
Almost immediately, Reb Velvel clashed with Ramaz, Klein and the

other Agudath ha-Rabbanim figures over their organization's manifest monopolies and alleged malfeasances in the area of kashruth.
Often asserting his greater knowledge in Torah and halakha, he
spent the next decade or more battling the East European rabbinic
establishment for control of that lucrative industry. Reb Velvel created first, the Agudat ha-Yehudim ha-Ortodoksim (1914) and then
his own Vaad ha-Kashruth (1918) to carry out his challenge.[29]

Reb Velvel's extensive difficulties with the Agudath ha-Rabbanim
however went deeper than religious and monetary competition over
kashruth. In the early 1920s Reb Velvel strongly questioned the
Agudath ha-Rabbanim's continued support for its favorite institution, the Rabbi Isaac Elchanan Theological Seminary. Representing
himself as a true opponent of secularism and modernization, he was
appalled to hear that under its president, Dr. Bernard Revel, plans
were being made to attach a college to the traditional yeshiva. How
could Ramaz, Klein, Levinthal and others, he asked, support a
school where philosophy and biblical criticism would be taught? At
best, these studies would take young men away from the sacred
books resulting in the production of religiously ignorant rabbis
unable to aide the religiously-barren American Jewish community.
Even worse was the possibility that these studies would destroy traditional faith at the yeshiva, making it but another version of the
hated Jewish Theological Seminary of America. Didn't his colleagues understand, Reb Velvel cried, that the yeshiva's proposed
move out of the Lower East Side was but an attempt to hide its activities from the traditional immigrant community?[30]

Finally, as the self-claimed upholder of tradition, the quintessential
"ultra" Orthodox Jew of the 1920s, Reb Velvel had much to say
about Zionism and American Orthodox support for the movement.[31]

Actually, as Joshua Hoffman's recent, comprehensive study of
Margolis has pointed out, Reb Velvel, a product of the Volozhin
yeshiva, was a supporter of early Hibbat Zion. Margolis would later
write that he then thought that the influence of rabbis like himself
would be beneficial to the movement, undermining the power of the
anti-religious. And the rabbi had faith that Zionism would aid the

persecuted Jews of Eastern Europe. Consequently, this self-described friend of Rabbi Samuel Mohilever attended the Second Zionist Congress in Basel in 1898. As an incipient Mizrachiite, Margolis believed that while Zionism was not the true redemption, its potential power to help unify the Jewish people could bring a positive response from God. He would also argue the permissibility of cooperating with the non-religious in the building up of the land. However, as the non-religious viewpoint continued to dominate the Zionist cultural revolution in the early years of this century, Reb Velvel became increasingly disenchanted with the movement.[32]

To be sure, Reb Velvel continued to allow that there were religious Jews who sincerely, if erroneously, supported the movement, hoping their work would aid the condition of their fellow Jews. He could respect their motives. He came, however, to have nothing but contempt for those seemingly religious ones (Mizrachiites?) who backed this irreligious and destructive movement for personal gain. Given the references to self gain and the rhetoric during his later battles in New York with the kashruth establishment, it is not surprising that his differences with religious Zionists became another front in his on-going war with the Agudath ha-Rabbanim.[33]

It is not known exactly when Reb Velvel accepted the Agudath Israel position. Indeed, Hoffman has shown that as late as 1913, he was still able to say, like the Mizrachi might have, that cooperation with the non religious on issues like anti-Semitism was possible and praiseworthy. It is clear, however, that by the early 1920s, Reb Velvel was theologically opposed to the Zionist cause. Zionists, he argued, should be seen as false messiahs. They were violating Talmudic dicta of not rising up against the nations of the world and had increased anti-Semitism which threatened Jewish survival. By then he was firmly proclaiming that "God will send at the end of days his redeemer to those who wait for him. For him and for no one else. And as he took us out of Egypt, so he will show us miracles soon and in our day."[34]

Predictably, Reb Velvel attempted to direct American Orthodox funds and support solely to the religious institutions of the old yishuv and not to the Zionist settlement in Palestine. The Agudath ha-Rabbanim had itself frequently pointed out that often the most religious did not receive Zionist funds. Such was the stance on Palestinian activities that Reb Velvel proposed for his Knesset ha-Rabbonim in 1921 at its first convention.

Reb Velvel wanted the Knesset ha-Rabbonim to stand for the many causes he held dear. It was to express his dismay over the low caliber and corrupt rabbis who dominated the Agudath ha-Rabbanim, offering an alternative to the truly religious Jew. Among other things, it was

> to avoid all forms of unpleasant publicity in sanctioning the marketing of kosher products and to prevent the dealers in such products from encouraging the services of rabbis to advertise their products, and to that end every community is appealed to and urged to support the Orthodox rabbis and to pay them living salaries so that they will not find it necessary to receive remuneration for sanctioning articles as kosher and be obliged to accept perquisites of a questionable source.

It would also "strengthen Jewish education in every city throughout the United States and Canada and extend every effort to have public funds collected for the cause of Jewish education expended on Talmud Torahs and Yeshivot."

On the foreign scene, of greatest interest to us, the Knesset was

> to help the government in Palestine which is working to establish a new community, but at the same time to leave rabbis of Palestine the work of establishing Judaism and culture . . . to support the old institutions . . . and to bring order out of the chaotic disorder among the various representatives who come to America to solicit funds for the old institutions in Palestine.

And, of course, through all its work it was "to bring about harmony and unity among the different elements which are working for Orthodox Judaism." Such at least were Reb Velvel's draft resolutions for the 1921 convention.[35]

The convention delegates were evidently not as compliant as he might have anticipated. As Hoffman has shown, on the issue of Palestine, they changed the wording in the resolution "to help the government in Palestine which is working to establish a new community" to read "to assist the British High Commissioner and [unnamed] Zionist authorities in Palestine." Unlike their leader Reb Velvel, who was, predictably, concerned most with the old religious community, the majority of delegates, at this juncture, were equally concerned with the development of the new yishuv. Interestingly enough, Hoffman has further discovered that two years later the Knesset seemingly had a change of heart when it expressed support for the Agudath Israel positions. Apparently, they reiterated that stance again in 1924. But then, in 1925, the Knesset, possibly for reasons not directly related to Zionism, sounded again very much like their Agudath ha-Rabbanim opponents when, at their convention in Lackawaxen, Pennsylvania, they sent greetings to the Zionist Congress in Vienna. Such, then, was the unsteady, fluctuating position of a non-Mizrachi American Orthodox group in the mid-1920s.[36]

The true beginning of strong, organized Orthodox opposition to Zionism in America is beyond the scope of this study. Well into the 1930s, and despite the fact that the leader of the Agudath ha-Rabbanim, Rabbi Eliezer Silver of Cincinnati, was himself personally an Agudist, the organized East European rabbinate in this country still advocated cooperation and unity among Mizrachi and Agudath Israel forces worldwide. In 1933, for example, Silver called for a "meeting in Eretz Yisrael of all heads of world Orthodoxy [to] unify the Mizrachi and Agudath Israel. We must no longer, suffer from disunity."[37]

Silver's efforts went unrewarded. From Europe he heard Agudath Israel leaders insist that "the Mizrachi leave the World Zionist Organization." In America he listened to the fears of Agudath ha-Rabbanim colleagues that their organization's pro-Mizrachi position was being undone.[38]

In 1939, the first permanent American branch of Agudath Israel was organized. Under Silver's presidency the new group closely aligned with its world movement. Efforts were made to move the indigenous East European Orthodox rabbinate into their ranks, and many did become Agudists in the 1940s. Most importantly, Agudath Israel ranks were swelled by the arrival in this country of refugee rabbis and lay Orthodox Jews fleeing Hitler and World War II. They would bring their own perspectives on modernity, secularism and Zionism and open a new chapter in the history of Orthodoxy in the United States.[39]

5

Jacob A. Riis: Christian Friend or Missionary Foe: Two Jewish Views

Jacob Riis Attacked and Defended

The Lucas–Riis Letters

On August 14, 1903, the *American Hebrew* excitedly reported that "a particular settlement house on the Lower East Side. . . . that has attracted much attention in the past few years, mainly owing to the fact that one of its patrons is a gentleman of international repute as an advocate and friend of the poor" was not living up to its announced "high and commendable purpose." Its work, they declared, "has not been of a strictly non-sectarian character, as has always been supposed. Children have gone to their homes singing religious hymns in honor of the Christ and the Virgin" taught to them by "Christians carrying on proselytizing work under our noses." They did not identify the patron or his mission by name but did record his following "passion(ate)" response to a reporter's query:

> Yes, the house is a Christian settlement . . . We have nailed the Cross to the door and it is going to remain there. If your Jewish mothers don't know where they are sending their children, it is about time that Christian influence stepped in and took care of these children.[1]

Two weeks later, the ghetto-based *Yiddishes Tageblatt* expanded upon its uptown contemporary's exposé and identified both the missionary and his institution. Under the headline, "Mothers Beware," downtown readers were informed that the "raison d'être for the existence of the King's Daughters (the settlement's original name) is to come to Christ and bring others to Christ." Immigrants were warned that "it is a Christian Settlement and our children must be kept away." The patron in whose honor the Settlement had been renamed several years earlier was once again quoted as arrogantly suggesting: "Let the Jewish women find out the nature of the house before they send their children there."[2]

These revelations may well have shocked many within the New York Jewish community, for until then muckraker and social reformer Jacob A. Riis had been publicly counted as one of the most knowledgeable and supportive friends of these new immigrants. The *American Hebrew* had described him just two years earlier as "a close observer in whom the philanthropic impulse has been ingrained by his journalistic experience." One month later, the same journal had praised him as "one whose judgment carries weight because of the fulness [sic] of his knowledge of existing conditions as well as the difficulties surrounding the solution of the problems involved."[3] That might well explain that newspaper's initial reticence to identify the New Yorker as an opponent by name. Indeed, respect for Riis' good works was so ingrained within local Jewry that, even after the exposés, some Jewish observers found it difficult to believe that Riis himself could be active in the missionizing seemingly going on in Henry Street. The *Hebrew Standard*, a vehicle which consistently spearheaded anti-conversionist drives, suggested that the reformer be given the benefit of the doubt by the Jewish community.

> As a sign of the times, we choose to take the most optimistic view of the situation. Having done this we may well ask, has not the impartial reviewer of the situation in which misery and degradation play so great a part permitted himself to become an agent of the soul savers whose personal Christianity resolves itself into a supreme effort to make conversions of children of Jewish parents.[4]

Riis, for his part, was quickly afforded the opportunity to refute newspaper allegations and to publicly disassociate himself from downtown conversionists. On August 26, 1903, just twelve days after the first charges appeared, Albert Lucas, secretary of the Union of Orthodox Jewish Congregations of America, wrote to Riis officially requesting that he issue a statement to the Jewish community explaining "the religious influence and work (if any) that is carried on at the Jacob Riis Home." But Riis' reply, which talked of "love for a young Jew in (whose) name the work at Henry Street began. . . and has been carried on all these many years" and which asserted that the "Gospel of Love shall be preached in that spot at least as long as we live," did little to allay Jewish suspicions. If anything, his failure to explicitly deny missionary objectives convinced Lucas, a grizzled veteran of many anti-conversionist fights, that in Riis, Jews were encountering the most pernicious type of anti-Jewish foe. Here was a widely-respected social servant—seemingly above public reproach—who secreted his soul-saving goals beneath the rhetoric of Christian love.[5]

Lucas was soon troubled further by Riis' unexpected publication of their correspondence in the *New York Evening Post* in mid-September. Now it seemed that Riis was intent on publicly obscuring his anti-Jewish stance. And when the same exchange of letters appeared sometime later both in the *American Hebrew* and in the *Churchman*, a missionary publication, Lucas was undeniably persuaded that Riis was at one and the same time seeking to confound the Jewish community while truthfully appealing to his real clients, supporters of missionary societies.[6]

These private and public exchanges convinced Lucas and other ghetto spokesmen that from then on Riis' activities would have to be closely monitored and downtowners frequently reminded that the well-known reformer was no friend of theirs. Accordingly, when a *Hebrew Standard* reader later inquired whether "the Jacob Riis Settlement . . . is one of the places where Christianity is forced upon Jewish children," the newspaper replied: "The Jacob Riis Settlement is one of the worst offenders among the proselytizing influences on the lower East Side." And when Riis subsequently publicly supported the opening of thirty Federation of Churches Summer Vacation schools in the ghetto, the downtown journal reacted predictably: "That Jacob A. Riis gives his endorsement is only what is to be expected from him. His view of Christianity is that it should be forced into the lives of all the 'lower half' whether it wants it or not." Lucas publicly defined Riis' motives in establishing "proselytizing missions" as "in exactly the same spirit as the missionaries . . . sent abroad for converting the savage heathens." And by 1906 the Riis Settlement, one of many so-described "proselytizing missions," had become the primary focus of Lucas-led anti-missionary activities. In March of that year, for example, the Jewish Centre movement was created on the lower East Side "to provide as many suitable centers as possible where Jewish children and youths shall receive under Jewish influence—religious, physical and moral training." They planned to establish their first refuge "in the immediate vicinity of the Jacob Riis Home." It also followed that Lucas and his stalwarts would be quick to support a neighboring Catholic priest in his own attack against Riis' sectarian settlement efforts in Spring, 1908.[7] Only then they were to find that the problem of opposing Jacob Riis had become somewhat more complicated. Now when attacked, the reformer piously denied any Christianizing motives whatsoever. More significantly, there were now Jewish spokesmen— most notably Rabbi Stephen S. Wise—who were prepared to testify to Riis' non-sectarian sincerity.

The Curry Incident

On Easter Sunday, 1908, Father James B. Curry, Rector of the St. James Roman Catholic Church on the Lower East Side denounced Riis and his settlement workers for allegedly "pauperizing the children and making grafters of their parents." He blasted them for "misleading the public and exaggerating conditions . . . to obtain money little of which reaches the poor." Most significantly, he pointedly accused Riis of seeking converts among Roman Catholic as well as Jewish children. In his remarks, which received front page coverage in the *New York Times*, Curry explained that Riis' original intention had been to proselytize only among Jews. But when, "several of the rich patrons of the Settlement House went there and found a number of young Jews, they made a protest against having the money used exclusively for Jews." From then on "the settlement folks decided to draw in a few St. James boys."[8]

These new revelations certainly came as no surprise to Lucas. Riis had now been proved an enemy of all poor immigrants. Still, the Curry protest was an important outsider's reminder to downtown Jews that the missionary threat continued. Lucas' letter of support for Curry published in the Times predictably reiterated his long standing perception: "Mr. Riis' settlement societies are proselytizing societies to the fullest extent and . . . endeavor to attract children from Roman Catholic and Jewish congregations." This time, however, Lucas closed with a word of advice for Riis. Speaking on behalf of both downtown's Catholics and Jews, Lucas suggested that there former "transfer his activities to Hell's Kitchen . . . We feel we are able to take care of ourselves."[9]

Riis had no intention of moving to midtown Manhattan. His Easter repose, or "The Peace of Quiet Week" as he called it, shattered by these new allegations, Riis was in no mood to take travel or other instructions from the "perennial Mr. Lucas." Angered and hurt by this renewed impugning of his reputation, Riis now staunchly and explicitly denied that "proselytizing" or "sectarianism" played a role in Henry Street activities. And also unlike five years earlier, Riis set out to publicly remove all doubt about the sincerity of his labors.[10]

Riis opened his defense by questioning the reliability of his critics. Riis countercharged that Curry was a liar and "the greatest hardship . . . the poor of the tenements have . . . to endure." And Lucas, he declared, was motivated by crass materialistic designs. Recalling his first encounter with downtown anti-missionary forces, Riis wrote:

> We invited a body of Jewish rabbis . . . to see if they could find any trace of religious instruction there. The upshot of that was a proposition to 'sell' our house to the Jews. One does not traffic in settlement houses as in stocks and bonds.[11]

Privately, Riis was even more vitriolic and racist when he identified Curry and Lucas as sub-humans. He wrote to his daughter ten days after the new controversy broke:

Have you heard anything . . . about the war that has raged over our settlement house? The Catholic priest and Jewish rabbi in the neighborhood have jumped as one *with all their eight feet* (emphasis mine) . . . declaring me a grafter and a proselytizer.[12]

Riis' unqualified denial and his strident counterattack were heard and accepted most warmly within Protestant "non-sectarian" social reform circles. *The Charities and the Commons,* an organ of the Charity Organization Society, declared: "We hold no brief for settlements when they are fairly criticized, but unless the newspapers have done him grievously wrong, Father Curry has borne false witness." The priest was advised to "emulate the settlement in their practical concern for . . . the young people of his parish rather than fulminate against his neighbors."[13]

Their sentiments were echoed, surprisingly, by a number of Jewish settlements house workers. David Blaustein, director of the Educational Alliance, led the rally to the defense of the Christian activist when he characterized the new charges "as a rule not justifiable." While admitting that some individuals did enter the welfare field to make human and other capital out of it, in this instance it clearly was not the case. Lucas' five year campaign to discredit Riis within his community also had seemingly made little impact on Henry Moskowitz, a Jewish leader of the downtown Ethical Culture Society who now responded that in his sixteen years of service he had never witnessed "any attempt at direct or 'insidious' proselytizing." And Charles Bernheimer, assistant headworker at the University Settlement, reported in Riis' defense that committed workers placed great importance upon the immigrant maintaining his ancestral faith. All settlements, he emphasized, "transmute . . . the morality of the fathers and mothers in Israel in (making) for the genteel, decent and honorable young man and woman."[14]

Such support did not satisfy Riis. Lucas and Curry could be discredited, but future liars and opportunists would arise unless the public understood exactly where he stood on the settlement/missionary issue. He searched for a vehicle which would "clear the air

for good." The *Outlook*, a Progressive periodical, published his definitive rejoinder in May 1908.[15]

The purpose of settlement house work, Riis there admitted, was
undeniably "religious," but only in the sense that it sprang "from
the impulse to help the brother . . . to quicken . . . the rebirth of
faith in an all-loving Father whose children we are, call Him what
we will." Proselytizing, on the other hand, was totally foreign to his
thought and action. Indeed, he argued, one of the House's goals was
to work with and not against existing local immigrant religious
institutions to better serve "the Jews and Catholics . . . who are the
real settlement."

Christianity, he acknowledged, did play a role in the House's life,
but only once a year, at Christmas. Then Riis claimed the privilege
"which nothing could make (him) surrender, to talk. . . of the peace-
and good will which He came to bring whose birthday we celebrate." And to graphically underscore the non-denominational
nature of this ceremony, Riis pointed out that once he had invited
Rabbi Stephen S. Wise to participate in the Yuletide ceremony. There
he had instructed his youthful listeners that "every Jew and every
Christian in our house should be as big as Rabbi Wise, to come up to
his ideal." These actions, Riis believed, were in no wise offensive to
downtown clients. Rather, they contributed to "bettering spiritually
the condition of Jews and Roman Catholics alike."'[16]

Rabbi Wise, Riis' co-celebrant in the Christmas ceremony, was one
Jewish leader who heartily endorsed Riis' multi-faceted apologia.
Opposed to Lucas' allegations and apparently untroubled by Riis'
published anti-Semitic opinions, Wise now redoubled his efforts to
convince his co-religionists that Riis was no missionary but a
thoughtful and sensitive friend of the Jews. Accordingly, Wise agreed
to participate in an inaugural "Maccabean Festival" which was held
at the Riis House that following December. It was there that Wise
reportedly declared that Riis' "unselfish desire to do good to grown
persons and children regardless of creed and without attempt at
proselytizing, had given him a new conception of Christianity."[17]

Soon after I came to New York, Riis came to me saying "I must have your help." He put it in all earnestness and simplicity, saying: "You know I have no wish to proselytize among your people. I want them to be the best of Jews and I want you to come down to the Riis Settlement and tell them so." And then his was the plan of having me come down to the Jewish boys and girls who foregathered at the Settlement and point out to them the heroic story of the Maccabees. Riis' eyes glistened as he himself spoke to me of the Maccabees. He could not have spoken with deeper admiration if he had been thinking of his Danish forebears . . . and we had the . . . celebration . . . This was Riis' way of answering those who protested against what they conceived to be his attempt to wean children from Judaism and win them to his own faith.[18]

The debate over Riis and his House within the New York Jewish community would continue for at least one more year. In December 1909, the Hebrew Standard angrily reported that the Lilies of the Valley Circle of Young Judea, a Zionist organization led by such luminaries as Professor Israel Friedlaender, Henrietta Szold and Rabbi Mordecai M. Kaplan, was holding its meetings at the Riis Settlement. Were these Zionists unaware, the periodical wondered out loud, that the Henry Street center was "persistent and nefarious in its proselytizing activities?" And didn't they understand that their presence in the House would be used by missionaries "to show that Jews were in favor of the work done at the Riis Settlement?"[19]

The Young Judeans responded that as an organization which exists "to counter missionary influence and to encourage Jewish programs" they had no fear either of the impact of meeting in non-Jewish surroundings nor of insidious cooptation by conversionists. But that was not even the case. Riis, they asserted, encouraged their efforts and "never interfered in the slightest way with the strictly Jewish programming of the circle." Their patron placed but one restriction on their efforts. "The study of Hebrew was denied," they calmly reported, "as the study of all foreign languages has never been permitted in the House." For them, as for Wise, Riis was no foe of Jews or Judaism.[20]

Exploring the Two Jewish Views

Albert Lucas perceived Jacob Riis as an insidious missionary foe. He was supported by newspaper editorials and joined in his struggle by a seemingly unlikely ally, a neighboring Catholic priest. Stephen S. Wise, on the other hand, saw the downtown reformer as a warm Christian friend. Jewish settlement workers and to a lesser extent Young Judeans echoed his words. How could a man so consistently reviled by one segment of New York Jewry retain the admiration and support of others within the same community?

Albert Lucas probably would have answered that the key was trickery. Riis, he would have said, was a missionary unchanged from 1903–1909 who through differing means of subterfuge convinced Wise and other gullible Jewish spokesmen that he was no soul saver. But to prove that a conspiracy was afoot, Lucas would have to first establish that Riis was a missionary. And such evidence was not then, and is not now, easily forthcoming. Since Riis never explicitly admitted, publicly or privately, that he was proselytizing, proof of his conversionist designs can and could be only inferred from statements and activities.[21]

Consider Riis' publication of the Lucas letters in the *Churchman*, the action which clinched the Jewish leader's suspicions. The downtowner undoubtedly would have argued that the choice of this publication reflected Riis' desire to have those who ordinarily followed and supported missionary groups understand that he was one of them. And had Lucas known of Riis' contemporaneous correspondence with other settlement house leaders, he would have further suggested that the Henry Street workers wanted financial more than moral support. The Lucas controversy had begun at the height of the institution's fund-raising season. And Riis was concerned that *Churchman* readers "who wish to contribute to our fund" be made aware of his good work downtown. Lucas would have sadly observed that for Riis the newspaper allegations could have not come at a more opportune moment. He was able to adroitly coopt Jewish complaints both to publicize the Christian work at his home and to raise funds from missionary sources to continue his nefarious labors.[22]

But does an appeal to Christians who support conversionists conclusively prove that the settlement workers making the pitch are themselves missionaries? Is it not possible that the acute exigencies of fund raising convinced a clever Riis to publish a most ambiguous letter in a conversionist journal permitting many potential backers to believe that his settlement was a missionary center. More convincing evidence would have to be offered to prove that Riis was precisely what Lucas said he was.

A document from the Riis family unpublished papers which suggests that cooptation motivated the settlement's invitation to Wise to participate in the 1908 Maccabean Festival might provide just such evidence. Consider this undated letter which was obviously composed in December 1908, written by Riis' wife to the Settlement's headworker:

> Don't be worried about the Jewish festival, Charles McDowell [a settlement trustee] thinks it is a fine idea and he is a good Christian and no one is a better Christian, if being a lover of Christ makes a Christian . . .[23]

Was Mrs. Riis reassuring Henry Street workers that the celebration of Hanukkah constituted no deviation from their longstanding promotion of Christian policies? Was the Jewish festival to be used ultimately as a way of bringing Jews to Christianity? Unfortunately, once again, bits of inferential evidence do not unquestionably substantiate the anti-missionary's understanding of Riis' motivations and tactics.

A change in Riis' approach to settlement house work might better explain the basis of the Jewish split over the downtown reformer. If the uncorroborated 1903 newspaper allegations were in fact correct, if Riis was then a missionary, it is possible that by 1908 and due specifically to fund raising considerations, he had been forced to backtrack and could no longer impose his religious views upon his youthful charges. It might then follow that each Jewish group knew a "different" Jacob Riis. Wise *et al.* knew, mistakenly revered, and vocally supported a man who had grudgingly abandoned his Christianizing goals. Lucas and his supporters, on the other hand, were either unaware of, or were unmoved by, any changes in their long-standing opponent.

This supposition would offer as evidence of Riis' change the tenor of his reaction to Jewish attacks in 1903 as compared with his response to the Curry-Lucas renewal five years later. In the former instance, the settlement patron was seemingly pleasantly surprised by the furor created and calmly planned the exploitation of this publicity. He took the initiative in publishing the Lucas letters and was apparently troubled only when the *Evening Post* buried his correspondence on the back page.[24] In 1908, Riis was publicly angered by the Curry-Lucas statements. And privately, he and his associates appeared very concerned over the conceivable negative impact of the affair. Contributors were writing in, bothered that Christianizing, graft and/or pauperization could be rife in the House. Here, quite unlike his first encounter with public criticism, Riis was seemingly compelled by outside pressure to defend his work and to widely disavow proselytism both to the public and to his supporters.[25]

This pronounced shift in public demeanor and private behavior, it is suggested, reflected the settlement's changed financial/ideological profile. In 1903, Riis was a missionary reaching out to a limited—albeit substantial—parochial Christian constituency. Over the next five years, the settlement's needs required that Riis broaden his charity base. Riis realized that new contributors might include affluent Jews and others who would never support a Christian mission.[26] Placing practicalities ahead of theology, he abandoned the proselytizing once regnant in his House. Having changed his orientation and squarely facing a $500 budget deficit, he was being unfairly accused; hence his anger and concern.[27]

But to prove that Wise *et al.* met and came to know a "new" Riis requires more than just the extant inferential evidence here available. Riis was certainly in 1908 more troubled than before. But the roots of his discontent cannot be determined. Riis' settlement records are significantly almost silent on any supposed change of tactics or approaches. There is but one reference, early in 1908, to a policy shift; a suggestion that consideration be given to the hiring of a "Jewish assistant."[28] But it cannot be determined whether that unrealized move was designed to meet Jewish and supporter needs and requests or to simply mislead Jewish opponents. Indeed, this same inferential evidence can be used to argue, with the same measure of uncertainty, that Riis was in 1908, to use Lucas' favorite term, as "disingenuous" as before. But now he was out to trick not only Jewish clients but Gentile supporters as well. He had broadened his charity base since 1903 with private assurances of non-sectarianism and consequently was obligated to publicly reassure potential critics both from within and without. Public apologias, private letters and most dramatically, the cooperation of an unwitting Wise was the answer.

Neither trickery nor change can conclusively explain the roots of the split Jewish view of the reformer. The more convincing argument is that the two groups of Jews who witnessed the same consistent pronouncements and activities defined Riis' sincere, if poorly conceived and communicated, ideas differently. But only Wise *et al.* correctly understood and accented Riis' ideas and intentions. For Riis never perceived himself as an active missionary with conscious designs upon Jewish souls. He was rather a committed believing Christian who felt strongly that universal Christian teachings were basic to settlement work and could contribute much towards the immigrants' Americanization and cultural upbringing.

A close reading of some of Riis' unpublished papers and less-publicized statements make evident just this commitment to Christianity within the settlement, short of proselytism. In an undated draft speech to settlement workers, written in a tone highly reminiscent of his 1908 public apologia, Riis observed: "Settlement work, Christian work . . . not sectarian not preaching but Christian. It is because you are a Christian that you are there searching for your brothers."[29]

To Riis, settlement Americanization goals could be reached only under Christian auspices. Discounting completely the "non-sectarian approach towards Americanization of the immigrants," Riis once declared at a settlement meeting that "social work . . . could not have developed except in a Christian country." But he was also quick to assert that a Christian environment did not necessitate making all clients Christians. "It is not to proselytize Hebrew children," he wrote, "but to teach Hebrew and Gentile children what Christianity means." And Christianity as expressed here meant the universal teachings of peace, good will and brotherhood as well as the essential American values of loyalty and patriotism, all exemplified by Jesus and transmitted through universalized Christian traditions.[30]

Riis sincerely believed that this devoutly Christian approach to settlement house work should not have pricked Jewish sensibilities. Were they all not engaged in the search for the best means of changing the newcomers? Dr. Wise and others had no trouble with his methods. Riis' social theology did, however, greatly disturb Lucas and his constituency who generally had little patience for Christian good works and who saw the missionary's subtle undermining of the immigrant's faith in the methods he used.[31]

This interpretation effectively clarifies the mystery of Riis' changed demeanor in response to Jewish attacks between 1903 and 1908. In the earlier instance, Riis did not feel threatened because he was simply asked to explain the nature of the religious activities at the settlement. And he thought that his references to "Gospel of Love" or to "his love for a young Jew" in no way implied that proselytism was the settlement's goal. Riis, in this view, sincerely believed his parting words to Lucas in 1903: "If there is anything in that [Christian settlement] spirit not commendable to your people, I am very sorry for you. I think you are wrong." Riis' publication of the Lucas letters may well have reflected fund-raising priorities, but not as a missionary center. That many downtown Jews misunderstood his statement was, for Riis, either a separate issue or unimportant.[32]

In 1908, the encounter with immigrant criticism was quite different. Riis was now publicly and explicitly attacked as a missionary. He was startled and angered that his message of Christian concern had been misconstrued. But more importantly, he was also accused of misusing funds designated for the poor and of breaking the spirit of dependent families. This latter attack, coming at a time when settlements were being widely criticized for their alleged insensitivity to client needs, constituted a most serious challenge both to his and his institution's basic integrity. The proselytism charge was now one of several pressing allegations which required concerted public and private defense.[33]

This interpretation helps us understand the motivation which led the several professional Jewish social workers to actively support Riis' apologia. For them, the Curry-Lucas attacks undeniably represented the expansion of an ongoing crisis of confidence between them and their fellow Jewish immigrant clients. Lucas must have long been a thorn in their side too. He was a most vocal critic of the lack of Jewishness in German-run philanthropic efforts on the Lower East Side.[34]

Rabbi Wise's own affinity for Riis' cause also grew out of a longstanding commitment to the settlement house movement. But it was strengthened greatly by his close personal relationship with the reformer and clinched by his belief that the mixture of universal Christian and American social values in settlement work in no way threatened to undermine the Jewishness of ghetto clients.[35] From that vantage point, Wise could participate in a Yuletide-Christmas celebration without apprehensions. The rabbi may have well seen this joyful mixture of Christian and Jewish holidays as a major statement by his Gentile colleagues that Judaism too possessed universal and American values worthy of exhortation to immigrant clients.[36]

Rabbi Wise was not alone in his belief that Christianity's universal messages as taught to downtowners posed no real barrier to Jewish continuity. Consider, for example, the reaction of two other well-known Americanized, religiously liberal Jews to downtown protests over Christmas celebrations in the public schools. While downtown leaders feared that "missionaries find the task made much easier when the minds of our children are impregnated with a sympathy for Christianity through the celebration of Christmas," uptown spokesmen like Rabbi Maurice Harris of Harlem's Temple Israel declared that he was "sorry to see a week usually associated with peace and good will made one of discord." He protested against "the well-meaning but indiscreet people who rushed into print with grievances. . . which made the judicious grieve."[37]

Similarly, at the height of the 1906 controversy over Christmas pageants in the New York schools, Rabbi Judah Magnes of Temple Emanu-El preached that "the true Hebrew, the real Hebrew resents the activity of those Hebrews who would strip Christmas of all its beauty." Turning to what Jews could derive from another's religious observance, he declared:

> Peace on earth. Good will to men; glory to God in the highest. Shall not the day come when, we, too, shall be able to sing this? Sing it as Jews, as men and women who have something to give to this world.[38]

When taken to task by downtown journalists for seemingly advocating that Jews actually celebrate the birth of the Christian messiah, Magnes denied that that was his intention. Although he would never suggest that Jews accept the "god-like life" of Jesus as the truth, he reiterated that "peace on earth, good will to men, this is a universal thought in which we as Jews could join."[39]

Albert Lucas would have nothing of his liberal Jewish colleagues' distinctions between the offensive parochial and acceptable universal teachings of Christianity. For him, Christianizing influences of any sort constituted the most pressing external threat to Jewish continuity in America. Lucas best expressed his position in response to a 1903 New York Sun editorial which criticized his attacks against Christian-run settlements and which saw nothing wrong in clubs "carried on in the love of Christ," if they "make a larger and truer life possible" for their Jewish clients.[40]

"The violence of my attacks upon the settlements," Lucas declared, "has grown with each new recruit to their number until today I look upon all assertions of 'unsectarianism,' 'undenominationalism' and 'altruism' with suspicion." Lucas further argued that "it is not from a genuine altruistic love of mankind, unmixed with proselytizing intentions that these Christians seek . . . the lives of our children." In all events, he concluded "no believer to . . . constitutional American institutions will ask. . . that our boys and girls shall forswear their own faith."[41]

Accordingly, although Lucas unquestionably believed that Riis was a missionary, the issue of the reformer's hidden motives was, ultimately, of secondary importance. Even if Riis and his fellows were sincerely committed only to the advocacy of universal Christian values in Americanization work, they would have still constituted a major threat to the immigrant community. As he saw it, Christian workers inculcated a disrespect for the Jewish heritage and paved the way both for individual conversions and mass disaffection from ancestral faith. For Lucas, downtown Jews were faced with a threefold agenda: overt missionaries had to be stopped, subtle conversionists identified and undermined, and immigrant Jews convinced that Americanized Jewish institutions—like his Jewish Centre—could teach universal and national virtues as well if not better than Christian settlements. Thus committed, he opposed all of Jacob Riis' efforts.[42]

Conclusion

Wise and his fellows may have well been correct in their understanding that Riis was no missionary foe. But were they also right in their depiction of him as a warm Christian friend? A review of his variegated reactions to his encounters with Jewish criticism suggests that they too may not have truly understood the reformer's propensities and attitudes.

Insensitivity towards the needs and fears of immigrant clients marked Riis' responses to Jewish indictments. He was either unaware or unconcerned that East European Jews, coming from a world where the Cross meant only conversion, if not deprivations and pogroms, could not differentiate between Christian methods and Christianizing goals. He made no attempt to acknowledge and dispel downtown apprehensions over the significance of crucifixes on the door, New Testament Bible stores and/or Christian holiday commemorations. He certainly never entertained the thought that good Americanization work could be done in a truly non-sectarian or Jewish environment. And he never explicitly placed distance between himself and self-declared missionaries operating down-town.[43]

This uncompromising attitude was first manifest at the very beginning of the controversy when he brusquely informed reporters that the Cross on the settlement door would never be removed. It reappeared soon thereafter, when he published the Lucas letters without comment in both the general press and in Christian and Jewish journals, leaving the documents open to a variety of inter-pretations or misconceptions. It was seen again, when he accused an advocate of Jewish social work and education of the crassest of materialistic designs. And it culminated in a published comprehen-sive apologia which spoke to fears of contributors, Progressives, Christian colleagues and Americanized Jews. Not a word was addressed to downtown clients or immigrant leaders. The Maccabee celebration may have been a step in the right direction. But a more sensitive patron would have met with his critics and attempted to explain away nagging misperceptions.

But that was not Riis' style. He could see no validity in immigrant protests over Christian teachings in the ghetto. If anything, he was moved more than once to anger and to expressions of anti-Semitism by Jewish activists. Consider his troubled and threatening response to Lucas' 1906 efforts to eliminate Christmas celebrations from the public schools:

> I have just written to Mr. Schiff . . . asking him to call off the Jews who are meddling with Xmas [sic] in the public schools warning them that *that* [emphasis his] was bad. I did not know they had any festivals in the schools but since they have, *the Jews* [emphasis his] must not ques-tion it. If they do, they will precipitate trouble they will be sorry for. The reply will come in an inquiry as to how many Jewish teachers there are in those same schools and what may be their influence upon the children if *that* [emphasis his] is their spirit. It is not, but once that dog is loosed, we shall have trouble as they had abroad and of peace and good will there will be an end. I for one will not stand it for a moment.[44]

Years of living among the immigrants and of reporting on the diffi-culties of their adjustment to America had not sensitized him to their fears of Christianity nor convinced him of the legitimacy of their conceptions of Americanization.[45]

It may be that Wise *et al.* were personally too close to the reformer to see these fundamental faults in his attitudes towards their fellow Jews. It is also possible that these same Americanized Jews engaged in social reform work suffered from the same myopia to immigrant sensibilities. But for us it is clear, whether his contemporary supporters acknowledged it or not, Jacob Riis though probably no missionary, was certainly no friend of those he was pledged to serve.[46]

6

Jewish Communal Divisiveness in Response to Christian Influences on the Lower East Side, 1900–1910

In 1905 there were no fewer than seven Christian missions on the Lower East Side devoted explicitly to luring Jewish children, and to a lesser degree Jewish adults, from their ancestral faith They were the People's Home Church, which proudly pronounced that "evangelism must be first in our experience," three settlements founded by the New York City Mission and Tract Society, and the independent Church Settlement House, the Grace Church Settlement, and the Jewish Bible Mission. In addition, the Federation of Churches and Christian Organizations of New York City sponsored eight daily summer vacation Bible schools in the predominantly Jewish (downtown) vicinity which enrolled more than 2,000 Jewish children in 1905. These Bible schools never openly proclaimed the conversion of the Jews to be an institutional goal. Indeed, the parent Christian Federation took great pains to explain that while "their inspiration is Christian, their management is human and their mission is not a proselytizing one." However, the summer schools frequently met in City Mission centers like God's Providence House and the People's Home Church, while their study-guides and curricula placed great emphasis on christological explanations of the Hebrew Bible and textual explication of the New Testament. Furthermore, the Mission Society saw its Bible school work as an important addition to its year round program, which produced, in its estimation, "good results." Christian teachings were also propagated to Jewish residents of the Lower East Side at Mott Street's Gospel Settlement and Chrystodora of 7th Street. These institutions, like the vacation Bible schools, did not openly admit to conversionist aims but advertised Christian religious services and Bible classes as a regular part of their social program. Finally, Christian influence was fostered downtown by the Jacob A. Riis and College Settlements, which held periodic— primarily Christmas and Easter-time—observances organized by founders committed to doing good Christian works among the ghetto poor.[1]

While it is impossible to determine how many Jews these organizations converted, it is clear that literally thousands of Jewish children attended these settlements and church centers and that in the minds of many downtowners the potential for missionary triumphs constituted a major communal problem. Newly arrived Americans, coming from an East European world where the Cross meant only conversion, if not deprivations and pogroms, drew upon their own unhappy experiences in fearing these American institutions. They were little attuned to the subtle distinctions between Christian charity and Christianizing goals. Some of those who had been in America somewhat longer—and it is their organized reaction to this problem that we shall detail presently—recognized the symbolic significance of the presence of missionaries and their fellow travelers in the ghetto. It said to them, as it had said to opponents of conversionists in their communities for almost a century, that Judaism and Jewish status were under attack. They believed that Christian instruction in their schools and settlements cast the Jewish faith as degenerate, unenlightened, and decidedly un-American. And they noted what Christian efforts in their community's midst said about their equality and minority status in this country. To be proselytized implied that Jews and Judaism were somehow subordinate to other groups and confessions in this legally nonsectarian country.[2]

These popular fears and concerns were heightened when press reports appeared about Christian institutions either forcing or tricking Jewish children into participating in Christian services as a first step toward their ultimate conversion. Such was the case when the New York World, in July 1905, described the alleged physical illtreatment of Jewish girls at a summer camp in Milford Haven, Connecticut, conducted by God's Providence House. Soon thereafter the

Yiddishes Tageblatt and the *Hebrew Standard,* which represented the views of immigrant Jewry, and the *American Hebrew,* which reflected the outlook of the more Americanized uptown Jews, all reported the story of youngsters who reportedly refused to participate in morning Christian prayers and were "placed in a garret and fed . . . on bread and water." Although subsequent investigations questioned whether the punishments were meted out because the campers balked against Christianity being imposed on them or were, rather, a result of the campers' "flagrant insubordination which had nothing to do with prayer," the incident provided Jewish editorialists and other observers with the opportunity to reiterate their long-standing grievance about Christians using the lure of fresh-air camps to expose Jewish children to Christian services and teachings without the knowledge and approval of their parents. Jewish journalists and some of their readers used the occasion to call for a comprehensive organizational response to what they would later term "masked institutions." The *American Hebrew,* for example, called for "American 'self-defense' work . . . to make impossible one-half of the missionary institutions" that it asserted touched "fully one tenth of the homes of the East Side." In a similar vein, the *Hebrew Standard* sought to "arouse the Jewish community to its sense of duty." Albert Lucas, the most celebrated opponent of missionary work of his day, asked: "How much longer is the Jewish community going to stand idly by? When will something be done to offset the missionizing influences in our Jewish homes?" Private citizen Walter H. V. Epstein had no answer. But in a letter to the editor of the American Hebrew, he cried out: "Young men and women of the East side . . . what are you going to do about it? Will you allow your little brothers and sisters to attend schools where the service of a God, not recognized by the Israelites, is forced upon them?"[3]

These calls for Jewish communal activities—together with the ongoing anger and upset about Christian missionizing recharged by the Milford Haven incident—led to the creation of a loose confederation of organizations on the Lower East Side headed by the Jewish Endeavor Society and the teachers of the Albert Lucas Classes. The Endeavor Society, which was organized in 1901 by the early students and first graduates of the Jewish Theological Seminary sought to provide the children of East European immigrants who were well on the road to Americanization with Jewish educational and cultural programs and with "dignified services" designed, in their own words, "to recall indifferent Jewry to their ancestral faith." For the Endeavorer Society, Christian missionary successes were proof that Old-World styles of prayer and learning, as embodied in the *landsmanshaft* synagogue and heder, could not be successfully transplanted in American soil. As an alternative to Christian after-school programs, they initiated in 1902 talmud torah classes with a modern curriculum that included Bible, history, religion, spelling and grammar, and so forth. Similar training was available at the Albert Lucas Classes explicitly constituted as an institutional bulwark against Christian missions. Working first out of Pike and then Rivington and ultimately Chrystie Streets' large synagogues, teachers recruited by their zealous antimissionary leader offered Jewish religious instruction in English exclusively" on an equal basis to boys and girls, earning for the schools—in the words of one friend—"a reputation for thoroughly practical instruction in Judaism."[4]

These independent activities were strongly supported by the recently founded Union of Orthodox Jewish Congregations of America. This organization, which was established in 1898 by leaders of many of America's earliest Sephardic and central European congregations—the most traditional Jews in this country prior to the arrival of the East European Jews—worked for "the protection of Orthodox Judaism [in this case immigrant Jews] whenever occasions arise in civic and social matters." Antimissionary work clearly fell within that purview. The union's zeal to meet the missionary challenge was further strengthened by the personal interest displayed by its foremost spokesman in this campaign. The union's first secretary, Rabbi Bernard Drachman, then professor of codes at the Jewish Theological Seminary, was the prime mover behind the student-run Jewish Endeavor Society. He had opposed missionaries a decade earlier and told his students to do the same. Orthodox Union president Henry Pereira Mendes had likewise long championed, and in the 1890s personally initiated, anticonversionist campaigns. And Albert

Lucas was since 1900 the energetic secretary of the Orthodox Union. The Orthodox Union leadership provided their younger colleagues working in the field with encouragement and financial support. The young Endeavor Society members, to their minds, were continuing a holy tradition of which they themselves had been proudly part. This coalition against the missionary foe was solidified further by the support Harry Fischel, Leon Kamaiky, Otto Rosalsky, and William Fischman gave to the cause. They were spokesmen for an emerging Americanized Orthodox leadership of East European heritage from within the ghetto itself.[5] Fischel, a builder and real estate developer, Kamaiky, a newspaper publisher, Rosalsky, a lawyer, and Fischman, a prosperous merchant, were each representative of a new elite within the immigrant community. Born in the Old World, they had come, as youths, to these shores in the early 1880s and had by the turn of the century succeeded in both establishing themselves economically and becoming attuned to the ways of the land. They offered themselves as financial patrons and/or social guides to their fellow immigrants and their children in adjusting to America. Like the younger Jewish Endeavor members, they saw conversionist inroads as glaring evidence that American Jews were increasingly uncomfortable with the religious styles and trappings of the past. They willingly supported communal programs to solve the socio-religious dilemmas that seemingly encouraged missionary successes.[6] In 1906 this coalition of groups concerned with Christianizing influence on the Lower East Side responded to the challenge through the Jewish Centres Association. The Association's tactics included the publication in the Yiddish and Anglo-Jewish press of the names and addresses of alleged missionary centers, the infiltration of Christian groups to ascertain their true ends, the instigation of public demonstrations in the streets against Christian Homes, demanding the return of Jewish children, and most dramatically, the planned creation on Henry Street of the first of what they hoped would be numerous Jewish Centres. These enlarged versions of the Albert Lucas and Jewish Endeavor Society classes would, they hoped, beat the conversionists at their own game through, as one contemporary described it, "a school for school, picnic for picnic warfare."[7]

These concerted antimissionary efforts failed, however, to gain either mass local backing or even unquestioned community support. Ghetto-based rabbis, for example, like those associated with the Agudath ha-Rabbanim (Union of Orthodox Rabbis of the United States and Canada), were explicitly critical of their work. And although the Association did succeed in garnering enough backing to establish one Jewish Centre on Henry Street, it closed after two years due to lack of funds. Lucas, the Endeavor Society, and their supporters observed to their dismay that while most—if not all—Jews worried about their children falling into the hands of proselytizers, when it came to actually fighting the missions, the coalition, in fact, stood alone.[8] Indeed, they found that their antimissionary work, which at first glance seemed to be a cause around which all Jews could rally, was often scorned and censured, when not ignored, by other groups.

Uptown German Jewish leaders denigrated "[Jewish Centre] religious enthusiasts" as having "done more harm in the world than all the rest of the workers for the betterment of mankind can overcome." And downtown rabbinic leaders simply stayed away.[9] Why was this so?

To be sure, uptown leaders shared the antimissionary coalition's concern about conversionists setting up shop in the ghetto. There is, for example, evidence that Jacob H. Schiff, who did not back Jewish Centre era battles, quietly bankrolled Adolph Benjamin—Albert Lucas's acknowledged teacher—during the former's battle against the apostate missionary Herman Warszawiak before the turn of the century.[10] Schiff and many of his German friends refused, though, to fund Jewish Centre activities because they perceived that Lucas and his supporters were intent on doing more than just driving the missionaries out of the Lower East Side. In their eyes, Lucas and his group opposed almost all outside efforts to Americanize the Jew. They were seen as prepared to denounce with equal intensity as *personae non gratae* Christian settlement house workers and Christian public school teachers as well as the so-called "subtle conversionists." And the Germans recognized that their names too appeared on the list of those who were unwelcome in the ghetto. Uptowners, moreover, accurately understood that the Jewish Centre people represented a new type of immigrant opposition to their acculturation efforts. These activists were not newcomers unversed in American ways. The term "greenhorn" certainly could not be hung upon their Orthodox Union mentors. The Jewish Centres Association's work was, in fact, informed by the belief that the process of immigrant acculturation to the English language and American cultural values was both inevitable and a positive good. Where the Association differed from the uptowners—and the source of tension between the two groups—was the Association's belief that other persons advocating Americanization did not have the best interests of the Jews and Judaism at heart. Only they, Association stalwarts publicly asserted, understood how to reconcile Judaism and Americanization, only they were committed to making the immigrant proud of his heritage and at home in America.

The Association thus sought to deny Christian groups any role in the Americanization of Jewish immigrants. Avowed missionaries, subtle conversionists, devout Christian social workers who spoke only of their desire to do Christ's work among the poor, school officials who organized Christmas pageants, and Christian schoolmarms who taught that Jewish traditions were barriers to becoming good Americans—all were seen as equally threatening to Jewish continuity. Though the Association recognized that only avowed conversionists and their subtle missionizing colleagues were explicitly dedicated to formal missionary activity, it viewed all of these Christian workers as united in their depiction of Judaism as a degenerate system unworthy of perpetuation in America.[11]

However, to the Association's way of thinking, Christians were not the only Americanizers who sought to undermine the Jewishness of their clients. Members and supporters of the Jewish Centres Association publicly questioned the intentions of Jewish settlement house patrons, some of whom were the very uptowners whose support they were seeking for their communal work. They asserted that German-run institutions, particularly the Educational Alliance, purposely undermined Jewish identification and attachments because settlement house workers believed they blocked rapid and complete adaptation to American life. Such were the sentiments of A. H. Fromenson, an editor of the *Yiddishes Tageblatt* and a charter member of the Jewish Centres Association, who defined the term "Jewish institution" in such a way as to exclude the Educational Alliance. A "Jewish instituion," he wrote, "is one which stands for Jewish ethics and Jewish ideals and engraves its Jewishness over its doorposts." The Educational Alliance, which is "ashamed of the name 'Hebrew Institute' graven over its portals . . . and which stands for something 'broader' than Judaism—an invertebrate, anemic, condescending, patronizing sentimentalism . . . has lost for all the regenerative work on the East Side the full means of its usefulness." Some critics even suggested that Jewish settlements were nothing more than "in reality a less pernicious method of Christian missionizing."[12]

Jewish Centre affiliates saw themselves as the only Americanizers working in the ghetto with an appropriate institutional solution to the dilemma of how to make the immigrants more attuned to the ways of this country without destroying their ties with their ancestral past. Thus, they scoffed when the Educational Alliance attempted to "cope with the irreligiousness of so many of our young people" through its People's Synagogue. The Jewish Centres Association denounced the synagogue's English-language service, with its Reform Jewish liturgical bent, as straying too far from the historical and residual sociological underpinnings of Judaism to be effective. They, in effect, told their potential German benefactors that although their financial support was certainly appreciated, they had little respect for their approach to meeting Americanization problems.[13]

Beyond whatever personal offense the patrons of the Educational Alliance felt, they remained convinced that these parochial zealots were unworthy of support because they misread the intentions of their fellow Americanizers. As the older uptown elite saw it, a broad spectrum of organizations and individuals, Jewish and Christian, with good motives and intentions, were successfully helping Jewish immigrants adapt to their new surroundings. Only the few groups with explicitly nefarious goals had to be kept from interacting with ghetto youngsters.[14]

These German Jews included themselves among those "attempting," as Louis Marshall, a long-time patron of the Educational Alliance, put it, "to inculcate ideas of self-respecting citizenship in conjunction with the true Jewish spirit." And if their religious activities did not conform to their critics' narrow definition of Judaism, Jewish settlement supporters were quick to assert that the Jewish East Side itself was "by no means of one opinion on religious matters," nor significantly, was the settlement constituency ever entirely Jewish. "There are quite a goodly number of Christians living in our midst," one observer remarked, "whose rights and privileges deserve our due respect." Their downtown critics, Marshall suggested, wanted to see the settlements Americanize only Jews and teach—when they spoke of religion—one parochial form of that faith, which would create "a ghetto in fact as it is today in name." They, on the other hand, were facilitating mass East European acculturation without denigrating Judaism's basic universal moral and ethical teachings. The Educational Alliance, its friends averred, "deserve[d] credit for pursuing a policy which not altogether free from sectarianism cannot be open to charges of religious bigotry and small-mindedness."[15]

Educational Alliance backers believed, moreover, that their policy of teaching religion's universal message, devoid of "bigotry and small mindedness," also characterized the intent and labors of many of their Christian counterparts. Indeed, some felt that immigrant Jews could learn American ways not only from Christians but from the universal teachings of Christianity as well. Such was the attitude of Rabbi Stephen S. Wise, who rallied to the defense of the muckraking settlement house leader Jacob A. Riis when the latter was accused in 1908 by the Jewish Centres Association of subtle missionizing in his "non-sectarian" settlement house. For Wise, Christmas observances, which greatly angered Jewish Centre men, were not a problem. Yuletide commemorations that celebrated not so much the birth of Christianity's messiah but rather the American principles of brotherhood, peace, and gooduill were no more inappropriately sectarian than the moral religious instruction offered at the Educational Alliance.[16] At the time Wise had come to Riis's defense, he had been supported by a number of Jewish settlement house workers who saw the attack as part of a broader battle over how "Jewish" their labors should be. They were under siege from Association quarters over their nonsectarian educational policies, which allegedly said nothing positive to immigrant clients about their ancestral heritage. And while they slavishly followed an approach that the Jewish masses did not want or need, Riis, said the association, used the same "non-sectarian" calling as a missionizing subterfuge. Rabbi Judah L. Magnes reacted in an almost identical fashion to Wise in response to Jewish Centre protests against Christmas activities in the public schools. Magnes saw such pageants as highlighting the universal teachings of "peace on earth, good will to men . . . a thought in which we as Jews can join."[17]

However, in the case of overt conversionist activity and the perpetuation of blue laws that recognized Christianity as the established faith of the American people, uptown Jews took a less tolerant stance. Indeed, uptowners, led bv Marshall and some Reform rabbis, fought valiantly, if unsuccessfully, over the course of a generation to see Sunday laws changed.[18] The same Louis Marshall who was unmoved by Christmas celebrations in the schools was angered when New York State School Regents penalized Jewish students by scheduling promotion examinations on Sabbath and holidays, thus forcing pupils to decide between Jewish observance and educational advancement. And the same Jacob Schiff who made contributions to Jacob A. Riis's good works actively opposed overt conversionists having their way in the ghetto.[19] For them, when missionaries seemed to have their way and Jews were punished for observing their faith , vocal responses were clearly necessary. However, even when uptoun and downtown Jews perceived matters in the same light, the former failed to react affirmatively to calls for cooperative efforts. One contemporary source suggested that this reluctance stemmed from the "rich Jewish community's . . . unmistakeable tendency to stay clear of movements that have their origins or are in the hands of downtown Jews." But even beyond the issue of power sharing, another fundamental difference of opinion divided Jewish groups. The Germans frequently expressed the opinion that the tactics employed by the ghetto-based activists undermined Jewish status in America.[20]

Overt, noisy anti-Christian work was viewed in many uptown quarters as "rousing anti-Jewish feeling . . . [as likely] to bring about a *Juden Hetze* here" in the United States.[21] In attempting to drive Christian schools from the ghetto, Jews showed themselves ungrateful to those sincere Christians offering them assistance in becoming good Americans. And in persecuting the avowed missionaries, Jewish activists were seen as denying Christians their basic constitutional rights. Such was the stance taken by the *New York Sun* toward the Milford Haven furor. An editorial titled "Does This Not Look Very Much Like Bigotry?" castigated Lucas and his fellows for describing Christians doing good work in the ghetto as promoters of "anti-Jewish sentiments": Who, except the bigot, they argued, would object to "Christians stepping in" and working until "there will be no more suffering to relieve." Placing the missionaries within and their "bigoted" opponents without the spirit of the American Constitution, they continued, "In this country of religious freedom shall anybody be debarred from inculcating the precepts of religion and from practicing its charity?"[22]

Uptowners wanted to avoid acrimonious debate over the Jewish Centres Association's implicit critique of Christianity. Antagonism from gentile newspapers, in their view, would not enhance Christian support for their own campaigns against the blue laws. Nor did they want to debate publicly the implications of the *Sun's* closing salvo, which further legitimized Christian missions to Jews: "Jews, no less than Christians, must accept the truth of the saying of Jesus. 'Let your light so shine before men that they may see your good works and glorify our Father in Heaven.'"[23]

For one Jewish critic of the Association's tactics, the more efficacious method of dealing with offensive Christian works was "quiet, dignified house-to-house work . . . to end the ignorance on the part of the parents and self-indulgence on the part of the children." Public "welfare is dangerous and ridiculous."[24]

Lucas and his confederates would have nothing of the uptowners' understanding of Americanization nor of their defensive, self-effacing posture toward criticizing the dissemination of Christian views. In their view, the nonsectarianism of settlement houses substantially undermined Jewish consciousness, while the unwillingness of German Jews to recognize the perniciousness of Christian "non-sectarianism" contributed to missionary successes. In addition, they were appalled by their coreligionists' careful maneuvering in this area of Jewish-Christian relations. For them, it was silent testimony to a lack of will or courage on the Jews' part. Thus, there was little more that could be said and little basis for cooperation. German Jews considered the instances of Christian missionary successes a limited problem that had to be dealt with judiciously. The Association saw widespread conversionist activity and anticipated even greater success in the wake of an unbridled Americanization gone wild, a communal malady for which they held German Jews partly responsible. And convinced as they were that if missionaries were not stopped American Jewry's future would be endangered, Association leaders were not about to trim their ideological or tactical sails to garner German approbation and support. They would stand against the Christian missions even without the uptowners' financial backing.[25]

The Jewish Centres Association coalition also found, much to their dismay, that active spiritual and logistical support for their crusade was also not forthcoming from the immigrant Orthodox religious leadership. To be sure, members of organizations like the Agudath ha-Rabbanim shared the Association's concern over lost children, and they certainly had no respect for the concept of non-sectarianism in Jewish life. Nor did they care how their views were received in the gentile world. They were ultimately less concerned about American law respecting the immigrants than about new Americans observing Jewish law. And so, immigrant synagogues and rabbis stood apart from the anticonversionist campaigns, thereby causing Lucas to lament more than once "the blind obstinacy of the 'majority' rulers of the synagogues, who wrap themselves in the

'Yehus' of their own piety and blind themselves with the 'Yods' of their own phylacteries."[26]

The unwillingness of immigrant rabbis to support the Jewish Centres stemmed, ironically, from their perception that groups like the Endeavor Society and the Lucas Class leaders, rather than constituting a major part of the solution to conversionism, were in reality a significant part of the problem. Rabbis and their lay supporters would not open their synagogues for Jewish school activities designed to counter missionary activities and later would not fall in behind the Henry Street Centre because, to their minds, the Christian downtown, the German Reform philanthropists, and the Centre activists were all guilty of spreading, each to a varying degree, the anti-Jewish ideology of Americanization. The immigrant rabbis saw the missionaries as the most nefarious of these groups because they used Americanization ideas and techniques to Christianize the immigrants. But all the so-called "Jewish" organizations were also dangerous: they sought to destroy the ancestral teachings and observances of Judaism in their zeal to assimilate the immigrants. The uptowners offered a foreign conception of the faith that they promoted as legitimately Jewish, and the Association which fostered the study of Judaism in English, modified the sociology of synagogue life, and offered religious education on an equal basis to girls and boys, as well as deviating from traditional procedures and attitudes in other ways that also undermined the links with Jewish tradition. Indeed, in their rejection of the new methods of Jewish education that emerged in part from the antimissionary campaigns, immigrant synagogue leaders implicitly suggested that these modernist departures paved the way for missionary successes by acknowledging and accommodating the doubts in young minds about the resilience of transplanted ways in America. For them, as with all other Jewish groups that reacted to Christian influences downtown missionary response—or nonresponse—was part of a broader ideological understanding of Americanization. As they saw it, Americanization had to be resisted whether it emanated from Christian, German, or even from association "Orthodox" sources.[27]

Consequently, the Agudath ha-Rabbanim failed to develop in the first decade of the twentieth century any specific program to counteract downtown Christian influences. Antimissionary work was not among the many communal problems noted by the Agudath ha-Rabbanim, for example, at its founding. Nor did that issue come before its early conventions. They touched on the conversionist issue only inferentially, when they considered means of transplanting older European forms of Jewish education to American soil. But then, even if they had been disposed to fight conversionists with weapons similar to those of the association activists, these still unacculturated Jews were manifestly ill-equipped by language and training to do so.[28]

Thus the battle against Christianity's influence on the Lower East Side, which at first glance seemed to be a cause around which Jews of all stripes could unite, was in the end as divisive as any other in communal politics. Only that segment of New York Jewry that accepted the incompatability of acculturation and yet was ambivalent about the promise and pitfalls of the process possessed both the energy and cultural capability to oppose what they defined as the conversionist threat. They were clearly suspicious of all Americanizers other than themselves and who were relatively unconcerned about how their public protectors were received outside their own community, found the portals of the uptown charity establishments closed to them. The doors of downtown synagogues were also barred to them because they were seen by others as Americanization advocates foreign to their own immigrant community.

7

Why Albert Lucas Did Not Serve in the New York Kehillah

In 1910 Albert Lucas was one of the most renowned members of the New York Jewish Community. This English-born and -educated communal worker was the dynamic secretary for the Union of Orthodox Jewish Congregations of America. There, among American-born traditionalists of German and English extraction, he earned an enviable reputation as an advocate of "Orthodox Judaism whenever occasions arose in civil and social matters." The repeal of Blue Laws, the protection of the rights of Sabbath observers in the civil service and the elimination of all signs of sectarianism from the public schools were all issues Lucas championed.[1]

Lucas was also famous as a defender of Jews of all denominations against overt and subtle forms of anti-Semitism. He staunchly and publicly responded to a Police Board President's allegations that "ignorance, prejudice and stubborness hindered every desire to raise the condition of the poor of the Jewish quarter." He was also the quintessential anti-missionary fighter of his day. Lucas exposed the true designs of subtle conversionists, retrieved Jewish children from missionary homes, and constantly utilized the newspapers to educate Jewish parents of the dangers of Christian settlements.

Lucas also founded and personally ran a group of Jewish mission schools out of downtown synagogues. There he showed himself to be an innovator in Jewish education. He was among the first to offer systematic Jewish religious training to girls, and he strongly advocated English as the most appropriate language of instruction in Jewish schools. Lucas truly personified the turn-of-the-century notion of an "American Orthodox" or an "American Traditionalist." He was convinced that immigrant acculturation to the new society was both inevitable and warranted. All his life he was openly committed to helping Russian immigrants reconcile their growing American identity with fading ancestral ties.[2]

Finally, Lucas was a man honored for his organizational skills in the creation of city-wide Jewish coalitions. In 1906 he successfully brought those who shared his opinions—both American-born uptown residents and Russian-born ghetto denizens—into joint partnership, to stop missionary activity and to promote modern Jewish education. Orthodox Union rabbis Henry P. Mendes and Bernard Drachman, and downtown spokesmen, Harry Fischel, Isidor Hershfield, Otto Rosalsky, and William Fischman—all called Lucas friend, colleague and leader.[3]

In 1910 Lucas' fellow Orthodox associates joined with members of uptown's German Reform elite and, under the leadership of Rabbi Judah L. Magnes of Temple Emanu-El, established the New York Kehillah. This voluntary, umbrella communal organization placed the perpetuation of Jewish identity—specifically through innovation in Jewish education—at the top of its broad communal agenda. Anti-missionary work, opposition to Sunday laws, protection of Sabbath observation against discrimination—all the other concerns Lucas held dear—were now issues addressed by this powerful uptown-downtown coalition. Even the Kehillah's initial raison d'être—a quest for community in response to a Police Commissioner's anti-Semitism—intersected with Lucas' interests. With his background, organizational experience and apparent disposition, Lucas should have become a major force in the organization's attempts to synthesize Judaism and Americanization. And yet, while Mendes, Drachman, Fischel *et al.* served with distinction in the Kehillah's powerful Executive Committee or on its important Religious or Educational Committees, Lucas was destined to play no active role in that vital city-wide organization. What was it about Albert Lucas that precluded his service in the Kehillah?[4]

The roots of Lucas' ultimate non-participation in the Kehillah must be sought in the early stage of his public career, when he first demonstrated a great commitment to Americanization and anti assimilation work, as well as a real organizational genius, on the one hand, but a lack of talent to attract other leaders of the New York Jewish community to his point of view, on the other hand. In June 1903, he keynoted the Third Orthodox Union convention with a wide-ranging discussion of the problems of Jewish education. The Orthodox Union at that moment had arrogated to itself a dual organizational mandate: the promotion of a synthesis of Americanization and Orthodox Judaism and an opposition to the teachings of Reform. Lucas spoke strongly on both themes when he asserted that he and his convention listeners alone possessed the proper understanding of America, the immigrant Jew and Judaism's requirements to respond appropriately to second-generation difficulties. Unacculturated, Yiddish-speaking downtown leaders, he suggested, clearly understood Judaism's theology and knew how the faith was perpetuated in Europe, but they lacked sufficient comprehension of their own sons' and daughters' changing needs and identity.

Lucas focused on one particular aspect, when he upbraided the heder's failure to provide young Jewish girls with adequate religious instruction. "It would be a fatal policy for us," he declared, "to neglect the instruction of our girls in a true conception of the tenets of our faith. . . . It is not against the dicta of rabbis to teach religion to girls."[5]

Reform German leaders, in Lucas' view, also had little to say to disaffected ghetto youngsters. Uptowners, to be sure, identified with America and saw themselves as Jews. But they knew little of Jewish tradition and were proven failures in "their methods of imparting religious education." Their own assimilated children, he observed, had lost contact even with their religion's most universal and ethical teachings, leaving them bereft of both Jewish knowledge and a contemporary Jewish way of life.[6]

On the other hand, he felt his Orthodox Union was uniquely fit for the task: they neither resisted America nor were they assimilationists. America would have to be served. Modern Jewish education would, perforce, utilize the public school's educational techniques, emphasizing "religious instruction in the vernacular" and offering schooling to both boys and girls. But Americanization also would have to be monitored. Acculturation, most decidedly, could not be allowed to go so far as to permit the infusion of Christian religious ideals and observances into Jewish consciousness.[7]

It was regarding this issue that Lucas redoubled his criticism of the uptowners. The Orthodox Union, he averred, stood well-nigh alone within organized American Jewry in opposing the insidious undermining of ancestral identity by zealous missionaries and sectarian schoolmen. Reform Jews, he charged, cowardly refused to help in closing the missions. They were content to tell Jewish parents "to keep their children away," and they were afraid to fight Christians proselytizing in the public schools. Uptowners advised those who would oppose school sectarianism "to leave well enough alone, rather than to mention a subject so fraught with difficulty." Lucas proudly concluded that to him and his organization had fallen the lonely but high tasks of battling the conversionists on downtown streets, of challenging the public schools every Christmas, and of taking the lead in upgrading Jewish education.[8]

Lucas' uncompromising arrogation of the role of champion of immigrant Jewish identity did little to endear him to established uptown leadership. His subsequent activities, which included the publication in metropolitan and Jewish newspapers of the names and addresses of offending Christian institutions downtown, a public "expose" of muckraker Jacob A. Riis' alleged conversionist schemes, and the organization of a Christmas-time boycott of public schools, only heightened their distaste for him. Even those who somewhat agreed with his estimations of the conversionist problem were appalled by his zealous demeanor and his lack of discretionary tactics. One such observer remarked that, while "there is a great deal of truth in what Mr. Lucas says about the missions schools on the East Side . . . he becomes a trifle too wrought over the issue." Jewish groups, this observer argued, should not attempt to close Christian missions nor engage in "a sort of 'stand-pat,' school for school, picnic for picnic warfare. Quiet, dignified house-to-house work" he argued, should characterize downtown efforts; Lucas, he asserted, "is a trifle heated and too melodramatic to cope with the situation."[9]

There were others, moreover, who perceived Lucas as nothing more than a troublemaker whose actions threatened Jewish status in America. One uncharitable uptowner declared that "religious enthusiasts [like Lucas] have done more harm in the world than all the rest of the workers for the betterment of mankind can over come." Lucas' pronounced activities, he further argued, "would bring upon the Jewish community the concerted efforts of those that they are pleased to call the enemy."[11]

Lucas had little time for these criticisms and was not concerned at all with mollifying the uptowners. He was preoccupied with the basic yet enduring problem of getting the Orthodox Union's messages across to the downtowners he was pledged to serve. Proselytism in its varying forms posed to his mind the most profound challenge to Jewish continuity, and some ghetto dwellers, Lucas observed, were unaware of, if not unconcerned with, the extent of Christianity's subtle methods to win their children. "Religious apathy or at least indifference of the parents" were, he felt, constant impediments to "fighting the missionaries." Other recent immigrants understood the conversionist threat but questioned the Union's religious reliability in responding to the challenge. A distinct cultural communications gap separated the English-born Lucas and his native-American traditionalist followers, from those Russian Jews who feared that proposed modern educational practices would by themselves undermine Jewish continuity. One immigrant critic reportedly even suggested that ulterior conversionist motives lay beneath Lucas' own pedagogic innovations:

> A man who speaks correct English and never went to cheder, who, moreover, pronounces Hebrew in a queer outlandish manner . . . what can he know of Jewish religious teaching! When that man's name is "Lucas" and when you remember that Lucas is only another form of Luke; bearing in mind, also, that Luke was an apostle . . . the suspicion that the said Lucas must be a missionary, masking his nefarious purposes under a pretense of Judaism, becomes unavoidable.[12]

This air of suspicion had profound practical ramifications. While the Orthodox Union supported the Lucas-administered Jewish mission schools that dotted the Lower East Side, the downtown synagogue leaders, who were asked to open their buildings for these classes, were much less enthusiastic. Lucas reported that "everyone encountered the opposition of the elders in control of the synagogues, to allow their buildings to be used for religious instruction, if English were the medium."[13]

Lucas' innovative solution to this dilemma was to seek to organize an uptown-downtown traditionalist coalition, linking Orthodox Union leaders with a small but crucially important new brand of East European Jewish leadership. He was among the first to recognize that a generation had passed since the start of large-scale Russian Jewish migration to these shores. The unacculturated first arrivals of the early 1880s were beginning to bring forth articulate, English-speaking lay leaders who were often affluent and ready to redirect Jewish group energies toward solving the problem of assimilation. They called themselves orthodox yet they did not share the abhorrence of Americanization by the religious Yiddish-speaking Jews. Like the Orthodox Union, they perceived the community's greatest future struggles as centering around the immigrant's reconciliation of conflicting Jewish and American identities. Lucas hoped that this new elite of Russian Jewish origin would help transmit, amplify and legitimize the traditional teachings of the European Jewish heritage in the new American milieu. Lucas trusted that these newly Americanized would also lend significant financial support to his institutional projects. He sought "East Side men whose names are almost unknown outside their neighborhood, whose donations to charitable and sociological organizations amount in two instances to $12,000 to $15,000 yearly."[14] Once established, this uptown-downtown coalition would be able to develop a network of Jewish mission schools throughout the ghetto which would be independent of existing congregations and finan cially solvent. These institutions, "the eyes and ears of the ghetto," could help Lucas track missionary comings and goings. And they would be temples of modern Jewish pedagogy, implanting in the hearts of youngsters a love for Judaism with respect for their new country.[15]

In 1906, after three years of planning, struggle and cooptation, Lucas' dream was realized when the Jewish Centres Association was created with the publicized goal of building "a center next door or in the vicinity of every Christian mission institution on the East Side." These schools were expected to embody all of Lucas' ideas and initiatives. Jewish children would be provided "the same light, cheerful rooms, cleanliness and wholesome food that Christian workers offer." Strides would be made in the upgrading of Jewish education. And the Jewish Centres would endeavor to shut down the Christian competition by persistent exposes of offending institutions.[16]

The Jewish Centres Association was the realization of an anticipated alliance of uptown and downtown traditionalists. Rabbi Henry Pereira Mendes of the Spanish-Portuguese Synagogue, the founder of the Orthodox Union, and his Jewish Theological Seminary colleagues, Bernard Drachman, Aaron Eiseman and Israel Davidson, all lent moral support and personal advise to the movement. Union laymen, N. Taylor Phillips, New York City Controller and scion of one of American Jewry's oldest families, and physician Dr. Abraham Wolbarst, American-born of German ancestry, led the list of uptown Centres directors. Builder and real estate tycoon, Harry Fischel, successful merchant and manufacturer, William Fischman, Judge Otto Rosalsky, lawyer Isidor Hershfield, and newspaper editor Leon Kamaiky spoke most often for the East European contingent. The older Americans brought long-standing organizational and personal experience to this new endeavor. Rabbis Mendes and Drachman, for example, had fought missionaries as early as the 1880s. The newly acculturated drew upon more recent individual efforts toward synthesizing Judaism with American values. Fischel had been a director of the Machzikei Talmud Torah since 1892; there he had been instrumental in providing religious classes for girls. Since 1902 Fischman had been president of the fledgling Downtown Talmud Torah. Lucas was convinced that this coalition possessed the prestige, experience and, most importantly, the sensitivity to downtown problems and proclivities needed to effectively direct the immigrant second generation through the trials of acculturation.[17]

The Jewish Centres Association's first year seemed to confirm its founder's highest expectations. In July 1906, the first independent Jewish mission was established at 272 Houston Street. A young men's and young women's auxiliary, seventy persons strong, assisted in Lucas' classrooms, and by the end of the summer an average of forty-five youngsters were attending its daily kindergarten. Sewing classes averaged twenty-two students every day, and forty-five boys and girls were steadily studying the Bible. True to his program for "paralleling the methods of Christian missionaries," kindergarten teachers were instructed "in every instance where the singing of sectarian hymns would be possible . . . to use Jewish hymns and melodies." Lucas boasted that his children often left his school singing the parodied nursery song, "This is the way we go to Shule every Shabbos morning."[18]

Soon, however, disconcerting voices were heard from the Jewish Centre. The coalition had apparently grown too quickly, without assured long-term financial backing. Board members were called upon both to increase their own contributions and to find new contributors. Lucas, for one, was concerned that additional supporters would not come forward. "There still exists," he complained, "to far too great an extent the self-spirit of only looking out for the opportunity of satisfying one's own spiritual requirements."[19]

The spring of 1907 brought sad verification to Lucas' bleak predictions. A $1,000 operating deficit threatened to halt education work right "before the summer vacation." As the prime season for conversionist labors approached, Lucas even desperately considered the idea of accepting money from the Executive Director of the Federation of Churches to keep the Centre open. "If a Christian organization," he declared, "is willing to provide the funds for the work to be done by Jews, then I am willing to accept their proffered help . . . I am not afraid of 'tainted money'." The Jewish Centre did survive its second summer, only to close its doors for good at the end of 1907.[20]

The failure of the Jewish Centre convinced many coalition members that grand communal initiatives could not succeed without more broadly based financial support. That required the necessary inclusion of uptown Reform Jews in future projects. But was this old elite concerned with the issues which so exercised Association activists? Fischel, Mendes and their colleagues believed so, and they thus rejected Lucas' earlier expressed belief that the famous philanthropists were insensitive to the problems of Christianity and the entire dilemma of acculturation. They certainly did not agree with the *Hebrew Standard's* post-Jewish Centre warning that cooperation with the Jacob Schiffs and Louis Marshalls of the New York community would lead to the surrender of the community into their hands and the inevitable abandonment of dearly held concerns. This downtown organ, which consistently backed Lucas' initiatives and attitudes and gave the earliest support for the Jewish Centre, argued in 1907 that Reform Jews "were more anxious to stand with the Gentiles than to be on brotherly terms with fellow Jews." Uptown "watchwords . . . diplomacy, expediency and advisability," it averred, "were euphemisms disguising their lack of moral backbone and courage." In its view, only those traditionalists "who would dance to their fiddling, are admitted to their counsel."

A year later, Fischel, Mendes et al. acted upon their confident perception when a new large-scale communal endeavor began to appear upon the New York Jewish horizon. Police Commissioner Thomas Bingham's September 1908 allegation that "fifty percent of the criminal classes in New York City were Jews" precipitated calls from many quarters for a truly unified Jewish response. Toward that end, on September 5, 1908, just four days after the much publicized canard appeared, a meeting was held in Clinton Hall on the East Side which attracted "a broad, middle grouping of the Jewish organizational spectrum." Jewish Centre veterans were prominent among those arguing that "alliance with uptown leaders . . . [was] indispensable for effective action."[22]

Two weeks later, Union traditionalists and new elite members appeared with Temple Emanu-El Rabbi and Kehillah champion Judah Magnes and announced an October conference that would be dedicated to linking all "Jewish organizations of New York." That conference and subsequent meetings and discussions further confirmed Association members' impressions that Reform Jews possessed anti-assimilationist sensibilities, as they witnessed the range of Kehillah concerns and emphases grow from initial "protest and defense" to more permanent and profound "community building." The merger of old and new elites, crossing all denominational lines, was formalized in April 1909, when Fischel, Kamaiky, Fischman, Mendes. Phillips and Drachman joined Magnes, Schiff, Marshall *et al.* on the initial Kehillah executive committee. Several years later, Hershfield and Rosalsky joined the Jewish community's power base.[23]

Albert Lucas would have nothing to do with this movement toward inter-denominational cooperation. Alliances, in his view, could be formed only with those who truly understood the nature of Christianity's long-standing threat to Jewish identity. And as late as 1907, he felt uptown Jews had yet to show him any real comprehension of what his continuing battles were all about. Lucas had only to think of Judah L. Magnes', the Kehillah's champion, opinion, expressed only a year before the Kehillah's founding, that Christianity could play a positive role in the Jewish immigrant's life. In response to Lucas's own Orthodox Union-run Christmas-time boycott of New York City public schools, Magnes had declared that "the true Hebrew, the real Hebrew, resents the activities of those Jews who would strip Christmas of all its beauty." The Jews, Magnes then continued, could learn much from the Yuletide sentiment:

> Peace on earth. Good will to men, glory to God in the highest. Shall not the day come when we, too, shall be able to sing this? Sing as Jews, as men and women who have something to give to the world.[24]

Lucas also knew that Magnes' viewpoint was not unique among uptown Jewry. Maurice Harris, Magnes' Reform rabbinical colleague and a future Kehillah executive committee member, had echoed similar sentiments when he expressed sorrow "to see a week usually associated with peace and good will made one of discord [by] the well-meaning but indiscreet people who rush into print with grievances that make the judicious grieve."[25]

Lucas thus felt justifiably concerned that if American traditionalists like himself cooperated with Reform uptowners, great sums of money might be forthcoming for Jewish communal projects, but the all-important basic problems which the Jewish Centres Association addressed would be ignored or abandoned. So disposed, Lucas witnessed the growth of the Kehillah with great concern and suspicion.[26]

By 1909 Lucas realized that most of his former supporters were destined to align themselves with the new city-wide endeavor. Even the Orthodox Union, which had spawned all his efforts, was on record as offering at least half-hearted support for cooperative activities with members of other denominations. In February 1909 the Union decided to give the new communal initiative a chance "if the Kehillah can help not merely Judaism but Orthodox Judaism." A Committee of Twelve was appointed to represent Union interests at the March 1909 Founding Conference, although delegates were instructed "to oppose the Kehillah becoming a part of the American Jewish Committee," the symbol of uptown power and influence. With the merger seemingly inevitable, Lucas wisely undertook a tactical rear-guard action to limit Reform Jewish power within the new coalition. His plan was to attend the Kehillah's Founding Convention as one of the three hundred delegates representing over two hundred New York Jewish organizations and there, on the convention floor, to rally those of Orthodox leanings in support of an amendment to the Kehillah's constitution calling for the election of fifty members to the governing executive committee instead of the proposed twenty-five. He hoped to garner the votes necessary to pack that all-powerful organ with those who, to his mind, understood the needs of downtown masses.[27]

"Pandemonium" reportedly broke out when Lucas activated his plan, only to have his nemesis, convention chairman Magnes, rule his motion out of order. When calm was restored, the chair's decision was appealed, and to Lucas' dismay the ruling was supported by a 99 to 77 vote. Now shown to be in the minority, Lucas was resigned to sit back and watch as many of his former Jewish Centre colleagues entered into what he feared was an unequal partnership with German brethren.[28]

Sometime later, Lucas' traditionalist friends gave him an opportunity to monitor the Kehillah from within, when he was elected to the organization's less-powerful Advisory Council. Lucas accepted a spot within a contingent which was to gain a reputation within Magnes' circle as "a populist, irresponsible body thirsting for power" which "provided favorable soil for Kehillah critics." But his heart was not in it; he served there inactively for only one year. Lucas preferred to carry on alone. He maintained his own style of anti-missionary organization and educational work through his mission schools which operated, as in the beginning, out of downtown synagogues through World War I.[29]

Albert Lucas' career is illustrative of a generally unrecognized type of Orthodox Jew in turn-of-the-century America. He accepted Americanization as irresistible and even warranted, but distrusted most Americanizers, be they liberal Jews or Christians. As such, he had little in common with those in the downtown community who sought to resist acculturation and who were destined to lead a vociferous opposition to later Kehillah modern educational initiatives. Lucas was clearly unlike those who Fischel once characterized as "of the 'old-fashioned' type who believed that the only way to give children a Jewish education is by teaching them in the same way as they were taught twenty-five years ago and who have always held back progress . . . at all times."[30]

And yet Lucas was also very different from Fischel, who both accepted Americanization and trusted the uptowners. Lucas' inability to see German Reform Jews as allies in any grand anti-assimilation endeavor stemmed from his unique understanding of whence emanated the most overriding cause of second-generation disaffection. Lucas believed that assimilation first took hold when American-Christian society forcibly attempted to extend the boundaries of acculturation to unacceptable limits. Missionaries and school sectarians snared relatively few Jews to complete conversion, but engendered widespread disrespect for Judaism. Consequently, stopping Christianity's institutional and ideational impact upon the immigrant's life was, for Lucas, the essential first step in controlling disaffection. Unfortunately for him, most of his Jewish Centre colleagues

came to see his life-long concerns as symptomatic of larger assimilatory processes. Fischel, for example, believed that fault lay initially
and primarily with the Jews of America for not making the faith of
their parents more attractive to those becoming one with American
society. For the Kehillah's most outspoken Orthodox supporter, the
solution began with more and better forms of modern Jewish education.

This difference in perspective carried over directly to their respective attitudes toward the uptown elite. If improved education was
the key and conversionism only a symptom, and if the Germans
showed a willingness to help bankroll modern pedagogic initiatives,
then there existed a clear potentiality for cooperation in anti-assimilation work. So disposed, Fischel later would have little difficulty
with Magnes' 1912 self-effacing suggestion that missionaries have a
"right to exist" so long as Jews failed to respond adequately to their
children's needs. Lucas, on the other hand, was undoubtedly
appalled by the Kehillah's declaration that "we cannot fail to see the
justice of the contention that until we are prepared to do our duty
the responsibility of caring for the children of the city must be
assumed by non-Jewish organizations." As he saw it, quietism
toward Christianity and distaste for his noisy and intense campaigns
were no way to solve the central concern of American Jewry.[31]

Fear of the new society he had chosen to accept separated Lucas
from those who made up the Kehillah. Lucas saw Christianity on
the Lower East Side as representative of Christian anti-Semitism at
work and a clear indication of the hazards of Jewish minority status
in the United States. To stay silent, or even to be discreet toward the
roots of Christianity's impact upon the immigrant, testified to a lack
of will or courage on the Jews' part. Lucas said as much when he
declared: "It is not from a genuine altruistic love of mankind,
unmixed with proselytizing intentions, that these Christians seek . . .
the lives of our children . . . No believer in . . . constitutional American institutions will ask . . . that, our boys and girls forsake their
own faith."[32]

Kehillah activists were more sanguine about America. Conversionism, in their view, would be opposed whenever it appeared, but the

prime focus of communal attention would be internally directed. They would strive above all to make all uptowners and downtowners jointly aware of their social and educational obligation: to Americanize Jewish youth.

8

In Search of the Other Jewish Center: On the Writing of the Social History of American Orthodoxy, 1900–1918

In his inaugural sermon as founding rabbi of The Jewish Center in March 1918, Mordecai M. Kaplan, great innovator that he was, sought to articulate the uniqueness of his new endeavor. In his published remarks he asserted that for too long philanthropically inclined, newly affluent East European Jews had only been concerned with the physical and social fate of their poor coreligionists downtown. The communal institutions they had built ignored their own Jewish needs. The time had come, he argued, and The Jewish Center was the place for

> the higher and enlightened form of selfishness . . . in us. Frankly . . . we are establishing The Jewish Center for the purpose of deriving from it for ourselves pleasures of a social, intellectual and spiritual character . . . We are not building an institution for the doing of uplift work. This time we feel that we are as much in need of being uplifted as they for whose benefit the city is dotted with communal institutions.[1]

An historian, possessed of an orientation fundamentally different from that of an institution builder, immediately casts a jaundiced eye at such claims of uniqueness. His skepticism is heightened when he knows from his own research that at least two major institutions, in neighborhoods adjoining Kaplan's own, and with which Kaplan had more than a passing personal or professional relationship, had set about, in the very year prior to the rise of The Jewish Center, comparable social educational work for newly affluent Jews. In 1915 the Special Joint Committee of the Social, Finance and Membership and Neighborhood Committees of the Young Mens' Hebrew Association in Yorkville declined to extend its programming into neighboring and poor Jewish East Harlem, preferring to serve the more affluent Upper East Side. Of course, had Kaplan, former educational director of the Y, known of this class bias he undoubtedly would have responded that the problem with the Y was that while they catered to more affluent Jews, they did not give them Jewish enough programming, hence the need for his new Jewish Center.[2]

Kaplan would have had more difficulty defining Harry Fischel's efforts in 1913 as insignificant or irrelevant compared to his own attention to the rich. In that year, the builder-philanthropist created the so-called rich man's annex of the Uptown Talmud Torah at then-fashionable 115th Street and Lenox Avenue. Fischel believed that Jews, who were so concerned with the conditions of the poor, were "negligent when it comes to their own children's Jewish education . . . permitting them to become respectable ignoramuses," and so he started a school "to give proper Jewish instruction along the most modern lines to the children of the so-called 'baalbatim'—that is men whom God has given sufficient means to pay for the instruction of his (sic) children." Kaplan could certainly have said that his initiative—by virtue of its complete integration of sanctuary, school and ancillary activities—advanced Fischel's efforts. But could he really claim uniqueness in addressing the needs of the newly elite rich?[3]

And what would he do with the fact that there was a Jewish Centers Association (sp. Centres) in New York, apparently offering modern Orthodox services to the next generation, in existence more than ten years before his uptown group organized? Several brief newspaper accounts from 1906 spoke of a branch of the Jewish Centres Association in Jewish Harlem and indicated that there were other Jewish Centres groups downtown. Who were the founders and members of this movement and how did they compare in constituency and mission to Kaplan's later efforts? Answers to questions about an association or movement that no previous historian had ever looked at, it seemed to me, would help gauge the level of hyperbole in Kaplan's proud statement as well as the roots of the famous

West Side institution. As it turned out, the search for the "Other Jewish Center" shed relatively little light on Kaplan's antecedents, but it unearthed much information about the social history of relations to the larger Jewish community and attitudes towards the gentile world among the future American Orthodox "baalbatim" who Kaplan hoped to reach at The Jewish Center.[4]

An initial survey of the catalogues and reports of holdings in major Jewish archives revealed, not unexpectedly, the most meager shred of institutional documentation on this most ephemeral organization. All records relative to the Jewish Centres Association apparently were lost—assuming extensive documentation ever existed-save a series of letters from that organization's founder, Albert Lucas, to Louis Marshall from 1903–1908 (the years of the Centres' life as indicated by newspaper accounts) stored in Marshall's papers in the American Jewish Archives.

Who was this Albert Lucas, a figure who, previous to my studies, was unknown to historiography? Fortunately, his contemporaries considered him to be a leader of some import which offered a start to my investigations. A compilation of biographical sketches of Jewish communal workers published by the *American Jewish Yearbook* in 1905–1906 identifies the British-born Lucas as Secretary of the Union of Orthodox Jewish Congregations of America and "organizer and superintendent of. . . religious classes. . . in downtown synagogues in which girls as well as boys are taught the Jewish religion in the English language exclusively; purpose, to counteract the Christian missionaries."[5]

What connection could Marshall, a Reform lay leader, have with the Jewish Centres Association, an initiative headed up by an official of the Orthodox Union and possibly linked ultimately to a major Orthodox synagogue? The putative connection was twofold: Marshall, as a leading Jewish philanthropist, backed organizations across the denominational spectrum. (To his great credit, when sent minutes of meetings from groups he supported, he was sure to retain them for his files and ultimately for historians.) Additionally, when Kaplan's Jewish Center was dedicated, Marshall was one of the featured speakers, standing in the pulpit with spokesmen for the

Orthodox Union. It seemed plausible that a research trip to the American Jewish Archives in Cincinnati might reveal the linkage between the two Jewish Centers.[6]

The Marshall letter file for 1903–1908 told a very different tale. It revealed the story of a private debate and public battle between Lucas and a famous historical figure linked closely to Jews and Judaism of that time, a conflict out of which arose the Jewish Centres Association. The earliest document detailing this controversy was a letter dated September 3, 1903, from Lucas to Marshall. It begins with a reference to enclosed "copies of letters which have passed between Mr. Jacob A. Riis and myself," with Riis' letter described as "about as disingenuous a communication as could have been written." Lucas accuses Riis of leading through his "settlement. . . missionaries among the children in Pike Street;" Lucas was turning to "some men of weight in our community in order to properly bring this matter before the public," requesting that they "meet with a few of us who are conversant with this question and to decide what is best to be done. . . . We will have to offer bribe for bribe, and spend dollar for dollar, in order to hope for any permanent success." Lucas closed with a handwritten appeal: "If you could spare the time for me to call upon you and talk this over, I should appreciate it very much."[7]

That Lucas, identified previously as a missionary fighter, would identify an enemy and seek support in the wider community was not surprising. It was his choice of target, Jacob Riis, author of the classic *How the Other Half Lives,* supposedly a long-time friend of the immigrant and frequently praised by contemporary Jews, that was unexpected and thus was exciting to me as a researcher. It indicated that Lucas, alone or through the OU, was taking on an acknowledged friend of the Jews, accusing him of anti-Semitic behavior. But I did not know how Marshall and his people of "weight" reacted to that stance and how did all of this relate to the 1906 Jewish Centre story.[8]

As a start towards answering these questions, an examination of the Anglo-Jewish, Yiddish and the general press for the years 1903–1908 revealed a story line for a controversy that was very much in the public eye. Beginning in 1903, Lucas publicly accused Riis of secretly proselytizing Jewish children within his supposedly nonsectarian settlement house on Henry Street. When Riis—to Lucas' mind—failed to respond appropriately to an official request from the Secretary of the Orthodox Union to explain reports of events at his immigrant home, downtown activists moved against the so-called "masked institutions." Indeed, Riis and his house were often mentioned by the Orthodox Union in its anti-missionary work which included publishing in the Jewish press the names and addresses of alleged missionary centers, infiltrating Christian settlement groups to determine their true ends, and instigating street protests to drive offenders out of the Jewish neighborhood. Remarkably, the Orthodox Union's efforts, under Lucas' guiding hand, even led them into a coalition with a local downtown Catholic priest who shared the Jews' concerns about what the Protestant Riis was doing to all immigrant children. Most importantly for us, the locus of all this activity was the well-publicized Jewish Centres Association. One Jewish Home was created across the street from Riis' establishment, and a branch of the Jewish Centres offering modern Jewish educational and traditional services was built in Harlem.[9]

The published sources indicate that Lucas was not alone in his endeavors. There were, as Lucas had told Marshall, "a few of us conversant with this question." Indeed, it was effectively an OU operation, as Lucas gathered lay and rabbinic leaders of the Union into his Centres movement, and he linked uptown American Orthodox Jews of German/Central European extraction with a rising and acculturating class of East European Jews. Newspaper reports identified Union President Rabbi H. P. Mendes—apparently Lucas' rabbi and patron from the Spanish-Portuguese Synagogue—as an advisor to the inner circle, along with Rabbi Bernard Drachman of the uptown Zichron Ephraim and professor at the Jewish Theological Seminary, then the seat of the OU. These same accounts list some twenty-four directors of the Centres, for about ten of whom we can find brief biographies in the *American Jewish Yearbook* and like sources. If this ethnic, professional and class data is at all representative, Lucas' Orthodox Union colleagues were an impressive group.

They included the Deputy Controller of the City of New York, N. Taylor Phillips, scion of one of American Jewry's oldest families and a member of Mendes' congregation. Uptown Orthodoxy's ranks were swelled by the presence of physician Dr. Abraham Wolbarst. The downtown majority included two newspaper editors—essential for an operation like Lucas'—A. H. Fromenson of the *Yiddishes Tageblatt* and Leon Kamaiky of both the *Tageblatt* and the *Morgen Zhurnal;* Judge Otto Rosalsky; builder and real estate tycoon Harry Fischel; merchant and manufacturer William Fischman; and lawyer Isidor Hershfield.[10]

Clearly missing from that list is Marshall and his friends, to whom Lucas had directed his plaintive "bribe for bribe" call. In fact, although the Jewish Centres movement could boast of Leon Kamaiky, its one charter member from the American Jewish Committee (also founded in 1906), the true charity leaders and power magnates of New York Jewry showed little interest in the Lucas activist campaign. Their absence was of no small moment for the initiative. Although Lucas boasted when his movement began that he could rely on "East Side men . . . whose donations to charitable and sociological organizations amount in two instances to $12,000 to $15,000 yearly," after just one year, disconcerting reports spoke of the lack of assured long-term financial backing. In May 1907 a chastened Lucas would have to admit that "there still exists to far too great an extent the self-spirit of only looking out for the opportunity of satisfying one's own spiritual requirements." Sadly for Lucas, ongoing funding from those who might have supported his Centres was never forthcoming. After a summer of struggle in 1907, the Jewish Centres Association downtown and its branch in Harlem closed their doors permanently at the end of the year.[11]

Why were Lucas' calls for help ignored? His anti-missionary work should have been of interest to what he called Jewish "men of weight." Both Marshall and Jacob Schiff, for example, had supported similar campaigns. The Educational Alliance itself, the very hub of German Jewish socio-philanthropic work was born in 1887 in response to the conversion threat. It is here that the absence of internal documentation from Lucas' camp hinders our search for a full history of the Jewish Centres. Ideally, letter files, minute books and organization memoranda would identify the people approached for help and the methods used to raise contributions. The responses from those people would indicate why philosophically and/or practically Lucas' work was low in their list of priorities. Moreover, minutes from meetings would highlight the willingness or unwillingness of directors to alter policies and tactics to enlarge their support base. No records remain—at least to my knowledge—which could answer these questions.[12]

Did such files ever exist? Thinking that records on Lucas' work might have survived outside established archives—sources in American Jewish history have been known to be housed for generations in makeshift vaults and closets of synagogues—I made an effort to learn more about Lucas, his family and associates. Aided by a reference to Rabbi Mendes in one of Lucas' letters to Marshall and my knowledge that he was of British Sephardic extraction (indicated by a newspaper profile and the AJYB biography which stated that his wife's maiden name was Nieto), I asked at New York's Spanish-Portuguese Synagogue, the American Orthodox congregation that Mendes served, whether Lucas had been a member and, if so, whether he had any descendants. The congregation has membership records for that period—few congregations do—and there was a membership card for Lucas. Unfortunately, the brief data on Albert and Rebecca Lucas indicated that they had no children. Equally disappointing, there evidently was no estate. A check of the probated wills on file in the counties he lived in, uncovered none for him. They apparently died as paupers: congregational records indicate they were buried at the expense of the synagogue. They left no family or scholarly legacy. What of their ostensible sponsoring organization, the Orthodox Union? Remnants of ninety years of records from an institution that dates back to 1897 miraculously found their way to the Library of the American Jewish Historical Society in Waltham, Massachusetts. There are minutes of committee meetings and other activities beginning in 1923, but not a sheet of paper on early twentieth century missionary work—an item high on the agenda then—has survived the OU offices' several moves over the decades.

Did Lucas' friends have a greater sense of history and leave us information on the Jewish Centres Association? Harry Fischel's family knew the historical significance of their ancestor and donated his papers to New York's Agudath Israel Orthodox Jewish Archives. However, these files contain nothing on this early activity. Finally, what of Lucas' rabbi and OU president, H. P. Mendes? Mendes had a forty-six-year tenure at the Spanish-Portuguese Synagogue. But scholars have been left to study—apart from synagogue minutes—only four "scrapbooks kept by Mendes' mother, Eliza de Sola Mendes during the early years of the ministry of her son," housed at the American Jewish Archives and two boxes of "sermons, addresses, correspondence and personal materials," deposited at the Jewish Theological Seminary of America. None of these documents relate to Mendes' relations with Lucas.[13]

Ironically, it is primarily from the well-maintained papers of Lucas' enemy, Jacob Riis, and of the offending institution, the Jacob A. Riis Neighborhood Settlement, that we begin to gain some inkling as to what went wrong with the Jewish Centres' initiative. From documents housed at the New York Public Library and the Library of Congress we learn that Jacob Schiff was a supporter of the Riis home as early as 1902, a year before the controversy broke. These sources also confirm that American Jewish Committeeman Nathan Bijur, German Jewish philanthropist Nathan Straus, and Miriam K. Wildberg of the Columbia Council of the Council of Jewish Women were also either friends or associates of the settlement leader. Each penned a warm, personal letter of condolences to Riis on the occasion of the death of his first wife, Elizabeth. Schiff's relationship with Riis is confirmed by a letter among his papers (which, like Marshall's, are extant at the American Jewish Archives) that speaks of the $2,100 Schiff, his son-in-law Felix Warburg and a Mr. Seligman contributed in 1906 (the year the Jewish Centre was founded) to build a gymnasium across the street from Lucas' operation, on the premises of the Riis settlement home designated for use by Jewish clients. Unfortunately, these same papers—like Marshall's—do not say why no funding was available for the Lucas endeavor. But they do raise strong questions again about why anti-missionaries like these uptown notables stayed clear of the Jewish Centres Association campaign. [14]

For the answer to that question, the Riis papers again prove most useful. Putting aside Riis' vitriol over being attacked by Jews—he made anti-Semitic characterizations of Lucas and resorted to racist stereotyping of his Catholic friend—the personal papers reveal a disturbed Riis uncomprehending how his Christian efforts on behalf of the Jewish poor could be misconstrued as conversionist. As he saw settlement work, the missionaries' sole raison d'être was the baptism of Jews: their success or failure could be quantified by their yearly tallies of converts. He, on the other hand, wanted to help young Jewish immigrants become good Americans, and from his perspective that could best be achieved by their learning universal Christian values. In other words, for him, knowing Jesus helped implant the range of virtues from cleanliness to manliness to patriotism to godliness. Of course, in believing this, he did not take into account how a Jewish group like the OU and Lucas and the Jewish parents and youngsters he sought to serve would react viscerally to a center with crucifixes on the front door and to his statements that "yes, the house is a Christian settlement . . . We have nailed the Cross to the door and it is going to remain there. If your Jewish mothers don't know where they are sending their children, it is about time Christian influence stepped in and took care of the children."[15]

It is entirely possible that Riis' Jewish friends understood—or made—the same distinctions he made and thus did not see him as the missionary enemy and threat that Lucas did. The probability that New York Jewry's ultimate men of weight, to again borrow Lucas' terminology, felt that way is heightened by the fact that Rabbi Stephen S. Wise, one of their leading Reform spiritual guides, was an outspoken public supporter of Riis and even made several interfaith appearances at the Henry Street settlement home to back up his remarks. If the German Jewish elite observed and were moved by Wise's point of view, they had to ignore the subtle anti-Semitic implications of Riis' remarks. What Riis was suggesting was that

Christian values alone, however universalized, were the best way, if not the only way, of making Jews into good Americans. Did not Jewish tradition preach the same commonsense values? Lucas might have made that point if Marshall, Schiff and their friends had let him through the door. But as far as we know, such audiences did not take place. [16]

Was it only Lucas' campaign against Riis that undermined support from the communal elite? After all, a quick survey of the Lower East Side would have shown that many felt that Riis at his worst was only a small part of the problem. There were, for example, at least seven missions devoted explicitly to luring Jewish children—and to a lesser degree their parents—away from Judaism. Lucas was aware of, and indeed spoke out against, centers like the People's Home Church that proudly proclaimed that "evangelism must be first in our experience." Why did not Marshall, Schiff, and the others back Lucas when he was "right" and become directly involved with the Jewish Centres Association thereby moving it, with their accumulated wisdom and money in the appropriate directions? Here again, the absence of internal documentation makes answering this question difficult.[17]

Contemporary newspaper accounts do, however, suggest a number of explanations. Lucas failed not only because of his harsh treatment of Christians, but also because of his intemperate words towards his fellow Jews, in fact, the very same affluent Jews he hoped to reach for contributions. To begin with, there were Jews who questioned the Lucas forces' confrontational tactics in opposing missionaries. Jewish Centres people were comfortable trying to drive Christians of all stripes from the ghetto; many Jewish observers were not. One spoke of "rousing anti-Jewish feeling [as likely] to bring a *Juden Hetze* here in the United States." Another agreed, stating that "public warfare is dangerous and ridiculous" and suggested that "Lucas is a trifle heated and too melodramatic to cope with the situation." A third denigrated [Jewish Centres] "religious enthusiasts" as having done "more harm in the world than all the rest of the workers for the betterment of mankind can overcome."[18]

Lucas was unmoved by these attacks, responding that while "some may even be inclined to believe that it would be better to leave well enough alone, . . . if we, as a sect feel that we are laboring under any injustice, we must base our claim for the removal of such disability upon no sympathetic ground but upon the broad, plain and undebatable plea of our rights as citizens." He countered by asking: "How much longer is the Jewish community going to stand idly by?. . . When will something be done to offset the missionizing influence in our Jewish homes?" He melodramatically chided his coreligionists, stating that "our brethren in Russia are suffering enough in 'Honor of the Holy Name,' it should be an inspiration to our weak-kneed brethren here." And he agreed with the sentiments expressed by a contemporary that "the rich Jewish community's . . . unmistakable tendency [is] to stay clear of movements that have their origins or are in the hands of downtown Jews." For American Jewish Committeemen, whose own conservative organization was born out of a desire to moderate ill-tempered voices speaking on behalf of the Jewish community, Lucas' radical tactics and strident rhetoric were undoubtedly the wrong approach.[19]

But there was more. Concomitant with his plaintive calls for money for his antimissionary work, Lucas and his associates publicly pilloried German-American Jewish leaders for their support for institutions that, to the Orthodox Union leader's mind, did not promote Jewish identity strongly enough. They even had nasty words to say about their potential patrons' own commitment to the Jewish faith. Yiddish newspaper editor A. H. Fromenson, a Jewish Centres charter director wrote in 1904:

> [A] Jewish institution is one which stands for Jewish ethics and Jewish ideals and engraves its Jewishness over its door posts. [The Educational Alliance is] ashamed of the name "Hebrew Institute" graven over its portals . . . and which stands for something broader than Judaism-an invertebrate, anemic, condescending, patronizing sentimentalism. . . . [It] has lost for all its regenerative work on the East Side the full means of its usefulness.[20]

For himself, Lucas had the following to say about Reform Judaism just two months before his initial 1903 solicitation of Marshall: "I have always considered [Reform] useless for anyone who desired permanently to improve the conditions of Judaism." He continued sarcastically that "they succeed in making such good Jews and Jewesses out of their children that the proprietors of private schools usually request the parents of such Jewish scholars . . . to withdraw them not through religious bigotry but because of the dangerous example these Christ-less Christians show to observant Christian children."[21]

In light of these statements, it is remarkable that AJC people did not write off everything associated with Lucas' name. In fact, if Marshall is typical, there was some German support for purely educational activities downtown run under Lucas' name. Between 1903 and 1908, Marshall made an unspecified contribution to Lucas' religious classes which were started as an anti-conversionist move and supervised by the activist. We also have to assume that Marshall's name on a document announcing a testimonial dinner in 1908 in honor of the "public spirited work of Albert Lucas" was simply good-heartedness on the uptowner's part. But backing for Lucas' attacks against Jacob Riis who was not unquestionably a missionary—or turning to Lucas to drive out even the avowed conversionist—was not for Marshall.[22]

Statements and actions by Lucas and some of his closest associates must have caused tension within OU ranks as well. The failure of the Jewish Centres initiative may have been a cruel object lesson for Orthodoxy's own *balabatim*. Men like Fischel and Hershfield may have shared Lucas' perception that the great men of wealth were reluctant to share power with downtown movements, but they also may have learned that great communal objectives could not be achieved without significant German help. Moreover, some may have come out of this abortive anti-missionary campaign with a new perspective on the roots of the problem. Not totally unlike the Germans, they may have come to suspect that while overt conversionists did cause problems for Judaism and Jewish status, their successes—which were actually quite limited—were part of the larger problem of assimilation among second-generation youngsters. The wiser course was to expand the horizons of Jewish education, a position which, not incidentally, German Jews could approve. They may have come to think that by demanding that everyone focus on missionaries, Lucas—his sterling qualities notwithstanding—was a barrier to intra-Jewish communication and cooperation on the enduring question of assimilation.

Such possibilities could only be fully verified by the long-lost files of the Jewish Centre and the early Orthodox Union. However, the probability that these thoughts motivated factions within the OU is heightened by a look at how OU people responded to the next, even larger community-wide endeavor, i.e., the New York Kehillah. Extant organizational records closely document this initiative: Kehillah files survived because its chairman, Rabbi Judah L. Magnes, had the good sense to take them with him when he settled in Palestine in the early 1920s, becoming the first head of the new Hebrew University. From the Central Archives for the History of the Jewish People in Jerusalem come documents that speak of Orthodox Union cooperation with German leadership in the field of education, an alliance with which, as we will presently see, Lucas wanted no real part.[23]

The Kehillah was born initially out of the desire by most uptown leaders for a unified Jewish response to New York Police Commissioner Thomas Bingham's September 1908 allegation that "fifty percent of the criminal classes in New York City were Jews." Very early on, as the movement formed to fight this anti-Semitic allegation, it became clear to Kehillah founders that their emerging alliance had great potential for addressing, in a substantive way, many of the largest needs of New York Jewry. The problems of anti-Semitism and of criminality were both important, but so were the issues of unemployment and industry, poverty and philanthropy, and above all, education to counter assimilation. But to achieve their lofty goal of, in effect, reconstructing an organized Jewish community in voluntaristic America, the leaders needed the cooperation of all elements of the Jewish polity. Towards that end, the Orthodox Union was among many groups approached for the uptown-downtown endeavor.[24]

For the Orthodox Union, participation in the Kehillah promised financial support for interests very dear to them. In fact, at an OU meeting in March 1909 where the question was candidly raised of "how the Kehillah can help not merely Judaism but Orthodox Judaism," Rabbi Mendes spoke excitedly of some seven "special [Orthodox] requirements with which the Kehillah would be concerned":

> Jewish observance, religious schools, religious centres to counteract the activities of Christian attempts to convert our children, decorum [in the synagogues?], the elevation of men and women to the consciousness of religious life, religious duty and religious aspirations, regulation of *Schechita, Milah, Kiddushin, Gett* etc. and most importantly, the regulation of talmud torahs and yeshivas.[25]

But cooperation with the Kehillah, which was dominated by German Reform Jewish leaders, required a great measure of Orthodox Union faith in their colleagues' goodwill. It meant ignoring a blistering series of editorials in the downtown organ, *The Hebrew Standard,* one of which argued that, in the immediate post-Jewish Centres period, Reform Jews "were more anxious to stand with the Gentiles than to be on brotherly terms with fellow Jews" and that only those traditional Jews "who would dance to their fiddling are admitted to their counsel."[26]

Evidently the OU as an organization and many former Jewish Centre supporters harbored no such fears. The OU appointed a Committee of Twelve to represent Union interests at the Kehillah's March 1909 founding conference, although their delegates were clearly instructed to be wary of German Jewish power. They were told "to oppose the Kehillah becoming a part of the American Jewish Committee," the symbol of uptown influence and control. Former Jewish Centres directors Fischel, Kamaiky, Fischman, Mendes, Phillips and Drachman joined the initial Kehillah executive committee. Several years later Hershfield and Rosalsky joined the Kehillah, the Jewish community's power base.[27]

The failure of the Jewish Centres may have had an important effect, on a number of levels, on Orthodox cooperation with the Kehillah. It reminded them that they alone could not adequately support their most profound "special requirements." But equally important, that experience may have made them ask what were their most profound needs. Not surprisingly, their answer was not so different from that of the uptowners. The list of "special requirements" enumerated by the OU places antimissionary work itself in third place. It could be seen as a subsidiary of the most frequently reiterated problems of schooling, of raising men and women "to the consciousness of religious life duty . . . and . . . aspirations." In other words, *the issue,* which united the entire community, was the larger fight against assimilation.

Further evidence is provided by Kehillah records which delineate the actual priorities established by the Jewish community and show the extent to which Orthodox Union leaders assented to its hierarchy of concerns. Notwithstanding intermittent carping from Lucas' friends at *The Hebrew Standard* that the Kehillah was essentially ignoring the issue, antimissionary work was one of the Kehillah's expressed concerns. In January 1910, the 25-man Executive Committee of the Kehillah, which included at least seven Orthodox Union members, referred antimissionary work to its Committee on Religious Organization, a group that included old-time conversionist fighters and OU/Jewish Centres supporters Rabbis Mendes and Drachman. In typical Kehillah style, one that advocated close study of problems before devising solutions, the committee was given the mandate of "investigating conditions" and of offering recommendations for possible action.

A month later the committee's report seemed to breathe new life into the Jewish Centres concept when it argued that continuing conversionist activities required "multiplying Jewish schools"—congregations were to be "induced to set up religious schools"—and "forming Jewish centers such as one of the officers [of their committee] attempted to form some years ago." The officer noted for his hands-on experience was not Lucas but Isidor Hershfield. Over the next few years (essentially 1910–1913) Hershfield, with the help of some Kehillah insiders like Bernard G. Richards, "agitated the issue" of missionaries and the Jewish Centres within the Kehillah.[29]

Hershfield, among others, followed the issue as the original Committee on Religious Organization report was referred by the Executive Committee to the Kehillah's Committee on Education in June 1910. There the initial findings were accorded a somewhat mixed reception. It was argued that although missionaries were largely unsuccessful, there was a need for Jewish Centers for a variety of social ills, including not only conversionists but also "cheap shows and movies." Still, Hershfield and Richards were made a subcommittee on Jewish Centers to move the project further. They announced in August 1910 that "after its own investigation the Kehillah was now to pick up the work of the Jewish Centres Association."[30]

A month later, however, after initially sensing support for the project within the Jewish community, Hershfield and Richards allowed that while the response to their announcement "indicates more support for Jewish Centers than previously . . . the response held out little hope for financial support." Both now suggested that Jewish Centers be made a low priority. They called for "more publicity and mass meetings at which time an organization for establishing Jewish Centers must be launched. As for the Kehillah, it would be able to give only moral support to such an organization."[31]

Despite this less than enthusiastic support for Jewish Centres, the Kehillah did remain concerned about missionary successes. For the next two years (through 1913) intermittent reports were received about conversionist successes and calls went out for Kehillah responses. Investigations were made and plans were suggested, but dramatic Kehillah initiatives were not undertaken.[32]

As an interesting sidelight to this period of low concern over missionaries, it may be noted that the individual most frequently suggested as a hands-on leader of the Kehillah anticonversion work was a young man named Elias A. Cohen. The son of an Orthodox lay leader, David Cohen, and destined to become in his own right an important New York Conservative Jewish spokesman, Cohen had been, just a few years earlier, a club member at the Jacob A. Riis Settlement House. Had Marshall known of this association he would have said—and Riis may have agreed—that Cohen's experience there had not destroyed his Jewish allegiances. Of course, Lucas would have opined that having witnessed what went on in Henry Street, this "survivor" was resolved to stop future missionaries. What we do know is that Cohen's approach was quite different from Lucas'. Cohen would write about anticonversionist work in 1911 that "a noisy investigation would not help the situation at all and only patient work and absolutely definite information is of any use to us."[33]

Ultimately, however, the most definitive statement of where anti-missionary work stood on the Kehillah's agenda was articulated by the Committee on Religious Organization in April 1912. The committee possessed, as previously noted, important Orthodox Union representation, and allowed that while "some of the Christian societies [downtown] are frankly missionaries, other Christian societies, however, with the best of intentions . . . carry on religious work . . . particularly during the summertime . . . Such activity has created a large amount of indignation among Jewish parents." Kehillah policy was "to bring this situation to the attention of various Christian societies and on the part of some we are glad to say, we have met with an intelligent response." But, sounding very much like I have suggested Marshall and Schiff thought in the 1903–1908 period, they continued:

> We cannot fail to see the justice of the contention that until we are prepared to do our duty the responsibility of caring for the children of the city must be assumed by non-Jewish organizations. This is a problem that can be met only when we ourselves as a community come to realize our great responsibility for the thousands and thousands of Jewish children who are allowed to roam about our streets without proper Jewish influence.[34]

For this committee, as for the Kehillah, providing proper Jewish influence through education was the high priority while fighting missionaries was of secondary importance.

Lucas would have scoffed at this report and its implications as he would have been saddened by Cohen's cautious perspective. For him it would have been bitter verification that his own friends had lost sight of the real battle and had permitted themselves to be coopted

by the uptowners. They were certainly "doing the Germans' fiddling," articulating the uptowners' rhetoric, having lost contact
with the clear and present needs of youngsters in danger. For Lucas,
the Kehillah's position on conversion was ultimate justification for
his not joining the organized Jewish community's leadership. When
the initial Kehillah structure was developed, colleagues on the Executive Committee convinced Lucas to join the Advisory Board. Lucas'
view was that the Kehillah was top-heavy with German power and
that the AJ Committeemen would dominate positions and policies.
In truth, friendly pressures had their impact even on Lucas and he
accepted that calling, but his heart was not in it. After one year of
inactive service he resigned. One can I imagine that Kehillah feet
dragging on missionary work, as Lucas would have perceived it,
must have taken its toll on whatever enthusiasm he had for the
Kehillah experiment. Lucas would maintain his own antimissionary
activities and educational work through his missions schools out of
downtown buildings through World War I.[35]

But clearly Lucas' opinion—and that of his friend, editorial writer
A. H. Fromenson—was the minority view within the OU's upper
ranks. Men like Fischel, Drachman and Mendes and worthies like
Kamaiky, Rosalsky and, of course; Hershfield possessed a broader
perspective on what had to be done on behalf of second-generation
Jews. Antimissionary work was on the Kehillah agenda through
1913, but modern Jewish education and the broader task of meeting the acculturation needs of youngsters became and remained the
foremost concern of the organized Jewish community. That essential
work brought them into ongoing contact and alliance with the German Reform leaders and towards trust that they shared a common
concern for the future of Judaism among second-generation Jews.
As members of the Kehillah Executive Committee over a decade,
they were constantly being informed about, when they themselves
did not actually participate in, the innovative educational endeavors
of that young Orthodox rabbi, Mordecai M. Kaplan. Thus it is not at
all surprising that OU/Jewish Centre backers were among those who
supported Kaplan when he struck out on his own in 1918 through
The Jewish Center to address the Jewish needs of uptown Jews and

to test his larger assumptions about what had to be done to keep the next generation close to Judaism. It is also understandable that given Kaplan's desire to emphasize the profoundest American message while upholding the validity of Jewish ways, that the American Jewish Committee men too would be with him.

OU/Kehillah lay leaders Mendes, Fischman, Rosalsky and Samuel Lamport participated in the dedication of The Jewish Center in March 1918. Reform Kehillah spokesmen Marshall and Judah Magnes shared in the celebration. Harry Fischel of the OU, the Kehillah, the "rich man's annex" of the Uptown Talmud Torah and so many other endeavors was undoubtedly an honored guest. He would have come across the Park from his home at Congregation Kehilath Jeshurun. His own rabbi, Moses Sebulun Margolies (Ramaz) of the OU and the Agudath ha-Rabbanim, a supporter of Kehillah educational plans, was also on the Jewish Center program. It is unknown whether Albert Lucas received an invitation to sit in the audience.[36]

9

From Exception to Role Model: Bernard Drachman and the Evolution of Jewish Religious Life in America, 1880–1920

Introduction

In 1885, newly ordained Rabbi Bernard Drachman returned from rabbinical school in Breslau, Germany and found an American Jewry uninterested in his professional services. "There was no room, no demand in America," he would later recall, "for an American-born, English-speaking rabbi who insisted on maintaining the laws and usages of Traditional Judaism." To be sure, there were vacancies in Reform pulpits. And these German-American "congregations of standing and importance," as Drachman described them, wanted young men of education and refinement possessed not only of ordination but a Ph.D from a European university. They desired their leaders to have the general culture their congregants valued and to stand for a Judaism radically redefined to meet modern conditions. But Drachman would not countenance such a calling. To be a Reform rabbi meant officiating in synagogues that had broken dramatically with the traditional approach to divine services and identifying with other rabbis who, that same year, had adopted the Pittsburgh Platform, a denationalized, universalistic reading of Judaism.[1]

Drachman did share basic theological beliefs with his newly arrived East European brethren, but he was also not a viable candidate for a ghetto-based *shtibl*. Rabbis, in the immigrants' view, were born in Russia and trained in East European yeshivas, not at Western European seminaries.[2] For them, wide cultural interests were at best unnecessary and at worst cast doubts upon the candidate's loyalty to Judaism.[3]

Drachman had to seek employment among American-born Jews who respected his training and shared his theology: those of the second-generation that desired to follow "the traditional ritual and customs of the synagogue." Such acculturated Jews were attracted to this young rabbi because they saw in him a spiritual guide who integrated loyalty to Judaism with American mores. He could show them how to be true Americans without abandoning their traditions. Such individuals comprised Newark's Ohab Shalom Congregation, from whose pulpit in 1885 Drachman began to preach his traditional conception of Judaism. But his definition of loyalty to tradition soon led him into conflict with those he was elected to lead. Early in his tenure, the synagogue voted, over his objections, to allow mixed seating during services. The rabbi refused to accept this violation of traditional ritual practice and resigned from the congregation.[4]

Undaunted, Drachman continued his search for a post where he could minister to Americanized Jews who willingly observed, at least within the confines of the sanctuary, the teachings of American Orthodoxy. Drachman's five year quest for "fertile soil for the development of the harmonious combination of Orthodox Judaism and Americanism" ended in 1889. He was elected "rabbi for life" of Manhattan's fledgling Congregation Zichron Ephraim.[5]

Thirty years later, young American-born, English-preaching traditional rabbis found an American Jewry eagerly applauding their efforts. Interest in a Judaism rooted in, as Drachman described it, the reconciliation of "the basic concepts of traditional Judaism and its modern conditions" was clearly on the rise. To be sure, the demand for rabbis like Drachman did not emanate from Reform congregations, nor from ghetto-based storefront synagogues. While immigrant rabbis continued to hold sway with the religious masses on East Broadway, the days of the hegemony of East European Orthodox rabbis among traditional Jews were numbered. The immigrants' own children, seeking religious expressions faithful to tradition but in consonance with America, would emulate the teachings and examples of Drachman and others like him in the proceeding decades.

The years between Drachman's first quest for a job and the beginnings of the American congregational search for men like Drachman were a period of profound change in the history of American Jewry. The concept that traditional Judaism could live in harmony with American culture, that its combination of the Jewish past with the American present constituted the strongest response against disaffection, was slow in emerging and slower still in gaining widespread approbation. It had to battle with Reform teachings which argued that traditional ideas and practices were unnecessary vestiges of a benighted past. And it also had to wait while Americanization undermined the old-world Orthodox belief that the East European religious system could flourish upon American soil. Those who promoted the tradition/America admixture struggled to define how much of each would best cement long-range allegiance to Judaism. It was only at the end of this period that the balances were set, establishing patterns which have since dominated the religious outlook of affiliating, acculturated Jews in this country

Americanized Jewry in the 1880s

Bernard Drachman's observation that at the time of his ordination "Reform Judaism, mainly in the form established by Dr. Isaac M. Wise, had conquered almost the entire field of American Jewish life" was only partially correct. To be sure, by 1875 a national Jewish congregational association (Union of American Hebrew Congregations [UAHC], 1873) and a theological seminary (Hebrew Union College [HUC], 1875) had been formed by Wise. And he soon thereafter established a national rabbinic alliance (Central Conference of American Rabbis [CCAR], 1889). These institutions, which Wise hoped would represent and serve all American Jews, were the mainstays of Reform national hegemony in the late 19th century.[6]

Liberal Jewish ritual practices were also widespread. Few German-American congregations adhered punctiliously to European Orthodox practices, as the immigrants of the 1840s-1850s had transformed their houses of worship by 1880. Services had been shortened, English was universally used in prayer, and vernacular sermons were common. The times of Jewish services were in conformity with this country's work schedule. Men and women sat together in family pews, and in the most radical of congregations readers were accompanied by instrumental music and men wore neither hats nor prayer shawls. Some even substituted Sunday for Saturday as the Jewish Sabbath.[7]

But a congregation's abandonment of Orthodox strictures did not necessarily lead to association with Reform. Many synagogues adopted the most radical of practices without affiliating with like-minded congregations. Other synagogues which broke more subtly with the past by adopting mixed seating and abridging the services referred to themselves as Conservative-Orthodox. Although estranged from Orthodoxy, they were not comfortable with Reform. Even those congregations that officially joined the UAHC under the leadership of CCAR rabbis did not always follow Reform teachings. For example, New York's Temple Israel appears, at first glance, to have been a prototypical late nineteenth century Reform congregation. When founded in 1869 in then rural Harlem, this small German immigrant congregation followed all Orthodox rituals and practices save separate seating. This noteworthy departure from tradition was not intended to signal an ideological break with the past; it was done simply because "there was no gallery available for the women" in the rented quarters. The Temple's services were liberalized some ten years later when an organ was introduced. This move caused more traditional members to secede from the congregation, creating the not uncommon sight of a small nineteenth century Jewish outpost serviced by two competing, fledgling synagogues.

Temple Israel moved formally into the Reform camp in the early 1880s when it joined the UAHC, abandoned the siddur and, in 1894 adopted the CCAR's *Union Prayer Book*. And yet remnants of Orthodox practice long persisted. Worshippers wore skull caps during services, and the Temple continued to observe the religious Second Holy Day of Festivals. These concessions to tradition reflected, in the first instance, the personal discomfort some men may have felt facing God bareheaded. In the second case, tacit congregational recognition of a religious distinction between Jewish life in Palestine as opposed to the Diaspora—a fundamental break with the anti-rabbinic spirit of the Pittsburgh Platform—suggests that Harlemites probably understood neither the historical significance of the Second Holy Day nor what their national group had to say.[8]

A local congregation's failure to practice what its movement preached was a problem for more than just Reformers. Inconsistent synagogue practices troubled both liberal and more traditional spokesmen. In voluntaristic America, Reform national synods could adopt policies, and individual Orthodox rabbis could attempt to transmute age-old traditions. But neither could be assured that anyone—even those who felt close to their leaders—either understood or was consistently committed to following their directions. Ancestor worship was the most important factor for many Jews when making their religious choices. For others, an affinity for the new took precedence over the things hallowed in the past. And always, the demands of observance conflicted with their identities as Americans. So while Reform had the national organizations and traditional practices were largely ignored, no one movement possessed the unqualified allegiances of American Jewry.[9]

The organizational emergence of Reform also neither stifled nor silenced those rabbis who advocated more traditional conceptions of Judaism. Despite their lack of popularity or effectiveness among the laity, these rabbis still had the power to struggle against the more liberal clergy. And battle they did, especially after the adoption of the Pittsburgh Platform. The Platform did not deal "a mortal blow to Orthodox Judaism" as one contemporary critic claimed.[10] What it did do was to change the attitudes of several leading American rabbis towards cooperation with Isaac M. Wise *et al.* in pursuit of ideological and liturgical consensus. It spurred those troubled by the declaration to structure a new coalition and a new institution to perpetuate their understanding of the faith.

Before 1885, Historical School rabbis or American Conservative spokesmen such as Marcus Jastrow, Benjamin Szold, Aaron Wise, and Alexander Kohut had found common cause with Isaac M. Wise and other segments of the Reform movement in the attempt to stem widespread disaffection from Judaism. All were committed to the evolution of a unified approach to synagogue life. Some were even involved in the development of the HUC as an American seminary. The ideological and practical bases for affinity were there: After all, each of these men served in congregations which deviated from traditional practice in their use of instrumental music, a modern prayer book, and in seating patterns. And these rabbis were joined with Wise in supporting interpretations of Jewish history and theology at variance with contemporary Orthodox teachings. Compromise and cooperation were the hallmarks of this interdenominational encounter through the early post-Civil War years.[11]

This informal consensus of liberal Jewish leaders showed signs of strain in the early 1880s. Rabbis of varying theological stripes began to debate each other in virulent newspaper polemics. Testiness on ideological issues might well have reflected growing Reform confidence in the future hegemony of their movement and a concommitant restiveness on the part of Conservatives about the power of their point of view. Certainly, the famous *treif* banquet of 1883 did little to maintain harmony among Jewish leaders. At a dinner in honor of the first HUC graduating class, Historical School guests— defined here as those who observed kosher dietary laws—were appalled that shrimp was served as the first course. For them, the menu was symbolic of how far their confreres had moved from tradition. It was also proof of how oblivious Wise's group was to their needs as ritually observant Jews.[12]

But it was the Pittsburgh Platform, adopted in July 1885, which altered conclusively the relationship among religious leaders in America. Wings of the Reform movement coalesced in Pittsburgh. Wise came together with Kaufman Kohler, David Philipson, Emile G. Hirsch and other so called Radical Reformers in adopting a deritualized, denationalized reading of Judaism rooted in an optimistic view of the world and committed to expressing Jewishness through advocacy of progressive good works.[13] Historical School people could no longer cooperate with a Reform now so divorced from traditional teachings. Following the Pittsburgh conclave, Conservative leaders determined to form a new coalition and organization.

The Jewish Theological Seminary of America linked Historical School men like Jastrow, Kohut and Szold with the Orthodox Drachman, H. P. Mendes, Henry Schneeberger and Sabato Morais, the Seminary's first president. The organizers emphasized the linkages that united leaders and downplayed the ideas and practices which separated them. Common educational training provided an immediate basis for cooperation. They had been trained at Western European theological seminaries. Some had studied together in Zecharia Frankel's Breslau Seminary. Others had been classmates in Azriel Hildesheimer's Berlin Seminary. All emerged from their training convinced that a Judaism unprepared to harmonize itself with modern conditions and contemporary popular desires would not survive in America. They differed on the degree of change required, but they believed that the Reform solution was no answer: that would lead to the extinction of Judaism. So they met in January 1886, and in 1887 founded a seminary which Morais prayed would save "Historical and Traditional Judaism . . . by educating, training and inspiring teachers-rabbis who would stand for the Torah and Testimony." Alumni of this New York institution would use "their knowledge of Jewish learning, literature, history, ideals and Jewish Science" to teach all others how Jews could live "as a power for human uplift and as a factor in the evolution of world civilization in both Americas."[14]

But was anyone listening to them or for that matter to their Reform antagonists? As with the Pittsburgh Platform, it is clear that these rabbinic endeavors affected only a small minority of American Jews. Most continued to live their lives as Americans unmoved by the growth of religious institutions. Untouched by the rabbis, some found a place for Judaism in their lives, others simply assimilated. Reform synagogue officials were aware that their influence upon the laity was diminishing as the century closed. One spokesman observed that co-religionists "think that all Judaism requires is to join the YMHA and attend its entertainment."[15] Orthodox spokesmen, likewise, were not impressed with the commitment of their adherents. Lewis N. Dembitz, an Orthodox lay leader at the end of the century, may have said it best when he described most of his fellow Orthodox Jews as "persons who do not lead a Jewish life, but read the olden prayers."[16]

Accordingly, for all its institutional growth, Americanized Jewry of the 1880–1900 period was in trouble. Disaffection was taking its toll. Fortunately for the faith's survival in this country, a new migration of Jews was arriving from Eastern Europe bringing a fresh vitality to religious life. For them, the theological and practical distinctions which sometimes linked and at other times separated Reform, Conservative and Orthodox Jewish expressions were purely academic. To the religious immigrants, all were foreign, American forms of religion antithetical to their way of thinking. These immigrants believed that they were bearers of the true Judaism, one which survived centuries of persecutions and the most recent Czarist pogroms and which was potent to resist the disintegrating power of freedom. But soon they too encountered America, and the old ways and values were quickly and profoundly questioned.

East European Orthodoxy in America, 1880–1920

"America is a treif land where even the stones are impure. . . ." "Whoever wishes to live properly before God must not settle in that country." The Ridbaz (Rabbi Jacob David Willowski) and the Hafetz Hayim (Rabbi Israel Meir Ha-Kohen Kagan) were not without grounds for their respective admonitions to their East European flocks. Late nineteenth century America *was* no place for the practicing and professing Jew who wished to maintain the teachings and usages of traditional Judaism, at least not those forms that were known and honored in Eastern Europe. The land of freedom militated daily against the recreation on these shores of the religious civilization that had survived centuries of tyranny. America, the *Ridbaz* observed, was a place "where groups with varying viewpoints came to be settled and no one recognizes any authority." Communal discipline, organization and religious structure, the very bedrock of the Russian Jewish community, did not exist in voluntaristic Amer-

To be sure, there were a number of well-known and learned Eastern European-trained rabbis in America by the 1880s prepared to show Jews how to hold fast to the faith in this alien land. Rabbis Abraham Joseph Ash, Moses Weinberger and Joseph Moses Aaronsohn of New York and Chicago's Joseph Lesser were among those who settled in America. And although they preached to anyone who would listen of the Jew's obligation to observe the Sabbath, of the necessity to provide children with a comprehensive Jewish education and of the community's responsibility to monitor and to supervise the provision of kosher meat, etc., they lacked the power to coerce their parishioners. In open America, no ecclesiastical power could mandate religious observance. No tithe could be enforced to support institutions.

And in an unregulated, free enterprise system, anyone could open a butcher shop, sprinkle saw dust on the floor, paint the words "Baser Kasher" on the window, and declare himself an authorized slaughterer and overseer of meat preparation. When day was done a butcher could officiate as a *mohel* (circumcisor) or *mesader kidushin* (marriage ceremony official) with or without any rabbinical authorization or training. These moonlight activities caused dire projections to be made of a twentieth century American Jewry made up of halakhically illegitimate children in a world where priests *(kohanim)* married divorcees and where men and women divorced and remarried without securing a rabbinical writ of divorce. Such was the libertine world religious Jews were admonished to avoid.[18]

Millions of Jews paid little heed to these warnings. Other voices spoke more forcefully to them. One voice was that of the Czarist government whose century of government-inspired persecutions that oppressed Jews undermined their confidence in their own communities. Nineteenth century Russian Jews were thus prepared for their break with rabbinic authority in America while still in Europe. Russian attacks on Jews and their communities caused many to lose their unqualified faith in their kehillahs as protectors and their rabbis as guides. Jews who were undecided whether to try a new life where Judaism was "unknown" or to stay in the declining East

European center were aided in breaking with the past by the sounds of Enlightenment and radicalism that spoke of progress and change. So aware, they could now hear strongly the sirens of advancement and opportunity from a far-away America. And although many who left did so with trepidation about the fate of their Judaism in the New World, the depressed circumstances of their European lives made them willing to take a chance that their faith could survive relocation in the land of freedom.[19]

Some Jews on the boat to the United States decided that no real chance was being taken. Upon arrival they commited themselves willingly to rapid assimilation. They wanted to build a new life in America, to become totally one with American society as soon as economic and social circumstances permitted. However, this quest to disassociate themselves from their ancestral roots could not be effected for at least one generation. While a Jew could publicly proclaim upon arrival on Delancey Street, in the heart of the Lower East Side ghetto, that he officially renounced his Jewish identity, with whom could he then assimilate on his downtown block? Approximately twenty years would elapse before he could make his boast stick, although the desire was there even before his actual encounter with the realities of American life.[20]

Most religious Jews arrived in this country prepared to see their old traditions preserved in this new land. If not for reasons of faith, they clung to European ways as a defense against the shocks caused by first encounters with a foreign American culture. But sincere commitment to ancestral teachings and practices foundered on the rocks of Americanization. Those who in America ceased observing the Sabbath or disdained sending their children to separatistic Jewish schools or deferred to gentile courts and authorities and not to rabbis in their personal or business dealings did not seek to separate themselves from their people and their past. They simply followed the road and procedures set down by America for its immigrants' advancement and acceptance in this new world. In so doing they found that the observance of Judaism's law and the reestablishment of the old ways was impossible.

Sabbath observance is an example. While European preachers rhapsodized that "more than the Jews preserving the Sabbath, the Sabbath preserved the Jews," they did not have to deal with America. This country promised that any man who worked hard and well could get ahead. Six days of work were certainly mandated for all with lofty aspirations. The seventh day was for rest and prayer. But America's Sabbath was on Sunday, a reality driven home weekly by onerous Blue Laws. The Jew had to decide whether to work five days, jeopardizing his economic rise, or labor six days and violate his faith's holy day. That is, of course, if his sweatshop boss even offered him the choice. Many entrepreneurs in the ghetto simply said, "If you don't work Saturday, and maybe secretly on Sunday, don't report for work on Monday." Faced with this choice, masses of immigrant Jews broke the Sabbath to accelerate their economic advancement in America.[21]

Americanization wrought comparable violence with long-standing Jewish educational ideals. This country preached social acceptance for all, conditional on the immigrant's accepting the American way of life, but not requiring conversion to the majority faith. In such a context, Jewish schools, which taught Hebrew and Yiddish but not English; Jewish traditions and not the culture of the host society; keeping Jews physically separate from gentile teachers and students—such schools could have no enduring place.[22] The non-sectarian American public school was the place to be, even if in selecting it, Jewish parents understood that there no effort would be made to instill a sense of belonging to Judaism in their children.[23]

A separate Jewish court system, likewise, could have little success within free America. Constitutional law subjected Jews, like all other citizens, to this country's civil and criminal codes. Disputing Jews could submit their grievances, if both sides agreed to abide by the ultimate decision, to a rabbinical board for arbitration. But the enforcement of these decrees required the continuous good will of the parties, particularly the losing side. Moreover, rabbinic courts had no power, other than their indignation, moral suasion and limited social pressure to bring recalcitrant defendants to the bar.[24]

But even as immigrant Jews lessened their ties to the Jewish civilization of the past, many retained an affinity for the religious rituals from Russia. And they were accustomed to their fellow immigrant rabbis even if they did not hearken to the preachings. The popularity of the *landsmanshaft* synagogue, the ephemeral store-front congregation in the ghetto where Jews converged to pray and socialize as they had in their old home town, did not mean that its members rejected American ways. The *landsmanshaft* was simply a way-station along the path to acculturation, a comfortable, nostalgic reminder of the good old days. It preserved an identity and a consciousness to fall back upon as one made strides in America. Nonetheless, it was within these precincts that the residual vitality of East European Orthodoxy was daily expressed, even if the worshippers' lives outside the sanctuary ran increasingly apart from what the faith taught.[25]

Americanization, to be sure, did not affect with equal speed and intensity all East European religious immigrants. There were some who resisted the calls of the new life and strove mightily, if unsuccessfully, to simulate Russian religious conditions in voluntaristic America. The establishment in 1886 of Yeshiva Etz Chaim on the Lower East Side was one such step in this direction. Its founders hoped the world of East European learning would take root. But their early insistence that students pay but marginal attention to English and American studies doomed the school to widespread unpopularity among the ghetto population. Etz Chaim would have to change its orientation, as we will see, to even begin to make an impression within the downtown community.[26]

Rabbi Jacob Joseph was not given that second chance to influence his fellow immigrants. In 1887, the Association of American Orthodox Hebrew Congregations brought this Lithuanian-born, Vilna-trained disciple of Rabbis Hirsch Leib Berlin and Israel Salanter to the United States and installed him as chief rabbi of New York City. The immigrant lay leaders who chose Rabbi Jacob Joseph hoped that this prestigious scholar would not only put an end to the disorganization and lack of discipline endemic to American Jewish life, but that he would also lead a potent counter attack against the lures of

Americanization. For them, the establishment of a chief rabbinate was symbolic proof that a transplanted European religious civilization could bear fruit in this country.

They were sadly mistaken. Rabbi Jacob Joseph's American career was an abject failure Ironically, they who hired him and placed such confidence in their candidate played no small role in his downfall. While Association members recognized Rabbi Jacob Joseph's authority and relegated to him enormous responsibility, they and the larger Jewish community accorded him no power to put his policies into effect. He could oversee kashruth in meat markets, but he could not make abbatoir owners accept his regulations. Nor could he stop other New York rabbis from seeking the butchers' allegiances by asserting their own authority as "Chief Rabbi of the Congregations of Israel" or as "Chief Rabbi of the United States." Nor for that matter could he stop his Association from levying fees upon butchers for his services, raising cries of corruption if not *korobdka* (an infamous Czarist tax) from the Socialist press and other unsympathetic organs. While Rabbi Jacob Joseph could throw his weight behind the need to invigorate Jewish education, he could not stop parents from sending their children to the public schools. Nor did he even succeed in upgrading the ghetto *melamed's* private heder, that hallow institutional shell of the European educational model. Finally, while the rabbi could address fiery Yiddish exhortations to Jewish masses, demanding that they observe the Sabbath, he could not stop his flock from working on Saturday as he preached from his Sabbath pulpit. Rabbi Jacob Joseph died in 1902 with the dream of successfully transplanting European modes to America no closer to realization than when he started fifteen years before.[27]

Still, the dream that the old ways could permanently take root in America, with but the most modest of changes, and that order could be brought to the religious community survived Rabbi Jacob Joseph's demise. It lived on and, indeed, intensified through a new institution, the Agudath ha-Rabbanim (Union of Orthodox Rabbis of the United States and Canada), an organization born in New York on July 29, 1902, the very day of Rabbi Jacob Joseph's funeral. This organization of East European rabbis from immigrant Jewish centers as geographically scattered as Montreal, Toronto, Bangor, Omaha, and Denver tacitly recognized that Americanization and voluntarism were forces too powerful for any rabbi or ad hoc organization to alone combat effectively. The fight against America required, interestingly enough, that the rabbis appropriate an American institutional pattern, unknown to them in Eastern Europe. In forming a union, colleagues were asked to surrender a degree of personal autonomy to the discipline of their coast-to-coast organization. For example, the association mandated that no rabbi occupy a pulpit in a city served by a fellow member without board approval. In return, delegates expected that their organization would develop strategies, promote policies and monitor institutions created to solve the dilemmas which so confounded Rabbi Jacob Joseph.[28]

The rabbis were quick to address the concerns of Jewish education. For them, solutions lay not in the modifications of existing forms of Jewish pedagogy but in greater communal commitment to them. Etz Chaim and similar schools elsewhere on the continent were still the ideal North American teaching institutions. But great pains had to be taken to monitor their students lest they fall into more Americanized ways. Towards that end, the rabbinical organization early on arrogated to itself the privilege of supervising "the subjects taught in the yeshiva . . . lest the students regard the yeshiva simply as a stop over before they pursue secular subjects." They also expressed boundless approval of the Rabbi Isaac Elchanan Theological Seminary (RIETS), the first upper-level Torah center in America, founded in 1897 by, among others, future members of the Agudath ha-Rabbanim. The organization in 1903 formally recognized RIETS and committed itself to improving the school's tenuous financial situation. Three years later, ties between the school and the rabbinical association were further cemented when a Semicha (ordination) Board was formed under Agudath ha-Rabbanim control. Men ordained at RIETS would have the same training, qualifications and orientation as candidates educated in Europe. These graduates would join hands with their elders in leading a renaissance of traditional Jewish practice.[29]

But how to broaden their appeal beyond their own limited constituency and induce the drifting younger generation into a commitment to intensive Jewish education? And how to raise public esteem and funds to support the advanced Torah institution? The rabbis from Eastern Europe hoped that personal suasion and public exhortation would stimulate the residual sentiments of the immigrant generation. They believed that if parents could be drawn back to Torah, their children would follow.

The Agudath ha-Rabbanim similarly addressed the vexing problem of Sabbath observance. They publicly identified those establishments, particularly butcher shops and bakeries, that violated the Sabbath. They encouraged Jews not to patronize such concerns and exhorted all public violators and the Jewish community at large to return to traditional behavior. Interestingly, the rabbinic organization here appealed outside its own circumscribed constituency to Jewish union leaders that the "Sabbath day off' be a demand in owner-worker deliberations. They further politicked to convince "Jewish charitable organizations to set up divisions to seek employment for Sabbath observers," all, however, to no avail.[30]

The rabbis expended no little effort to ensure proper supervision of kosher meat and other food stuffs. It was their hope that all aspects of slaughtering and meat inspection and "the supervision of . . . wine, Passover liquor and matzot" should be under the watchful eye of a local member of their organization. It prayed that when a rabbi found "it necessary to publicly disqualify a butcher for violating the kashruth laws, then no other rabbi may reinstate the butcher." If two rabbis disagreed about the reliability of a butcher, a third party would be called upon, presumedly under Agudath ha-Rabbanim conditions. The willingness of colleagues both within and without their organization to follow directions and restrictions was crucial to success in this area. But here economics and American voluntarism conspired to thwart the rabbis' plans.[31]

Kosher supervision concessions were more than merely a source of honor, responsibility or even power in the American Jewish community. A rabbi's control of a particular butchery was a most important source of steady income, a chance for personal income many were unwilling to share and unable to do without. Rabbis did not trek to western outposts like Des Moines and Sioux City, Iowa with the primary goal of building great Jewish communities. Rather they were drawn by the large stockyards of these cities and the monetary rewards to be earned as kashruth overseers. There they jealously guarded their prerogatives. Others who resided shorter distances from New York or Chicago were no less protective of their concessions. "Chief Rabbis" who brought order to meat industries within locales but a few hours from the immigrant hubs also held to their jobs for dear life.[32]

The rabbinical organization did not request nor require that members surrender concessions to their national ecclesiastical board. If anything, their arm was there to protect the legitimate rabbis' control, to weed out frauds and impostors and to limit competition among rabbis that undermined public confidence in kashruth.

It was on the last point of policy, the limitation of competition clause, that the Agudath ha-Rabbanim was undone. Independent rabbis constantly demanded a piece of the action. They publicly pilloried the organization as an oligarchy and accused opponents of price-fixing and exploitation. Popular confidence in the East European rabbinate often foundered on the kashruth rivalry as Jews witnessed their rabbis battling with each other. Sometimes rabbis not part of the Agudath ha-Rabbanim accused those who affiliated of trafficking in horse meat. Other times, two Agudath ha-Rabbanim men fought in open disregard of their organization's non-encroachment policies. The most celebrated internecine struggle of the early twentieth century involved Rabbi Jacob David Willowski, who somehow, against his own best advice, found his way to America and showed up in Chicago. Honored upon his arrival by his colleagues as *zekan ha-Rabbanim* (senior rabbi), Willowski attempted to impose his authority upon the Midwestern domain of Rabbi Zvi Album. When the latter resisted, their ensuing city-wide battle occasioned bitter polemics and even fist fights by supporters of each faction. Willowski should have known better. In voluntaristic America, everything went.[33]

If economics and voluntarism waylaid kashruth plans, American-ization undid their educational and Sabbath observance objectives. Like Rabbi Jacob Joseph before them, Agudath ha-Rabbanim mem-bers were manifestly unable to solve the problem of how to promote greater commitment to the Sabbath when those to be influenced were out working on Saturday and not in *shul* to hear plaintive plat-itudes. Preachings also failed to shake the immigrants' growing belief in the equality, if not superiority, of American culture with Jewish tradition. Rabbinic exhortations and organizational propa-ganda may well have convinced some to submit voluntarily to their authority. But for many more, the guilt over non-adherence to tradi-tion even when evoked by the most respected of European preachers was still no match for the drive for personal advancement and the desire for social acceptance. The faith of immigrants in America would not permit them to endorse all-day schools even when the rabbinic organization authorized the use of English as the language of religious instruction in locales where Yiddish was unknown and mandated the hiring of "graduates from the Normal Schools in the City Boards of Education" to teach secular subject in all-day schools. The European rabbis' idealized heder/yeshiva system, even when modified, did not fulfill the immigrants' educational wishes.[34]

Still, despite their failure to reverse the tide of Americanization within their community, Agudath ha-Rabbanim members, when they were not battling each other, retained a noticeable degree of respect, if not popularity, among first generation Jews. The religious Yiddish newspapers, particularly the *Morgan Zhurnal*, reported on their speeches and conventions and published their broadsides. And these journals reported that rabbis often packed downtown syna-gogues. Interest in the words but not the teachings of these rabbis was rooted in the same social dynamics which gave rise to and sus-tained the *landsmanshaft* synagogue system. The East European *rov* reminded his listeners of the better elements of the old home but no one was under any obligation to follow his commands. Downtown Jews moving away from consistent traditional practices still tipped their hats as their *rabbanim* walked by.[35]

Their American-born children had no hats to tip. Their parents' respect, if not admiration, for those Russian figures who held fast to their European faith was totally lost upon the second-generation Jew. The youngsters likewise had no affinity for their fathers' *landsmanshaft* synagogue, rooted as it was in a European civilization they did not know and in an estrangement from America they did not experience. They were American-born and bred, Yankees through and through, uncomfortable with and unwarmed by the people and institutions of their parents' past. For them, the social shells no less than the religious strictures of European Judaism were irrelevant to their lives. East European rabbis had little to say and *landsmanshaft* synagogues had even less to offer to this new generation. But maybe Bernard Drachman and a new type of Orthodox synagogue could.

Judaism for the Americanized East European Immigration, 1900–1910

Even as Rabbi Jacob Joseph and later, the Agudath ha-Rabbanim struggled to recreate European Jewish conditions upon American soil, other voices were heard in the ghetto arguing the impossibility of long-term Jewish resistance to the dominant culture. These critics asserted that even in the unlikely event that rabbinic exhortations and proclamations could turn the immigrants themselves away from America and back towards the old Jewish way of life, affinity with and allegiance to the past could not be transmitted to the next generation. Even if parents could be drawn back to the Torah of Europe, their children would not follow. Second-generation Jews, they explained, had minds of their own, and their minds were filled with the wonders and potential of America. For immigrant youngsters, a Judaism cemented in European symbols, values and traditions was nothing more than an unnecessary barrier potent only to hold them hack, if they were foolish enough to adhere to its antiquated forms, from achieving and growing as Americans.

And yet those who challenged the assumptions of East European rabbis did not despair for the future of Judaism beyond the *landsmanshaft* generation. Those who joined hands in organizations like the

Orthodox Union [OU], the JTS' Jewish Endeavor Society, and the modern Talmud Torah movement—we will call them American Traditionalists—shared the belief that even as acculturation destroyed the underpinnings of transplanted Judaism, Americanization, when harnessed, was no threat to Jewish survival. The key to continuity was the integration of as many American mores, styles and principles as possible into Jewish observance and teaching without destroying the essence of Jewish faith and tradition. But that required that they take a long hard look at Jewish civilization as brought over from Europe and determine which aspects of that culture were inviolable and which ultimately might be modified or jettisoned. And, of course, once having done so, the next equally important step was to convince downtowners that their prescriptions for survival did not, in fact, constitute untenable reforms of Judaism. These American Traditionalists addressed their concerns with undaunted optimism; their courage, as we have already indicated, was born out of their sense of acute necessity. To their minds, failure to change would relegate the faith of their fathers to extinction.

There was nothing in their people's tradition, they asserted, that mandated that Judaism be taught to children in the Yiddish language, nor that the religious school day could not start after the public schools let out, nor that the ethics of the fathers not be made relevant through the use of the most up-to-date American pedagogic methods. If these were the prices that had to be paid to convince American Jewish boys and girls "to perform all the duties, to think all the thoughts and to feel the emotions which are the historical heritage of those of the household of Israel," so be it. Now, eight to ten hours a week of Jewish schooling with periods devoted to "Jewish geography," "Bible baseball," recreation and the like would not be sufficient to produce from these schools a generation of American-born scholars able to expound upon rabbinic texts. But who was kidding whom. The call of the yeshiva, they reminded all, was being heard only by the most devoted few; the public schools reigned supreme. The Jewish community, the American Traditionalists concluded, had to decide whether to accept modern, supplementary education as a norm and survive or to continue resisting co-existence with the public schools and perish.[36]

American Traditionalists had a similar message for the unregenerated downtown synagogue. Noise, commotion, commercialism, non-uniform prayer books and unsanitary precincts, they stressed, were not holy unto the Lord. America's demands that its houses of worship be quiet and decorous and its services be conducted in both a holy tongue and English, highlighted always on the Sabbath by a sermon, did not violate Jewish teachings. Nor did halakhah preclude synagogues from establishing Saturday afternoon services as the central prayer meeting of the week. As long as the devotions were offered along strict Orthodox lines, there was no reason, American Traditionalists argued, that men and women not be encouraged to come to synagogue when they could most easily attend. Rabbinic pleas for greater Sabbath observance, they explained, would reach a wider audience at an afternoon hour, particularly among those people who wanted to pray and be with other Jews on Saturday, after the end of America's workweek. Downtown synagogues, the modern critics continued, could choose to resist making the prayers more widely intelligible and could refrain from bringing the services closer to the life situations of the next generations, but only at the peril of witnessing their congregations' decline upon the death of their immigrant stalwarts.[37]

Even as American Traditionalists assured their listeners that most American ways and methods could be integrated with Jewish tradition, they also readily admitted that America unbridled and unchallenged still constituted a grave threat to Jewish continuity. They understood that whatever the cohesive value of the Saturday afternoon services, they were still but a fall-back position in response to America's demand that men and women violate their holy day to advance. And while they acknowledged the popularity and applauded the methodologies of public school education, they readily recognized that these temples of Americanization more often than not denigrated the Judaism of its students when they were not promoting Christianity as America's religion in their supposedly theology-free precincts.

American Traditionalists were, accordingly, resolute, through both lobbying and newspaper editorial writing, in their opposition to blue laws that supported the economics of non-observance. And they were forthright—through petitions and pickets—in their public appeals to boards of education at Christmas and Easter to assure that schools live up to their non-sectarian creeds. They stressed that as believers in America, they ultimately possessed powers far greater than the Agudath ha-Rabbanim to resist America when pernicious. They could do more than exhort. They knew how to reach out to government. That was the American way.[38]

Bernard Drachman, not surprisingly, was one of the staunchest and most outspoken advocates of the American Traditionalist point of view. For him, aid to the immigrants in reconciling conflicting identities constituted a new start for a long career dedicated to the harmonization of "the basic concepts of Judaism with its modern condition." He was joined in his mission to downtown by like-minded rabbis and laymen like H. P. Mendes, Sabato Morais, Henry Schneeberger and Lewis Dembitz, founders all in 1898 of the OU. This national congregational organization was in essence the brain-child of the more traditionally-observant elements from the 1887 JTS coalition. Ten years later, they were again ready to "protest against declarations of Reform rabbis not in accord with the teach-ings of our Torah." But in reality, their primary goal was the defense of "Orthodox Judaism whenever occasions arise in civic and social matters," primarily to help immigrants adjust religiously.[39]

But how to reach those they were pledged to serve? For all their sensitivity towards the needs of the "rising generation in Israel," OU founders were still Western European outsiders with limited social contacts downtown. Fortunately for them, almost a generation had passed since Drachman stood alone to face that dilemma. Enough time had elapsed for there to have emerged within East European immigrant society a small coterie of activists prepared to work with, and financially support, the OU. Significantly enough, people like author Judah David Eisenstein, Yiddish newspaper editor Kasriel Sarasohn, banker Sender Jarmalowski, builder Harry Fischel and businessman Jonas Weil had gained on their own much of what they and their uptown traditionalist colleagues hoped all other East European immigrants ultimately would achieve. They had come to America as young men and had rapidly adjusted to their country— some had become somewhat famous, others had accumulated modest fortunes—without abandoning ancestral traditions.[40]

Fischel was probably the proudest of the lot. Apt to refer to himself as "the East European Jacob Schiff" (Schiff was a famous German-American Jewish philanthropist), he was quick to recall how as a new immigrant he risked unemployment, if not starvation, to stay true to the Jewish Sabbath. For him cooperation with the OU represented an expansion of his own personal activities in the upgrading of Jewish education. As a director of the Machzikei Talmud Torah, he had been instrumental since 1892 in providing religious classes for girls, a dramatic step at that time.[41]

Others came into the coalition after first backing the chief rabbi. Even as Eisenstein and Sarasohn still personally supported the declining Rabbi Joseph until his death, they also looked to the OU for new directions towards Jewish survival. Two downtown activists had been in the uptowners' camp all along. Jarmalowski, who immigrated before 1881, was an original trustee of the 1887 Seminary. And Jarmalowski and Weil were both instrumental in Drachman's gaining his first enduring pulpit at Congregation Zichron Ephraim, a synagogue for acculturated East European Jews who, having made it uptown long before their time, established in Yorkville, Manhattan a decorous, architecturally pleasing Orthodox synagogue.[42]

Rabbi Dr. Philip Hillel Klein's support of the OU lent additional credibility to its efforts. A most uncommon East European rabbi, the Hungarian-born Klein, ordained by Rabbi Azriel Hildesheimer of Berlin and the holder of a Ph.D. from the University of Jena, arrived in the U.S. in 1890 and immediately assumed the post of rabbi of the First Hungarian Congregation Ohab Zedek in New York. Though destined to sit on the Presidium of the Agudath ha-Rabanim, the very symbol of resistance to Americanization, Klein's greater sympathies were with Drachman, Schneeberger and Mendes with whom he joined at the founding of the OU. Ten years later, he would again display his affinity for the American Traditionalists when he agreed to share his pulpit with Drachman, who became an English-speaking rabbi of Congregation Ohab Zedek when it moved up to Harlem.[43]

With Klein and Fischel and his friends heralding their policies downtown, OU leadership turned to the youthful members of the Jewish Endeavor Society (JES) to conduct the actual day-to-day social and religious work. The Endeavorers were Drachman's disciples, recruited out of his JTS classroom, inspired to lead their own "indifferent generation back to ancestral faith." Men like Charles Kauvar, Herman Abramowitz, Julius Greenstone, and Mordecai M. Kaplan, future leaders all of second-generation American Conservative and Orthodox congregations around the country; gained herein valuable anti-assimilation field experience as they organized "dignified youth services," modern educational programs and attractive social and recreational activities on the Lower East Side and later in Harlem and in Philadelphia. Following their teacher's advice, the Endeavorers sought to admit America into their Orthodox services as much as Jewish law would permit and to eliminate customs which would embarrass and disillusion worshippers. Recognizing the growing unfamiliarity with Hebrew, they instituted supplementary English prayers and considered substituting English translations for the traditional prayers. A weekly English sermon on topics related to the American Jewish experience became standard. Drachman, Mendes and other OU rabbis were often guest preachers and congregational singing in English and Hebrew was encouraged. Yiddish played no role in rabbinic discourse or lay discussion, and all overt signs of commercialism were eliminated.

Endeavorer educational, social and cultural programs were also instituted with American values and influences in mind. Their talmud torah classes, for example, proffered a varied curriculum of bible, history, religion, spelling and grammar taught after public school and on Sundays by volunteers. And their co-curricular social and cultural activities were explicitly designed to keep Jewish children off the streets even longer, away from the pernicious influences of missionaries and Christian settlement workers who promoted solutions to youthful identity problems inimical to Jewish survival.[44]

Their enthusiasm and commitment to the disaffected notwithstanding, the OU was neither immediately nor universally accepted by the communities it sought to serve. Its members and policies clearly were unacceptable to the Agudath ha-Rabbanim. For men like Willowski even such a seemingly innocuous sociological accommodation as the English sermon was a challenge "to the continuance of the Jewish religion." Moreover, as most East European rabbis saw it, OU leaders were poorly qualified religious leaders; after all, uptowners were trained in Berlin or Breslau and not in Vilna or Volozhin. The Agudath ha-Rabbanim felt that OU members, bereft of a constituency in their home neighborhood where Reform held sway, were trying to infiltrate another's community. OU leaders and their misguided followers were depicted by their detractors as little different from other evil assimilation agents (missionaries, Christian social workers, German Jewish philanthropists, etc.) who swooped into the ghetto, brandishing their American banners.[45]

Agudath ha-Rabbanim leaders also pointedly accused the American Traditionalists of not even living up to their own announced mandates. They were seemingly committed to stopping Reform and promoting Orthodoxy, and yet in 1904, OU leaders willingly sat with officials of the Reform Emanu-El Brotherhood, Temple Israel, and the West Side Synagogue. There they considered a report drafted by the interdenominational Board of Jewish Ministers to coordinate the endeavors of the JES and other less traditional young people's synagogues which operated out of German-sponsored, Reform influenced settlements. In the view of the East European rabbis, the OU was lending unfortunate recognition to deviants and thereby; threatening Jewish continuity.[46]

To be sure, OU spokesmen themselves were not of one mind on the question of cooperation with less traditional elements on non-theological issues. And disunity within OU ranks over whether Reform input and money could be trusted undermined further this organization's effectiveness. One school of thought, headed by Fischel and including the other newly affluent and recently acculturated attracted to the cause, argued that the Orthodox community had neither sufficient manpower nor resources to successfully battle assimilation alone. To their minds, if German philanthropists and their rabbis showed interest in the revitalization of Orthodox education and demanded only that the methods of instruction be the most up to date, there was no reason to reject their assistance out of hand. As Fischel and his coterie saw it, the Reform Jews' theological opinions were their private concerns, irrelevant to discussions of how best to recapture immigrant children to their faith. Schiff, Louis Marshall and others were not seen by their OU friends as promoting Reform Judaism among the downtowners. What the Germans did want was for their potential clients to speak, behave and in this case learn like Americans, sentiments which the Fischel group shared.

Others within the Orthodox camp did not share this faith in German reliability and thus disdained cooperation. A small contingent led by the then famous ghetto anti-missionary fighter and OU Secretary Albert Lucas argued that the great philanthropists could not be trusted to keep their hands off the substance of Jewish education. As Lucas saw it, the Germans were so intent on showing that immigrant Jews and their Judaism were totally compatible with America that it would only be a matter of time before they would push the talmud torahs to teach "an inverterbrate, anemic, condescending, patronizing sentimentalism." Lucas was convinced of German untrustworthiness not so much by the theology of Reform, although he had many nasty things to say on that subject, but rather by their unwillingness to strongly support his crusade against neighborhood missionaries. For him, leaders who were cautious in speaking out against America when most threatening could not be allies in Jewish communal work. So disposed, he consistently fought, well beyond 1910, for OU go-it-alone policies. Lucas stridently condemned the Schiffs and Marshalls as those "more anxious to stand with Gentiles than to be on brotherly terms with fellow Jews." And he minced few words in denigrating those within his own OU "who would dance to their [German] fiddling."[47]

Ultimately, OU initiatives were stymied more by mass unresponsiveness than by either Agudath ha-Rabbanim excoriations or disunity within their own ranks. Even as immigrant Jews observed fewer and fewer of the mitzvoth they retained still the belief that the one true Orthodoxy was that transplanted from Europe. Such was undeniably the mind-set of the immigrant father who chastised his son for attending Endeavorer services conducted by Mordecai M. Kaplan in the Henry Street Synagogue one Saturday afternoon. "You are a *shaigetz* (for attending)", the father reportedly declared, "and Kaplan is a bigger *shaigetz* for conducting the prayers." The Henry Street synagogue, Kaplan would later recall, was declared treif because the services were offered in "an orderly fashion." Immigrant parents were slow to be convinced that changes were permissible within the confines of Jewish law.[48]

But what of their children? Youngsters, in the hundreds, did attend OU services, lessons and game periods, but many more stayed away. Some, under the sway of unyielding parents, honored their elders' request that they stay clear of this new religious lifestyle. Many more left to their own devices were simply unmoved by the Endeavorer's appeals as they followed the road towards assimilation.

The OU, like Drachman, would have to wait for youngsters to leave their parents' homes to truly and permanently become a mass-based force in the life of American Judaism. But these turn of the century efforts were certainly not in vain. They laid the groundwork for later, more profound and popular anti-assimilation work and provided those who would work in the field with their first on-the-job training, which would hold them in good stead.

American Judaism on the Road to Suburbia, 1910–1920

The time for the coming of age of Jewish anti-assimilation work was the 1920s. The place was the early suburbs of the 1920s that witnessed the greatest building boom in this nation's history as new, better built neighborhoods were constructed in this country's many great metropolises. Second-generation Jews, and some of their parents, possessed of money and social confidence flocked to these new residential areas. It was within these new communities that Americanized Jews faced the problems of assimilation on an increasingly widespread basis. Residing in these more heterogeneous environments, the Jew who wanted to drift away finally got his/her chance. All were not lost, though, in the early inter-war years. Conservative and American Orthodox synagogues arose in these mixed settlements. Their synagogue centers were headed by English-speaking rabbis and proffered a wide array of social, cultural and recreational activities which constituted a significant bulwark against Jewish social disintegration.[49]

Some rabbis, as previously noted, knew what to do from their early experiences with the Endeavorers. Others had apprenticed in the synagogue centers, Young Israel synagogues and Conservative Temples that had been established in the 1910s, predominantly in neighborhoods on the outskirts of the immigrant settlements. In these posts, they ministered to a maturing, economically mobile second generation on the road out of the ghetto. There these rabbis experimented with plans and techniques for the harmonization of Judaism and Americanism totally in consonance with the philosophy of their spiritual mentor, Bernard Drachman.

In February 1913, the JTS harvested the first fruits of its 1902 reorganization project when the rabbinic and lay representatives of some twenty four congregations met in New York to found the United Synagogue of America (USA). Brought to the metropolis by Seminary head Solomon Schechter, they were charged with promoting a middle ground between assimilation and Old World Judaism clearly distinct from Reform and slightly different from that of the OU American Traditionalists. To be sure, a goodly number of the delegates were from the German-American congregations long in the Seminary-Conservative constellation. From pre-Schechter days they had struggled against disaffection and Reform in middle-class American neighborhoods. But the stars of the conclave, with whom lay the future of the Conservative movement, were the rabbis of "Schechter's Seminary." Post-1902 graduates like Joel Blau, Israel Levinthal, Herman Rubenovitz and Louis Egelson had all lived up to their schools' expectations. They had become heads of congregations in communities outside of the ghetto (Manhattan, Brooklyn, Boston and Washington D.C. respectively), responsive to the needs of mobile, second-generation East European Jews and prepared to do whatever was needed to keep the acculturated loyal to the synagogue.[50]

These men who patiently laid the ground work for Conservatism's interwar growth were truly the type of rabbi the young Drachman had wanted to be. They were ready and able to help laity integrate loyalty to Judaism with life in the American society around them. Seminary graduates owed Drachman a spiritual, when not personal, debt of gratitude even if Drachman was no longer associated with their alma mater. Drachman, the organizer of the Endeavorers, where many of these men had interned, had broken with President Schechter over irreconcilable theological and philosophical differences, even as Drachman and his Conservative opponents retained an abiding, common belief in the necessity of assisting East European youngsters, grow up comfortably as both Americans and Jews.[51]

But if Drachman was saddened that his disciples, now on their own and away from downtown, adhered to liberal interpretations of Jewish belief and modes of synagogue practice different from his— he was most troubled by rabbinic accommodation of lay demands for linked seating—he could be heartened by the fact that Endeavorer ideas lived on within a new American Orthodox group. The same years which witnessed the slow coalescing of Conservative congregations into a United Synagogue also saw the rise of the Young Israel (YI) movement within New York's Lower East Side and soon beyond, as American Orthodoxy too prepared for the 1920s–1930s.

Like the Endeavorers before them, Young Israel, which also began on the Lower East Side "to bring about a revival of Judaism among the thousands of young Jews and Jewesses. . . whose Judaism is at present dormant," was led by JTS students. Inspired from within the Seminary by former Endeavorer Mordecai M. Kaplan and by Schechter's second-in-command, Israel Friedlaender, and advised from without by Drachman, future rabbis like Moses Rosenthal and Samuel Sachs sought "to awaken Jewish young men and women to their responsibilities as Jews" through the by-then well-established balance of classes, educational forums and Americanized Orthodox services. The fidelity of Conservative leadership to Orthodox ritual strictures, specifically the separation of the sexes during prayer, was clearly mandated by the locus of their activities. Remembering the battles of just a few years earlier over Endeavorer services, Young Israelites understood that their clients, or maybe better, their parents, would be cool to profound breaks with the past. Indeed, sensitivity of Seminary people to the feelings of potential downtown critics was so acute that when Rabbi Joseph Hertz (a pre-Schechter JTS graduate and later Chief Rabbi of Great Britain) spoke at YI sabbath services, he lectured Friday night in English and Saturday morning in Yiddish.[52]

This careful approach had its rewards. Four downtown synagogues, including, not surprisingly two OU affiliates which had backed earlier Endeavorer efforts, trusted the Orthodoxy of the YI and opened their doors to it. More importantly, the YI did better than its predecessors in attracting a solid lay constituency of "young businessmen and professionals" to its program. In fact, it was they who helped the YI grow beyond the old Endeavorer mixture of educational and strictly religious programming towards the social synagogue center it soon became. Fired with an approach to congregational life which would hold it in good stead for more than a generation, the YI sponsored dances, athletics, boat rides, etc., standard events at non-sectarian or Christian settlement houses. Harry G. Fromberg, an early lay leader, explained the thrust of anti-assimilation work:

> The time has come when the man and woman in America must be taught to feel that he or she need not be deprived of the innocent social pleasures so long as it is done in accord with Jewish rites and principles. It is the aim of the synagogue to make the young people feel that being Jews need not deprive them of their social activities and pleasure.[53]

Rabbi Herbert S. Goldstein could not have agreed more. In fact, his Institutional Synagogue (IS) more than either the YI or the Conservative synagogues of early suburbia constituted pre-World War I

Jewry's most profound effort to put second-generation Jews at ease within religious precincts. Goldstein's congregation in Harlem was founded on the principle that the synagogue had to offer the second-generation Jew much more than modern services if it hoped to compete with assimilation. Like the Young Israelites, he understood that settlement house and YMHA programs so popular among youngsters, though often devoid of Jewish content, had to be brought into synagogue life. Within the IS, dance classes, gymnasium activities, libraries and art exhibits would be infused with Jewish symbols. It was presumed that once drawn into synagogue life by the ancillary activities and there surrounded by Jewish teachings of all kinds, the IS member would be drawn ultimately into the sanctuary and towards greater religious dedication and affiliation.[54]

The roots of Goldstein's Orthodox synagogue efforts could be traced back to the OU American Traditionalist coalition. Drachman and his generation of American Orthodox rabbis were his friends. His first teacher was Endeavorer stalwart and JTS faculty member Mordecai M. Kaplan, even as the younger rabbi articulated his theological differences with his senior. Fischel was his father-in-law and chief financial backer. Together they constructed the prototype Conservative and OU Jewish Center synagogue of inter-war days in the years immediately preceding the mass Jewish move towards suburbia.[55]

The coming of age of American Traditionalist ideals, personalities and institutions was not lost upon its early old-line opponents in the Agudath ha-Rabbanim. By the end of our period, elements within East European ranks came to accept Drachman's now generation-old understanding that a Judaism unchanging in America was doomed to failure. Accordingly under the influence of rabbis like Klein and Moses Sebulun Margolies, Goldstein's senior rabbi in a Yorkville synagogue prior to the birth of the IS, RIETS was slowly transformed from a transplanted East European yeshiva into an American Orthodox rabbinical seminary. Needless to say, the emergence of Fischel and other East European laymen as major benefactors played no small role in the changes as did the pressure from the students themselves for a more American curriculum. But at the heart of the move was the perception by many in the old Orthodox camp that the future of their children could not be left to the assimilationists or to the mercies of the Seminary rabbis.[56]

Rabbi Bernard Revel was appointed in 1915 to lead a reorganized RIETS. His mandate was to produce Orthodox rabbis knowledgeable in the ways of America and able to preach in English homilies attractive to fellow second-generation Jews—worthy opponents of JTS graduates. To instruct his students in the bedrock Talmudic curriculum he brought in the rabbis of the Agudath ha-Rabbanim. But to teach his rabbis the ways of America his choices were H. P. Mendes, Herbert S. Goldstein and, most fittingly, Bernard Drachman. By the early 1920s RIETS men too would be on the road to suburbia, taking their messages to second-generation Jews, in competition with JTS graduates but united in their dedication to assist their fellows in reconciling American and Jewish identities.[57]

10

A Generation Unaccounted For in **American Judaism**

A generation of Jewish religious activism, innovation and experimentation is unaccounted for in Nathan Glazer's seminal periodization in *American Judaism.* This lost generation consists of the minority of committed young people of East European heritage who reached their majority between 1900 and 1920. While still living in their parent's immigrant neighborhoods or in second settlement enclaves, they experienced and sought to solve for themselves and their fellows many of the problems of disaffection from Judaism caused by Americanization. They placed their faith in a synagogue transformed to address the social needs and cultural proclivities of their own "rising generation in Israel" while they pledged that their movements would preserve the traditions their parents cherished. In so doing, they started anti-assimilation work that Glazer feels began only in the 1920s and within the newer second-generation communities of that later era. The organizational loci for these efforts were the Orthodox Union, the Young Israel, the Institutional Synagogue and the reborn Jewish Theological Seminary, and to a limited extent, the Union of Orthodox Rabbis—groups that Glazer either ignores or considers either too immature, unable or unwilling to respond positively to the critical issues around them. A close look at these unacknowledged pioneers of American Judaism in the twentieth century—who they were, what they did, how they were received, and what became of them and their movements—may also refine our understanding of the nature of interwar Judaism and Jewishness, an understanding largely derived from the view first sketched for us thirty years ago by Nathan Glazer.

As Glazer has it, the period 1880–1920, the era of East European migration, witnessed the steady erosion of the faith and religious commitment of immigrant Jews. While he notes, somewhat hyperbolically, that there were among the immigrants "*thousands* of Jews with a *fabulous* knowledge of traditional law and usage" (my emphasis), he admits that they and the hundreds of thousands of their less lettered fellows were unable to resist the pressures America applied to give up their old ways.

Additionally, Glazer suggests that because most newcomers did not hold concrete Jewish dogmas their commitment to Judaism declined. The masses of Jews had been socialized in Europe to follow the practices of Judaism, not to think them through or to justify to others the bases of the faith. Consequently, when the Jew who "was brought up to observe the commandments . . . came in touch with a kind of thought which questions fundamentals," he found himself "at a loss." Nonetheless, the immigrant's intellectual disaffection from the past was not always observable in the ghetto. Residual social, cultural, and psychological affinities still kept him tied to Jews and Judaism while still downtown. Glazer explains that

> a non-believing Jew might still, from habit, observe the dietary laws, go to synagogue now and then (and when he went, so thorough was the East European training, he often knew most of the prayers by heart), say Kaddish . . . for his father and so on.[1]

Glazer is also quick to note that there were those within ghetto society—maybe those who were the most learned—who attempted to resist the tide of Americanization. He records the several flawed and ultimately unsuccessful efforts by Orthodox Jews in the late 1880s to recreate East European conditions. Glazer sympathetically characterizes both the chief rabbi experiment, an effort to use rabbinic authority and charisma to bring order to the business of kosher meat and the early history of the Etz Chaim Yeshiva, an attempt to produce here "prodigies of rabbinic learning" as heroic efforts to recapture and reassemble the past in America. But each, he reminds us, foundered on the rocks of American voluntarism.[2]

Continuing this all-too-familiar and basically correct narrative, Glazer emphasizes that whatever residual effect nostalgia, guilt or education had upon the first generation, none of these forces influenced the children of immigrants. As he sees it, it made little difference whether a parent exposed his child to the best Talmud Torahs or provided him with no formal training, the result was the same. Here the sociologist argues powerfully:

> Those who had the best Talmud Torah educations were as likely to drop all religious observance in late adolescence or early adulthood as those who received none. The hundreds and thousands of synagogues organized by East European Jews were the work of the immigrants themselves; the children had no part in them and wished none.[3]

Significantly, Glazer does allow that during this period of Judaism's rapid decline there were two efforts initiated outside of downtown society to meet the religious problems and needs of the children of immigrants on their own American terms. But as he has it, one was still in its nascent stage as World War I came and went, and the other was stillborn.

The former, the resuscitation of the Jewish Theological Seminary under the impact of East European migration and with the help of German Jewish philanthropy began in 1902. Playing on the established community's fears that the new American youth, becoming divorced from the old Jewish ways, would inevitably gravitate toward the radical movements in their midst, Dr. Cyrus Adler was able to convince Jacob Schiff, Louis Marshall and others to refinance a then moribund institution rededicating it to producing American-born, English-speaking, traditional rabbis who could minister and control their own kind. Solomon Schechter, as Glazer accurately tells it, was brought over from England, and under his leadership the long process began which led to twentieth century Conservatism. However, Glazer notes ironically that "initially, the Seminary had little influence on the East European Jews, aside from offering an avenue of upward mobility to some of its youth." Glazer dates the beginnings of Conservatism's impact, once having defined a Conservative synagogue as one that was "neither Reform nor East European Orthodox," from the calling together in 1913 of sixteen congregations into the United Synagogue of America.[4]

The latter attempt to reach the children of the new Americans, the Orthodox Union, founded in 1898, was even "much less successful." Dr. H. P. Mendes, rabbi of the Spanish and Portuguese Synagogue of New York, founded the OU to strengthen the few remaining American Orthodox congregations by aligning them with "the great number of East European Jews." He hoped that together they could appeal to the younger generation. But, according to Glazer, since the East European congregations would not recognize the Seminary's authority to ordain rabbis—and the JTS was the institution that spawned Mendes' communal work—cooperation proved impossible: "The East European congregations soon ran away with the organization." Glazer considers the Orthodox Union and the Agudath ha-Rabbanim (Union of Orthodox Rabbis), founded in 1902, as the two pre-World War I old-time efforts to institutionalize opposition to new religious ways. But he notes that in voluntary, disorganized America "the majority of congregations and rabbis of the East European immigrants joined neither group."[5]

For Glazer, whatever dismal chances Jews had of surviving as a religious group in American life before World War I were reduced even further during the watershed decades of the 1920s and 1930s. "The rapid dissolution of the Jewish religion" was seemingly the faith's fate in this country's areas of second settlement, those areas of middle-class apartment houses toward the outskirts of cities to which upwardly mobile second-generation Jews flocked before the Great Depression. And in the early suburban areas of third settlement, the most heterogeneous neighborhoods of all, to which the most affluent and acculturated Jews moved, religious life was in further decline. To be sure, Glazer recognized that within these new

> zones of American Jewish life . . . elaborate synagogues were built and for the first time the synagogue as a large communal structure . . . (was) not weak. But it was nevertheless true that the overwhelming majority of the immigrants' children had deserted Judaism. They did not convert, but they were indifferent or hostile to the traditional religion.[6]

It was in this period of Jewish decay that Conservatism became important. While Glazer is quick to note that neither Conservatism, nor for that matter Reform to its left nor Orthodoxy to its right, was particularly successful in halting the apparent inevitability of mass assimilation, he argues that the denomination that the Seminary spawned offered the most cogent and attractive alternative to disaffection then available. By emphasizing Jewishness for wavering second-generation Jews more than Judaism, Conservative leaders were able to maximize their potential constituency as East European adjustment to America was completed. But a successful Jewish revival under major Conservative and other influences would await a subsequent era.[7]

By emphasizing American Judaism's failures, Glazer makes clear for historians that all subsequent discussions of the evolution of Jewish religious life in this country must acknowledge at their outset how large and continuous have been the losses to assimilation. Glazer makes us understand that even as this rabbi or that layperson strove to develop new forms of Jewish expression or to produce relevant American Jewish programming to accommodate the social and behavioral needs of potential followers, many, if not most, Jews were totally unresponsive to these calls back to faith, so great was the pressure of Americanization. Still, I wonder if in declaring assimilation victor over persistence—as surely it was—for at least the first 200 years of American Jewish history, Glazer made the error of writing a victor's history, underplaying and post-dating the vitality and variety of the responses from anti-assimilationists.

Take, for example, what was left out of his discussion of disaffection on the Lower East Side. Beginning in 1900, spurred on by frequent editorials and articles in the New York Anglo-Jewish press, the *Hebrew Standard* and the *American Hebrew* that explored the problems of the "rising generation in Israel," a loose coalition of young downtowners and their elders from both within and without the ghetto arose to meet the challenge of assimilation. The thrust of their efforts was the creation of new-style, American "young people's synagogues," as they were called, offering "dignified services to recall the indifferent in Jewry back to faith." Basically, that meant forming congregations that reflected, through governance, aesthetics and ritual, their members' growing identities as Americans and ambivalences about their Judaism.[8]

In the young people's synagogues, it was averred, Jews would pray as Americans do—Gentile friends could join or watch and no one would be offended or ashamed—without doing violence to the ritual core and religious content of the ancient service. There the young person's senses would not be assaulted by the unseemly noise, movement and commotion of the store-front immigrant synagogue. Nor would the young downtowner be put off by gross commercialism, for example, the selling of synagogue honors, that shattered the solemnity that was supposed to characterize an American religious ceremony. Instead the members would be encouraged to join a revitalized community in congregational singing even as his or her attentiveness to the proceedings would be heightened further by the English-language prayers that supplemented the traditional siddur. And of course, all would remain still, men on one side of the *mechitza*, women on the other during prayer and the weekly English sermon offered by both lay and, most significantly, rabbi-in-training leaders on social and historical topics of the day.

But probably it was the young people's synagogues' innovative approach to recall, today called outreach, even before a potential member set foot in the synagogue that maximized their appeal. They openly and positively adjusted their synagogue's clock and calendar to accommodate the social and economic realities of their community while remaining most sensitive to the calls of the Jewish past.

They understood, for example, that it was an unavoidable, if lamentable, fact of life that their young people violated the holiness of the Sabbath every week by working. They realized that all calls from on high—and there were transplanted East European rabbis and *maggidim* who regularly chastised the offenders in the strongest terms—would have no dramatic effect upon the masses of violators. To be sure, young people's synagogue leaders also did not countenance this patent breaking of Judaism's most hallowed of commandments. But, they would not condemn the transgressors as they opposed their acts. Instead, they made every effort to convince Jews that when they were able to follow the traditions, the synagogue was prepared to accept and to service them. That meant that the young people's synagogue made the Saturday afternoon *mincha-maariv* service the major service of the week. The following argument was offered to youthful downtowners. In the best of all possible Jewish worlds, all would honor the Sabbath and attend synagogue three times that day, if not every day. But given the reality that Jews were working steadily until the American work week concluded on Saturday afternoon, it would be both unrealistic and ultimately self-defeating to demand attendance in the synagogue Saturday morning and to excoriate those who did not. But when work was done, Jews were invited to be with their own kind in the modern synagogue, and through reciting the old prayers with the useful English additions, and while socializing with other Jews they would acquire a positive American Jewish identity, the most potent bulwark against assimilation.[9]

Admittedly, it is impossible to determine how successful this shift in approach within the American synagogue was in attracting back that lost generation. Glazer is, of course, right: So many Jews simply ignored all efforts to attract them, But the activists' acceptance into the Orthodox synagogue of their fellow Jews regardless of what their religious life-styles were outside the sanctuary also constituted a noteworthy milestone in the evolution of American Judaism in the twentieth century. The makers of this change in synagogue life, the uptown-downtown coalition, were invariably affiliated with the Orthodox Union and/or the JTS, the very organizations which, as noted previously, Glazer considered as either too immature, unable, or unwilling to respond effectively to assimilation. For American Sephardic Rabbis H. P. Mendes and Henry S. Morais and their German-American colleagues Bernard Drachman, Henry W. Schneeberger and others, efforts on behalf of ghetto youth were ambitious reflections of the Orthodox Union's avowed mandate "to protect Jews in their civic and religious life," They raised funds within their own congregations for youth synagogues and they worked with and inspired the young men and women who ran the new synagogues downtown. They were thus the patrons of the Jewish Endeavor Society even as they offered their services periodically as guest lecturers or preachers. Incidentally, they also frequently went to Albany in the hope of doing away with the onerous blue laws which contributed so mightily to widespread non-observance of the Sabbath.[10]

Not surprisingly, their efforts downtown were far from universally accepted. But here Glazer's understanding of the roots and dimensions of the problem is only partially accurate. Most East European synagogues and their rabbis did not back OU initiatives. But it was not so much the OU's organizational base at the Seminary that spawned opposition to them. After all, the Agudath ha-Rabbanim itself averred that the founders of the 1887 Seminary—and Mendes, Drachman and Schneeberger among them—"were full-hearted for the faith of Israel and its Torah" even if they were not great Talmudists. Rather, the opposition was based on the Europeans' inability to recognize the necessity for sociological change if Judaism were to survive in America. They would continue to hark back to the romanticized civilization they knew and left behind in Eastern Europe: in Russia young people's synagogues were unknown. This opposition to change, even as institutionalized through the Agudath ha-Rabbanim, did not however, lead either to the stifling of the OU's activities nor to "East European congregations [running] away with the organization."[11]

The efforts of the Orthodox uptowners survived and grew because there were other elements within the religiously heterogeneous Lower East Side community who not only actively supported all OU efforts but quickly became powers within that organization. In 1900, there was already emerging downtown what may be called a new East European elite of men of letters and of some wealth. People like builders Harry Fischel and Jonas Weil, lawyer and later judge Otto Rosalsky, newspaper editors and writers Leon Kamaiky, Kasriel Sarasohn and Judah David Eisenstein had all come to America at the very beginning of the era of East European migration. None was yet forty by 1903 and all had spent the better part of their lives in the United States. Each had clearly become Americanized and yet had somehow retained his religious affinities. They were role models for what the larger, younger cohorts of their generation could become as American Jews. They easily found common cause with the Orthodox from uptown. For their part, Mendes and Drachman welcomed this participation and enthusiasm for their anti-assimilation crusade.[12]

The OU also welcomed supporters from a seemingly very unlikely source as downtown proved to be even more religiously diverse than might have been expected. Early on, Rabbi Dr. Philip Hillel Klein, a leader of the Agudath ha-Rabbanim and head of a large Hungarian-American Congregation downtown, broke with his rabbinical organization's positions against the OU both by joining the American group and by opening rooms in his synagogue for their late Sabbath afternoon sessions. By 1910, Klein was joined in his dissent by at feast two other East European rabbis, Moses Sebulun Margolies and Bernard Levinthal, even as all three remained significant leaders of the resisting Agudath ha-Rabbanim.[13]

But even with this wide ranging if not especially deep support, the OU campaign could never have seen the light of day without the ongoing efforts of the foot soldiers in the anti-assimilation struggle. Young, American-born men and women of East European heritage drawn from the streets of the Lower East Side sought to help themselves and their fellows develop a place for Judaism within their American lives. Their drives found institutional expression as early as 1900 through the Jewish Endeavor Society, which became the unofficial youth division of the OU. Most significantly, the male leaders of the Endeavorers were drawn from, or found their way to, the student body of both the old Seminary (pre-1902) and Schechter's Seminary. It was there that future United Synagogue leaders like Herman Abramowitz, Mordecai M. Kaplan, Charles Kauvar, Julius Greenstone, and Joel Blau began their careers, as Glazer would have it, as "Conservative" rabbis except that by all accounts and self-definitions, separate seating, other rituals and the like, the synagogues were American Orthodox.[14] That some of these Seminary-trained activists remained close to American Orthodoxy long after they left their school and internships on the Lower East Side, helps refine another topic in Glazer's work: the evolution of a distinctly Conservative response to "the rapid dissolution of the Jewish religion."

As indicated previously, there were, as early as 1900, synagogues attracting acculturated immigrants and their children that were "neither Reform nor East European Orthodox." But the Endeavorer congregations displayed none of the features readily associated with the Conservative synagogue that Glazer knew. Nor, for that matter, did most of the American synagogues—a far more preferable term— built either in the ghetto or areas of second settlement in New York and other cities by the time of the founding of the United Synagogue. A close look at the ritual practices and ethnic composition of 17 of the 24 charter members of that national organization shows that the 13 congregations that changed the service the most— authorizing mixed seating, offering instrumental music on the Sabbath and/or changing the starting times of prayers on Friday or Holiday nights—were synagogues founded in the nineteenth century by American Jews of Central European extraction. A few had been at some point near Orthodoxy, the majority were Conservative congregations of long-standing. In the meantime, two congregations headed up by Seminary graduates and attracting East European Jews joined the United Synagogue while remaining American Orthodox: They offered Endeavorer-style services to the acculturated even if their synagogues were in Rochester, New York and Kansas City and not the Lower East Side. Only two American congregations composed of rising East European Jews and their children seem to have shown true signs of affinity for what would become twentieth-century Conservatism by instituting family pews. But in one of those cases mixed seating was as far as the congregation would subsequently move in liberalizing the service.[15]

In that instance, Charles Kauvar, rabbi of Denver's Beth Hamidrash Hagodol and a former Endeavorer, made every effort to maintain "traditional Judaism in an American setting." During his fifty years in the Rocky Mountain congregation, he did not countenance any additional changes in ritual, creating what would later be called the "Traditional" synagogue. Interestingly enough, during the interwar period and beyond he was considered a colleague by rabbis of both the Rabbinical Assembly (Conservative) and Rabbinical Council of America (Orthodox).[16]

While the United Synagogue welcomed all sorts of congregations bent on addressing the problem of assimilation, outside its purview, two other initiatives, unqualifiably American Orthodox in character, were being established with at least indirect help from the Seminary, one within the ghetto, the other without. In 1913, concomitant with the founding of the United Synagogue and the problem of youth disaffection from Judaism unresolved downtown, a second institution to "bring about a revival of Judaism among the thousands of young Jews and Jewesses . . . whose Judaism is at present dormant" was inaugurated. Like the JES before them, the early leaders of the Young Israel movement were Seminary students. Significantly, student rabbis Moses Rosenthal and Samuel Sachs looked for advice from former Endeavorer and now Seminary professor Mordecai M. Kaplan in developing programs "to awaken Jewish young men and women to their responsibilities as Jews." Young Israel activities began as a balance of classes, educational forums and lectures and Americanized Orthodox services.

Two years later, when the first permanent Young Israel (Model) Synagogue was created, one of the lay people—and Young Israel was destined to be a lay-led movement for most of its first two generations of existence—succinctly articulated his group's American Orthodox approach:

> [A model synagogue is to be created] where every atom of our time-honored tradition could be observed and at the same time prove attractive particularly to the young men and women; a synagogue where, with the exception of prayer, English would be spoken in delivering sermons and otherwise, complete congregational singing instituted, "schnoddering" eliminated and decorum to an extent of almost 100% maintained.[17]

Young Israel emphasized its purely social agenda in 1918:

> The time has come when the man and woman in America must be taught to feel that he or she need not be deprived of the innocent social pleasure so long as it is done in accord with Jewish rites and principles,

it is the aim of the synagogue to make the young people feel that being Jews need not deprive them of their social activities and pleasures.[18]

Rabbi Herbert S. Goldstein, JTS class of 1914, could not have agreed more with these sentiments. In fact, his Harlem-based Institutional Synagogue, even more than either the Young Israel or United Synagogue congregations constituted the most wide ranging Jewish religious response to assimilation during this time. While at the Seminary, Goldstein had been exposed to Kaplan's evolving idea that the synagogue had to offer the second-generation Jew more than modern services if it hoped to stymie assimilation. Practically, settlement house programs often criticized for their lack of Jewish content, had to be brought into the synagogue. Religious goals remained the same: Jews had to be moved toward stronger affiliation with their people and with God. But synagogue life could be approached through any number of portals. Dance classes, gymnasiums, libraries, art exhibits could all be coopted to make the Jew comfortable in that setting. From there, it was hoped he would find his way towards greater religious commitment.[19]

Arguably, it was there that the Institutional Synagogue created, before the end of the First World War, the prototype of the Conservative Synagogue Center while maintaining the core of the Orthodox rite and without doing violence to the traditional time for prayers and the liturgy of the service. In any event, the American synagogue before 1920, whatever its success in attracting the assimilating, expressed itself in a variety of forms, few of them characteristically Conservative. Ultimately, of course, the full-fledged Conservative temple, synagogue center and all, appeared and truly became the largest exponent of American Judaism against the forces of assimilation. The time for that maturation was, as Glazer says, the 1920s and 1930s and the places were the areas of second and third settlement. But Conservatives were not out there alone with unique sociological methods fighting the good if losing fight against disaffection. The heterogeneity of expressions which had previously characterized the American synagogue did not end with the close of European hostilities; only the balances of popularity were altered as

Jewish demography changed. American Orthodoxy still had its roots in downtown areas even as it still had to put up with its East European critics. But at least in the hub there were few Conservatives to battle. The areas of second settlement were heartlands for both Conservatism and American Orthodoxy. Certainly such areas as Brooklyn with its fourteen Young Israel branches were most hospitable to American Orthodoxy as it was to some seventeen Conservative temples. It was in the areas of third settlement to which the majority of American Jews would ultimately move, and particularly outside New York City, that Conservatism really began to hold sway.

Still, it is noteworthy that American Orthodox congregations bearing the "Conservative" appellation of "Jewish Center" could also be found in those regions. And in suburbia there were also numbers of nascent Reform congregations attracting their own segment of Jews of East European ancestry those who wanted an even more modern, liberal service. All denominations appealed to the Jewishness of their people with the hope of capturing them back toward observance.[20]

Still, Glazer is unqualifiably correct in his evaluation of synagogue success in this era. No matter how organizationally strong American Jewry appeared to be during the inter-war period, it was manifestly weak in commitment as disaffection took its great toll. One indicator of the dimensions of that problem is the "Back to Synagogue" project in 1933, when the Orthodox Union willingly joined the United Synagogue and the Reform Union of American Hebrew Congregations to reclaim Jews to religious life regardless of their denominational expression. But this cooperative effort was minimally successful. The denominations would have to await the post-World War II "Jewish revival" for a fresh start and not incidentally greater bases for inter-Jewish competition and non-cooperation.[21]

11

Time, Place, and Movement in Immigrant Jewish Historiography

The theories developed in the 1920s by Robert Park, Ernst W. Burgess, and, most importantly for us, Louis Wirth to explain twentieth-century American Jewish immigrant life were influenced strongly by an uncritical acceptance of an early and tendentious depiction of the texture of medieval Jewish life. And they ascribed static patterns of immigrant behavior, based on observations of life in one city and among one particular immigrant group, to all new Americans and all localities in the United States. Yet these scholars' works, all from what came to be known as the Chicago school of sociology, stood unchallenged for more than two generations and even today still inform most discussions of time, place, and movement in immigrant, immigrant Jewish, and second-generation ethnic historiography.

Writing as they did at the opening of the interwar period, when nativism and calls for "Hundred-percent Americanism" transcended the streets to pervade the academy and, ultimately, American governmental policy, theirs was an optimistic message, arguing from social science the possibility of immigrant assimilation into a broad American polity. They wrote with confidence of the wide applicability of their research findings, for such was the legacy of 1910s Progressivism, of which they still felt a part. They were of the tradition that believed that if you create a study model and study it well, you can predict beyond the initial example and readily project your findings to other places and times.[1]

It was Burgess who in 1923 offered a model, drawn from Chicago, which tightly linked immigrant economic conditions and mobility with well-defined residential concentrations. His "Concentric Zone

Theory" divined that all twentieth-century American cities possessed four areas of settlement, spinning off and out of a downtown central business-financial district, an area that was initially the core of the city. New York's Wall Street area might immediately come to mind to illustrate the Chicagoan's point. Back in the seventeenth and eighteenth centuries, the Battery Park to Wall Street area was all of New York City, except that Battery Park—which is, in fact, landfill—was not yet in existence. Most of the area north of Wall Street was farmland. And, of course, Brooklyn, Long Island, of which Queens is a part, and the Bronx were either legally or geographically separate from the city. Obviously by the nineteenth century Wall Street had become what it is today and in significant part what Burgess described as a classic Central Business Zone. This district was characterized as home to very few residential inhabitants, for it served as the central retail district, the financial hub, and the locus of civic and political activities.[2]

The Central Business Zone was encircled by what Burgess called the Area of First Settlement or the Zone in Transition. Other terms, euphemisms like "Little Italy," "The Ghetto," and "The Black Belt," were also used by the sociologist. Simply put, it is a slum area. As Burgess explained it: this section was once, in the early nineteenth century, a "suburb" of private homes and lands, But now, as a long-term victim of the burgeoning of the late-nineteenth-century city, it was pockmarked by tenements and blighted by factories and sweatshops near and in the buildings where the poorest immigrants and blacks had to reside. They had no choice: they must be near their work, for they labored intolerably long hours and could not afford rents elsewhere. At best it was an area "from which the most enterprising of aspiring individuals hope and ultimately do escape." At first glance, this description seemingly could be applied to the Lower East Side. It certainly was true of Chicago's Near West Side, Burgess's actual study area. And as the sociologist had it: what was true in the Windy City held by extension for all other cities.[3]

Those on the way up economically, "skilled" and "thrifty" factory and shop workers or, more often than not, their children, are moved and placed by Burgess into the Zone of Workingman's Homes or the

Area of Second Settlement, a "region of escape from the Ghetto." It is a better-built neighborhood, with elevator apartments predominating, and nice brownstones highlighting the neighborhood. Burgess called his Lawndale section of Chicago "Deutschland" and intimated in passing what it meant socially for immigrants to live there by describing the district as a place where Russian Jews attempted to imitate the German Jews.

For Burgess, great American cities were home to two final concentric economic zones. The area of third settlement, the so-called better residential zone, situated toward the outskirts of the city, is home to the great American middle class; the place and status toward which the best of the immigrants and surely their children are heading. Residents of these neighborhoods, where private homes predominate, are often professional people; minimally they are high school educated and are employed in white-collar occupations.

Finally, 1920s American cities were said to have slowly emerging commuter zones—this country's first twentieth-century suburbs— sitting astride the city limits. If you wanted to live in this private home district, the sociologist made clear, you had better have money and an automobile, and it would help significantly if you were a WASP. For himself, Burgess was troubled that in the commuter zone, residential restrictions were based on more than economics.

The historical interpretive narrative attached by Burgess to his zone theory was that all immigrants entered into first-settlement areas and over time moved up and out toward the outskirts of the city. For him, an immigrant's residential address would tell it all. He was in certain agreement with what one of his Progressive contemporaries said in a popular vein about newly successful New York Jewish businessmen: "The further uptown they move, the larger one may be sure is his bank account." And as a 1920s Progressive himself, he was also certain that what was becoming true of immigrants would ultimately be true too of intra-American migrants as well; blacks from the south would join Jews and others on the road to suburbia, if only the WASPS out there would accept those who were making it. Burgess had no sense of aspiring and achieving blacks being stopped early on in the move outward.[4]

Burgess left it to his colleague Robert E. Park to describe and predict what this inevitable immigrant march to suburbia meant to the new American's sense of ethnic, religious, or racial cohesion. Park argued that first-settlement areas were homes to slowly changing traditional societies made up of individuals who held to transplanted European identities. Second-settlement neighborhoods were made up of the acculturating in the throes of breaking away from the old ways. In fact, the most dramatic expression of their new self-definition was their physical move from the ghetto. Still in all, these migrants were not fully at home in America. They were marginal people, still struggling both with their new national identities and with the greater impersonality and decreased social stability that comes with new affluence, Americanization, and declining propinquity to their own kind.

The reconciliation of marginality, it was predicted, would come in the third and latter areas of settlement. There, if Americans would only allow immigrants (or, for that matter, blacks) to settle, the acculturated newcomers would feel totally part of American society, live among all types and peoples, and contribute to the advancement of our homogenized nation.[5]

Altogether, Burgess and Park offered their interwar society an optimistic, progressive vision of the resolution of America's racial, immigrant, and ethnic problems. All minority groups were destined to move up the economic and residential ladder and seek out their earned positions, if those who preceded them would only let them, Equally important, these newcomers to America and/or to the city were ripe for the warranted values of assimilation and would, again if given a chance, identify totally with the majority society.

It remained for Burgess's and Park's student Louis Wirth to focus his teachers' observations and predictions about cities, social life in ghettos and beyond that pale, and movement toward affluence, integration, and assimilation upon the quintessential immigrant/minority group, the Jews. And it was here in Wirth's full-length monograph on Chicago Jewry, *The Ghetto*, published in 1928, that the work of the Chicago school fully entered American Jewish historiography.

It could almost have been anticipated that Wirth would find that the city his midwestern Jews encountered corresponded in most of its salient features to the model developed by Burgess. They were both studying Chicago, and when Wirth took teachings out of the seminar room to the streets for his observations, predictably he was able to see, and ready to show, that each Jewish section had its own physical and economic character and served as home to a particular class of Jew. Wirth's affinity for what Park had to say about the social qualities found among Jews in each of these settlement areas was even greater. Not only could he verify by his own observations what he had learned at the university about Jewish life in the contemporary' ghetto, he could project his findings widely because it appeared to him that what Jews were then doing in Chicago was in full consonance with Jewish history.

He had learned, seemingly from the reading of two early histories of medieval Jewry, that Jewish life in the historical, involuntary ghettos of the past was closed, unchanging, and stultifying. Moreover, he had been brought to understand that "the Jew as long as he finds himself enclosed by ghetto walls is not only helpless, but is extremely naive about the world around him." Thus, when he saw the same behavior patterns in Chicago he was prepared to say that although America did not prescribe specific ghetto areas for Jews, Jews bound by their history gravitated to ghettos not only "because of accessibility and low rents but also by tradition." One can see Wirth's sense of the European ghetto being replicated in America when he wrote:

> The [American] Ghetto is a complete world, but it is a small and narrow one. It has its intellectuals, but their intellect is of a circumscribed sort. What it lacks in breadth of horizon, it makes up in emotion. . . . It is almost completely cut off from the world as if it were still surrounded by a wall and its inhabitants were still locked behind ghetto gates.[6]

Clearly American Jewish historiography would have evolved quite differently if Wirth had had access to what we now know of the variegated social, intellectual, and economic profile of medieval Jewry. Without historical precedent to buttress his assumptions, he might have been able to see the difficulties of projecting widely such an overarching understanding-the very problems that we shall raise momentarily. Unfortunately, Wirth's teachers, Israel Abrahams, author of *Jewish Life in the Middle Ages,* and David Philipson, author of *Old European Jewries,* had neither the skills nor the objectivity of our contemporaries. Abrahams, the English Liberal Jewish leader, and Philipson, his American Reform counterpart, were consistently intent on contrasting the closed nature of medieval Jewish life, complete with a depiction of the Jew as culturally and socially backward, with the newly open, vibrant, modern Jewish society, home to the worldly Jew; a transformation achieved due to Gentile largesse, a bounty of emancipation. So they argued that so long as Jews were kept apart from Gentiles, Jewish life suffered. Now, in the modern period, thanks to the opening of society, Jews were changing, improving, and Gentiles could expect that greater freedom and acceptance of the Jew would inevitably lead to Jews taking an even greater earned place in the contemporary liberal world.[7]

If early Jewish historiography skewed what Wirth knew of the historical ghetto, contemporaneous American and American Jewish historiography offered literally no other studies of immigrant or immigrant Jewish life and few examinations of the American city against which Wirth's understanding, and for that matter his mentors' conceptualizations, could be fairly compared. American historians writing in the generation which immediately preceded the appearance of Marcus Lee Hansen's seminal work *The Immigrant in American History* showed little positive interest in detailing and evaluating the contribution and character of new Americans. Indeed, when they did write about immigrants—and remember, their studies were at least several steps removed from those whom they were studying, and furthermore, most American historians had not the linguistic ability or cultural skills to get close to the immigrants—their tracts were rife with what one historian has called the "Mayflower complex," the very nativist disposition against which Burgess, Park, and Wirth had struggled.[8]

American Jewish historians, for their part, were consumed by their own "Mayflower complex," their attempt through filiopietism and apologetics to argue the early presence of the Jews in the United States, even before the arrival of the Mayflower. So directed, the well-meaning amateurs who peopled the American Jewish Historical Society had no time for the realia of the immigrant period that had just ended. Even the amateur historian closest to the immigrants, a man who spoke their language and knew their ways, newspaper editor Peter Wiernik of the *Morgen Zhurnal*, offered no conceptualizations as grounding for his interesting relating of facts,[9]

In fact, if Wirth *et al.* had been looking for popular approbation for their sense of Jewish migration and settlement patterns, they would have had to look no farther than the classic and best-selling immigrant novel of their time, Abraham Cahan's *The Rise of David Levinsky*.[10] But then again, who was looking? So, untouched and uncriticized, Chicago school theories acquired the status of a true conventional wisdom through the end of the Second World War.

The 1950s brought with them a new popular vision of the ideal American society; and as a by-product of the rise to ascendancy of the teachings of cultural pluralism, there came the first substantial questioning of the Chicago school's conceptualizations and predictions. Cultural pluralists had, of course, long argued—from at least the days of the young Horace Kallen around World War I, and against both assimilationists and nativists—that the greatness of America lay not in the homogeneity of its people, but rather in its heterogeneity. But it was not until the buoyant, expansive, victorious early postwar days that this most progressive of American ideologies eventually superseded the melting pot advocates and Anglo-Saxon conformity conceptualizations in the popular mind. For cultural pluralists, the ideal American is one who upon his/her arrival in America makes every effort to conform to American ways and aspires toward economic greatness in order to make his/her ultimate contribution to this country. Along the way, much of his/her unusable past—those aspects of European heritage that would set him/her fully apart from all others—are jettisoned. At the same time, this growing American is certain to hold fast to aspects of ancestral culture or religion, particularly if these pieces of his/her past can be dressed up in American garb. It is this individual, proud of Americanism and comfortable with his/her roots, who has the greatest chance of aiding this country's growth. Moreover, American culture itself benefits by the infusion of Jewish or Italian or Polish or Irish symbols or elements. Simply put, we live together, learn from each other, and most important, learn to tolerate diversity in culture and society.[11]

Within this emerging atmosphere, it was inevitable that the 1920s theories that had predicted and maybe even hoped for total assimilation as the ultimate result of the Americanization process would be questioned. And in fact, in the early 1950s, two major works, Will Herberg's *Protestant-Catholic-Jew* and Marshall Sklare's *Conservative Judaism*, did just that, arguing that the later areas of immigrant settlement (the neighborhoods closest to or within suburbia) were still home to Jewish identification. As they told the story of immigrant progress and acculturation—in their case, primarily Jewish progress and acculturation—new Americans moved inexorably forward from the types of ghettos and identities described by the Chicago school toward the newer and better neighborhoods. (Significantly, Sklare's affinity for the Wirth definition of Near West Side Jewish life was predetermined by the fact that his prime study area was also Chicago.) In these second and third settlement neighborhoods, Jews increasingly behaved and achieved as other Americans did, just as the earlier theorists had predicted. But as good 1950s cultural pluralists, Herberg and Sklare also argued that the abandonment by Jews of old ways as they moved toward suburbia did not leave them devoid of group identities. Rather, they created new ways of linking up with their own kind and their own common past totally in consonance with American mores. Concretely this meant that the immigrant's transplanted European Orthodox identity, which succored the new arrival even as it had difficulty dropping roots in free America's hostile soil, ultimately could not survive the Americanization and movement of its adherents. But fortunately for the survival of Judaism and the good of America, after a slow start among the marginal, conflicted Jews in second-settlement areas, where a residual Orthodoxy still held on, in the third suburban settlement areas, Conservatism came into its own, providing the new

American Jews with just the right mix of their past and present, enabling them to remain true to Judaism and making them good Americans. For himself, Herberg added one additional gloss to this description of 1950s Judaism. Out in suburbia, he argued, all religious denominations—Protestants, Catholics, and Jews—were in the process of creating an American civil religion which emphasized shared values as Americans and which played down historical differences. To be sure, Jews still believed differently than did their Christian counterparts, and their weekly religious calendar was uniquely their own. But ultimately that was a problem only for theologians. Meanwhile, socially, aesthetically, and even architectually, synagogues were increasingly like churches, and more importantly, churches were like synagogues, as American Judaism, with Conservatism being the quintessence thereof, took its honored place as an equal in a culturally pluralistic America.[12]

In time, as the more intensely ethnic 1960s began to unfold, cultural pluralism's teachings raised voices in other rooms in the academy. Immigrant and then social historians began to light their own fires, directing their attacks at the start of the Chicago school's immigrant trail. They offered substantial revisions of Burgess, Park, and Wirth's views, focusing primarily on the physical dynamics of downtown life, and from there looked closely at when and how immigrants moved out of and beyond ghetto limits.

Moses Rischin, author of the classic *The Promised City* (published in 1963), offered the most telling early critique. True to the teachings of his mentor, Oscar Handlin, and attuned, as was his senior, to the message, enunciated to all by the late Hansen, that the new Americans had to be studied from their own perspective, Rischin set out to detail the saga of the daily life and trials of adjustment of the immigrant on the Lower East Side. Totally conscious of what Wirth had written, years later he would recall: "When in my second year of graduate study I first read his book, I was quietly incensed that so simplistic a sociological formula should have gone virtually uncontested and attained universal currency." Rischin was soon to point out, utilizing the nuts-and-bolts methodologies of the urban historian, how large, variegated, and economically diverse was Jewish life downtown. Hard-nosed examinations of downtown's growth, physical characteristics, population density, and demographic data led him to reveal that both the poor and those Jews on the way up resided each in their own subenclaves in the larger area known to outsiders as the Lower East Side. Why didn't these Jews with new money take their affluence and move uptown as they "should have"? True, downtown was the classic slum neighborhood—indeed it had more than even Chicago's share of tenements and dilapidated buildings. But Rischin discovered that New York's "Zone in Transition," to borrow Burgess's phrase, was also a neighborhood which over time frequently changed for the better. Rischin's study of early-twentieth-century New York real estate trends helped him understand how a "less crowded quarter (south of East Broadway) where private dwellings, front courtyards and a scattering of trees (recalling) a time when Henry, Madison, Rutgers and Jefferson street addresses were stylish" could come into existence. A consideration of metropolitan urban renewal policies permitted him to hint to us how the 1890 to 1900 public parks movement created a more salubrious setting for some downtowners. All of this, he understood, created a class of denizens of better buildings who were in a first-settlement area when seen from a wide-lens aerial map, but whose bank account tallys were clearly those of second- and third-settlement residents. These "allrightniks" stayed downtown possibly because they liked the soul of the old neighborhood or wanted to live near their factory, particularly if, as boss, they did not have to report to work at six a.m. It is equally possible, and this point must be pondered further, that immigrant affluence and acculturation did not go hand in hand. The Jew making it economically might not have been ready to tread out of the ghetto.[13]

Burgess, Park, and Wirth were no longer alive in 1963 to rebut Rischin's refutation. Had they lived, they might have posed the following question: Could it not be that New York, by virtue of its size or its situation as the major point of immigrant entry, is the idiosyncratic exception that does not undo the Chicagoans' rule? As it turned out, the next generation of immigration research addressed this query. Inspired in large measure by Rischin's lead, scholars have demonstrated how immigrants, from Jews to Italians to Irish, from New York to Poughkeepsie to Boston to Marblehead and many towns in between, simply did not behave economically or residentially in predictable fashion.

One widely evidenced finding was that it was the poor, sometimes more than the rich, who left the ghetto, and that they did so in search of jobs rather than as a reflection of having made it. Another, closely derivative finding has been that so-called second settlements often manifest first-settlement physical characteristics and are home to a floating urban poor. Simply put, as I found from looking at Harlem, just as there were factory owners living in better-built apartments on Madison Street, so were there employable painters living in what became dilapidated tenements on 105th Street and Third Avenue. So much of the 1970s urban-immigrant historiography underscored the impossibility of ascribing static patterns of immigrant economic behavior to specifically designated geographical locations. And if what was true of New York was not always applicable to all other places, certainly the Chicago-based paradigm can no longer be used to describe immigrant patterns of settlement and movement.[14]

But what of the residual strength of the Chicagoans' theory in setting the agenda for historiography on social acculturation and, out of that, for understanding of Jewish denominational history? Wirth had posited, and Sklare had accepted as true, a stereotypical view of the texture of Jewish identification downtown. Ghetto dwellers were all supposedly ill-attuned to the ways of America. Their soon-to-be-tenuous religious identities were rooted in their transplanted European past. The institutional locus of their affiliation was, of course, the ephemeral, if useful, storefront synagogue; a place toward which the Americanizing Jew would increasingly feel uncomfortable. But then again, as the Chicago theorists and Sklare have it, by the time the downtowner started losing his faith in that old-line *shul*, he was already on the way uptown. Certainly downtown could not be a place where attempts at the reconciliation of American and Jewish identities might take place. For Sklare, that synthesis would take place well beyond downtown limits. For the Chicagoans, attempts at new redefinitions of Judaism would never take place.[15]

My own contributions to this historiographical discussion suggest quite a different pattern of behavior. Just as the Lower East Side proved in reality to have been home to variegated economic classes of Jews, so was downtown a center for many shades of European and American styles of Jewish identification. Indeed, there is a significant correlation between the economic and socioreligious diversity downtown and what we will call "American time" constituting a key factor in effecting this recognizable heterogeneity. My findings raise, I believe, ultimate questions about the applicability of Wirth's work and to some extent of Sklare's as well, beyond Chicago and maybe even within Chicago.

To be sure, the type of European-style synagogue Wirth saw, and Sklare understood, did predominate on the Lower East Side, In the ephemeral storefront synagogue, Yiddish was the vernacular of discourse and conversation, and Hebrew was the language of prayer. The informality of worshipper interaction was readily observable to any passerby, for Jews looked to these synagogues not only as places where they could meet God, but, equally important, as a venue where they could communicate with their own kind as beginning Americans seeking to solve the mysteries of the new country. *Maskil* and downtown literatus Judah David Eisenstein probably evoked the contemporary scene best when he described the early days of his own synagogue, the Beth Hamedrosh Hagodol. "Our synagogue," he wrote, "maintained a socially religious atmosphere, combining piety with pleasure; they called their *shul* a *shtibl* or prayer club room; they desired to be on familiar terms with the Almighty and abhorred decorum; they wanted everyone present to join and chant the prayers, above all they scorned a regularly ordained cantor."[16]

Certainly, as Eisenstein notes, these synagogues were more than just bastions of ethnic camaraderie, for a portion of the new arrivals were quite pious. Our historian noted the existence within the synagogue of a daily *Hevrah Mishnayot* and a *Hevrah shas* (talmud study classes), and he observed that the religious reliability of the *shohet* (ritual slaughterer) employed by the *shul* was scrupulously monitored, as was the congregation's baking of matzah, Moreover, this particular synagogue was, both in 1879 and then in 1887, intimately involved in the ultimately flawed scheme to create an enduring chief rabbinate in New York, the institutionalization of transplanted European identity and piety. [17]

Wirth and Sklare would have had no difficulty with this description, for it ended with the emphasis on the final failure of the transplanted tradition. They would quickly have noted, and I would concur, that this form of European Judaism had great problems surviving the Americanization of the first generation and the rise to maturity of the second generation. Wirth and Sklare would move the Americanized away from the synagogue and up and out of the ghetto.

I am not so ready to move these Jews away and out so fast, if at all. Rather, I would have a significant cohort stay in the first-settlement area considerably longer and there engage in seemingly uncharacteristic new immigrant behavior: the attempt at positive reconciliation of Jewish and American identities.

The first signs of this behavior, which was supposed to obtain later and in second- and third-settlement areas, began in the mid-1880s and in synagogues like the now-maturing Beth Hamedrosh Hagodol. There and then three concomitant changes took place in the religious life-style of those on the road to acculturation, all related to, or reflective of, Jews' desires to feel more comfortable and respectable in the synagogue.

The earliest East European congregations looked to relocate *within* their neighborhoods, as soon as congregational finances would permit, from their storefront homes to grand landmark synagogues. This was done either by renovating former churches, by purchasing buildings previously occupied by German congregations, or by building their own new religious edifices. For itself, and as an example, Beth Hamedrosh Hagodol, which began in 1852 in an attic on Bayard Street, purchased in 1885 the Norfolk Street Baptist Church and moved into the Gothic Revival building. In these buildings of which they could be proud—they could show them off to Gentile friends; that is, of course, if they possessed such American compatriots—services were conducted largely as they had been in the past, but the demeanor of the worshippers was noticeably different. To be sure, men still sat separately from their wives, the siddur was followed without abridgement, and the time of prayers was not altered. However, gone now was the "prayer club intimacy" that had earlier characterized synagogue life. Decorum, always the first call of acculturating groups in dressing up their services, was strongly emphasized. The maintenance of order was furthered by the assignment of seats or pews. This new formality, ostensibly doing what they thought Americans did, was intensified further in the late 1880s when four of New York's landmark East European congregations embarked upon what one historian has aptly described as "the chazan craze."[18]

The same Beth Hamedrosh Hagodol people who as newly arrived immigrants had scorned cantors were ready as Americanized Jews, in the late 1880s, to pay the "well-known cantor, Israel Michaelowsky, a large salary." They did so to keep themselves competitive with their sister congregation, Kehal Adath Jeshurun, which in 1886 shocked downtown society by engaging Rev, P. Minkowsky for the then staggering sum of $5,000 per annum. The Suvwalker and Kalvarier *shuls* were also impressed, and they too went out and hired men "of foreign melodies."[19]

For Americanizing immigrants—significantly, Eisenstein called them "the young reformers"—these cantors were well worth the investment. They brought elegance and respectability to the services. Moreover, for synagogue leaders, failure to acquiesce to this new trend was tantamount to institutional suicide. They understood that immigrants on the way up socially and economically would not pray in synagogues beneath their station.

Who were these change-makers? Clearly they were Jews living downtown who had made their first money. In fully voluntaristic America, someone had to have paid the $85,000 cost of constructing Kehal Adath Jeshurun's Moorish-style sanctuary-center on Eldridge Street. And in many ways they were Americanizing. For additional evidence beyond their synagogal behavior, look to the fact that they they knew enough about this country, and felt comfortable enough with American ways, to engage the Herter Brothers, a Christian architectural firm, to construct their synagogue. Why did these Jews on the way up persist downtown? Several social, psychological, and logistical considerations must be underscored. For some, the desire to be innovators, leaders, and powerful within their own ethnic community may have kept them close to the synagogue and the sanctuary's eastern wall. For them, Americanization did not lead on a straight line to assimilation. For others, it was their sense of the incompleteness of their own social acculturation even as they were clearly doing well economically in America that kept them in proximity to their own kind. Finally, for almost all "allrightniks" there was a very basic question in the New York of the 1880s and 1890s: where, if they wanted to go, could they take their new affluence and identity?[20]

As alluded to earlier, the history of the physical growth of the metropolis in the nineteenth and twentieth centuries was quite different from Chicago's. In New York, because of real estate and transportation problems, second-settlement neighborhoods came into being quite long after large numbers of rising immigrant Jews might have had use for them. In essence, by 1890 there were East European Jews in New York well ahead of their fellows in Americanization and of their city in their residential desires. How did this happen and where did these "overachieving" new Americans come from? To answer this question requires an understanding of "American time" and of the periodization of East European Jewish migration.

Understandably, the standard periodization, which marks the start of East European migration to America at 1881 and the rise of second-generation Jewry of Russo-Polish heritage with 1921, has great merit. The pogroms of 1881 inaugurated a steady stream that brought 2.25 million Jews to these shores over the next forty years. And the 1921 date is very useful because it recognizes both the importance of government quota legislation and the social coming of age of the majority of the next generation of Americans. Still, this static dating, for all its value, obscures two historical realities that are very important to us. There were between 40,000 and 45,000

Jews of Russian-Polish descent in this country before 1881. (Their presence was noted a generation ago by Professors Jacob Rader Marcus and Salo Baron in their predating of the period to 1852 and 1863 respectively.) By 1890, these Jews had been here long enough to have arrived economically as well as to have raised a second generation that was reaching its majority. These old-new immigrants and their children might have relocated uptown and worked there for the development of a new American Judaism, if only there had been second-settlement neighborhoods ready.[21]

They would have been joined in their hegira by a second, distinct, and often overlooked cohort of East European Jews, migrants of the early 1880s who either had made it financially or had matured as Americans stronger and faster than did their fellows. Clearly these immigrant overachievers did not need the predicted or assigned amounts of American time to reach a higher level of economic and social mobility. In effect, they could not wait until the 1900s to be part of the mass aggregate of acculturating and upwardly mobile Jews so noticed by historians as the ones who created the large-scale demand for housing in New York that ultimately wrought new neighborhoods and new forms of Judaism uptown. But they had to wait on the Lower East Side, and as they did, they conducted important early experiments on the reconciliation of Judaism with America.

What became of these innovators and their experiments after the new, post-1900, second-settlement neighborhoods were constructed in New York? Sklare would have those with the new ideas on the road out toward suburbia, where the real action against assimilation was seemingly about to begin. (In so doing, of course, Sklare would render this discussion of 1890s Lower East Side activity as merely an early footnote to a later process that took place elsewhere.) Once again I am not so prepared to immediately move all Jews with new ideas away from the Lower East Side, even if they had money, social confidence, and new neighborhoods beckoning.

Religious innovation and experimentation continued to characterize downtown life; indeed it intensified, through the World War I period, even as parallel efforts obtained (predictably, for Sklare) in uptown neighborhoods. Young people's synagogues on the Lower East Side, whether they bore the name Jewish Endeavor Society (pre-1910) or Young Israel (post-1913), offered both late first- and rapidly maturing second-generation Jews the panoply of social and religious services characteristic of the "American synagogue" and normally encountered first only in the suburban area. In truth, the fundamental difference between the ghetto's American synagogues and those situated toward or in suburbia lay not in their appreciation of America but in the fidelity to Jewish tradition. Simply plotted, the degree of deviation from Jewish ceremonial, calendar, clock, and liturgical past became increasingly acute as synagogues were built farther and farther from the hub. But the commitment to offering American social options to Jews was basically the same wherever institutions were built before World War I.[22]

By whom and for whom were these synagogues built? They were built by Jews who had begun their American careers in *shtibls* in the 1870s to 1880s, and who had watched how the pressures of the new land undermined the commitment of their friends, even as they had their own problems with some aspects of the past while remaining true to the essence of the tradition. These builders were resolved, at latest by the turn of the century, to help their own generation and, most importantly, their children make their own positive reconciliations. We know from the memoir literature that positions like these were taken by Jewish innovators both in the ghetto and without, and by Jews who wanted both to occupy and to share the sanctuary's eastern wall. Sharing of the wealth and honor was more endemic to uptown. (As a subsidiary' point, it should be noted that there was opposition to their stance both downtown and uptown; a note to ponder as we look at the persistence or lack of persistence, under American time and through areas of settlement, of the oldest ways.) The synagogues downtown were built for second-generation youngsters who might be more acculturated than affluent. These second-generation Jews from poor downtown homes could find no currency, relevance, or solace in the *shtibl,* but hoped to possibly hold on to something of their Jewishness, if only they could be shown how, Their more affluent friends, maybe a classmate at

CCNY, may well have shared their sentiments, seeking (sometimes successfully) to find a synagogue to their liking uptown. Their sisters, secretaries, or stenographers may also have been attracted to these American places of worship, as they too were often estranged from the storefronts they so rarely attended. Invariably, these synagogues were ministered to by young second-generation American-trained rabbis or rabbinic interns, students at the Rabbi Isaac Elchanan Theological Seminary and the Jewish Theological Seminary of America, with careers as American Orthodox or Conservative rabbis ahead of them. In all, these synagogues were built by and for the wide diversity of economic and social shades and classes that made up the immigrant American Jewish community of East European heritage. Some of these Jews were here longer and were less successful than their fellows. Other came here later and were quicker in their rise. Some were ultimately anxious to assimilate and made their move as soon as circumstances permitted. Others held closely or loosely to a variety of Jewish traditions and expressions. Some of these Jewish life-styles were typically New York-like. But so many more had to be found both in innercity and outer-ridge communities elsewhere. All are worthy of study and characterization as the historiography of immigrant life from downtown to beyond further matures.[23]

fred.

12

A Stage in the Emergence of the Americanized Synagogue among East European Jews: 1890–1910

When in 1880, an East European immigrant Jew attended synagogue, he prayed and socialized in a *shtibl*.[1] While participating in the services there, he could step back from the new world of America into the sounds, smells, and past of his East European Jewish heritage.[2] The ethos of the earliest Russian, Polish, Rumanian or Hungarian congregations could be sensed immediately upon entry into the storefront or tenement loft. Synagogues like New York's Beth Hamedrosh Hagodol, wrote historian Judah David Eisenstein, had a "socially religious [atmosphere] . . . combin[ing] piety with pleasure . . . [with worshippers] . . . on familiar terms with the Almighty . . . abhorr[ing] decorum . . . want[ing] everyone present to join and chant the prayers; [and] above all scorn(ing) a regularly ordained cantor."[3]

As the years passed and the East European presence in most large American cities intensified, a visitor to the immigrant neighborhood, seeking out this style of religious practice among the poor, would not even have to enter the synagogue's portals to know he had found the people of Kiev or Minsk or Bialystock in America. By the mid-1880s, storefront signs bearing the names of the locality from whence their Jews had emigrated proliferated downtown. The *landsmanshaft* quality of congregations was more consciously articulated as the new Americans sought out friends from their home town with whom they might pray and socialize. Synagogue names like "Beth Hamidrash . . . ," Kehal Adath Jeshurun," or "Ohab Zedck" which did not immediately identify the country, let alone the

265

province or town of members' origins, grew less common as every shtetl, it seemed, had its sons and congregation in America.[4]

By 1920, when the child of an East European Jew attended synagogue, he or she more often than not prayed, and socialized afterwards, in an Americanized congregation. There while sitting still during services and participating when told to do so they could taste the world of their parent's religious past through familiar hymns and the unchanged basic prayers without doing violence to their growing identities as Americans. The tenor of religious life in these new commodious sanctuaries could be sensed immediately upon entry through high columned doors. They had the sights and sounds of an American institution. Worshippers were handed a uniform prayerbook and men were often requested to wear identical silk-lined skull caps. Newcomers were admonished to remain quiet during services—the cantor, and increasingly the rabbi, had to be heard—as they were escorted to their seats by ushers. Congregants particularly looked forward to those portions of the devotions that were rendered in English. If they were regular synagogue attendees, they might also enjoy the moments set aside for congregational singing or responsive reading. That too helped them feel at home in the synagogue. And all sat back and awaited the sermon offered by their rabbi trained in an American university as well as a traditional seminary.[5]

These new synagogues for a new generation of Jews have widely been seen as products of the 1920s. It has been argued that concomitant with their arrival both physically and economically in new and better-built neighborhoods towards the outskirts of their cities, Jews built stylish synagogues to combat assimilation in new heterogeneous environs. The modern service was projected as only part of its attractiveness as ancillary activities of all types for the entire family dotted the congregational bulletin board.[6]

The first, however, of these Americanized synagogues well predate the 1920s. Their origins extend back to the turn of the twentieth century and to the very immigrant neighborhoods that spawned the acculturating Jew. There and then groups of young adults of East European heritage disaffected from their father's *shtibls* started experimenting with changing synagogue life to meet their need to identify as Jews and as Americans. These innovators were helped by segments of their parent's own first generation. A new elite of East Europeans who had risen above their station sooner than most bankrolled their efforts. And they found guidance and thoughtful leadership from within the faculty and ultimately, the student-rabbis of the Jewish Theological Seminary of America. In the first decade of the new century, innovators called their organization the Jewish Endeavor Society, (JES) effectively the youth wing of the nascent Union of Orthodox Jewish Congregations of America. A similar-style group, the independent Young Israel, began operations in 1913. These synagogues were defined by their founders as Orthodox, a view borne out by the fact that men and women sat separately, the sexes partitioned by a wall or curtain known as a *mechitza;* the siddur (the unabridged, unmodified traditional prayerbook), was used; no instrumental music, like an organ that might be used in a Conservative or Reform synagogue, was allowed, and Saturday and holiday evening services began at sundown. (Non-Orthodox congregations often made alterations in the starting time of services to meet the changing work and social needs of members.) Largely out of these early initiatives evolved the ideas, techniques and personnel that would lead and direct the Americanized synagogue of the 1920s and beyond.[7]

But even the earliest fully-acculturated synagogues have in their debt one almost universally-unacknowledged precursor, the proto-American synagogue of the 1890s. Also situated on the Lower East Side, it was moving away from, but not yet free of, the world of the *shtibl* of which it was once a part. Far from "abhorring decorum," it had its problems combining "piety with pleasure" and in defining and enforcing uniformity of behavior. It reflected the sensibilities of the new affluence of its members as well as their particular stage of Americanization, but clearly did not look far enough ahead to where its next generation was heading. As a result, it served both as a worthy propaedeutic for the first generation leaders destined to work with the JES and the Young Israel as well as a foil, even more than the *shtibl,* against which post-1900 workers contrasted their efforts. For historians, its experience illuminates the complex process of immigrant decision-making in determining which aspects in traditional culture and religious ritual might be maintained and when and how other less useable elements may be jettisoned as the newcomers became more attuned and committed to patterns of American social behavior.

Several downtown congregations seemingly fit that model. There was, to begin with, Beth Hamedrosh Hagodol, Eisenstein's old synagogue. By the 1890s, after some thirty years of existence and growth, housed now in a spacious sanctuary, it had become concerned about maintaining quiet in the synagogue and had hired a melodious cantor. Quite a change from its storefront days, but most characteristic of the proto-Americanized synagogue. Interestingly enough, their efforts, which were mirrored in part by their neighboring Ohab Zedek Congregation and the Suvwalker and Kalvarier synagogues, caused Eisenstein to characterize them as "reformers." But Kehal Adath Jeshurun of Eldridge Street is the synagogue that best typifies this signal stage in the evolution of the twentieth century synagogue. (Kehal Adath Jeshurun also left us their minute books in an until-recently sealed synagogue vault; a critically important month-by-month account of the synagogue's organizational activities.) It is to that institution's history that we turn our attention.[8]

The analysis begins, through the help of its minute books, in 1890. Kehal Adath Jeshurun was then some thirty years old and downtown's first rich man's congregation was ensconced in a magnificent Moorish-style three-story edifice built just three years earlier at a cost of $85,000. The sanctuary with its hand-carved holy ark imported from Italy and the members, which included banker Sender Jarmalowski and real estate man David A. Cohen, had truly come a long way since the synagogue serviced early Rumanian immigrants who offered their devotions in rented halls on Pearl and then Allen Streets. Now on Eldridge Street, it readily displayed the first characteristic of a proto-American synagogue: an affluent membership.[9]

Laymen like Cohen or Jarmalowski or Isaac Gellis, who made his fortune as a sausage manufacturer, were large scale contributors to congregational and communal campaigns. They frequently made the synagogue long-term loans, apparently interest free, of $1,000 to $2,000 to pay off debts. And in one case, in 1891, Gellis opened up his abattoir and donated 1000 lbs. of meat for the poor of the neighborhood. Extending charity beyond their home was also on the leaders' agendas when in 1894 Kehal Adath Jeshurun opened its doors to the homeless at Passover; a nineteenth century precursor of a late twentieth century phenomenon and problem.[10]

Not all members had $1,000 or $2,000 to lend their synagogue; few families downtown could afford the $10 a month it cost to escape a cold-water tenement for "the privacy of a three- or four-room flat." Still the rank and file of cigar and cloak manufacturers, businessmen and storekeepers who applied for membership in the congregation in the 1890s apparently had, or had access to, $150–$200 to purchase a permanent seat in the sanctuary. Ownership of a seat was not only a sign of status and of belonging, it was also an investment. There was a resale value for seats as the synagogue became more famous. Acquiring a renowned cantor—as we will presently see—helped in this regard. Sometimes seats were willed to children; other times members traded up for better, more expensive seats as financial circumstances allowed. In any event, whether members had the dollars or had to borrow them, Kehal Adath Jeshurun in its heyday was clearly for Jews who as one contemporary observer might have put it, "have risen above their station."[11]

The best of Kehal Adath Jeshurun were not phenomenal entrepreneurial success stories; they had not made their money overnight. Rather they were men of substance who raised money needed to build and maintain their synagogue, and made occasional contributions to their wider community. Their stories indicate how early in the mid-nineteenth century East European Jews began arriving and started their rise in this country.

As useful as 1881, the infamous year of Russian pogroms, is as a benchmark for the beginning of East European migration, there were between forty thousand to forty-five thousand Jews of East

European descent in this country before 1881. That means that Jews arriving in the late 1860s and 1870s, like those who built Kehal Adath Jeshurun which operated first out of downtown halls, had enough time in America to emerge in the 1890s as a downtown elite on Eldridge Street. That was certainly true for Cohen, Gellis, and Jarmalowski.[12]

David A. Cohen arrived in the United States from Suvwalk, Lithuania as a lad of fourteen in 1868. Following the paths first blazed by the still dominant German-Jewish immigrants he became a traveling peddler. In his slow but steady rags to riches rise he moved from trading in tinware to clothes manufacturing. By the 1890s he was president of Gold and Cohen Inc. realtors on Lower Broadway.[13]

Isaac Gellis came to these shores a year after Cohen as a young man of nineteen. A native of Mennel, Russia, and a butcher by trade, he became "a pioneer in the manufacturing of kosher provisions" on Henry Street on the Lower East Side.[14]

Sender Jarmalowski arrived just a few years later than his friends and started out somewhat ahead of most East European immigrants. But in his case too, amassing a fortune took not only considerable effort but also time. Born in 1841 in Grajewo, Poland, he left his yeshiva and home as a boy to seek his fortune in the west. His first stop was Hamburg, Germany, where he worked in banking and as a ticket agent for steamship lines crossing the North Atlantic to Castle Garden. In 1873, he apparently took note and inspiration from his employers' advertising and bought his own way to America. Upon arrival in New York, he opened a small banking concern on Canal Street—the first of its kind by an East European. It was not until the beginning of the twentieth century, however, that Jarmalowski, then in both real estate and banking became renowned for his wealth. Eisenstein, who was related to Jarmalowski through marriage, wrote that the "word on the street was that Jarmalowski was worth over three million dollars."[15]

But were these leaders, and their fellow congregants as Americanized as they were affluent? As members of a proto-American synagogue, they would be by definition considerably more attuned to this country than *landsmanshaft* Jews and somewhat less than the Endeavorers, the Young Israel and other later fully-Americanized congregations. Their synagogue structure and congregational ambience reflected their being in the midst of cultural change.

There was, to begin with, their studied ambivalence as to what constituted proper behavior within the sanctuary. As an Americanizing congregation, it made every effort at least leaders did—to effect quiet during services. The unarticulated but constant fear which they shared with all fully Americanized congregations was that Christians might pass the synagogue and witness Jews behaving in an Oriental manner. (*Landsmanshaft* Jews, on the other hand, were not yet concerned that they were acting less than Occidentally.) Accordingly, trustees at Kehal Adath Jeshurun were engaged to monitor who entered or left the sanctuary: admission was sometimes reserved for "respectable people." Ushers were installed to maintain order in the aisle. Spittoons were purchased to help keep the sanctuary clean in response to that most unsightly of habits. And an elaborate system of fines was drawn up for members who failed to heed the leaders' admonitions about idle conversation. All these measures frequently failed to still Jews in prayer or even to quell patently riotous behavior when controversies stirred the congregation.[16]

There is an unusually instructive and entertaining short vignette in the minutes of 1897 describing in sparse, clipped terms one such untoward occurrence.

> A complaint was received against Avrohom Wallenstein that during evening services of Sukkoth [Tabernacles], he struck a well-known person who regularly prays in our midst. Resolved, that he is no longer to pray in our Beit Hamidrash [literally "house of study, in this case, daily prayer meeting room] or in our Shul [main sanctuary]. The secretary is to write him a letter.[17]

Apparently, fisticuffs were frequent in the synagogue, although congregational summary justice, as in this case, was somewhat unusual. When David Cohen heard about the Wallenstein case, he became immediately exercised because when he "was gravely insulted in our synagogue . . . [when] I was president of the congregation . . . not a single officer uttered a word regarding this."[18]

Cohen notwithstanding—he resigned in protest only to return shortly—other synagogue leaders perceived themselves as appropriately dismayed about breaks in order. But in truth, they themselves contributed to commotion in synagogue life by their failure to move against the *schnoddering* system of fund raising. Americanized congregations understood that quieting the habitual gossiper—not to mention showing the mean and combative to the door—would not insure the decorous solemnity they desired if the prayers and the reading of the Torah were frequently interrupted by the auctioning off of synagogue honors or the solicitation of funds from honorees. Leaders of *landsmanshaft* synagogues did not care. In their already noisy rooms, interruptions for public announcements of gifts and honors was a frequent and time-honored fund-raising practice. For itself and by definition, the proto-American synagogue had not fully internalized the Americanized approach which disdained *schnoddering*. The minutes from 1896 indicate members were obliged to be called to the Torah—a basic synagogue honor—at least three times a year and donate at least $4.00.[19] Jews often discharged their duties with dignity and propriety. But sometimes, as in the case of Israel David Gutman's "disturbance of the peace at the Bima [reader's desk] on the Sabbath," the delays and indignities caused by the calling out of donations led to quarrels among worshippers.

Apparently on that fateful Saturday in January 1899 as the Torah reading came to a close, Gutman was given the honor of raising the Torah from the reader's desk (for all to see). However, as was customary, before he could fulfill his duty, he had to wait for the calling out of offerings and the recitation of prayers on behalf of those who had been called previously to the Torah or for the sick in the congregation. That particular Sabbath, a bar mitzvah boy and a bridegroom had been previously called up. Their families wished to make offerings in their honor, and there were the regulars who wanted prayers made for the ill. Apparently the boy's and the bridegroom's families "picked a quarrel" with each other (over who would go first?). While cooler heads were trying to calm things Gutman broke with protocol and raised the Torah before any offerings were made.

Was the hot-tempered Gutman simply impatient with proceedings that Sabbath? Did he have his own grievances against the bridegroom or the bar mitzvah's family? Or was he a rebel against the entire *schnoddering* scene? The minutes are silent on his specific motivation. What they do tell us is that the synagogue leaders were aghast. In addition to taking Jewish law into his own hands by raising the Torah before the appropriate time, Gutman had also "caused the shul a few dollars in damages." No further offerings could be made that morning. When asked by the president the reason for his impetuous act, Gutman reportedly "answered the president with the greatest rudeness and with the basest swear words which cannot even be written down on paper." Fearing riot, "because among so many people, the worst can happen," the president remained silent. Remarkably, no action was taken against the ill-mannered member. The minutes only report seemingly that "the congregation can certainly not expect any great honor to result from this."[20]

Kehal Adath Jeshurun really did not learn from that incident. The members may have perceived the fight as an aberration—although there had been fights comparable to that one before—and fund-raising through *schnoddering* was a long-standing tool, a valued tradition they were loathe to undermine. It would not be until 1915 that the synagogue would move towards doing away with it by limiting the time and number of offerings acceptable and determining that "if someone has a bar-mitzvah it must be announced one month before to the sexton whether he is requesting [the privilege of designating honorees] for the entire Sabbath or only the Maftir" (the concluding portion of the weekly Torah reading). The last decision may have gone a long way towards reducing commotion at the reader's desk.[21]

Ultimately however, proto-American congregations like Kehal Adath Jeshurun placed their drive for solemnity—not to mention, class and fundraising—on the prayer-shawled shoulders of their well-paid cantor. They reasoned that the "respectable people" who laid down their hard-earned dollars to be in the pews—and to be seen in the sanctuary, as they imagined "real" Americans did—would be sure to behave appropriately when the Rev. Pinchas Minkowsky or the Rev. Yitschok Herlands etc., accompanied by their choirs, appeared in the pulpit. Quiet would be a return on the worshippers' investment since tickets were sold for sabbaths and holidays year round, not just for the High Holidays as is the custom in most congregations today. For congregational leadership it was a decision of no small moment, when they moved to bring in "a regularly ordained cantor." The significance or power of the cantor—he challenged the *schnoddering* system and the sale of permanent seats as *the* way to raise funds and to project synagogue status—was sometimes evident in the quality of the contract he extracted from the landmark congregation. At the very height of the cantor craze during the late 1880s and early 1890s, when virtuosi manned the altars all over the neighborhood in open competition for the dollar, Pinchas Minkowsky, clearly having the upper hand over the trustees, received the following very favorable terms from Kehal Adath Jeshurun. A five year contract guaranteed him $2,500 per annum above and beyond whatever costs Kehal Adath Jeshurun incurred in helping recruit his choir. To gain his services, the congregation agreed to buy out his contract from his former synagogue in Odessa at the cost of 1,000 rubles. Kehal Adath Jeshurun also reimbursed the cantor for both his own travel expenses and those of his wife and children. And musicians of his stature and their families did not travel in steerage. They traveled "from Odessa to Brehmen or to Hamburg, by second class railroad and by first class ship from Hamburg and second class from Brehmen." To set themselves up in an apartment (surely not a tenement), the congregation "provide[d] the sum of $300 for household goods." Finally, Minkowsky was granted six weeks vacation, wherein he could appear as a guest cantor elsewhere, if he so chose, or simply rest up for the busy season of the High Holidays.[23]

Minkowsky's successors did not do nearly as well with the trustees. The thirteen cantors from 1892 to 1910 certainly did not demand a yearly bonus of $500 as Minkowsky did, an additional honorarium which he sometimes actually received. As the frenzied demand for cantors subsided considerably in 1893, $500 was closer to the annual salary a good downtown cantor could expect. Still, whatever the going rate, Kehal Adath Jeshurun remained competitive. As late as 1897 they found themselves in a struggle with Congregation Agudath Achim Krakover over the services of a Cantor Saperstein. Over the years, the Cantor's Committee spent considerable time and effort auditioning cantors, offering candidates for congregational election, negotiating contracts with them and their choirs, monitoring their performance in the pulpit, calling them to task for malfeasance in office and discharging incumbents, and conducting searches. A proto-American synagogue had to have the best possible performer money could buy. The dignity, call it the honor, of its American status-seeking congregants depended on it.[24]

With it all, a cantor's moodiness and the congregational leadership's testiness could also break the solemn, formal mood all were ostensibly trying to create. In August 1901, Cantor Avrohom Menovitch arrived late to services and found that the congregation had designated a lay leader to begin the recitations without him. Ready to take over, Menovitch discovered, not once but twice, that the "cantor" would not yield to him. It was not until the beginning of the Sabbath Additional Prayers *(Musaf)* that the synagogue officials "honored the cantor with leading the prayer service." Clearly annoyed, Menovitch attempted to even the score. Instead of praying, with his accustomed panache, "the Blessing for the New Month," a cantorial showpiece, Menovitch simply rattled off the prayers "quickly and carelessly and it was an embarrassment to the brothers." The ensuing "big uproar among the brothers" led to a special meeting in which the Cantor asked "the congregation's pardon," promising "that in the future such a thing will not happen again."[25] Where was The rabbi through all this noise, *schnoddering*, and commotion? Kehal Adath Jeshurun had no ordained, official spiritual leader either in the wings or up front throughout its heyday (1887–1915). If and when the congregants looked for guidance, they contented themselves with two *maggidim* (itinerant preachers) who were hired (1905–07, 1907–1910) more to entertain than to lead. Moreover, these unheeded guides were strictly bound by the controls placed upon them by lay authorities, who made clear by their contracts how powerless they wanted a rabbi to be. In clearly spelling out who ruled the *shul*, this quintessential proto-American congregation adumbrated the changing relationship in America between rabbi and immigrant.

Kehal Adath Jeshurun was not the first downtown congregation without a rabbi. But for most rabbiless *shtibls*, it was a question of economics rather than a stand against authority. In the *shtibl*, it was the cantor that they did not want. Other proto-American congregations installed rabbis in their pulpits; some even engaged renowned sages as their leaders, even if they did not always or even regularly follow his strictures. The First Hungarian-American Congregation Ohab Zedek (established 1873) was home to Rabbi Dr. Philip Hillel Klein; Beth Hamedrosh Hagodol, as it got on its feet, brought into its pulpit a series of important rabbis, including Rabbi Abraham Ash, and later, Rabbi Shlomo Elchanan Jaffe. Notably, that oldest East European synagogue was the seat of Rabbi Jacob Joseph's administration when he served as Chief Rabbi of New York (1887–1902).[26]

Kehal Adath Jeshurun did not oppose Rabbi Joseph's implied suzerainty over all religious Jewry. They agreed to the principle that he was supposed to control the upgrading of kosher food supervision, lead in encouraging greater observance of the Sabbath and inspire greater Jewish commitment to religious education, among his various communal functions. Indeed, Jarmalowski was on the selection committee which recruited the sage from Vilna. The congregation was one of the fifteen congregations which organized the Association of American Orthodox Hebrew Congregations that conducted the search. It may be supposed that this synagogue's leaders rendered the proper formal respect to the leader as he strode by or into a pulpit, although Rabbi Joseph spoke but once at their synagogue (at a funeral) during his checkered fifteen year tenure downtown.[27]

But in many ways, the Eldridge Street congregation displayed a decided independence from rabbinic authority. Their method of operation was to ignore or circumvent Rabbi Joseph's decrees rather than to confront or dismiss them. In 1891, Rabbi Joseph, sincerely anxious to insure the kashruth of matzahs baked for the Passover, decreed that synagogues "post no circulars . . . relating to Passover [i.e., bakery ads for their products] unless his name is affixed." Kehal Adath Jeshurun congregants were also concerned that members eat the right foods on the holiday. But they were unwilling to cede to Rabbi Joseph the power to determine from which bakeries Jews should buy. Their solution was to declare that no circulars at all would be posted that year "regardless of whether or not they have a kashruth certificate from a rabbi." Later on, the congregation subtly put additional distance between itself and Rabbi Jacob Joseph when it voted to monitor closely the prices charged for matzah under the Chief Rabbi's control. If it should be determined that the costs were too high, "the congregation should bake the matzahs at their own expense."[28]

For Kehal Adath Jeshurun members, their distance from rabbinic authority did not reflect an underlying desire to break with Jewish law They simply felt that in America, the laity made the decisions in ecclesiastical as well as in secular matters This attitude, or arrogance, was surely evident in 1905, when the congregation finally hired a *maggid* to complement its cantor. Their interest was in hiring a sermon giver not a rabbi, a bombastic, pyrogenic homiletician, not a guide on Jewish practice or law.

The newcomer was charged with offering a daily Torah discourse to the regulars who attended afternoon-evening services. More importantly, he was obliged to offer a major presentation every Sabbath, holiday and Sunday, and to make himself available "to preach when an important event occurs for the benefit of our congregation " In an era and society that valued highly the well delivered spoken word a *maggid's* performance was judged on his ability to move his audience to tears by his admonitions, to anger by his polemics, and to laughter by his asides The men in the pews and their wives in the balcony wanted the catharsis skilled forensics could induce. Just as they liked to sit back and enjoy the performances of the cantors, so they were ready to listen and discuss later what the preacher had to say. How much real thought they gave to following the pulpit message offered from on high was another matter entirely.[29]

Synagogue trustees had their own barometers for measuring a *maggid's* performance: they sold tickets for his pulpit extravangances, particularly for his Sunday show—the true day of rest for downtown masses—and they could judge by their ticket sales how well they were doing. Lay leaders made it clear that although preaching was the only function desired of the *maggid,* they would determine the subjects he could address. Kehal Adath Jeshurun's 1905 contract with Rabbi Moshe Mordecai Rivkind specified that "the maggid is not permitted to bring up matters pertaining to the state without the permission of the president, . . . nor to insult any persons in his lecture." The synagogue's contract with Rivkind's successor, Rabbi Binyamin Meir Levy specified that "if the maggid wishes to discuss political matters, he is to ask the president."[30]

The synagogue also made it clear to the *maggid* that he was their employee when they dictated that he "may not issue any [writs of] divorce without the permission of the president," that "all charities received at a sermon or eulogy belong to the shul and the maggid has no claims to them," and that "in his private business matters, such as kashruth certification . . . he is not to use his title as rabbi of the shul." The final element, as will be noted soon, was of no small moment to Rabbi Rivkind. It undercut his ability to project his authority—and to receive honoraria—outside of Eldridge Street itself.[31]

Rabbi Rivkind signed the contract, for an annual salary of $300—considerably less than the cantor—but he acted outside the synagogue as if he was in fact in charge at home. The issue of the *maggid's* independence came to a head in December, 1906 when the trustees received a troubling note from "representatives of all three Orthodox synagogues in Paterson, New Jersey." Apparently, to standardize kashruth regulation in their town, a committee of "ten well-known rabbis" was formed to oversee proper slaughtering and preparation of meats. These officials proceeded to render a judgment "regarding Kashruth and ritual slaughters" that dismayed "a party of socialists." Maybe they were socialists or maybe they were simply Jews unhappy with the ruling. In any event, Rivkind was brought to town and paid $20 to declare on his authority as "the greatest

Rabbi from Eldridge Street Shul and the United States . . . that the halachic [Jewish legal] ruling of the ten rabbis was null and void, because they are all good-for-nothing scoundrels and other base expressions regarding the rabbis." The lay leadership back home on the Lower East Side was aghast at this arrogation of status and authority. In the presence of the Paterson Committee, Rivkind was asked to explain how he could have spoken out "without asking or obtaining permission of the president." Although certainly in violation of his contract, Rivkind did not back down. He answered that "neither the president, nor anyone else could tell [me] how to conduct [myself] as a rabbi. I am a rabbi and I remain a rabbi. As of today, I am resigning as rabbi of your congregation."[32]

There is no discussion of any attempt to keep him save a notation, one month later, of a battle with Rivkind before a rabbinical court, possibly over severance issues. In April, 1907, Kehal Adath Jeshurun moved on to its next *maggid*, Rabbi Levy, who was offered the same or worse terms as Rivkind. Levy apparently kept to his business of preaching and was probably very good He stayed three years, even receiving a raise in 1909, and a small rental increase a year later. He fulfilled the needs and fit the tastes of his constituents until congregational tastes apparently changed, for beginning again in 1910 Kehal Adath Jeshurun did without a *maggid*. Nevertheless, he was remembered warmly. When he died suddenly in 1914, it was "resolved that a notice be placed in the *Tageblatt* and a decision will be made at the next trustees meeting as to a date for a eulogy." For that final tribute they probably had to engage a guest *maggid* if lay leadership preferred not to deliver it.[33]

Kehal Adath Jeshurun people were, for the most part, happy, content and surely in control of their synagogue. They had taken some bold steps away from the ambience sociology and governance patterns of the Old World synagogue and its New World transplant, the *landsmanshaft* synagogue, even if, as noted previously, they still had a way to go—whether it was their handling of decorum or their fund-raising procedures—to be truly part of the Americanized Jewish religious scene. But clearly, when at its best, this proto-American congregation fulfilled two of the prime functions so often identified with—and in effect showed the way for—its fully Americanized descendent. Speaking to upwardly mobile American Jews, the proto-American congregation suggested that the synagogues could be a showcase of their affluence and sense of American values and techniques, a place their hypothetical Gentile friends could visit and admire. It also could be flexible and amenable to change in the way Jewish ritual and prayer proceeded and in the way synagogue life was ruled. Though none of the lay leaders who loved to sit back and listen to a cantor or a *maggid* ever suggested that something might be amiss with the way the Jewish law ordered the services, theirs was the mind-set later so commonly seen in Conservative, Reform and Orthodox synagogues. Time spent in prayer, no matter how reverent one's demeanor, was to be joyfully savored. Worshippers were, in a word, to be entertained, and their social and personal needs strictly accommodated. That approach subsequently offered Judaism the best chance of attracting the drifting next generation of American-born Jews back to an interest in religion.

But as only a prototype of the Americanized synagogue, Kehal Adath Jeshurun was remarkably not in touch, however, with that essential, overriding reason for change. The immigrant leaders of the synagogue did little to insure that future generations would feel the same impulses towards the *shul*. Ironically, the affluent bought permanent seats for, or willed them to, their children. But they did not work to see that their descendents would want to use their pews. It was here, in their myopia towards the needs of their youngsters, even more than in their inability to always maintain order—later synagogues also had these problems, sans fisticuffs—that Kehal Adath Jeshurun, behaved still like a *landsmanshaft* synagogue, and was thus less than a sure home for the next generation of Jews.

In the approach towards education, Kehal Adath Jeshurun's congregation had a warm spot in their charitable hearts for downtown schools. They frequently contributed to yeshivas and talmud torahs. and held appeals during services for the fledgling Yeshiva Etz Chaim in 1891. Some years later they would permit students from Yeshiva Etz Chaim "to study in their Beit Hamidrash." They frequently bought tickets for charity picnics and the like for the more American-style Machzikei and Montefiore Talmud Torahs. And once they even entertained opening up the synagogue to an outside group "once a week in order to meet for the purpose of giving children religious instruction." But not until 1901 did the congregation get around to "discuss[ing] the founding of a Talmud Torah . . . for the children of members [as] a good thing for Judaism and also a benefit for our congregation." These deliberations led ultimately to the establishment of a small school, but apparently there was less than great enthusiasm for the endeavor. The minutes of 1903 note that the future of the school was debated and "it was decided in the meantime, until the next meeting to keep only two teachers and to resolve the matter at the next meeting." At that subsequent gathering, "the congregation withdrew its plan to spend shul monies." It was left to the two teachers "to continue classes, at their own expense for six months" (possibly charging tuition themselves?). There was but one further discussion of education within the synagogue. In 1907 a committee was established to explore the propriety of opening "once again . . . a children's school and to work out plans for its location."[34]

Significantly, this shortsightedness was not lost on those Endeavorers whose emphasis were heavily on education for the next generation. In fact, they were sometimes dismayed and disturbed that the selfishness or enjoyment—seeking of downtown synagogue leaders undermined their own efforts. One outspoken Endeavorer, writing in 1903, explained that their young, and not-yet-affluent cohorts frequently sought out space from Kehal Adath Jeshurun and its sister landmark synagogues for their major Saturday afternoon services. With no buildings of their own, they looked at those hours approaching sundown, particularly during the long days of summer, as the best time to attract workers, who labored on the Sabbath, for prayers and comraderie. Unfortunately for them, afternoon-evening was also prime time for the *maggidim* and the modern educators lost out.

Services were successful but unfortunately a *maggid* usually appeared on the scene followed by his hosts and naturally the services had to make room for the Yiddish preachers.[35]

Innovators working on behalf of the next generation would have to look for help beyond the synagogues themselves to individual bene-factors who could see past the enjoyment of their seats "near the Eastern wall," to sponsor synagogues which were quieter, more American and more responsive than their own. Jarmalowski was one such member. In 1887, it will be recalled, he cooperated with the Association of American Orthodox Hebrew Congregations in bringing an Eastern Europe Chief Rabbi to America. By 1897, he was ready to join hands with the fully American Orthodox Union in sponsoring the Union including its Endeavorer youth division. In so doing he took that fundamental step beyond his peers who were comfortable with the new religious world within which they were living, but were not yet fully attuned to the future challenges facing Jews in this country.

In sum, Kehal Adath Jeshurun, our emblematic proto-American synagogue of the 1890s-early twentieth century, was a half-way house for American Judaism as it evolved from exponent of East European traditions and culture to reflector of this country's social patterns and the needs of the acculturated. Like the *landsmanshaft* synagogue, it was committed to meeting the socio-religious wants of that first generation who intially knew only of past European tradi-tions. But different from the East European transplant, it recognized and was willing to respond to the changes American mores were making upon the life-style, economic profile and self-definition of their advancing first-generation constituents. It was, in that impor-tant respect, not unlike the fully-Americanized synagogue of the future. But as a half-way house it was less than what was needed, because it was for only one generation. The synagogue failed to directly and comprehensively address the even more complicated decisions second-generation Jews were making in divining what aspects of their ethnic past might survive within their American future. The proto-American synagogue's myopia in reading the needs of first generation Jews so well but missing those of their children were surely noted by the individuals who would shepherd twentieth-century American Judaism to full maturity. They would learn from this signal omission. The direct link between the proto-American synagogue of the 1890s–1910s to the American synagogue of inter-war years was extended when forward-thinking people like Jarmalowski went beyond their desire for convenience to active commitment through educational programming to the younger generation. Through their altruism and benefactions they buttressed the work of the young rabbis and teachers-in-training downtown and helped the fully-Americanized synagogue become a reality. [36]

13

Consensus Building and Conflict over Creating the Young People's Synagogue of the Lower East Side

It was a moment of both satisfaction and expectation for Elias L. Solomon when, on February 3, 1904, he rose at a public meeting of the New York Board of Jewish Ministers to report on the activities of the Jewish Endeavor Society (JES). Just two days earlier, "the movement for the erection of a Young People's synagogue on the lower East Side" had taken a major stride forward when a conference that he had chaired, organized by the Endeavorers, had unanimously resolved "that the service they desired was an orthodox one, with the sermon and some prayers in English, and with the Singer Prayer Book."

This had been no mean feat for the twenty-five-year-old, Vilna-born, CCNY-educated, Jewish Theological Seminary student and the coterie of classmates he led. Many individuals and organizations downtown were concerned that second-generation Jews, born in this country, were rapidly drifting away from synagogue life and basic Jewish commitments. He and his friends had convinced the seemingly disparate and often competitive thirty-five organizations in attendance, including the immigrant Congregation Agudath Achim Cracow, the Zionist Council of Greater New York, the New Era Club of the Educational Alliance, the Young People's Auxiliary of the Machzikei Talmud Torah, and the Reform Emanu-El Brotherhood that JES's approach to synagogue life had the best chance of attracting back to Judaism "the well-intentioned young man and woman reared in this city with American ideas and American views [repelled by] the various existing shules . . . suitable only for the old generation." Solomon was now advancing one step further his cause of "recall[ing] . . . indifferent Jewry to their ancestral faith." He was seeking interdenominational approbation from New York's most prestigious Americanized Jewish clergy. These respected leaders were, not incidentally, the rabbis of uptown's best-known philanthropists, the Jews most capable of granting Endeavorer efforts the consistent financial support they required.[1]

As Solomon, wary of opponents, surveyed the room in search of allies, he might have caught the eye of Seminary president Solomon Schechter and JTS executive committee member Simon M. Roeder. Concerned that he present himself well before these eminences, he was confident of their support because the Jewish Endeavor Society had the deepest of ties to the Seminary. Bernard Drachman, professor of Bible, Hebrew grammar, and Codes, would later assert that the JES was "the fruit of my efforts . . . to influence the students of the Seminary and other youths and maidens in the same period of life, to organize a movement for the winning of adolescents for Traditional Judaism." Whatever Drachman's input, it is clear that Seminary students, both men and women, had been the backbone of the Society since its founding in 1900.[2]

Solomon could count among his closest male associates JES founders and board members rabbis Charles Kauvar, Phineas Israeli, Herman Abramowitz, and Mordecai M. Kaplan, all recent graduates of the Seminary rabbinical school. Also, Solomon was not unmindful of the contributions of Seminary Teacher's Course students Ida Mearson, Irene Stern, and Frances D. Lunevsky to Endeavorer educational programs. Mearson, chairman in 1904 of the JES Religious Schools Committee, had been principal for two years of Endeavorer Religious School for Children #1 on Chrystie Street. Likewise, Stern was principal of School #4 on Lexington Avenue in Harlem, while Lunevsky was JES secretary to the board. Seminary linkage to the Endeavorers was further confirmed when one or another Seminary leader—Drachman, Louis Ginzberg, Israel Friedlaender, or Schechter himself—lectured to their group. Just two days earlier, Joseph Mayer Asher, the Seminary professor of homiletics, had given Solomon's

JES conferees heartening "words of encouragement" when their proceedings had come to an end.[3]

Confident that Schechter and Roeder would be proud of his manner and diction (the Russian-born, Jerusalem-reared Solomon had worked hard under JTS tutor of elocution Grenville Kleiser to speak an unaccented English), Solomon shifted his gaze to senior rabbis of whose support he was far less assured. Samuel Schulman and Maurice H. Harris were spiritual leaders of Temple Beth-El of Fifth Avenue and Temple Israel of Harlem, respectively, both staunch advocates of classical Reform Judaism. Would they acquiesce to the Board of Ministers projecting an American Orthodox service as the way to reach the next generation of Jews?[4]

Solomon did more than merely hope that they would. In a nuanced letter to the editor of the *American Hebrew*, published just before the February 3 meeting, he had taken pains to reach out to potential supporters in formulating a definition of JES activities that would suggest the commonalities between Orthodoxy and Reform. In arguing the merits of an "orderly, dignified [Orthodox] service, accompanied by congregational singing and an English sermon," he had said that "the *Orthodox* young people represented by the Jewish Endeavor Society have for the last four years been clamoring for a *properly reformed service*" (emphasis mine). He had suggested that "given a service, orderly, dignified, accompanied by congregational singing and an English sermon, what objections can even the Reformers raise against it?"[5]

Looking further around the room on February 3, 1904, Solomon would have seen two of New York's most renowned Jewish communal workers, Lillian Wald of the Henry Street Settlement and Henry Moskowitz of the downtown branch of the Ethical Culture Society. Though Solomon may have mused that these two old hands at social work practice should have been impressed with the acumen and perspicacity of a young man able to bring together thirty-five disparate groups, he had to have wondered what interest and support these secularized Jews would manifest for a traditional Jewish initiative.

Solomon's eyes narrowed as his stare met that of his certain opponent in the room, Rabbi Joseph Silverman of Temple Emanu-El. Just six weeks earlier, Silverman had begun offering a decidedly Reform religious alternative to "the young men and women of the East Side [who are] . . . repelled rather than attracted by the antiquated mode of life led by their orthodox parents." His English-language services, held at his newly established Emanu-El Brotherhood on East Fifth Street, had featured an organ and a choir and utilized the Union Prayer Book. Although soon Silverman had substituted the Singer (English-Hebrew) siddur for the Union Prayer Book and had eliminated the organ and choir, reportedly in response to downtown criticism, Solomon perceived those modifications as merely tactical retreats. He was also not impressed that a lay leader of the Emanu-El Brotherhood, a Mr. J. Levinson, had signed Monday's conference memorandum. Solomon suspected that a push for Reform hegemony in youth religious work was still in the offing, and he was unconvinced that Emanu-El's rabbi would countenance an established Orthodox ritual for this neighborhood-wide intiative.[6]

To Solomon's great pleasure, his remarks were well received by the Board of Ministers meeting. Speaker after speaker, from Schechter to Wald to Moskowitz, "with a single exception," rose to support Solomon's point of view. Wald even brought words of support for the effort from "Christian ministers [who] had told her of the need of a religious center to which they might direct persons who come under their observation." That unsolicited source of backing probably surprised the representatives in attendance from the Union of Orthodox Jewish Congregations. These Orthodox Jews, who wanted backing for their antimissionary efforts against downtown Christian social groups that did not refer Jewish clients to Jewish organizations, would be looking for disingenuous ulterior motives in that statement. Despite JES's high profile against Christian activities in the ghetto, Solomon was undoubtedly gratified that Wald's remarks only raised a few eyebrows and did not divert discussion from the announced topic. At evening's close it was resolved that because the need for "religious centers or settlements" was a real one, "one or more should be started under the Board of Ministers and that therein the Jewish Endeavor Society and other bodies should find fields for their activities." Rabbi Silverman was the sole dissenting voice. As anticipated, he rose to offer a motion in "favor of a Reform Synagogue." His move, seconded only "as a matter of courtesy," was voted down unanimously.[7]

Although none of the assembled identified this meeting as the landmark it was, a consensus was reached in outline on an approach to worship acceptable to almost all Americanized religious elements for answering the needs of second-generation East European Jews; the dissenting voices in a seemingly unified opinion on how to address a basic religious problem came from the newly-arrived East European Orthodox rabbinate identified with the Agudath ha-Rabbanim (Union of Orthodox Rabbis of the United States and Canada) and one lone voice in the Reform camp.

Emerging from that meeting, Solomon had good reason to trust that the imprimatur of this alliance would afford the Endeavorers critically necessary financial support. Simultaneously he had to have wondered if this interdenominational agreement would help or hinder the efforts of the JES to sell its modern synagogue concept to suspicious immigrant elements downtown. Truth be told, in JES's four years of existence, its services had been received with mixed reviews on the streets of the Lower East Side.

There were, to be sure, synagogues like Congregation Shaare Zedek of Henry Street and "the Norfolk Street" Synagogue (possibly Beth Hamedrosh Hagodol, but more likely Congregation Ohab Zedek) that periodically opened their doors to JES services and classes. In every instance, these relationships had not long endured. To that date, the JES had been turned away, not because downtowners questioned or rejected its religious philosophy, but rather because of its inability to compete with the *maggidim* (itinerant preachers) who rented the limited meeting space available in downtown synagogues. Arnold Eiseman, Endeavorer board member and Solomon's JTS classmate, explained his group's dilemma: "The services were successful but, unfortunately, . . . a 'maggid' usually appeared on the scene followed by his hosts and naturally the services had to . . . make room for the Yiddish preacher."

At the Monday conference, a trustee of the Pitt Street Congregation Agudath Achim Cracow, a Mr. Leinkram, offered that synagogue's *beth midrash* to the JES. The offer might have reassured Solomon that now the community would be more supportive, but he also had to have known that with the Reformers on board, it was essential for the JES to project fidelity to Orthodoxy if it was to gain the confidence of downtown. Potential critics were certainly watching.[8]

One immigrant Yiddish press editorialist may have been giving vent to this wariness when he wrote that "the public will want to know the character of the service [and] the tendency of the resident minister who is to conduct the services and preside over the activities." While this moderate writer was not *a priori* about to withhold "support for the People's Synagogue Association," he did assert that "it will have to refrain from giving offense to the Orthodox tastes and susceptibilities on the East Side and refrain also from any attempt to substitute old forms for new."[9]

Accordingly, the Endeavorers took care in addressing the knotty question of how much English could be used in the service without violating Orthodox strictures (and, at the same time, without undermining their interdenominational coalition). While Solomon and his group advocated the need for an English-language sermon and a Hebrew-English siddur, they also emphasized that they did not "care to put the stamp of approval on the ignorance of the Hebrew language . . . by conducting services in English." While that statement did not fully close off the possibility that some of the prayers might be in the vernacular, at least the core of the service would be in Hebrew. Responding to doubts concerning the intelligibility of the service to those with minimal Jewish or Hebraic backgrounds, the Endeavorers offered to hold classes to help "young people acquire sufficient knowledge . . . to follow the services." "One need not be a profound Hebrew scholar," they averred, "to participate in the Orthodox service. "[10]

Not incidentally, this stance did not sit well with the editors of the *American Hebrew*, a publication read by many of the JES's uptown coalition partners. The *American Hebrew* openly feared that the

Endeavorers' approach "of retaining Hebrew as the backbone of the service" would fail to serve the religious needs of their second-generation constituency. "The great multitude of young people downtown never enter a synagogue because . . . they know nothing of it." On a more philosophical tack, the editors of the *American Hebrew* entered the longstanding debate over the place of the vernacular in services by arguing that "sufficient Hebrew to enable a person to *follow* [emphasis theirs] the service does not appeal to us; some of the service must reach the heart and that is only possible when the language of prayer is understandable to the person."[11]

The Endeavorers were soon to find that their position was actually more traditional than that of at least one outspoken lay leader of the Orthodox Union. (Like the Seminary, the Orthodox Union had longstanding ties with the JES.) Lewis N. Dembitz, Orthodox Union vice-president, entered the fray with the remark that "on the language question . . . both of you [the *American Hebrew* and the Endeavorers] are wrong." But as he developed his rambling thoughts, it became clear that he was less sympathetic to the JES than to their interlocutors. Dembitz dismissed the objection that "putting any of the *obligatory parts* [emphasis mine] of the ritual in English. . . would drive off the parents of the young folks entirely." He evoked as his prooftext for a minimal use of English in the service "the express words of the Mishna (*Sota,* vii:1) that the Prayer and the 'Shema' is lawful in any language." But he was not opposed to a possible alternative direction more akin to JES's. "Perhaps," he wrote, with the needs of the older generation in mind, "the matter might be compromised by only having a Methurgeman [translator] for the prophetic lessons and some parts of the Sedrah and by singing some English hymns." Dembitz's advice was to let "the matter take shape according to the tastes and desires of those who attend the services." If all could not agree on every detail for a single Orthodox service, he concluded, "downtown is big enough for two or three such synagogues."[12]

The JES's intention to adhere to a strict version of Orthodoxy—stricter than Dembitz's—was often lost on downtown's older generation and its rabbis, who did not appreciate the delicacy of the JES stance. Years after his involvement with the JES, Mordecai M.

Kaplan would remember the unhappiness of an immigrant father who chastised his son for attending Endeavorer Saturday afternoon services in the Henry Street Synagogue. "You are a *shaigetz* [for attending], " the father apparently said, "and Kaplan is a bigger *shaigetz* for conducting the prayers." The "orderly fashion" of the prayers, Kaplan allowed, had in itself rendered the JES "treif."[13]

Rabbi Jacob David Willowski must have seen Endeavorer sensitivities on the use of English as a meaningless gesture, in no way protective of the sanctity of Orthodox tradition. This well-known and outspoken East European *rov*, the Agudath ha-Rabbanim's *zekan ha-rabbanim* (senior rabbi), remonstrated against the use of English even in sermons, not to mention in the prayers. In his *She'elot u-Teshubot Bet Ridbaz*, he derided such homiletics as containing "no guidance for the Jewish people, . . . mak[ing] them like the rest of the nations . . . [and] open[ing] the gates leading to . . . Reform Judaism. "[14]

The Agudath ha-Rabbanim, according to at least one reputable source, may have been in less than full concurrence with the senior rabbi's perspective. Later in 1904, the *Yiddishes Tageblatt* pilloried the European rabbis for "declaring as blasphemous the use of English in the Jewish pulpit"; the *American Hebrew* damned them for "resolv[ing] to boycott any of their colleagues who dared to preach in English." Orthodox immigrant *literatus* Judah David Eisenstein was quick to clarify and amplify the Agudath ha-Rabbanim's position: "The Union of American Orthodox Rabbis," he averred, never condemned "preaching and teaching in English." In fact, he continued, "several of their own members often preach in English." Eisenstein explained that the real problem exercising local religious Jewry and necessitating unequivocal rabbinical condemnation was the arrogation of the term "orthodox" by Seminary figures, who, of course, were involved with Jewish immigrants and their children.[15]

Reading the denigration of professors Schechter and Ginzberg, JES leaders surely had cause for concern about the impact of such denunciations upon their own efforts downtown. While the Agudath ha-Rabbanim had never publicly questioned the personal religious reliability of Solomon and his fellow Seminary men and women, Solomon had to know that it would be a large step for the

European rabbis to approve Endeavorer activities. English-language sermons might be deemed halakhically appropriate on principle but not when they were given by so-called expounders of the Higher Criticism," men who were *"kofer ba-Torah* [heretics] [who] would not have a share in the World to Come."[16]

For all these real and potential encumbrances, Solomon and the Endeavorers had to have believed that credit earned among the large, youthful constituency downtown would ultimately carry them to success. They were admired for their record in battling missionaries. Their services constituted an effective way to combat those scandalously entrepreneurial "temporary synagogues" that brought "shame to every self-respecting man and woman" every High Holiday season. The JES exemplified the pride of an emerging body of young Jews who attended "our universities, acquiring the universal knowledge which their fathers seldom possessed," and who were eager to better themselves. Everything considered, they had to believe that if they could keep their coalition together, with its promise of ongoing support and financial encouragement, their long-awaited, permanent religious center would become a reality.[17]

To the Endeavorers' certain dismay, the consensus developed with the help of the Board of Ministers did not long endure. Rabbi Joseph Silverman seems to have been the major undermining force. He continued to work for an Emanu-El and Reform role, if not hegemony, in religious youth work. Soon after being voted down at the Board's public meeting, Silverman went on the offensive, claiming that his initiative was "the first attempt to meet the religious needs of the younger generation which is not attracted to the services of the older generation." Predictably, Elias Solomon was quick to upbraid the seeming disingenuousness of the Reform leader. The Endeavorer reminded his listeners that the JES started young people's services four years before the Emanu-El Brotherhood and he asked rhetorically, "Is this the standard of ethics which the great adopt unto themselves, to be different from that which they set up for the lower level to follow?"[18]

One downtowner, identifying himself only as "an East Sider," could not have been more direct. "Dr. Silverman," he contended, "has come downtown to compete with the Jewish Endeavor Society." It is "hardly a dignified proceeding on the part of the rabbi of Emanu-El . . . now when success is in sight . . . to step in to reap the glory."[19]

Silverman had, apparently, more than bluster. Possibly behind the scenes, Emanu-El's rabbi was working to get the Ministers to grant equal recognition to his efforts. The success of his infighting became noticeable at an April 8, 1904, meeting of the Board of Jewish Ministers, when a committee of seven reported on final plans for the Young People's Synagogue. Among the recommendations were that the "number of *synagogues* [note the plural] be determined by the desire of the neighborhood and according to the state of funds [and that] as experimental places of worship the Jewish Endeavor Society Synagogues and Emanu-El Brotherhood be approved."[20]

To be sure, the suggestion that the Ministers authorize two very different initiatives was reported out of committee only after great debate. A newspaper account of the in camera deliberations stated that "the voting for one synagogue instead of two or more, had been 3 against 3, and that the chairman (Mr. Isaac S. Isaacs) had given the casting vote against one synagogue." It is unknown what motivated the president of the West End (Reform) synagogue to break the tie. But at least one influential member of the committee of seven, a Mr. Bullowa, was an Emanu-El Brotherhood representative.[21]

The adoption of this report did not preclude additional interdenominational cooperation in support of a permanent Endeavorer synagogue downtown. In fact, a substantive enabling resolution was appended to the report, which referred to an ongoing "People's Synagogue Association," a central council, and so forth, to coordinate future efforts. In practice, the designation of both the JES and the Brotherhood as "experimental places of worship" meant competition between them and denied the aspiring downtown youngsters their requisite financial support. When all was said and done, the Emanu-El Brotherhood was legitimized to project its "model" Reform services as an answer to second-generation religious disaffection and to the "lures . . . of the music halls and gambling dens where vice . . . beckons to destruction."[22]

Over the next months and years, the Emanu-El Brotherhood proceeded with "delicate caution" in addressing its downtown constituency: it offered a predominately English-language service but required men to keep their heads covered during prayers and prohibited smoking in its meeting rooms on the Sabbath day. Rabbi Silverman was seemingly less concerned with downtown sensitivities than were his board members. He even contemplated passing a collection plate around during Friday-night services. A remonstration from the first East European Jew on his board in line with the Brotherhood's publicly announced intention to "be strongly conservative so as not to repel the elders" seems to have stopped him.[23]

These policies and efforts achieved an early modicum of success for the Brotherhood as it grew from "an experimental place of worship" to being a recognized fixture on the Lower East Side. By 1910, the *American Hebrew* printed, without comment or critique, a report on the fifth annual meeting of the Brotherhood, replete with the hyperbole that they are "doing excellent pioneer work in a direction not hitherto attempted and in a section of the city not covered by similar organizations."[24]

As the Emanu-El Brotherhood proceeded on its own, the Board of Ministers' plans "for a permanent building [for an umbrella Young People's Synagogue] after a year's work of experimental synagogues" lost momentum and ultimately any chance of coming to fruition. Regardless of whatever deliberations were held, initiatives toward a Board of Ministers-sponsored synagogue were dropped after 1908.[25]

Left to their own devices, JES leaders and members still continued to struggle to make their synagogue activities and classes a permanent reality in the downtown neighborhood. Despite this disappointment, Endeavorers displayed no loss in enthusiasm for their labor in the succeeding months. In April 1905, for example, an unnamed author, signing his letter to the *American Hebrew* only as "Endeavorer," announced with "a feeling of happiness" that "after an interval of two long years" an organization "that is quietly but surely teaching the tenets of the Jewish religion to the younger generation" would be resuming Sabbath afternoon services. The Endeavorers' friend, Mr. Leinkram, and "the broad-minded trustees and members" of the Pitt Street Synagogue seemed to have worked out a way for the synagogue to be the site for a "service that would be as severely Orthodox as the rest, and at the same time, to exclude those features that are objectionable to the younger people. "[26]

As it turned out, "Endeavorer" spoke too quickly. In the few days between the receipt of his letter and its publication, the congregation changed its mind, necessitating the *American Hebrew* to place an asterisk next to "Endeavorer's" missive calling attention to a footnote referring to a "change of program due to the bigoted refusal of said Congregation to fulfil its promises to the Society." Elsewhere in the weekly, they explained that

> notwithstanding the hearty endorsement of the society and its workers . . . by Rabbis Henry Pereira Mendes and Bernard Drachman [of the Orthodox Union] . . . a number of the members of the congregation, including the President, and many of the younger element tried very hard but in vain to obtain use of the synagogue. At a meeting of the congregation held last week, a committee from the society was in attendance but not allowed to speak.[27]

Although there are no extant records to ascertain why the Endeavorers were silenced at the meeting and again were turned down, it is not unreasonable to surmise that they had fallen victim once more to what an angry *Yiddishes Tageblatt* editorialist had earlier described as "the petty politicians and blind fanatics [who] cannot be brought to their senses."[28]

Though rebuffed, the JES persevered as late as 1908, in its semi-monthly Sunday evening lecture series. That year, Endeavorer alumni Mordecai M. Kaplan and Elias L. Solomon (now ordained rabbis) were among the invited speakers. Bible and Hebrew classes for young adults conducted by Jewish Theological Seminary studentLouis I. Egleson also met twice a month. Meanwhile, Egleson's classmate Joseph L. Schwartz served as principal of a Sunday School for girls. Through it all, JES continued its "appeals to the Jewish public for a home of its own." But the dream of "a Synagogue, particularly for young people, where regular services will be held on

Sabbath and Holidays, with a sermon in English," was never realized.[29]

The demise of the Jewish Endeavor Society (circa 1910) may have resulted primarily from the graduation from the Seminary of Elias L. Solomon's generation of JTS students, who moved on to more substantial Jewish leadership careers. Such was the view of Endeavorer mentor Bernard Drachman, who would later write that the "Jewish Endeavorer Society ceased to exist [because] . . . so many of its leading spirits and chief workers found their life work in other fields and other places and were unable to devote their efforts to its service." In fact, Endeavorer alumni, drawing in part upon the invaluable "field experience" gained on the Lower East Side, were destined, over the next fifty years, to make significant contributions to the maintenance of Jewish identification among second- and third-generation Jews.[30]

After graduation from the Seminary in 1904, Elias L. Solomon assumed the pulpit of Congregation Beth Mordecai in Perth Amboy, New Jersey. A year later, he moved to the Bronx's Congregation Kehilath Israel, which was to be a founding member of the (Conservative) United Synagogue of America in 1913. In 1919, Solomon became English-speaking rabbi of a Manhattan Orthodox synagogue, Yorkville's Kehilath Jeshurun. He was called to the pulpit of Congregation Shaare Zedek on New York's West Side in 1922, a position he would hold for the next thirty-four years. He had sunk enduring roots in the emerging Conservative movement.[31]

To be sure, the second-generation Jewish community on the Lower East Side was not left bereft of those endeavoring to effect "a revival of Judaism among the thousands of Jews and Jewesses . . . whose Judaism is at present dormant." There was Rabbi Silverman and his Brotherhood. And by 1910, as if compelled by the idea of multiple synagogues and the spirit of competition engendered by the Board of Ministers' actions, Stephen S. Wise of the Free Synagogue offered his version of a model Reform to downtown masses. For Wise, too, the Lower East Side was an open field for approaching those who "had not forsaken their Orthodox Jewish moorings and yet were eager . . . to hear the word and message of an intensely loyal Jewish liberal." His implicit message was that existing Reform initiatives had not hit their mark.[32]

Wise's religious efforts—he used a hand organ and passed the plate around on the Sabbath and prayed and preached with his head uncovered—may have sparked new Orthodox efforts to reach the unaffiliated. According to one account, the "sons of . . . pious Jews" founded the Young Israel Synagogue in 1912 because "they feared Wise's invasion," even as "they were a trifle drawn to his eloquence and sophistication." Another view has it that these worthy successors to the Endeavorers, as Rabbi Drachman characterized them, simply emerged, like the Kaplans and Solomon before them, out of JTS classes "to awaken young Jewish men and women to their responsibilities as Jews in whatever form these responsibilities are conceived." This appeal soon translated itself into a complex of classes, forums, lectures, and, of course, Americanized Orthodox servlces.[33]

As the Young Israel and the Lower East Side efforts of the Free Synagogue took shape and as the Emanu-El Brotherhood continued its work in the years before 1920, no consensus developed on the type of services to be offered to young downtown Jews. The February 1904 Board of Ministers concordat would remain a unique, never-repeated moment. Nonetheless, even as they consistently differed in their approach and policies, all these Young People's Synagogues were united in a common goal and fate. Theirs was the challenge to motivate second-generation Jews to look beyond the road to assimilation toward an American Jewish religious identity with which they could be comfortably at home.

14

The Winnowing of American Orthodoxy

He is the type of Jew seen less and less in today's metropolitan area Orthodox congregations. He is the infrequent Sabbath worshipper who drives to services on holy days but stealthily parks his car around the corner from *shul* so as not to embarrass himself nor offend his more observant neighbors. His kitchen at home is kosher insofar as biblically forbidden foods are never or rarely served (someone should study the phenomenon of the "chazer pot" in otherwise kosher kitchens), and meat and milk meals and dishes are kept separate. However, he is not overly concerned with the religious reliability of his butcher. The words "Basar Kasher" on the window, sawdust on the floor, and some sort of rabbinic certificate on the wall are proof enough that meats sold within these Jewish precincts were prepared with punctilious regard for ancient and rabbinic ordinances. Moreover, for him, glatt kosher meats are more an economic hardship than a religious *desideratum*. His commitment to kashruth at home does not extend to cheeses, breads and milks. Indeed, he is probably unaware of halakhic considerations in the production of these foods. Outside his home, kashruth observance may be limited to the avoidance of pork and shellfish dishes and possibly, all non-kosher prepared meats. This "fish-out" eater is, or course, totally at home in his neighborhood kosher delicatessen or restaurant regardless of whether that Jewish settlement is open on the Sabbath or employs a full-time *mashgiach* (kashruth overseer).

This Jew and his wife do not follow traditional Jewish family purity laws, though his wife may have gone to the mikveh once prior to their marriage. They know of no religious prohibitions limiting the mixing of the sexes socially. They like social dancing both

299

within and without the synagogue, and they may be dismayed that once very popular events like the "synagogue social" no longer appear on Orthodox congregational calendars.

Now in their sixties and seventies, this type of Jew a generation or so ago was the rule, not the exception, in Orthodox congregations. Indeed, throughout the inter-war period, these American-born children of immigrants were Orthodoxy's rank and file. They kept the Orthodox synagogue alive and in the battle against the more liberal denominations between the end of the era of immigrant Orthodoxy (circa 1880–1920) and the rise of the present generation of resurgent modern and refugee Orthodoxy. Indeed, these Jews, who defined their Orthodoxy more as an institutional identification than as an all encompassing system of beliefs and rituals, may well have made their denomination the largest among affiliating Jews until at least 1945. And yet, American Jewish religious historiography has rarely even noted their existence, let alone their significance. To be sure, thirty years ago sociologist Charles Liebman included them in his undifferentiated category of America's "non-observant Orthodox." But the processes which kept them loyal to Orthodox organizational life and the changes both within and outside their movement that ultimately led to their winnowing away have not been addressed directly.[1]

Received historical truth has it that the 1920s witnessed an abrupt change in the fortunes of both Orthodoxy and Conservatism in America. Prior to that time, it has been argued, Orthodoxy transplanted from Europe retained a tenuous hold upon the masses of religiously-identifying immigrant Jews. It was an Orthodoxy, to be sure, stripped of its traditional communal coercive powers and unable to keep the disaffected in line. Still, it served a major socio-religious purpose for the many new Americans who sought stability and the comforting reminders of home and shtetl while experiencing the anomie of the new country's environment. Literally thousands of small *landsmanshaft* synagogues gave immigrant Orthodoxy its most enduring institutional expression. It was there that Jews from every East European locale were able to pray and socialize with their own kind even as they preserved the customs of Zhitomir, Bialystock and Vilna. Significantly, the Orthodox immigrant's commitment to the faith of the fathers often did not extend beyond the precincts of the *shtibl* and their culinary practices. Simply put, immigrant Jews went to *shul* Friday night to be among friends and to pray to God and ate only kosher foods because they knew of no other cuisine, but they went to work on Saturday morning to advance themselves in America. However, as memories of Europe began to recede, social attachments to the *landsmanshaft* system inevitably loosened. Still, when they went to *shul* they expected services to be authentically Orthodox in the European style.[2]

This form of religiously inconsistent behavior based on nostalgia and the communal elements in synagogue life was incomprehensible to the immigrants' children who were not only Americans but were also imbued early on with the drive for economic mobility and social acceptance. They steadily drifted away from Orthodoxy, their European-based religious identity powerless to stem the tide of assimilation. The ludicrous attempts by leaders of ghetto-based synagogues to attract the "lost generation" back to Judaism through the appointment of charismatic chief rabbis, who stammered Yiddish-language messages to English-speaking listeners, failed utterly. Clearly unpopular with young people by the outbreak of World War I, immigrant Orthodoxy was in danger of losing even its most consistent immigrant generation supporters. Creeping acculturation, if not the actual demise of long time backers, threatened the persistence of that expression of Judaism.[3]

Orthodoxy's credibility crisis, the historical tradition continues, reached acute proportions when Jews exited from the immigrant ghettos beginning in the early 1920s. As long as Jews had lived downtown, disaffection and assimilation were limited by the homogeneous population of the ghetto environment. Although a Delancey Street Jew in 1900 could announce publicly that he officially renounced his Jewish identity, with whom, on his Jewish block, would he than assimilate? Twenty years later, however, the disaffected Jew could make his boast stick, because Jewish demography had changed. The decade immediately preceding the Great Depression witnessed American history's greatest building boom. In each of this country's great cities, new outer-borough or suburban neighborhoods were built to relieve the tremendous overcrowding wrought by the mass influx of poor whites and blacks into the inner cities during wartime.

Middle-class groups of all ethnic and religious stripes flocked to these new residential areas. Immigrant Jews and their children, those possessed of the economic wherewithal to make the move, joined the intra-city migration, settling for the first time in their American experience in mixed neighborhoods. There they clearly had the choice of either continued identification with their faith and people or of complete assimilation into general society. Moreover, during that national era which emphasized conformity of all peoples to American ways, significant external pressure was placed upon the Jew to look and behave like all others. It was there and then, we have been told, that Orthodoxy, European in form and demeanor, unresponsive both to the American environment and to its peoples' changed economic and demographic profile, lost its residual currency with the Jewish masses.[4]

Fortunately for the survival of Judaism, the received truth has taught us, Conservatism was on the scene. (it had been awaiting its chances to serve since 1900, but until that time, most immigrants were not Americanized enough to want it, and their children were not old enough to need it.) Conservatism offered an increasingly large number of Americanizing Jews and their now mature children an alternative to an outdated, irreconcilable Jewish identity and assimilation, presenting its potential communicants with a compelling, sociologically sophisticated mixture of liturgical traditionalism and ideological liberalism tailored to the new neighborhood life, it emerged during the inter-war period as American Jewry's numerically-predominant denomination, or so we have been told.

Conservative synagogues respected and accommodated the American Jews' desire to pray seated next to their wives as good American family men, even as congregants wished to participate in a service which conserved many of the time-honored melodic and liturgical elements of the siddur. Seminary-trained rabbis accorded tacit acceptance—Conservative legal approval came later on—to family decisions to drive to services on Sabbaths and holidays because the sanctuary was miles away from their homes. Synagogues changed the times of Friday and holiday night prayers, recognizing that outer-borough commuters employed in inner city trades, professions and emporia could not always easily attend sundown services. And they provided congregants with an array of ancillary services—dances, movies, lectures, athletics all within their synagogue centers. Furthermore, the Conservative Movement cast all these developments in the mold of older Jewish philosophical and practical traditions, facilitating the communicants' continued identification with the faith's useable past while living and praying as American. So conceived and instituted, the Conservative Movement—some 260 United Synagogues of North American congregations strong by 1928—lured those masses of Jews who readily abandoned Orthodoxy away from complete assimilation and back towards Judaism.[5]

Inter-war's Orthodox rank and file would not have agreed with this widely-accepted narrative. For them, abandoning the piety of immigrant Orthodoxy and the comfort of the *landsmanshaft* did not leave them either bereft of a Jewish identity or in search of a new religious way of life. To begin with, though they had moved to new, better-built residential areas towards the outskirts of the city, they still resided in highly-homogeneous Jewish neighborhoods. As one most perceptive Jewish urban historian has shown, the streets of New York's Astoria and the Grand Concourse were no less Jewish than those of the ghetto's Allen and Delancey. One could be Jewish and, indeed, marry Jewish by living and socializing on one's Jewish block. Jews of this period met their own kind in schools, at the work place, at public and private social clubs and the like. They did not always need the synagogues to serve as the rallying central Jewish institute, though to be sure the Conservative synagogues of that time offered themselves as such. Like their fathers before them, once acculturated they saw the synagogue primarily, if not exlusively, as a place where one came to pray. And Jews came to pray when they felt the personal need in times of family crises, in commemoration or in memorial of significant life cycle events, or during the High Holy Days. At these times, Orthodox Judaism's rank and file wanted to pray in the most authentic, legitimate (read "effective") way. And that meant in an Orthodox synagogue, albeit one possessed of some modern accoutrements.[6]

For this constituency of Jews, the transfer of their allegiance to emerging Conservatism—or for that matter to fledgling Neo-Reform—required that they both needed and were committed to those liberal expressions of Judaism. But neither the need nor the commitment was yet strongly in place within their religious mind-set. The Jews of Flushing, New York, did not need their synagogues to postpone wintertime *erev shabbes* service from early sundown to after dinner because of the propinquity of their homes to stores and otherwork places in the 1920s-1930s. The Manhattan-based merchant could get home to Queens in time to attend services scheduled according to Judaism's clock; that is, of course, if he had a driving commitment to attend services at all after a hard week in the American workplace.

Moreover, Orthodox Jews did not need to sit next to their wives during prayer services, though if they had had their druthers they probably would have preferred to do so. But to their minds the joys of mixed seating were not substitute for the serenity they felt in knowing that their prayers in days of crisis or of judgments were being offered to the Almighty in his most traditional of houses.

Rank and file Orthodox Jews ultimately could not accept Conservative teachings and religious procedures as legitimate, even as their personal behavior ran far afield of what Orthodoxy preached. So disposed, hedging their bets in this world and the world to come, they searched for a type of synagogue that would not embarrass them as Americans—although travel back to the Lower East Side *shtibl* to observe papa's *yahrzeit* was not uncommon—but would at the same time keep the lines of communication open to Providence.

Fortunately for them, they found American Orthodox synagogues ready to accommodate their religious needs and social desires. offering acculturating East European Jews "dignified services" noteworthy for their insistence upon decorum, weekly sermons in the vernacular, and supplementary English-language prayers while retaining the core of traditional *tefillah* and Orthodoxy's understanding of time and seating configurations, Orthodox synagogues, in fact, had been waiting for them as early as 1900. In 1901, the Jewish Endeavor Society, founded by the early students and first rabbis produced by the pre-Solomon Schecter Jewish Theological Seminary, set up shop on the Lower East Side, in Harlem and in Philadelphia "to recall indifferent Jewry [those disaffected from the *landsmanshaft* synagogue] back to their ancestral faith." Some 10 years later, the Young Israel movement was inaugurated "to bring about a revival of Judaism among the thousands of young Jews and Jewesses whose Judaism is at present dormant." And in 1917–1918, the Institutional Synagogue and The Jewish Center Synagogue were established in Harlem and New York's West Side, respectively, to serve the acculturated resident one-step removed from the ghetto. Their New York-based institutions inspired comparable synagoguel ife-styles in cities and communities nationwide.[7]

Significantly, in each of these pre-World War I endeavors, potential communicants were offered more than just the chance to pray as an American. Displaying features later and more widely seen as characteristic of the Conservative synagogue center, these institutions promoted a wide range of ancillary synagogue activities—lectures, dances, movies, athletics. Moreover, no questions were asked about one's personal observance outside of synagogue precincts. Synagogue leaders understood that theirs was the task of "drawing back" towards tradition those disaffected, regardless of their clients' religious commitment at the moment of encounter.[8]

These early activities were, however, only minimally successful. Like their early Conservative counterparts, American Orthodox too found that most immigrants were not Americanized enough to want their services, and their children were still too young to need them. Additionally, so long as these American Orthodox worked where old-world Orthodoxy still held sway among the faithful, the modernizing encountered frequent, stridently expressed opposition from transplanted Russian *rabbanim*. Rabbi Jacob David Willowski, the so-called *Ridbaz*, was probably the most famous opponent of sociological change. He once declared that adoption of even the seemingly innocuous English-language sermon "would leave no hope for the continuance of the Jewish religion." But there were others also. As one JES member explained: "Our services were successful but unfortunately a *maggid* usually appeared on the scene followed by his hosts and naturally, the services had to move to make room for the Yiddish preachers." Inspired by the *maggid's* public comments, a family's raised eyebrows may have deterred some young people, albeit uncomfortable with their fathers' *landsman-shafts*, from joining, with a clear conscience, the rabbinically castigated new religious societies.[9]

Still, the idea that the Orthodox synagogue must accommodate its constituency, accept all who seek its precincts, and make them comfortable there as Americans and as Jews, regardless of their personal religious observance, were ideas that survived into the 1920s. And between the wars these ideas became articles of faith for out-borough or suburban congregations, led by American-trained rabbis produced by the Rabbi Isaac Elchanan Theological Seminary (RIETS), the rabbinical-training arm of what is today Yeshiva University.

But RIETS did not begin as a seminary for the training of American rabbi. When founded in 1897, it was a transplanted East European Yeshiva providing immigrant students and scholars with an opportunity to continue their religious learning. Only after a decade of pressure from, among others, Americanized Orthodox East European lay leaders, was RIETS reorganized as the Rabbinical College of America. Under the leadership of Rabbi Bernard Revel, the school slowly began to produce rabbis knowledgeable in American ways and able to preach in English homiletic messages attractive to fellowsecond generation Jews—worthy opponents of JTS graduates.[10]

Once in the field—either in Young Israel or Orthodox Union (OU) congregations situated outside of the inner city—these young Orthodox rabbis quickly discovered not only that most potential communicants were moving away from personal, all-encompassing Orthodoxy, as already had been the case in the ghetto, but that the newly popular, traditional denominations accepted them without question. Accordingly, they recognized that if they took a hard line towards members' non-observance, either through pulpit excoriation or through the denial of membership or synagogue honors, and if they ignored demands to push ritual and the synagogue's ancillary activities to the limits of Jewish law, they would find themselves without a congregation and without a pulpit. To help Orthodoxy's rank and file within the synagogue and to prevent them from looking into the more liberal denominations, inter-war American Orthodox rabbis followed the congregations's desires—even if they did not agree with them at the outset—to bestow synagogue membership and honors upon individuals known to be Sabbath violators and even to welcome into congregational lists men who had married out of the faith. And it was patently understood that the rabbi would come down from his study to greet members when they attended mid-week synagogue socials. The rabbi might also dance with the synagogue president's wife at the congregational banquet, if lay politics ordained a waltz with the rabbi. Inter-war, Orthodox Jewry thus found their synagogues a most accepting and accommodating environment. The Orthodox synagogue was there when they needed it. It was organized and maintained along American lines and made no great demands upon their personal religious deportment.[11]

This "half-baked laity, with a confused and distorted view of Judaism whose personal observance of mitzvoth has vanished to a great extent," as one St. Louis-based rabbi defined his community's rank and file, was comfortable enough with the Orthodox synagogue to constitute the single largest element in inter-war Orthodoxy. More than the remnants of immigrant Orthodoxy and those later-to-be-called "modern Orthodox," this, at first, a small contingent of the acculturated who deemed Orthodoxy important—if not central—to their private as well as their public lives, populated the estimated 900 Orthodox Union synagogues in 127 cities in twenty-seven states coast to coast. And to a lesser extent they predominated in the thirty-two New York and East Coast, out of ghetto-based Young Israels, whose members seemingly practiced more consistently what they prayed. Indeed, if one adds to the Orthodox rank and file a third, equally understudied segment of American Jewry—those Jews who joined the so-called "traditional Orthodox synagogue" which proliferated outside of the East Coast and which followed all Orthodox synagogue rituals and traditions, save separate seating—one would probably find that that mixed aggregate (rank and file Orthodox and traditional synagogue members) all recognized as "Orthodox" by the OU might well substantiate the 1937 boast that it represented "the largest Jewish religious group numerically in the United States."[12]

Certainly in New York City, outside of Manhattan, even when one excludes the "traditional Synagogues" from the calculations, Orthodox synagogues more than held their own. In the 1920s and 1930s, Queens and Long Island were served by eleven USA congregations and by an estimated nineteen OU synagogues. In the Bronx, eleven Conservative Temples were matched by as many Orthodox synagogues and in Brooklyn's new Flatbush, Bensonhurst and Borough Park neighborhoods, the Brooklyn Jewish Center and sixteen other Conservative congregations competed with fourteen Young Israel affiliates. Significantly, in this and in other cities, both USA and OU Congregations bore the names "Jewish Center," highlighting the similarity of the services offered in both institutions. Nationally, when one adds the traditional Orthodox to the outer-city rank and file Orthodox total, similar statistics emerge.[13]

The winnowing of Orthodoxy's rank and file began after World War II. It was equally a result, on the one hand, of changes in Jewish demography, sociology and religious psychology and, on the other, of the increasingly exclusionary attitudes taken by the Orthodox synagogues towards the marginally observant. To begin with, the post-war Conservative and Neo-Reform approaches to synagogue life, far more than those of the 1920s–1930s, suited well Jewish suburban-sprawl life. Now men and women truly worked far away from their homes, and their homes were many miles from their temples. Thus, whereas the 1920s Jewish merchant working in Manhattan could conceivably have closed his store and made it home to Astoria for Friday evening services, his son or daughter, a 1950s–1960s Wall Street attorney living in Levittown, Long Island definitely could not. And why, for that matter, should they have tried? Unlike their ancestors, they were psychologically comfortable as followers of legitimate middle-class expressions of Judaism which formally countenanced their driving to services and encouraged family participation in all synagogue rituals. Armed with their denomination's imprimatur, post-World War II Conservative and Reform Synagogue members felt no guilt regarding their un-Orthodox behavior. Unlike his father—as we portrayed him at the outset—who drove to Orthodox services and parked his car out of sight of others, the Levittowner unabashedly left his car in the Temple's parking lot. Finally, when they arrived—whether they were Conservative or Neo-Reform—they felt very much in touch with Judaism's ancient revered traditions; the prayers sounded like those in the American Orthodox synagogue. God, they were reassured, would harken to their petitions and supplications even if the older formulas were accompanied by an organ or guitar.[14]

But what of their "parents" and, to a lesser extent, those of the younger generation still unconvinced of the legitimacy and efficacy of liberal denominational theory and practice? They followed the Orthodox synagogue as it too moved from outer-borough or outer-city limits to the new suburbia, with the anticipation that *shuls* would continue to accept and accommodate their deviant religious behavior. And in some localities, particularly in towns and suburbs removed from New York and its environs, their expectations were fulfilled. Where Orthodoxy became a beleagured minority in the heartland of Conservatism and Neo-Reform, synagogues and rabbis followed the now time-honored tradition of overlooking members' heterodoxy. Not so the synagogues and rabbis of New York and other post-war Eastern Orthodox hubs. There, to an ever increasing degree, the resolute, minimally committed Orthodox as opposed to those desirous of becoming more personally observant, the so-called *baalei teshuvah* of all ages, were no longer admitted to and/or were made to feel uncomfortable with synagogue life.[15]

In New York and elsewhere, RIETS graduates and others of even more traditional yeshiva training stood strongly against mixed social activities and functionally dismantled other ancillary features. Moreover, they subtly, when not overtly, disenfranchised minimally committed members by establishing as norms for full congregational integration the punctillious adherence to kashruth, Sabbath and family purity laws. These contemporary Orthodox rabbis could take hard-line approaches without risking their position because for the first time in American synagogue history there now existed within their communities a large, growing coterie of mostly younger Jews who shared and desired this strict orientation .[16]

These committed cohorts were more often than not the modern Orthodox *triumphalist* children of interwar Jewry's small modern Orthodox *survivalist* contingent. They did not consider themselves a threatened minority seeking out a *minyan* among their brethren. Better educated than their elders and those in the provinces, these products of post-1945 Jewish day schools were more secure in, or at least were better able to compartmentalize Jewish traditions and American mores, than were their talmud-torah/heder-educated parents, even as the definitions of modern Orthodox behavior moved steadily to the right. And convinced as they were that they and their fellow day-school graduates could insure Orthodoxy's continuity without the assistance of those less committed than themselves, they felt no impulse to worship with those who had drifted from their Jewish norms. They certainly did not have their parents' close personal and social links with and sensitivity towards the less observant. (Remember that a generation or so ago, modern and rank and file Orthodox children sat side by side in large synagogues or communal talmud torahs. Today, day schools are for the modern Orthodox and the children of *baalei teshuvah*, and Orthodox talmud torahs, at least in New York, are dying.) Moreover, the committed cohort's conceptions of the synagogue—their synagogue agendas—were fundamentally different from those of the older rank and file. For the triumphalists' younger generation, the synagogue was not primarily a ritual, commemorative and memorial domain. Nor was it really a center for the intensification of Jewish identity. Rather it was a home where the already committed could assemble, study and pray—the synagogue's age-old function even in the most modern of architectural settings—helping them increase their familiarity with tradition beyond what they had learned of it in school.[17]

The increasingly confident stance of those educated in day schools was strengthened by the slow movement into their neighborhoods and into their synagogues of another highly committed, newly emerging constituency: refugee Orthodoxy's second generation. These individuals were the now grown children of the immigrants who fled to America from Germany and Eastern Europe during and after Hitler's reign with their devotion to the maintenance of Eastern European Orthodoxy well-nigh intact. Their parents were the Jews who, during the classical period of East European migration, had heeded the admonition of the Hafetz Hayim that whoever hopes for the continuity of Judaism will not come to America.[18] Arriving in this country during the late 1940s-early 1950s, these refugees set about under the guidance of survivor *roshei yeshiva* to transplant the so-called yeshiva world in the United States. The remarkable institutions they created were matched only by their ability to keep so many of their second-generation children closely bound to their father's faith, an accomplishment unique in the annals of American Jewish history.[19]

And yet the children of Orthodox refugees were not totally immune to Americanization, at least, not to its economic aspect. Young graduates of transplanted yeshivas aspired towards economic mobility. They wanted to be doctors, accountants, lawyers, computer scientists, and other positions and professions which clearly required secular education, even if they ultimately felt more comfortable in the yeshiva. Fortunately for them, they sought professional higher education during an era when American universities permitted individuals to graduate from their schools without large-scale exposure to the assimilatory liberal arts. Schools—public and private, Ivy League too—even gave transfer credit for yeshiva education, not only because the business of education changed, but just as importantly, because of America's quest during and since the cold-war era to train the best and the brightest. Americanization, consequently, was no longer a prerequisite for advancement in American society. Accordingly, in the 1960s and after, children of refugees rose from ghetto poverty to affluence in the fashionable middle- and upper middle-class urban and suburban neighborhoods without losing their commitment to Orthodoxy, fundamentalist in content and slightly American aesthetic in tone. There they linked arms with—and indeed have influenced significantly—their day-school-trained co-religionists in creating a contemporary synagogue life committed to the study of traditional law and its maintenance with modern conveniences. Indeed, when these Jews talked about socio-religious ancillary activities, their concerns were with eruvim (enclosures permitting carrying on the Sabbath day) which allowed observant parents to wheel baby carriages to services, thus enabling the Orthodox family to stay together while praying together—albeit on opposite sides of a *mechitza.*[20]

This new era Orthodox synagogue tacitly winnowed out the aging rank and file Orthodox Jew. To be sure, the less observant elderly "member" still perceived the Orthodox sanctuary as God's most—or only—authentic house. But he found that God's—or rather Orthodox Judaism's—requirements become stricter than ever. Glatt kosher meats, *cholav Yisroel* cheese, *mikvehs* and *eruv* building campaigns were the issues central to the younger, more educated members' lives. The synagogue's agenda projected concerns foreign to him. The older rank and file Jew had been moved from the core of his denomination to the periphery, and he is today destined for extinction. His descendants have already found—or will find—their places in more liberal denominations or among the assimilated. They may, of course, find their ways towards affiliation with the rising numbers of committed Orthodox. But the entry requirements for such initiates are becoming more stringent day by day.

15

The Ramaz Version of
American Orthodoxy

Ramaz's Rabbinical Chroniclers

The Rabbis Lookstein, Joseph and Haskel, the former, the late
founder of the Ramaz School, the latter, a member of its first class
and today principal of the day school, marked many of the mile-
stones in their institution's history with brief, heartfelt, impressionistic chronicles of their educational work. The forums for their
reminiscences traditionally were school dinner-dance journals cele-
brating the tenth or the thirtieth or the fortieth anniversary of
Ramaz. Other times, they looked back when the school concretized
plans for a remodeled building or broke ground for a new educational center. On these occasions, they offered the following recount-
ing—which we will presently summarize—of the school's history.
And if they "sentimentalize(d)" or "exaggerate(d)" in their "absorb-
ing chapter in the chronicle of Jewish education in this land," they
averred that it was not due "to willfulness but to love."[1]

Ramaz was established as "a Progressive Day School offering a
comprehensive Jewish and secular education to boys and girls of elementary school age," with a student body of six and a teaching staff
of two, in 1937. It was a time when "darkening shadows were
descending upon European Jewry," during an era where Jews here
in America felt less at home than any time before or since. It was
also a period where "when one carried a Jewish book outdoors, one
turned the cover against one's body, so that no one would know it
was a 'Jewish book.' "And although Rabbi Joseph never mentioned it
in print, his son was certain to note that the school was born within
one of New York's most anti-Semitic neighborhoods: Yorkville on

New York's Upper East Side was then home to the German-American Bund, a pro-Nazi group.[2]

What the elder rabbi did frequently recall was that initially there was significant opposition to his plans, not from anti-Semites, but from his own Jews within his home congregation, Kehilath Jeshurun, the synagogue that would sponsor the school for the next fifty years. After all, critics argued, America was itself then in the throes of a seemingly unrelenting Depression. A new school project at that point might not be economically feasible. And besides which, even if monies could be raised to found Ramaz, naysayers continued, was not all-day intensive Jewish education patently separatistic, maybe un-American, and decidedly declassé? As Rabbi Haskel retold that part of Ramaz's story most recently, he candidly remarked that (despite opposition) "Joseph H. Lookstein was determined to start a school. If the congregation would help him, he would stay, if not he would leave and go someplace else. The lines were clearly drawn."[3]

Rabbi Joseph should not have been surprised by this opposition even as he quickly and permanently stilled their voices. Lack of enthusiasm for Jewish education for their children had long characterized the behavior of that class of uptown Jewry: wealthy, acculturated first- and second-generation Americans. Lookstein himself might well have known that already a generation earlier, Harry Fischel, one of his congregation's most famous lay leaders, had publicly upbraided his fellow pew-dwellers for the following most paradoxical attitude: Newly affluent "baalbatim" were the ones who financed modern talmud torahs and bankrolled the few all-day schools and yeshivas then in existence. They were blessed daily for providing the children of the poor with quality Jewish education. At the same time, they were slow or reluctant to send their own children to the very schools they had built. "They were negligent when it comes to their own children's education," permitting them to grow up as "respectable ignoramuses." And now Rabbi Lookstein was asking Jews who reputedly thought twice before sending their kids to a Jewish afternoon school to turn around and support an "unnecessary" day school for the "children of the more affluent [who] are not being attracted to Torah."[4]

Subtle arm-twisting by the rabbi and possibly the calling in of those social and moral credits any forceful rabbi accumulates over the years—and Rabbi Joseph had few peers in his ability to wade in and through the rough-and-tumble world of synagogue politics—probably carried the day in the board room. But to make Ramaz a permanent success, to attract "the Jewish children then attending private schools" in the uptown area, Ramaz's initial target student population, he had to immediately and convincingly disabuse affluent parents of their prejudiced but not entirely false notions about the type of school he was inaugurating, "Day schools," "yeshivas," or "Jewish academies"—all these terms were used interchangeably by Lookstein in the early days—he pleaded, did not necessarily have to be "ghetto schools in underprivileged neighborhoods for *underprivileged* [emphasis his] youngsters possessed more of an European than an American atmosphere culturally isolate[d] and tempt[ed] by religious sectarianism." Lookstein understood, from the very start, that the reputation and ultimate survival of his school hinged not solely, if even primarily, on how well students and graduates did in the halls of Jewish study, but more importantly, on how comfortable, integrated, and successful the Ramaz person was in the wider, outside world.[5]

Every effort was therefore made to "remove from [students] the consciousness of being different." Lookstein pledged that his youngsters would not pay a social penalty for spending their school day in Jewish surroundings. Ramazites were encouraged to "mingle with other American children" in neighborhood playgrounds whenever possible, on Sundays and during Christmas (renamed Winter) and Passover/Easter vacations. The school would not be in session during these American days of rest and recess. To do otherwise, Lookstein argued, would injure students both psychologically and religiously. The principal wrote that Jews in America "simply must be given one day where they can do as they please and enjoy as they do with other children. That day is Sunday." He was certain and fearful that "the child's mind interprets [school during Christmas] as a penalty and it may well turn him against his school and what it stands for." He also knew that if he kept his school open at Yuletide when affluent "families go off on vacations," Ramaz would be tarred as just like the "ghetto schools" so many of his Jews had steadily avoided.[6]

To stand apart and thereby to be attractive, Ramaz also would have to clearly and consistently demonstrate its commitment to the integration, if not supremacy, of secular studies within the day school curriculum. As Lookstein saw it, earlier American yeshivas "grudgingly dispensed" general knowledge, one might suggest primarily because students demanded such training to enable them to compete within American society. Lookstein implied that had the founders and leaders of the old-style schools had their druthers, secular studies would have been held to the barest minimum. At Ramaz, the rabbi promised, "general knowledge would be freely offered;" just fulfilling "the requirements of providing a general education" would simply not suffice. To emphasize how important it was for the school to excel as an advocate of the broadest cultural horizons for its students, Lookstein made it clear that he wanted both his general and Jewish studies instructors, teachers and rabbis alike, to reflect his positive views. In fact, the Talmud instructors could even be called upon to assist in the general studies programs. "A teacher might be a specialist in Talmud instruction. Why cannot his talents, if he has them," Lookstein asked, "be used for dramatic or musical performances, even if occasionally the theme of the performance is not 'Jewish.'" And within this one classroom, rabbis would at all times reflect the American goals of the school. "Teachers," the principal argued, "must possess more than Jewish learning, [they] must in appearance, speech and training exemplify the bearing of an American Jewish gentleman."[7]

The mutual respect the teaching of the secular and the learning of the religious would have for one another could be seen at a glance in any Ramaz school schedule. Secular and Jewish studies classes would alternate one after the other through the entire school day. In "ghetto schools," English teachers more often than not "moonlighted" in the late afternoon after completing their own full public school teaching day. Elsewhere, a literal changing of the guard took place at 4 p.m. as the garbardine-clad rabbis were replaced by teachers in sport coats. Such would never be the scene at Ramaz. All teachers dressed in similar fashion, and every effort was made to avoid hiring moonlighters. It was felt that when history or science or literature was taught by someone holding a second job—no matter how skilled and dedicated he/she might be—that immediately spoke volumes about the priorities of the school.[8]

Finally, the constituency Lookstein addressed had to be convinced that Ramaz, no less than the private schools around it, would more than adequately prepare their youngsters for successful professional and business careers and lives. For them, the most telling indicator of the validity of Lookstein's approach would be the admission of their children to the prestigious schools of their choice after their years at Ramaz. When Ramaz was young and maintained only an elementary school (1937–45), that might mean the selection of one of their girls for the academically strong Hunter College High School. When the high school began graduating its young men and women (starting in 1949), the placement of Ramaz's best at Columbia and Barnard and occasionally at Yale, Harvard, or Radcliffe was closely observed.

Ramaz would, therefore, be certain to publicize widely its Ivy League record. Rabbi Joseph could, of course, begin by noting that his own son had gained admission to the 1949 freshman class at Columbia College. That would underscore his own personal affinity and commitment to that social and education value. At the same time, Lookstein had to make clear to all who might approach his school that there was an even higher goal to a Ramaz education. For him, the Ramazite had not only to be equipped with the academic abilities to succeed in Harvard classrooms, but had also to be provided with the social skills to interact well with Jews and Gentiles of all kinds in the Yard and, most importantly, have the confidence and sensitivity to remain committed to Orthodox religious life as he strode proudly through the higher echelons of American society. Echoing his father's deepest prayer, Rabbi Haskel sounded Ramaz's creed best when he wrote that the school seeks "to fuse two traditions within one wholesome, integrated, respectful and dignified young man at whom the Jewish and non-Jewish world would look with pride and admiration and say: Here is a product of a Yeshiva education."[9]

By the rabbis' own accounts, Ramaz's notions of and commitment to its students' comfort, integration, and success as Jews within American society, once established in the late 1930s, dominated the school's outlook during the thirty-five year principalship of Rabbi Joseph (1937–71). In the last fifteen years or so and under Rabbi Haskel's stewardship, a fourth dimension, or by-word, has been added to the Ramaz creed: an articulated dedication to "menschlichkeit."

To be sure, as we have just noted, Ramaz, during the senior rabbi's tenure, always desired to have each student turn out to be "a mensch," although the Yiddish phraseology was never used. The school's leadership demanded that "a yeshiva ought to train its students with certain proprieties and that a mood of dignity should prevail in the halls." And Ramaz students were taught all the social graces. In the 1950s that meant social dancing classes. Along these same lines, in the 1960s, the school recommended—but did not enforce—a uniform dress code for students (blue blazer with gold emblem and gray trousers or skirts). In all instances, Ramazites were to look and behave like gentlemen and gentlewomen.[10]

In the 1970s, however, under the impact of turmoil within American society and enduring crises facing Soviet Jewry and Israel, the school began to seek to instill a profound dedication to "menschlichkeit" (defined here as Orthodox social responsibility and activism) within its students. Or as Rabbi Haskel proudly put it: "we are (now more than ever) more self-conscious of what our responsibilities are." At home, on the American scene, Ramaz, during the early 1970s, encouraged its students to be highly informed and, if moved, to become involved in the great national debate over the propriety and morality of the Vietnam War. Even closer to home, youngsters were trained to be activists on behalf of Soviet Jewry. The Student Struggle for Soviet Jewry (SSSJ) found ready footsoldiers in the yeshiva's student body. Probably the most publicized example of Ramaz out in the streets was its daily prayer vigil in 1983 in front of the Soviet U.N. Mission on behalf of refusenik Anatoly Shcharansky.

Menschlichkeit, of course, also included demonstrating, within schoolrooms and without, love and concern for the survival of Israel.[11]

But could street protesting peacefully coexist with the comfortable, integrated, and successful lives Ramaz had always promised its students? Rabbi Haskel never commented on the comforts gained while on the march, but he strongly averred that his youngsters' integration and future success were never in doubt in these unconventional classrooms. In 1971, he would write that "under the right auspices, students can learn more about what education really means when walking in a protest march for an hour, than they can in a week of study in a class." For himself, Rabbi Joseph, by 1979, would be echoing his son's words when he exclaimed that "participating in a demonstration for Soviet Jewry is as important as attending classes in any course . . . marching enthusiastically and proudly in an Israel Independence Day Parade is a lesson in history, in freedom and in Jewish solidarity."[12]

Had he lived into the 1980s, Rabbi Joseph would also have been pleased with the fourth aspect of menschlichkeit that was first articulated by his son during this last decade. As "the world is changing," Rabbi Haskel would write in 1984, "and becoming less tolerant, less open, more exclusionary and very often more self-righteous," Ramazites are being trained as Orthodox advocates of "love for all Jews and [are taught] to feel responsible for them, wherever they may be and however they may live." Practically that might mean, for example, that in the 1980s, Ramaz students would stand loyally and gladly with Conservative day school students and Reform youth group members in protest marches. And when they got back to Yorkville, they would then study within the classroom that which linked and that which ultimately differentiated them from their fellows. Their teachers, likewise, would stand arm and arm with rabbis of the more liberal denominations in support of causes that touched all Jews. As Rabbi Haskel saw it, this new aspect of menschlichkeit was not really new. His "open, tolerant school" was precisely what his "father of blessed memory wanted Ramaz to be." Only in Rabbi Joseph's heyday, advocacy of such a basic element in the Ramaz creed did not have to be so explicitly articulated.[13]

Implicit, when not totally explicit, in the Looksteins' sketches of their school's history, is their proud sense of how different Ramaz was and is from all the American yeshivas that preceded it, and how today it stands as a model institution for forward-looking Orthodox groups to emulate. Ramaz, it would seem, was the first to attract a different type of student previously unseen on day school rolls. He, or just as likely she, was not only more affluent than all the others, but came from a family whose commitment to full-time Torah education was by no means absolute. The better public schools and private education were always options for Ramaz parents. No wonder the Looksteins had to frequently reiterate their faith that the youngsters in their care would not lose out by studying with their own kind. "Ghetto school" parents backed yeshiva initiatives precisely to keep their youngsters as separate as possible from Gentile institutions and life-styles. Their basic concern was whether they could afford the tuition to keep their boys apart.

From these initial grand distinctions stemmed, beginning in Rabbi Joseph's days, two additional, fundamental areas of difference. In socializing its students within, and to some degree without, American society, the utmost latitude was given both inside and outside the classroom towards appreciating American cultural symbols and mores as their own. Rarely did Ramaz officials define American behavior patterns as essentially Gentile and therefore to be avoided. In the other, earlier, schools, good American fun was forcefully downed as "what the Gentiles do" and therefore to be avoided. Not surprisingly, Ramaz also stood out in its conception of what should be its ideal product. In Yorkville, the quest, felt so strongly earlier and elsewhere, to produce talmudic prodigies out of American schools was replaced firmly by the goal of raising up young men and young women, possessed of a well-rounded Jewish education, adhering to the preachings of Torah, while at the same time—if not more importantly—comfortable, integrated, and successful in the American world. Seemingly, given the option of trying to mold renowned men of Torah out of a most parochial Jewish environment or graduating future famous American Jewish men and women, Ramaz consciously essayed to produce the latter.

But even as Rabbi Joseph saw himself as attracting and molding a different brand of yeshiva graduate, Rabbi Haskel, it is suggested, has redefined the school's mandate and ideal type by expanding the categories of difference separating its charges from most other yeshiva youngsters. Ramaz would never say that hours spent on social activism are a religiously indefensible waste of time more appropriately spent studying Torah in the House of Study. Indeed, the Yorkville school's leaders might even suggest that the street can be not only a classroom, but also a synagogue, where Jews of all stripes may discharge the highest of religious duties. In Ramaz's view, so many other schools have, in the most contemporary of days, drawn too narrowly into their books and their selves.

In sum, the school's own chroniclers have consistently suggested that there exists a distinct Ramaz version of American Orthodoxy and Orthodox education that if not still unique is at least a model different from all earlier and most other present-day norms. In essence, there is a "Ramaz plan" that might be followed. They have left it to their friends and foes alike to define and determine how close they have come to reaching their goals in producing what one very recent rabbinic supporter described as "a group of alumni who have successfully achieved the synthesis of two cultures." For the historian, there remains the more rewarding task of exploring, underscoring, and questioning the accuracy of the rabbis' implied assertions. How truly distinctive, both in its inception and over the years, has been the Ramaz version of American Orthodoxy? What are, or have been, the norms against which the school's experience must be compared? And have there been over the two and one-half generations, particularly this last score of years, instances wherein attempts were made to minimize the school's uniqueness: to be, if you will, "more like a yeshiva," even if under Rabbi Haskel new areas of difference have been emphasized. A second look at aspects of Ramaz's history, moving us beyond the journals and into school records, student and parent publications, and other ephemera, may ultimately help us closely limn the nature of the Ramaz version of Orthodoxy.[14]

A Different Student Body

Rabbi Joseph Lookstein's assertion in June 1937 that "hitherto the parochial school has had a special appeal [only] for the children of the middle class and poorer Jewish homes" is not completely accurate. At least in the two decades that immediately preceded Ramaz's founding, "the inalienable right . . . of a child from a rich Jewish home [to receive] a full and comprehensive Jewish education" was being addressed partially at two Brooklyn-based schools, the Hebrew Institute of Borough Park (aka Yeshiva Etz Hayim) and at the Yeshiva of Flatbush. It is also certain that Ramaz could not have been the first all-day Jewish school to have on its rolls children from homes that were less than fully Orthodox. Etz Hayim, for one, founded in 1916, was known in its neighborhood both as a school which included "the children of baalbatim [affluent lay leaders] of the local Orthodox synagogues" and "as Orthodox in character but somewhat less than Orthodox in observances than the traditional yeshiva." And the word on the Yeshiva of Flatbush (founded in 1928) was, by virtue of, if nothing else, its being the first coeducational yeshiva in the United States, that it too attracted to its rolls youngsters from the best Brooklyn Jewish families but not all of them were particularly Orthodox. Certainly both schools were different in constituency, both economically and socioreligiously, from the earliest yeshivas established a generation and a half earlier on the Lower East Side and in other Jewish neighborhoods of the time.[15]

The oldest yeshivas in America, the Yeshiva Etz Chaim and the Rabbi Jacob Joseph School of downtown Manhattan, the Yeshiva of Harlem and the Yeshiva Toras Chaim of uptown, and the Yeshiva Rabbi Chaim Berlin and the Mesivta Torah Vodaas of Brooklyn clearly had been the "ghetto schools" against which Rabbi Joseph juxtaposed Ramaz. These ghetto schools, even if they were not precisely in the worst of neighborhood, were run on a shoestring and had the poorest of immigrant Jewish children as their students.

Moreover, the religious families that sent their children to these transplanted East European institutions were unacculturated, and the schools made every effort to keep their students that way. For them, a major part of being Orthodox was a studied seclusion from the ways of America. As Rabbi Joseph suggested, these schools "grudgingly dispensed" American learning to their students and did more only when pressured by the students themselves, who despite everything wanted to know about the new country around them.[16]

The crowd at Brooklyn's Etz Hayim and Flatbush in the 1920s was fundamentally different from the Lower East Side Orthodox of the pre-World War I period. To begin with, they were far from the poorest of Jews. They lived in one of the up-and-coming Jewish neighborhoods of the pre-Depression era. Secondly, they were not afraid of American ways and means. And they wanted any school to which they would send their youngsters to reflect their positive appreciation of general culture. Certainly in this regard they were very much like the vast majority of Jewish families, even Orthodox families, who during that era sent their youngsters to public schools. But, at the same time, they were obviously very different from both the majority of Jews and the completely separatist Orthodox. They were at home within America, but they feared what comfort, and possibly acceptance, in America might mean to their own children's attachment to the Jewish people. It was that perception, so common in today's Jewish world, that day schools must promote acculturation, even as they limit assimilation, that pushed these clearly committed but far from totally Orthodox parents to send their sons and daughters to a Jewish school in the 1920s. One contemporary observer put it this way: "Many parents send their children to a yeshivah primarily to engender in them a love for their people and its cultural heritage." And not incidentally, that feeling of belonging was expressed through "a strong attachment to the Zionist way of life."[17]

Where Ramaz differed from the modern Brooklyn schools was primarily in the percentage of rich youngsters on its rolls, and beyond that, most significantly, in the lower level of Jewish knowledge and commitment of its parent body. Ramazites were, on the whole, a class of Jews economically the next cut above the Brooklyn "baalba-tim." Socially, they were somewhat more Americanized than even the most acculturated Flatbushite, and, as noted, religiously they were significantly less aware and involved. In essence, they were the first day school constituency to have to be recruited to intensive Jewish learning and convinced of the value of Orthodox practice. Remember, Etz Chaim of Manhattan's people built their own school to shield their children from America. Likewise, Flatbush and Borough Park parents were fired with a drive to ensure Jewish continuity even if the maintenance of old forms of Orthodoxy was not their highest priority. The "discriminating parents" at Ramaz, on the other hand, seemingly would have been equally happy to have their children sit among the children of New York's best families in the city's elite private schools. These families were Orthodox primarily in the sense that their synagogal affiliation was with an Orthodox synagogue. Their lives bespoke how many were the cultural alternatives available to the affluent Jew.[18]

Evidence of where Ramazites stood both socially and economically in America and within the spectrum of Jews calling themselves Orthodox during at least the first generation or so of the school's existence (1937–1960) is provided by the articles and notices that appeared in the Ramaz Parents' Council newspaper. Clearly many Ramaz families were comfortable with a school that could speak proudly of "tuxedos and dancing shoes" and of "the appearance of Miss Mimi Benzell the noted opera singer who gave unstintingly of her talents" at its major fundraiser of the year, a dinner dance at the Hotel Astor, while at the same time, and on the same page of the newspaper, it could express concern over "Parties, Dating and Going Steady" among its students. For these parents, an Orthodox school religiously liberal enough to sponsor an event that featured mixed social dancing and a female vocalist—policies unheard of in earlier and other existing school—and socially sensitive enough to deal openly with the reality that their teenagers behaved more or less like other youngsters around them—earlier and existing schools rarely confronted these problems positively—was totally in step with their activities and world view as upwardly mobile Americanized Jews. At the same time, other school newspaper notes suggest that many of these same parents were unaware of, or unconcerned with, the core demands an Orthodox school naturally makes upon the faithful.[19]

In November 1952, for example, Dr. Benjamin Brickman, long-time supervisor of the school, in an article pointedly entitled "School and Home: An Educational Team," made it abundantly clear that there was just so much the school could do to promote religiosity among its students within the four walls of the classroom. If what the children learned of Orthodox teachings was not integrated in their families' lives, he argued, no progress would be made. "Without any intent whatever to 'preach,'" Brickman suggested that "the 'shabbos party' on Friday afternoon [must be] a wonderful prelude to an actual sabbath-like Friday night. Otherwise it is just play-acting and emotional clashes begin to disturb the child."[20]

Consider whether such an article would have ever appeared in a comparable organ of an old-line yeshiva. (It is unlikely, of course, that such schools would ever have utilized such an American educational device.) The families that affiliated with those earlier schools were decidedly *shomer shabbes,* and if some possibly were not, they certainly kept their heterodoxy to themselves. Moreover, in the unlikely event that the nonobservance of the minority became public knowledge, it is certain that the *roshei yeshiva* would not have been reticent about preaching to transgressors. At Ramaz, nonobservance was clearly a known fact of life. And it was characteristic of Ramaz's definition of Orthodoxy and approach to its promotion that offenders were handled with kid gloves. In this case, the method was to convince parents of the psychological value of there being one religious formula for a family (read: Orthodoxy).

Two years later, it was clear again that many forms of non-Orthodox behavior were still endemic to Ramaz. At that point, the school spoke and preached somewhat more strongly of parental obligations to the school and to the faith. But the critique was still offered in the most genteel fashion. The newspaper reprinted an article by Milton A. Saffir, director of the Chicago Psychological Guidance Center, entitled "When School Teaches Practices Not Observed at Home." Through this piece and on the authority of a physician and not a rabbi, Ramaz offered non-Orthodox parents three alternatives in reconciling their practices with school traditions.

> If they disagree with the fundamentals of a particular school's orientation toward Judaism, they should not send their child to that school. If they accept the basic principles, they should explain their own departures . . . to the child in the same way that they justify their way of living to their own conscience. . . . If . . . the parents' omission . . . is no more than laziness, indifference or inconvenience, they might as well begin observing them for the sake of their child's education.[21]

Taking the most optimistic view of why many Ramaz families were not observing *mitzvot* basic to Orthodoxy, the school would continue to teach the modern value of commandments and promote their observance. In October 1955 Brickman wrote on "Daily Worship and Synagogue Attendance" and noted that "without regularity of worship and synagogue attendance [in the home], the study of prayers [in the school] may remain merely an intellectual pursuit." Significantly, four years later, Brickman composed an almost identical article on "Daily Worship" as part of a conscientious attempt "to bridge the gap between parents and school . . . [on] many activities and practices at Ramaz based on educational and ideological principles which may not be known to our parents."[22]

Most assuredly, however, although the majority of Ramaz families were both affluent—"the professional class . . . children of doctors, lawyers and teachers"—and seemingly marginally Orthodox, significant numbers were not. Economically speaking, by his own designs Rabbi Joseph had determined from the very outset that while Ramaz sought to attract children of the affluent, and would acquire the appellation of a "rich man's school," a considerable proportion of the student body would be scholarship youngsters. In 1937, in an early statement on the subject, Rabbi Joseph prayed that his school not become "a school for social snobs." It made sound Jewish, social, and pedagogic sense for silkstocking youngsters to sit with, learn from, and in turn teach "children from deserving Jewish families." Lookstein envisioned originally that "twenty percent of the students will be free scholarship students." As it turned out, a significantly larger percentage of such pupils filled the Ramaz rows from almost the very start. And after a generation of operation and service (1958), Ramaz could boast that 54 percent of its students received "financial aid."[23]

One reason why there was always room for so many scholarship youngsters was that, for the longest time, Lookstein's initial target student body, the young people closest to home, the Yorkville crowd of Park, Madison, and Fifth Avenue Jews, did not avail themselves of his offer. New York's richest Jews and their friends backed his concept with their dollars. But true to form, they were very slow in sending their own youngsters to Ramaz. After the first class of six, an unrepresentative prototype made up of the son of the rabbi, the daughter of the ritual director, the daughter of the congregation's treasurer, and three other children from families close to the school and the endeavor, Yorkville for the next thirty-five years would contribute a bare minimum of students. Not until the early 1970s would the Kehilath Jeshurun vicinity become the prime feeder neighborhood to Ramaz.[24]

But maybe the rabbi had expected too much of his neighborhood and of New York's richest Jews. He knew that his then aging and declining congregation—one estimate remembers it being home "in 1935 to but forty families"—might provide Ramaz with some money, but had no children to enroll. Indeed, the Ramaz initiative may have been in part an attempt on the part of the forward-thinking rabbi to revitalize his own congregation through the day school. In any event, the numbers suggest that among Yorkville Jews of the time, large and impressive Conservative and Reform temples, like the Park Avenue Synagogue and Temple Shaaray Tefila, with their respective afternoon and Sunday school programs and the like, and, of course, the ever present option of disaffection from Jewish life, were more captivating than Ramaz (and Kehilath Jeshurun).[25]

Fortunately for Lookstein, his call to the rich was heard by the affluent in other neighborhoods. The economically heterogeneous West Side of Manhattan began in 1938 and continued until 1973 to be Ramaz's foremost "feeder" neighborhood. That meant that youngsters with the addresses 336 Central Park West and 580 West

End Avenue attended the school in 1939. And a generation later, children from homes just up those blocks at 110 Riverside Drive, 156 West 86th Street, and 670 West End Avenue wore their blue blazers on the crosstown bus. Significantly, there was, beginning in the 1940s, a local yeshiva, the Manhattan Day School, available to them. It was not a "ghetto school." But it did not have Ramaz's élan. One early Ramaz parent explained her decision to send her son across town this way: "The school on the West Side took every child that wanted to come in, if they could afford it or not. The classes were overcrowded and poorly supervised. . . . [Rabbi Lookstein] wanted the gold knockers on the door, he wanted the children from the Upper Middle Class."

Meanwhile, up from the Bronx came youngsters in the 1940s with good, socially respectable Grand Concourse addresses. A generation and a half later, no Ramazites came from that neighborhood, as it had become a Jewish neighborhood of the past. The 1970s rich Ramaz students from the Bronx sported addresses like Kappock Street or Fieldston Road in the new Jewish Riverdale section.[26]

Significantly, these neighborhoods also produced Ramaz's scholarship youngsters. Remember, New York's neighborhoods differ socially and economically square mile by square mile and sometimes block by block. Thus, the West Side cohort in 1939 included, too, youngsters from the less-desirable, but by no means slum, apartments on 104th and Broadway. In 1970, children with addresses like 771 Amsterdam Avenue and 250 West 104th Street, increasingly not the best of neighborhoods, were also part of Ramaz. Likewise in the Bronx, 1940s working-class subneighborhoods like Morris and Walton Avenue and the more northerly Gun Hill Road sent on their boys and girls. And in the 1970s, Kingsbridge and the Van Cortlandt Park section, just a mile or two from Riverdale, but sometimes thousands of dollars away in adjusted gross family income, also fed students to the day school.[27]

Ramaz students also turned out to be a highly diversified religious crowd. As suggested earlier, some families had to be reminded year after year to have their boys wear "street caps to and from school" as yeshiva youngsters did, and not go around bareheaded as did all others. Other families needed no such reminders; they already lived the religious life Ramaz was teaching and sometimes even more. Probably the most observant Ramazites—exclusive of the children of Orthodox rabbis, whose families could be counted on to be religious—were the scions of poorer families from the outer boroughs most identifiable by their practice of sending both their sons and daughters to the Ramaz elementary school but only their daughters on into the high school years. In these cases, a combination of the limits of geography and commutation, attitudes about intensive Jewish education for girls, and the availability of scholarship monies to attend a school honored for its excellence in general studies moved families towards Ramaz.[28]

Take as a hypothetical case, a *shomer shabbes* family living on Walton Avenue in the Bronx in the mid-1940s. Employment opportunities and social circumstances had placed them in a borough where there was only one well-established elementary-level yeshiva ready to educate sons and but three then-ephemeral schools for daughters. The Yeshiva Rabbi Israel Salanter, founded in 1923, could be counted upon to prepare young men in biblical and talmudic subjects for admission after bar-mitzvah into the high school program of the Rabbi Isaac Elchanan Theological Seminary (aka TA, the Talmudical Academy of Yeshiva University). This school could not, however, assure anyone that young men would receive the highest-quality general education. It was not like the Bronx's Yeshiva Torah V'Emunah and the Yeshiva Rabbi Chaim Ozer, schools characterized by one contemporary critic as "not allowing sufficient time . . . for instruction in secular subjects which is in violation of State law." But it also was not Ramaz. At Salanter it was reputably less an ideological predisposition against the secular and more the unavailability of funds to provide students with the best English teachers possible that gave it its reputation.[29]

If our modern-thinking second-generation Orthodox family was unhappy with the educational imbalances at Salanter, what could they say in favor of Morris Avenue's Yeshiva Academy for Girls (founded 1943, folded 1949) and the borough's new Beth Jacob Schools (East Bronx branch founded 1946, West Bronx founded

1947)? The earlier school presented itself as a girls' version of Salanter but succeeded neither in the general nor the religious studies.
The contemporary critic reported here in 1946 that "there is practically no organization in the school. The Executive Director. . . is a
recent arrival himself in the school and inherited a very disorganized and chaotic state of affairs. [He has] no understanding of the
problems and requirements of a modern school." For itself, Beth
Jacob would have a grand future ahead as a bastion of Torah education for young women. But its emphases, here more ideologically
based, would not be towards producing academically well rounded
American Jewish students. The family may have pined for the more
"Jewish" borough of Brooklyn with its more than a dozen boys' and
some nine girls' schools of varying ideological stripes. There, if they
wanted their children exposed to comprehensive secular studies
while they studied Torah in a single-sex school environment, they
had the all-boys Etz Hayim and the all-girls Shulamith School. And,
of course, if they were more religiously liberal, they had the even
more Americanized Yeshiva of Flatbush, America's first coed
yeshiva, with a curriculum that was not so dissimilar from
Ramaz's.[30]

Permitting us to project further about our somewhat idiosyncratic
family, we can suggest that they would have particularly appreciated
Flatbush's approach to Jewish studies, and to their pleasure, they
would find much more of the same at Ramaz. Possibly, they were
akin to Orthodox *maskilim* several generations removed, scions of
that hybrid of the nineteenth-century Jewish Enlightenment, who,
while maintaining traditional Jewish practice, developed wider
unorthodox cultural horizons and desired to learn as Jews the best
of all worlds. In practical educational terms, that meant that these
moderns applauded a school that taught not only Torah and Talmud but also the Prophets and Writings, Jewish history, and the living Hebrew language and literature. At Ramaz, these "softer"
Jewish disciplines, as the most Orthodox yeshiva people might have
characterized them, took their honored and equal place next to the
Pentateuch and Tractates.[31]

Finally, our hypothetical Bronx Orthodox family would have had to have possessed two additional social qualities to have chosen Ramaz for their youngsters. They would have to have been both tolerant and thick-skinned. After all, their own religious commitments notwithstanding, they were sending their children to classes with reputedly nonreligious youngsters. Such families would have to be unconcerned that their own children might be pulled the "wrong" way. Moreover, they would have to be oblivious to remarks made to and about them by other, more Orthodox acquaintances who might question the Bronxites' own Orthodoxy: They were sending children to a heterogeneous school with an unorthodox curriculum.

The winnowing out from Ramaz of some of these uncommon Orthodox families took place after children graduated the school's eighth grade. At that very important educational and social turning point, sons were often moved out and on to the far more Talmud-intensive, academically adequate, and single-sex TA, while daughters remained in the more religiously, socially, and educationally diversified Ramaz. For one East Bronx family that during the late 1950s to early 1960s sent three daughters through Ramaz High School and their one son only through eighth grade, the thought processes in choosing and staying in school(s) went basically like this: As a most tolerant Orthodox family, they had no problems with their children associating with all types of Jewish students. Significantly, they were Young Israelites, true and through, and believed strongly in that movement's time-honored policy of acceptance of diversity within the community. Though certainly not hard-core *maskilim*, they saw value in their children's exposure to wide-ranging Judaic disciplines. And as good Americanized Jews, they were always impressed with Ramaz's general studies curriculum. And remember, where they lived the only other options were Salanter or worse and Beth Jacob of the East Bronx.

When it came to high school, however, the family's different educational expectations for their daughters and son impacted directly on their choice of school. Although their son had in a sense gotten off to a "slow start" in his training in Talmud—Ramaz students started studying Talmud later and spent fewer hours per week on the subject than did fellows at Salanter—still they had hopes that their bright young man would now, after his bar-mitzvah, make up for lost time at the Talmudical Academy and minimally learn how to study a page of the Talmud on his own, the sure sign of a proficient layman. Possibly, their son would choose later on to study for the rabbinate, but they were far from sold on their son pursuing a career as a rabbi. Clearly, they had different hopes for their daughters: The girls would continue to be exposed to the manifold Jewish and general educational riches offered at Ramaz and there prepare for college, careers, and someday to build their own loyal Jewish homes. To be sure, there was an Orthodox educational alternative available to them: the Manhattan branch of the Central Yeshiva High School for Girls (founded 1959). This girls' "counterpart" to the Talmudical Academy proffered a Ramaz-like mixture of courses and an adequate pre-university educational program. (Interestingly enough, Ramaz, by virtue of its more liberal approach to Orthodox education, offered its girls courses in Talmud, and thus had the chance of producing distaff *talmedei chachamim,* while the religiously traditional Central only offered Mishnah for the most advanced students.) But our East Bronx family kept their girls where they were through graduation. To their minds, Ramaz simply offered a much better academic program. Besides which, their girls did not want to leave their friends behind.[32]

Significantly, the single-sex religious environment offered by Central did not sway them from Ramaz. For many Orthodox families, the problems of coeducation increased dramatically as their children reached the teen ages and moved with their male and female friends from the classroom to the movies and the ballroom. At Ramaz, high school students of both sexes not only studied together-even the most traditional of subjects-they were taught the social graces together and were encouraged to attend school-run dances. Welcome Freshmen, Sophomore Tea, and Senior Prom were all part of the school's social scene until at least the mid-1960s. Central segregated its Orthodox girls both within the classroom and without; there were no mixed dances held on that all-girl premises.[33]

On one level, our East Bronx family, by being unperturbed and unmoved by these realities, was following a by-then time-honored American Orthodox policy of studied unconcern and/or confidence that their daughters, even when exposed to mixed environment and potentially troubling circumstances, would remain as Orthodox as were they. Remember, long before Beth Jacob or Ramaz or even, for that matter, Salanter, during the heyday of the original "ghetto schools" truly on the Lower East Side, the most religious boys were directed to obviously single-sex yeshivas. Their sisters attended public schools with youths of all races and creeds. And although now the option of all-girl education was clearly available, the family was not so moved. Maybe too their "complacency" had something to do with their own biographies and life-styles as second-generation American Orthodox Jews: As youngsters, they too had gone to synagogue socials. And if the truth be told, this ritually observant *shomer shabbes* couple still enjoyed waltzing at their own Young Israel annual dinner. From that perspective alone it was clearly all right for their daughters not only to learn these skills but to practice same at school-sponsored and chaperoned events. At the same time, of course, they also had no problem with their son attending the more traditional Talmudical Academy, where no such social skills or dances were officially countenanced.[34]

It is certainly noteworthy that just a few years earlier there were girls at Ramaz from "even more" Orthodox families that did not take the same "laissez-faire" approach towards dance classes and proms. And yet they chose Ramaz for their daughters, even in some cases enrolling them at the school after eighth grade. In 1954, for example, a young woman from the Bronx enrolled by way of the Yeshiva Rabbi Moses Soloveichik. She had attended what might be called a partially coeducational school: there boys and girls sat together during general studies throughout the elementary grades. However, religious studies classes were sex-segregated beginning in the sixth grade. All things being equal, this young woman's family would have been pleased had their daughter attended Central Yeshiva. The dilemma was that at that early date, Yeshiva University, which ran this school, had yet to build its Manhattan branch. There was only the Brooklyn school, and daily commutation to Bedford Avenue in Flatbush was logistically impossible. To be sure, there was a newly established Beth Jacob school on St. Nicholas Avenue open for such a student, but that school was simply not right for them. Ramaz, on the other hand, was both a reasonable and a reachable alternative to public school education.

As it turned out, four other Soloveichik School families felt the same way, and together they entered the highly heterogeneous Ramaz School. There these five like-minded students frequently found that their families' definitions of appropriate public Orthodox behavior differed from that of most of their schoolmates. These differences always manifested themselves in areas of social dancing and the like. True to their beliefs, they absented themselves from these activities. And true to Ramaz's own accepting and liberal position, these youngsters were not forced or pressured to conform. These patently Orthodox students took advantage of Ramaz's quality general and Hebraic studies curriculum. But in other ways, they stayed apart.[35]

Just a few years later, Ramaz's student body began to display a different type of heterogeneity when children from religiously observant but decidedly non-Orthodox homes began appearing at the school. Scions of many of New York's leading Conservative rabbinic and Jewish Theological Seminary professorial families found Ramaz educationally sound, logistically convenient, and ideologically acceptable. Had these Manhattan, Bronx, and Lower Westchester-dwelling families had their druthers, they probably would have been happier enrolling their youngsters in a Conservative Solomon Schechter day school. But with no such schools available until very recently, where else but to Ramaz could these so intensely Jewish families send their sons and daughters? For them, there was never any doubt about the quality of Ramaz's general studies, nor of its ability to prepare its graduates for the wide university world, not to mention the high degree of sexual equality that obtained in the Yorkville classroom. To be sure, some Conservative families would have been happier still if Ramaz had been more egalitarian in its approach to worship. When daily services were held, a *mechitza* separated the sexes, boys alone were counted towards a minyan and it was they who led the services. But the unmistakable reality that for all its pedagogic and social liberalism, Ramaz is still, after all, an Orthodox institution, has not dissuaded Seminary worthies from enrolling their youngsters. In fact, in recent decades, concomitant with the intensification of the Conservative movement's active concern over women's rights in Judaism, have witnessed a substantial increase in the number of Seminary families involved with Ramaz.[36]

Thus, on balance, with the exception of these Conservative youngsters who would not have been comfortable in any other Orthodox school and Ramaz's silk-stocking youths who might not have attended any Jewish school at all, Ramaz has had many of the types that attended and did attend (sister at Ramaz, brother at TA) the earlier and stricter yeshivas. And if the truth be told, even the most traditional of yeshivas had their percentage of students from less than the "best" Orthodox homes, but as previously noted, deviance there was rarely acknowledged. Where Ramaz really was different was in the proportions of religious versus nonreligious youngsters and most significantly in the school's explicit acceptance and accommodation of diversity. In a word, Ramaz had many of the students other schools tolerated, but even more so, and they were welcomed as such.

Different Cultural Symbols

From its very inception and in so many ways, Ramaz was the most Americanized of yeshivas. Its policy consistently was that, unless proven otherwise, this country's social mores and cultural patterns were always worth emulating. As such, there was only the most minimal of anxieties over whether in acting as their fellow citizens did, Ramaz students were in fact following in the "ways of the Gentiles"; a behavior pattern Orthodox Jews studiously avoided. The earlier schools and even some of the more progressive interwar yeshivas more closely guarded the lines among what was patently Jewish and unqualifiedly good, what was clearly American and might be experienced to a degree, and what was dangerously Christian and had to be evaded. Take, for example, how different Ramaz was in its idiosyncratic and suggestive calm over the American "national-religious" observance of the Christmas season.

Throughout American Jewish history, and particularly during the generation that immediately preceded Ramaz's founding, Christmas posed a major challenge to the maintenance of Jewish identity. For example, in the supposedly nonsectarian public schools, Yuletide symbols and stories about the baby Jesus, manger pageants, and the like, all reminded youngsters, Gentile and Jewish alike, that if America was not legally a Christian country, it was certainly a majority-Christian civilization. From their own perspectives, Jewish leaders used the crisis of Christmas to emphasize for their coreligionists both the differences between themselves and the Christian world and the Jews' ultimate minority status in free America. Practically that meant, that if the public schools were closed on this national holiday that in fact accommodated Christian religious sensibilities, Jewish schools had to be open: Jews could not grant tacit recognition to another faith's supremacy in this country.[37]

Ramaz, on the other hand, apprehended the Christmas season much long the same nontheological lines as did most Americans. They saw late December as a time where many Americans, particularly more affluent ones, took some time off for a winter vacation. Practically speaking, the public schools were closed, granting Jewish teachers employed in that system a week to play with their children or to visit with friends. The Gentile friends of Jewish children were also on holiday. Why, Ramaz asked, should Jews not be part of this national hiatus? Indeed, to do otherwise, to hold classes in the pre-New Year week and particularly on December 25th, would effectively demonstrate how different Jews were rather than how comparable they were to other American people. Thus for the Yorkville group, since the Christmas scene in America had been altogether secularized—not incidentally, many Christian leaders, to their own dismay, had to agree—there was no reason why Jews could not behave here like everyone else.[38]

If here Ramaz was so different from even its sister Americanized schools, there were many other equally suggestive social areas where other yeshivas in fact shared, followed, or approached Ramaz's understanding and acceptance of this country's life and ways. Though always the most American of yeshivas, Ramaz was rarely totally idiosyncratic in its acceptance of American mores. Indeed, that by the late 1960s, many schools that once agreed in principle with Ramaz, would then find what the Yorkville school continued and still explicitly accepted as no longer appropriate for them, points out not so much how distinctive Ramaz's version of American Orthodoxy was from its inception, but rather how different it became over time. The case-study model here being offered, centering around approaches to extracurricular activities, specifically athletics and mixed social dancing under Orthodox schools auspices, highlights just this changing phenomenon.

Clearly these sorts of recreational activities stem from American and not Jewish sources. True, one can tendentiously co-opt Maimonides' teaching that physical fitness is warranted to infer a medieval precedent for engaging in modern sports. Still, the fact remains that recreational calls to Jewish youths developed directly out of their encounter with the new host society. These activities were, for all to see, essentially American, but were they also the tabooed "ways of the Gentiles"?[39]

Historically speaking, immigrant youngsters were first exposed to sports and recreations, and with them, not incidentally, conceptions of American views of what was manly and womanly, along the streets of the downtown hubs and in the settlement houses. The founders of the "ghetto schools," totally in keeping with their philosophy of studied separatism from America, saw no place in the Jew's world for these Christian ways. Athletics took boys away from their Torah studies. Equally important, sports promoted the wrong type of man—the coach, the manager, and not the rabbi, the scholar—as the appropriate role model for their youngsters. Mixed social dancing was even more problematic. It brought boys and girls into direct social and physical contact. For them, the fact that America permitted teenagers to hold hands and bodies while dancing (and possibly after dancing as well) meant nothing. Jewish traditions of modesty, as they understood them, proscribed such behavior. The same could be said of questionable social contacts when athletic activities naturally developed into spectator sports. There not only did boys and girls sit together and socialize during games, but they often behaved in manners inappropriate for religious youth.[40]

Predictably, Ramaz explicitly defined athletics, sports, and social dancing as good American fun and not foreign ways. To be sure, they would admit that these activities were almost unknown in other times and places in Jewish history. But that truth did not render them *ipso facto* unkosher. Moreover, it was clear to them that American Jewish youngsters, regardless of what the tradition might say about appropriate behavior patterns, were playing, spectating, and dancing. Not incidentally, the parents of Ramaz's affluent, initial target constituency—and, for that matter, probably most other American Orthodox Jews of all social and economic ranks—fox-trotted and waltzed and played and watched ball. As they saw it, for Ramaz to rule out these extracurricular activities would have been tantamount to declaring the Yorkville initiative a "ghetto school" regardless of how modern its classrooms were, and how American its calendar. Besides which, no matter what schools might say, do, or not do, youngsters would find each other in some playground, dance floor, or worse. Wasn't it preferable, Ramaz concluded, to have teenagers at chaperoned games and dances where limits might be more realistically set. By the way, wasn't that also the American way?[41]

Remarkably enough here, Ramaz's appreciation of this cultural situation, at least for the years before the 1960s, was shared to a degree by almost all contemporary yeshivas, even those that in general had little good to say about Ramaz's educational and social philosophy. The prime difference, as we will presently see, was that whereas Ramaz was explicitly accepting of what these recreational/social events meant, other schools offered only implicit nods towards what they could not stop and were much more reserved in their formal approbation of what might go on.

In 1951, for example, sports, active and spectator, officially became part of New York yeshiva life when, under the auspices of Yeshiva University's Community Service Division, the Metropolitan

Jewish High School League was established. This conference initially joined together on the basketball hardwood boys' teams from the coed and most pedagogically progressive Ramaz, the single-sex, Talmud-intensive but general educationally modern Manhattan and Brooklyn TAs, the less secularly responsive Rabbi Jacob Joseph Yeshiva (RJJ), and three old-line "ghetto schools," the Mesivtas Chaim Berlin, Torah Vodaas, and Tifereth Jerusalem. Ramaz's older sister school, Flatbush, and their younger sibling, the Hebrew Institute of Long Island (HILI), would join the league just a few years later. There was also begun, early on, a girls' division linking Ramaz, Flatbush, HILI, and Brooklyn and Manhattan Centrals.

Once again, the affinity of Ramaz, Flatbush, and HILI for such an arrangement was not surprising. American public and private schools, which in this regard were their models, routinely sponsored athletic events. The participation of the TAs, RJJs, and Centrals, on the other hand, seems at first glance somewhat out of step with their school philosophies. And the membership of the Mesivtas in the league was well-nigh at total deviance from their approach to education and to America. What, for example, were the single-sex Yeshiva University High Schools doing countenancing their students attending, let us say, the Ramaz game where not only did pupils of both sexes sit together but where Ramaz female cheerleaders, in their short skirts, performed during time-outs and half-time? What of the TA/Central's conservative conception of Jewish definition of modesty? Should not the TA have demanded at least that there be no exposed thighs at the game and, maximally, that boys' games be viewed only by male students, and girls', by females? Such a demand would have easily permitted TA fellows and Central gals, as good American athletes, to compete to the best of their abilities and without the unwarranted distraction of the opposite sex.

And what of the joining of RJJ and the even more separatist Mesivtas into this most American of games? Shouldn't they have downed athletics for its clear contribution to *bitul torah* and emphatically opposed spectator sports for their creation of a patently immodest milieu? And yet the record shows that in the first decade of the league all schools played against each other, and whatever the results were, they all tacitly took the more liberal Ramaz-like view of the sporting scene.

Similar-style questions can be leveled, at least at the TAs, for their attitude towards their youths attending social dances sponsored by Ramaz. Clearly this American mixing of the sexes institutionally was not for them, although there is some evidence that chaperoned coeducational Saturday night parties, off school premises, were part of the BTA/Central scene under the watchful eyes of the girls' parents. At the same time, those youngsters who did attend the Yorkville-based functions did not risk the censure of their rebbes. That a BTA student-newspaper gossip column in 1951 could talk about a "TA senior who had such a hard time with his girl at the Ramaz dance" tells much about how open, known, and routine was the sight of the fox-trotting Yeshiva University High School student. And as far as Mesivta students were concerned, some too may have deviated from the European norms, but they did so more surreptitiously.[42]

The lines of demarcation in this social context between Ramaz and other yeshivas, and even more significantly among Ramaz, the TAs, and the Mesivtas, became much clearer in the 1960s. Ramaz cheerleaders still dressed the same way even if Saturday night dances were becoming passé and thus by their own lack of momentum were no longer an issue. TA officials still looked the other way as Ramaz girls sashayed by: They stayed in the Jewish league and thus continued to offer no formal opinion on the appropriateness of these events. But the Mesivtas moved on and out. Although it is impossible to say that Mesivta boys did not, on their own, attend these games—just as they may have been coming to dances earlier— open, spectator sports were clearly defined by school leaders as off-limits to their Orthodox boys.

But withal, a degree of acquiescence to these American social ways did endure at least into the 1970s. Condemnation of the social environment of basketball games did not immediately carry over to the game itself. For a while, this American pastime would continue to be part of their world through an Inter-Mesivta League where games were played in front of all-male audiences. There, even the most Orthodox of groups tacitly admitted that boys in this country liked to play ball, and no matter how unnecessary it might be, on balance, when monitored as closely as possible, it was countenanced as a less-harmful *bitul torah* than many other contemporary social and cultural pursuits. Even in the Mesivta, it was reasoned, boys will be boys.

The Ideal Product

In November 1953, the Ramaz Parents Council newspaper proudly reported that "the Ramaz infiltration of Morningside Heights and its daily newspaper became complete last month" when Columbia University's *Daily Spectator* ran a picture of four Ramaz graduates, newly arrived on that Ivy League campus, standing, freshman beanies and all, in front of the cupola in Vam Am Quadrangle. It was further reported that the featuring of the day school foursome in an article on freshman orientation at Columbia was orchestrated by the *Spectator's* associate editor, a 1952 Ramaz graduate. Four other Ramazites had a part in this pleasant conspiracy, serving as they did on the newspaper's staff.

Six months later, the same school organ reported that "the newsroom at the Columbia *Spectator* presents a picture not unlike a Ramaz alumni meeting" and remarked that the aforementioned associate editor "is really a B.M.O.C." (a big man on campus, to use 1950s parlance). In subsequent years, similar proud comments would be made to the parent and student bodies about the progress of the men and women of Ramaz in the Halls of Ivy.[43]

Ramaz officials readily confirmed that such notices were posted "with malice aforethought" to bolster confidence in the school among those parents whose belief in the academic rewards of a Ramaz Jewish day school education was less than complete. "The school is often asked," they emphasized,

what kind of adjustment a Day School student makes at his college or university. How does he do in his extracurricular activities? Well here is one answer. Five boys . . . all graduates of our school, have achieved the recognition of their fellows in a highly competitive field. What more can we ask for?[44]

In fact, Ramaz did ask for more. It expected that its young men at Columbia (and young women at Barnard) would, of course, do well in the classroom, thus upholding the school's high academic reputation. Equally important, the Looksteins expected that while learning all they could about the beauties of the secular world, they would remain true to Orthodox faith commitments. Probably the school was proudest when its Columbia men, "just to keep things integrated," were "the leaders in the organization of a daily *minyan* in the Columbia dorms."[45]

To be sure, Ramaz did somewhat more than just hope and expect that its Ivy League fellows would remain Jewish. Early on, Rabbi Joseph Lookstein was often a guest speaker at Inter-Collegiate Zionist Federation of America meetings at Columbia, possibly at the behest of Haskel Lookstein, Ramaz's first Ivy League student, who in the early 1950s was educational vice-president of the Zionist society. Rabbi Joseph also made himself available to student groups headed up by former Ramazites at other secular universities throughout the metropolitan area.[46]

In extolling the compatibility of the Ramazite with Ivy League lifestyles, the school implicitly discounted three widely held fears maintained by other Orthodox educational groups. Clearly it had little use for the concerns long articulated by the "ghetto schools" that college would religiously contaminate yeshiva boys by exposing them to secular subjects. (The solution to this "problem" officially and consistently offered by schools like Mesivta Torah Vodaas and Chaim Berlin, etc., had always been: If you can avoid it, don't go to college at all. But if you must go, for purely careerist reasons, enroll at night after a day insulated in your yeshiva and pick your courses carefully to avoid contamination.) Ramaz's whole approach, as we have noted, had always been to welcome, accept, and learn from secular realms and ideas in producing the modern American Orthodox intellectual.[47]

Lookstein's group also did not share the anxieties harbored by parents of, let us say, TA boys or Central girls, who were less fearful than the Mesivta Torah Vodaas people about what their children would learn but were more troubled about how they would live Jewishly on a secular college campus. These elders were in touch with the immediate, pre-World War II history of the American university that showed little concern for the Orthodox Jewish students' commitments to maintain their religious identities.

They remembered how Orthodox youngsters were marked absent and penalized if they absented themselves from classes on Jewish holidays and the Sabbath. They were aware that that era's social environment had made it unthinkable for an Orthodox boy to even consider wearing a *kipah* on campus. And remember, hats were not worn indoors. Gentlemen did not do that. Moreover, they had seen how in trying to fit in—maybe they wanted to write for the school newspaper, join the debating team, or the dramatics society, all of which met or worked on Friday night—Orthodox Jewish youths unlearned the holy lessons their prior yeshiva education had given them. For these parents, who respected and appreciated the secular but were fearful of the world of the college campus, the option of a Yeshiva College, founded in 1928, was a godsend. There youngsters could learn as other collegians did, while studying the Torah rigorously. And they could have good college fun under Orthodox auspices without misgivings and tensions.[48]

Ramaz's leaders were far more sanguine about the survivalist abilities of their former charges. For them, the Ivy League school was not a great challenge to faith that had to be avoided, but a profound proving ground for their approach to Jewish education. And the Looksteins believed that if they had done their job right—and they were confident from young Haskel's school days forward that they had—no harm to Judaism would come from this exciting secular environment.

To be sure, Ramaz's equanimity was heightened immeasurably by an old foe now slowly becoming a friend: the American university itself. It is coincidental, but nonetheless highly significant, that Ramaz began sending its first youngsters off to college in the early

1950s at the very point where the Ivys and others were beginning to respect, at least officially, the Jewish holidays and Sabbath. Total social acceptance within the dorms and on the student councils for the Orthodox Jews' somewhat idiosyncratic behavior would come a generation later. (By the 1970s, kosher dorm suites were readily available at Columbia, Princeton, long a bastion of genteel academic anti-Semitism, built its own kosher dining club.) Still, there was enough good news coming out of the deans' offices in the 1950s and 1960s to reassure the most religious of Ramaz parents that their sons could go to Columbia, their daughters to Barnard, and all would be well. And as far as social isolation was concerned, by the late 1950s, there were enough observant youths on campus to permit the founding and maintaining of specifically Jewish clubs and societies, like the ones Rabbi Joseph addressed, providing students with a social and cultural context for their Jewish allegiances. Not incidentally, the founding of Yavneh, the national Orthodox students organization on college campuses, took place at Columbia in the early 1960s under the leadership of Ramaz graduates.[49]

There was, however, a third fear held by other Orthodox elements that Ramaz could neither reject out of hand nor parry with the help of a changing, progressive American society. That was the very real concern that the student who went to the university, even if he remained true to the faith, would never truly become learned in the Torah, would never become a *talmid chacham.*

It was here that Ramaz, in its lack of concern with this anxiety, demonstrated how very different it was from so many other yeshivas. In a sense, the ideal product of the "ghetto schools" had been and was the rabbi raised on American soil but trained to stay apart from American culture who could hold his talmudic own with the Torah scholars of Europe. At the TA and beyond that at Yeshiva College, the ideal products were both the Torah scholar and the practicing rabbi and the committed layman with the highest possible credentials in Torah learning and with more than a reasonable affinity for the modern world. In a word, Yeshiva College at its best was to be more than a school for rabbis. Ramaz's ideal product was the committed Orthodox Jewish layman possessed of a modicum of facility with Torah sources and well-integrated into the modern world. It was explicitly not a pre-rabbinical school. And the record shows that it did not raise up many men who would later become rabbis. As of 1987, the school could number fewer than ten Orthodox rabbis, including Rabbi Haskel Lookstein, the founder's son. Rather, it was an institution for "the development of an informed and responsible Jewish laity." Accordingly, for at least the first generation and a half of its existence, Ramaz did not emphasize the goal of Torah education beyond high school days. Of course, if the Ramaz alumnus desired such continued training, there were, increasingly, credit-bearing Jewish studies courses available on their general college campuses. And there was the option of a junior year abroad, at Israeli institutions like the Hebrew and Tel Aviv Universities.[50]

A Different Responsiveness

Over the past score of years, the Ramaz School has remained essentially still the most economically and religiously heterogeneous of Jewish all-day schools. Affluent youngsters with Park Avenue addresses—as that first of Rabbi Joseph's dreams began to be realized in the late 1960s—have shared lab tables with scholarship children from throughout the Tri-State area. Most Ramaz families still feel comfortable on the social dance floor; at least they do at the school's annual dinner dance. And the most recent study of Ramaz families showed that late 1980s students were just about as kosher and as Sabbath-observing as those who attended the school a generation or more ago.[51]

At the same time, in several subtle and yet distinctive ways, under Rabbi Haskel's leadership, the school has become more "like a yeshiva." Mixed dancing classes and seasonal socials no longer occupy Ramaz's academic and extracurricular calendar. And Ramaz cheerleader attire has become more modest. These noticeable changes, of course, may have to do both with a new religiosity in the school as well as the changing mores and trends within American society. After all, there is still a mixed-voice school choir on campus, a somewhat less noteworthy if no less offensive deviation

from Orthodox practice elsewhere. And Ramaz classrooms, cocurric-
ular retreats, and extracurricular activities are still avowedly coeducational. What is undeniably reflective of a changed, more "yeshiva-
like" atmosphere at Ramaz is the redefinition of what constitutes the
school's ideal product. The best of Ramaz's graduates today is the
young man or young woman who attends an Ivy League school,
preparing there for a professional career, keeping the Sabbath and
kashruth while on campus, *after* having spent a year or more in
intensive post (high school) graduation Torah learning at a yeshiva
in Israel. This trend, which began in the mid-1970s, has been consistently supported by the school's administration. Rabbi Haskel, for
one, proudly declared in 1982:

> Yeshivat Har Etzion and then Harvard or Princeton; Michlala and then
> Barnard; Orot and then the University of Pennsylvania; Bet Midrash
> l'Torah and then Columbia; Kerem b'Yavneh and then Yeshiva—This
> is *Torah* and *Derekh Eretz* on a level which could hardly have been
> dreamed of in 1937 but which is a yearly reality for Ramaz students.[52]

Rabbi Haskel's inclusion of Yeshiva in this elite company is very
noteworthy. Ramaz students still do not enroll in large numbers at
Yeshiva College or Stern College directly out of high school. Ramaz
still emphasizes an Ivy League direction for its students, even as
Yeshiva has improved dramatically over the last generation as an
academic institution. But it is clear from here that when Ramazites
turn up at Yeshiva/Stern, by way of Israel, they are advertised as
well-respected Ramaz products.[53]

But withal and ironically so, the last years have also witnessed, in
another equally suggestive way, Ramaz becoming even less like
other yeshivas around it. Under Rabbi Haskel's leadership, Ramaz,
far more than other yeshivas, has emphasized the interrelatedness
of overt Jewish activism with Torah book learning, in forming the
character of the true "Man of Torah." The code word for this new
emphasis, "menschlichkeit," began to pervade Ramaz's halls in the
late 1960s.[54]

Menschlichkeit, as noted previously, does not mean here having
all the right social skills and behavioral graces. Rabbi Joseph's

school had always taken close note of that requirement. It meant rather seeing the great causes facing the Jewish people as the active, participatory responsibility of the yeshiva student. Ramaz has raised few barriers to its students' taking part with a full heart in Jewish and even in general social protest activities. Other yeshivas have articulated serious reservations about the limits of such behavior.

Take as a first example of difference, Ramaz's attitude, as opposed to that of other yeshivas, towards the Orthodox Jew's involvement in the discussions and protests that ensued just a generation ago over the Vietnam War.

Ramaz permitted and even encouraged its students to express themselves on this national tragedy and debate. For them, that was part of what it meant to be a good American. Equally important, that was also part of what it meant to them to be a good Jew. To punctuate this position, Ramaz conducted *y'mai iyun* (in a sense, teach-ins) to acquaint its youngsters with the issues and, most significantly, to explore how the war affected their lives as Jews. Rabbi Haskel declared Ramaz's October 1969 Moratorium Day program "the finest in any school. A representative of the Conservative Party and a Ramaz alumnus debated the issues . . . [and were] peppered by questions from the floor." After the assembly, school was adjourned as students were "informed where other Moratorium events were being held throughout the city."[55]

In designating these sessions *y'mai iyun,* Ramaz was utilizing a terminology normally reserved for straight Torah studies, thus according to this contemporary discussion of hawks and doves the high calling of *mitzvat talmud torah* (the commandment of studying the Torah). No other yeshiva so totally integrated the present-day scene with the teaching of American values and Jewish traditions.

In fact, many other yeshivas harbored serious qualms about such activities. Questioners included those who believed that these world issues were patently not the concern of the Jew, certainly not the interest of the Man of Torah. Moreover, the using of the street as a classroom and the turning of the classroom into a debate forum was deemed a *bitul torah* (an unconscionable waste of time). Additionally, some argued, in a quasi-philosophical, mystical vein, that if yeshiva students truly wanted to save the world, the best way to achieve same would be by sticking to their books. The merit, they allowed, that would come to all by uninterrupted study by *talmedei chachamim* might somehow have the power to save mankind. One such spokesman offered this analogy: Asking Men of Torah to actively involve themselves in the national debate was tantamount to taking medical researchers from their laboratories while they were engaged in research that could end an epidemic to administer impermanent inoculations to the general population.

Given this point of view, the only possible rationale for leaving the *beth midrash* would be the exigencies of a *sha'at ha-dechak* (an emergency situation facing the *Jewish* people that required hands-on attention). And even then, when Orthodox Jews did take action, they had to be most careful that they did not commit a *chilul ha-shem* (a desecration of God's name) by associating with the wrong people (radicals or even nonobservant Jews).[56]

Ramaz, for its part, was no less concerned with desecration, although its conception of what actually constituted that act was somewhat narrower. Where it disagreed most profoundly with other yeshiva groups was in its acceptance of the widest range of Jewish colleagues in fights for good causes. This difference of opinion was most clearly dramatized in Ramaz's response to an almost universally acknowledged *sha'at ha-dechak*: the 1970s American Jewish struggle on behalf of Soviet Jewry.

By the late 1960s, it was abundantly clear to almost all Orthodox Jews, and to American Jewry in general, that the spiritual persecution of Soviet Jewry had reached a *sha'at ha-dechak*. And in most circles, there was general approbation for nonviolent street protest as a means of gaining wide media attention and popular support for the human rights cause. To be sure, the nascent Jewish Defense League believed that nonviolence was not a strong enough response. And elements, interestingly enough, within both the Jewish establishment and the old-line Orthodox community felt that quiet diplomacy was the best response. But both of these opinions were held by a minority of committed Jews.[57]

For Ramaz, there was no question but that peaceful activism was the way to proceed. Beginning in 1970, it opened its doors to the largely Orthodox Student Struggle for Soviet Jewry (SSSJ), and continued to do so over the next fifteen years. In fact, Ramaz youngsters once again outside of the classroom, were among the sturdiest foot soldiers for the SSSJ when they conducted in 1983 an ongoing morning prayer vigil for refusenik Anatoly Shcharansky. For the school, this act was the highest possible manifestation of menschlichkeit. Equally important, over the past generation and on into today, Rabbi Lookstein and the school have cooperated fully with legitimate protest groups not linked with American Orthodoxy. For the Yorkville contingent, it made no difference whether those standing shoulder to shoulder with them on the picket line were Conservative or Reform Jews or their leaders, all were engaged in the holy mission of *pidyon shevuim* (redemption of the captives).[58]

To Ramaz's dismay, this point of view was not universally held by Orthodox Jews. The counterargument, of course, was that although saving Soviet Jewry is unquestionably a *sha'at ha-dechak* and truly worthy of Orthodox attention, the most traditional Jews should go it alone in presenting their case: cooperation with Conservatives and Reformers on this nonspecifically religious issue, it is argued, tends to add legitimacy and recognition to these "deviances" when attention is turned to purely halakhic realms.

That viewpoint was expressed dramatically in 1985 when a group of 120 Orthodox, Conservative, and Reform rabbis, sat down and were arrested *en masse* in front of the Soviet Mission to the United Nations. Many of Lookstein's colleagues, leaders of other yeshivas and Orthodox Jewish communal organizations, participated in this community-wide protest. But many others stayed away, so strong was their sense of denominationalism.[59]

For a disappointed Haskel Lookstein, this noncooperation constituted continuing evidence that even if in his own outlook, in his school's Torah classes, and in the messages being given to his students in and beyond Ramaz's hallowed halls, the school today is more like a yeshiva than the academy of his father's day, when all is said and done, it remains so very different and apart from the "yeshiva world." In a sense, as the 1980s closed, Ramaz displayed some of the behavioral characteristics tacitly acceptable to the yeshiva world thirty years ago. But that world had itself moved significantly away from those early, tentative, early post-war moorings. And so, the Ramaz version of American Orthodoxy remained distinctive, and if emulated by some, was more often than not, a minority opinion within this country's Orthodox community.[60]

Notes

The following abbreviations are used:

AH	*American Hebrew*
AJA	*American Jewish Archives*
AJH	*American Jewish History*
AJHQ	*American Jewish Historical Quarterly*
AJYB	*American Jewish Yearbook*
EJ	*Encyclopaedia Judaica (Jerusalem and New York, 1971–72)*
HS	*Hebrew Standard*
JARSP-NYPL	*Jacob A. Riis Settlement Papers-New York Public Library*
JARP-LC	*Jacob A. Riis Papers-Library of Congress*
JARP-NYPL	*Jacob A. Riis Papers-New York Public Library*
JHSP-AJA	*Jacob H. Schiff Papers-American Jewish Archives*
JCR	*Jewish Communal Register, New York: Kehillah (Jewish Community), 1917–1918*
LMP-AJA	*Louis Marshall Papers, American Jewish Archives*
MA	*Judah L. Magnes Archives. Jewish Historical General Archives, Jerusalem, Israel; copy of file at American Jewish Archives, Cincinnati, Ohio.*
Min CED	*Minutes of the meeting of the Committee on Education of the Jewish Community of New York*
Min ECK	*Minutes of the Executive Committee of the Kehillah*
Minutes	*Minutes of the Eldridge Street Synagogue, 12–16 Eldridge Street. New York, 1890–1916*
MJ	*Morgen Zhurnal*
OU	*Orthodox Union*
PAAJR	*Proceedings of the American Academy for Jewish Research*
PAJHS	*Publications of the American Jewish Historical Society*
RA	*Archives of the Ramaz School*
RM	*Ramaz Mirror*
UJE	*Universal Jewish Encyclopedia (New York, 1939–43)*
YT	*Yiddishes Tageblatt*

Notes to Introduction

1.   See Moshe Davis, *The Emergence of Conservative Judaism: The Historical School in Nineteenth Century America* (Philadelphia, 1963), pp. 18–19 for his characterizations of Orthodoxy and Historical School Judaism. See also, pp. 334, 335, 351, 354 for his categorization of Dembitz, Drachman, Mendes and Morais as members of the Historical School.

2.   Marshall Sklare, *Conservative Judaism: An American Religious Movement* (Glencoe, Ill., 1955), p. 44, Will Herberg, *Protestant-Catholic-Jew: An Essay in American Religious Sociology* (Garden City, 1955), p. 183.

3.   Abraham S. Karp, "New York Chooses a Chief Rabbi," *PAJHS* (March 1954): 127–198.

4.   For Sklare's understanding of the geographical progress in the rise of Conservative Judaism see pp. 47–48. See also Nathan Glazer, *American Judaism* (Chicago, 1957) pp. 81–85, 91–92.

5.   Jeffrey S. Gurock, *When Harlem Was Jewish, 1870–1930* (New York, 1979), pp. 98–108, 116.

6.   It should be noted that sociologist Charles Liebman was the first to critique Davis' definitions and portrayals of Orthodoxy and Conservatism in America as they relate to Mendes, Drachman and the like. Liebman spoke, I believe correctly, of an Orthodoxy that was distinctive from both the Historical School and the old-line Orthodoxy of Rabbi Jacob Joseph. See Liebman's, "Orthodoxy in Nineteenth Century America" *Tradition* (Spring/Summer 1964): 138–147 and Karp's rejoinder "The Origins of Conservative Judaism," *Conservative Judaism* (Summer 1965): 32–48 which is supportive of Davis' view. My work on the American Orthodox rabbinate acknowledges Liebman's work even as it identifies and explores further American Orthodoxy as an ongoing group and phenomenon that has existed for more than century in competition with Historical School and Conservative Judaism.

Notes to Chapter 1, *Resisters and Accommodators: Varieties of Orthodox Rabbis in America, 1886–1983*

1.   Moshe Davis. *The Emergence of Conservative Judaism* (Philadelphia, 1963), p. 237; Bernard Drachman, *The Unfailing Light* (New York, 1948), pp. 177–182; Cyrus Adler; "Semi-Centennial Address," in *The Jewish Theological Seminary of America: Semi-Centennial Volume*, ed. Cyrus Adler (New York, 1939), pp. 5–7; Henry Pereira Mendes, "The Beginnings of the Seminary," *ibid.*, pp. 35–42.

2.   The dividing lines between "Orthodox" and "Conservative" rabbis involved in this initiative were much less the differences in their rabbinical training than in their philosophy and practices in American pulpits after ordination. The similarity in their rabbinical training, whether they are indicated in the text as "Orthodox" or "Conservative," is evidenced by the following comparisons. Among those of Ashkenazic origins, both Drachman and Kohut were graduates of the Breslau Seminary, the former in 1885, the latter eighteen years earlier. Schneeberger was ordained by Azriel Hildesheimer in Berlin in 1871, Aaron Wise was ordained by the same man a few years earlier when Hildesheimer was still in Eisenstadt, Hungary.

Wise and his older colleague Kohut significantly were students at the Pressburg Yeshiva in Hungary, the school of Rabbi Moses Sofer (the *Hatam Sofer*), before gaining ordination among more modern, liberal exponents of traditional Judaism. Bettelheim was ordained in the 1860s by Rabbi Shlomo Yehudah Leib Rappaport, the famous traditional rabbinical pioneer of the Haskalah and supporter of *Wissenschaft des Judentums*. Marcus Jastrow, ordained by Rabbis Moses Feilchenfeld of Rogasen and Wolf Landau of Dresden, clearly received at least as traditional a training as the other American-serving rabbis, both Orthodox and Conservative. Probably the most traditionally trained rabbi in the group was Rabbi Moses Maisner. He was ordained by Rabbi A. S. B. Sofer of the Pressburg Yeshiva. Drachman described his colleague as a "strong adherent of Orthodox teachings who served Adath Israel Synagogue of New York." See *AJYB* 5664 (1903–4), p. 77 and Drachman, p. 179. Importantly, all the rabbis here mentioned, including Maisner were recipients of Ph.D.s from recognized Central European universities. See below for a discussion of the levels of Orthodox training received by those who defined themselves as Orthodox in the America of the 1880s. For now, the heterodoxy of practice among those defining themselves as Conservative is evidenced by the fact that Kohut of New York's Ahavath Chesed, Wise at the city's Rodef Shalom, and Jastrow at Philadelphia's Rodef Shalom all came to pulpits which had already broken with totally distinct Orthodox practices. Bettelheim was rabbi in the Baltimore Hebrew Congregation, which used the Jastrow-Szold prayerbook and permitted mixed seating during the services. Significantly, his Orthodox colleague Schneeberger served that city's Congregation Chizuk Emunah, whose members had broken away from the Baltimore Hebrew Congregation over the issue of mixed seating.

Among the Sephardic rabbis, the Mendeses, father and son, were members of a British-based rabbinical house. Both received secular training at English-style schools and universities and were trained for the rabbinate primarily at home through family tutors. Their father and grandfather was London Rabbi David Aaron De Sola. Meldola De Sola of Montreal, another of the fourteen Seminary founders, was also a grandson of David De Sola. Sabato Morais, commonly acknowledged as the greatest guiding spirit behind the Seminary, was privately trained for the rabbinate in Italy and ordained by Rabbi Abraham Baruch Piperno of Leghorn. Henry S. Jacobs, born in Kingston, Jamaica, rabbi of Ashkenazic Congregation B'nai Jeshurun of New York in 1886, also claimed Sephardic heritage and received similar training. He was ordained by Rabbi N. Nathan of Kingston and served at Shearith Israel (New York) for two years before moving on to B'nai Jeshurun. There he was more comfortable with the abridged Torah reading and other variations which made that congregation, in the words of its historian, "classified as Conservative-Reform, together with Jastrow of Philadelphia and Szold of Baltimore."

Rabbis Weil and Davidson are the remaining rabbis mentioned in the sources as involved with the founding of the Seminary. I have been unable to find any background information on these two figures except for the random remark in an *AJYB* listing of rabbis and cantors in 1903–4 that a Rabbi D. Davidson served Congregation Agudath Jesharim in New York City. For more details on these rabbis, see

Davis, pp. 329–366; Israel Goldstein, *A Century of Judaism in New York* (New York, 1930), pp. 160–163; Isaac Markens, *The Hebrews in America* (New York, 1888), pp. 275–308; Isaac Fein, *The Making of an American Jewish Community: The History of Baltimore Jewry* (Philadelphia, 1971), pp. 118–119. David De Sola Pool and Tamar De Sola Pool, *Old Faith in a New World* (New York, 1955), pp. 192–194, 425; Guido Kisch, ed., *Das Breslauer Seminar: Jüdisch-Theologisches Seminar (Fraenkelscher Stiftung) in Breslau 1854–1938* (Tübingen, 1963), pp. 381–403.

3.   This denominational historiographic point of view is clearly most reflected in Davis's *The Emergence of Conservative Judaism.* See also on this trend, Herbert Parzen, *Architects of Conservative Judaism* (New York, 1964), pp. 18–25.

4.   Mendes, pp. 35–41. See also on the purposes of the early Seminary, Davis, p. 237; Adler; pp. 5–7; and Drachman, pp. 177–182. There is a significant difference of opinion among both historians and contemporary observers as to the relative strength of the so-called Orthodox as opposed to the Conservative factions in the organizing of the Seminary. Clearly reflecting later denominational tensions and prejudices, Drachman's autobiography suggests that Kohut "was the only rabbinical representative of Conservative Judaism." See Drachman, p. 179. Cyrus Adler, in his contribution to the Jewish Theological Seminary festschrift, talks of a highly heterogeneous grouping "reflecting varying views." See Adler; p. 5. Davis's work suggests a view of these events similar to Adler's. In like manner; Drachman is clear in his understanding of the early Seminary as having an "uncompromising adherence to the tenets of Orthodox Judaism (although the term 'Orthodox' is not used." See Drachman, pp. 181–182. Davis emphasizes the heterogeneity of opinion which pervaded the Seminary. For our purposes it is clear; however; that the self-defined Orthodox leaders in the institution saw their work as strictly Orthodox, albeit looking, as Drachman put it, "for the harmonious combination of Orthodox Judaism in America which to me was the true concept of Judaism." See Drachman, p. 206.

5.   Abraham J. Karp, "New York Chooses a Chief Rabbi," *PAJHS* (March 1954), pp. 129–194. Jonathan D. Sarna, trans. and ed., *People Walk on Their Heads: Moses Weinberger's Jews and Judaism in New York* (New York, 1982), pp. 22, 111–114.

6.   The suggestion that the rabbis here engaged in organization building viewed themselves as Orthodox rabbis creating Orthodox institutions in America is evidenced either by their contemporary statements or by their later activities. Morais, for example, argued during the deliberations over the founding of the Seminary that it should be called "The Orthodox Seminary." See Davis, p. 235. Drachman, as noted previously, argued that "although a certain proportion of the organizing delegation and participating rabbis belonged to the Conservative wing of Judaism, the principles of the Seminary . . . were those of uncompromising adherence to the tenets of Orthodox Judaism." See Drachman, p. 181. The Mendeses and Schneeberger were founders-leaders of both the Seminary and the later Union of Orthodox Jewish Congregations of America, which was formed in 1898 to promote "Orthodox Judaism whenever occasions arise in civic and social matters." See Israel M. Goldman, "Henry W. Schneeberger: His Role in American Judaism," *AJHQ* (December 1967): 179, and *AH*, January 4, 1901, pp. 231–233. Additionally, not only did the men see themselves as Orthodox, but they were perceived as such by

some significant contemporary observers. Rabbi Joseph H. Hertz, a student of Morais, eulogized his teacher as "the trusted leader of Orthodox Judaism in America." See J. H. Hertz, "Sabato Morais: A Pupil's Tribute," in Adler; p. 47. Drachman himself referred to Morais, H. P. Mendes, and Schneeberger as "splendid representatives of the Orthodox ministry." See Drachman, pp. 177–182. But probably the most significant "testimony" to Morais's Orthodoxy is the appreciation of him expressed by the Agudath ha-Rabbanim, which, as we will immediately see, represented transplanted East European forms of Orthodoxy in America. Its *Sefer ha-Yovel shel Agudath ha-Rabbanim ha-Ortodoksim de-Artsot ha-Brit ve-Kanada* (New York, 1928) recounted the history of the Jewish Theological Seminary and stated that "the founder of the Seminary, Dr. Sabato Morais, was indeed an upholder of the old traditions, and the early students who emerged from there were full-hearted for the faith of Israel and its Torah." The *Sefer ha-Yovel* then contrasts Morais's upholding of old traditions with the later "conservatives, so-called 'upholders of old traditions' who did not deserve to be called such." See *Sefer ha-Yovel*, p. 18. To be abundantly fair; it should be noted that the publication of Davis's book sparked an important historiographic debate as to how the designations "Conservative" and "Orthodox" may be used in dealing with nineteenth century figures. One of the most spirited exchanges was between Abraham J. Karp and Charles Liebman on the question of Morais's designation as Orthodox. Liebman claimed that "Morais . . . must be reclaimed to Orthodoxy," based upon his textual-based understanding that when Morais used the term "enlightened conservatism" he was referring to modern forms of Orthodoxy. If "conservatism" did not mean Orthodoxy, it is unlikely he would have used the term "Orthodox" in his defense of the Seminary to Reform Rabbi Richard Gottheil as an "Orthodox institution which will win many converts to intelligent conservatism." Liebman also notes historiographically that in other writings Davis characterized Morais as "the unflagging champion of traditional Judaism." For Liebman "the first head of the Seminary was apparently fond of the term 'conservative' as a synonym for Orthodoxy." Karp, on the other hand, while admitting that Morais called himself Orthodox and "espoused the cause of Orthodoxy," he displayed many un-Orthodox philosophical and practical features uncharacteristic of "the Orthodoxy of a rabbi living in the 19th century." Morais, for example, worked with non-Orthodox elements in both nontheological, communal endeavors and in the founding of Maimonides College. Morais also chose as his colleagues on the advisory board of the Seminary men like Jastrow, Szold, Kohut, etc., for Karp "hardly an Orthodox rabbinic body." Most significantly, Karp quotes Morais as advocating liturgical change and philosophical departures deviating from Orthodox belief. Our suggestion is that Morais may be characterized as an Orthodox rabbi based on his self-definition and activities, his acceptance as such by his American Orthodox colleagues, and most notably his acceptance by the Agudath ha-Rabbanim. Clearly Karp is right in arguing that Rabbi Hayim Soloveitchik of Brest-Litovsk, Isaac Elchanan Spektor of Kovno, or even Samson Raphael Hirsch of Frankfurt am Main might not have called Morais an Orthodox rabbi. But that conceivable nonrecognition does not make him a Historical School rabbi by default. Rather, he and his generation of Orthodox rabbis Drachman, Schneeberger, *et al.* as we will see below, are spiritual, when not actual, antecedents of the "Orthodoxy espoused and practiced by the Rabbinical Council of America in the present decade of the 20th century," a basis of judgment of Orthodoxy which Karp feels cannot be used in evaluating Morais. See on this debate, Charles Liebman, "Orthodoxy in Nineteenth Century America," *Tradition* (Spring–Summer 1964): 132–140, and Abraham J. Karp, "The Origins of Conservative Judaism," *Conservative Judaism* (Summer 1965): 33–48. There is, of course, no historical debate or question concerning the Orthodox affiliation of Rabbi Jacob Joseph.

7.   Karp, pp. 143–144; Max S. Nussenbaum, "Champion of Orthodox Judaism: A Biography of Sabato Morais" (D.H.L. diss., Bernard Revel Graduate School, Yeshiva University, 1964), pp. 1–10; *JE*, vol. 8, pp. 486–487. The elder Mendes, though not a university graduate, was well versed enough in secular culture to run Northwick College, a school for Anglicized Jewish youths.

8.   Drachman, pp. 3, 100, 151, 165, 167, and *passim*.

9.   Goldman, pp. 153–159 and *passim*.

10.   The elder Mendes was born and raised in Kingston, Jamaica, where he established the Beth Limud School of Kingston. He resigned that post when he moved on to England for his "family-based" rabbinical training. After service in a pulpit in Birmingham he was elected to a pulpit in London, where he built Northwick College, a Jewish boarding school. H. P. Mendes attended his father's school, which drew to its student body the children of Anglicized upper-middle class families of varying religious commitments. It offered them a combined secular and religious curriculum. On the Mendeses' early training and associational patterns, see *JE*, vol. 8., p. 468, and Eugene Markovitz, "Henry P. Mendes: Builder of Traditional Judaism in America," (D.H.L. diss., Bernard Revel Graduate School, Yeshiva University, 1961), pp. 4–5. Morais, similarly, had a broad associational pattern with Jews of all stripes as well as non-Jews. He counted among his closest Jewish friends Emanuel Felici Veneziani, who was destined to be named Chevalier of the Crown of Italy, Israel Costa, later Chief Rabbi of Leghorn, and Raffaelo Ascoli, lawyer and writer. His membership in the Order of Free Masons of Italy testified to his associational history with non-Jews, particularly Italian patriots, in his youth and young manhood. See Nussenbaum, pp. 7–10. For an example of Morais's communication, if not participation, on nontheological issues with Reform rabbis, see Nussenbaum, p. 150, for a discussion of Jastrow, Mendes, and Joseph Krauskopf mediating an 1890 Philadelphia cloakmakers' strike. The Mendeses showed their interdenominational orientation in their activities in the founding and early leadership of the New York Board of Jewish Ministers, later the Board of Rabbis. See Markovitz, pp. 133–153, for discussions of their combined antimissionary and promodern Jewish education work.

11.   Drachman, pp. 100, 206. Drachman insisted in an appended note to his autobiography, that he did not agree with the view which saw Hildesheimer's Berlin Seminary as Orthodox and by analogy his education as less than Orthodox. For him, Breslau, which advocated "the bindingness of Jewish law," and Berlin, which advocated "the harmonious union of Orthodox faith and modern culture," were both Orthodox institutions. He did, of course, note that some other Orthodox

respected even the Orthodoxy of Hildesheimer. For him, Breslau and Berlin were both "in fundamental harmony with the basic concept of Traditional Judaism and its adjustment to modern conditions."

12. Although the committee that chose the chief rabbi was concerned about the "various shades of Orthodoxy . . . in America," Rabbi Jacob Joseph himself never spoke out publicly in criticism of the legitimacy of the Orthodox ordination claimed by his English-Sephardic and American-born Ashkenazic colleagues. Indeed, there is some evidence that at least one of his contemporaries both recognized the existence of an American Orthodoxy uptown that was different from theirs and was pleased with its activities. Weinberger, in a letter to a friend in Hungary, spoke of "uptown congregation named Orach Chayim, whose members are enormously wealthy and completely German. . . who go there daily for the afternoon prayers and to engage in Torah study." See Sarna, p. 116. Polish-born Abraham Neumark, trained at rabbinical seminaries in Berlin and Breslau, was spiritual leader of that congregation. His educational profile is clearly not unlike Schneeberger's or Drachman's. See Ben Zion Eisenstadt, *Anshe Hashem b'Arzeis Ha-Bris* (St. Louis, 1933), p. 21, for Neumark's biography.

Despite this "character witness," additional questions could have been raised, and would still be cogent today, as to the acceptability of the ordination of the Seminary Orthodox group to those of East European heritage. Critics of the Sephardim would have relatively little difficulty with the ritual and philosophical Orthodoxy of those who ordained Morais and Mendes. But they might question the levels of knowledge of traditional Talmud and rabbinic sources achieved by their colleagues. The Sephardim might be seen as Orthodox but not as highly revered or respected as Orthodox rabbis. Observers seeking to denigrate Schneeberger's legitimacy might also criticize his early training and facility with traditional texts. And questions could be raised about his teacher Hildesheimer. Though widely seen as an Orthodox rabbi by German Jewry, it is clear that he moved his seminary from Eisenstadt to Berlin because of opposition to him emanating from Hungarian rabbis, disciples of the Hatam Sofer, who deplored his modernism. See on Hildesheimer *EJ*, vol. 8, col. 478, and Leo Jung, ed., *Jewish Leaders (1750–1940)* (New York, 1953), pp. 220–221. However; it also should be noted that Hildesheimer was "orthodox enough" for the committee which selected Rabbi Jacob Joseph to solicit his opinion about possible candidates for the chief rabbinate of New York. See Karp, p. 137.

Bernard Drachman's case presents far more problems. He might be "disqualified" from the Orthodox rabbinate on the basis of his early training as well as the background of his teachers. At the Breslau seminary, Drachman counted as his teachers a most heterogeneous faculty which included Heinrich Graetz, Manuel Joel, Israel Lewy, David Rosin, Jacob Freudenthal, and Baruch Zuckerman. All of these scholars were advocates of the philosophy of *Wissenschaft des Judentums*, and friends, colleagues, or disciples of Zachariah Frankel. Although Drachman claimed for himself a belief "in the bindingness of the authority of tradition upon the individual conscience," he was ordained by Joel, a recognized contemporary supporter of Frankel, who clearly questioned the untrammeled validity of the oral law. See on the history of the Breslau seminary, Isaac Heinemann, "The Idea of the Jewish Theological

Seminary 75 Years Ago and Today," in Kisch, pp. 85–101. At all events, I believe that Drachman proved his Orthodoxy not so much at the Breslau seminary but immediately thereafter, when he left one of his earliest pulpits, at New York's Congregation Bikur Cholim, over the issue of the synagogue trustees' demand that he support their initiative toward mixed seating in the services. That act, more than philosophical pronouncements and educational background, might ultimately prove to be the most effective historical guideline between American Orthodoxy and American Conservatism in the nineteenth century.

Even if Rabbi Jacob Joseph could havè accepted this appreciation of Drachman as Orthodox, he might still have had difficulties with the ongoing affiliation of Drachman and his associates with the Jewish Theological Seminary. They all called their work Orthodox, but an examination of the institution's earliest curriculum would raise additional questions. Not only were they part of a most heterogeneous faculty but they were training rabbis in a way more reminiscent of Breslau, if not Geiger's Berlin, than of Volozhin. The Bible was "the principal text book of the Seminary . . . selected portions of the Talmud form[ed] a part of each year's instruction," Jewish history would be taught primarily for "its bearing upon the history of the world," and all graduates were to be required to have a secular education. Additionally, words like "critical accuracy" and "Historical Judaism" were used to describe the approach toward study, phrases that could be construed as supporting either American Orthodoxy or Conservatism but certainly not the Orthodoxy of East European Rabbi Jacob Joseph. See Davis, pp. 240–241, for the Jewish Theological Seminary statement on curriculum.

13. Karp, p. 188.

14. Benjamin Kline Hunnicutt, "The Jewish Sabbath Movement in the Early Twentieth Century," *AJH* (December 1979), pp. 196–215.

15. Clearly Mendes, Morais, *et al.* had no cause to denigrate the legitimacy of Rabbi Jacob Joseph's Orthodox ordination. But they did outspokenly question his effectiveness as an American Orthodox rabbi. H. P. Mendes wondered out loud, "will he be able to take up the fight against the encroaching steps of Reform in America? Do not give way to false hopes. Those who come after you will be Americans, full-blooded Americans like your brethren in faith uptown." And Morais chimed in, "[Rabbi Joseph) is not a cultured man. He does not possess the knowledge nor the literary attainments which a rabbi should possess." See *American Israelite*, March 30, 1888, and *New York Herald*, July 31, 1888, quoted in Karp, p. 153.

16. It is interesting to note that in attempting to recreate rabbinic authority in America, specifically on the kosher meat issue, Rabbi Joseph ultimately had to turn to his uptown American Orthodox colleagues H. P. Mendes and Drachman for help in bringing the wholesale butchers into line. Drachman and Mendes aided their downtown associate, although for them meat monitoring was not the highest communal concern. See Karp, p. 169.

17. Sarna, pp. 51–56.

18. The Orthodox rabbinate in America, of course, predates the 1880s. Rabbi Abraham Rice of Baltimore is generally acknowledged as the first ordained rabbi to serve in this country. A student of Rabbis Abraham Bing and Wolf Hamburger of

the yeshiva in Wuerzburg, he arrived in the United States in 1840 and served in Baltimore, Maryland. He was joined in the American Orthodox pulpit in 1853 when Rabbi Bernard Illowy arrived from Hungary. A student of Rabbi Moses Schreiber of Pressburg and later the recipient of a Ph.D. from the University of Budapest, Illowy served in pulpits in New York, Philadelphia, and New Orleans before becoming Rice's Baltimore-based colleague in the 1860s. Representatives of the East European Orthodox rabbinate in the United States pre-1887 include Rabbis Abraham Joseph Ash of New York, Abraham Jacob Lesser of Chicago, New York's Joseph Moses Aaronsohn and, of course, Moses Weinberger. Ash served Beth Hamedrosh Hagodol intermittently from 1860 until his death in 1887. His passing helped precipitate the search which led to Rabbi Jacob Joseph's selection. Rabbi Lesser, trained at yeshivas in Mir and Minsk, came to the United States in 1880 and served in Chicago until 1900, when he moved to Cincinnati. Rabbi Aaronsohn was, in the words of one contemporary Hebrew journalist, Zvi Hirsch Bernstein, "the first Orthodox rabbi in America with the exception of Rabbi Abraham Joseph Ash." See on these early rabbinical figures, Fein, pp. 54–55, 95, and *passim*; Israel Tabak, "Rabbi Abraham Rice of Baltimore," *Tradition* (Summer 1965), pp. 100–120; David Ellenson, "A Jewish Legal Decision by Rabbi Bernard Illowy of New Orleans and Its Discussion in Nineteenth Century Europe," *AJH* (December 1979), pp. 174–195; Sarna, pp. 4–5; Judah D. Eisenstein, "History of the First Russian-American Jewish Congregation," *PAJHS* (1901): 3–74; *Sefer ha-Yovel*, p. 137; Zvi Hirsch Bernstein, "On Jews and Judaism Thirty-Five Years Ago," *Yalkut Maarabi* (1904), p. 129. Of course, such notables as Rev. Gershom Mendes Seixas and Rev. Isaac Leeser served as ministers/hazzanim and spokesmen for traditional Judaism in this country from the late eighteenth through the mid-nineteenth century without the benefit of ordination.

19. For a graphic representation of the information extant on these founding members, see Benzion Eisenstadt, *Chachme Yisrael beAmerika* (New York, 1903).

20. *Sefer ha-Yovel*, pp. 13–21.

21. The *Sefer ha-Yovel* reports that the organizational meeting at Ramaz's home in Boston took place "at the time of the Zionist meeting" in that city (undoubtedly the Federation of American Zionists meeting), raising the question of what impact Zionism's secular nature made on the founding of the Agudath ha-Rabbanim. The winter of 1901–1902 is, of course, a significant time-frame in general Zionist history. In December 1901, at the Fifth Zionist Congress, a resolution was passed favoring a program fostering global Zionist national education, the launching of secular Hebrew culture as part of the Zionist movement. Religious Zionists angered by the resolution's total omission of any religious orientation to the Zionists' Jewish cultural activities met four months later under the leadership of Rabbi Isaac Jacob Reines to organize as an independent body to protect the interests of religious Jews in the Zionist movement. The World Mizrachi movement would soon emerge out of these latter deliberations. Looking at America, the limited historiography on the early years of Zionism in this country indicates that East European Rabbis Margolies and Philip Hillel Klein, along with—and significantly so—Drachman and Mendes, were among the early backers of Hovevei Zion in New York. The Hebrew

and Yiddish press of the day noted that these rabbis addressed Zionist cell meetings. Additionally, the *Encyclopedia of Religious Zionism* indicates that Rabbis Dov Baer Abramovitz, Abraham Eliezer Alperstein, Joseph Grossman, Bernard Levinthal, and Margolies—all charter members of the Agudath ha-Rabbanim—were consistent supporters of Mizrachi both here and abroad. Thus it is not surprising to find Levinthal, Ramaz, and others attending the New England conclave in May 1902. And although that convention did not deal with the Mizrachi question of East Europe, the problem of religious Judaism being overlooked might well have been on their minds when a resolution to condemn Dr. Emil G. Hirsch for asserting that "the Sabbath is dead" was considered out of order by some Zionist delegates who asserted that "the Zionist movement does not recognize religious questions." That may well have made some impact upon the Orthodox rabbis there at the convention. Of course, Sabbath observance would become a basic plank of the Agudath ha-Rabbanim's program.

In any event, it is important to note that both the organization and its member rabbis as individuals, though resisting of Americanization, were not anti-Zionist. In 1903, at the Agudath ha-Rabbanim's second annual convention, "Zionism was unanimously accepted as part of the Conference program." A year later, a eulogy for Theodor Herzl was pronounced by Rabbi Margolies at the third convention. As late as 1936, the Agudath ha-Rabbanim could congratulate the American Mizrachi on its twenty-fifth anniversary. The era of anti-Zionism among Orthodox rabbis in America dates from a later period, clearly much later than the rise of organizational anti-Zionism of the Agudath Israel in Eastern Europe. See below for a discussion of postwar anti-Zionism among Orthodox rabbis. See on the foregoing discussion, *AH*, May 30, 1902, pp. 39–41; *AJYB* 5664 (1903–1904), p. 161, and 5665 (1904–5), p. 282; Hyman B. Grinstein, "Memoirs and Scrapbooks of Joseph Isaac Bluestone," *PAJHS* (1939): 53–64; Samuel Rosenblatt, *The History of the Mizrachi Movement* (New York, 1951), pp. 1–20; Pinchas Churgin and Leon Gellman, *Mizrachi: Jubilee Publication of the Mizrachi Organization of America (1911–1936)* (New York, 1936).

22.   There is some disagreement in the sources about the date of the meeting in Ramaz's home. The *Sefer ha-Yovel* states that the meeting was held in the month of Adar (February–March) at the time of the Zionist convention in Boston. That year, the Zionist convention in Boston met at the end of May. Our working assumption is that the Adar date is mistaken.

23.   *Sefer ha-Yovel*, p. 24.

24.   *Ibid.* For an English translation of the Agudath ha-Rabbanim's constitution, see Aaron Rakeffet-Rothkoff, *The Silver Years in American Orthodoxy: Rabbi Eliezer Silver and His Generation* (Jerusalem and New York, 1981), p. 316.

25.   Gurock, *When Harlem Was Jewish* (New York, 1979), p. 23.

26.   Judah David Eisenstein, *Ozar Zikhronothai: Anthology and Memoir* (New York, 1929), pp. 77, 118. "Biographical Sketches," *AJYB*, 1903, p. 180. Eisenstein, the early historian of the East European Jewish religious community in the ghetto, recorded for posterity Rabbi Widerwitz's public appreciation of who made him chief rabbi of the United States: "The sign painter," he reportedly asserted. And to the question of "why of the entire United States?" he replied, "because it is impossible to

bring together all American communities to dismiss me." Despite this humorous epigram, it should be noted that Widerwitz was nonetheless a scholar who had published. while still in Russia, the works of Rabbi Mendel of Lubavitch and who, according to Eisenstein, published numerous scholarly articles. Rabbi Segal was even more of a serious scholar than Widerwitz. Indeed Segal authored a most significant work of American halakhah, *Eruv ve-Hotzaah* (1901), a tract which argued the permissibility of carrying in New York's East Side on the Sabbath. His position was based on the reality that the Jewish Quarter was enclosed on three sides by water and the fourth side was considered legal "as a closed door" by virtue of the elevated railroads linked by raised columns north to south in Manhattan Island. Eisenstein tells us, significantly, that the "Hasidim who followed him carried their *taleisim* on the Sabbath." Eisenstein, p. 118. Of course, Widerwitz's and Segal's difficulties with Rabbi Jacob Joseph stemmed not from varying interpretations of "Sabbath texts" but rather the competition over the right of supervision in the crucially important "workaday" world of kosher meat supervision. See below for more on the split within the East European Orthodox rabbinate in America over the power of kosher regulation. It is also possible that Segal and Widerwitz, of Galician and Hasidic orientation, did not fit in the Agudath ha-Rabbanim's predominantly Lithuanian, non-Hasidic group of rabbis.

27. English-born Joseph Asher was educated secularly at Jews' College grammar school, Owens College, Manchester, and Trinity College, Cambridge University. As such his training was quite similar to that of the Mendes family. But he received his rabbinical training in Kovno, Russia, and was ordained by Rabbi David Tevel Katzenellenbogen of Kovno/Suwalk, qualifying him at least theoretically for Agudath ha-Rabbanim membership. Clearly his position as professor of homiletics at the Seminary, not to mention his role as rabbi and preacher at Conservative Congregation B'nai Jeshurun in New York before moving on to the Orthodox Orach Chaim in the same city, did not help his chances of being invited to joined. Asher identified closely with the Mendes-Drachman strain of Orthodoxy. So did his predecessor at Orach Chaim, David Neumark. As noted above in n.12, the Polish-born Neumark was trained in the Breslau and Berlin rabbinical seminaries before coming to the United States and linking up with the American Orthodox group. Philadelphia-born Henry S. Morais was the recipient of an American secular education and was trained for the ministry by his father, Sabato Morais. He served congregations in Syracuse, New York, and Newport, Rhode Island, before beginning a very significant tenure at Congregation Mikve Israel in New York.

Henry Speaker (1895), David Wittenberg (1895), Bernard M. Kaplan (1897), Leon H. Elmaleh (1898), Morris Mandel (1898), Menahem M. Eichler (1899), Michael Fried (1899), Emil Friedman (1899), David Levine (1900), and Israel Goldfarb, Phineas Israeli, Hillel Kauvar, and Nathan Wolf, all of the 1902 pre-Schechter rabbinical graduating class round out the list of so-described "full-hearted (American Orthodox) rabbis." All also played an important role in the Jewish Endeavor Society, to be discussed below. See for biographical descriptions: "Biographical Sketches," *AJYB* 5664 (1903–4), p. 42; Adler, pp. 76–78; Eisenstein, *Anshei Shem*, p. 21.

28. *Sefer ha-Yovel,* p. 18.

29. Mendes, Abramovitz, Drachman, Greenstone, Kauvar, Morais, and Schnee-berger were all officers and trustees of the Orthodox Union in 1903. See *AJYB* (1903–4), p. 159. The decision to oppose the activities of the Orthodox Union was part of a blanket relection by the Agudath ha Rabbanim, at its third convention, of Rabbi Mendes's appeal to them to cooperate in (a) bringing "to the notice of the rabbis the fact that certain marriages legal in Jewish law are illegal according to the law of the State," (b) regulating the practice of milah, i.e., "mohelim not paying sufficient regard to surgical cleanliness," and (c) opposition to the "Cincinnati College" of the Reform movement. The Agudath ha-Rabbanim responded that they would abide by the state's laws and did not need to be reminded. They also averred that mohelim under their influence always used great caution in the operations. Most significantly, they rejected cooperation with Mendes in opposing Reform. They demurred that Seminary rabbis (now post-1902) "are not fit for the position of rabbi on account of lack of proper and sufficient preparation." Finally, the Orthodox Union was not recognized as a valued ally in the fight to perpetuate Judaism. The Agudath ha-Rabbanim noted that "our principal aim has always been directed to form and build up a union of real Orthodox congregations." See *AH,* July 8, 1904, p. 204, July 30, 1904, p. 262, and Markovitz, "Henry Pereira Mendes: Architect of the Union of Orthodox Jewish Congregations of America," *AJHQ* (March 1966): 380–381.

The Agudath ha-Rabbanim's nonacceptance of Seminary graduates post-1902 is understandable considering the change of administration and emphasis at the start of the Schechter years. Non-recognition of the Orthodox Union, an organization led by the Orthodox leaders of the old Seminary, cannot easily be based on the sudden invalidity of the Seminary. Rather, one might argue it was due to (a) unwillingness of the Agudath ha-Rabbanim to share leadership, (b) holding the American Orthodox to be guilty by association for working with Conservative leaders, and (c) the presently to be discussed Americanizing thrust of the Union, which the Agudath ha-Rabbanim rejected.

30. *AH,* January 4, 1901, p. 231.

31. Indirect impressionistic evidence supporting this view of the Orthodox Union rabbis as searching for a constituency to lead may be found in Drachman's autobiography. Commenting upon the lot of the American Orthodox rabbi around the turn of the century, he lamented: "It seemed for a time. . . . that there was no room, no demand in America for an American-born, English-speaking rabbi who insisted upon maintaining the laws and usages of Traditional Judaism. . . . Reform Judaism had conquered almost the entire field of Jewish life. . . . There were a few Orthodox congregations whose members were American-born . . . But there were no vacancies. Groups of East Europeans . . . adhered to Orthodox traditions of their native lands and wanted rabbis of that type." See Drachman, p. 167. In truth, the leaders of the Orthodox Union were interested not so much in leading first-generation immigrants but in struggling for the second generation.

32. *Sefer ha-Yovel,* pp. 25–26; Rakeffet-Rothkoff, pp. 317–319. See Rabbi Zalman Jaccob Friederman, "Takanot Hachomim," *Ha-Peles* (1902), pp. 469–471 for

another look at how the Agudath ha-Rabbanim understood the picture of Jewish education at its inception, Hapgood focuses upon the career of Vilna-born Rabbi Moses Reicherson (1827–1903), a great Hebrew grammarian. Arriving in New York in 1890, he authored articles for *Ner Maaravi, Ha-Pisgah,* and *Ha-Ivri* and edited *Ha-Techiya.* But his talents went almost unnoticed in New York, and he died a "melamed in the Uptown Talmud Torah." See Eisenstein, p. 106, Hutchins Hapgood, *The Spirit of the Ghetto* (New York, 1902), pp. 55–57.

33. *Sefer ha-Yovel,* p. 26, and Rakeffet-Rothkoff, p. 319. To be sure, not long after its founding, the Agudath ha-Rabbanim moved slightly off its staunchly separatistic stance. At its second convention, held in August 1903, leaders agreed both to work toward a systematic curriculum for "all talmud torahs and hedarim" in this country and to give financial aid to talmud torabs in smaller communities. Mention was also made of the need to establish Hebrew schools for girls. Equally important, it was decided to hire "graduates from the normal schools in the employ of the City Boards of Education" to teach secular subjects in the all-day yeshivas, a concession to United States law if not custom. A year later at the third convention, held in July 1904, authorities leading talmud torahs and yeshivas "were requested to institute lectures for the young on Saturday and Sunday afternoons." No mention was made of the language of discourse or the topics for discussion. In any event, for the Agudath ha-Rabbanim the ideal form of Jewish education remained the transplanted heder/yeshiva system from East Europe. See *AJYB* 5664 (1903–4), p. 160; 5665 (1904–5), p. 282.

34. *AH,* May 30, 1902, pp. 37–38.

35. *HS,* October 18, 1901, p. 4; *AH,* January 18, 1901, p. 284; February 8, 1901, p. 379; April 5, 1901, p. 596; Drachman, pp. 225 ff.

36. *AH,* December 6, 19o1, p. 118; February 7,1902, p. 375; May 2,1902, p. 725; December 25, 1903, p. 205. For more on the history of the Jewish Endeavor Society, see my "Jewish Endeavor Society," in Michael Dobkowski, ed., *American Jewish Voluntary Organizations* (Westport, Conn., forthcoming). Clearly the Jewish Endeavor Society was a critical first step toward what would emerge as the Young Israel Synagogue in the 1910s. See on that my "The Orthodox Synagogue," Chapter 2 of this volume.

37. Ironically the JES stood for one of the causes which most interested the Agudath ha-Rabbanim, putting the imposter rabbi and his "mushroom Synagogue" out of business. See *AH,* October 17, 1902, p. 608, for the Society's position on the privately owned and operated "congregations" which sprung up overnight yearly around High Holiday time ostensibly offering services to non-seat holding downtowners in "rented rooms, saloons and dance halls." With reference to *maggidim,* we have the comments of one Endeavorer that his "services were successful but unfortunately a 'maggid' usually appeared on the scene followed by his hosts and naturally the Services had to make room for the Yiddish preacher." See *AH,* January 16, 1903, p. 298. For more on JES cooperation with Reform congregations, see my "Consensus Building and Conflict," Chapter 13 of this volume.

The foregoing description of Agudath ha-Rabbanim opposition to the JES is based exclusively upon observations made by Society proponents about the tenor of criticism which greeted their efforts on the Lower East Side. We are thus hearing only from Agudath ha-Rabbanim critics possessed of their own particular biases. A major bibliographical issue which must be addressed beyond this work is the specific opinions of individual Orthodox rabbis over (a) the permissibility of substituting vernacular prayers for the original Hebrew, (b) what are the obligatory prayers which had to be recited in the original, and (c) whether Yiddish-language sermons were inviolable and whether there exist certain "secular" topics that ought not to be discussed from the pulpit.

38.   *Sefer ha-Yovel*, p. 26; Rakeffet-Rothkoff, pp. 319–320; *AJYB*, 1903, p. 160; Drachman, p. 229. When Drachman's association was first founded, Rabbi Jacob Joseph was one of the individuals who initially cooperated with him. Eisenstein, p. 77. And by the mid-1920s there are indications that the Agudath ha-Rabbanim had come to work not only with Orthodox Union people but with more liberal Jews and non-Jews in promoting the five-day work week. See Hunnicutt, pp. 196–225. But that era of semicooperation began a full generation after Drachman's organization came into being.

39.   Again it should be noted here that Drachman's organization worked with Reform Jews from its very inception, which might have discredited that organization *a priori* in Agudath ha-Rabbanim eyes. See Hunnicutt, pp. 199–200.

40.   See *HS*, October 24, 1902, p. 4; *AH*, February 7, 1902, p. 400; *HS*, June 12, 1903, p. 10, for examples of turn-of-the-century Orthodox Union lobbying efforts.

41.   For Mendes's early anticonversionist efforts, see Markovitz, "Henry P. Mendes," pp. 53–54. On the Orthodox Union's early 1900s antisectarianism campaigns, see Leonard Bloom, "A Successful Jewish Boycott of the New York City Public Schools," *AJH*, December 1980, pp. 180–188; Gurock, "Jacob A. Riis: Christian Friend or Missionary Foe: Two Jewish Views," Chapter 5 of this volume; idem, "Why Albert Lucas of the Orthodox Union Did Not Join the New York Kehillah," Chapter 7 of this volume. Parenthetically, my two aforementioned articles note the strong differences in opinion between Orthodox Union leaders and Reform Jewish spokesmen on how to deal with Christianity's impact on the immigrant Jew.

42.   Jacob David Willowski, *Sefer Nimukei Ridbaz: Perush al ha-Torah* (Chicago, 1904). For more on Willowski's United States career, see Aaron Rothkoff, "The American Sojourns of Ridbaz: Religious Problems within the Immigrant Community," *AJH* (June 1968): 557–572. For his conflicts with other Orthodox rabbis, see below.

43.   See Arthur Goren's authoritative history of the Kehillah, *New York Jews and the Quest for Community* (New York, 1970), particularly chapters 2 and 3, for the evolution of the "Jewish Community" idea and varying group reactions to its formulation.

44.   *AH*, January 4, 1901, p. 235; *IIS*, March 5, 1909, p. 12; *Min ECK*, April 7, 1909; *MA*, P31/1398; *Min CED*, April 10, 1910; *MA*, P3/1662.

45.   Goren, p. 50.

46. *Min ECK*, December 12, 1909; *MA*, P3/1398; *Min ECK*, October 8, 1912; *MA*, P3/1400; *Min ECK*, October 10, 1910; *MA*, P3/1399; *Min ECK*, May 14, 1912; *MA*, *P3/*1400; *JCR*, pp. 292–293, 1187–1188.

47. *JCR*, pp. 1187–1188; *Min ECK*, April 17,1909; *MA*, P3/1398; *Min ECK*, December 11, 1911; *MA*, P3/1400.

48. Rabbi Philip Hillel Klein was born in Hungary in 1848. He received his earliest training from his father; Rabbi Zeev Zvi Klein, a disciple of the *Hatam Sofer.* At the age of fifteen he began studying with Rabbi Hildesheimer while the latter still resided in Eisenstadt. Like his mentor, Klein ultimately migrated to a more cosmopolitan setting, in his case, Vienna, where he studied secular subjects while teaching at a yeshiva led by Rabbi Zalman Shpitzer. In 1869, at the age of twenty-one, he was ordained by Rabbi Zvi Benjamin Auerbach of Halberstadt at Hildesheimer's Berlin Rabbinical Seminary. Klein ministered in Liebau, Russia, before migrating to the United States in 1890. See *Sefer ha-Yovel*, p. 140. Klein served with Drachman on the committee on resolutions at the second Orthodox Union convention in 1901. He was also honored at that occasion with the privilege of delivering the opening prayer to the delegates. See *AH*, January 4, 1901, p. 235. For Klein/Drachman's Harlem career; see Drachman, pp. 277–279; Gurock, *When Harlem Was Jewish*, p. 119; and First Hungarian Congregation Ohab Zedek, *Golden Jubilee Journal* (New York, 1923), *passim*. Drachman for his part, in his autobiography, lauded Klein as "a rabbi of the old ghetto-type, on a par with the great Talmudists of Poland and Russia, but he was a university graduate as well." See Drachman, p. 280.

49. See *EJ*, vol. 2, col. 959, and *AJYB* 5664 (1903–4), p. 79, for basic biographical information on Ramaz. For Ramaz's pulpit career and an in-house look at his relationship with Kaplan, pre-1910, see Joseph H. Lookstein, "Seventy-Five Yesteryears: A Historical Sketch of Kehilath Jeshurun," *Congregation Kehilath Jeshurun, Diamond Jubilee Year Book, 1946* (New York, 1946), pp. 17–236. For a complete examination of the Ramaz-Kaplan-Kehilath Jeshurun relationship, see Gurock and Jacob A. Schacter, *A Modern Heretic and a Traditional Community: Mordecai M. Kaplan, Orthodoxy and American Judaism* (New York, 1996).

50. *AH*, January 31, 1908, p. 344; February 28, 1908, p. 444; *HS*, February 14, 1908, p. 1; *Min ECK*, December 11, 1911; *MA*, P3/1400.

51. *Min ECK*, October 8, 1912; *MA*, P3/1400; *Min ECK*, December 10, 1912; *MA*, P3/1400. Moses S. Margolies and Philip H. Klein to Executive Committee of the Jewish Community (Kehillah of New York), October 1, 1912, in *Min ECK*, October 21, 1912; *MA*, P3/1407; *JCR*, pp. 292–293.

52. Klein to Bernard G. Richards, *MA*, P3/1414; *Min ECK*, August 11, 1914; *MA*, P3/1410.

53. For a history of the Uptown Talmud Torah's Americanization efforts and problems before and during the Kehillah era, see Gurock, *When Harlem Was Jewish*, pp. 99–108.

54. See *HS*, June 18, 1915, p. 1, for Goldstein's major statement on the role of the Orthodox rabbinate in America.

55. For more on Goldstein's career in Yorkville and beyond, see Isaac Berkson, *Theories of Americanization* (New York, 1920); A. Joseph Epstein, "The Early History of the Central Jewish Institute, 1915–1920" (M.A. thesis, Bernard Revel Graduate School, Yeshiva University, 1977); Aaron Reichel, "An American Experiment: The Institutional Synagogue in Its First Score of Years" (M.A. thesis, Bernard Revel Graduate School, Yeshiva University, 1974).

56. "Biographical Sketches of Jews Prominent in the Professions, etc., in the United States," *AJYB* 5665 (1904–5), p. 152; Marvin Feinstein, *American Zionism, 1884–1904* (New York, 1925), pp. 132, 170–171, 209.

57. Moses Rischin, *The Promised City: New York's Jews, 1870–1914* (Cambridge, Mass., 1962), pp. 103, 239–240. Masliansky's memoirs indicate that prior to assuming his job at the Educational Alliance, he reportedly told Louis Marshall, "It is the goal of the Educational Alliance to warm the immigrant Jewish soul with his traditions which he has preserved over the thousands of years of his travails in Diaspora, because he will never become a good American if he loses his Judaism. . . we must Americanize the older generation and Judaize the younger souls." See Zvi Hirsch Masliansky, *Masliansky's Memoirs: Forty Years of Life and Struggle* (New York, 1924). See also for more on Masliansky, his *Sermons*, trans. by Edward Herbert, rev. and ed. by Abraham J. Feldman (New York, 1926), and *Droshes* (New York, 1908–9).

58. *AH*, January 4, 1901, p. 235. *JCR*, p. 72, indicates that as late as 1917–1918, three years after Klein and Margolies left the Kehillah's executive committee, Masliansky remained on that powerful cooperating board.

59. Eisenstadt, *Doros ha-Aharonim*, 2nd ed., vol. 2 (Brooklyn, 1937), p. 59; *MJ*, August 7, 1908, p. 5; August 19, 1908, pp. 7–8.

60. *MJ*, June 5, 1911, p. 5; June 3, 1910, p. 5; Hurwitz was more than just a school principal. He was a prolific writer in the field of Jewish education, authoring both textbooks for students and a philosophical tract on the goals of Jewish education in America. Among his books for youths and schoolchildren were *Dinai Yisroel Minhagav, Otzar ha-Yahadut, Hagim Zemanim,* and twenty-two other similar primers. His approach to Jewish education was best expressed in a tract entitled *Ha-Dat ve-ha-Hinuck* (1927) in which he argued that Jewish educational goals in America had to be different from those prevailing in Europe. He advocated a balanced curriculum of Jewish history, Bible, prophets, and Hebrew language and literature in addition to the traditional study of Talmud, ideas very much in keeping with those of the Kehillah innovators.

61. *MJ*, September 22, 1910, p. 7; June 5, 1911, p. 5; *YT*, April 1912, p. 7. Given Hurwitz and Masliansky's attitudes, which clearly differed in many ways from those of the Agudath ha-Rabbanim, an organization which neither joined, it is not surprising that both helped found the Jewish Ministers Association of America (Agudas ha-Rabbanim ha-Matiffim) in 1916. Hurwitz was the organization's first secretary, and Masliansky was a charter member of the organization, which included in its membership such American-born or Americanized rabbis as Drachman and Moses Hyamson. See *JCR*, pp. 1189–1192. Noteworthy also is the fact that this organization was not the first attempt to bring Orthodox rabbis of varying

backgrounds together. In 1896, Mendes attempted to establish an Orthodox Rabbinical Council of New York City. There were ten names in its charter of organization: Mendes, Drachman, and Meisner of early Seminary officialdom, plus seven other worthies: Rabbi Morris Wechsler, in 1895 spiritual leader of Congregation Brit Shalom of New York, and Rabbi Wolf Friedman, possibly the rabbi of Congregation B'nai Israel Anshe Sameth, and five otherwise unidentifiable rabbis named Bloch, Gur, Marcus, Yanowsky, and Tzinzler. See on this early group, Markovitz, pp. 374–375, and for brief biographical sketches, see *AJYB* 5664 (1903–4), pp. 55, 104. Hurwitz and Mashansky did, however, stop short of joining the interdenominational Board of Jewish Ministers, an organization joined by Mendes, Drachman, and younger colleagues Hyamson and Goldstein. See *JCR*, pp. 298–300.

62. *AJYB* 5664 (1903–4), p. 74; Naomi W. Cohen, *Not Free to Desist: The American Jewish Committee, 1906–1966* (Philadelphia, 1972), p. 563; Alex Goldman, "Bernard L. Levinthal: Nestor of the American Orthodox Rabbinate," in *Giants of Faith: Great American Rabbis* (New York, 1964), pp. 160–176; *Sefer Kavod Chachomim* (Philadelphia, 1935), *passim*. It is interesting to note that among the dignitaries offering greetings in honor of Levinthal's anniversary were such ideologically diverse communal leaders as the Jewish Theological Seminary's Cyrus Adler; identified there as head of the American Jewish Committee, Morris Rothstein of the Zionist Organization of America, Conservative Rabbi Julius Greenstone, American Orthodox Rabbi David De Sola Pool, and East European trained Yeshiva University worthies Joseph B. Soloveitchik, Moses Soloveitchik, and Bernard Revel. The Agudath ha-Rabbanim also sent greetings.

63. *Sefer Kavod Chachomim*, p. 75; Goldman, p. 167.

64. A clear thrust of the above presentation is the historiographical necessity of full-length studies of these exceptional East European rabbis who, as we will see, so influenced the next generation of Orthodox rabbis. For example, although Rabbi Levinthal supported Americanization efforts and as such should have been a role model for the next generation of Orthodox rabbis, an "oral tradition" about him, which needs amplification, maintains that he jealously protected his prerogatives in centralizing Philadelphia pulpits and keeping younger RIETS men out for more than a generation. Ramaz on the other hand, as we will see later; supported the goals of the newer colleagues.

65. There are, of course, instances where American Orthodox rabbis cooperated with East European colleagues in the hope of ensuring the latters' hegemony of kashruth supervision. As noted previously, Drachman and Mendes in 1888 helped Rabbi Jacob Joseph control the wholesale butchers of New York. And in that same year, both English-speaking rabbis conducted appeals in their synagogues to help save Rabbi Joseph's failing association. In the 1890s accusations were leveled against Drachman claiming that he was both awarding "tens of thousands of *heksherim* to *shohatim* and butchers who did not observe the Sabbath" and planning to usurp Rabbi Jacob Joseph's position as chief rabbi. Critics pointed to Drachman's Vaad ha-Rabbanim Mahzike Hadath (Rabbinical Council–Strengtheners of the Faith) as the source of the problem. Drachman replied that his organization had a

broad agenda for protecting observant Jews, not just kashruth, and that he had been brought into this area of controversy by problems of Jewish consumers.

If one accepts Drachman's apologia, it may be understood that kashruth supervision was not at the top of his communal concerns. At most he saw himself as a protector of Jewish consumers in the broader economic sense. Harold Gastwirth notes, for example, that in April 1899, Drachman was involved in the founding of the Orthodox Hebrew Society, dedicated to dealing with problems of Sabbath observance, Sunday blue laws, and Christian missionaries, but not kashruth. The Orthodox Union's list of concerns in its early generation did not prioritize kashruth supervision. To be sure, in 1905 the Orthodox Union discussed the idea of certification of retail stores, and five years later talked about a set of universal requirements governing kashruth. But neither idea was acted upon. See on these Orthodox Union positions, *YT*, January 19, 1905, p. 8, and *AH*, March 25, 1910, p. 535. And, of course, as we have noted previously, Orthodox Union rabbis deferred to the Agudath ha-Rabbanim in Kehillah days and activities. For these and more details on the American rabbis' early relationship with Agudath ha-Rabbanim rabbis over kashruth, see Harold P. Gastwirth, *Fraud, Corruption and Holiness: The Controversy over the Supervision of the Jewish Dietary Practice in New York, 1881–1940* (Port Washington, N.Y., 1974), pp. 55–82.

66. Clearly much more needs to be known about what motivated East European-born rabbis to depart far away from the immigrant centers. In the case of Rabbi Matlin, *Sefet ha-Yovel*, p. 146, suggests that "illness and weakness forced him to move to western mountain states," but the choice of Sioux City, a town of at most several hundred Jews, was undoubtedly not a random selection. The growth of kashruth supervision as a profession was facilitated greatly in the post-1880 period by advances in the agricultural and railroad industries. The introduction of the refrigerator car "made it possible to slaughter the cattle and dress the meat in the west, thus substantially reducing the cost of shipping as compared with that of transporting a live animal." See Gastwirth, p. 27. At all events, it is important to note that the vast majority of East European rabbis did not move out of touch with the immigrant centers. Then as now, the lack of contact with colleagues and superiors, the unavailability of religious training facilities and spouses for their children, and the myriad of religious activities which require a Jewish community, seemingly kept these rabbis close to "home." A statistical analysis of the sixty charter members of the Agudath ha-Rabbanim residing in thirty-one American cities in 1902 reveals the following: A full quarter lived in New York City alone, and another third had settled in cities with Jewish populations in excess of fifty thousand. Only five rabbis ministered in cities with less than five thousand Jews: Providence, Rhode Island, Portland and Bangor, Maine, Des Moines, and Omaha. Thus Rabbis Grodzinsky and Zarchy were the only ones working in small towns remote from the Baltimore-Boston seaboard, east-of-the-Alleghenies segment of America which thirty-five of the sixty called home. (Rabbi Matlin moved out of New York after 1902.) The geographical homogeneity of this group is further highlighted by the fact that only five of the sixty lived west of St. Louis. Rabbi Zarchy, who during his career served

in Lexington, Kentucky, was the only one of the sixty to preside south of the Mason-Dixon line.

Twenty-seven years later, the pattern of East European rabbinic settlement had not changed appreciably. There were 313 members of the Agudath ha-Rabbanim working out of eighty-six cities. But 152 of them—approximately one-half—lived in New York. An additional fifteen resided in Chicago, America's second-largest Jewish city. Nine more were based in Baltimore. Surprisingly, only five were centered in Levinthal's Philadelphia, a city often seen as a bastion of Conservative Jewry. All in all, 207 of the 313 rabbis made the Baltimore-Boston seaboard their homes. Noteworthy also is the fact that the Agudath ha-Rabbanim had members in thirteen New Jersey cities within approximately three hours of New York and Philadelphia, and members in thirteen Massachusetts cities within approximately three hours of Boston or New York. An additional seventeen rabbis were based in Western Pennsylvania and western New York State. An equal number ministered west of St. Louis, including four in Los Angeles, four in Minneapolis St. Paul, and three in San Francisco-Oakland. Des Moines was by that time led by a Rabbi N. H. Zeichik, and Rabbi M. H. Braver worked out of Sioux City. Omaha continued to be served by Hirsch Grodzinsky, an individual whose perseverance alone is deserving of further study. The South could only boast of four rabbis, two in growing Atlanta and one each in Lexington and Norfolk, Virginia. Certainly the Agudath ha-Rabbanim's members did not comprise the totality of the East European rabbinate in America. But the sixty subjects in 1902 and 313 in 1929 constitute enough of a sample to make these reasonable judgments. All these statistics verify our Suggestion that the East Europeans stayed close to the immigrant hubs until well into the twentieth century.

67. See Gastwirth, pp. 55–90, for the most complete discussion of Rabbi Jacob Joseph's difficulties with his competitors. The Willowski-Album dispute has been studied through the published writings of each. Album authored *Sefer Divrei Emet*, 2 vols. (Chicago, 1904–1912), where he defended his position. Willowski's introduction to his *Nimukei Ridbas: Perush al ha-Torah* (Chicago, 1903) offers his side of the story, along with a wide-ranging indictment of religious practice in America. That work, along with Weinberger's 1887 tract, ranks high within the rabbinic "protest" literature of the immigrant period. For the best secondary account of the dispute, see Rothkoff, pp. 557–572. See also on the Ridbaz-Album battle, Gastwirth, pp. 90–92.

68. Gastwirth, pp. 92–118.

69. Gilbert Klaperman, *The Story of Yeshiva University: The First Jewish University in America* (London, 1969), p. 53. Klaperman notes significantly that although the school's New York State Certificate of Incorporation clearly states that among the objects of the school's concern was "preparing students of the Hebrew faith for the Hebrew Orthodox Ministry," the true agenda of the school was more in line with its public newspaper announcement in January 1897, which made no reference to training for the pulpit as a reason for establishing the school. See Klaperman, pp. 52–54.

70. It should be noted, however; that from its inception RIETS was never totally sealed off as an institution. Secular studies, albeit at this point a peripheral, necessary evil, were offered at the school seemingly to attract native-born students away from public school education. These students, we will immediately see, changed significantly the focii of the school. See Klaperman, pp. 52–54, 75.

71. It is important to note that not all of the RIETS faculty members were Agudath ha-Rabbanim members. Rabbi Joseph's nemesis, Hayim Yaacov Widerwitz, frequently lectured at the yeshiva. See Klaperman, pp. 69–70, 80.

72. *Ibid.*, pp. 88–89.

73. The comparison of native-born to foreign-born students at RIETS here noted is taken from Klaperman's study, which is in turn based on an article by I. Cohen, "Yeshiva Rabbi Isaac Elchanan," in the journal *Aspaklaria* (Adar, 1907). More scientific analyses of the nativity, not to mention the actual real numbers, of students at the institution are rendered impossible by the unavailability of RIETS records from its inception until its merger with Etz Chaim in 1915. Thus, estimates of student enrollment in the early years are derived entirely from contemporaneous newspaper sources, memoirs, and interviews with early students and their families, dutifully recorded by Klaperman.

74. This projection of the nature of student interest in studying at RIETS is based upon our knowledge of what was taught at the school and a sketchy awareness of what became of some of the members of the early class of 1901. Klaperman reports that of the twelve or so students known to have been in the school as of 1901, five later attended medical school, one became an English-language journalist, only two became Hebrew teachers, and one was destined to serve as a rabbi. See Klaperman, p. 78.

What is more interesting and unfortunately unknown is the question of where these students came from. Our understanding of immigrant history in this country tells us that most children of new Americans were sent to the public schools, and some were also afforded a supplementary Jewish education. What made the families of RIETS students different, allowing them to a great extent to ignore the usual tool of Americanization? More needs to be known about this significant self-selecting group.

75. The nature of the student demands and the formal decision of the directors to elect Ramaz are known from contemporary newspaper sources. See for a complete discussion of these accounts, Klaperman, pp. 93–106. The unavailability of internal documentation makes it, however; impossible to know why the directors (seven rabbinic, thirteen lay) moved to stem the protest. One possible explanation is that fear of encroachments by the Jewish Theological Seminary upon the fledging Orthodox institution may have moved their hands. Klaperman reports that just a year before the strike three RIETS students had presented themselves to Dr. Solomon Schechter to discuss the possibility of their enrolling in the newly reoriented Conservative Seminary. It should be remembered, of course, that one of Schechter's mandates was to train East European Jews to minister to their Americanizing brethren. Fear of possibly losing good men to the more liberal denomination may have moved the hand of the RIETS directors. That same fear, as we will

presently see, may have influenced the Agudath ha-Rabbanim to support the 1915 merger and reconstitution of RIETS.

76. See Klaperman, pp. 99–133, for a discussion of the tumultuous seven years between the student strike and the establishment of the Rabbinical College of America. Several times during that era, RIETS was threatened with closing. Student unrest continued, for substantive changes in curriculum were slow in catching on. Some students expressed their displeasure by actually moving on to the Seminary. As late as 1913, the ever-present and supportive-of-change Ramaz criticized RIETS's "unrealistic curriculum as a cause of student defection." See Klaperman, pp. 171–172. It was also a time which saw a rising group of concerned Orthodox laymen like David A. Cohen and Harry Fischel, who preached a practical synthesis of "Orthodox Judaism and Americanization." Fischel for one was quite forthright in asserting, upon the Rabbinical College's founding, that its goal was "to educate and produce Orthodox rabbis who will be able to deliver sermons in English, to appeal to the hearts of the younger generation."

It should also be noted that during these years, Rabbis Jaffe and Masliansky were among the prime movers of a Yeshiva LeRabbanim, "a yeshiva to train rabbis." See Klaperman, pp. 117–118. Masliansky's participation is not surprising, given his already noted attitude toward Judaism and Americanization. What Jaffe, who showed no previous interest in types of synthesis, was doing there is hard to explain. Klaperman suggests that "Rabbi Jaffe was the stormy petrel on the rabbinic scene known as an impetuous non-conformist who rushed in without fear when his mind was made up." See Klaperman, p. 117. Jaffe, defined in this essay as one of the Agudath ha-Rabbanim's opponents of accommodation and cooperation, is another of the oft-mentioned rabbinic figures worthy of further study.

77. For a complete biography of the early years of the first president of Yeshiva University, see Aaron Rothkoff, *Bernard Revel: Builder of American Jewish Orthodoxy* (Philadelphia, 1972), pp. 27–39 and *passim*.

78. *Ibid.,* pp. 38–39. The close spiritual and personal ties between the Seminary and Dropsie were cemented through the activities of Cyrus Adler, president of both Dropsie, from 1908, and of the Seminary, from 1915. See also Ira Robinson, "Cyrus Adler, Bernard Revel and the Prehistory of Organized Jewish Scholarship in the United States," *AJH* (June 1980): 497–505, for a discussion of the relationship between the Orthodox leader; Conservative leadership, and the rise of Jewish letters in this country.

79. See *Rabbinical College of America Register 5678 (1917–1918)* (New York, 1917), reprinted in Klaperman, p. 254, for a listing of the faculty positions held by Drachman and Mendes. See also Drachman, p. 368, for his description of his teaching duties at the yeshiva. Significantly, Drachman notes that he never taught Talmud at RIETS because it was the special domain of the East European rabbis, who were "inclined to consider Occidental and most especially American rabbis as inferiors." See also *Rabbi Isaac Elchanan Theological Seminary Register 5685* which lists Goldstein as assistant professor of homiletics. An interesting subject for examination is the progression of the line of homiletics instruction at American Jewish theological seminaries from Drachman at the seminary through Mendes and Goldstein

and ultimately to Rabbi Joseph H. Lookstein at Yeshiva University and its relationship to the greater history of denominational life. For more on this issue see below.

80. For a listing of the members of the Rabbinical College Committee, see *Rabbinical College Register* in Klaperman, p. 254. An intriguing question emerging here concerns Jaffe's relationship with Goldstein, his former student, who went from him to the Seminary and then into the American Orthodox pulpit and ultimately to Revel's institution.

81. As was true of all previously noted important rabbinical political decisions in America, not all East European rabbis followed the organization's apparent line of thinking. See below for a discussion of early opposition to the new RIETS initiated by, among others, Rabbi Gabriel Wolf Margolis. This tentative reconstruction of Agudath ha-Rabbanim attitudes is based upon several of the organization's activities in response to episodic changes toward Americanization undertaken at RIETS. In 1905, the Agudath ha-Rabbanim called for its right to supervise both religious and secular studies and to monitor student behavior. Indeed in 1902 it attempted to make the RIETS building, to be built ultimately on Montgomery Street, the center for its organization as well. See on this Klaperman, pp. 171, 207. See also his remark that "the Agudath ha-Rabbanim had long challenged the desirability of a secular education for rabbis." Of course the theme of fear of the Seminary is, as previously noted, a subject open for much more extensive study.

82. In 1917–18 *Rabbinical College of America Register* lists seventeen "alumni" of that institution. The 1924–25 RIETS *Register* counts thirty-three graduates since "the reorganized Seminary" came into existence. Clearly the latter group, who were ordained under the new curriculum, must be characterized as American-trained rabbis. As for the earlier group, Rothkoff suggests that the men ordained before the reorganization "had received the greatest part of their rabbinic training in European yeshivot." See Rothkoff, p. 51. These earlier rabbis might be seen simply as having finished their education in the United States, constituting in effect the next generation of Agudath ha-Rabbanim membership. Unfortunately, more detailed background information on these first graduates is unavailable, since the yeshiva's student records for those years are no longer extant.

83. Of the seventeen pre-1918 alumni listed, seven were noted as having positions in New York or Brooklyn synagogues or schools. Four others found pulpits in the Baltimore-Boston areas, and an additional three resided in Western Pennsylvania or upper New York State. Omaha, Seattle, and Canton were home to the remaining three rabbis. The latter listing also indicates that yeshiva graduates continued to settle in the New York area or in the outlying areas already served by Agudath ha-Rabbanim members. Of the thirty-three pre-1925 graduates, twenty-four found jobs in the New York-Brooklyn synagogues and schools. The Baltimore-Boston axis attracted two others, and western Pennsylvania and upstate New York became home to four others. The remaining three rabbis lived in Omaha, Ottawa, Canada, and Savannah, Georgia.

84. Rakeffet-Rothkoff, p. 107.

85. Rothkoff, p. 171.

86. Conflicts arose primarily when a young yeshiva graduate either simply assumed a full-time position or more problematically, as we will see below, accepted such deviations from Orthodox ritual in his synagogue as a low or nonexistent *mechitza* (partition separating the sexes in prayer). There were also instances, on the other hand, where East European rabbis would contact the yeshiva for an American rabbi to help conduct High Holiday services. The younger colleague would preach in English. See for an example, Rabbi Silver's 1939 letter of thanks to Rabbi Revel for sending him a rabbinical student assistant, quoted in Rakeffet-Rothkoff, p. 176.

87. See Rothkoff, pp. 169–180, for examples of pressure placed on Revel by Agudath ha-Rabbanim members. In 1930 Silver sent a questionnaire to many of the American-trained Orthodox rabbis to ascertain through some twenty-two specific questions their behavior patterns in the rabbinate, their relationships, if any, with rabbis of the more liberal denominations, their interests in the kashruth industry, etc. Rakeffet records sample reactions to these inquiries, which ranged from "the respectful to the polemical." Some were pleased that the established Agudath ha-Rabbanim was interested in their activities. Others perceived Silver's questions as an invasion of their privacy. See Rothkoff, pp. 99–105. These questions and answers, saved in the Silver Archives, remain still an invaluable trove for a social and attitudinal history of the early American Orthodox rabbinate.

88. Full membership in the Agudath ha-Rabbanim would be accorded to those trained to "adjudicate all areas of Jewish law" *(yadin yadin)*. Associate memberships would be offered to those possessing only *yoreh yoreh*, the power "to decide matters of ritual." For these working definitions see Rakeffet-Rothkoff, p. 104.

89. *Ibid.*, pp. 43–95, for a detailed biography of Silver's early years and the stages of his American rabbinic career.

90. This understanding of Revel's behavior is predicated upon documentation extracted from Rothkoff's biography. That volume notes that Revel frequently received letters from young rabbis in the field complaining about the inroads Conservative Judaism was making into their constituencies. Indeed, supporters of Yeshiva were very concerned that an Agudath ha-Rabbanim rabbi would drive congregants to the more liberal denomination. Rothkoff reports that Revel received a telegram in 1937 from laymen who wanted an American Orthodox rabbi to remain in a pulpit over the objections of an East European *rov*. The young rabbi, they said, was passing "the legacy of the Torah to our children . . . and our elder learned rabbi by his conduct setting a bad example to our young ones causing them to shift to Conservatives." See below for more on Conservatism's impact. At the same time, Revel had to continue to have the approbation of the East European rabbis to keep the religious reliability of his school at status quo. This led to the perceived fence-straddling position. For documentary evidence supporting this thesis, see Rothkoff, pp. 166–178.

91. For a discussion of the individuals and groups who came together to form the RCA in 1935, see Louis Bernstein, *Challenge and Mission: The Emergence of the English-Speaking Orthodox Rabbinate* (New York, 1982), pp. 9–12.

92. De Sola Pool and Jung were throwbacks to the Drachman/Mendes era or style of American Orthodox rabbis, based on their training at Western European seminaries and at secular schools and not East European yeshivas or at early RIETS in America. De Sola Pool, born in London in 1885, was trained at that city's Jews' College before studying in Berlin at Hildesheimer's seminary. He arrived in the United States in 1907 and assumed Shearith Israel's pulpit, a position he would hold until his retirement in 1956. For more on his life and career; see his own history of his congregation, *An Old Faith in a New World: Portrait of Shearith Israel, 1654–1954* (New York, 1955). Leo Jung was born in Moravia in 1892. He moved to London in 1912, when his father, Meir Jung, was elected rabbi of the London Federation of Synagogues, only to return to Central European yeshivas before receiving ordination in the Berlin Rabbinical Seminary in 1920. He migrated to the United States that same year and after two years' service in Cleveland, assumed the Jewish Center pulpit in 1922. For more on Jung's career; philosophy, and approach to the American rabbinate, see his autobiography, *The Path of a Pioneer: The Autobiography of Leo Jung* (London and New York, 1980). See also Nima H. Adlerblum, "Leo Jung," in *The Leo Jung Jubilee Volume*, ed. by Menahem M. Kasher, Norman Lamm, and Leonard Rosenfeld (New York, 1962), pp. 1–40, and his collected sermons and essays, most specifically *Foundations of Judaism* (New York, 1923), *Crumbs and Character* (New York, 1942), *The Rhythm of Life* (New York, 1950), *Harvest* (New York, 1955), and *Heirloom* (New York, 1961). Goldstein, as noted before, had Jaffe's *semicha* and seminary ordination. It is not surprising that these men, each serving affluent, acculturated pulpits, gravitated toward each other and toward the Orthodox Union. The Jewish Center; of course, had been founded in 1918 by Kaplan, who had not yet formally broken institutionally with Orthodoxy. The prototype of the predominantly Conservative Jewish Center Synagogue was created under Orthodox auspices, and it is clear that Jung's congregation was keenly aware of the tensions between Orthodox and Conservative rabbis over leadership of the acculturated Jewish community.

93. The names of these rabbis and their agendas are derived from the *Program of the Third Annual Convention of the Rabbinical Association of the Rabbi Isaac Elchanan Theological Seminary, August 8–9, 1931*. Significantly, the convention dealt with four major issues: "The Problem of Placement," "The Relation of the Rabbinical Association to Existing Rabbinical Organizations," "Our Part in the Maintenance of the Yeshiva," and "The Cultural Program of the Yeshiva." A study of the some twenty-five or so men listed as committee members of the association, their backgrounds and their pulpit experiences, would cast much light on the growth of the early Orthodox rabbinate. We would like to know of the levels of conflict and cooperation which they encountered both with the Agudath ha-Rabbanim to their right and the Conservative colleagues to their immediate left.

94. For the many details on the evolution of RCA policies toward kashruth regulation, see Bernstein's chap. 4 on kashruth, pp. 91–121.

95. *Ibid.*, p. 92 and *passim*.

96. Marshall Sklare, *Conservative Judaism: An American Religious Movement* (Glencoe, Ill., 1955), is the standard and best starting point for understanding that

movement's growth and development. See also, on the sociological-theological mix which made Conservative Judaism so attractive, Will Herberg, *Protestant-Catholic-Jew* (Garden City, 1955). And for an insightful look at the growth of Conservative Judaism within the New York metropolis, see Deborah Dash Moore's *At Home in America: Second Generation New York Jews* (New York, 1981).

97. *Ha-Pardes*, published in Chicago by Rabbi Samuel Aaron Pardes beginning in 1927, made public many of the ordinances and exhortations promulgated by the Agudath ha-Rabbanim against synagogue modernization efforts. This organ reported that at the 1930 convention of the Agudath ha-Rabbanim, both Conservative and Reform rabbis were described as "enticers" seeking to lead Jews astray, and a prayer was proffered that Jews be saved from these forms of idolatry." More significantly, that same year the Agudath ha-Rabbanim opposed Orthodox synagogues conducting late Friday night lectures on "secular" subjects, since they emulated the more liberal denominations and might confuse the careless into believing all denominations were basically the same. In 1931, Silver denounced the Conservatives for teaching "a new Torah" and argued the necessity of his organization's continuing to pillory the activities of the deviationists. Of course, the Agudath ha-Rabbanim was publicly most exercised by the Conservative rabbinate's incursions into the realms of kashruth and marriage regulation. The liberal-traditionalists' attempt to solve the agunah problem in the 1930s was described as an "abominable act which threatens the future of the Jewish people." The Agudath ha-Rabbanim also declared all associations with Conservative rabbis in communal efforts off-limits to its members. See on these proclamations, *Ha-Pardes* (June 1930), p. 26; (December 1930), p. 6; (June 1931), p. 28; (May 1934), p. 2; (June 1935), pp. 2–5. See above p. 355 for fuller title. See also Agudath ha-Rabbanim de-Artzot ha-Brit ve-Kanada, *Le-Dor Aharon* (New York, 1936), for a full-length polemic against Conservative activities in the areas of marriage and divorce.

98. Bernard L. Sheintag, "Rabbi Joseph H. Lookstein: A Character Study by a Congregant," in *Congregation Kehilath Jeshurun Diamond Jubilee*, pp. 53–57 and *passim*. Lookstein's election as a student rabbinical assistant in 1923 followed the resignation of Rabbi Elias L. Solomon, a Seminary graduate and destined to be a leader of the Conservative Rabbinical Assembly. It marks, on a one-synagogue microcosmic level, the beginning of the competition between RIETS and Seminary men. Until then, when looking for a university-trained, English-speaking rabbi, the upwardly mobile, acculturated congregation had to look for Seminary men like Kaplan, Goldstein, and Solomon. Solomon, significantly, did not have the "benefit" of either prior Orthodox ordination before Seminary graduation, as in Goldstein's case, or subsequent ordination, as in Kaplan's case, before assuming an Orthodox pulpit. With Lookstein, one might argue, the congregation could have the correctly trained rabbi they wanted, prepared both sociologically and halakhically. This change is certainly worthy of further investigation and explication.

99. Lookstein's gift for the homily can be discerned through an examination of his compiled sermons. See his *The Sources of Courage* (New York, 1943), *Faith and Destiny of Man: Traditional Judaism in a New World* (New York, 1967), and *Yesterday's Faith for Tomorrow* (New York, 1979).

100. Haskel Lookstein, "Joseph: The Master of His Dreams" in *Rabbi Joseph H. Lookstein Memorial Volume*, ed. Leo Landman (New York, 1980), pp. 16–17.

101. Joseph H. Lookstein, "The Modern American Yeshivah," *Jewish Education*, (April 1945), pp. 12–16. The Ramaz School was not the first modern day school in twentieth century America. The Yeshivah of Flatbush preceded it by more than a decade. And, of course, more separatistic yeshivas like Etz Hayim and the Rabbi Jacob Joseph School, the latter attended by Lookstein himself, date back to 1886 and 1902 respectively. For more details on the history of American yeshivas, see Alvin Schiff, *The Jewish Day School in America* (New York, 1966).

102. It may be suggested that the contentment of Lookstein's congregation was also based on the geographical proximity of the members' residences to the work and business district of New York and their socioeconomic profile. Based in Yorkville, they were still living in the inner city, making commutation from work to home to synagogue without violating the Jewish Sabbath clock a logistical possibility. And as an upper-middle-class group, congregants may have been able to more easily adjust their work and life schedules to remain consistent with ancestral time traditions. Of course, more investigation needs to be done to explain their attitudes toward nonegalitarian Synagogue seating patterns.

103. That each of the dilemmas noted here posed a real problem for the American Orthodox RCA members during the interwar period is evidenced by the fact that questions requesting guidance on each issue were submitted by members to either the RCA Standards and Rituals Committee or to its Halacha Commission during the first fifteen years of that organization's existence. In submitting questions to their peers, members of the RCA made a significant statement of independence from senior East European-trained authorities. See Bernstein, pp. 39–51, for the RCA proclamations on these social-theological questions.

104. Bernstein, p. 15. It may be suggested that men trained as American Orthodox rabbis in the interwar period at RIETS and at the HTC can be classified into four categories when looking at that rabbinate's relationship with the Conservative rabbinate. There were those, like Lookstein, who competed with the Conservatives as Orthodox simulators without making theological accommodations. There are those noted here who liberalized ritual without formally going over to Conservatism and who remained in the RCA. Category three includes those who, either for financial considerations or out of sincere theological belief, left the Orthodox rabbinate and joined the RA. And there are those RIETS men in limbo who served mixed-seating congregations and felt comfortable neither in the RA nor in the RCA. Each of these varieties of RIETS alumni needs further amplifications.

105. During the first quarter-century of its existence, the HTC ordained some 132 rabbis and graduated some 200 Hebrew teachers. It also trained meat slaughterers who undoubtedly served midwestern communities. By the milestone year of 1947, the HTC complex included a Rabbinical Department, a Teachers Institute, a school for shochetim, and four prep-school classes, and served as co-sponsor of the Chicago Jewish Academy, a "Ramaz-style" day school. The alumni of this institution, men like Maurice Solomon of Kansas City, Manuel Laderman of Denver, Colorado, New York's Simon G. Kramer, and Baltimore's Uri Miller, who became head of

the RCA, clearly made their mark upon American Jewry and have yet to be studied. We also need to know more about the background, training, and philosophy of Rabbis Saul Silber, Isaac Ha-Levi Rubinstein, Ephraim Epstein, and Abraham Cardon, who helped found the school. Noteworthy also is the fact that Rabbi Oscar Z. Fasman, an early ordainee, became in 1946 "the first American-born person to lead an institution granting Orthodox rabbinic ordination." See Saul Adelson, "Chicago's Hebrew Theological College," *Jewish Life* (December1947), pp. 43–48, for a brief discussion of the history of that school. See also Eliezer Berkowitz, "A Contemporary Rabbinical School for Orthodox Jewry," *Tradition* (Fall 1979), pp. 56–64, for a discussion by an HTC faculty member about the goals of modern theological seminaries. See also, for a brief autobiography of Fasman, his "After Fifty Years, an Optimist," *AJH*, (December 1979), pp. 159–178.

106. Bernstein, pp. 14–15.

107. *Ibid.*, pp. 142, 135.

108. Rakeffet-Rothkoff, pp. 105–106.

109. Bernstein, pp. 128–129. The Agudath ha-Rabbanim suggested that the some "twenty percent" of the RCA members who were "more or less acceptable," i.e., at least separate-seat congregations, be admitted as full members. The others might become associates but without full privileges. Negotiations took place between RCA and Agudath ha-Rabbanim leaders in 1939 but to no avail.

110. See Rakeffet-Rothkoff, pp. 264–271; Klaperman, pp. 171–177; and Bernstein, pp. 10–11, for discussions of the history of Yeshiva from the demise of Revel to the election of Belkin.

111. A thorough biography of Belkin is clearly warranted but remains to be written. Basic biographical materials and short discussions of his philosophy are to be found in Leon Stitskin, "Dr. Samuel Belkin as Scholar and Educator," in *Studies in Judaica in Honor of Dr. Samuel Belkin as Scholar and Educator*, ed. by Leon Stitskin (New York, 1974), pp. 3–18, and Hayim Leaf, "Dr. Samuel Belkin—Scholar, Educator and Community Leader" (Hebrew), in *Samuel Belkin Memorial Volume* (New York, 1981), pp. ix-xx. The former article also contains a partial list of Belkin's writings.

112. Rabbis Jung and Lookstein were key figures in the battle to prevent the imposition of Agudath ha-Rabbanim hegemony. Both were members of the Yeshiva board and were appointed to the executive board during the interregnum period. More importantly, they were the rabbis of Manhattan's two most affluent Orthodox congregations from where were derived many of the major financial contributors to the institution. Lookstein was also instrumental in galvanizing the RCA's official response to the Agudath ha-Rabbanim's challenge.

113. The Halacha Commission was a seven-man board led in the early 1940s by Rabbi Simcha Levy, a RIETS alumnus and rabbi in Perth Amboy, New Jersey. The other six men included both RIETS and HTC graduates. For more details on the issues faced and decisions rendered by the commission, see Bernstein, pp. 34–71.

114. It should be noted that by 1940, Rabbis Klein and Margolies, two of the most famous pre-World War I rabbis, who undoubtedly would have backed RCA activities, had passed away. Margolies's last connection with RCA rabbis was at

their organizing meeting in 1935, where he gave his blessing. Margolies's policies were continued and developed further by Lookstein, his student, pulpit successor, and grandson-in-law. Significantly, Levinthal, who survived his fellows, did not show great enthusiasm for the younger rabbis, though he seemingly shared their point of view about America. Of course, Rabbi Soloveitchik clearly surpassed his earlier colleagues in support of the American rabbinate. Besides his practical backing, he gave the idea of harmonizing Judaism and Americanism a broader philosophical grounding.

115. Aaron Lichtenstein, "R. Joseph Soloveitchik," in *Great Jewish Thinkers of the Twentieth Century*, ed. and introduction by Simon Noveck (Clinton, Mass., 1963), pp. 282–285. There is no full-length biography or autobiography of Soloveitchik's career or thought. Indeed, as Lichtenstein pointed out a generation ago, most of Soloveitchik's teachings have been orally presented and not published. Lichtenstein continues that "although Soloveitchik has published very little, he has written a great deal. . . . R. Soloveitchik himself once described it as a 'family malady.' Soloveitchik attributes this familial reluctance to the demands of perfectionism." See Lichtenstein, p. 287. More recently some of Soloveitchik's lectures and essays have been compiled. See, for example, Abraham R. Besdin, ed., *Reflections on the Rav: Lessons in Jewish Thought, Adapted from Lectures of Rabbi Joseph B. Soloveitchik* (Jerusalem, 1979), and Joseph Epstein, ed., *Shiurei ha-Rav: A Conspectus of the Public Lectures of Joseph B. Soloveitchik* (New York, 1974).

116. Rothkoff, pp. 118–122. Rabbi Moses Soloveitchik headed up a RIETS faculty of rabbis from Eastern Europe seemingly possessed of close ideological affinities to, if not membership in, the Agudath ha-Rabbanim. It would be interesting to know of the relationship both within the seminary and subsequently without between the East European teachers and the American students. To what extent did the teachers back or influence Agudath ha-Rabbanim policy, and to what degree did they support the American-born students? In other words, did Rabbi Joseph Soloveitchik's soon-to-be-discussed attitude toward his American disciples constitute a break in the RIETS faculty atmosphere?

117. Lichtenstein, p. 285.

118. *Ibid.*, p. 286; Rothkoff, p. 214; Rakeffet-Rothkoff, pp. 267–271. Joseph Soloveitchik's contact with Yeshiva University did not abruptly begin in 1941. In 1936, he delivered a series of lectures on philosophy at Yeshiva College. See Rothkoff, p. 129. He taught general philosophy in the college during the early years of his tenure at the university. In 1940, he organized with Revel a Boston branch of RIETS; an institution which did not survive his moving to New York. It should, however; be noted that Soloveitchik did not give up his position of leadership and authority in Boston when he began his formal connection at Yeshiva. He commuted for the next forty years between New York and Boston.

119. It should be noted that when Joseph Soloveitchik was appointed, there was some student opposition to the choice. See Rakeffet-Rothkoff, pp. 269–270. In the chaotic interregnum days, fears were raised that Soloveitchik would be the pawn of the Agudath ha-Rabbanim and help them dismantle the institution which Revel had built.

120. Lichtenstein, p. 282.

121. Joseph B. Soloveitchik, "Tribute to Rabbi Joseph H. Lookstein," in *Rabbi Joseph H. Lookstein Memorial Volume*, pp. vii-viii; letter; Joseph B. Soloveitchik to Israel Klavan, May 23, 1952, quoted in Bernstein, p. 49. It may be suggested that the use of the term "vague probability" can be applied to almost all situations where a RIETS man found himself in a "traditional" pulpit not affiliated with the Rabbinical Alliance or the United Synagogue. This approach closely follows the inclusionist policy of defining as within the fold all who have not formally joined the competing denomination. In truth, many famous present-day RCA rabbis began their careers in such mixed-seating pulpits, effected change over time, and ultimately rose to prominence in their movement. Clearly the history of Orthodox rabbis in less-than-Orthodox pulpits remains for future research.

122. Translated text of a Soloveitchik interview with the *Jewish Day*, November 19, 1954, quoted in Bernstein, p. 59.

123. We have noted that during Rabbi Jacob Joseph's unsuccessful career; his nemesis, Rabbi Segal, attracted followers from among Galician and Hungarian Jews who felt uncomfortable with the leadership of the Lithuanian Rabbi Joseph. They formed the association of the Congregation of Israel of Poland and Austria. Clearly the issue of ethnic subdivision within immigrant Orthodox Jewry remains to be examined beyond the limits of the present work.

124. See above for our discussion of East European rabbinic noncooperation in the area of kashruth.

125. Margolis was the author while still in Europe of *Agudat Erov* (Vilna, 1895), a commentary on the Passover Haggadah, *Shem Olam* (Vilna, 1901), a series of funeral orations, *Toras Gabriel* (Jerusalem, 1902), a commentary on Genesis and Exodus, and *Ginze Margaliot* (n.p., 190[?]), a commentary on the Book of Esther. In this country he published *Hiruzei Margoliot*, 2 vols. (1919). For Margolis's biography and bibliography, see Eisenstadt, pp. 240–241.

126. Margolis's account of his difficulties over kashruth with the Agudath ha-Rabbanim is recorded in his *Hiruzei Margoliot*. See Pt. II, pp. 378, 381–385, 394–395, 400. See Gastwirth, pp. 118–122, for both sides of the story.

127. *Sefer Knesseth ha-Rabbanim*, vol. 2. (New York, 1924), pp. 22–23.

128. *Ibid.*, pp. 44–45. Margolis was, of course, not the only outspoken critic of the schools Revel built and refashioned. Rothkoff points out that the founding of Yeshiva College as a bona fide liberal arts college particularly troubled a group called the Rabbinical Board of New York, which in January 1932 complained that Yeshiva was devoting too much time to secular studies and taking away from the hours of talmudic study. From within Yeshiva, complaints were often heard from roshei yeshiva that funds which should have gone to RIETS were being diverted to the less-talmudic Teachers Institute and to the "secular" college. To be sure, many Agudath ha-Rabbanim members, as we have noted, had their own difficulties with the directions RIETS took. But they stayed within RIETS as its ordaining body.

129. Volume 1 of *Sefer Knesseth* consists primarily of letters of support for the organization drafted by individual rabbis, reprinted articles on organizational conventions from the Orthodox New York newspapers, the *Yiddishes Tageblatt* and the

Morgen Zhurnal, and the resolutions and speeches made and given at Knesseth conventions during the early 1920s. (It seems as if the Knesseth was defunct by the end of that decade.) The sources note in passing that 135 members affiliated as of 1921. Of these, forty-three names and thirty-six addresses of rabbis can be derived from the text. Not surprisingly, all the rabbis about whom we have information served in communities where Agudath ha-Rabbanim members resided and in proportion to the opponents settlement patterns. A natural basis for rabbinical competition thus seemingly existed. Of the thirty-six for whom we have addresses, thirteen were New York- or Brooklyn-based, fourteen lived along the Baltimore-Boston seaboard, and seven in Boston or environs alone. (It should be remembered that Margolis was a chief rabbi in Boston prior to moving to New York.) Three others resided in Cincinnati, and St. Louis, Kansas City, Omaha, and Montreal were home for the others. It also should be noted that six Knesseth members appeared as Agudath ha-Rabbanim affiliates in the latter's 1929 *Sefer ha-Yovel*. These sources give one the impression that the Knesseth was at best a loose confederation. Members may have held varying degrees of commitment to it and opposition to the Agudath ha-Rabbanim. We have noted the similarities in the groups' platforms. When the Knesseth died, it was probably not a large step "back" into the Agudath ha-Rabbanim's fold.

The looseness of the organization even on the ideological level can be seen with reference to its approach to Zionism. Although Margolis, as late as 1922, still opposed Zionism theoretically, the organization he led took a somewhat different stance. See on this aspect of Margolis and his organization, Gurock "American Orthodox Organizations in Support of Zionism, 1880–1930," Chapter 4 of this volume.

Finally, membership in the Knesseth ha-Rabbanim may be related, interestingly enough, to the rise of Prohibition legislation in the United States. Under Internal Revenue Commission regulations, to be allowed to utilize wines for sacramental purposes, a rabbi had to show that he was a member of a recognized rabbinical body. Illegal kosher wine "peddling," of course, often became an abuse of this system. In any event, the Knesseth gave rabbis a home base for legal or possibly illegal wine handling. See *Sefer Knesseth*, pp. 74–76.

130. Helmreich, *The World of the Yeshiva* (New York, 1982), p. 24. It should be noted that even in its European-style infancy RIETS always offered some basics in secular studies.

131. Belkin's participation in this school warrants fuller explication. It was certainly an institution quite unlike the university he would later lead. Helmreich notes two basic sources on the life and career of Levenberg, "Rabbi Yehuda Heschel Levenberg," *Olameinu* (January 1975), pp. 14–15, and Isaac Ever; *Harav Yehuda Heschel Levenberg: Zayn Leben und Kamf* (Cleveland, 1939).

132. Helmreich, pp. 26–37. Significantly, when Mesivta Torah Vodaas was founded in 1917 in the acculturated, middle-class Williamsburg, Brooklyn neighborhood, the school's curriculum was quite modern and American. Classes were conducted in English and Hebrew, and Talmud was not the cornerstone of study. Rabbi Mendlowitz transformed the yeshiva almost overnight, modeling it after the

Hungarian *yeshivot* of his youth. See Alexander Gross, "Shraga Feivel Mendlowitz," in *Men of the Spirit,* ed. Leo Jung (New York, 1964), pp. 533–561, for a discussion of this rabbi's career; including his activities in the founding of Torah Umesorah (National Society of Hebrew Day Schools) in 1944. Yeshiva Rabbi Chaim Berlin began as an elementary yeshiva in 1906. It did not rise to advanced status until the leadership era of Rabbi Hutner, ca. 1940.

133. Israel Meir Ha-Kohen Kagan, *Niddehei Yisrael* (Warsaw, 1894), pp. 129–130, quoted in Rakeffet-Rothkoff, p. 18.

134. Helmreich, pp. 39–44 For a hagiographic biographical sketch of Rabbi Bloch, see Chaim Dov Keller; "He Brought Telshe to Cleveland," in *The Torah World: A Treasury of Biographical Sketches,* ed. Nisson Wolpin (New York, 1982), pp. 262–276. For a similar treatment of Rabbi Kotler; see Shaul Kagan, "From Kletzk to Lakewood," in *ibid.,* pp. 184–205. *The Torah World* is a collection of interesting short biographies of yeshiva-world luminaries culled from the pages of the *Jewish Observer,* the voice of the Agudath Israel in America. They give the reader of sense both of that group's understanding of history and of its reverence for its leaders.

The Mirrer Yeshiva (U.S., 1946) and the Kamenetz Yeshiva (U.S., 1960), both in Brooklyn, are other examples of refugee yeshivas. Rabbi Eliezer Yehudah Finkel and his son-in-law, Rabbi Chaim Leib Shmuelevitz, were the leading figures in the migration of the yeshiva community from Mir; Poland, to Shanghai, China, where it remained through 1945, when part of the school settled in Jerusalem. Rabbi Abraham Kalmanowitz, who preceded them to America, brought the rest of the yeshiva to Brooklyn. See on that episode, Eliyahu Meir Klugman, "Rosh Yeshivah in Mir-Poland, Mir-Shanghai and Mir-Jerusalem," and Chaim Shapiro, "The Last of Its Kind," in *The Torah World,* pp. 239–261. Rabbi Reuvain Grozovsky was a prime mover in the settlement of a Kamenetz community in America before taking a post at Mesivta Torah Vodaas. See his biography by Nisson Wolpin, "From Kamenetz to America" *ibid.,* pp. 206–222. Helmreich notes three other ideologically similar "advanced yeshivas in America," Brooklyn's Beth ha-Talmud Rabbinical College, the Talmudical Academy of Philadelphia, and the transformed Rabbi Jacob Joseph Yeshiva. The latter institution, a long-time elementary yeshiva, acquired refugee rabbis in the late 1940s–1950s, earning it that elevated status. See Helmreich, pp. 48–49

135. *EJ,* vol.7, cols. 1399–1400; Ernst J. Bodenheimer with Nosson Scherman, "The Rav of Frankfurt, U.S.A.," in *The Torah World,* pp. 223–238; Charles Liebman, "Orthodoxy in American Jewish Life," *AJYB* (1965), pp. 67–85; Israel Rubin, *Satmar: An Island in the City* (New York, 1972), pp. 39–42; Solomon Poll, *The Hasidic Community of Williamsburg* (New York, 1962), pp. 27–31. Clearly neither these books nor the present study begin to elucidate the multiplicity of differences among the various Hasidic sects in America. Our emphasis here has been solely on the commonalities of institutional structure and of allegiance to the figure of a rebbe/leader.

The placement of the Breuer community, for the purposes of this study, in the category of leader-oriented sects is based primarily on their its members' sense of allegiance to the late Dr. Breuer and to his successor, Rabbi Shimon Schwab, although the followers of these two men would never apply the Hasidic term "rebbe," with all its quasi-mystical connotations, to them. And, of course, Breuer people take a theoretical attitude toward the permissibility of secular studies quite different from that of Hasidim. Indeed one of the major thrusts of Hirshian philosophy was a belief in the possibility of synthesizing Western knowledge with Jewish tradition. That should at first glance have made the Breuer people quite comfortable with their Yeshiva University neighbors in Washington Heights. See on Hirschian philosophy and practice in twentieth century Germany, Herman Schwab, *History of Orthodox Jewry in Germany* (London, 1950).

And yet, as Liebman pointed out a generation ago, Hirschians in America have tended to align themselves with the Lithuanian yeshiva world. Liebman argued in 1965 that the community finds itself increasingly overwhelmed by the fervor of the yeshiva world" (including its negative attitude toward secular education). See Liebman, p. 72. It is also noteworthy from a bibliographic perspective that Rabbi Breuer's biography is included in *The Torah World* collection.

136. The denigration of RIETS's approach and curriculum by refugee-yeshiva rabbis dates back to before the war; when in 1938 Rabbi Elchanan Wasserman, then head of the Polish Baranowicz Yeshiva, visited the United States and publicly praised Mesivta Torah Vodaas while refusing to set foot in RIETS. Three years earlier, Rabbi Kotler; also on tour of America, refused a similar invitation from Revel. See Rothkoff, pp. 155–156. In 1950, at its second American convention, the Agudath Israel designated Mesivta Torah Vodaas, with Silver's acquiescence, its number-one funds beneficiary ahead of Yeshiva University. See Rakeffet-Rothkoff, p. 272. And in 1944, the Igud ha-Rabbanim was formed. This organization, made up primarily of graduates of the more traditional yeshivas in America, challenged the RCA/Yeshiva University and Agudath ha-Rabbanim association. See Liebman, pp. 75–76. Of course, one of the greatest targets of yeshiva-world acrimony was Rabbi Joseph Soloveitchik. Though no one ever questioned his scholarship or Orthodoxy, refugee-yeshiva people clearly were not comfortable with his approach toward RIETS and modernity in general. Liebman notes a graphic illustration of how Soloveitchik was viewed by others. In 1962, at Rabbi Kotler's funeral, Soloveitchik was not called upon to eulogize his fellow Torah giant, while men like the Satmar Rebbe and Rabbi Moses Feinstein were both accorded that high honor and obligation. See Liebman, p. 85.

137. For a study of the conflict between the Mizrachi and Agudath Israel during wartime and post-World War I Poland, see Ezra Mendelsohn, *Zionism in Poland: The Formative Years 1915–1926* (New Haven and London, 1981), pp. 24–25, 56–57. He notes there the Agudath Israel's "basically pre-modern Jewish identity" and its perception that religious Zionists were making it possible for the masses to "abandon their Judaism and still, in their own minds at least, remain Jews." For the Agudah's evaluation of its own history, see Joseph Friederman, "A Concise History of Agudah Israel," in *Yaacov Rosenheim Memorial Volume* (New York, 1968), pp. 1–66.

138. Rakeffet-Rothkoff, pp. 157–162. For more on the Agudath Israel's position on Zionism in theory and practice and the rise of the Yishuv, see Isaac Breuer; *Das*

Judische Nationalbeim (Frankfurt am Main, 1925), Yaacov Rosenheim, *Agudist World-Position* (New York, 1941), and Agudas Israel World Organization, *The Jewish People and Palestine* (London, 1947).

139. Rakeffet-Rothkoff, pp. 155–165.

140. *Ibid.,* pp. 175–183.

141. *Ibid.,* p. 290. In reality, however; Rabbi Kotler's Yiddish-only exhortation remained just a theoretical statement. Torah Umesorah, the National Society for Hebrew Day Schools, founded in 1944 by Rabbi Mendlowitz and headed by Rabbi Kotler until his death in 1962, which has done much to promote day schools and elementary-level yeshivas throughout the United States, has always adopted a multilingual (Hebrew, English, and Yiddish) approach to Jewish educational instruction. In essence, Kotler too had to recognize certain limitations in establishing Torah education beyond the particular immigrant youth constituency. See Liebman, pp. 72–73. And for a history of that educational movement, see Doniel Zvi Kramer; "The History and Impact of Torah Umesorab and Hebrew Day Schools in America" (Ph.D. diss., Bernard Revel Graduate School, Yeshiva University, 1976).

142. Rakeffet-Rothkoff, pp. 140–142. Silver once referred to these new leaders as "zealots" and deplored their "zealotry."

143. *Ibid.,* pp. 292–295.

144. Bernstein, pp. 141–156, discusses the disputes within and without the RCA over the ban and the options which presented themselves for response.

145. Helmreich, pp. 233–235. The Hebrew Theological College too had been influenced by Aaron Soloveitchik, younger brother of the Rov, who in 1966 left RIETS and headed up the HTC. For more than a decade he strengthened that institution's rabbinical department, and most significantly, as Liebman found out, "Reb Aharon has resisted pressures . . . to urge students to accept positions in synagogues with mixed pews in the hope of instituting *mehizot* later on." See Liebman. "The Training of American Rabbis," *AJYB*, 1968, pp. 25–26. However; in the late 1970s, he left HTC to found the Brisker Yeshiva of Chicago. For an example of present-day RIETS reverence for men like Rabbi David Lifshitz, see Noah Goldstein, "HaRav Dovid Lifshitz, Shlita," in the publication of the RIETS Rabbinic Alumni *Chavrusa* (April 1982), p. 4.

146. The traditions of Mendes or a De Sola Pool of both serving a Sephardic Orthodox congregation and becoming involved in broader communal affairs is continued today on a less publicized basis by Rabbis Louis Gerstein and Marc Angel from the home-base of Shearith Israel in New York. There are, however; other Sephardic rabbis who serve congregations outside the metropolis. The men who minister in New Rochelle, New Jersey, Houston, San Francisco, Los Angeles, and the recent Syrian immigrant community in Brooklyn stay clear of larger organizational ties. They serve immigrants who came here either before World War I or after World War II. These men, trained at Yeshiva University, stay clear of all existing Ashkenazic rabbinic combines. Their feeling is that in joining such organizations they would lose their distinctive Sephardic heritage and with it their popularity in their own ethnic community. They also have their own immigrant rabbis to contend with. For more on this understudied Jewish group, including its

denominational orientation, see Marc Angel's "The Sephardim of the United States: An Exploratory Story," *AJYB* 1973: 77–138.

147. *Intermountain Jewish News*, February 24, 1956, as quoted from Bernstein, p. 145.

148. *EJ*, vol. 11, col. 1581; vol. 13, col. 1494; vol. 14, col. 935; See also I. J. Karpman, *Who's Who in World Jewry* (Tel Aviv, 1978), p. 619 and *passim*. Clearly the military chaplaincy forces the Orthodox rabbi to interact daily and ceremonially with Jews of all denominations. A subject which demands further investigation is to what degree RIETS more than other yeshiva men volunteered for this somewhat religiously problematic service during wartime as well as beyond. The role of the chaplain in world conflict, including the area of difficulties with civilian and military authorities in protecting Jews, also should be examined. Toward that end, see Emanuel Rackman, "Mah Lamadu Anu Rabbanei ha-Tzava," *Talpioth* (April 1947), pp. 273–278.

It should also be emphasized strongly that when it came to saving Jews from Nazism or dealing with problems of refugees in general, the RCA rabbis had no monopoly upon concern and activity. During World War I, the Agudath ha-Rabbanim was in the forefront of the Central Relief Committee, which helped the displaced Jews of Eastern Europe. And though they placed a particular emphasis on helping Orthodox Jews, they helped all of their brethren and *cooperated* with American nontraditional groups. The same also can be said about the activities of the Agudath Israel and the refugee scholars in the establishment of the Vaad Ha-Hatzala, which tried to rescue Jews from Nazism and which also cooperated in relief and rescue efforts. See on this subject Rakeffet-Rothkoff, pp. 186–215, and Efraim Zuroff, "Rescue Priority and Fund Raising as Issues During the Holocaust: A Case Study of the Relations between the Vaad Ha-Hatzala and the Joint, 1939–1941," *AJH* (March 1979), pp. 305–327. The significant difference between their approach and that of the Americanized rabbis is that during the acute crisis the latter worked very often *within* existing interdenominational organizations and continued their support in calmer days. The differences here are very much akin to the differences between the attitudes of the Mizrachi and the Agudath Israel toward Palestine and Israel in the post-1930 era.

149. It is important to here note a very different type of split within Orthodox rabbinic ranks over attitudes toward activities outside the purely religious realm. In the 1960s, Rabbi Meir Kahane, a Brooklyn-based rabbi, founded the Jewish Defense League. That organization challenged the RCA establishment rabbis and their less-traditional partners in interdenominational, umbrella organizations over their perceived "soft" policies toward meeting the challenge of Russian Jewry. For more on Kahane as rabbi, leader, and rebbe, see Janet Dolgin, *Jewish Identity and the JDL* (Princeton, NJ, 1977).

150. Although the three men noted here and Berman are the most famous American Orthodox cooperators, they are by no means unique. A perusal of the *AJYB* and other sources over the last two generations indicates that RIETS/RCA men like Gilbert Klaperman, Sol Roth, and Frederick Hollander have all been presidents of the New York Board of Rabbis. Interestingly, the present executive director

of that group is Paul Hiat, a RIETS/RCA man. Orthodox presidents of the SCA beyond the first generation of Goldstein, De Sola Pool, and Lookstein include Joseph Karasick, Theodore Adams, and Walter Wurzberger. Of course, innumerable RCA men have served as presidents of local boards of rabbis.

151. Anne Lapidus Lerner; "Who Has Not Made Me a Man: The Movement for Equal Rights for Women in American Jewry," *AJYB* (1977): 3–38; Charlotte Baum, Paula Hyman, and Michel Sonya, *The Jewish Woman in America* (New York, 1976).

152. The debate within the American Orthodox rabbinate over women's role can be followed to some extent through the pages of *Tradition*, an RCA publication, and other contemporary journals. See, for example, Saul Berman, "The Status of Women in Halachic Judaism," *Tradition* (Fall 1973): 5–28; Michael Chernick, "The Halachic Process-Growth and Change," *Sh'ma* (April 1976): 92–94; A. M. Silver; "May Women Be Taught Bible, Mishnah and Talmud," *Tradition* (Summer 1978): 74–83; R. P. Bulka, "Women's Role: Some Ultimate Concerns," *Tradition*, (Spring 1979): 27–37; Emanuel Rackman, "The Principle of Polarity," *Judaism*, (Winter 1980): 9–11; Avraham Weiss, "Women and Sifrei Torah," *Tradition* (Summer 1982): 106–118; Saul Berman and Shulamith Magnus, "Orthodoxy Responds to Feminist Ferment," *Response* (Spring 1981): 5–18. See also *the Jewish Press*, December 10, 1982, p. 3, for the Agudath ha-Rabbanim's condemnation of women's services.

153. "Norman Lamm," *Current Biography*, 1978, pp. 27–30.

154. *Jewish Week-American Examiner*, July 3–16, 198 I; *Young Israel Viewpoint*, (September 1982); *Jewish Week-American Examiner*, October 4, 1981, p. 3; "Yeshiva University President Urges Orthodox Community to Broaden Its Horizons," undated press release, Union of Orthodox Jewish Congregations of America; Norman Lamm, "Modern Orthodoxy Identity Crisis," *Jewish Life*, May-June 1969, p. 7, quoted in Helmreich, p. 320.

Notes to Chapter 2, *The Orthodox Synagogue*

1.   Hyman B. Grinstein, *The Rise of the Jewish Community of New York* (Philadelphia, 1946), pp. 377–378. For important discussions of the phenomenon of intermarriage in the nineteenth century that notes the role synagogue legislation played in the decline of Jewish numbers, see Moshe Davis, "Mixed Marriage in Western Jewry," *Jewish Journal of Sociology*, 15, no. 2 (1968), pp. 180–181; Malcolm H. Stern, "The Function of Genealogy in American Jewish History," in *Essays in American Jewish History* (Cincinnati, 1958), pp. 83–84.

2.   Grinstein, *Rise of the Jewish Community*, pp. 375–381.

3.   The use of the term "Orthodox" to describe the synagogue practices of early nineteenth century congregations is, of course, somewhat anachronistic. One can only begin speaking accurately of Orthodox congregations when there are Reform and Conservative congregations to which they can be compared. Until the rise of *the liberal* denominations in American Judaism, all synagogues observed the base-level, later to be called Orthodox, practices of separate seating, unabridged or unmodified services as prescribed in the siddur, services unaccompanied on the Sabbath and holidays by instrumental music, and the staging of services at times

386   American Jewish Orthodoxy in Historical Perspective

corresponding to Judaism's traditional clock and not America's time schedule. For the purposes of this study, nineteenth-century congregations truly begin to be called Orthodox when they manifest, into *the rise of liberal denominations*, an adherence to these fundamentally important ritual practices. These basic liturgical elements also can be effective, if somewhat imperfect, criteria, for designating late nineteenth- to twentieth-century synagogues as Orthodox. For us, a synagogue will be called Orthodox in the later era if it follows these practices, or failing on one or more characteristics, does not self-consciously or formally see itself as part of the more liberal denominational camps. It should be remembered that not until 1913 and the founding of the United Synagogue of America (Conservative) did there exist three national bodies to which congregations could belong. Of course, even after 1913 not all congregations in the United States affiliated with one or another of these groups. We will also see later that not all self-declared Orthodox congregations accept these elements as a strict enough basis for defining denominational life. Nor have all Orthodox leaders accepted as Orthodox those groups that deviate somewhat from these norms, but have not joined the Conservatives or Reformers.

4.   In 1820, there were but six U.S. congregations; all were Orthodox and all but one practiced the Sephardic ritual. Thirty years later, there were approximately thirty-seven American synagogues situated in eleven states. Almost all of these synagogues were founded as Orthodox German or Polish congregations and the vast majority of them had yet to break with Orthodoxy, hence the periodization for the first, pre-Reform stage of our study. The date of 1800 was chosen on the assumption that for a comparative study of exclusionary and inclusionary policies, one needs a critical mass of congregations, which simply did not exist before the nineteenth century.

5.   Edwin Wolf II and Maxwell Whiteman, *The History of the Jews of Philadelphia from Colonial Times to the Age of Jackson* (Philadelphia, 1975), pp. 224, 234–235, 240–241, 45a. In its decision of 1829, Rodeph Shalom went beyond the limits of inclusionary policies. If indeed a pledge to "raise children as Jews" stopped short of their formal conversion—a rare phenomenon to be sure in early nineteenth-century America—the synagogue seemingly admitted to its larger fold the legally non-Jewish children of intermarrieds.

6.   Isaac M. Fein, *The Making of an American Jewish Community: The History of Baltimore Jewry from 1773–1920* (Philadelphia, 1971), pp. 55–56. Buffalo Jewry's first congregation, Beth El, also attempted in its earliest years to impose "church discipline" through a system of fines. See Selig Adler and Thomas Connolly, *Prom Ararat to Suburbia: The History of the Jewish Community of Buffalo* (Philadelphia, 1960), p. 60.

7.   Bertram W. Korn, *The Early Jews of New Orleans* (Waltham, 1969), pp. 196–197. A similar policy of leniency seems also to have characterized the history of Richmond's Beth Shalome, and probably for the same reason. Richmond Jewry's historian has noted "that unlike the earlier Sephardic congregations established in the New World, Beth Shalom did not compel religious observance by their members. See Myron Berman, *Richmond Jewry, 1769–1976, Shabbat in Shocke* (Charlottesville, Va., 1979), pp. 38–39. It should be noted, however, that the New Orleans

congregation's very lenient approach lasted only until 1841 when, in part as a result of the influx of German Jewish immigrants, who seemingly broadened the community's Jewish marriage base, regulations were passed denying membership to intermarrieds. See Korn, p. 248.

8.   Morris U. Schappes, A *Documentary History of the Jews in the United States 1654–1875* (New York, 1950), p. 175.

9.   Questions may be raised concerning the designation of the reforms suggested initially by those who would found the Reformed Society of Israelites as still "within Orthodox Judaism." Clearly, their group's later activities, when on their own, cast doubt on whether their original idea of not "abandoning the institution of Moses" meant the maintenance of Orthodox teachings and core practices. But were their original demands outside Orthodoxy's widest pale? Indeed, with the possible exception of the shortening of the service proposal, these amendments were almost exactly the same as those, which we will see later, were offered in the early twentieth century by, among others, the Jewish Endeavor Society and the Young Israel within that era's Orthodoxy. Of course, as we will also see, not all Orthodox Jews of those days accepted these opinions as legitimate. In other words, this initial petition belongs as much within the history of the modernization or Americanization of Orthodoxy as to the beginning of Reform.

10.   Schappes, A *Documentary History*, p. 175.

11.   To be fair, other pre-1850 congregations had exclusionary policies toward intermarrieds on their books. However, questions must always be asked about how scrupulously they were enforced. For example, Cincinnati's earliest congregation, K. K. Bnai Israel (1824), also disqualified intermarrieds from synagogue membership. See James G. Heller, *As Yesterday When it Is Past: A History of Isaac M. Wise Temple—K.K. B'nai Yeshurun—of Cincinnati* (Cincinnati, 1946), pp. 26–28. As we will soon see, splits took place in congregations over laxity in enforcing religious behavior. However, Beth Elohim was designated the most exclusionary congregation of its time by virtue of the welter of regulations that governed the lives of those who accepted its leadership.

12.   Charles Reznikoff and Uriah Z. Engleman, *The Jews of Charleston: A History of an American Jewish Community* (Philadelphia, 1950), p. 115–128; Barnett A. Elzas, *The Jews of South Carolina* (Philadelphia, 1905), pp. 147–159. On the Charleston experiment in reform, see also Lou H. Silberman, *American Impact: Judaism in the United States in the Early 19th Century*, R. G. Rudolf Lecture in Jewish Studies, Syracuse University (March 29, 1964).

13.   Allan Tarshish, "The Charleston Organ Case" *AJHQ* (June 1965): 411–449.

14.   Grinstein, *Rise of the Jewish Community of New York*, p. 43.

15.   *Ibid.*, p. 40. On the quick end of Sephardic hegemony in America and continued institutional primacy into the nineteenth century, see Stern, *Function of Genealogy*, pp. 74–75.

16.   Grinstein and Jick differ as to the degree of amalgamation and muting of ethnic differences that took place in New York among Sephardim and Ashkenazim before the 1820s. The former speaks of the united community, whereas Jick describes New York Jewry as "a small, relatively homogeneous group." See Leon

Jick, The *Americanization of the Synagogue, 1820–1870* (Hanover, N.H., 1976), p. 26, Grinstein, *Rise of the Jewish Community of New York*, p. 49.

17. Jick, *Americanization of the Synagogue*, p. 24. Clearly the controversy over religious laxity was part of a broader list of complaints the recently arrived immigrants had with the American synagogue. Other significant complaints included the immigrants' disapproval of costly, obligatory synagogue offerings—which probably the poorer element could not afford—the unequal distribution of honors, poor educational services, the increased significance of the Hazzan as religious functionary, etc. See the entire list of particulars in Grinstein, *Rise of the Jewish Community of New York*, pp. 40–44.

18. Grinstein, *Rise of the Jewish Community of New York*, pp. 49–53.

19. Berman, *Richmond Jewry*, pp. 139–140; Heller, *As Yesterday When It Is Past*, p. 25; Fein, *Making of an American Jewish Community*, p. 55; Jick, *Americanization of the Synagogue*, p. 43.

20. To be entirely accurate, Philadelphia's Mikve Israel, alone among its sister Sephardic congregations, did take small, faltering, and clearly unenthusiastic steps toward Americanizing its services when in 1843 it finally officially permitted its Hazzan, Isaac Leeser, to deliver a weekly sermon in English. Leeser had introduced this practice more than ten years earlier and did not get much congregational support. His move toward modernization was reportedly "frowned upon with disdain." See Jick, *Americanization of the Synagogue*, pp. 60–61, as quoted from Maxwell Whiteman, "Isaac Leeser and the Jews of Philadelphia," *PAJHS* (1959), 48, no. 4, 213. See the discussion later in the chapter on Leeser and his efforts to develop a more responsive American Orthodox synagogue during the era of Reform.

Among the Ashkenazim of Baltimore Hebrew Congregation before 1850, we note, as did Jick, the somewhat strange behavior of congregants opposing Rabbi Rice when he attempted to control their Sabbath observance patterns, clearly an indication of lay permissiveness. At the same time, they also opposed Rice's attempt to Americanize the service by eliminating *piyutim*. See Jick, *Americanization of the Synagogue*, p. 72, as derived from Adolph Guttmacher, A *History of the Baltimore Hebrew Congregation* (Baltimore, 1905), p. 27.

21. Jick, *Americanization of the Synagogue*, pp. 86–88, 90–94; Grinstein, *Rise of the Jewish Community of New York*, pp. 355–356; Fein, *Making of an American Jewish Community*, pp. 56, 62–63; Adler and Connolly, *From Ararat to Suburbia*, p. 67; Hyman L. Meites, *History of the Jews in Chicago* (Chicago, 1924), p. 40; Morris A. Gutstein, A *Priceless Heritage: The Epic Growth of Nineteenth Century Chicago Jewry* (New York, 1953), pp. 164–166. Bylaws of the United Hebrew Congregation of St. Louis (1843) quoted in Jick, p. 50. *Minutes of United Hebrew Congregation of St. Louis* (April 15, 1855, July 17, 1859), quoted in Jick, *Americanization of the Synagogue*, pp. 151–152.

22. The statistics on synagogues discussed here are derived from Jick, *Americanization of the Synagogue*, who in turn obtained his information from Engleman, "Jewish Statistics in the U.S. Census of Religious Bodies (1850–1936)," *Jewish Social Studies*, 9, 2 (April 1947): 54–64, and from three nineteenth-century sources: Jacques I. Lyons and Abraham De Sola's A *Jewish Calendar for Fifty Years* (Montreal,

1984); Israel Joseph Benjamin, *Three Years in America, 1859–1862*, vol. 1, trans. Charles Reznikoff (Philadelphia, 1956), p. 82, which records highly impressionistic statistics; and *Statistics of the Jews in the United States* (Philadelphia, 1880).

23. That the stages in the rise of Reform in America followed closely the Americanization of German Jews in the nineteenth-century is central to Jick's thesis in *The Americanization*. For at earlier discussion of the problems of nineteenth-century Judaism in this country, see Moshe Davis, *The Emergence of Conservative Judaism: The Historical School in 19th Century America* (Philadelphia, 1965), pp. 6–7.

24. Adler and Connolly, *From Ararat to Suburbia*, pp. 94–95; B. G. Rudolph, *From a Minyan to a Community: A History of the Jews of Syracuse* (Syracuse, 1970), p. 72; Stuart E. Rosenberg, *The Jewish Community in Rochester, 1843–1925* (New York, 1954), p. 87; Fred Rosenbaum, *Architects of Reform: Congressional and Community Leadership: Emanu-El of San Francisco, 1844–1980* (Berkeley, 1980), p. 28; Fein, *Making of an American Jewish Community*, pp. 114–118; Israel Goldstein, A *Century of Judaism in New York: B'nai Jeshurun, 1825–1925, New York's Oldest Ashkenazic Congregation* (New York, 1930), pp. 158–160.

25. A continuum existed among nineteenth-century Americanized synagogues that ranged from the Orthodox, who permitted English-language sermons and emphasized decorum, through the most radical of Reform temples. Within that continuum there could also be found—among innumerable other phenomena and variations—synagogues whose ritual was totally Orthodox except that mixed seating was permitted; I have characterized this as a hybrid type of religious behavior. Conservative Jewish congregations, according to this definition, were more liberal still. They could be characterized as those permitting instrumental music in an abridged service, conducted according to the modern prayerbooks edited by nineteenth-century authors. But they were less liberal than their contemporary reform counterpart, by virtue of their continued observance of second days of holidays and the custom of men wearing hats during services—ceremonials that characterize Orthodoxy. Clearly, these denominations are not easily defined in the abstract; they are best identified by comparison. We have noted here and earlier some of the variables.

26. Adler and Connolly, *From Ararat to Suburbia*, pp. 94–95; Rosenberg, *Jewish Community in Rochester*, pp. 87–98; Rosenbaum, *Architects of Reform*, p. 28. The behavior patterns of these hybrid congregations closely adumbrates the activities of twentieth-century so-called traditional Orthodox congregations, situated particularly in the Midwest, which permit mixed seating but maintain all other Orthodox procedures and practices. These synagogues are discussed later in the chapter.

27. Fein, *Making of an American Jewish Community*, pp. 110–118.

28. Israel M. Goldman, "Henry W. Schneeberger: His Role in American Judaism," *AJHQ* (December 1967): 179–190. The dozen or so German congregations that stayed Orthodox were not the only such institutions in the United States before 1880. In Cincinnati, for example, in the very heart of the Reform center, Congregation Shearith Israel founded in 1855 sustained its Orthodoxy until 1885, when a graduate of Hebrew Union College, Dr. David Davidson, assumed the pulpit. In the 1860s, Rabbi Bernard Illowy, an Orthodox rabbi late of Baltimore, New Orleans,

and four other American cities, served as the rabbi. Although Heller, *As Yesterday When It Is Past*, pp. 199–200, notes its existence, nothing has yet been published on Shearith Israel, a topic for future consideration. Furthermore, when the Union of Orthodox Jewish Congregations—to be discussed shortly—was founded in 1898, some fifty-one congregations sent representatives to the inaugural meetings. The congregations attending could be described as including Conservative, traditional, and strictly Orthodox—although to what proportions remains to be determined. On the founding of the Orthodox Union (OU), see *AH*, June 10, 1979, p. 173.

29. Adler and Connolly, *From Ararat to Suburbia*, pp. 96, 100, 103; David and Tamar De Sola Pool, *An Old Faith in the New World: Portrait of Shearith Israel, 1654–1954* (New York, 1955), pp. 99–101, 112; Grinstein, *Rise of the Jewish Community of New York*, p. 366.

30. Fein, *Making of an American Jewish Community*, p. 118; Berman, *Richmond Jewry*, pp. 41, 61–63; Herbert T. Ezekiel and Gaston Lichtenstein, *The History of the Jews of Richmond from 1769–1917* (Richmond, 1917).

31. To be accurate, Leeser's first foray toward achieving a union of congregations to offset rampant disaffection from Judaism took place in 1841, when in the wake of the Damascus Blood Libel and several years before Wise's arrival, his proposal was offered. In 1849, Leeser's fears of "the threat an unrestrained Reform movement posed to the character of American Judaism" seemingly coincided with Wise's ambition for a unified American Jewry under his sway. See Jick, *Americanization of the Synagogue*, pp. 105; Davis, *The Emergence of Conservative Judaism: The Historical School in Nineteenth Century America* (Philadelphia, 1953), pp. 119–120, 128–129, 133.

32. Zichron Ephraim, although a nineteenth-century American Orthodox synagogue, was of a different ethnic kind. It was one of the first congregations made up primarily of East European and not German Jews. Sender Jarmulowsky, the founder of the first bank run by East European Jews, was a member. This congregation adumbrated a larger tradition, which came to the fore in the first decade of the twentieth century.

33. Davis, Emergence of *Conservative Judaism*, p. 237; Bernard Drachman, *The Unfailing Light: Memories of an American Rabbi* (New York, 1948), pp. 177–182; Henry Pereira Mendes, "The Beginning of the Seminary," in Cyrus Adler, ed., *The Jewish Theological Seminary of America: Semi-Centennial Volume* (New York, 1939), pp. 35–41.

34. *AH*, June 10, 1889, p. 172; January 4, 1901, pp. 231–234. More work needs to be done on the respective ritual and ideological positions and the ethnic orientations of the some fifty-odd congregations that founded the Orthodox Union. A preliminary examination reveals a mixture of American Orthodox of German extraction, typified by Chizuk Amuno and Shearith Israel of Baltimore; East European ethnic Orthodox with clearly some Americanized leanings—adumbrations of the future—exemplified by Zichron Ephraim, Sephardic synagogues led by New York's Shearith Israel; and, significantly, a number of synagogues "where organ and pews were in vogue." I would estimate that more than one-half of the congregations noted were Orthodox synagogues composed of German-American Jews.

35. *AH*, June 20, 1898, p. 172.

36. The Beth Hamidrash established in 1852 is the antecedent of the more famous Beth Hamedrosh Hagodol, founded in 1859 and still existing (1996) on Norfolk Street. The Congregation Beth Hamidrash Livne Yisrael Yelide Polin, established in 1853 and characterized by Grinstein as a mixed Russian-Polish congregation, also drew members from the original Russian Jewish synagogue. See Grinstein, *Rise of the Jewish Community of New York*, pp. 474, 477–478.

37. A differentiation is being made here among varieties of so-called Polish Jews arriving in this country. The Russo-Polish Jews arriving before and after 1852 were clearly less acculturated in the ways of the West than, say, Polish Jews from Posen, who were Central European in their attitudes and outlook. They constituted the beginnings of a new migration, which, of course, reached tremendous proportions after 1881. They, along with Jews from other parts of the Russian Empire, Romania, and Hungary, made up the new immigration of East European Jews.

38. Judah David Eisenstein, "The History of the First Russian-American-Jewish Congregation: The Beth Hamedrosh Hagodol," *PAJHS*, 9 (1901), pp. 64–72.

39. The official name of that synagogue is Congregation Kehal Adath Jeshurun M'Yassy (Jassy of Romania). This synagogue has been frequently mislabeled a Polish or Russian congregation. For more on this synagogue's history, see above, chapter 12.

40. It is impossible to determine how many East European congregations existed in the United States before the era of mass migration. The early Union of American Hebrew Congregation pamphlet, *Statistics of the Jews in the United States* (Philadelphia, 1880), upon which Jick based his assertion that there were some 275 synagogues then in the United States, lists nary an East European institution. Eisenstein in his memoir, *Ozar Zichronothai* (New York, 1929), p. 31, states that there were 152 congregations in this country. How many of these were East European is not indicated. My cursory survey of extant communal histories has indicated to me that at least twenty East European congregations existed in America before 1880.

41. In counting the number of East European synagogues that existed in America before 1880, I have omitted the most ephemeral of synagogues, later to be called "mushroom synagogues," which sprang up under sometimes unethical auspices every Jewish High Holiday season. In Milwaukee, for example, the first East European congregations were these "sporadic congregations" characterized by one contemporary as "Shaarey Harevach (Gates of Profit) to whose establishment the smartest preparations were being made." See Louis J. Switchkow and Lloyd P. Gartner, *The History of the Jews of Milwaukee* (Philadelphia, 1963), p. 192. Attempts to deal with this nefarious trafficking in religion in the twentieth century are discussed later in the chapter.

42. Gutstein, *A Priceless Heritage*, p. 35. Some congregations went even further in their theoretical requirements for membership. To be a member of Chicago's Congregation Ohave Sholom Mariampoler Chevrah Kadisha (burial society) or Chevrah Mishno U'Gmoro (Talmud society), candidates not only had to be Sabbath

observers, but were expected to refrain from shaving their beards. See Gutstein, p. 203.

43. Rabbi Hirsch Falk Vidaver Levy quoted in Albert Ehrenfried, A *Chronicle of Boston Jewry from the Colonial Period to* 1900, (n.p., 1963), p. 430.

44. Congregation Ohab Zedek, *Golden Jubilee, 1873–1923* (New York, 1923), n.p.

45. Gerard Wolfe and Jo Renee Fine, *The Synagagues of New York's Lower East Side* (New York, 1978), pp. 25, 43, 52, 96.

46. Wolfe and Fine, *Synagogues of New York's Lower East Side*, pp. 43–97; Jonathan D. Sarna, trans. and ed., *People Walk on Their Heads: Moses Weinberger's Jews and Judaism in New York* (New York, 1982), pp. 13–14. Sarna aptly describes this change toward greater formality as a "shift from participation toward performance." Although much has been written about the sociological implications of mixed seating, work needs to be done on the adoption of pews or assigned seats.

47. Eisenstein, "History of the First Russian-American Congregation," pp. 69, 73–74.

48. *Ibid.,* p. 73.

49. Sarna, *People Walk on Their Heads*, pp. 105–106. Weinberger's sentiments were undoubtedly seconded by the Beth Hamedrosh Hagodol group identified by Eisenstein as *hasidim* who as early as 1861 opposed "the reformed element [in that congregation who] wanted to introduce decorum and a musical cantor." See Eisenstein, "History of the First Russian-American Congregation," p. 69. Divisions over the necessity of hiring a cantor led to a temporary split in that congregation long before the cantor craze of the 1880s.

50. For the best primer on the subjects noted here, see Moses Rischin's classic, *The Promised City: New York's Jews, 1870–1914* (Cambridge, 1963), especially the chapters entitled "Tradition at Half-Mast" and "The Great Awakening."

51. Abraham J. Karp, "New York Chooses a Chief Rabbi," *PAJHS* 44, no. 3 (March 1954), pp. 129–198. The public announcement of the selection of the Malbim was published in the *Jewish Record* (Philadelphia). It noted that twenty-four synagogues signed the call and twenty-five others were prepared to cooperate.

52. The proliferation of *landsmanshaft* synagogues continued unabated up to World War I and the effective end of immigration. So great was the splintering of worshiping New York Jewry into this myriad of regional and local congregations that by 1917 the New York Kehillah could estimate that there were approximately 730 Orthodox synagogues in New York alone, the vast majority East European. What is also significant, the Kehillah noted that one-half of the Jewish population was unsynagogued totally, and that included the thousands who were hoodwinked yearly by unscrupulous mushroom synagogue operators. There were plenty of seats for "interested worshipers" but most of these seats went unused throughout the year. See *JCR*, pp. 117–121. For a short treatment of the complex history of the social, cultural, and religious role played by the *landsmanshaft* synagogue, see *Di Yiddishe Landsmanshaften fun New York* (New York, 1938).

53. This continued affinity for the old style of services even as Jews broke with the social-religious system that supported the immigrant synagogue came to the fore primarily in the form of opposition to innovation within Orthodoxy.

54. The attitude of second-generation Jews toward old-style religion is documented by their reaction to the post-1900 innovations sponsored by, among other groups, the Jewish Endeavor Society and the Young Israel.

55. Karp, "New York Chooses a Chief Rabbi," pp. 129–198.

56. Sarasohn's devotion to the harmonization of Judaism with Americanization through his newspaper was expressed through his development of the first English-language page in the *Yiddishes Tageblatt*. It was expressly dedicated to second-generation Jews and was full of information of a communal nature. It was in these pages that American Orthodox synagogues would, after 1897, get their message across to their acculturated potential members. On this and other Yiddish newspaper, see Mordecai Soltes, "The Yiddish Press: An Americanization Agent," *AJYB* 26 (1924–25), pp. 165–372.

57. For a biographical treatment of Klein and his affinity for Americanization, see above, chapter 1.

58. The downtown contingent was actually made up of some six congregations. They included Mishkan Israel, Chebra Kadisha Talmud Torah, Chebrah Kadusha Talmud Torah, Emuno Israel, B'nai Jacob, and Zichron Torath Moshe. Also included in the New York Orthodox camp were a small number of recent German immigrant Orthodox congregations, such as Adas Israel and immigrant Sephardic congregation Nefuzoth Israel. More needs to be done on these varieties of immigrant Orthodox synagogues, which are often left unnoticed. See *AH*, June 10, 1898, p. 172.

59. In 1901, Rabbi H. P. Mendes, president of the Orthodox Union, reviewed his organization's first three years of activities. Although Mendes reiterated that the Union was born to fight against Reform Jewish teachings and activities, it is clear that most of the organization's time, as noted by Mendes, was spent acting "in the interest of Orthodox Judaism whenever occurrences arose in civil or social matters as well as religious affairs." See *AH*, January 4, 1901, pp. 231–234.

60. Bernard Drachman, *The Unfailing Light: Memories of an American Rabbi* (New York, 1948), pp. 213.

61. Joseph H. Lookstein, "Seventy-Five Yesteryears: A Historical Sketch of Kehilath Jeshurun," *Congregation Kehilath Jeshurun, Diamond Jubilee Yearbook* (New York, 1946), pp. 58. For a more complete discussion of the nature of the American Orthodoxy espoused by the Jewish Theological Seminary in its pre-Solomon Schechter days, see above, chapter 1.

62. Jeffrey S. Gurock, *When Harlem Was Jewish, 1870–1930* (New York, 1979), pp. 23, 25, 26, 92–93, 95. Ohab Zedek also maintained the upgraded role of the cantor in the Americanized congregation when it hired Rev. Joseph (Yossele) Rosenblatt as its *chazan*. See Samuel Rosenblatt, *Yossele Rosenblatt: The Story of My Life as Told to His Son* (New York, 1954). Joining the three congregations noted above were two other East European uptown synagogues, Ateres Zwie and Nachlath Zwie, early arrivals in what would become Jewish East Harlem.

63. *AH*, June 10, 1898, p. 172.

64. *AH*, January 4, 1901, p. 233.

65. *HS*, October 18, 1901, p. 4; *AH*, January 18, February 8, March 5, 1901, pp. 284, 379, 596; Drachman, *Unfailing Light*, pp. 225ff.

66. *YT*, March 13, 1902, p. 2; *HS*, March 21, 1902, p. 4; *AH*, June 24, 1904, p. 160, as described in Gurock, *When Harlem Was Jewish*, p. 117.

67. *HS*, April 23, May 26, 1905, pp. 4, 4; also April 14, 1905, p. 4, as described in and quoted from Gurock, *When Harlem Was Jewish*, p. 118.

68. *YT*, March 25, 1906, p. 8. See the "Incorporation Papers of Congregation Mikve Israel" on file in the Office of the New York County Clerk, as described in Gurock, *When Harlem Was Jewish*, p. 118.

69. Aaron Rothkoff, "The American Sojourns of Ridbaz: Religious Problems within the Immigrant Community," *AJHQ* 57, 4 (June 1968): 561–562. For an on-the-scene look at the attitudes of the Agudath ha-Rabbanim (of which the Ridbaz was a member) toward Americanization efforts, see its major publication, *Sefer Ha-Yovel shel Agudath ha-Rabbanim ha-Ortodoksim de-Artsot ha-Brit ve-Kanada* (New York, 1928). See also Gurock, "Resisters and Accommodators." I note there the difficulties the Agudath ha-Rabbanim had with the Endeavorers' willingness to cooperate with Reform leaders who were then initiating their own style of youth services downtown.

70. *AH*, September 30, 1904, p. 516; *HS*, October 7, 1904, p. 7, as derived from Jenna Weissman Joselit, "What Happened to New York's Jewish Jews: Moses Rischin's *The Promised City* Revisited," *AJH* 73, 2 (December 1983): 163–172.

71. *AH*, January 16, 1903, p. 295. Ironically, it should be observed that the JES stood for one of the causes that most troubled the most traditional of downtown religious authorities—namely, the battle to stop the proliferation of mushroom synagogues. See *AH*, October 17, 1902, p. 608, for the Endeavorers' view of this dilemma.

72. *HS*, June 29, 1906, p. 4; Drachman, *Unfailing Light*, pp. 276–277, as described in Gurock, *When Harlem Was Jewish*, pp. 118–119. Endeavorers faced the institutional headaches of the graduation and migration out of New York of their early Seminary student leaders, who seemed not to be replaced until the rise of the Young Israel several years later and by Drachman's removal from the Seminary during that same period.

73. Not all East European groups or rabbis opposed these efforts. Rabbi Shmarya Leib Hurwitz, for example, in an article entitled "The Necessity to Found Synagogues for Youths Here in America," *YT*, April 15, 1912, p. 7, declared that as long as *landsmanshaft*-style synagogue services remained disorganized, too long were held in physically unattractive structures, and featured rabbis or preachers who offered discourses on esoteric Talmudic topics, young people would stand apart from the synagogue. See also *YT*, March 7, 1910, p. 5, for a similar type of critique of the old-time synagogue within downtown society.

74. Youth-oriented synagogues under Orthodox auspices did not disappear totally during the hiatus between the JES and YI-Institutional Synagogues era. Modern Talmud Torahs ran youth services and the Kehillah itself toyed with the

idea of inaugurating "model synagogue" programs. Indeed, in 1911, they set up eight provisional synagogues during the High Holidays to attract youngsters. On those post-JES and pre-YI activities, see Shulamith Berger, "Youth Synagogues in New York, 1910–1913" (unpublished seminar paper, TS, Bernard Revel Graduate School, Yeshiva University, 1981).

75. *AH*, January 10, 1913, p. 303; *HS*, January 12, 1913, p. 9. Rosenthal, the YI's first president was in the JTS class of 1913. See *Jewish Theological Seminary Student Annual*, 1914, pp. 50–51, (1915), pp. 51–52, all quoted from and utilized by Shulamith Berger "The Early History of the Young Israel Movement" (seminar paper, TS, YIVO Institute, Fall 1982).

76. Davis, *Emergence of Conservative Judaism*, pp. 324–326; Herbert Parzen, *Architects of Conservative Judaism* (New York, 1964), pp. 26–29ff *HS*, January 30, 1913, p. 12.

77. *AH*, January 10, 1913, p. 303 and *HS*, January 12, 1912, p. 9; *MJ*, January 10, 1913, p. 4, all derived from Berger, "Early History." The *Morgen Zhurnal*, for example, was a harsh critic of the contemporaneous New York Kehillah. See Arthur A. Goren, *New York Jews and the Quest for Community: The Kehillah Experiment, 1908–1922* (New York, 1970), pp. 127–128 and *passim*.

78. *AH*, January 10, 1913, p. 303. One source suggests that the YI idea did not originate with Seminary students at all, but with a troika of downtown youths who wanted more than their parents' *landsmanshaft* Judaism, but who were unimpressed by initiatives like Rabbi Stephen S. Wise's ghetto-based Free Synagogue. Soon thereafter, they linked arms with the Seminary students and leaders. Interestingly, they contacted Rabbi Judah L. Magnes for assistance. Two years earlier the Kehillah leader had called for a "presentation of Judaism which shall overcome the formalism and sterility of old-time Orthodoxy and shall yet avoid the extremes and extravagances of Reform. See David Warsaw, "A History of the Young Israel Movement, 1912–1937" (Master's thesis, Bernard Revel Graduate School, Yeshiva University, 1974), p. 9ff.

79. *HS*, September 29, 1916, p. 11.

80. *HS*, January 18, 1918, p. 9; Benjamin Kline Hunnicut, "The Jewish Sabbath Movement in the Early Twentieth Century," *AJH*, 69, no. 2 (December 1979), pp. 196–225.

81. Gurock, *When Harlem Was Jewish*, pp. 135ff. *YT*, 19, July 27, 1915, p. 8; Ira Eisenstein and Ira Kohn, ed., *Mordecai Kaplan: An Evaluation* (New York, 1952), *passim* as discussed, by Gurock, *When Harlem Was Jewish*, pp. 124–125.

82. Gurock, *When Harlem Was Jewish*, pp. 127–133.

83. Mordecai M. Kaplan, "Affiliation with the Synagogue," *JCR*, pp. 120–121.

84. *AH*, February 5, 1904, pp. 378, 384; *HS*, January 31, 1902, p. 8; Rischin, *Promised City*, p. 102, 242; Carl Hermann Voss, ed., *Stephen S. Wise: Servant of the People* (Philadelphia, 1970), p. 34.

85. Of the twenty-four charter-member congregations in the United Synagogue at the time of its founding in 1913, no more than two can be characterized as both Conservative in ritual, mixed seating, etc., composed of East European Jews and attractive to them. Some thirteen were nineteenth-century, formerly Orthodox or

Conservative congregations composed of German Jews. Two others were headed by Seminary rabbis and attracted East European constituents, but like the Endeavorers and the YI, did not break ritually from American styles of Orthodoxy. See the analysis of the early U.S. congregations, The United Synagogue of America, "Report of the Second Annual Meeting (1914)," pp. 17–20. Parenthetically, it should be noted that a number of the once-Orthodox Union congregations moved on to the United Synagogue in the late 1910s. Why and how they moved has yet to be considered.

86. For discussions of the rise of Conservative Judaism and the emergence of Neo-Reform during this period, see Leon A. Jick, "The Reform Synagogue," and Jack Wertheimer, "The Conservative Synagogue" in *The American Synagogue: A Sanctuary Transformed* (New York, 1987).

87. It is suggested here, as well as in most historical accounts, that the locus of East European rabbis and their congregations was the inner city. One must note, however, that *landsmanshaft*-style synagogues did survive the pre-World War I migration to satellite ghettos such as New York's Harlem or Brownsville. See Gurock, *When Harlem was Jewish*, and Alter Landesman *Brownsville: The Birth, Growth and Passing of a Jewish Community in New York* (New York, 1969), for examples of that phenomenon. How far beyond these areas and for how much longer than 1880–1920 did immigrant religious civilization survive remains to be studied. In all events and from whatever location, East European rabbis were outspoken in their condemnation of Conservative activities. See *Ha-Pardes*, June 1930, p. 26; December 1930, p. 6; June 1931, p. 25; May 1934, p. 2; June 1935, pp. 2–5. See also, Agudath ha-Rabbanim de-Artzot ha-Brit ve-Kanada, *Le-Dor Aharon* (New York, 1936). The battle against Conservative Judaism in Cleveland is discussed in Aaron Rakeffet-Rothkoff *The Silver Era in American Jewish Orthodoxy* (Jerusalem and New York, 1981), pp. 112–114, 326–347. For the Conservative rabbi's side of the story, see Solomon Goldman, *A Rabbi Takes Stock* (New York, 1931).

88. It remains to be determined how many Conservative congregations in the period from 1920 to 1940 were formerly Orthodox.

89. Gilbert Klaperman, *The Story of Yeshiva University: The First Jewish University in America* (London, 1969); Aaron Rothkoff, *Bernard Revel: Builder of American Jewish Orthodoxy* (Philadelphia, 1972), pp. 43–71; *The Rabbi Isaac Elchanan Theological Seminary Register* 5685 (1924–1925) (New York, 1925).

90. Rothkoff *Bernard Revel*, p. 169.

91. See Gurock, "Resisters and Accommodators." See also Bernard Sheintag, "Rabbi Joseph H. Lookstein: A Character Study by a Congregant, in *Congregation Kehilath Jeshurun*, pp. 53–57; and Leo Jung, *The Path of a Pioneer: The Autobiography of Leo Jung* (London and New York, 1980). The very useful term "respectable Orthodoxy" was coined by Jenna Weisman Joselit. Finally, it may be suggested that the Yorkville and West Side adherence to Orthodoxy might be due to a combination of the geographical proximity to their work and to the congregants' socioeconomic status. As upper middle-class Congregations, members there may have been able to more easily adjust their work and life schedules to remain consistent with ancestral traditions. Of course, more investigation needs to be done to explain their attitudes toward non-egalitarian synagogue seating patterns.

92. That each of these problems and others posed real problems for American Orthodox synagogues and their rabbis is indicated by the fact that between 1935 and the 1950s questions on each of these concerns were submitted by members of the Rabbinical Council of America (the organization of Americanized, English-speaking rabbis, founded in 1935) to their Standards and Rituals Committee or to their Halacha Commission. See Louis Bernstein, *Challenge and Mission: The Emergence of the English Speaking Orthodox Rabbinate* (New York, 1982), pp. 39–51 and *passim*.

93. *OU,* April 1943, p. 5; February 1945, p. 11.

94. Bernstein, *Challenge and Mission,* pp. 14–15.

95. Orthodox Union figures are derived from the organizations noted as members published in their organ, the *Orthodox Union,* which ran from 1933 to 1946. In 1935, for example, the paper noted that a convention of Orthodox synagogues at the Far Rockaway Jewish Center on Long Island (which included Queens) was attended by the center's nineteen member congregations; hence that number. See *OU* October 1935, p. 7. The *Orthodox Union,* a major untapped source for the social history of this period, also highlights two other issues for consideration in making such calculations. A number of U.S. synagogues in 1929 appear as members of the OU in the 1930s. That means that either synagogues drifted back and forth between movements or held dual memberships. In addition, it appears that the term "Jewish Center" applied both to American Orthodox and to Conservative congregations of that era. Statistics on the New York-based Young Israel Movement are derived from a pamphlet, *Young Israel: Its Aims and Activities,* published by its National Council circa 1935.

96. In 1925 the YT had thirty-two affiliates, twenty-four situated in New York City proper.

97. *OU,* July 1937, p. 2; December 1942, p. 5; April 1944, p. 6. Significantly, each of these writers contrasted the strength of Orthodoxy in New York with their own powerlessness in the country. Some made the point that all New York wanted from the hinterlands was money and never gave any logistical support for the growth of the movement elsewhere. I derived the unofficial statistics on the OU from synagogues listed as members in the Orthodox Union.

98. *OU,* January 1941, p. 12; January 1935, p. 1.

99. Israel Maier Ha-Kohen Kagan, *Niddehei Yisrael* (Warsaw, 1884), pp. 129–130, quoted in Rothkoff *Bernard Revel,* p. 18.

100. For interesting, albeit hagiographic, biographical sketches of the transplanted Yeshiva rabbis and of Dr. Breuer, see Nisson Wolpin, ed., *The Torah World: A Treasury of Biographical Sketches* (New York, 1982). This volume is a collection of articles culled from the pages of the *Jewish Observer,* the organ of the Agudath Israel. In particular see the discussion on Rabbi Aaron Kotler in Shaul Kagan, "From Kletzk to Lakewood," pp. 184–205; and on Rabbi Bloch of Cleveland's Telshe Yeshiva in "He Brought Telshe to Cleveland," pp. 262–276. For information on Dr. Breuer, see Ernst J. Bodenheimer with Nosson Scherman, "The Rav of Frankfurt, U.S.A.," pp. 223–238. On the settlement patterns and sociology of the Hasidic groups, see Israel Rubin, *Satmar: Island in the City* (New York, 1972). The Breuer

and the Lithuanian Yeshiva groups were placed with the Hasidim because they, too, viewed their religious leaders as true chief rabbis. However, the influence of each rabbi on daily lives varies greatly from group to group.

101. William Helmreich, *The World of the Yeshiva: An Intimate Portrait of Orthodox Jewry* (New York and London, 1982), p. 284.

102. Shubert Spero, "Orthodox Judaism," in *Movements and Issues in American Judaism: An Analysis and Source Book of Developments since 1945*, ed. Bernard Martin (Westport, Conn., 1978), p. 88; Charles Liebman, "Orthodoxy in American Jewish Life," *AJYB* 66 (1965), pp. 58–61.

103. Rabbi Moses Scherer, president of the Agudath Israel, summed up best the changed educational orientation of Orthodox Jews from interwar days to today when he said: "When I was a youngster, it was very possible for someone to be an Orthodox Jew without continuing (intensive Jewish education) beyond elementary school. . . . Today it is unthinkable that one can really be an Orthodox Jew unless he had at least graduate Yeshiva high school." See this statement in William Helmreich's "Old Wine in New Bottles: Advanced Yeshivot in the United States," *AJH*, 69, no. 2 (December 1979).

104. Alvin I. Schiff, *The Jewish Day School in America* (New York, 1966), pp. 48–86; Samuel Heilman, *Synagogue Life: A Study in Symbolic Interaction* (Chicago, 1973); and Heilman, *The People of the Book: Drama, Fellowship and Religion* (Chicago, 1983).

105. See Helmreich, *The World of the Yeshiva*, pp. 220–238, for his important discussion of college education and the yeshiva world students. Also see pp. 272–275, for a description of the economic and demographic patterns. Interesingly enough, although the new-era Orthodox see themselves as resisting if not being merely unimpressed with American societal phenomena and change, they have been consciously, or unconsciously, affected by American social patterns. The eruv issue is a graphic example. The idea that families and not just grown men should go as a unit to services is an American religious phenomenon. The role and status of women in the Orthodox synagogue are discussed later in the chapter.

106. The estimate of 1,000 present day synagogues has been offered by Marc Lee Raphael, in *Profiles in Faith: American Judaism* (New York, 1984). This work is based on his close examination of synagogue lists extant in the New York offices of the Orthodox Union and is thus to be considered highly reliable. Less reliable statistics that magnify the numbers of synagogues and constituents by the OU are published without revision yearly in *AJYB*. For an important discussion of the reliability of earlier estimates, see Liebman, "Orthodoxy in American Jewish Life," pp. 22–26.

107. Bernard Martin, "Conservative Judaism and Reconstructionism," in *Movements and Issues in American Judaism: An Analysis and Source Book of Developments since 1945*, ed. Bernard Martin (Westport, Conn 1978), p. 102. The relative strengths of Conservatism, Reform, and Orthodoxy in three cities are discussed in Morris Axelrod, Floyd S. Fowler, and Arnold Gurin's *A Community Study for Long Range Planning* (Boston, 1967); these authors found that 44 percent of the synagogues in Boston at the time were Conservative affiliates, as opposed to 27 percent Reform and 14 percent Orthodox. Sidney Goldstein and Calvin Goldscheider, *Jewish*

Americans: Three Generations in a Jewish Community (Englewood Cliffs, NJ 1968), found that in Providence 54 percent were Conservative, 21 percent Reform, and 20 percent Orthodox. See also Michael Meyer, "Reform Judaism," in *Movements and Issues*, p. 159; Spero, "Orthodox Judaism," p. 85; Liebman, "Orthodoxy in American Jewish Life," pp. 34–36.

108. Anne Lapidus Lerner, "Who Has Not Made Me a Man: The Movement for Equal Rights for Women in American Jewry," *AJYB* (1977): 3–38; Charlotte Baum, Paula Hyman, and Sonya Michel, *The Jewish Women in America* (New York, 1976). The debate within American Orthodoxy can be followed to some extent through the pages of *Tradition*, an RCA publication. See for example, Saul Berman, "The Status of Women in Halachic Judaism," *Tradition* 14, 2 (Fall 1973): 5–28; Michael Chernick, "The Halachic Process—Growth and Change," *Sh'ma* 6, 112 (April 1976): 92–94; A. M. Silver, "May Women be Taught Bible, Mishna and Talmud," *Tradition* 16, 2 (Summer 1978): 7483; Avraham Weiss, "Women & Sifrei Torah," *Tradition* 20, 2 (Summer, 1982): 106–118: Saul Berman and Shulamith Magnus, "Orthodoxy Responds to Feminist Ferment," *Response* 12, 2 (Spring 1981): 5–18. See also the *Jewish Press*, December 10, 1982, p. 3, for the Agudath ha-Rabbanim's condemnation of women's services within Orthodox synagogues.

Notes to Chapter 3, *How "Frum" Was Rabbi Jacob Joseph's Court? Americanization Within the Lower East Side's Orthodox Elite, 1886–1902*

1. "Broadside of Association of the American Orthodox Hebrew Congregations, April 1888" published in Appendix 3 of Abraham J. Karp, "New York Chooses A Chief Rabbi," *PAJHS* 44, 3 (March 1955): 191.

2. "Broadside," in Karp, 191. The sad saga of Rabbi Jacob Joseph's career in New York has attracted the attention of almost every historian of that city's Jewry as well as most chroniclers of the general history of American Judaism. Relying on the excellent account of the Rabbi's travails, offered by Abraham Karp in 1955, the focus of accounts invariably centers on the chief rabbi's failures to control the kashruth industry he set out to regulate. While this debacle was truly Rabbi Joseph's undoing, it was, to my mind, not the sole or even the major goal or story of his administration. Rather, if the aforementioned broadside is to be believed, kashruth regulation was important—along with effectively controlling marriage and divorce procedures—in terms of putting Orthodoxy's house in order towards the pursuit of a loftier goal of returning immigrant youngsters to the world of Torah Judaism they remembered from Eastern Europe. This present study looks at the nature and degree of commitment harbored by the Association and the chief rabbi's circle towards these values. Unfortunately for the chief rabbi the goals of transplantation were submerged beneath the morass of his troubles controlling meat production. On "brazen outlaws" in control of synagogue life, see Moses Weinberger, *Ha-Yehudim ve-ha-Yahadut be-Nuyork* (New York, 1887). This work has been translated into English as *People Walk on their Heads: Moses Weinberger's "Jews and Judaism in New York,"* Jonathan D. Sarna, trans. (New York, 1982), 44.

3.   "Broadside" in Karp, 191. For a discussion of the interrelatedness of the founders of Etz Chaim with the leadership of the Association, see Jeffrey S. Gurock, *The Men and Women of Yeshiva: Higher Education, Orthodoxy and American Judaism* (New York, 1988), 12–13. On the founding of Ets Chaim and its early curriculum, see Gilbert Klaperman, *The Story of Yeshiva University: the First Jewish University in America* (London, 1969), 17–34. For specific reference to Rabbi Joseph's visit and his favorable views of the school, see YT, July 27, 1888: 1 noted in Klaperman, 28.

4.   Weinberger, Sarna trans., 104, *Ha-Ivri*, September 17, 1897: la; October 15, 1897: le quoted in Klaperman, 40. For *Ha-Ivri* editor Gerson Rosenzweig's approbation and relationship with Etz Chaim, see Klaperman, 29.

5.   On the founding of and course of study at the Yeshiva Rabbi Yitzhak Elchanan, the relationship between those founders, the Association and Etz Chaim group, and the mutual affection the Yeshiva and the Agudath ha-Rabbanim had for each other, see Gurock, *The Men and Women of Yeshiva*, 18–21.

6.   See above, Chapters 1 and 2.

7.   Thirty years ago, Abraham Karp, in his seminal study of Rabbi Jacob Joseph's career noted in passing that the "wealthy Orthodox businessmen . . . in control of the Association [were] worldly in outlook [and] wanted a scholarly chief rabbi to be accepted by the larger Jewish community and the non-Jewish world. To be a master of Talmud was important, but equally important were general culture and knowledge of the tongue of the Americanized element of the community." See Karp, 139. But he did not pause to fully evidence the truth of that assertion. We will presently note how correct Karp's intuition was as we study lay and rabbinic attitudes within that court.

8.   "Broadside" in Karp, 191.

9.   On the curriculum of Etz Chaim in its earliest days, see Gurock, *The Men and Women of Yeshiva*, 11–12, 15 and Klaperman, 24–25.

10.   It should be noted that Rabbi Moses Weinberger, whom we have noted, was very close to, and in sympathy with, the goals of the Association opened a second downtown all-day Orthodox school in 1895. His Yeshivat Or ha-Hayyim was really a "high school" taking students up towards the age where they might be ordained. Maybe it was, as Shnayer Z. Leiman, who uncovered this school's history suggests, the first advanced yeshiva in America. In all events, like Etz Chaim, it too had the goal of devoting little attention to secular subjects. However, starting as it did almost a decade after Etz Chaim and possibly learning from Etz Chaim's example, this school recognized the unavoidable desire of American students to learn about their new society. Accordingly, they provided some exposure to secular subjects since they knew "full well that American students will not confine their study to the four ells of Halakhah" so long as these teachings did not conflict with the traditions and required the religious heads of the school to make sure that the nonessential secular subjects not become too important for pupils. See, on this ephemeral institution, Shnayer Z. Leiman, "Yeshivat Or ha-Hayyim: the First Talmudical Academy in America," *Tradition* 25, 2 (Winter 1990): 77–88.

11.   See Ira Eisenstein, "Mordecai M. Kaplan," *Great Jewish Thinkers of the Twentieth Century* (Clinton, 1963), 253. See too Simon Noveck, "Kaplan and Milton

Steinberg," 147. On Kaplan, Fuenn and Kohut see, *The Journals of Mordecai M. Kaplan* (hereafter *Journals*) I, 256 (January 30, 1917), 256–58 (February 1, 1917). These references from the journals on file in the Rare Book Room of the Jewish Theological Seminary of America are published with the authorization of its Chancellor, Dr. Ismar Schorsch. My thanks to Chancellor Schorsch for his permission. For just a taste of the issue of the impinging of modern ideas within the traditional world of Eastern Europe, most specifically the controversies that surrounded the question of introducing vernaculars and secular subjects in East European yeshivas, with a particular focus on the Volozhin Yeshiva, see Meier Berlin, *M'Volozhin Ad Yerushalayim* (Tel Aviv, 1939), 88–101; Moshe Tzenovitz, *Etz Hayim: Toldot Yeshivas Volozhin* (Tel Aviv, 1972), 317–44, Shaul Stampfer, "Three Lithuanian Yeshivas in the Nineteenth Century" (Ph.D. diss., Hebrew University, 1981), 79–80, 120–21; Jacob J. Schacter, "Haskalah, Secular Studies and the Close of the Yeshiva in Volozhin in 1892," *The Torah U-Madda Journal* 2 (1990): 91–96.

12.   For more references to Israel Kaplan's early life and training, see *Journals* 4: 217 (January 17, 1929); 6: 181 (October 4, 1929); 19: 264 (March 7, 1959). For more specifics on Israel Kaplan's relationship with Rabbi Relnes, see William Berkowitz, "Interview with Mordecai M. Kaplan" in *Dialogues in Judaism* (Northvale, 1991), 31 where Kaplan refers to his father as a "student-colleague" of Reines. The Mordecai M. Kaplan Archives in Wyncote, PA also contain two letters written by Reines to Kaplan in 1908 which reflect their friendship.

13.   Ehrlich was the author of the three-volume Hebrew *Mikra ci-Feshuto* (Berlin, 1899–1901) and the seven-volume *Randglossen zur hebräischen Bibel* (Leipzig, 1908–1914). On the Kaplans' relationship with Ehrlich, see *Journals* 15: 239 (June 24, 1949); 19: 104 (June 13, 1958); 254 (February 7, 1959). Ira Eisenstein, 255; Mordecai M. Kaplan, "A Founding Father Recounts," *Alumni Association Bulletin*, Teachers Institute and Seminary College of Jewish Studies, Jewish Theological Seminary of America (1959) and "The Influences That Have Shaped My Life," *The Reconstructionist* 8, 10 (June 26, 1942): 30.

14.   There is some discrepancy within the sources about how long Kaplan studied at Etz Chaim and at what point in his schooling he left for public school. One account has him at Etz Chaim for a year and a half. Other sources suggest his stay was almost three years. In all events, by age 12, he was off to the Jewish Theological Seminary. On Kaplan's early education, sec Berkowitz, 32; Kaplan, "The Influences," 29; idem, "Response," *Proceedings of the Rabbinical Assembly of America* 15 (1951): 214. The only contemporaneous source that criticizes rabbis from Eastern Europe—but not Israel Kaplan specifically —for sending their sons to public schools is Weinberger's pamphlet that describes the reason he established his school, Yeshivat Or ha-Hayyim, referred to in note 10. See on this, Leiman, 83–84.

15.   Lloyd P. Gartner, "From New York to Miedzyrecz: Immigrant Letters of Judah David Eisenstein, 1878–1886," *AJHQ* 52, 3 (March 1963): 236.

16.   *Ibid.*, 242–43.

17.   It is unclear from Elsenstein's rhetoric what he meant precisely by the term "the conservative faith." One possibility, in keeping with rest of the sentence that describes "conservative faith" as including "even the most minor mitzvah of the

commandments of the Torah," suggests that the term conservative is used as an adjective referring to what we might more properly call traditional Orthodox practice. However, it is noteworthy that in an earlier part of the essay when he describes the nature of Orthodoxy in America he never used the word "conservative" in his description. The other possibility, of course, is that Eisenstein is referring to the same "Conservative" Judaism that he pilloried earlier In the essay. If such be the case, it suggests a certain degree of ambivalence towards Conservatism on Eisenstein's past and certainly points towards him being tolerant of the Seminary producing what we might call traditionally-oriented Conservative rabbis.

18. Judah David Eisenstein, "Yesod ha-Seminar ha-Chadash," in *NuYorker Yiddishe Zeitung* (New York, 1888) reprinted in Hebrew translation in Eisenstein, *Ozar Zichronothai* (New York, 1929), 206–11.

19. For a listing of the members of the original Board of Trustees of the Jewish Theological Seminary Association, see "Certificate of Incorporation of the Jewish Theological Seminary Association," in Moshe Davis, *The Emergence of Conservative Judaism: The Historical School in Nineteenth Century America* (Philadelphia, 1965), 386–87.

20. For information on Lewin, see "Certificate of Incorporation," in Karp, 189–90 and *Proceedings*, title page.

21. Germansky and a S. Bernstein of 89 Division Street are listed as "Subscribers" to the JTSA throughout most of the 1890s. See *Proceedings* for the listing. Germansky and a Moses Bernstein also of 89 Division Street—very possibly the same person as S. Bernstein—are listed as founders of the downtown yeshiva. See "Certificate of Incorporation, Rabbi Isaac Elchanan Theological Seminary Association," in Klaperman, 244.

22. See Karp, 169 for a discussion of Rabbi Joseph and these uptown rabbis.

23. It must be noted that the transplanted East European rabbinate in this country was never monolithic. As I have indicated in "Resisters" and elsewhere, a number of important rabbis both inside and outside of the Agudath ha-Rabbanim were more favorably disposed towards the questions of Americanization. But as an organization, the Agudath ha-Rabbanim took a harder stand than seen earlier within Rabbi Joseph's court. See on the variety of hard line positions taken by that rabbinical group, Gurock, "Change to Survive: The Common Experience of Two Transplanted Jewish Identities in America," in *What is American about American Jewish History*, Marc Lee Raphael, ed. (Williamsburg, Va., 1994). For the text of the organization's charter which, nonetheless, does note some slight concessions on the question of English in their favored schools and which speaks also of training Jewish youngsters who attended public schools, see *Sefer ha-Yovel shel Agudath ha-Rabbanim ha-Ortodoksim de-Artsot ha-Brit ve-Kanada* (New York, 1928), 25–26.

24. For a concise synopsis of the history of the transformation of the old Seminary into the institution associated with Dr. Schechter, see Marc Lee Raphael, *Profiles in Judaism: the Reform, Conservative, Orthodox and Reconstructionist Traditions in Historical Perspective* (San Francisco, 1985), 88–91. For references to contemporaneous criticism of the new leaders of the Seminary and their orientation, see *AH*, June 17, 1904, 130; July 1, 1904, 174, 180.

25. On the controversies that surrounded Willowski, see Aaron Rothkoff, "The American Sojourns of Ridbaz: Religious Problems Within the Immigrant Community," *AJHQ* 57:4 (1968): 557–72; Karp, "The Ridwas: Rabbi Jacob David Willowsky, 1845–1913," *Perspectives on Jews and Judaism: Essays in Honor of Wolfe Kelman* (New York, 1978), 215–37. See also Jenna W. Joselit, *New York's Jewish Jews: the Orthodox Community in the Inter-War Years* (Bloomington, 1990), 30–31.

26. *AH*, July 1, 1904, 180. It needs to be noted that despite Eisenstein's backing of Wlllowski and his attack on the graduates of the pre-Schechter Seminary, the first years of the twentieth century did not necessarily witness a full fledge retreat on the part of this very complex ghetto-based Jewish observer from his favoring acculturation within Orthodoxy. For as late as 1897, Eisenstein was among the founders of the Orthodox Union, headed up by the American Orthodox rabbis and lay people who were active at the Old Seminary. And that group promoted in its own way modern Orthodox services which included English language sermons. What can be certain is that he was no longer favorably disposed towards Seminary graduates—even those who finished really before Schechter came on the scene. It is most probable that Eisenstein was not fully committed to every aspect of any organizational agenda, be it the Orthodox Union or the Agudath ha-Rabbanim. In all events, Eisenstein's public critique remains an indication of Agudath ha-Rabbanim's influence upon the community.

27. *AH*, December 9, 1904, 93.

Notes to Chapter 4, American Orthodox Organizations in Support of Zionism, 1880–1930

1. Shlomo Noble, "Pre-Herzlian Zionism in America as Reflected in the Yiddish Press," in *Early Zionism in America*, Isidor S. Meyer, ed. (New York, 1958), 39.

2. Hyman B. Grinstein, "The Memoirs and Scrapbooks of the Late Dr. Joseph Isaac Bluestone of New York City," *PAJHS* (1939), p. 55.

3. Marvin Feinstein, *American Zionism, 1884–1904* (New York, 1965), pp. 29, 42–43.

4. Melvin I. Urofsky, *American Zionism from Herzl to the Holocaust* (Garden City, N.Y., 1976), pp. 76–79, 84.

5. Urofsky, pp. 93–94. Grinstein and Feinstein record the diversity of Orthodox approaches to Zionism but do not make clear the difference between the groups. See Feinstein, pp. 31, 43, 54–55, 97, 127, 245–248, 268–269 and Grinstein, pp. 57–62. See also Grinstein, "Orthodox Judaism and Early Zionism in America" in Meyer, pp. 219–224. Unique among the general histories of Zionism in America, Evyatar Freisel (*Ha-Tenuah ha-Tziyonit be-Artzot ha-Brit, 1897–1914* [Tel Aviv, 1970], p. 90) does not make a strong statement about Orthodox opposition to Zionism in America. He does, however, allow that "in the Jewish street during this time period (circa 1897) there were extremist Orthodox organizations that opposed Zionism no less and possibly more than the Reform."

6. On the founding of the Agudath ha-Rabbanim see above, chapter 1.

7.   For the text of the Agudath ha-Rabbanim's inaugural charter see *Sefer ha-Yovel shel Agudath ha-Rabbanim ha-Ortodoksim de-Artsot ha-Brit ve-Kanada* (New York, 1928), pp. 25–26. For just a taste of the controversies that surrounded the question of introducing vernaculars and secular subjects in East European yeshivas, with a particular focus on the Volozhin Yeshiva, see Meier Berlin, *MeVolozhin ad Yerushalayim* (Tel Aviv, 1939), pp. 88–101, Moshe Tzenovitz, *Etz Hayim: Toldot Yeshivat Volozhin* (Tel Aviv, 1972), pp. 317–344, Shaul Stampfer, "Three Lithuanian Yeshivas in the Nineteenth Century" (doctoral dissertation, Hebrew University, 1981), pp. 79–80, 120–121.

8.   *Sefer ha-Yovel*, pp. 25–26.

9.   Although, as Ehud Luz points out, "few Mitnaggedic rabbis in Lithuania . . . were attracted to Hibbat Zion" and "the movement faced wall-to-wall opposition from Hasidic rebbes," the intensity of opposition to the nationalist movement clearly increased over time. In the early 1880s, some Lithuanian rabbis were not put off by Zionism's attempt to move the Jewish people away from the tradition of national passivity, and thus supported the Hibbat Zion as they had supported the old Yishuv. However, by the 1890s as the movement grew and Orthodoxy did not predominate, issues surrounding the background, life-styles and orientations of leadership put off additional Orthodox rabbis. By the turn of the century, full scale opposition was articulated as the concerns transcended issues of life-style and the Orthodox felt that Zionism intended to replace traditional Judaism with secular nationalism as an ideology to be followed by the masses of Jews. From there, would eventually emerge the Agudath Israel. Thus, there were two Orthodox camps by the 1910s: the Mizrachi and the Agudath Israel. See on this subject Ehud Luz, *Parallels Meet: Religion and Nationalism in the Early Zionist Movement (1882–1904)* (Philadelphia, 1988), pp. 30, 45, 48–49, 65–66, 114–115, 211, 225–226, 286. See also Avraham Baruch Steinberg, *Sefer Da'at ha-Rabbanim* (Warsaw, 1902) and Shlomo Zalman Landau and Yosef Rabinowitz, *Sefer Or LiYesharim* (Warsaw, 1900) for contemporary polemics against Zionism from Orthodox figures.

10.   *Sefer ha-Yovel*, p. 21–22; *AJYB* 5663 (1902–3), p. 102; 5664 (1903–4), p. 124; 5665 (1904–5), p. 240, 282; 5666 (1905–6), pp. 133–134;5670 (1909–10), p. 150; "Minutes of the Fourth Annual Convention of the Federation of American Zionists," *The Maccabaean* (June 1901), pp. ix, xxx; "List of Delegates", *The Maccabaean* (June 1902), pp. 337–338.

11.   For a discussion of the Agudath ha-Rabbanim's negative views of Reform rabbis and non-cooperation with their American Orthodox colleagues, see above, chapter 1.

12.   *AH*, July 8, 1904, p. 204; 7/30/04, p. 282; *The Maccabaean* (June 1901), pp. xxii–xxiii; *AJYB* 5663 (1902–3), p. 102; 5664 (1903–4), pp. 124, 159, 161; 5665 (1904–5), p. 240; 5666 (1905–6), pp. 133–134; 5667 (1906–7), p. 109; 5670 (1909–10), p. 150. To be sure, the influence of rabbis Klein, Schaeffer and Ashinsky cannot be minimized in understanding the partial rapprochement. They were the three Agudath ha-Rabbanim leaders and members who also held memberships in the Americanized Orthodox Union. See below p. 10 and Note 14 for more on these pivotal rabbis.

13. Ephraim Shimoff, *Rabbi Isaac Elchanan Spektor: Life and Letters* (Jerusalem, 1961), pp. 122, 126–128, 144–145; Judah Appel, *Betokh Reshith ha-Tehiya* (Tel Aviv, 1935);Samuel K. Mirsky, "Isaac Elchanan Spektor" in *Guardians of our Heritage (1724–1953)*, Leo Jung, ed. (New York,1958), pp. 311–312; Yitzhak Rivkind, *Ha-Neziv ve-Yihuso le-Hibbat Zion* (Lodz, 1919), pp. 8–10; Joseph Litvin, "Naphtali Tzevi Berlin (the Netziv)" in *Men of the Spirit*, Leo Jung, ed. (New York, 1963) pp. 294–295; Y. Nissenbaum, *Ha-Dat ve-ha-Tehiyyah ha-Le'-ummit* (Warsaw, 1919–1920), pp. 92–118; E.M. Genechovsky, "Samuel Mohilever" in *Men of the Spirit*, pp. 423–432.

14. The other two founders or early members of the Agudath ha-Rabbanim who were also either Honorary Vice Presidents, members of the Executive Committee or delegates to the early 1900 meetings of the FAZ, the men who were not trained or ordained by the three luminaries, were Ramaz and Dr. Philip Hillel Klein. The two senior members of the group, one trained in West-Central Europe (Klein) and the other in Bialystock were both clearly through their actions and pronouncements sympathetic to the world views of Spektor, Berlin and Mohilever. For more on Klein and Margolies, see above, chapter 1.

Finally, four other founders and early members of the Agudath ha-Rabbanim were among the founders of Mizrachi in America, a logical step given that at least two of them. I.L. Levin or Detroit and Isaac Ginsburg of Rochester were Spektor/Berlin disciples.

That these rabbis constituted a next generation of leaders is evidenced from the facts that of the seventeen rabbis about which we have biographical information (of a list of nineteen names) all were born within the same twenty year time period, nine of the seventeen attended yeshivas in the same decade of the 1860s.

The basic biographical information that informs this survey was derived from "Minutes of the Fourth Annual Convention of the Federation of American Zionists," *The Maccabaean* (June 1901), pp. ix, xxx; "List of Delegates," *The Maccabaean* (June 1902), pp. 337–338; *Sefer ha-Yovel*, pp. 138, 140–142, 151, 161; *AJYB* 5663 (1902–03), p. 102; 5664 (1903–04), p. 124; 5665 (1904–05), p. 240, 282; 5666 (1905–06), pp. 133–134, 149; 5670 (1909–1910), p. 150. For more on Masliansky, see above, chapter 1 of this volume, and Moses Rischin, *The Promised City: New York's Jews, 1870–1914* (Cambridge, Mass., 1962), pp. 103–239, 240.

15. *Die Welt*, December 31, 1897, pp. 10–11; Friesel, p. 30.

16. These rabbis who supported Zionism were trained in Europe and departed for America at a point in the early history of Zionism when levels of opposition to the movement within Orthodoxy were relatively low. See Note 9 for the chronology on the evolution of anti-Zionism among East European rabbis. Of course, one must clearly calibrate their degree of Zionism. The message of European Religious Zionism heard by these rabbis did not include a commitment to aliyah. As noted above, they departed for America and not Palestine in the 1880–1890 period. In this ironic regard, they were much akin not only to the masses of non-ideologically committed immigrant Jews who voted for America and not Zion with their feet, but also to their liberal American Jewish religious counterparts and the secular American Zionists who would come to support an American form of Zionism that did not

include personal commitment to migration. Few of the Agudath ha-Rabbanim worthies ever left America. Their support was largely in the realm of positive exhortations for the movement, fund-raising and in calls for unity among differing
Orthodox elements on this crucial question. It may be suggested that here too we
see a subtle Americanization operating on the most Orthodox of Jews in the United
States.

17.   *AJYB* 5666 (1905–06), p. 134.

18.   Friesel, pp. 246–247; Urofsky, pp. 92–93; Yonathan Shapiro, *Leadership of
American Zionist Organization, 1897–1930* (Urbana, 1971), pp. 25–28; Grinstein,
pp. 58–60. For background information on rabbis and lay people who were leaders
of the FAZ, OU and/or the Agudath ha-Rabbanim see *AJYB* 5663 (1902–03), p.
102; 5664 (1903–04), p. 124; 5665 (1904–05), p. 240, 282; 5666 (1905–06),
pp. 133–134, 149; 5667 (1906–07), p. 109; 5669 (1908–09), pp. 23, 41; 5670
(1909–1910), pp. 150, 168–169; 5671 (1910–1911), pp. 223, 252; 5672
(1911–1912), pp. 220, 241; 5673 (1912–1913), pp. 222, 245; 5674 (1913–
1914), p. 366; 5675 (1914–1915), pp. 282, 298, 310; 5676 (1915–1916) pp.
293, 310; 5677 (1916–1917), pp. 227, 245, 258; 5678 (1917–1918), pp. 336,
347, 354; 5679 (1918–1919) pp. 316, 324; 5680 (1919–1920), pp. 318, 325,
327.

19.   Urofsky sees the OU as the incipient Orthodox liaison with the FAZ that
went its own way into the Mizrachi. In reality, OU leaders were long-term constituents of the FAZ while Agudath ha-Rabbanim members moved slowly towards separatist Religious Zionism. See Urofsky, p. 94.

20.   Whatever problems roshei yeshiva—many of whom were good Agudath
ha-Rabbanim men—had with the Teachers Institute, they were not caused by the
Zionist orientation of the school, but the *Wissenschaft* aspects and the religious reli-
ability of some of the teachers. See Gurock, *The Men and Women of Yeshiva: Higher
Education, Orthodoxy and American Judaism* (New York, 1988), pp. 77–81. On
Reines' Lida yeshiva, see Geulah Bat-Yehuda, *Ish ha-Me'orot: Rabbi Yitzhak Yaacov
Reines* (Jerusalem, 1988), chapter 43.

21.   Israel Rosenberg, "Galui Da'at," *MJ*, translated and in *Sefer Ha-Yovel*, pp.
57–58.

22.   *Sefer Ha-Yovel*, pp. 81–82.

23.   *Sefer Ha-Yovel*, pp. 78–79.

24.   *Sefer Ha-Yovel*, pp. 71–75.

25.   *Sefer Ha-Yovel*, pp. 76–77.On the founding and structure of the Agudath
Israel, see, Gershon Chaim Bacon, "Agudath Israel in Poland, 1916–1939: An
Orthodox Jewish Response to the Challenge of Modernity", (Ph.d. dissertation,
Columbia University, 1979), pp. 41–43. See also Isaac Lewin, *Unto the Mountains*
(New York, 1975), pp. 71–74.

26.   *Sefer Ha-Yovel*, pp. 76–77.

27.   *Sefer Ha-Yovel*, p. 110.

28.   Gershon Greenberg, "Separation and Reconciliation: American Orthodoxy
and the Concept of Zion," *Proceedings of the Ninth World Congress of Jewish Studies*
(Jerusalem, 1986), pp. 127–129.

29. On Margolis in Boston and in conflict with rabbis in New York, see Harold Gastwirt, *Fraud, Holiness and Corruption* (Port Washington, N.Y., 1974), pp. 92–93, 119–122 and *passim*. For a comprehensive examination of many aspects of Margolis' career and ideas see, Joshua Hoffman, "The American Rabbinic Career of Rabbi Gavriel Zev Margolis" (M.A. thesis, Bernard Revel Graduate School, Yeshiva University, 1992).

30. See *Charuzei Margoliot* vol. II, (New York, 1918), p. 394 and *Sefer Knesset ha-Rabbonim*, vol. 2 (New York, 1924), pp. 44–45 for Margolis's views of RIETS.

31. Once again, the description of Margolis as an "ultra" is mediated by our understanding of what that term means in the American context. For example, as Hoffman's study indicates, like the Agudath ha-Rabbanim that he opposed, Margolis did not take a totally unyielding position against secular studies per se. He himself was knowledgeable of military and political history among other non-Jewish disciplines.He apparently agreed that English was appropriate in Talmud Torah schools. He also supported the Rabbi Jacob Joseph School in the early 1910s and was a signatory to a fund-raising letter which said that students from that American yeshiva could qualify for college entrance. See Hoffman, pp. 80, 124.

32. *Ha-Peles* (Berlin, 1903),pp. 330–336 discussed in Hoffman, pp. 5, 9.

33. On Margolis' tolerant, Mizrachi-like attitude see *Charuzei Margoliot*, vol. 2 p. 363, quoted in an earlier version of Hoffman's work. See Hoffman, "Rabbi Gavriel Zev Margolis and the Knesset ha-Rabbonim" (unpublished seminar paper, Bernard Revel Graduate School, Yeshiva University, 1989.), p. 41.

34. *Sefer Knesset ha-Rabbonim*, vol. II, pp. 11–21, 22–23 for his views on Zionism in the 1920s noted in Hoffman, "Rabbi Gavriel Zev Margolis . . .," p. 37. See also chapter 1, above.

35. On Margolis' intentions in founding the Knesset ha-Rabbonim see, *Sefer Knesset ha-Rabbonim ha-Ortodoksim be-America*, vol. 1 (New York, 1921), p. 2 and p. 9 for Margolis' draft resolutions. An English rendering of the convention resolutions. some of which differ from Margolis' drafts were published in the *Kansas City Jewish Chronicle*, March 4, 1921, pp. 1, 4. We have used that translation in this article (for most of the resolutions, the variations are insignificant) and have discussed the one area, Zionism, where the differences are substantive. See also Hoffman's discussion, "The American . . .," pp. 87, 101–105.

36. *Kansas City Jewish Chronicle*, March 4, 1921, pp. 1, 4. See, the *Jewish Daily Bulletin*, September 3, 1925, p. 8 for the 1925 convention greeting. See on these documents, Hoffman, "The American . . .," pp. 105–108. Hoffman hypothesizes that the 1925 greeting to the Zionist Congress reflected Margolis' group being in agreement with the secular Zionists in opposing a plan to colonize Jews in the Crimea that been advocated by the Joint Distribution Committee and the Knesset's greatest rival, the Agudath ha-Rabbanim.

37. For Silver's remarks see, *Ha-Pardes*, December 1933 quoted in Aaron Rakeffet-Rothkoff, *The Silver Era in American Jewish Orthodoxy* (Jerusalem and New York, 1981), p. 156.

38. Rakeffet-Rothkoff, pp. 156–157.

39. Rakeffet-Rothkoff, pp. 161–164.

Notes to Chapter 5, *Jacob A. Riis, Christian Friend or Missionary Foe: Two Jewish Views*

1.   *AH*, August 14, 1903, pp. 407–408.

2.   *YT*, August 26, 1903, p. 8.

3.   *AH*, July 17, 1901, p. 284; August 2, 1901. p. 387.

4.   *HS*, November 9, 1903, p. 6.

5.   *New York Evening Post*, September 18, 1903. p. 16. Soon after receiving Riis' reply, a concerned Lucas wrote to Louis Marshall, another long-time opponent of missionaries, and characterized Riis' response as "about as disingenuous a communication as could have been written." Lucas argued that Jews would have to offer "bribe for bribe" to stop conversionists. Albert Lucas to Louis Marshall, September 3, 1903, LMP-AJA.

6.   *AH*, September 25, 1903, p. 614; *The Churchman*, September 26, 1903, p. 351; Albert Lucas to Louis Marshall, September 17, 103, LMP-AJA. Riis may have unclouded ever so slightly Jewish knowledge of what exactly was going on in the Settlement when be spoke with uptown Rabbis H. P. Mendes and Joseph Asher and granted their request to be told the names of Jewish children attending his home and whether they came with their parents' consent. There was no reported discussion of the curriculum taught on Henry Street. There is also no indication either in the Jewish press or in the Riis Neighborhood House Papers whether such a visit ever took place. The Mendes papers (AJA) are totally silent on this incident. See, Minutes and Reports, Executive Committee, Jacob A. Riis Neighborhood Settlement, Executive Committee Meeting, November 13, 1903. JARNSP-NYPL. One should also note that despite the negative publicity generated by the exposés, Jewish children seem to have continued to attend the Riis Home in significant numbers. See, Minutes and Reports, Boys' Department, Jacob A. Riis Neighborhood Settlement, Report of F. W. Maaloe, Director of Boys and Men's Work, January 1904, JARNSP-NYPL.

7.   *HS*, April 20, 1906, p. 8; May 25, 1906, p. 8; *AH*, August 5, 1905, p. 266; March 30, 1906, p. 578. Although Riis was now frequently seen as no friend of the Jews, when be succeeded in clearly non-sectarian work (e.g. pleading for children's playgrounds in Chicago), he was praised by the Jewish press. See, *YT*, June 3, 1905, p. 8.

8.   *New York Times*, April 13, 1980, p. 1; see also *New York Sun*, April 13, 1908, p. 4; April 15, 1908, p. 4.

9.   *New York Times*, April 14, 1908, p. 1.

10.   *New York Times*, April 15, 1908, p. 5; *The Outlook*, May 9, 1908, p. 69.

11.   *New York Sun*, April 15, 1908, p. 4; *New York Times*, April 15, 1908, p. 5.

12.   Jacob Riis to Kate, April 24, 1903, JARP-NYPL. The 1908 attack on Riis seems to have disturbed greatly many members of Riis' family. One of them could not fathom "that a man who gives himself as he does should be hated by anyone." See Marietta to Kate, April 1908, JARP-NYPL.

13.   *The Charities and the Commons*, April 18, 1908, pp. 89–90.

14. Blaustein quoted from *New York Sun*, April 16, 1908, in *The Charities and the Commons*, April 25, 1908, pp. 140–141; see also *AH*, May 9, 1908, p. 566.

15. Jacob Riis to Miss Charlotte A. Waterbury, April 28, 1908, JARP-NYPL.

16. *The Outlook*, May 9, 1908, pp. 69–71. This full-length apologia was followed one month later by a shorter open letter "To our Supporters" detailing the course of the 1908 controversy. Lucas and Curry were described as having "not the remotest idea of what we are trying to do here, though they are our near neighbors." It also noted Wise's appearance at the House a year earlier. This document was to be reproduced in the thousands of copies to be used if they were ever again attacked. See, Jacob A. Riis to Miss Waterbury, June 18, 1908, JARP-NYPL. See also "To Our Supporters," June 1908, JARP-NYPL.

17. *New York Times*, December 21, 1908, p. 2.

18. Stephen S. Wise to Rev. Newell Dwight Hollis, D.D., June 12, 1914, JARP-NYPL.

19. *HS*, December 24, 1909, p. 8.

20. *HS*, December 31, 1909, p. 8. In spite of the protests the Riis Settlement House continued to serve and was appreciated in its service by its Jewish clients. Controversy and condemnations never placed the House as out of bounds for Jewish youths. A Souvenir Journal commemorating the twenty-eighth anniversary of the Settlement lists the alumni of each of the young men's clubs housed at the Settlement. Among them are the Riis and Wingate Clubs organized in 1907—after the first exposé—and which numbered twelve and thirteen boys with Jewish-sounding names as former members. The Seminole and Spartan Clubs, established in 1913, boasted of twelves and nineteen Jewish former members, respectively. See *Souvenir Journal Jacob A. Riis House* (New York: 1920), JARP-NYPL. Indeed, one Jewish former client Elias A. Cohen was destined to be a leader in Jewish religious communal affairs. See Elias A. Cohen letter to Roger Williams Riis, undated, 1938, JARP-NYPL.

21. There is unfortunately no recorded public reaction from Lucas to the statements made by Wise, Blaustein, et. al. at the time of the Curry controversy or to the 1909 debate. The Lucas papers are not extant and the Wise papers contain no correspondence with Lucas.

22. Riis to Mrs. Julian Heath, September 24, 1903, JARP-NYPL.

23. Mary Riis to Miss Charlotte A. Waterbury, undated, JARP-NYPL.

24. Jacob A. Riis to Mrs. Julian Heath, September 21, 1903, JARP-NYPL.

25. Charlotte A. Waterbury to C. E. Halberstadt, April 20, 1908, JARP-NYPL; H. S. Braucher to Clara Field, April 22, 1908, JARP-NYPL; see also Riis' letter circulated "To Our Supporters" (June 1908) JARP-NYPL, which reviewed the entire Curry affair with a decidedly apologetic tone.

26. Jacob Schiff, Felix Warburg and a Mr. Seligman were all important Jewish benefactors of the Settlement in 1908. Indeed two years earlier the three had raised $2,100 to build a gymnasium designated for use by Jewish clients. See Jacob A. Riis to Jacob Schiff, November 20, 1906, JHSP-AJA. Nathan Bijur, Nathan Straus and Miriam K. Wildberg of the Columbian Council of the Council of Jewish Women were also either Jewish friends or associates of the settlement leader. Each penned a

warm letter of condolence to Riis in May 1905 at the death of Riis' first wife, Elizabeth. See Nathan Bijun to Jacob A. Riis, May 19, 1905; Nathan Straus to Jacob A. Riis, May 18, 1905; Miriam K. Wildberg to Jacob A. Riis, June 11, 1905, JARP-NYPL. Riis' relationship with Schiff needs further elucidation, for although Schiff never expressed himself on the Settlement's ideological position, not in 1903 nor in 1908, it is clear that he was a financial supporter of Riis' Home as early as 1902. See Jacob A. Riis to Mrs. Julian Heath, December 18, 1902, JARP-NYPL, which discusses a Schiff contribution to the Riis building fund. Could it be that as Schiff's influence grew in the Settlement, Riis became more sensitive to Jewish concerns? Unfortunately, the few extant Schiff papers from that period note just one instance of the Jewish patron reacting to activities in the Riis House—fund raising in 1906. There was no discussion of the ideology then taught at the House. See Jacob H. Schiff to Jacob A. Riis, undated, 1906., JHSP-AJA. As previously noted, Schiff never entered the public debate over Riis' settlement activities.

27. *The Outlook*, May 9, 1908, p. 88. This issue which contains Riis' complete public response to Curry-Lucas also includes a plea for funds to offset a $500 deficit.

28. Mary Riis to Miss Charlotte Waterbury, undated, 1908, JARNSP-NYPL.

29. Jacob A. Riis, "To Settlement Workers," (n.d.), JARP-NYPL. See also Riis, "Pamphlet," (n.d.), JARP-NYPL.

30. *YT*, July 1, 1904, p. 8; *The Outlook*, May 29, 1909, p. 8.

31. Riis's crucial definitions of narrow sectarianism, non-sectarianism and Christian non-sectarianism in settlement work is seen clearly in a specific provision of his will. Fearful that the House not "fall into narrow sectarian ways," he appointed a seventeen-member board of advisors to insure that upon his death the settlement ideology would remain Christian non-sectarian, to wit, "that they keep it faithful to the zeal and spirit of our Christian faith, that thou love thy neighbor as thyself be he Christian, Jew or pagan." Interestingly, no Jews were included as projected advisory board members, although Schiff was a trustee of the will. See Jacob A. Riis, "Will," November 7, 1911, JARP-LC.

32. *New York Evening Post*, September 16, 1903, p. 16.

33. From 1902 on there were yearly criticisms of the settlements, Jewish and non-Jewish, published in the Yiddish and Anglo-Jewish press. Settlements were accused of undermining the religious faith of Jews, of alienating children from their parents, of failing to check criminality, of encouraging criminality by restricting the natural exuberance of youths and, of course, of promoting proselytizing. See, as examples of discussions of this subject, *HS*, April 11, 1902, p. 6; July 6, 1903, p. 8; October 18, 1907, p. 8; *YT*, July 15, 1903, p. 5; July 22, 1903, p. 8; *AH*, May 27, 1904, p. 507; June 3, 1904, p. 75; December 7, 1906, p. 108.

34. For discussions of the origins and purposes of the Albert Lucas Religious Classes, the forerunner of the Jewish Centre, established downtown both to counter missionaries and to promote more intensively Jewish programming for children than then offered by existing German-run settlements, see *HS*, June 26, 1903, p. 8; July 21, 1905, p. 8; May 13, 1905, p. 8; *AH*, April 14, 1905, p. 645.

35. Rabbi Wise learned first hand of Riis' deep social commitment based on religious faith from an earlier Christmas time incident in Portland, Oregon, where he was a rabbi in 1904. Arriving in town on a lecture tour, Riis was "getting a little troubled about where to get in a little kindness to someone in need before Xmas [sic]." Riis subsequently found a woman suffering from rheumatism and with Wise's assistance raised monies from local philanthropists to cover expensive medical treatments. Riis himself donated one third of his honorarium from his lecture at Wise's synagogue to this good cause and joyously recorded this event in a letter to his wife back in New York. Undoubtedly impressed by this sincere act of piety, Wise agreed to help that poor woman's family celebrate their Christmas. See Jacob A. Riis to My Sweet Darling Lamb, December 18, 1904, JARP-NYPL. For the rabbi, participation in that seasonal observance certainly did not reflect a belief in a parochial Christian faith. It was rather a natural outgrowth of his support for good social work done in the name of another man's faith.

Wise's ongoing support for Christian social activism in the New York ghetto is reflected in the appearance of such well known social gospelers as Walter Rauschenbush, Edward Everett Hale and John Haynes Holmes in the Free Synagogue pulpit. Riis himself spoke there in 1907 and 1912. Indeed, the activities of the Free Synagogue paralleled and were influenced by those of these Christian activists. One might also suggest that Wise's apparent serenity towards the issue of Christian teachings, universal or not, within the immigrant community had something to do with his own belief that the message of Jesus, as opposed to the teachings of Christianity, had something to teach both Jews and Christians. Wise first expressed this view in 1900 when he suggested that Jewish Sunday School instruction include Jesus as a Jewish prophet. He reiterated this idea in several sermons in Portland in 1905. And later on in his career, his sermon "A Jew's view of Jesus" caused a major stir within American Jewish ranks. See Stephen S. Wise, "Is it Possible to Have a Fellowship of the Churches," *Beth Israel Pulpit*, March 1905, pp. 31–45, and Melvin I. Urofsky, "Stephen S. Wise and the Jesus Controversy," *Midstream*, June/July 1980, pp. 36–40.

36. In the early years of his career, Wise frequently preached on Judaism's ability to teach the ideals of morality, ethics and social justice as well as Christianity. See, for example, Stephen S. Wise, "The National Church Federation," *Beth Israel Pulpit*, November 1905, pp. 108–118. And Riis, to be sure, made a point at the Chanukah celebration of noting what Christians could learn about brotherhood, loyalty and patriotism from the Maccabees. See *The Outlook*, May 29, 1909, p. 8.

37. *HS*, December 15, 1905, p. 5; *AH*, January 11, 1907, p. 256.

38. *AH*, December 28, 1906, p. 201; *HS*, December 28, 1906, p. 4.

39. *HS*, December 28, 1906, p. 8.

40. *New York Sun*, August 2, 1905, reprinted in *HS*, August 4, 1905, p. 8.

41. *HS*, August 4, 1905, p. 5.

42. One of the major problems which Lucas faced—apart from the identification of who his foes actually were—was the question of fund raising to continue his struggle. Could it be that Lucas really knew that Riis was not a missionary, but used his well-known figure as a focus for his own pecuniary purposes? Unfortunately,

the total absence of Lucas' papers makes the determination of this conceivable hidden agenda the moot problematic of all. See on his fund raising problems, *HS*, July 8, 1904, p. 10; July 21, 1905, p. 8. For a critique of Lucas' zealousness by one contemporary downtowner see, *AH*, July 28, 1905, p. 235.

43.   In his frequent attempt to rouse downtown Jews from their complacency about Christian work downtown, Lucas often evoked the imagery of what the Cross meant to Jews in Eastern Europe. He would remark that at a time when Jews still in Russia were suffering martyrdom, New York Jews were oblivious to Christian incursions within this free country. See, for example, *HS*, December 15, 1905, p. 5.

44.   Jacob A. Riis to Jane Robbins, December 26, 1906, JARP-LC.

45.   This interpretation of Riis' attitudes towards immigrant Jews contradicts Richard Tuerk's article which argues that as Riis got to know the immigrants better he grew in sensitivity to their problems. Tuerk characterizes Riis as having been "blatantly anti-Semitic" when he wrote *How the Other Half Lives* in 1890. However, "as the American public became increasingly antagonistic towards the immigrants . . . Riis became more compassionate and even militant in his defense of immigrants in general and Jews in particular." This growth argument is based almost exclusively upon Riis' published writings and pays little attention to Riis' private papers. See Richard Tuerk, "Jacob Riis and the Jews," *New York Historical Society Quarterly* (July 1979): 179–199. Our work follows the older historiographical view of Riis as concerned with the poverty of Jews but unaware of client ideas and social needs. See, for examples of this interpretation, Isidore S. Meyer's review of Hutchins Hapgood, "The Spirit of the Ghetto," *AJHQ* (June 1970): 545; Irving Howe, *World of Our Fathers* (New York: 1976), pp. 396–397; and Lewis Fried, "Jacob Riis and the Jews," *American Studies* (Spring 1979): 5–25. This latter work delves into much of Riis' private papers and views in understanding Riis' Christian view of social work and his insensitivity to different views of how to approach immigrants. He only notes in passing Jewish response to Riis.

46.   Riis' anti-Semitic references were clearly restricted to un-Americanized, immigrant Jews and may have reflected his frustration at the slowness of their assimilation. As noted previously he hod nothing but the highest regard for Jacob Schiff, Wise and other Jewish uptown notables.

Notes to Chapter 6, *Jewish Communal Divisiveness in Response to Christian Influences on the Lower East Side, 1900–1910*

1.   Robert A. Woods and Albert J. Kennedy, eds., *Handbook of Settlements* (New York, 1911), pp. 235–43; M. Katherine Jones, comp., *Bibliography of College, Social and University Settlements* (New York, 1896), pp. 22, 28; College Settlements Association, *Second Annual Report of the College Settlements Association for the Year 1891* (New York, 1892), pp. 13–14; Federation of Churches and Christian Organizations in New York City, *Eleventh Annual Report of the Federation of Churches and Church Organizations in New York City* (New York, 1906), pp. 2, 19, 44, 45, 57; New York City Mission and Tract Society, *Annual Report for the Year 1905* (New York, 1906), pp. 10, 12, 22, 25.

2. New York City Mission and Tract Society, *Annual Report 1905* pp. 12, 25. One statistical indication of the popularity of Christian-run settlements among Jewish Youngsters is the *Eleventh Annual Report of the Colleges Settlements Association October 1, 1899–October 1, 1900* (New York, 1900), p. 41, which notes that approximately 1,000 children were enrolled in their kindergarten, domestic work classes, clubs, and summer excursions during that year. If these figures are at all reliable and are projected for other similar groups, their impact on Jewish youth was considerable. One should also note, however, with reference to the numbers actually converting that the De Witt Memorial Church's proud declaration that some thirty-one Jews had seen the light in 1905, if accurate, reflected a not particularly cost-effective operation based on an expenditure of $7,500 of the City Mission's yearly budget of $33,000. See for background on the history of American Jewish responses to Christianity in their midst prior to 1905, Jonathan D. Sarna, The American Jewish Response to Nineteenth Century Christian Missions," *Journal of American History* 68 (1981): 35–51.

3. *New York World*, July 3, 1905, p. 12; *YT*, July 12, 1905, p. 8; *AH*, July 14, 1905, p. 181; *HS*, July 21, 1905, p. 8; *YT*, July 21, 1905, p. 8; *AH*, July 21, 1905, p. 207; *AH*, July 28, 1905, pp. 234, 236. This 1905 event was by no means the first example of published reports of Christian influence on Jewish children complete with the assertion that Jewish parents had no knowledge of the Christianizing influence. Nor was it the first time calls were heard for a comprehensive Jewish response. If anything, this present "horror story," as one contemporary called it, simply recalled the almost decade-long festering issue and thus constituted the culmination of calls for activity. Prior protests involved the Pro-Cathedral (1901), the City Mission's notorious proselytizer Herman Warszawiak (1902), the Gospel Settlement (1903), and the same God's Providence House (1903). And the Lower East Side was also bestirred by the downtown campaign against Jacob A. Riis of 1903 for his alleged secret proselytizing at his Henry Street Settlement. This 1905 event is most striking, as we will see presently, by its impact upon the New York press and its leading to a semipermanent Jewish institutional response. See on the pre-1905 legacy of missionary conflict which involved many of the actors in the 1905 drama, *AH*, December 6, 1901, p. 143, February 21, 1902, p. 432; April 25, 1902, p. 696; *HS*, August 14, 1903; *AH*, May 22, 1902, p. 23. See my "Jacob A. Riis: Christian Friend or Missionary Foe: Two Jewish Views," *AJH* 71 (1981): 29–47, for the sources describing that controversy.

4. *AH*, January 18, 1901, p. 284; *AH*, February 18, 1901, p. 375; *AH*, May 4, 1901, p. 596; *AH*, June 13, 1902, p. 105; *YT*, November 2, 1903, p. 8; *HS*, March 13, 1903, p. 4; *AH*, March 22, 1903, p. 631; *AJYB* 5666 (905–6), p. 85. For a short history of the Jewish Endeavor Society, see my "Jewish Endeavor Society," in *American Jewish Voluntary Organizations* ed. Michael Dobkowski (Westport, Conn, 1985).

5. See *AH*, December 4, 1904, p. 231, for a discussion of the early purposes of the Orthodox Union and for a listing of the members of the organization's early board of directors. See above, chapter 7, for an analysis of the Jewish ethnic composition of the Union in its formative years. See Drachman's autobiography, *The*

Unfailing Light (New York: Rabbinical Council of America, 1948), pp. 225–26, for his account of his relationship with the Endeavor Society. See Eugene Markovitz, "Henry P. Mendes: Builder of Traditional Judaism in America," (D.H.L. diss., Yeshiva University, 1961), pp. 53–54, for a discussion of that leader's early antimissionary work.

6.   Basic biographical information on these and other new elite members was derived from "Biographical Sketches of Jews Prominent in the Professions etc. in the United States," *AJYB* 5665 (1904–5): 52–213; "Biographical Sketches of Jewish Communal Workers in the United States," *AJYB* 5666 (1905–6): 32–118, and *JCR*, *passim*. For more on Fischel and the other new elite Eastern Europeans, see Herbert S. Goldstein, ed., *Forty Years of Struggle for a Principle: The Biography of Harry Fischel* (New York, 1928), pp. 38–39 and *passim*. See also Arthur A. Goren, *New York Jews and the Quest for Community* (New York, 1970), pp. 32, 38, 65, 127, 201, 274.

7.   *AH*, July 28, 1905, p. 235; August 5, 1905, p. 266; *HS*, December 15, 1905, p. 9; *YT*, January 11, 1905, p. 8; *AH*, March 30. 1906, p. 578; *HS*, March 30, 1906, p. 4.

8.   The history of the rise and rapid fall of the Jewish Centre must be followed through newspaper accounts appearing primarily in the Anglo-Jewish press. Unfortunately neither Lucas nor the coalition left records of their activities. See on that institutional experiment, *AH*, February 17, 1905, p. 399; August 5, 1905, p. 266; April 20, 1906, p. 671; *HS*, March 30, 1906, p. 8; September 21, 1906, p. 4; May 11, 1906, p. 20; August 31, 1906, p. 8; September 28, 1906, p. 3; May 11, 1906, p. 20; May 17, 1906, p. 8; June 21, 1901, p. 28; June 30, 1907, p. 11; July 19, 1907, pp. 8–9.

9.   *HS*, July 8, 1904, p. 10.

10.   See David Max Eichhorn, *Evangelizing the American Jew* (New York, 1978), p. 179, for the suggestion that Schiff bankrolled Benjamin.

11.   See Leonard Bloom, "A Successful Jewish Boycott of the New York City Public Schools," *AJH* (December 1980): 180–88, for one published secondary account of the role members of this coalition—particularly Lucas's followers—played in a protest against school sectarianism. See also the author's "Jacob A. Riis," which discusses the issue of how one differentiates among forms of Christian influence in the ghetto. See below for further discussion of conflicting Jewish attitudes toward Christianity's multifarious influences downtown.

12.   *HS*, May 27, 1904, pp. 551; *YT*, December 30, 1903, p. 8. For other, similar criticisms of the Educational Alliance emanating from groups associated with the Jewish Centre, see *HS*, January 24, 1902, p. 6; *AH*, August 26, 1904, pp. 377–78; September 23, 1904, p. 491.

13.   *AH*, January 24, 1902, p. 6; February 29, 1904, p. 278. Clearly the Jewish Endeavor Society was not alone in the early years of this century in promoting American-style services attractive to those becoming uncomfortable with *landsman-shaft*-style Orthodoxy. Great public debates ensued as to what synagogue functions had to remain unchanged and what ceremonials could be abridged or discarded. Fromenson spoke out strongly for the legitimacy of the Jewish Endeavor Society's changing the trappings of synagogue life and against both the old-line Orthodox,

who opposed all changes, and Reform elements behind the Emanu-El Brotherhood and People's Synagogue, which wanted to go further than the JES in making changes. Fromenson, Lucas, S. P. Frank and other Orthodox Union leaders—later to be Jewish Centre Leaders—also participated in the great debates held in 1904 on the possible unification of all these youth synagogue efforts. On this issue and on these groups, see above, chapter 13.

14. See Morton Rosenstock, *Louis Marshall: Defender of Jewish Rights* (Detroit: Wayne State University Press, 1965), p. 268, and Charles Reznikoff, ed., *Louis Marshall: Champion of Liberty* (Philadelphia, 1957), pp. xxv, xxxviii-xxxix, 936–54, 967–71, for discussions of his anti-blue law work. See above p. 000, no. 50, for the Lucas-Marshall letter of 1903. Marshall probably also had strong words to say about Lucas's definition of the Reform Judaism which Marshall practiced: "Christless Christianity . . . useless for anyone who desired permanently to improve the conditions of Judaism." See *HS*, June 6, 1903, pp. 1, 3, for Lucas's attack against Reform Judaism.

15. *HS*, January 31, 1902, p. 8; *AH*, June 3, 1904, p. 76; June 10, 1904, p. 103; September 9, 1904, p. 431. See also *AH*, January 29, 1904, p. 349, for a discussion of uptown's understanding of the ghetto dwellers' religious needs.

16. *Outlook*, May 9, 1908, pp. 69–71. *New York Times*, December 21, 1908, p. 2. Stephen S. Wise to Newell Dwight Hillis, June 12, 1914, JARP-NYPL, all quoted and analyzed in chapter 7, below.

17. David Blaustein, director of the Educational Alliance, Henry Moskowitz, a Jewish leader of the Ethical Culture Society downtown, and Charles Bernheimer, assistant head worker of the University Settlement, were among the vocal defenders of Riis. For their attitude and on Magnes's point of view, see below, Chapter 7.

18. Uptown lay and religious leaders were in the forefront of the movement which led to the introduction, first in 1907, of the Strauss/Levy Sabbath Observance Bill which, interestingly, repeatedly failed to win passage through the 1910s. See on the early attempts at this bill's passage, *HS*, April 24, 1908, p. 6. See *AH*, December 7, 1906, p. 114, for an account of the criticism of avowed missionary work by Dr. Joseph Silverman of Temple Emanuel and Dr. Samuel Schulman of Temple Beth Fl. Significantly, neither responded to the *Hebrew Standard* editorial of the next week urging support for the Jewish Centres in reaction to the same Christian statements which exercised these Reform leaders. See *HS*, December 14, 1906, p. 8. See also Silverman's statement "United States Not a Christian Nation," reported in *HS*, March 2, 1906, p. 4.

19. For evidence of Schiff's backing of Riis's activities, see Jacob A. Riis to Julian Heath, December 9, 1902, JARP-NYPL, which discusses Schiff's contribution to a Riis building campaign. See also an undated Jacob H. Schiff to Riis letter, found in the Schiff Papers, American Jewish Archives, Cincinnati, which notes Schiff's contribution to a 1906 campaign. Significantly, Schiff did not express himself publicly on the Riis question in 1908.

20. *AH*, May 22, 1903, p. 23.

21. *HS*, January 8, 1909, pp. 1–3.

22. *New York Sun*, August 2, 1905, quoted in *HS*, August 11, 1905, pp. 6–7.

23. *Ibid.*

24. *AH,* July 28, 1905, p. 235. See also on anti-activist criticisms, *HS,* July 8, 1904, p. 10.

25. *YT,* December 30, 1903, p. 8; *HS,* August 11, 1905, p. 8; *AH,* December 29, 1905, p. 210.

26. *AH,* August 21, 1903, pp. 439–40.

27. For discussions of the ideological reservations transplanted eastern European religious leaders and their downtown lay supporters had toward the JES, Albert Lucas Classes and all other types of American Judaizing influences see *YT,* March 25, 1903, p. 8; November 20, 1903, p. 8; *AH,* January 16, 1903, p. 298; September 4, 1903, p. 503; June 5, 1903, p. 81; October 2, 1903, p. 634; May 13, 1904, p. 794. There are also some sources that suggest that downtown ghetto Orthodox groups saw American Jewry as in consort with Christian conversionists. See on this view *HS,* January 8, 1909, pp. 1–3; and Goren, *New York Jews,* p. 284. Lucas's critique of the immigrant religious leadership was that they took a too narrow view of immigrant problems. They were seen as intent only on insulating themselves from contemporary problems, not involving themselves in reaching large numbers of disaffected Jews.

28. The nonintersection of antimissionary concerns and conceptions of Jewish education in America is seen in the declarations of the Agudath ha-Rabbanim recorded in its *Sefer ha-Yovel shel Agudath ha-Rabbanim ha-Ortodoksim de-Artsot ha-Brit ve-Kanada* (New York, 1928), pp. 25–26. See also on early Agudath ha-Rabbanim conventions which discussed Jewish continuity and religious education with no reference to the missionary problem, *AJYB* 5664 (1903–4): 160; 5665 (1904–5): 782; and *AH,* July 8, 1904, pp. 204–5.

Notes to Chapter 7, *Why Albert Lucas Did Not Serve in the New York Kehillah*

1. *AH,* January 4, 1901. pp. 231–233. The Orthodox Union represented the rabbinical and lay leadership of American traditional Judaism in the United States at the turn of the century. Its predominantly American-born German/English Jewish ethnic composition is substantiated by the following background information on the place of birth, time in America, and educational training of 19 of the 24 members of the 1900 Orthodox Union Board of Trustees. Fifteen of the members were either born here or in England, or came to America from Central Europe before 1870. All fifteen received their major educational training in American or British schools. Not surprisingly, nine were early rabbis, supporters or students of the pre-Solomon Schecter Jewish Theological Seminary of America. Of the remaining four members, men born and trained in Eastern Europe, two, Kasriel Sarasohn, editor of the *Yiddishes Tageblatt,* and Hebrew teacher Julius Buchhalter, were part of a small *Haskalah* circle which began settling in New York in the early 1870–1880s. Rabbi Philip Hillel Klein and Mr. Isidore Hershfeld were the remaining East European-born leaders. Klein was one of the first East European-trained rabbis to accept the realities of Americanization and to cooperate with American-born colleagues in

modernization efforts. Hershfield was the first of the more recently arrived East European lay activists to join Lucas in his Americanization/Judaizing work. For a complete listing of the members of the early Orthodox Union board, see *AH*, January 4, 1901. p. 235. And for more details on the lives and careers of these early leaders, see "Biographical Sketches of Rabbis . . .," *AJYB* 5664 (1903–4): 40–108; "Biographical Sketches of Jews Prominent in the Professions . . .," *AJYB* 5665 1904–5): 52–217. See *AH*, February 7, 1902, p. 400, March 22, 1903, p. 631 and *HS*, June 12, 1903, p. 10 for accounts of the Orthodox Union's earliest campaigns on behalf of the rights of Orthodox Jews. For more on the Orthodox Union's early history, including the differences between it and the old-line Agudath ha-Rabbanim (Union of Orthodox Rabbis of the United States and Canada), see Eugene Markovitz, "Henry Pereira Mendes: Architect of the Union of Orthodox Jewish Congregations of America," *AJHQ* (March 1966): 370–374.

2.   *HS*, August 9, 1901, p. 4; August 14, 1903, p. 4; *AH*, August 21, 1903, pp. 439–440; *AH*, July 14, 1904, p. 181; July 21, 1904, p. 207; *HS*, August 4, 1905, pp. 8–91 *AH*, August 18, 1905, pp. 322–323. For background information on mission schools like Lucas', see Alexander Dushkin, *Jewish Education in New York City* (New York, 1918), p. 89 and *passim*.

3.   *AH*, February 17, 1905, p. 399; August 5, 1905, p. 266; *HS*, March 30, 1906, p. 8, September 21, 1906. p. 4.

4.   *HS*, May 28, 1909, p. 11; Bernard G. Richards to H.P. Mendes, January 4, 1910. *MA*, P3/1399; Report of Religious Committee, Kehillah. February 8, 1910. *MA*, P3/1878, Bernard G. Richards to Elias A. Cohen, March 7, 1910. *MA*, P3/1394; *AH*, May 20, 1910, p. 66; Bernard G. Richards to Elias A. Cohen, March 11, 1910. *MA*, P3/1394; *Min CED*, June 10, 1910. *MA*, P3/1662; *Min CED*, September 12, 1910. *MA*, P3/1662; *Min ECK*, September 22, 1910. *MA*, P3/1399; *HS*, July 28, 1991, p. 4; *HS*, August 4, 1911, p. 4; *Min ECK*, March 16, 1911. *MA*, P3/1400; *Min ECK*, September 12, 1911. *MA*, P3/1400; *Min ECK*, February 13, 1912. *MA*, P3/1401.

5.   *HS*, June 26, 1903, pp. 1, 3.

6.   *Ibid.*

7.   *Ibid.*

8.   *Ibid.*

9.   *HS*, August 14, 1903, p. 10, *AH*, July 14, 1905, p. 181; August 21, 1903, pp. 439–440; July 21, 1905, p. 207; August 5, 1905, p. 266. For a complete discussion of Lucas' campaign against the noted muckraker and reformer, see above, chapter 5. For more on the Lucas-led Orthodox Union of the schools see, Leonard Bloom, "A Successful Jewish Boycott of the New York City Public Schools." *AJH* December 1980, p. 180–188. See also *AH* January 5, 1906, p. 24; December 7, 1906, p. 114 for more on Lucas' many activities.

10.   *AH*, July 28, 1905 p. 235.

11.   July 8, 1904 p. 10. See also *HS*, January 8, 1909. for another account of uptown opposition to Lucas' tactics. The fear that anti-missionary work could evoke anti-Semitic responses from the Christian community was evidenced by an editorial published in the *New York Sun* on August 2, 1905. In a comment "Does

This Not Look Like Bigotry," Lucas and his followers were called "religious bigots" for his activities. Christians, the newspapers declared. had the religious freedom to teach their faith to Jews. More important. they argued "Jews no less than Christians. must accept the truth of the saying of Jesus 'Let your light so shine before men that they may see your good works and glorify your Father in Heaven." See on this editorial and its attending controversy *HS*, August 4 1905 pp. 8–9; *AH*, August 18, 1905 pp. 322–323.

12.   *HS*, July 8, 1904, p. 10; January 8, 109, pp. 1–3.

13.   *AH*, March 17, 1905, p. 485. For more examples of Lucas' frustrations with downtown religious and synagogue leaders. see *HS*, August 21. 1903. pp. 439–440: *HS*, August 14, 1903, p. 16; July 14, 1905, p. 181; December 15, 1905, p. 9.

14.   See below, p. 172 and note 17.

15.   *AH*, March 17, 1905, p. 485; *HS*, August 14, 1903. p. 10; July 14. 1905. p. 181, *HS*, December 15, 1905, p. 9; January 8. 1908. p. 3.

16.   *AH*, February 17, 1905, p. 399; August 5, 1905, p. 266; *HS*, March 30, 1906, p. 8, September 21, 1906. p. 4.

17.   *HS*, May 11, 1906, p. 20. Background information was obtainable on ten of the twenty-four initial directors of the Jewish Centre. Its first President was a Mr. Lubetkin who reportedly "about 20–21 years (earlier) had worked in the closing of Christian missions." Phillips, Wolbarst, William Prager and A.H. Fromenson, editor of the *Yiddishes Tageblatt* and originator of that newspaper's English page dedicated to the second generation Jews, were the identifiable American-born, or long-time U.S. resident members of the board. Fischel, Fischman. Rosalsky, Hershfield and Kamaiky were the most famous downtown representatives. These new elite members were all either of Russian descent or of related ancestry. By 1905, all had yet to pass their fortieth birthday and all had spent, by that date. the greater part of their lives in this country. See "Biographical Sketches of Jews Prominent in the Professions etc. in the United States." *AJYB* 5665 (1904–5): 52–213: "Biographical Sketches of Jewish Communal Workers in the United States." *AJYB* 5683 (1903–4): 169–218; *JCR, passim*. For more on Drachman's and Mendes' early anti-missionary and pro-modern Jewish education activities. see *HS*, February 7, 1902, p. 400; March 22, 1903, p. 631; *HS*, June 12, 1903, p. 10; Markovitz, p. 374. See also Drachman's autobiography *The Unfailing Light*, New York, 1948. For more on Fischel and the other new elite of East European, see Herbert S. Goldstein, *Forty Years of Struggle for a Principle* (New York, 1928), pp. 38–39 and *passim*. See also Arthur A. Goren, *New York Jews and the Quest for Community* (New York, 1970), pp. 32, 38, 65, 127, 201, 274.

18.   *HS*, August 31, 1906, p. 8; September 28, 1906, p. 3; May 11, 1906, p. 20; *AH*, April 20, 1906, p. 671.

19.   *HS*, May 17, 1907, p. 8; June 21, 1907, p. 2; August 30, 1907, p. 11.

20.   *HS*, July 19, 1907, pp. 8–9.

21.   *HS*, November 31, 1908, p. 8; December 6, 1907, p. 8; December 13, 1907, p. 8; December 20, 1907, p. 8; December 27, 1908, p. 8.

22.   Goren, *op. cit.*, pp. 25, 31. See also *YT*, September 6, 1908, p. 6.

23. Goren, pp. 38–42. *AH,* October 2, 1908, p. 535; October 23, 1908, p. 615; *Min ECK,* April 17, 1909. MA, P3/1398. *JCR,* p. 72.

24. *AH,* December 28 1906 p. 201; *HS,* December 28 1906 p. 4.

25. *AH,* January I1 1907 p. 256.

26. *HS,* January 31, 1908 p. 8.

27. *HS,* March 5, 1909, p. 12; April 2, 1909, p. 12; Goren, pp. 53–54.

28. *HS,* April 2, 1909, p. 12.

29. *HS,* April 9, 1909, p. 4; Goren, p. 129; Dushkin, p. 89.

30. Jeffrey S. Gurock. *When Harlem Was Jewish* (New York, 1979), pp. 108–109. For more on the split within Orthodox opinion which led to Fischel's statement, see Goldstein, pp. 110–116.

31. *HS,* February 11, 1910, p. 4; Report of the Executive Committee and Proceedings of the Third Annual Convention of the Jewish Community (Kehillah), New York, April 27–28, 1912, p. 13.

32. *HS,* August 11, 1905, p. 8; *AH,* December 29, 1905, p. 210; *YT,* December 30, 1903, p. 8.

Notes to Chapter 8, *In Search of the Other Jewish Center: On the Writing of the Social History of American Orthodoxy, 1900–1910*

1. Mordecai M. Kaplan, "The Jewish Center," *AH* March 22, 1918, 529–31.

2. Jeffrey S. Gurock, When *Harlem Was Jewish, 1870–1930* (New York, 1979), 123–24, 152. See also Young Mens' Hebrew Association of New York, "Meetings of the Special Joint Committee Consisting of Members of the Social, Finance and Membership and Neighborhood Committees," meeting of March 14, 1915 (YlVO Archives). For Kaplan's contemporary negative comments on the Jewishness of the Y movement, see *YT,* July 19, 1915, 8 and *YT,* July 21, 1915, 8, as noted in Gurock, *ibid.,* 152.

3. *MJ* August 11, 1913, 5 and *MJ,* October 12, 1913, 4, as discussed in Gurock, *ibid., 106.*

4. For a passing reference to the Jewish Centres uptown in Harlem see *HS,* June 29, 1906, 4.

5. "Biographical Sketches of Jewish Communal Workers in the United States," *AJYB* 5666 (1905–1906), 32, 85.

6. On Marshall's support for Orthodox institutions and for evidence that he kept reports sent to him, see Gurock, *op. cit.,* 105, 108, 190. See *AH,* March 22, 1918, 545 for a report on Marshall at the founding of The Jewish Center.

7. Albert Lucas to Louis Marshall, September 3, 1903 (Louis Marshall Papers, AJA).

8. For positive Jewish opinions of Jacob A. Riis, see *AH,* July 1901, 284 and August 2, 1901, 387.

9. For a complete discussion of the evolution of the Jewish Centres out of the Riis-Lucas controversy of 1903, see above, chapter 5.

10. *HS*, May 11, 1906, 20. For biographical information on the directors and friends of the Jewish Centres, see "Biographical Sketches of Jews Prominent in the Professions etc. in the United States," *AJYB* 5665 (1904–1905): 52–213; "Biographical Sketches of Jewish Communal Workers," *AJYB* 5666 (1905–1906): 169–218; *UJE* VI (1939): 301.

11. See Naomi W. Cohen, *Not Free to Desist: The American Jewish Committee, 1906–1966* (Philadelphia 1972): 563 for an AJC listing which includes Kamaiky. On the Jewish Centres see *HS*, May 17, 1907, 8; June 21, 1907, 2; August 30, 1907, 11; July 19, 1907, 8–9.

12. On support by Marshall, Schiff and other German Jewish leaders for anti-missionary endeavors and particularly their involvement with the Educational Alliance, see Morton Rosenstock, *Louis Marshall: Defender of Jewish Rights* (Detroit, 1965), 268; Charles Reznikoff, ed., *Louis Marshall: Champion of Liberty* (Philadelphia, 1957), xxv, xxxviii-xxxix, 936–54, 969–71, and S. P. Rudens, "A Half-Century of Community Service: The Story of the New York Educational Alliance," *AJYB* (1944–1945): 73–86.

13. See Albert Lucas to Louis Marshall, November 1, 1903 (Louis Marshall Papers, AJA) for references to Lucas and Mendes. For Mendes' papers see "Scrapbooks kept by Eliza de Sola Mendes during the Early Years of the Ministry of her son, Rabbi Mendes in New York," AJA, Box 60, Homiletics and Sermons, and H. P. Mendes Papers, Boxes 81–1–2, Jewish Theological Seminary of America. For sources on Fischel see his papers in the Orthodox Jewish Archives of the Agudath Israel of America, New York City. Information on OU holdings in Waltham is provided by the Library of the American Jewish Historical Society's card catalogue. The AJHS has no complete, published list of sources. I am grateful to Mr. Victor Tarry of the Spanish Portuguese Synagogue for his assistance in tracking down Lucas' membership card. Thanks are also due to my friend, attorney Lawrence Newman, for endeavoring to find Lucas' apparently nonexistent will.

14. On Riis' Jewish friends see Jacob A. Riis to Jacob H. Schiff, November 20, 1906, Jacob H. Schiff Papers, AJA; Nathan Bijur to Jacob A. Riis, May 19, 1905, Nathan Straus to Jacob A. Riis, May 18, 1905, Miriam K. Wildberg to Jacob A. Riis, June 11, 1905, Jacob A. Riis to Mrs. Julian Heath, December 18, 1902, JARP-NYPL.

15. On Riis' anti-Semitic remarks about his opponents see *The New York Times* (April 15, 1908), 5; Jacob A. Riis to Kate, April 24, 1903, *JARP-NYPL*. For an analysis of Riis' distinctions between missionaries and Christian work see above. See also *AH*, August 14, 1903, 407–8.

16. On Wise's personal affinity for Riis and his comfort with Riis' thoughts see J. Gurock, *ibid.*, 35–36.

17. For sources on the range of actual missionary and Christian groups operating downtown during the first decade of the twentieth century, see above, chapter 6.

18. *HS*, January 8, 1909, 1–3; *AH*, July 28, 1905, 235; *HS*, July 8, 1904, 10.

19. *HS*, June 26, 1903, 1, 3; *AH*, May 22, 1903, 23; *HS*, August 14, 1903, 8; *HS*, December 15, 1905, 8.

20. *HS*, May 27, 1904, 50–51. For similar criticisms of the Educational Alliance emanating from groups associated with the Jewish Centres see *HS*, January 24, 1902, 6; *AH*, August 26, 1904, 377–78; and *AH*, September 23, 1904, 491.

21. *HS*, June 26, 1903, 1, 3.

22. Albert Lucas to Louis Marshall, November 17, 1908; Jacob Goldstein, Conrad J. Saphier and N. Taylor Phillips to Sir (or Madam), December 14, 1908, LMP-AJA.

23. For background on the migration of Kehillah papers from New York to the Central Archives in Jerusalem see the introduction to Hadassah Assouline, ed. "Judah Leib Magnes Papers 1890–1948 (incl.: archives of the New York 'Kehillah' 1908–1922)" in *Ginzei Am Olam: The Central Archives for the History of the Jewish People, Jerusalem* (Jerusalem, 1979).

24. On the founding and organization of the Kehillah, see Arthur A. Goren, *New York Jews and the Quest for Community* (New York, 1970), 25–42 and *passim*.

25. *HS*, March 5, 1909, 12.

26. *HS*, December 6, 1907, 8; December 13, 1907, 8; *HS*, December 20, 1907, 8; *HS*, December 27, 1907, 8.

27. *HS*, March 5, 1909, 12; *HS*, April 2, 1909, 12. See also *JCR* (New York, 1917–1918), 72.

28. Bernard Richards to H. P. Mendes, January 4, 1910 (*Judah Leib Magnes Papers 1890–1948*). On the *Hebrew Standard* criticisms of Kehillah activities on missionaries, see *HS*, December 17, 1909, 4; February 11, 1910, 8; February 25, 1910, 13; March 11, 1910, 8.

29. "Report of the Religious Committee, February 8, 1910" (*Judah Leib Magnes Papers 1890–1948*).

30. "Minutes of the Meeting of the Committee on Education of the Jewish Community of New York, June 10, 1910" (*Judah Leib Magnes Papers 1890–1948*). See also the announcement appearing in *HS*, August 26, 1910, 8.

31. "Minutes of the Meeting of the Committee on Education of the Jewish Community of New York, September 12, 1910" (*Judah Leib Magnes Papers 1890–1948*).

32. *HS*, July 28, 1911, 4; August 4, 1911, 3; Bernard G. Richards to Louis Posner, Chairman of Advisory Committee, September 22, 1910; Bernard Richards, Secretary to Samuel Bloch, November 3, 1910; circular letter from Louis Posner, Chairman Advisory Committee, dated November 16, 1910 (*Judah Leib Magnes Papers 1890–1948*).

33. For evidence of Cohen's involvement with the Riis home see, Elias A. Cohen to Roger Williams Riis, 1938 (Jacob A. Riis Papers, New York Public Library). For Cohen's views on antimissionary tactics see, Elias A. Cohen to Bernard G. Richards, May?, 1911 (Judah *Leib Magnes Papers 1890–1948*).

34. *Report of the Executive Committee and Proceedings of the Third Annual Convention of the Jewish Community (Kehillah) of New York, April 27–28, 1912*, 13.

35. For a discussion of the circumstances that surrounded Lucas' very brief association with the Kehillah, see above, chapter 7.

36. *HS*, March 22, 1918, 545.

Notes to Chapter 9, *From Exception to Role Model: Bernard Drachman and the Evolution of Jewish Religious Life in America, 1800–1920*

1.   Bernard Drachman, *The Unfailing Light: Memoirs of an American Rabbi* (New York: 1948), pp. 132–153, 167, 177. For the text of the Pittsburgh Platform. see Nathan Glazer, *American Judaism* (Chicago: 1957), Appendix A.

2.   For a complete discussion of Drachman's education and religious training and how it differed from that of an East European rabbi, see above, chapter 1.

3.   Drachman, p. 167.

4.   Drachman, pp. 197–200.

5.   Drachman, p. 206.

6.   Drachman, p. 167.

7.   The understanding that nineteenth-century Reform temples began as Orthodox and liberalized their rituals as their members became Americanized has been most effectively argued by Leon Jick in his *The Americanization of the Synagogue, 1820–1870* (Hanover, N.H. 1976). The best way to study the changes in synagogue life is to examine as Jick did, the many annalistic communal histories which tell of the rituals of hundreds of congregations. On the breaks with Orthodoxy and the changed orientation of congregations, see above, chapter 2.

8.   Gurock, *When Harlem Was Jewish, 1870–1930* (New York, 1979), pp. 10–12, 20–21.

9.   Jick understands Reform as evolving from within the laity. See specifically his statement that the Pittsburgh Platform was virtually unnoticed by contemporary laity.

10.   Gurock, "Resisters and Accommodators," Chapter 1 of this volume.

11.   The most extensive study of those religious groups which compromised and cooperated with Reformers is Moshe Davis, *The Emergence of Conservative Judaism: The Historical School in Nineteenth Century America* (Philadelphia, 1963), pp. 149–230.

12.   Davis, pp. 219–220; Michael A. Meyer, "A Centennial History" in Samuel Karff, ed., *Hebrew Union College Jewish Institute of Religion at One Hundred Years*, (Cincinnati, 1983) pp. 41–43.

13.   For more on the Pittsburgh Platform and those who participated in its promulgation see David Polish, "The Changing and the Constant in the Reform Rabbinate," *AJA* (November 1983): 270–272 and *passim*. On the similarities in background and in attitudes towards modernization among those American Orthodox and Conservatives in the late Nineteenth Century, see chapter 1.

14.   *The Jewish Theological Seminary of America: Semi-Centennial Volume* (New York: 1939), pp. 37–38, 41.

15.   On the B'nai B'rith as an alternate secular form of Jewish identity, see Deborah Dash Moore, *Bnai Brith and the Challenge of Ethnic Leadership* (Albany, 1976).

16.   Gurock, *When Harlem*, p. 12; *AH*, June 20, 1898, 172.

17.   Jacob David Willowski, *Sefer Nimukei Ridbaz: Perush al ha-Torah* (Chicago: 1904). For more on Willowski, who, as we will see, eventually ended up for a while

in the U. S., see Aaron Rothkoff, The American Sojourns of Ridbaz: Religious Problems Within the Immigrant Community." *AJHQ* (June 1968): 557–572. Israel Meir Ha-Kohen Kagan, *Niddehei Yisrael* (Warsaw, 1894), pp. 129–130, quoted from Aaron Rakeffet-Rothkoff. *The Silver Years in American Jewish Orthodoxy* (Jerusalem, 1981), p. 18.

18. Rothkoff, pp. 562–564. Jonathan D. Sarna, ed. *People Walk on Their Heads: Moses Weinberger's Jews and Judaism in New York* (New York, 1981), pp. 26–27; Willowski, pp. 3–4; Harold P. Gastwirth. *Fraud, Corruption and Holiness: The Controversy over the Supervision of Jewish Dietary Practice in New York City 1881–1940* (New York: 1974), pp. 1–13.

19. Moses Rischin, *The Promised City: New York's Jews, 1870–1914* (Cambridge, 1962), pp. 19–50, particularly the section on "Torah, Haskala and Protest," Salo W. Baron, *Steeled by Adversity: Essays and Addresses on American Jewish Life* (Philadelphia, 1971), pp. 275–276; Isaac Levitats, The *Jewish Community is Russia, 1772–1844* (New York, 1943), pp. 20–102.

20. See below, chapter 14.

21. Benjamin Kline Hunnicutt, "Jewish Sabbath Movement in the Early Twentieth Century" *AJH* (December 1979): 196–197 On the choice between Sabbath observance and mobility in one immigrant's career, see Herbert S. Goldstein, *Forty Years of Struggle for a Principle: The Biography of Harry Fischel* (New York, 1928), p. 12. See also Ben Eliezer, *Letters of a Father to His Son* (London, 1928), pp. 214, 216–217.

22. Emanuel Gamoran. *Changing Conceptions in Jewish Education* (New York: 1925), pp. 59–144; Gedalyahu Alon, "The Lithuanian Yeshivas" (translated from the Hebrew by Sid Leiman) in Judah Goldin ed., *The Jewish Expression* (New York: 1970), pp. 448–464; Rischin, p. 31; Louis Greenberg, *The Jews of Russia* (New Haven: 1946–52), vol. 1, pp. 32–36; Levitats, pp. 69–86.

23. On the affinity of immigrant Jews for the public school, see Jacob A. Riis, "The Children of the Poor," in Robert A. Woods, et. al., *The Poor of the Great Cities* (London, 1896), p. 102; Selma Berrol, "Education and Mobility: The Jewish Experience in New York City, 1880–1920" *AJHQ*, (March 1976), 257–272 and idem., "School Days on the Old East Side," *New York History*, (April 1976), 201–213.

24. For a discussion of Jewish court systems in nineteenth century Russia, see Levitats, p. 196–207. On Jewish voluntary courts of arbitration in New York, albeit of a somewhat later period, see Israel Goldstein, *Jewish Justice and Conciliation: History of the Jewish Conciliation Board of America* (New York, 1981).

25. Hyman B. Grinstein, "The Efforts of East European Jewry to Organize Its Own Community in the United States," *PAJHS*, (December 1959), 73–89; *Di Yiddishe Landsmanshaften Fun New York* (New York, 1938).

26. Gilbert Klaperman *The Story of Yeshiva University The First Jewish University in America* (London: 1969), pp. 11–23.

27. Abraham J. Karp "New York Chooses a Chief Rabbi," *PAJHS*, (1955): 129–194; Gastwirth, pp. 55–90.

28. For an organizational account of its founding, see *Sefer ha-Yovel shel Agudath ha-Rabbanim ha-Ortodoksim de-Artsot ha-Brit ve-Kanada* (New York, 1928), pp. 13–

24. On the observation that the Union was rooted in an American organizational form, it must be noted that in Eastern Europe, ad-hoc ephemeral rabbinical organizations existed in the 1860s and beyond to fight the rise of Reform. Similar organizations were formed to combat Zionism. And *Ha-Levanon*, an anti-Enlightenment journal, articulated their opposition. But an inter-communal or supra-communal organization comparable to the eighteenth century Vaad Arba Artzot did not obtain until the 1910s when the Agudath Israel was founded. Interestingly, as we will soon see, the idea that the Agudath ha-Rabbanim was an American model organization was espoused by a major critic, Rabbi Gabriel Z. (Velvel), Margolis in the 1920s who challenged the Agudath ha-Rabbanim as a Union not unlike labor unions. Yet he too adopted another American model, Knesseth Ha-Rabbonim, a congress if you will, to combat Americanism and his enemies in the rabbinate.

29. *Sefer ha-Yovel*, p. 26; Rakeffet-Rothkoff, p. 319; Klaperman, pp. 52–54, 69–70, 75, 80.

30. *Sefer ha-Yovel*, p. 26; Rakeffet-Rothkoff, pp. 319–320; *AJYB* 5664 (1903–4): 160; (1904–5): 282.

31. *Sefer ha-Yovel*, p. 27; Rakeffet-Rothkoff, pp. 320–321. For a comprehensive discussion of the settlement patterns of East European Orthodox rabbis in the United States at the turn of the century and beyond, see above, chapter 1. See also *Sefer ha-Yovel*, p. 146 and Gastwirth, p. 27.

32. *AH*, January 10, 1913, p. 303; *HS*, January 12, 1913, p. 9. Rosenthal, the YI's first president, was JTS class of 1915. Sachs, the YI's second president, was JTS class of 1915. See *Jewish Theological Seminary Student Annual* (1914), p 50–51, (1915), p 51–52, all quoted from and utilized by Shulamith Berger's "The Early History of the Young Israel Movement" (typescript seminar paper, YIVO Institute, Fall 1982); *HS*, January 30, 1913, p. 12.

33. The Willowski-Album dispute may be studied through the writings of each man. Album wrote *Sefer Divrei Emet*, 2 vols. (Chicago, 1904–1912), where he defended his position. Willowski's introduction to his *Nimukei . . .* offers his side of the story. See also Rothkoff, pp. 557–575 and Gastwirth, pp. 90–92.

34. *AJYB* 5664 (1903–4): 160 and (1904–5), p. 282.

35. For a discussion of the ideological bent of the *Morgen Zhurnal see* Mordecai Soltes, "The Yiddish Press: An Americanizing Agent," *AJYB* (1924–1925): 165–372.

36. See *AH*, May 30, 1502, pp. 37–35 for a description and text of Drachman's articulation of the OU stance on the problems of Jewish education to the New York Board of Jewish Ministers.

37. *HS*, October 18, 1901, p. 4; *AH*, January 15, 1901. p. 284; February 8, 1901, p. 379; April 5, 1901, p. 395; Drachman, pp. 223ff.

38. See *HS*, October 24, 1902, p. 4; *AH* February 7, 1902, p. 400; *HS*, June 12, 1903, p. 10 for examples of early 1900s OU lobbying efforts. On the OU's anti-sectarianism campaigns, see Leonard Bloom, "A Successful Jewish Boycott of the New York City Public Schools," *AJH*, (December 1980), 180–188; See also above, chapter 5.

39. *AH*, January 3, 1901, p. 231; *AJYB* (1903–4): 159. Eugene Markovitz, "Henry Pereira Mendes: Architect of the Union of Orthodox Jewish Congregations of America," *AJHQ* (March 1966), 380–381.

40. For a statistical analysis of the background of East European leaders in the OU, see above, chapter 7.

41. Herbert S. Goldstein, ed., pp. 52–54 and *passim*.

42. Drachman, p. 213; Davis, p. 386.

43. See above, chapter 1 for a biographical treatment of Klein.

44. *AH*, December 6, 1901, p. 118; February 7, 1902, p. 375; May 2, 1902, p. 725; December 25, 1903, p. 205. For more on the history of the Endeavorers, see Gurock, "Jewish Endeavor Society" in Michael Dobkowski, ed. *American Jewish Voluntary Organizations* (Westport, Conn.: 1986), pp. 228–231. The OU also supported a number of other, independent youth synagogue initiatives. On the story of congregations Shomre Emunah and Mikve Israel of New York, see Gurock, *When Harlem Was Jewish*, pp. 117–118.

45. *AH*, September 30, 1904, p. 516; 115, October 7, 1904, 7 as derived from Jenna Weisman Joselit, "What Happened to New York's Jewish Jews: Moses Rischin's The Promised City Revisited," *AJH* (December 1983): 163–172.

46. See above, chapter 13.

47. See above, chapter 7.

48. Mordecai M. Kaplan, *Journal* (unpublished diaries, Jewish Theological Seminary of America) v. 15, September 17, 1950. The Endeavorers also had difficulties with downtown *maggidim* (itinerant preachers) who competed with them for space in downtown synagogues for their Saturday afternoon sermons. On *maggidim*, see *AH*, January 16, 1903, 295.

49. For the best account both of the migration patterns of second generation Jews out of the inner city and towards suburbia in this nation's largest metropolis and of the levels of ethnic group persistence as opposed to assimilation achieved by these Jews, see Deborah Dash Moore, *At Home in America: Second Generation New York Jews* (New York, 1981). On the rise of Conservative Judaism in these areas, see Marshall Sklare, *Conservative Judaism: An American Religious Movement* (New York, 1954) and Will Herberg, *Protestant-Catholic-Jew: An Essay in American Religious Sociology* (New York, 1955).

50. Jack Wertheimer, "The Conservative Synagogue," in *The History of the Synagogue in America* (New York, 1987). See also Herman H. and Mignon L. Rubenovitz, *The Waking Heart* (Cambridge, 1967), pp. 29, 32. Needless to say, in the beginning Conservative rabbis sometimes experienced difficulties in attempting to implement seemingly innocuous changes like the abolition of the selling of mitzvoth; see Herbert Rosenblum, "The Founding of the United Synagogue of America, 1913" (diss., Brandeis University, 1971), pp. 129, 134.

51. Drachman, pp. 261; *AH*, October 1, 1909 as noted in Rosenblum, 124.

53. *AH*, January 10, 1913, 303 and *HS*, January 12, 1912, 9.

54. Gurock, *When Harlem Was Jewish*, pp. 127–133, 135ff; *YT*, July 19, 1915, p. 5; July 21, 1915, p. 5; Ira Eisenstein and Ira Kohn, ed. *Mordecai Kaplan: An Eval-*

uation (New York, 1932), *passim* as discussed by Gurock, *When Harlem Was Jewish,* pp. 124–125.

55.   Interestingly enough a year after his student established the IS in Harlem, Kaplan built The Jewish Center on New York's West Side with a similar synagogue mandate in mind.

56.   For a discussion of Klein's and Margolies' attitudes towards Americanization, see above, chapter 1. On the early history of RIETS and its transformation, see Klaperman, pp. 73–149.

57.   Aaron Rothkoff, *Bernard Revel: Builder of American Jewish Orthodoxy* (Philadelphia, 1972), p. 27–39 and *passim*.

Notes to Chapter 10, *A Generation Unaccounted for in* American Judaism

1.   Nathan Glazer, *American Judaism* (Chicago and London, 1937, rev. ed., 1972), pp. 62, 69–70.

2.   Glazer, pp. 70–72.

3.   Glazer, pp. 72–73.

4.   Glazer, pp. 73–77.

3.   Glazer, pp. 77–78.

6.   Glazer, pp. 81–85.

7.   Glazer, pp. 91–92. For Glazer's discussion of the era of Jewish revival in the decade 1945–1956, see Chapter VII.

8.   *HS*, March 28, 1905 p 4.; *AH*, April 5, 1901, p 597; April 28, 1905, p. 4; *HS*, March 21, 1902, p. 4. The proceedings would be heightened further by the English language prayers that supplemented the traditional siddur. And of course, all would remain still, men on one side of a *mechitza*, women on the other during prayer and the weekly English sermon offered by both lay and, most significantly, rabbi-in-training leaders on social and historical topics of the day.

9.   *HS*, October 18, 1901, p. 4; *AH*, January 18, 1901, p. 284; February 8, 1901, p. 379; April 5, 1901, p. 596; Bernard Drachman, *The Unfailing Light: Memories of an American Rabbi* (New York, 1948), pp. 225ff.

10.   *AH*, January 4, 1901, pp. 231–234; December 6, 1901, p. 118; February 7, 1902, p. 375: May 2, 1902, p. 725; December 25, 1903, p. 205.

11.   Glazer, pp. 77–78; *Sefer ha-Yovel shel Agudath ba-Rabbanim ha-Ortodoksim de-Artsot ha-Brit ve-Kanada* (New York, 1928), p. 18. For a discussion of the opposition by a leading member of the Agudath ha-Rabbanim to one respect of the young people's synagogue, the English-language sermon, see Aaron Rothkoff, "The American Sojourns of Ridbaz: Religious Practice within the Immigrant Community," *AJHQ,* (June 1968), pp. 561–562.

12.   For biographies of these new elite members and their relationship with the Drachman-Mendes faction in the orthodox Union, see above, chapter 7.

13.   For biographies of Klein, Margolies and Levinthal and a discussion of their affinities for Americanization, see above, chapter 1.

14. For a brief history of the Jewish Endeavor Society, see Gurock's "The Jewish Endeavor Society," in *Jewish American Voluntary Organizations*, Michael Dobkowski, ed. (Westport, Conn., 1986), pp. 228–231.

15. The United Synagogue of America, *Report of the Second Annual Meeting* 11914), pp. 17–20, indicates that there were twenty-four charter-member congregations in the USA, not sixteen as Glazer suggested; Joseph P. Shultz, ed., *Mid-America's Promise: A Profile of Kansas City Jewry* (Kansas City, 1982), p. 19: Stuart E. Rosenberg, *The Jewish Community in Rochester, 1843–1925* (New York, 1954), p. 169ff.; Samuel P. Abelow, History of *Brooklyn Jewry* (Brooklyn, 1937), pp. 78–79; Alter Landesman, *Brownsville: The Birth. Development and Passing of a Jewish Community in New York* (New York, 1969), p. 214.

16. Allen Dupont Breck, *The Centennial History of the Jews of Colorado, 1859–1969* (Denver, 1969), pp. 88–90; Michael W. Rubinoff, "C. E. B. Kauvar: A Sketch of a Colorado Rabbi's Life," *Western States Jewish Historical Quarterly* (July 1978): 293.

17. *AH*, January 10, 1913, p. 303, *HS*, Jamuary 12, 1913, p. 9. Rosenthal, Young Israel's first president, was JTS class of 1913. Sachs, Young Israel's second president, was JTS class of 1915. See *Jewish Theological Seminary Student Annual* (1914), pp. 50–51, and (1915), pp. 51–52, all quoted by Shulamith Berger, "The Early History of the Young Israel Movement," typescript (YIVO Institute for Jewish Research, Fall 1982). See also *HS*, September 29, 1916, p. 8.

18. *HS*, January 18, 1918, p. 9.

19. Jeffrey S. Gurock, *When Harlem Was Jewish, 1870–1930* (New York, 1979), p. 135ff.; *YT*, July 19, 1915, p. 8; July 21, 1915, p. 8.

20. To be sure, exact figures on the number of congregants affiliated with each movement are nonexistent. We do have an exact count of the congregations in the USA for 1929; see The United Synagogue of America, *Report of the 17th Annual Convention* (1929). The USA did not report the number in the 1930s and early 1940s. Orthodox Union figures were compiled from the appearance of members' names in the *Orthodox Union*, which ran from 1933–1946. For example, in 1933 the paper reported a convention of Orthodox synagogues on Long Island at the Far Rockaway Jewish Center (note the term Jewish *Center*) attended by 19 member congregations. A factor which must be considered in making such calculations is the fact that a number of synagogues which were members of USA in 1929 appear as members of the OU in the 1930s. This means that synagogues either drifted back and forth between movements or held dual memberships. Statistics on the Young Israel movement are derived from a pamphlet, *Young Israel: Its Aims and Activities* (1935?). For a broader analysis of these trends, see below, chapter 14.

21. *OU*, January 1935), p. 1.

Notes to Chapter 11, *Time, Place and Movement in Immigrant Jewish Historiography*

1. For a comprehensive examination of the outlook of the Chicago school, with particular reference to its affinity for Progressive-assimilationist thought, see

Fred Matthews, "Louis Wirth and American Ethnic Studies: The World View of the Enlightened Assimilationist," in *The Jews of North America*, ed. Moses Rischlin (Detroit, 1987), pp. 123–143, esp. pp. 123–129.

2.   On the geography of New York City from the seventeenth to the late nineteenth century, see Charles Lookwood, *Manhattan Moves Uptown: An Illustrated History* (Boston, 1976), pp. xvii–xxi and *passim*; Bayard Still, *Mirror for Gotham* (New York, 1956), pp. 78–125, 205–257; Ira Rosenwaike, *Population History of New York City* (Syracuse, 1972), pp. 81–88.

3.   For a graphic description of the Lower East Side as a slum area, see Robert De Forest and Lawrence Veiller, eds., *The Tenement House Problem: Including the Report of the New York State Tenement House Committee of 1900* (New York, 1903), pp. 69–118 and *passim*, see also pp. 131–134 for a discussion of Chicago conditions.

4.   Burton I. Hendrick, "The Jewish Invasion," *HS*, February 15, 1907, p. 14; Ernst W. Burgess, "Residential Segregation in American Cities," *Annals of the American Academy of Political and Social Sciences* 42 (1923): pp. 105–107 idem, "The Growth of the City: An Introduction to a Research Project," in Robert E. Park, Ernst W. Burgess, and Roderick D. McKenzie, *The City* (Chicago, 1925), pp. 47–67.

5.   Robert E. Park and Ernst W. Burgess, *Introduction to the Social Sciences, including an Index to Basic Sociological Concepts* (Chicago, 1921), pp. 229, 311–315; "Behind Our Masks," *Survey Graphics*, May 1926, p. 135; Robert E. Park and Herbert A. Miller, *Old World Traits Transplanted* (New York, 1921), pp. 203–205. See also the work of Paul Frederick Cressey, another member of the Chicago school, "Population Succession in Chicago, 1898–1930," *American Journal of Sociology*, July 1938, p. 61.

6.   Louis Wirth, *The Ghetto* (Chicago, 1928), pp. 105, 222, 226

7.   Israel Abrahams, *Jewish Life in the Middle Ages* (London, 1895), pp. 16, 309, 340. See also Abrahams, *Jewish Life Under Emancipation* (London, 1917), p. 46 and *passim*; idem, "The Spiritual Zionism of 'One of Our People,'" *Jewish Chronicle*, May 25, 1906, p. 46; idem, "Palestine and Jewish Nationality," *Hibbert Journal*, April 1918, pp. 445–465; David Philipson. *Old European Jewries* (Philadelphia, 1894), pp. 21–22, 195–196, 199–201. See also idem, *The Reform Movement in Judaism* (New York, 1917).

8.   Bernard Weinryb, "Jewish Immigration and Accommodation to America Research Trends and Problems," *PAJHS* (1957): 366.

9.   For a discussion of the early stages in American Jewish historiography see Jeffrey S. Gurock, *American Jewish History: A Bibliographical Guide* (New York, 1983) pp. xv–xviii See also Peter Wiernick, *History of the Jews in America from the Discovery of the New World Until the Present Day* (New York, 1912)

10.   Abraham Cahan, *The Rise of David Levinsky* (New York, 1917).

11.   Horace P. Kallen, *Judaism at Bay: Essays Towards the Adjustment of Judaism to Modernity* (New York, 1932); idem, *Cultural Pluralism and the American Idea: An Essay in Social Philosophy* (Philadelphia, 1956).

12.   Marshall Sklare, *Conservative Judaism: An American Religious Movement* (Glenece, Ill., 1955), pp. 47–83, esp. 47, 5762, 66–72; Will Herberg, *Protestant-Catho-*

lic-Jew: An Essay in American Religious Sociology (Garden City, N.Y., 1955), pp. 172–211, 239, 242, 245, 262.

13. Moses Rischin, *The Promised City: New York's Jews, 1870–1914* (Cambridge, 1962), pp. 78–94 and *passim*. On Rischin's critique of Wirth, see idem. "Responsa," *AJH*, December 1983, pp. 192–193, and his introduction to the John Harvard republication of Hotchins Hapgood's *The Spirit of the Ghetto* (Cambridge, 1967), pp. xxix-xxx. On Rischin, Handlin, and their ultimate spiritual mentor, Hansen see Rischin, "Marcus Lee Hansen: America's First Trans-Ethnic Historian," in Richard L. Bushman, ed. *Uprooted Americans: Essays in Honor of Oscar Handlin* (Boston, 1979). See also Deborah Dash Moore, "The Ideal Slum," *AJH*, December 1983, pp. 136–137, and idem. "The Construction of Community," in Rischin, *The Jews of North America*, pp. 106–107

14. Gurock, *When Harlem Was Jewish* (New York, 1979), pp. 30–40, 53–57. See also Stephen Thernstrom, *Poverty and Progress: Social Mobility in A Nineteenth Century City* (New York, 1970), pp. 85, 198–199; Clyde Griffin, "Workers Divided: Craft and Ethnic Differences in Poughkeepsie," in Thernstrom and Richard Sennet, eds., *Nineteenth Century Cities* (New Haven, 1969), pp. 59–131.

15. Sklare, pp. 43–48.

16. Judah David Eisenstein, "The History of the First Russian-American Jewish Congregation: The Beth Hamedrash Hagodol" *PAJHS* 9 (1901): 64–72.

17. *Ibid.*, p. 72; Abraham J. Karp, "New York Chooses a Chief Rabbi," *PAJHS* 44, no. 3 (March 1954): 129–198.

18. Gerard Wolfe and Jo Renee Fine, *The Synagogues of New York's Lower East Side* (New York, 1978), pp. 43–97; Jonathan D. Sarna, trans. and edt, *People Walk on Their Heads: Moses Weinberger's Jews and Judaism in New York* (New York, 1982), pp. 13–14.

19. Eisenstein, pp. 69, 73–74.

20. See above, chapter 2.

21. On the periodization of American Jewish history, see Samuel Joseph, *Jewish Immigration to the United States from 1881 to 1910* (New York, 1914); Jacob Rader Marcus, "The Periodization of American Jewish History," *PAJHS* (1958), pp. 125–133; Jeanette Meisel Baron, ed., *Steeled by Adversity: Essays and Addresses on American Jewish Life by Salo Wittmayer Baron* (Philadelphia, 1971), pp. 276–277.

22. See above, chapter 9 and Chapter 10.

23. See above, chapter 1 and Chapter 7. See also Jeffrey S. Gurock, *The Men and Women of Yeshiva: Higher Education Orthodoxy and American Judaism* (New York, 1988), pp. 18–43; Bernard Drachman, *The Unfailing Light: Memories of an American Rabbi* (New York, 1948); Herbert S. Goldstein, *Forty Years of Struggle for a Principle: The Biography of Harry Fischel* (New York, 1928).

Notes to Chapter 12, *A Stage in the Emergence of the Americanized Synagogue Among East European Jews*

1. Americanized synagogues, bearing the trappings and possessing the presence, style and decorum characteristic of the 1920s, which will be presently dis-

cussed. clearly predate that era. In fact. Americanized synagogues date hack to the eighteenth and nineteenth centuries, and their emergence corresponds closely to the earlier cycles of American Jewish immigration. In other words, it may be argued that during each of the Sephardic (1654–c. 1830), Central European (c. 1830–1881) and East European periods (1881–1920), Jews first founded synagogues that reflected their Old World roots. Then, over the course of time, as Jews made their social adjustments to this country, American synagogues emerged within that group reflecting the heightened social and economic status of communicants.

Often the Americanization of synagogues has been depicted as synonymous with the denominational liberalization of services. Namely, the least American of congregations, reflecting most the European mores of members, have been characterized as Orthodox. As members adjusted further to America they have been seen as adopting Conservative or Reform orientations. And while many synagogues and individuals did follow that straight line progression, more recent scholarship has shown that both in the nineteenth century as in the twentieth century—as will be presently indicated—not all Americanizing Jews, or Americanizing congregations moved straight towards liberalization of their religious orientation. In many instances. there were delays of generations among both people and institutions and in some cases, denominational change never took place. Accordingly, both in the nineteenth and twentieth century non-European style Orthodox congregations existed in this country that deviated from European social patterns without changing their denominational labels. In fact, a more useful way of categorizing congregations is to differentiate among varying types of American and non-American congregations. This article suggests stages, and focusses on one stage in the emergence of the Americanized synagogue among East European Jews. For treatments which utilize strongly the denominational designations for understanding congregational emergence see: Moshe Davis, *The Emergence of Conservative Judaism: The Historical School in 19th Century America* (Philadelphia, 1965) and Nathan Glazer, *American Judaism* (Chicago, 1957). For a pathbreaking view of nineteenth century Americanized v. non-Americanized synagogues that notes delays in the movement from Orthodoxy towards liberal Judaism in America see: Leon Jick, *The Americanization of the Synagogue, 1820–1870* (Hanover, N.H., 1976). See also more recent studies that draw upon Jick's model: Jeffrey S. Gurock, "The Orthodox Synagogue," and Jack Wertheimer, "The Conservative Synagogue" in *The History of the Synagogue in America*, ed. Jack Wertheimer (New York, 1988). On the standard periodization of American Jewish history and the East European period in particular see; Samuel Joseph, *Jewish Immigration to the United States from 1881 to 1910* (New York, 1914); Jacob Rader Marcus, "The Periodization of American Jewish History," *PAJHS*, 77 (March 1958), pp. 125–133; Jeanette Meisel Baron, ed., *Steeled by Adversity: Essays and Addresses on American Jewish Life by Solo Wittmayer Baron* (Philadelphia, 1971), pp. 276–277.

Of course, having noted 1881 as the "start" of the East European period, it should be emphasized that East European Jewish life and religious life clearly predate 1881. Intact, the earliest distinctive East European congregation, New York's

Beth Hamidrash, the antecedent of the more famous Beth Hamedrosh Hagodol, was founded in 1852. Indeed there were at least twenty East European congregations in America by 1880. By 1890, some of these congregations were showing proto-American characteristics. To be sure, there were East European Jews praying in this country before 1850. But prior to that time, Russian Jews, if they were synagogue-goers, attended congregations conducted along Central European. though increasingly Americanized, lines. See Gurock, "The Orthodox Synagogue," pp. 43–47 and notes.

Finally, the term *shtibl*, though usually applied to post-World War II immigrant Orthodox synagogue culture, dates back to at least the turn of the century. Eisenstein, for example, used it to describe his congregation. although he spelled it *stuebel*. See Judah David Eisenstein, "The History of the First Russian-American Jewish Congregation: The Beth Hamedrosh Hagodol," *PAJHS* 9 (1901): 69. See also Abraham J. Karp's important study of East European *landsmanshaft* style synagogue life, "An East European Congregation on American Soil Beth Israel Rochester New York 1874–1886," in *A Bicentennial Festschrift for Jacob Rader Marcus*, ed. Bertram W. Korn (Watham, Mass. and New York, 1976) pp. 263–303

2.   Although these types of synagogues looked to the outside world and were preceived by most of their attendees as transplanted institutions from Europe, to some very religious authorities American *shtibls* were in fact quasi-American institutions. One most articulate critics, Rabbi Moses Weinberger. objected to the power relationships and governance procedures in these *shuls*. See Jonathan D. Sarna, trans. and ed.. *People Walk on their Heads: Moses Weinberger's Jews and Judaism in New York* (New York and London, 1981), pp. 43–44.

3.   Eisenstein, "History of the First," pp. 64–72.

4.   The proliferation of *landsmanshaft* synagogues continued unabated up to World War I and the effective close of immigration. So great was the splintering of New York's religious Jewish community. for example, into this myriad of regional and local congregations that by 1917 the New York Kehillah could estimate that there were approximately 730 Orthodox synagogues in the city. the vast majority East European. See *Jewish Communal Register* (New York, 1917), pp. 117–121 and *passim*.

5.   My emphasis here is on the commonality rather than the differences in format and structure of the interwar synagogues attended by East Europeans whether they or later scholars designated them as Conservative or Orthodox. See Marshall Sklare, *Conservative Judaism: An American Religious Movement* (New York, 1972), pp. 92, 93, 105, 110. On the architecture and social structure of these synagogues see, Deborah Dash Moore. *At Home in America: Second Generation New York Jews* (New York, 1981), pp. 135–139.

See also Harry G. Fromberg, "The Tremendous Triumph of East Side Young Jewry in Religious Revival," *HS*, January 18, 1918, p. 9. *Jewish Center Bulletin*, October. 1935; and "For Dignity and Decorum at Religious Services," *The Orthodox Union* (December–January 1939–1940), p. 2. All are discussed in Jenna W. Joselit, "Of Manners, Morals and Orthodox Judaism: Decorum Within the Orthodox Synagogue," in *Ramaz: School, Community, Scholarship and Orthodoxy*, ed. Jeffrey S. Gurock (Hoboken, N.J., 1989), pp. 15–16.

6.   See Sklare. *Conservative Judaism*, pp. 67–72. for the most widely accepted periodization and locating of the rise of the twentieth century Americanized synagogue.

7.   See Gurock. "The Jewish Endeavor Society." in *Jewish American Voluntary Organizations*. ed. Michael Dobkowski (Westport. Conn., 1987). pp. 228–231; "A Generation Unaccounted for in *American Judaism*," *AJH*, 77 (December 1987): 251–259, "From Exception to Role Model: Bernard Drachman and the Evolution of Jewish Religious Life in America. 1880–1920." *AJH*, 76 (June 1987): 477–478, 480–484.

8.   For Eisenstein's statement on "reformers" see Eisenstein, "History of the First." p. 71.

9.   There is a disagreement in the sources as to the date of founding of the synagogue and its original ethnic character. Gerard Wolfe and Jo Rene Fine in *The Synagogues of New York's Lower East Side* (New York, 1978), p. 43 date the synagogue from 1856 and see it as home originally for Polish-Russian Jews. They also discuss the costs of building the 1887 sanctuary. Other sources. however, say it was founded somewhat later by Rumanian Jews. The Yiddish newspaper. *YT*, August 8, 1899, p. 5 suggests the synagogue was founded in the mid-1870s. Its contemporary, *Morgan Zhurnal* frequently referred to the synagogue as the Yasir synagogue. i.e.. from the town of Jassy. Rumania. This Rumanian influence is also seen in the legal name of the congregation, Kehal Adath Jeshurun M'Yassy. See *Congregation Kehal Adath Jeshurun M'Yassy v. Universal Building and Construction Co.*, New York State Supreme Court. Special Term, Pt. 4, January 21, 1910.

10.   Minutes, 12–16 Eldridge Street, New York, 1890–1916, April 27, 1891, December 13, 1891; January 1, 1893; April 15, 1894; April 24, 1894.

11.   Of the occupations listed for members and prospective members of the synagogue between 1890 and 1915. some 46 in all, 13 were businessmen, 5 manufacturers, 13 storekeepers, four bakers, one carpenter, one doctor and one lawyer. Though these occupational designations are not as reliable as census reports, they do indicate that a good proportion of members were white-collar workers and few blue-collar workers. At the same time there are clear indications that some of the synagogue's members were—or were occasionally—poor. See Minutes, April 30, 1894. for an example of the synagogue extending a low-cost loan to a member. For a discussion of the cost of living on the Lower East Side at the time see Moses Rischin, *The Promised City: New York's Jews, 1870–1914* (Cambridge, Mass., 1962). pp.79–80. See also Edward A. Steiner, "The Russian and Polish Jews in New York," *Outlook*, November 1902, p. 532. On the selling and willing of synagogue seats see Minutes, October 26, 1890; January 11, 1891; October 27, 1897.

12.   See Joseph, *Jewish Immigration, passim;* Marcus, "The Periodization," pp. 125–133; Jeanette Meisel Baron, ed., *Steeled bv Adversity*, pp. 276–277.

13.   For Cohen's biography see. *Morgen Zhurnal*, April 21, 1911, p. ld.

14.   For Gellis' biography see. the *New York Times*, March 23, 1906. p. 9. and the *Hebrew Standard*, March 30, 1906, p. 5

15. For Yarmulovsky's biography, see Eisenstein. *Ozar Zichronothai* (New York: 1929). p. 123.

16. Minutes, February 25, 1891; September 6, 1893; October 22, 1893 for examples of these attempts at decorum.

17. Minutes, October 4, 1897.

18. Minutes, October 18, 1897.

19. Minutes, April 1, 1896.

20. Minutes, January 2, 1899. See a comparable incident in the Minutes, December 7, 1890.

21. Minutes, February 14, 1915.

22. Eisenstein. "History of the First." p. 69: Minutes, February 25, 1891.

23. Minutes, January 17, 1892.

24. Minutes, December 7, 1890; January 11, 1891; January 13, 1891; January 5, 1892; August 13, 1893; May 24, 1896; August 15, 1897.

25. Minutes, August 11, 1901.

26. Congregation Ohab Zedek, *Golden Jubilee. 1873–1923* (New York. 1923). np.; Eisenstein, "History of the First. pp. 69–74; Abraham J. Karp. New York Chooses a Chief Rabbi," *PAJHS* (March 1955), pp. 129–198.

27. Karp, "East European Congregation." pp. 136, 190. Minutes, December 27, 1892.

28. Minutes, March 9, 1891; March 18, 1891; March 30, 1892. It is evident from looking at the dates of the few references in the minutes to Rabbi Joseph that Kehal Adath Jeshurun was quick to jump off the chief rabbi's bandwagon as the flawed experiment in rabbinical power in New York began to fail. Rabbi Joseph lived ten more years after he was mentioned in the minutes.

29. Minutes, February 2, 1905; April 12, 1905.

30. Minutes, February 2, 1905; April 12, 1905; May 23, 1905; April 14, 1907.

31. Minutes, April 12, 1905. I am grateful to my colleague, Dr. Jonathan D. Sarna for pointing out that the congregation's ban on Rabbi Rivkind possibly did not have to do with honoraria but rather with the synagogue's concern about writs of divorce issued without civil divorce a matter that brought the Jewish community into disrepute.

32. Minutes, December 20, 1906.

33. Minutes, January 30, 1907; August 1, 1909; April 14, 1907; July 5, 1914.

34. Minutes, March 1, 1891; April 26, 1891; August 28, 1892; June 3, 1894; May 26, 1895; June 16, 1895; June 5, 1897; January 30, 1898; September 30, 1901; October 2, 1901; April 15, 1903; May 3, 1903; January 20, 1907.

35. *AH,* January 16, 1903, p. 295.

36. On Yarmulovsky's involvement with Rabbi Jacob Joseph's selection see note 31. See *AH,* January 4, 1901, pp. 231–234 for information on Yarmulovsky's involvement in the Orthodox Union's leadership. His affinity for American values even as he supported the failed Rabbi Joseph is revealed in his participation in the early Jewish Theological Seminary of America. Others like him include Eisenstein, Harry Fischel, Jonas Weil and Kasriel Sarasohn—all young, new elite members of

proto-American synagogues who rose beyond their institutional protocols and proclivities.

Notes to Chapter 13, *Consensus Building and Conflict over Creating the Young People's Synagogue of the Lower East Side*

1.   "Religious Centers Downtown," *AH*, February S, 1904, 391; "Young People's Synagogue," *AH*, April 5, 1901, 596; "The Problem of the Ghetto," *HS*, May
9, 1902, 6. For a biographical sketch of Solomon, see *AJYB* 5665 (1904–5): 224.

2.   Bernard Drachman, *The Unfailing Light: Memoirs of an American Rabbi* (New
York, 1948), 225.

3.   For listings of JES hoard members, chairmen, and enumerations of those
who spoke before the group, see *Prospectus of Lectures Offered to the Public by the Jewish Endeavor Society* (1900–1901), (1902–1903), (1904–1905), (1905–1906),
(1907–1908) (Library of the American Jewish Historical Society). An examination
of the *Register of the Jewish Theological Seminary of America* (1903–1904), (1904–
1905), (1907–1908), (1909–1910) indicates that at least twenty-one of the forty-
six identifiable leaders of the JES between 1900 and 1910 were Seminary students.
Most of the men were rabbinical students. A few of the men and all of the women
were students around 1902 of a Seminary Teacher's Course, which seems to have
been an early coeducational incarnation of the Seminary's Teachers Institute.

4.   Kleiser's teaching position is noted in *AJYB* 5664 (1903–4): 145. For a
short biography of Harris and a description of the stance of his congregation, see
Gurock, *When Harlem Was Jewish, 1870–1930* (New York, 1979), 19–20, 94, 96;
see *AJYB* 5664 (1903–1904): 93, for a biographical sketch of Schulman.

5.   Elias L. Solomon, "To the American Hebrew," *AH*, January 29, 1904, 349.

6.   For the Emanu-El Brotherhood's initial statement of purpose, see its "Circular: Emanu-El Brotherhood, Its Aims and Purpose Taken from the Emanu-El Brotherhood Minute Book Board of Trustees Minutes, November 15, 1903," as published
in Myron Berman, "A New Spirit on the East Side: The Early History of the Emanu-
El Brotherhood, 1903–1920," *AJHQ* (September 1964): appendix 1, 78. For reports
on Silverman's quick change in plans, see *AH*, February 5, 1904, 378. The Singer
prayerbook to which reference has been made was *The Standard Prayer Book with
Authorized English Translation* by the Reverend S. Singer, first published in England
in 1890 and authorized by the Chief Rabbi, Dr. Nathan Marcus Adler. It offers the
complete Orthodox rendering of the prayers with a page-by-page English translation. For a brief history of the Singer prayerbook, see Vivian Silverman, "The Cente-
nary of the Singer Siddur," *Journal of Jewish Music and Liturgy* (5751–5752/1990–
1991): 43–45.

7.   "Religious Centers Downtown," *AH*, February 5, 1904, 391. On downtown, and particularly Orthodox Union, opposition to Christian influence among
immigrants and their children, see above, chapter 6.

8.   "Jewish Endeavor Society," *AH*, November 11, 1901, 660; "Jewish
Endeavor Society," *AH*, January 24, 1902, 313; "Jewish Endeavor Society," *AH*,

February 7, 1902, 375; Arnold Eiseman, "Letter to the Editor," *AH*, November 16, 1903, 298.

9. "Should Act Wisely," *YT*, April 22, 1904, 8.

10. Elias L. Solomon, "Letter to the Editor," *AH*, January 29, 1904, 349.

11. "Who Are the Unchurched," *AH*, January29, 1904, 346. For a discussion of Orthodox Jewish difficulties in Europe with the use of vernacular in the prayers, see Jakob J. Petuchowski, *Prayerbook Reform in Europe* (New York, 1968), 92–94.

12. "Religious Work Downtown," *AH*, February 5, 1904, 384.

13. Mordecai M. Kaplan, *Journal*, vol. 15 (unpublished diaries, Jewish Theological Seminary of America), September 17, 1950.

14. Jenna Weissman Joselit has pointed out that the often-combative Willowski not only wrote about the evil of English-language sermons, an opinion that was finally published in his *She'elot* in 1908, but also, at the very time of Endeavorer activities (circa 1904), when "invited to attend High Holiday services. . . he insisted on delivering the sermon himself" (in Yiddish). See Joselit, "What Happened to New York's Jewish Jews: Moses Rischin's *The Promised City* Revisited," *AJH* (December 1983): 168. On Willowski's activities and statements, see Jacob David Willowski, *She'elot u-Teshuvot Bet Ridbaz* (Jerusalem, 1908), 11, as quoted and discussed in Aaron Rothkoff, "The American Sojourns of Ridbaz: Religious Problems with the Immigrant Community," *AJHQ* (June 1968): 561–62.

15. "Fanaticism Run Wild," *YT*, April 29, 1903, 8; "A Word of Caution," *AH*, May 13, 1904, 794; Judah David Eisenstein, "The Orthodox Rabbis and the Seminary," *AH*, July 1, 1904, 180.

16. Judah David Eisenstein, "The Orthodox Rabbis and the Seminary," *AH*, July 1, 1904, 180. For specific criticism of the JES earlier on for inviting "Reform ministers" to their meetings, see Yehudi, "Our Duty to Our Faith," *HS*, November 1, 1901, 11.

17. "Jewish Endeavor Society," *YT*, November 2, 1903, 8; "Interaction of Uptown and Downtown," *AH*, March 21, 1902, 840; "A Remedy for Disgraceful Synagogues," *AH*, October 17, 1902, 608.

18. Joseph Silverman, "Religious Work of the Emanu-El Brotherhood," *AH*, February 5, 1904, 384; Elias L. Solomon, "The Endeavorers and the Brotherhood," *AH*, February 12, 1904, 416.

19. An East Sider, "Endeavorers and the Brotherhood," *AH*, March 19, 1904, 443.

20. "Young People's Synagogue," *AH*, April 8, 1904, 683.

21. "Young People's Synagogue," *AH*, April 8, 1904, 683. For a background sketch on Isaac S. Isaac's personal and institutional relationship to Reform Judaism, see *AJYB* 5665 (1904–5): 122. The importance of Mr. Bullowa on the committee may have indicated that it was he who ultimately reported the committee decision to the floor of the meeting.

22. "Young People's Synagogue," *AH*, April 8, 1904, 663; Berman, "A New Spirit on the East Side," 79.

23. See "Circular," in Berman, "A New Spirit on the East Side," 79. See also the interview with Louis Rosensweig summarized in Berman, 67.

24. "The Emanuel Brotherhood," *AH*, January 7, 1910, 265.
25. "Young People's Synagogue," *AH*, April 8, 1904, 663
26. "Jewish Endeavor Society" *AH*, April 4, 1905, 645
27. "Jewish Endeavor Society," *AH*, April 14, 1905, 645, 648.
28. "Do Something Quickly," *YT*, October 20, 1903, 8.
29. Jewish Endeavor Society, *Prospectus of Lectures* (1907–1908), 1–4.
30. Drachman, *The Unfailing Light*, 226.
31. For biographical data on Solomon, see *Register* (1904–1905), (1913–14), *AJYB* 5665 (1904–1905): 224; *UJE*, vol. 9, 640. Other important Endeavorers, most of whom became leaders of the United Synagogue, the Rabbinical Assembly, and, ultimately, the Conservative movement, include rabbis Herman Abramowitz, Charles Kauvar, Phineas Israeli, Aaron Drucker, Aaron Abelson, Israel Goldfarb, Jacob Dolgenas, Louis Egleson, Aaron Eiseman, and, of course, Mordecai M. Kaplan. Another well-known Endeavorer was Gabriel Davidson, who became executive director of the Jewish Agricultural Society. Biographical information on these important men's later careers is noted in Drachman's memoir and is available in the Seminary's frequent *Registers*, with the 1931–1932 (5692) *Register* being particularly useful. Unfortunately, to date I have been unable to track the later post-Endeavorer activities of the some fourteen women listed as leaders between 1900 and 1910. Most likely, if they pursued Jewish careers, they did so in the field of Jewish education, but there is no comparable listing of teachers from which information may be gleaned.
32. "For a Jewish Revival," *AH*, January 10, 1913, 303, quoted from Shulamith Berger, "Youth Synagogues in New York, 1910–1913" (seminar paper, YIVO Institute, 1981); Stephen S. Wise, *Challenging Years: The Autobiography of Stephen Wise* (New York, 1949), 102.
33. On the type of service held at the Free Synagogue, see Wise, *Challenging Years*, 103; and Melvin I. Urofsky, *A Voice That Spoke for Justice: The Life and Times of Stephen S. Wise* (Albany, 1982), 63. It should be noted that ephemeral youth-oriented Orthodox synagogues appeared during the hiatus between the JES and the Young Israel. Modern Talmud Torahs conducted youth services and the New York Kehillah toyed with the idea of "model synagogue programs. See above, chapter 2. The origins of the version that the rise of Young Israel is linked to Rabbi Wise's activities is based on two relatively late sources, *Young Israel Synagogue Reporter,* Fiftieth Anniversary Edition (New York, 1962) and David Stein, "East Side Chronicle," *Jewish Life* (January–February 1966): 31. This version was later repeated in Irving Howe, *World of Our Fathers: the Journey of the East European Jews to America and the Life They Found and Made* (New York, 1976), 197. Howe added the suggestion that the young people were drawn to Wise's eloquence. Urofsky, 64, tells the same story, relying on Howe. An earlier source on the Young Israel's origins is Hyman Goldstein, "History of the Young Israel Movement," *Jewish Forum* (December 1926): 529–30; Goldstein indicates that the primary sources make no reference to Wise's activities.

Notes to Chapter 14, *The Winnowing of American Orthodoxy*

1.   Charles S. Liebman, "Orthodoxy in American Jewish Life," *AJYB* (1965), pp. 34–36. Liebman identified non-observant Orthodox in the mid-1960s as members of Orthodox synagogues who showed no commitment to Jewish law, and he touched on some of the motivations keeping them in the Orthodox synagogue. Some are attracted by a famous rabbi or congregation. Others find nostalgic satisfaction in the old-style synagogue. Still others are unhappy with the perceived "coldness" of the more liberal services. This paper discusses the history of this significant contingent of synagogue-goers.

2.   By 1917, the New York Kehillah estimated that there were approximately 730 synagogues in New York City alone, most of them of the *landsmanshaft* variety. For a short treatment of the complex history of the social, cultural and religious role played by the *landsmanshaft* synagogue, see *Di Yiddishe Landsmanshaften fun New York* (New York, 1938). Even as Jews broke with the social-religious system which supported the immigrant synagogue, this continued affinity for the old style services came to the fore—as we will presently see—in the form of opposition to innovation within Orthodoxy. Finally, much has been written both in memoirs and in the scholarly literature about the disaffection of Jews from their traditions as part of the Americanization process. For the best primer on the subject see Moses Rischin's classic, *The Promised City* (Cambridge, 1963), especially the chapters entitled, "Tradition at Half-Mast" and the "Great Awakening." See also Nathan Glazer's *American Judaism* (New York, 1957), pp. 60–78.

3.   On attempts to recreate European conditions on American soil, see Abraham J. Karp, "New York Chooses a Chief Rabbi," *PAJHS* 44 (March 1955), pp. 129–198. See also Jonathan D. Sarna's important translation of Rabbi Moses Weinberger's protest against the demise of traditional behavior, *People Walk on their Heads: Moses Weinberger's Jews and Judaism in New York*, (New York and London: 1901) and Aaron Rothkoff, "The American Sojourns of the Ridbaz: Religious Problems Within the Immigrant Community," *AJHQ* 57, June 1968: 555–572.

4.   See Glazer's chapter "Judaism and Jewishness, 1920–1945," pp. 79–106 for the most articulate explanation of that tradition.

5.   Marshall Sklare, *Conservative Judaism: An American Religious Movement* (New York: 1954), pp. 66–128; Will Herberg, *Protestant-Catholic-Jew: An Essay in American Religious Sociology* (New York 1955), pp. 186–195; United Synagogue of America, *Report of the 17th Annual Convention* (May 19–21, 1929), pp. 14–16.

6.   For the best account both of the migration patterns of second generation Jews out of the inner city and towards suburbia in this nation's largest metropolis and of the levels of ethnic group persistence as opposed to assimilation achieved by these Jews, see Deborah Dash Moore, *At Home in America: Second Generation New York Jews* (New York, 1981).

7.   On the history of the Endeavorers see, Bernard Drachman, *The Unfailing Light: Memories of an American Rabbi* (New York, 1948), pp. 255ff; *HS*, October 18, 1904, p. 4; *AH*, January 4, 1901, p. 233; January 18, 1901, p. 284; February 8, 1901, p. 379; April 5, 1901, p. 596. On the founding of the Young Israel, see *AH*, January 10, 1913, p. 303; *HS*, January 12, 1913, p. 9. See also *Jewish Theological*

Seminary Student Annual (1914), pp. 50–51 and (1915), pp. 51–52, all quoted from and utilized in Shulamith Berger's "The Early History of the Young Israel Movement," (unpublished typescript seminar paper, YIVO Institute, Fall 1982). On the organizing of the Institutional Synagogue, see Jeffrey S. Gurock's *When Harlem Was Jewish, 1870–1930* (New York: 1979), pp. 135ff.

8.   One of the most imaginative ways in which the Endeavorers and Young Israel met the religious preferences of their prospective members was their emphasis on Sabbath afternoon services as their "key" service of the week, a service often followed by a lecture and/or social activity. The young synagogue leaders recognized that many of their potential communicants worked during the day and could only attend an evening service.

9.   Rothkoff, pp. 561–562; *AH*, September 30, 1904, 516; *HS*, October 7, 1904, p. 7, as derived from Jenna Weissman Joselit, "What Happened to New York's Jewish Jews," Moses Rischin's The *Promised City* Revisited," *AJH* 73, (December 1983): 163–172; *AH*, January 16, 1903, p. 295.

10.   Gilbert Klaperman, *The Story of Yeshiva University: The First Jewish University in America* (London, 1969); Rothkoff, *Bernard Revel: Builder of American Jewish Orthodoxy* (Philadelphia, 1972) pp. 43–71; *The Rabbi Isaac Elchanan Theological Seminary Register* 5605 (1924–25), (New York, 1925).

11.   That each of these issues posed real problems for the American Orthodox synagogues and their rabbis is evidenced by the fact that questions on each of these concerns were submitted by members of the Rabbinical Council of America (the organization of Americanized, English-speaking rabbis, founded in 1935) to their Standards and Rituals Committee or to their Halacha Commission from 1935 through 1950s. See Louis Bernstein, *Challenge and Mission: The Emergence of the English Speaking Orthodox Rabbinate* (New York, 1982), pp. 39–51 and *passim*.

12.   *OU*, April 1943, p. 5; April 1925, p. 11, for discussions by rabbis in the field of the low level commitment exhibited by their rank and file members. Significantly, contemporary rabbis outside of New York often contrasted the poverty of their pulpit life with that of the metropolis. The statistics on the number of Orthodox Union synagogues are derived from the listings of member organizations published in its organ, *The Orthodox Union*, a valuable source for the social and institutional history of inter-war Orthodoxy, published 1933–1946. See specifically *OU*, July 1937, p. 2, for its boast of numerical predominance. To be sure, exact figures on the number of congregations affiliated with each denomination are simply not available. However, as far as numbers of congregations are concerned, we have an exact account of the Conservative United Synagogue of America for 1929 in the aforementioned *Report of the 17th Annual Convention* (1927).

13.   In 1935 the *OU* noted the calling of a convention of Orthodox synagogues on Long Island (which included Queens) at the Far Rockaway Jewish Center attended by its nineteen member congregations. See *OU*, October 1935, p. 7. Statistics on the New York-based Young Israel Movement are derived from a *circa* 1935 pamphlet, *Young Israel: Its Aims and Activities*, published by its National Council. In figuring denomination affiliation and strength, note also that a number of 1929 USA congregations appear in the OU as part of the Orthodox group. That means

that synagogues either drifted back and forth between movements or held dual affiliation.

This argument clearly differs from the interpretations of Sklare and others who see Conservatism winning out over Orthodoxy in the inter-war period. Conservative Judaism's numerical hegemony began, according to this present study, as a post-World War II phenomenon. Though clearly the Orthodoxy of many Orthodox synagogues may have been watered down during this prior era, that does not mean that Conservatism dominated institutionally. As one contemporary 1940s Orthodox rabbi explained: "It is doubtful whether the conservative synagogue has gained much in an organized way [in his city]." There has been unquestionably an upsurge of conservative sentiment in the very ranks of Orthodox congregations. See *OU*, April 1943, p. 5.

14.   See again the previously noted studies by Sklare and Herberg on the growth of these movements. It is suggested here that the periodization of the rise and "conquest" of American Judaism is a post-World War II phenomenon. I am also emphasizing here the significantly changed attitude towards liberal Judaism of third and fourth generation Jews as opposed to that of earlier generations.

15.   The strength—or lack or it—of Orthodoxy in three cities, Boston, Milwaukee and Providence, is indicated in Morris Axelrod, Floyd S. Fowler and Arnold Gurin, *A Community Study for Long Range Planning* (Boston, 1967); Albert J. Mayer, *Milwaukee Jewish Population Study* (Milwaukee, 1967); and Sidney Goldstein and Calvin Goldscheider, *Jewish Americans* (Englewood Cliffs, 1968). See also Harold W. Polsky, "A Study of Orthodoxy in Milwaukee; Social Characteristics, Beliefs and Observances, in Sklare, *The Jews: Social Characteristics of an American Group* (Glencoe, 1960), pp. 325–335.

16.   Liebman noted a generation ago another dramatic change in Orthodox synagogues, what we might call the clericalization of the Young Israel. Most Young Israel synagogues are today headed by rabbis. In its nascent stage, however, the Young Israel synagogue was known for its lay leadership. See Liebman, pp. 58–61.

17.   For a basic history of the growth of the Jewish day school movement over the last generation, see Alvin I. Schiff, *The Jewish Day School in America* (New York, 1966), pp. 40–86. And for an anthropological study of the backgrounds, attitudes and social dynamics of the Jews attending these new era American Orthodox synagogues where talmudic learning has become increasingly important, see Samuel Heilman, *Synagogue Life: A Study in Symbolic Interaction* (Chicago, 1973), and *The People of the Book: Drama, Fellowship and Religion* (Chicago, 1983).

Rabbi Moses Scherer, president of the Agudath Israel, summed up best the change in the educational orientation of Orthodox Jews from inter-war days to today: "When I was a youngster, it was very possible for someone to be an Orthodox Jew without continuing [intensive Jewish education] beyond elementary school.. Today it is unthinkable that one can really be an Orthodox Jew unless he had at least graduated Yeshiva high school." William B. Helmreich, "Old Wine in New Bottles: Advanced Yeshivot in the United States," *AJH* (December 1979): 243.

18. Israel Meir Ha-Kohen Kagan, *Niddehei Yisrael* (Warsaw, 1894), pp. 129–130; quoted in Aaron Rakeffet-Rothkoff, *The Silver Era in American Orthodoxy* (Jerusalem and New York, 1981), p. 18.

19. For interesting biographical, albeit hagiographical, sketches of the transplanted Yeshiva rabbis who rebuilt communities in America, see Nisson Wolpin, ed., *The Torah World: A Treasury of Biographical Sketches* (New York, 1982). On the settlement patterns and sociology of Hasidic groups, see Israel Robin, *Satmar: Island in the City* (New York, 1982) and Solomon Poll, *The Hasidic Community of Williamsburg* (New York, 1962). For a thoughtful and comprehensive study of the sociology and mind-set of the Yeshiva world—most importantly, the yeshiva's development and maintenance of its sense of cultural superiority—see Helmreich, *The World of the Yeshiva: An Intimate Portrait of Orthodox Jewry* (New York and London, 1982), pp. 300–331.

20. See Helmreich, pp. 220–238, for his important discussion of college education and the students of the yeshiva world. And see pp. 272–275 for a discussion of economic and demographic patterns within that group. Interestingly enough, though the new era Orthodox see themselves as resisting, if not merely unimpressed with, American societal phenomena and change, they have been consciously, or unconsciously, affected by American social patterns. The *eruv* issue is a case in point. The idea that families, and not just grown men, should go to services is an American religious phenomenon.

Notes to Chapter 15, *The Ramaz Version of American Orthodoxy*

1.   Joseph H. Lookstein, "Ramaz at Forty," *Annual Dinner Dance Sponsored by Parents Council, January 16, 1977* (1977), p. 1.

2.   "Sunday School Is Not Enough" (undated flyer announcing the opening of the Ramaz School, 1937?) (RA); Haskel Lookstein, "Looking Back and Ahead: A View of Ramaz at Age Forty-Five," *Forty-Fifth Annual Dinner Dance Sponsored by the Ramaz School, January 17, 1982* (1982), p. 1. For more on the location of Bund activities in the 1930s, see Ronald Bayor, *Neighbors in Conflict: The Irish, Germans, Jews and Italians of New York City, 1929–1941* (Baltimore and London, 1978), pp. 70–71.

3.   Haskel Lookstein, "To Kehilath Jeshurun with Love," *Ramaz School: Forty-Eighth Annual Dinner Dance Sponsored by the Parents Council, January 13, 1985* (1985), p. 3; Joseph H. Lookstein, "Ramaz at Forty," p. 3; see also the typescript memoirs of George Jacobs, 1987 p. 14, RA.

4.   On the affluent second-generation Jews and their attitudes towards Jewish education, see Jeffrey S. Gurock, *When Harlem Was Jewish, 1870–1930* (New York, 1979), pp. 105–106; Joseph H. Lookstein, "Ramaz at Forty," p. 2.

5.   Joseph H. Lookstein, "The Ramaz School: History and Evaluation," *Testimonial Dinner Tendered to Rabbi Joseph H. Lookstein by the Parents Council, April 7, 1946* (1946), p. 1; idem, "Ramaz at Forty," p. 2.

6.   Joseph H. Lookstein, "Ramaz at Forty," p. 11.

7.   Joseph H. Lookstein, "The Ramaz School: History and Evaluation," p. 2; idem, "Ramaz at Forty," p. 4.

8.   Joseph H. Lookstein, "Ramaz at Forty," pp. 2, 7–8.

9.   *Ibid.*, pp. 8–9; Joseph H. Lookstein, "Did You Know," *Twenty-One, 1937–1958* (1958), p. 2.; Haskel Lookstein, "Where We Are Now and Where We Are Headed," *Annual Dinner Dance Sponsored by Parents Council, January 1971(1971)*, p. 2.

10   Haskel Lookstein, "Where We Are and Where We Are Headed," p. 1; *RM*, December 1951, p. 2.

11.   Haskel Lookstein, "Remember," *Forty-Seventh Annual Dinner Dance Sponsored by the Parents Council, January 15, 1984* (1984), p. 3.

12.   Haskel Lookstein, "Where We Are Now and Where We Are Headed," p. 6; Joseph H. Lookstein, "Rabbi Haskel Lookstein: An Evaluation and a Tribute," *Ramaz School: Annual Dinner Dance Sponsored by the Parents Council, December 21, 1979*, pp. 5–6.

13.   Haskel Lookstein, "Remember," pp. 1–2.

14.   Emanuel Rackman, "Modern Orthodoxy's Goal: Synthesizing Two Cultures," *Jewish Week*, January 2, 1987, p. 20.

15.   Joseph H. Lookstein to S. Erdberg, June 8, 1937 (RA); Moses I. Shulman, "The Yeshivah Etz Hayim Hebrew Institute of Boro Park," *Jewish Education*, Fall 1948, pp. 47–48; Noah Nardi, "A Survey of Jewish Day Schools in America," *Jewish Education* (September 1944), p. 25; Sidney Z. Lieberman, "A Historical Study of the Yeshiva High School Curriculum in New York City" (Ph. D. diss., Yeshiva University, 1959), pp. 162–163.

16.   Joseph H. Lookstein, "Ramaz at Forty," p. 4; Gurock, *When Harlem Was Jewish*, p. 106; idem, *The Men and Women of Yeshiva: Higher Education, Orthodoxy and American Judaism* (New York, 1988), pp. 8–17.

17.   Nardi, p. 25. On the nature of the Flatbush and Boro Park Brooklyn neighborhoods in the 1920s and 1930s, see Deborah Dash Moore, *At Home in America: Second Generation New York Jews* (New York, 1981), pp. 25, 72, 78; Egon Mayer, *From Suburb to Shtetl: The Jews of Boro Park* (Philadelphia, 1979), pp. 24–25.

18.   Joseph H. Lookstein to S. Erdberg, June 6, 1937 (RA); Joseph H. Lookstein to Vera Montgomery, October 14, 1937 (RA).

19.   *RM*, March 1956, p. 1.

20.   *RM*, November 1952, p. 2.

21.   *RM*, February 26, 1954, p. 2

22.   *RM*, October 1955, p. 2; February 10, 1959, p. 2.

23.   Joseph H. Lookstein to S. Erdberg, June 8, 1937 (RA); "Did You Know," p. 2; "Principal's Report, April 1945," *Minutes of the Board of Trustees of the Ramaz School*, p. 1, RA.

24.   By 1939, Kehilath Jeshurun's neighborhood was contributing a little less than thirty percent of the students. In that year, the Upper West Side, directly across Central Park, sent an additional thirty percent of the students. Forty percent came from the Bronx. Children from the Grand Concourse, Walton Avenue, Morris

Avenue, and environs hopped on the Lexington Avenue subway southbound to Yorkville.

By 1951, when the school first began compiling such statistics for itself, the percentage of students from Yorkville was down to less than ten percent. In that year, a full forty-five percent came from the Upper West Side; thirty-five percent came from the Bronx. The geographical distribution of the student body continued unchanged for the next decade. In 1961, Yorkville was still home to but eight percent of the students. Most still came from the West Side and the Bronx. It was not until five years later (1966), some thirty years into Ramaz's existence, that Yorkville began to make its move. In that year, 165 of the 683 Ramaz youngsters came from the home neighborhood. An additional five years later and the attractiveness of Ramaz to Yorkville parents was in full swing. The neighborhood had moved a bit beyond its 1939 proportion, with one-third of the students from Kehilath Jeshurun's vicinity. In 1973–1974, Yorkville finally became Ramaz's prime feeder neighborhood, as 225 of the school's 690 students came from that area. The Upper West Side was second with 211. No other neighborhood contributed more than fifty-seven students. Three years later, 1976–1977, Yorkville sent 338 of Ramaz's 749 students and the Upper West Side dropped slightly to 205. Since that time, the Yorkville percentage has remained constant. See "Ramaz School Register, 1951–1986" (typescript) RA; see also "Ramaz Academy Students, 1939" (typescript) RA.

25. See George Jacobs's recollections (1987).

26. See "Ramaz Academy Students, 1939"; see also, for addresses of Ramaz students in the 1950s and 1960s, *Pioneer* (1960), pp. 70–71; 1969, pp. 66–68. See also Jon Jucovy, "Oral History," manuscript version of "Memories of the Early Days of Ramaz" that appeared in *Ramaz Jubilee II: The Fifty-First Annual Dinner Dance Sponsored by the Parents Council . . . January 17, 1988*, n.p.

27. See "Ramaz Academy Students, 1939"; see also for addresses on Ramaz students in the 1970s, *Ramaz* (1973), n.p.; *ibid.*, (1974), n.p.

28. On the continuing problem of Ramaz students not wearing hats in the streets, see *RM*, December 1960, p. 3; March 1973, p. 6.

29. For information on the "ghetto"-type schools in the Bronx in the late 1940s, see "United Yeshivos, Board of Secular Education, Reports on Visits" (1946–1947) in the Shelley Safire Papers in the Yeshiva University Archive.

30. "Report on Visit to Yeshiva Academy for Girls, December 4, 1946," Shelley Safire Papers; see also Zevi H. Harris, "A Study of Trends in Jewish Education for Girls in New York City" (Ph. D. diss., Yeshiva University, 1956), pp. 150–151.

31. On the East European context for Orthodox *maskilim* schools, see Emanuel Gamoran, *Changing Conceptions in Jewish Education* (New York, 1925), pp. 193–194; On the nature of the Ramaz curriculum, see "Portrait of an Institute" (typescript, 1962), pp. 3–5, RA; Benjamin Brickman, "Yeshivath Ramaz at Thirteen," *Jewish Spectator* (October 1951), pp. 18–22. It is also noteworthy that beginning with Dr. Pinkhos Churgin, who helped Rabbi Joseph found Ramaz, the school maintained during its first two generations a close relationship with the Orthodox *maskilim* who made up the Teachers Institute of Yeshiva University. Children of that

school's faculty attended Ramaz, and some of the Teachers Institute students naturally gravitated to teaching positions at the Yorkville school.

32. On the curriculum at Ramaz as opposed to Central, see Lieberman, pp. 130–151, 230–245. Interview with former Ramaz parents, February 11, 1988. Names withheld at interviewees' request. Tape on deposit in Ramaz Archives.

33. On social dancing classes and dances on Ramaz premises, see *RM*, December 1951, p. 2. As far as dances at other schools are concerned, there is evidence that chaperoned Saturday night coed parties were part of the Central and TA social scenes in the 1950s but not on school premises nor with the direct approval of school officials. For more on this, see Gurock *The Men and Women of Yeshiva*, p. 284.

34. Ruchama Shain, *All for the Boss* (New York, 1984), pp. 30–31, 42. For more on the sociology of the Young Israel, see above, chapter 14.

35. Gurock, *The Men and Women of Yeshiva*, pp. 203–204.

36. A perusal of the 1985–1986 student-parent register of Ramaz indicates that some fourteen leading Conservative families have children at Ramaz. These families include Seminary faculty and deans, Conservative rabbis from Manhattan, Queens, and Long Island, and officials of the United Synagogue of America. Eleven of the fourteen families hail from Manhattan, which until recently had no Solomon Schechter school of any grade level. The emergence of the Abraham Joshua Heschel School on New York's West Side, and a new Schechter School at the Seminary itself has had some minimal impact.

37. On the difficulties Jews had with the public schools before Ramaz's era, see Leonard Bloom, "A Successful Jewish Boycott of the New York City Public Schools," *AJH*, December 1980, pp. 180–188; Moore, pp. 89–107.

38. Ramaz used the same sort of logic in organizing its school week along a Monday-Friday schedule. Other earlier schools had held classes on Sunday. This scheduling issue, obviously, did not hold the same emotional power as the Christmas recess did. See on Ramaz's rationale, Brickman, p. 20.

39. Maimonides, *Mishneh Torah*, Hilchot Deot 4:1 ff., 4:14–15.

40. On the immigrants' discovery of sports in America, the images it evoked, and the problems that ensued, see Gary Goodman, *Choosing Sides: Playground and Street Life on the Lower East Side* (New York, 1979).

41. On the importance of dancing and dance classes at Ramaz, see *RM*, December 1951, p. 2. The theme of the 1951 Fall Frolic was "The Roaring Twenties." And elsewhere in that newsletter it was reported that "not only are youngsters taught to dance, but they are taught the social amenities as well."

42. Evidence of the participation and persistence of all these schools during the 1950s is provided by the Ramaz *Pioneer*. The 1949 edition notes, two years before the league was established, games against the two TAs, RJJ, and the Mesivta Tifereth Jerusalem. The 1951 edition has Ramaz opposing MTA, BTA, RJJ, Mesivta Chaim Berlin, and Mesivta Torah Vodaas, and notes dances after the TA and RJJ games, as two sins were there compounded. The 1952 edition shows a league consisting of MTA, BTA, Mesivta Chaim Berlin, Mesivta Torah Vodaas, and RJJ. Ramaz cheerleaders are pictured in 1952 with longish skirts. Short skirts appeared in 1954 and remained the style for a generation or more. The 1952 edition is also

noteworthy for its report that a "tremendous [coed?] crowd" attended the Ramaz-Central game and for its comment that "it could have been the novelty of the game or could it?" The year 1953 is the last one for Mesivta Torah Vodaas, but Mesivta Chaim Berlin is listed as late as 1958. RJJ remained in the league until 1965. Then for two years it linked up with a number of Brooklyn Mesivtas in creating the short-lived Inter-Mesivta League, which closed its doors to girl fans. RJJ returned to the coed league in 1967. See on this subject, *Pioneer* (1949), p. 42; (1951), p. 38; (1952), pp. 40–42; (1955), p. 24; (1959), n.p; (1967), p. 27. See also on this subject, *TA Topics* 4, no. 1 (n.d. [1951?]), pp. 3–4.; interview with Paul Nodell, former basketball coach and after-game dance chaperone, October 28, 1987.

43. *RM*, November 1953, p. 2; May 1954, p. 2.

44. *RM*, November 1953, p. 2

45. *RM*, October 1954, p. 2.

46. *RM*, November 1951, p. 4.

47. Gurock, *The Men and Women of Yeshiva*, pp. 110–113.

48. *Ibid.*, pp. 82–86; Aaron Rothkoff, *Bernard Revel: Builder of American Jewish Orthodoxy* (Philadelphia, 1972), p. 71–94; Gilbert Klaperman, *The Story of Yeshiva University: The First Jewish University in America* (London, 1969), pp. 149–170.

49. Marianne Sanua, "Stages in the Development of Jewish Life at Princeton University," *AJH* (June 1987): 391–415; *AJYB* (1963): 448.

50. On the non-prerabbinic goals of a Ramaz education, see Brickman, p. 19. The number of rabbis who graduated initially from Ramaz is derived from a typescript master list of graduates available in the Alumni Office of the Ramaz School. As of 1987, there were at most fourteen rabbis who were once at Ramaz, of which at least four are Conservative rabbis. In addition, there were two cantors who are alumni; one of them is a woman.

51. For the geographical distribution of Ramaz students during the 1967–1987 period, see "Ramaz School Register," *Minutes of the Board of Trustees of the Ramaz School* (1967–1987) (RA). On the religiosity of late 1980s' Ramaz students as opposed to a generation earlier, see Nathalie Friedman, "The Graduates of Ramaz: Fifty Years of Jewish Day School Education," in Jeffrey S. Gurock, ed., *Ramaz: School, Community, Scholarship and Orthodoxy*, (Hoboken, N.J., 1989), pp. 83–123.

52. The 1984 Ramaz student yearbook, *Ramifications*, announced that "after a two year absence from the Ramaz scene, cheerleaders once again grace basket-ball games with their presence. Despite the conspicuous absence of the miniskirts of yesteryear." See *Ramifications*, 1984, p. 118. See also pp. 19–22, 28–29, and *passim* for discussions of choirs, retreats, dramatic presentations, and other coeducational activities. See also Haskel Lookstein, "Looking Back and Ahead." p. 3.

53. Concomitant with this shift on Ramaz's campus and extensions thereof, there has been a move among some other Orthodox families who have become implicit adherents to at least a part of Ramaz's version of American Orthodoxy even if their institutional allegiances, through their children's high school years, remain with Yeshiva University's schools. Although the ideal product of the Talmudical Academy is still the worldly and Torah-sophisticated Yeshiva College student, some of the TA's graduates do go off to the accepting and accommodating Ivy League

schools. There they do meet up with Ramazites-or reunite with them after both have spent a year in Israel-producing a close-knit Orthodox community on these campuses. See on this, Gurock, *The Men and Women of Yeshiva*, pp. 250–251.

54. See for a functional definition of "menschlichkeit," Haskel Lookstein, "Ramaz after Forty," *Ramaz School Annual Dinner Dance Sponsored by Parents Council, January* 22, 1978, p. 7.

55. On Ramaz students' recognition of the impact Vietnam was making on their lives, see *Ramifications* (1972), p. 69; see also *Ramifications* (1971), p. 62, for complaints about student apathy. On Ramaz's philosophy towards handling student discontent during the early 1970s, see Haskel Lookstein, "Education for the Now Generation," *Ramaz School Annual Dinner Dance Sponsored by the Parents Council, January* 25, 1970, pp. 1–8; on the emergence of a student-faculty-administration committee, see also *Ramifications* (1971), p. 63. On *y'mai iyun* at Ramaz that dealt with a wide range of contemporary social problems, see *Ramifications* (1973), pp. 5–6; 1974, pp. 19–26; 1979, p. 81.

56. Gurock, *The Men and Women of Yeshiva*, p. 223.

57. For an example of Orthodox rabbinical opposition to activism and for reliance on quiet diplomacy, see *Jewish Week*, December 18, 1987, p. 21.

58. The appearance of a speaker from the SSSJ discussing the plight of Soviet Jewry was first described as a "highlight of the year" in 1970. See *Ramaz* (1970), p. 9. See also *Ramifications* (1971), p. 63; 1975, p. 111; 1981, p. 18. On Ramaz protests on behalf of Shcharansky, see *Ramifications* (1983), pp. 10–11.

59. *New York Times*, March 6, 1985, p. 7.

60. It is noteworthy that in the spring of 1987, a group of Ramaz students petitioned the school's administration unsuccessfully to have a senior coed "social" activity on campus to commemorate their graduation. Denied, they proceeded to hold their own events off campus. In this regard, the school and its students were behaving somewhat like the TAs of the 1950s.

Index

447